T0299429

'At a time of unprecedented global change, where economic and political certainties have been swept away by a tidal wave of social, economic, technological and industrial revolutions, it is crucial that we understand the forces currently shaping the structure, conduct and performance of the global defence sector. This book offers the reader an expert, detailed yet eminently accessible analysis of the global defence industry as it adjusts to the challenging pressures of the new world disorder.'

Derek Braddon,
Emeritus Professor, University of the West of England

The Economics of the Global Defence Industry

This book makes an original contribution to our knowledge of the world's major defence industries. Experts from a wide range of different countries – from the major economies of North America and Western Europe to developing economies and some unique cases such as China, India, Singapore, South Africa and North Korea – describe and analyse the structure, conduct and performance of the defence industry in that country.

Each chapter opens with statistics on a key nation's defence spending, its spending on defence R&D and on procurement over the period 1980 to 2017, allowing for an analysis of industry changes following the end of the Cold War. After the facts of each industry, the authors describe and analyse the structure, conduct and performance of the industry. The analysis of 'structure' includes discussions of entry conditions, domestic monopoly/oligopoly structures and opportunities for competition. The section on 'conduct' analyses price/non-price competition, including private and state funded R&D, and 'performance' incorporates profitability, imports and exports together with spin-offs and technical progress. The conclusion explores the future prospects for each nation's defence industry. Do defence industries have a future? What might the future defence firm and industry look like in 50 years' time?

This volume is a vital resource and reference for anyone interested in defence economics, industrial economics, international relations, strategic studies and public procurement.

Keith Hartley is Emeritus Professor of Economics at the University of York, UK.

Jean Belin is Director of the IHEDN Chair in Defence Economics and Assistant Professor at the University of Bordeaux, France.

Routledge Studies in Defence and Peace Economics

Edited by Keith Hartley, University of York, UK and Jurgen Brauer, Augusta State University, USA.

Volume 11
Defence Procurement and Industry Policy
Edited by Stefan Markowski and Peter Hall

Volume 12
The Economics of Defence Policy
A New Perspective
Keith Hartley

Volume 13
The Economics of UN Peacekeeping
Nadège Sheehan

Volume 14
Military Cost-Benefit Analysis
Theory and Practice
Edited by Francois Melese, Anke Richter and Binyam Solomon

Volume 15
Analytical Peace Economics
The Illusion of War for Peace
Partha Gangopadhyay and Nasser Elkanj

Volume 16
The Economics of the Global Defence Industry
Edited by Keith Hartley and Jean Belin

Other titles in the series include:

The Economics of Regional Security
NATO, the Mediterranean, and Southern Africa
Jürgen Brauer and Keith Hartley

For a full list of titles in this series, please visit www.routledge.com/series/SE0637

The Economics of the Global Defence Industry

Edited by Keith Hartley and Jean Belin

LONDON AND NEW YORK

First published 2020
by Routledge
2 Park Square, Milton Park, Abingdon, Oxon OX14 4RN

and by Routledge
52 Vanderbilt Avenue, New York, NY 10017

Routledge is an imprint of the Taylor & Francis Group, an informa business

First issued in paperback 2021

British Library Cataloguing-in-Publication Data
A catalogue record for this book is available from the British Library

Library of Congress Cataloging-in-Publication Data
Names: Hartley, Keith, editor. | Belin, Jean, 1972- editor.
Title: The economics of the global defence industry / edited by Keith Hartley and Jean Belin.
Other titles: The economics of the global defense industry
Description: Milton Park, Abingdon, Oxon ; New York : Routledge, 2020. | Includes bibliographical references and index.
Identifiers: LCCN 2019029114
Subjects: LCSH: Defense industries–Economic aspects. | Military art and science–Economic aspects.
Classification: LCC HD9743.A2 E26 2020 | DDC 338.4/7355–dc23
LC record available at https://lccn.loc.gov/2019029114

ISBN: 978-1-138-60809-2 (hbk)
ISBN: 978-1-03-208580-7 (pbk)
ISBN: 978-0-429-46679-3 (ebk)

Typeset in Bembo
by Swales & Willis, Exeter, Devon, UK

Keith Hartley:
To my wife, Winifred and our family:
Adam, Rachel, Oliver and Imogen Hartley
Professor Lucy Hartley
Dr Cecilia Ellis and Martyn, Matthew Jacob, Kathryn Olivia and Sophie Elizabeth Ellis.

Jean Belin:
To my wife and our family: Emile and Lola.

Contents

Figures

Tables

Contributors

Jomana Amara is Professor of Economics, Naval Postgraduate School in Monterey, California. Her research interests include international economics, defense economics, health economics and public sector economics. jhamara@nps.edu

Laxman Kumar Behera is Research Fellow at Institute for Defence Studies and Analyses (IDSA), New Delhi. His research interests include Indian defence economy with a focus on defence industry, military spending, arms procurement and defence offsets. laxmanbehera@gmail.com

Jean Belin is Director of the IHEDN Chair in Defence Economics and Assistant Professor at the University of Bordeaux (GREThA, UMR CNRS 5113). His research interests include problems relating to the financing of the defence industry and the role of French defence firms in the National Innovation System. jean.belin@u-bordeaux.fr

Richard A. Bitzinger is Visiting Senior Fellow with the Military Transformations Program at the S. Rajaratnam School of International Studies (RSIS), Nanyang Technological University, Singapore 639798. His research interests include security and defense issues relating to the Asia-Pacific region, including regional defense industries and local armaments production, military modernization and force transformation, and weapons proliferation. isrbitzinger@ntu.edu.sg

Rob Bourke is a retired public servant and consultant based in Canberra, Australia. His research interests include defence policy for Australian industry. rob.bourke58@gmail.com

Michael Brzoska is Senior Research Fellow at the Institute for Peace Research and Security Studies at the University of Hamburg, Beim Schlump 83, 20145 Hamburg, Germany. He is also Associate Senior Researcher at SIPRI. His research interests include security implications of climate change. brzoska@ifsh.de

Raul Caruso is Associate Professor in Economic Policy, Department of Economic Policy and CSEA of the Catholic University of the Sacred Heart in

Milan, Italy, and Director of the European Centre of Peace Science, Integration and Cooperation (CESPIC) at the Catholic University 'Our Lady of Good Counsel' in Tirana, Albania. He is Editor in Chief of Peace Economics, Peace Science and Public Policy. His research interests include peace economics, military spending, economics of conflict and international political economy. raul.caruso@unicatt.it

Namhoon Cho is Senior Research Fellow at the Korea Institute for Defense Analyses (KIDA), 37 Hoegi-ro, Dongdaemun-gu, Seoul 02455, Republic of Korea. His research interests include North Korea's military, economy and denuclearization process. chonh@kida.re.kr

Christopher Mark Davis is Professorial Research Fellow, Oxford Institute of Population Ageing (OIPA), and Senior Research Fellow, Oxford School of Global and Area Studies, University of Oxford. His research interests include USSR and Russia in the areas of demography, health, ageing, the economy and defence economics. christopher.davis@wolfson.ox.ac.uk

J. Paul Dunne is Professor of Economics, University of Cape Town, Rondebosch, Cape Town 7701, South Africa. His research interests include economics of military spending, conflict and peace. John.Dunne@uct.ac.za

Antonio Fonfría, Facultad de CC. Económicas, Campus de Somosaguas, 28223 Pozuelo de Alarcón, Madrid. His research interests include defence economics, industrial policy, industrial organization, and international economics. afonfria@ccee.ucm.es

Raymond Franck of the Naval Postgraduate School, is Emeritus Professor, Naval Postgraduate School, USAF Academy. His research interests include defense acquisition practices and military innovation. cfranck215@aol.com

Keith Hartley is Emeritus Professor of Economics, University of York, UK. His research interests include defence economics, procurement, contracting, collaboration and measuring defence output. kh2@york.ac.uk

Kjetil Hatlebakk Hove is Senior Research Fellow at the Strategic Analyses and Joint Systems Division, Norwegian Defence Research Establishment (FFI), Box 25, 2027 Kjeller, Norway. His research interests include escalating costs and defence planning. Kjetil.Hove@ffi.no

Christopher W. Hughes is Professor of International Politics and Japanese Studies, University of Warwick. Department of Politics and International Studies, University of Warwick, Coventry, CV4 7AL. His research interests include Japan's international relations and security policy; Japanese defence policy; US-Japan alliance; Japan-North Korea relations; and political economy of Japanese defence industry. C.W.Hughes@warwick.ac.uk

Denis Jacqmin is Researcher at GRIP (Group for Research and Information on Peace and Security) in Brussels. GRIP, Chaussée de Louvain, 467,

1030 Brussels. His research interests include small arms and light weapons regulations, control of conventional arms transfers, and political and security developments in Ukraine. d.jacqmin@grip.org

Christoforos Kalloniatis, Major/Finance Corps in the Hellenic Army. He is an Academic Associate of the Department of Economics, University of Thessaly, and the Laboratory of Social & Political Institutions, Department of Sociology, University of the Aegean. Address: Neapoli, Mytilene, 81100 Mytilene, Greece. His research interests include defence economics and policy, EU Common Security and Defence Policy, public sector economics, environmental economics. ckallon@env.aegean.gr

Sarah Kirchberger is Head of the Center for Asia-Pacific Strategy and Security at the Institute for Security Policy at Kiel University, Holstenbrucke 8-10, D-24103 Kiel, Germany. Her research interests include China's military, especially naval, modernization and transnational military-technological cooperation in the Asia-Pacific. SKirchberger@ispk.uni-kiel.de

Collin Koh is Research Fellow at the Institute of Defence and Strategic Studies, S. Rajaratnam School of International Studies based at Nanyang Technological University, Singapore. His research interests include maritime and defence-industrial studies. iscollinkoh@ntu.edu.sg

Christos Kollias is Professor of Applied Economics at the Department of Economics, University of Thessaly, Editor of Defence and Peace Economics and Associate Researcher with the Hellenic Foundation for European & Foreign Policy. Address: 28hs Octovriou 78, Volos 38333, Greece. His research interests include defence economics, economic analysis of terrorism and crime, political economy, public sector economics and macroeconomic policy. kollias@uth.gr

Guy Lamb is Director of the Safety and Violence Initiative, University of Cape Town, Rondebosch, Cape Town 7701; and Research Associate, Centre for International & Comparative Politics, University of Stellenbosch, South Africa. His research interests include arms control, violence prevention, peacebuilding and policing. Guy.Lamb@uct.ac.za

Diego Lopes da Silva is Researcher at the Stockholm International Peace Research Institute (SIPRI). His research interests include military expenditure and arms production in developing countries. diego.lopes@sipri.org

Martin Lundmark is Associate Professor, Lecturer in Systems Science for Defence and Security, Swedish Defence University. His research interests include defence innovation, defence industry, defence exports, defence collaboration and strategic defence procurement. Martin.Lundmark@fhs.se

Julien Malizard is Deputy Director of the IHEDN Chair in Defence Economics and Associate Researcher at the University of Bordeaux (UMR

5113 GREThA). His research interests include defence budgets, the economic impact of defence activities and the arms trade. julien.malizard@fdd-ihedn.fr

Stefan Markowski is Professor and Chair of Management, University of Information Technology and Management, Rzeszow, Poland. His research interests include defence procurement, defence industry, military alliances and the economics of migrations. s.markowski@adfa.edu.au

Hélène Masson is Senior Research Fellow at the Foundation for Strategic Research (FRS, Paris) and in charge of the Defence & Industry Department. Her research interests include public policies in the field of armaments, business strategies, and defence export and cooperation. h.masson@frstrategie.org

Ron Matthews is Cranfield University Chair in Defence Economics at the UK Defence Academy, Shrivenham. His research interests include the broad spectrum of defence economics, especially offset and defence-industrial development. r.g.matthews@cranfield.ac.uk

Johannes Mohr is Non-Resident Fellow and PhD candidate at the Institute for Security Policy at Kiel University, Holstenbrucke 8-10, D-24103 Kiel, Germany. His research interests include Chinese outward direct investment, and the strategic impact of these investments. jmohr@ispk.uni-kiel.de

Eftychia Nikolaidou is Professor of Economics, University of Cape Town, Rondebosch, Cape Town 7701, South Africa. Her research interests include economics of military spending, conflict and peace; financial development and growth; and banking crises. Efi.Nikolaidou@uct.ac.za

Jon Olav Pedersen is Senior Research Fellow at the Innovation and Industrial Development Division, Norwegian Defence Research Establishment (FFI), Box 25, 2027 Kjeller, Norway. His research interests include processes of innovation in the defence industry. Jon-Olav.Pedersen@ffi.no

Christopher E. Penney is Senior Economic and Financial Analyst at Canada's Parliamentary Budget Office. His research interests include defence economics, the political economy of defence procurement, and methods in costing and financial risk analysis. Christopher.penney@parl.gc.ca

Antoni Pieńkos is Director of the Analysis Division at the Warsaw Institute for Strategic Initiatives, Warsaw, Poland. His research interests include defence-industrial cooperation in Europe, European naval forces, NATO and maritime security. antoni.pienkos@wiis.org.pl

Gil Pinchas, Coller School of Management, Tel Aviv University, P.O.B. 39040, Tel Aviv, 6997801, Israel. His research interests include optimal allocation and size of the defense budget; role and structure of the defense industry. gilpench@mail.tau.ac.il

Carlos Martí Sempere, Instituto Universitario Gral. Gutierrez Mellado. C/Princesa, 36. E28006-Madrid. His research interests include defence economics, industrial organization, innovation, system engineering and defence as a complex adaptive system. carlos.marti.sempere@gmail.com

Selami Sezgin is Professor of Economics, Eskisehir Osmangazi University, Department of Economics, Eskisehir, Turkey. His research interests include defence economics, economics of terrorism and public finance. selamisezgin@ogu.edu.tr

Sennur Sezgin is Associate Professor of Economics, Eskisehir Osmangazi University, Department of Economics, Eskisehir, Turkey. Her research interests include defence economics, economics of terrorism and political business cycles. sennursezgin@ogu.edu.tr

Binyam Solomon is Senior Defence Scientist at Defence Research and Development Canada (DRDC) and an Adjunct Research Professor at Carleton University. His research interests include political economy, defence management, peacekeeping economics and time series methods. Binyam.solomon@carleton.ca

Asher Tishler is Professor Emeritus, Coller School of Management, Tel Aviv University, P.O.B. 39040, Tel Aviv, 6997801, Israel. His research interests include mitigating the risk of advanced cyber-attacks; optimal allocation and size of the defense budget; productivity, wage and seniority; role and structure of the defense industry; and role of military intelligence. ashert@tauex.tau.ac.il

Robert Wylie is Visiting Fellow at the School of Business on the Canberra campus of the University of New South Wales, Canberra, Australia. His research interests include the functional dynamics of military technological innovation systems and the evolution of defence policy for Australian industry. r.wylie@adfa.edu.au

Preface

This book resulted from a meeting at a conference organised by Jean Belin, Chaire Economie de defense, IHEDN and held at the University of Bordeaux in 2015 (28–29 May, 2015). Following this conference, Keith Hartley and Jean Belin agreed to develop their collaboration through publishing a book on the world's defence industries. They agreed on a list of countries and authors. A publisher was found, namely, Routledge and the book became part of its Studies in Defence Economics Series.

Edited volumes take time to plan and organise. This volume was no exception and was especially challenging since it involved organising large numbers of authors from many countries world-wide. Initially, we planned that all chapters would be submitted by end-October 2018, allowing some time for comments and revisions with a final manuscript for the publisher by March-April 2019. Like all 'good' defence projects, there were the inevitable delays!

Many helped with this book. Our authors had to deal patiently with our many requests and we thank all of them for their support in preparing a volume of this size and complexity. Jurgen Brauer as co-editor of the Routledge Defence Economics Series was especially supportive in encouraging us to proceed with the idea. Keith Hartley also benefited from participation in a 2018 SIPRI Workshop on Arms Production Data, organised by Aude Fleurant of SIPRI. Finally, our thanks to the production staff, especially Christiana Mandizha, Helen Kitto and Colin Morgan, Production Editor.

Sadly, one of our authors died, namely Bud Udis. Professor Bernard Udis (1927–2018) was a distinguished economist, educator and scholar. After completing his doctorate at Princeton, he spent most of his academic career at the University of Colorado at Boulder. His research focused on economic and policy questions affecting the international defence marketplace and some of his publications became classics in defence economics.[1]

Note

1 This tribute was prepared by Raymond Franck.

1 The global defence industry

An overview

Keith Hartley and Jean Belin

Introduction: aims and objectives

This book makes an original contribution to knowledge and fills a major gap in the literature. Currently, there are no recent and up-to-date economics books dealing with the world's defence industries. The book has two further features. First, defence industries are important and major users of scarce resources but very little is known about these industries. Second, each author is an authority on their industry. By bringing together these specialists, each following a standard format, we make a unique and distinctive contribution to our knowledge and understanding of the global defence industry.

Criteria for selecting the countries

Various criteria were used to select the countries included in the study. The list of companies in the SIPRI Top 100 arms firms in 2016 provided the starting point. All countries listed in the Top 100 were included. Some countries were obvious candidates, such as the USA, Russia, the UK, France, Germany and Italy. It was also necessary to identify authors for each country's defence industry.

The editors selected authors on the basis of their knowledge, expertise, and availability. Some authors are leading defence economists; others are specialists from and for each nation. A further requirement was the publisher's word limit on the book's length which provided a constraint on the number of chapters and countries included in the book.

The SIPRI Top 100 arms producers is a comprehensive and publicly available database for arms producers and military service companies. It is published annually in the SIPRI Yearbook and is available in the SIPRI Database. It shows the names of each arms producer, its country of location, annual arms sales in current and constant prices, total sales, arms sales as a share of total sales, as well as total company profits and total employment. Subsidiaries are shown (SIPRI, 2018a).

The Top 100 includes private and public companies but not manufacturing or maintenance units of the armed forces. The Database contains financial and employment information on arms producing companies in Organisation for Economic Co-operation and Development (OECD) and developing nations (excluding China). The data are based on open sources and open information (e.g. company annual reports; articles in journals and newspapers). The Database was launched initially in 1989 and the current version contains data from 2002, including data for Russian arms companies. Collecting such data is a costly and time-consuming exercise for SIPRI but the result is a valuable and original contribution to knowledge. This book would not have been possible without the SIPRI Arms Industry Database. At the same time, this book's country studies of each nation's defence industry adds to the knowledge provided by the list of SIPRI Top 100 firms.

Table 1.1 shows the countries included in the book and the number of Top 100 arms companies by country in 2016. US arms companies dominated the number of Top 100 arms firms by country, accounting for almost 40% of the total. European countries accounted for a further 26% of the total numbers. Elsewhere, South Korea, Japan, India and Israel combined accounted for 20% of the total numbers in 2016.

Two countries, namely, China and North Korea, are included in the book, although neither are listed in the SIPRI Top 100. China is a major arms producer but little is known about its defence industrial base. Similarly, little is known about the arms industry of North Korea but its position in international relations made it a candidate for inclusion. The absence of published information on the defence industries of China and North Korea makes an original contribution to knowledge.

Two other countries were included even though they had no Top 100 companies, namely, Greece and South Africa. Greece is an example of a country whose defence industry is facing major financial and economic problems. South Africa is an example of a developing country and a country from the continent of Africa. Also, the South African company Denel was listed in the Top 100 arms companies until relatively recently.

It was not possible to include all countries. Notable exclusions comprised Belgium, the Czech Republic, Finland and the Netherlands. Nonetheless, these omissions are offset by the inclusion of the major European arms producers. Elsewhere, some South American and Asian nations are excluded (e.g. Argentina; Indonesia) but, again, these are balanced by the inclusion of other nations from these regions. Another notable omission is Iran where there is an absence of known specialists for that country. Overall, the key criterion in country selection was their representation in the SIPRI Top 100 arms producers. All countries with an arms producer in the SIPRI Top 100 in 2016 were included in the book.

The Top 100 list is not static and changes continuously. It is subject to new entry and exits reflecting increases and decreases in defence spending as well as new technology and industrial re-structuring. Firms merge to create new companies with new names and new business products (e.g. military outsourcing; emergence of drones and UAVs). Some large arms firms were only created relatively recently. For example, aircraft companies did not exist

Table 1.1 Top 100 arms companies by country, 2016

Country	*Number of Top 100 arms companies by country*
USA	38
China	Not known: see Chapter 3
Russia	10
UK	8
France	6
Trans-European	2
Italy	2
Germany	3
Spain	1
Greece	0
Poland	1
Ukraine	1
Switzerland	1
Sweden	1
Norway	1
Turkey	2
Israel	3
South Korea	7
Japan	5
Canada	1
Australia	1
Brazil	1
India	4
Singapore	1
South Africa	0
North Korea	Not known: see Chapter 27

Source: SIPRI (2018a).

Notes:

i) Top 100 ranked by arms sales and based on SIPRI Arms Industry Database, 2016. Subsidiaries are excluded.

ii) Trans-European companies are defined as companies whose ownership and control structures are located in more than one European country.

iii) China and North Korea are not listed in the SIPRI Top 100 arms companies: hence they are shown as not known.

in 1900 and aerospace firms and missile companies only emerged after 1945. Similarly, there were changes between 2016 and 2017. In 2017, there were 42 US arms firms in the Top 100, followed by 10 Russian and seven from the UK. The sole Norwegian firm in 2016 was no longer in the Top 100 in 2017 and the seven South Korean arms firms of 2016 were reduced to four firms in 2017 (SIPRI, 2018b).

The Top 100 also excludes specialist small arms firms which manufacture ammunition, rifles and light weapons. Estimates suggest that the small arms sector comprises some 1,000 companies and about 100 countries. However, some small arms production takes place in countries such as Brazil, Canada, China, Germany, India, Italy, Russia, Switzerland, Turkey, the UK and USA: these countries are included in this book. Also, some small arms production occurs in the Top 100 arms firms.

Outline of the book

Defence or arms industries (the terms are used interchangeably) invite questions about what we know; what we don't know; and what we need to know for further understanding and debates about policy choices for these industries. This book examines these issues starting with what is known about each industry.

Table 1.1 shows the countries included in the book. Authors for each chapter were asked to follow a standard format, namely, an introduction, summary of argument, industry description, case studies and conclusion. In more detail, each chapter uses the following standard format:

i) *A short statistical review* of national defence spending with data on annual defence R&D and procurement spending, defence equipment imports and defence equipment exports. Data are annual figures for the period 1980 to 2017 which covers years before and after the end of the Cold War. Where available, officially published data are presented; or where such data are unavailable, authors identify the data gaps; and where official data are not available, authors were asked to identify and review alternative data sources (e.g. trade association data; company data, etc.). In this way, the book identifies major gaps in the data on the world's defence industries.
ii) *Definition* of the national defence industry and data on its size and trends (e.g. annual sales and employment data for 1980–2017) as well as identifying the industry's major locations. This section includes a short historical overview of the industry and changes in industry definitions. Employment data distinguishes between direct and indirect numbers (supply chains), and proportions of R&D staff, skilled and unskilled (where available). The regional distribution of national defence industries is described with supporting data where available. Identifying the absence of official data on national defence industries will be an important research finding.
iii) *Industry structure* assesses whether the national industry is competitive, oligopolistic or a national monopoly, including the long-run trends in structure and the opportunities for competition. The leading arms firm and the top 10 major arms firms in 2016/17 are identified and if data permits, compared with the leader and top 10 in 1980. Entry

conditions are described, including any preference for national procurement. Again, where data allows, information on the national/global supply chain and trends is described and assessed.

iv) *Industry conduct* deals with price and non-price competition and long-run trends in conduct. Here, national procurement policy is introduced, including any preference for national equipment, the role of competition in procurement and the use of various forms of contract (e.g. cost-plus; fixed price and target cost incentives). Rules and the regulation of profitability are described and assessed.

v) *Industry performance*. Data on various performance indicators are reported and evaluated. These include defence industry productivity and profitability, exports and imports of defence equipment. Where possible comparisons are made with comparable civil industries (e.g. the whole economy; cars, pharmaceuticals, etc.). Other performance indicators include cost overruns and delays on major defence projects (e.g. aircraft carriers; submarines; tanks; combat aircraft). Examples are provided of any technical spin-offs and spin-ins. What are the strengths and weaknesses of each national industry?

vi) *Industry prospects* in the form of future challenges and its likely survival over the next 50 years (to 2070). What will the future industry look like: will its major firms survive; will new firms emerge; and in which product fields? Will new forms of business organisation emerge and will the future defence firm be radically different from today's arms firms (see Hartley, 2017)?

vii) Each chapter includes a critical evaluation of its national industry: its strengths, weaknesses and future prospects. Whilst a traditional structure-conduct-performance model is used, authors were asked to apply other analytical approaches (e.g. game theory; public choice models). Authors were encouraged to offer their own contributions and views on their national defence industry: its future challenges and prospects.

viii) The book ends with an overall conclusion with the editors identifying some common themes, problems, challenges and data availability.

The standard format for each chapter represents a 'counsel of perfection.' It is recognised that not all authors would be able to follow the guidelines and their actual performance will depart from the 'ideal.' Even such departures from the 'ideal' standard are informative.

Overall, interest in this area has strengthened in recent times as major global upheavals have called into question accepted economic and political conventions. Two developments have emerged. First, major developments within defence such as new technology and the revolution in military affairs (e.g. cyber warfare; space systems; drones and UAVs) as well as continued pressure to reduce defence budgets. Second, the emergence of new strategic threats such as global terrorism, so-called rogue states and nuclear threats from Iran and North Korea.

Conclusion

The book provides an authoritative, up-to-date and insightful study of one of the world's most important industries and one which can determine the future of our civilisation. It is a theme which is on a par with the global warming debate. The range of expert chapter authors provides the reader with access to the best knowledge currently available in this area. Each chapter follows a common format which allows comparisons between different countries and defence systems, so offering the reader a sum greater than its individual parts.

Little is known about the global defence industry and no single book exists which provides an up-to-date comprehensive coverage of the industry. Overall, the book fills a major gap in the literature: there are no rivals dealing with the economics of the global defence industry. Each chapter makes an original contribution to knowledge, each following a standard format to allow international comparisons. The book forms a main and supporting textbook for undergraduate and postgraduate courses in defence and peace economics, industrial economics, international relations, strategic studies and public procurement.

References

Hartley, K (2017). *The Economics of Arms*, Agenda, Newcastle.

SIPRI (2018a). *SIPRI Arms Industry Database 2016*, Stockholm, Stockholm International Peace Research Institute.

SIPRI (2018b). *SIPRI Arms Industry Database 2017*, Stockholm, Stockholm International Peace Research Institute.

2 The United States and its defense industries

Jomana Amara and Raymond Franck

Introduction

The defense industry in the United States represents a unique case due to its sheer size; its largest customer, the U.S. Department of Defense (DoD), and the non-defense industries engaged in defense related work. In 2017, with global defense expenditures estimated at $1.7 trillion, U.S. defense expenditures, at around $610 billion, accounted for approximately 36 percent of total global defense expenditures (SIPRI 2018a).

According to the *Defense News* Top 100 list for 2018, which ranks companies by defense revenue,[1] five and 39 of the top ten and top 100, respectively are U.S. companies (*Defense News* Top 100 List 2018). In addition, the Stockholm International Peace Research Institute (SIPRI) Arms Industry Database breaks out BAE Systems Inc. as a U.S. company subsidiary of BAE Systems U.K. and lists it in the top 10 in addition to six other U.S. companies.[2] In fact, the U.S. subsidiary to BAE Systems generates over 40 percent of its revenue (SIPRI 2018b). Among the top 10 companies, U.S. firms account for 69 percent of that group's defense revenue (Aitoro 2018).

The U.S. defense industry exported about $75.9 billion in 2017 (Mehta 2017). The United States spent $79.2 billion on research and development (R&D), and $124 billion on procurement—more than twice the amount that Google, Microsoft, and Apple spent on R&D and procurement combined. Worldwide spending for the same year was at $116 billion for defense R&D and $310 billion for procurement (Jane's IHS 2018a). The U.S. DoD sources the majority of its spending domestically due to the U.S. defense industry's high competency and the Buy America Act (procurement preference to domestic products with a punitive evaluation factor applied to most foreign products). In a 2007 report, DoD estimated that it awarded less than 0.5 percent of all contracts and about 1.5 percent of contracts for defense items and components to foreign contractors (DoD 2008).

The major exception is BAE Systems, a British firm that views the U.S. as one of its primary markets, and the most promising (BAE 2018, 19). BAE is a special case for a number of reasons. First, BAE participation in the U.S. market was facilitated by the longstanding "special relationship", between the

U.K. and the U.S. This has included close cooperation in defense acquisition programs, from the atomic bomb to the F-35. Among other things, this tradition of U.S.-U.K. cooperation helped BAE establish trust with DoD. The recent addition of the U.K. to the U.S. National Technical Industrial Base (DoD 2018, 11) will likely enhance this relationship

Second, BAE's strategy included acquisition of Sanders and Tracor, two key U.S. suppliers of highly classified military equipment.

Third, and related, BAE has a special security agreement with the U.S. Government; there's a "firewall" which prevents exchange of highly sensitive information between executives of the U.S. affiliate (all U.S. citizens) and the parent corporation in the U.K.

Finally, the statement "it is hard to tell whether BAE Systems should be flying the Union Jack or waving the Stars and Stripes" has been true for some time. Among other things, U.S. citizens hold a significant portion of its shares (Wayne 2006, C1).

Janes' World Defense Industry lists 271 U.S. companies as significant defense companies. Interestingly, Jane's does not list technology leaders such as Apple, Amazon, Alphabet, Microsoft, (first, second, third, and fourth most valuable companies worldwide, respectively), and does not provide data on the defense portion of their business, making it difficult to determine the size of the market with certainty (Jane's HIS 2018b). This lack of information exists despite the U.S. defense market's appeal. Jane's Market Potential Index (MPI) score (a scale from 0 to 5) assesses the appeal of 93 world defense markets based on a number of factors. The final market rating for the United States is 4.38, second after Japan's score of 4.39. The United States is the only nation ranked at 5 for overall defense investment and defense industrial capabilities.

The analytical foundation for this Chapter comes from works that explore the intersection of a game theory-enriched standard microeconomics and the literature on corporate strategy: e.g., *Competitive Strategy* (Porter 1980), *Co-opetition* (Brandenburger and Nalebuff 1996).

Our approach also reflects "contestability" (the inverse of barriers to entry; Baumol, Panzer and Willig 1988, esp. Chapter 10). Understanding barriers to entering the U.S. defense marketplace involves, *inter alia*, some knowledge of the large, complicated policy and regulatory structure which governs it. Accordingly, we devote considerable attention to that environment.

Economic environment of the U.S. defense industry

U.S. DoD spending

The U.S. defense industry depends for the most part on U.S. government expenditures. Figure 2.1 displays defense expenditures from 1980 to 2018, divided roughly into four separate periods: first, the Reagan buildup in the 1980s; second, the post-Cold War decline associated with a "procurement holiday;" third, various contingency operations following the World Trade

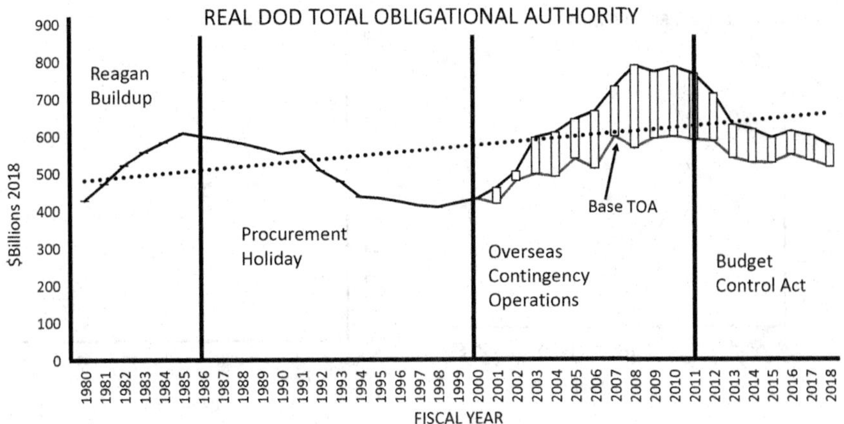

Figure 2.1 National defense Total Obligational Authority (TOA) in constant dollars (DoD Comptroller "Green Book" 2017).

Center attacks in 2001; and fourth, the Budget Control Act of 2011. As the dotted linear line in Figure 2.1 indicates, the data trends upwards over time. There is no trend, however, if the overseas contingency component is excluded.

In the post 9/11 era, the Total Obligation Authority (TOA) included allowances for various contingency operations, over and above the "Base" DoD TOA. The difference between the upper and lower line, the Base TOA, reflects this.

With the ending of the Cold War, U.S. defense budgets began a steady decline with no foreseeable end in sight at the time. With much new equipment in hand from the Reagan Buildup, the logical place to cut spending was in procurement, meaning that lesser defense budgets shown in Figure 2.2, and reported in Wayne (1998a), would most affect the defense industrial base.

DoD Procurement outlays have risen in keeping with the Reagan and "other contingencies" increases, the procurement holiday of the 1990s, the post-2001 increases (with an interesting spike in 2008 corresponding to the "surge" in Iraq), and then a downturn in procurement corresponding to the Budget Control Act of 2011.

Mergers in the defense industrial base

In 1993, Secretary of Defense Aspin and Deputy Secretary Perry concluded that some industrial consolidation was necessary and announced this to executives from major defense companies at a Pentagon dinner.[4] The main message was that the major defense players needed to consolidate to survive and the Defense Department would facilitate the process by

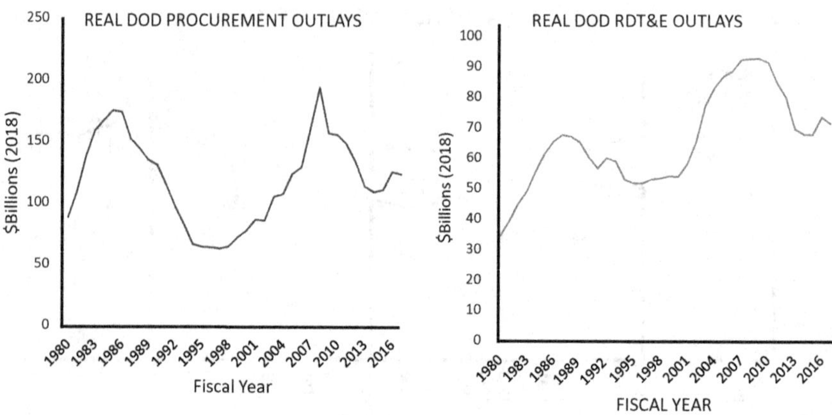

Figure 2.2 DoD procurement and research, development, technology, and evaluation (RDT&E) outlays in constant dollars (DoD Comptroller 2018).[3]

offering financial incentives and advocating consolidations in the event of antitrust challenges. The audience was receptive and as Norman Augustine (Martin Marietta CEO at the time) put it later: "You weren't going to survive unless you were willing to combine. So, there was not much of a choice" (Altoro 2016).

The Administration delivered. It provided strong advocacy for the Boeing-McDonnell-Douglas merger. It also allowed reorganization expenses as part of reimbursable costs, which amounted to a significant support, both direct and indirect, for the process (Gartzke 2010, 114, 116).

A large number of consolidations within the defense industrial base followed. One source (Tirpak 1998) estimated that 51 companies were combined into five. Reportedly the financial value of the consolidations totaled $55 billion (Wayne 1998b). The marquee mergers were Northrop with Grumman (in April 1994), Lockheed with Martin-Marietta (in August 1994), and Boeing with McDonnel-Douglas (in December 1996).

The era of very large mergers came to a rather abrupt end in 1998. With the proposed merger of Lockheed-Martin and Northrop-Grumman, and the advent of new leadership at the Departments of Justice and Defense, a consensus emerged that a merger between Lockheed-Martin and Northrop-Grumman went too far. Wayne (1998b) and Ricks and Cole (1998) provide excellent contemporaneous reporting of these events.

The authors of this chapter believe that one should view the "Last Supper" as ratifying, encouraging, and accelerating a long-term trend toward consolidation in defense industries. "Eye charts" showing defense corporations merging into ever smaller numbers have frequently depicted this phenomenon (e.g., Bialos, Fisher and Koehl 2009, 639).

The 1998 disapproval seems to have ended one era and started another. The Northrop-Grumman/Lockheed-Martin precedent discouraged mergers of very large companies. This prevailed for about two decades, during which time there was plenty of activity, but mostly involving larger companies acquiring smaller companies.

Recent experience, however, seems to indicate another era of large-scale consolidations. According to Harris Chairman and Chief Executive Bill Brown (Mattioli et al 2018b), "There's definitely a need for greater investment, which requires scale".

Despite all the activity, U.S. firms feature prominently in the worldwide top 10 revenue rankings. Table 2.1 shows snapshots of the rankings for U.S. firms, which appeared in at least one of the top 10 rankings. Five appeared in the top 10 for the 2018 rankings and seven in 2009 and in 2000. The Big Five—Lockheed-Martin, Raytheon, Northrop-Grumman, Boeing, and General Dynamics—have been regulars as top 10 defense firms.

United Technologies has been on the edge. Sometimes barely in the group and sometimes just out. General Electric, which ranked fifth in the 2000 list, has been absent in the other top 10 snapshots. It is, however, still a major defense producer *and* ranked 22nd in 2018. L3 Communications moved into the top 10 in 2009 but, in 2018, it moved back to 12th primarily due the sale of a division in 2017. Overall, the relative positions of the U.S. Big Five have remained fairly stable in recent decades as they adapt to market changes and remain industry leaders.

Table 2.2 shows a representative number of recent (as of 2018) and noteworthy mergers and acquisitions among the top 100 defense industrial firms. Five of the transactions involved companies that are both listed in the top

Table 2.1 Stability of revenue rankings for large U.S. defense firms (*Defense News* Top 100 List 2018)

Company	*2018 rank*	*2009*	*2000*
Lockheed-Martin	1	1	1
Raytheon	2	6	3
Northrop-Grumman	4	4	4
Boeing	5	3	2
General Dynamics	6	5	5
United Technologies	11	10	10
L3 Communications	12	9	46
General Electric (GE) or GE Aviation	22	18	5

Table 2.2 Some recent and noteworthy defense industrial mergers and acquisitions activity

Firms (with Defense News *Top 100 ranks published in 2018)*	*Type of transaction*[5]	*Transaction value*[6]	*Status (at Oct 2018)*	*Sources*
Boeing (5) & Embraer (69) Commercial[7]	Joint Venture	$3.7B (Boeing's 80 percent interest)	Awaiting approval from Brazilian government.	Boeing 2018
Boeing (5) & Millennium Space Systems	Acquisition	Undisclosed	Complete 2018	Erwin 2018
Boeing (5) & KLX	Acquisition	$3.2B	Announced 2018	Eakin 2018
General Dynamics (6) & CSRA (39)[8]	Acquisition	$7B	Completed 2018	Fuller 2017
Harris (19) & L3 (12)	Merger	$15B	Announced 2018	Mattioli, Cimilluca and Cameron 2018b
Harris (19) & Exelis	Acquisition	$4.6B	Completed 2015	Heilman 2015
Northrop-Grumman (4) & Orbital ATK (30)	Acquisition	$8B	Approved 2018	Mattioli, Cimilluca and Cameron 2018b
Rockwell Collins (41) & B/E Aerospace	Acquisition	$6B	Completed 2017	Rockwell Collins 2017
Trans Digm & Esterline Technologies	Acquisition	$4B	Announced October 2018	Esterline 2018
United Technologies (11) & Rockwell Collins (41)	Acquisition	$23B	Approved 2018	Bartz 2018

100 firms. Other mergers, such as Boeing's effort to acquire KLX, have significant transaction values.

The large-scale transactions are not limited to large defense industry players. The merger of Trans Digm and Esterline, for example, detailed in Table 2.2, does not involve any major defense industry players. Both are active, however, in the defense market and the transaction value is certainly significant at $4 billion.

In addition to the large size and value of the mergers, the rapid pace of multiple mergers and acquisition activity involving the same companies defines this period. Rockwell Collins, for example, acquired B/E Aerospace in 2017 and then United Technologies acquired Rockwell Collins the following year. It may well be that the era of no large defense industrial mergers is over—at least for a while. So, while Big-Five mergers are still off limits, other consolidations are apparently now in play.

Boeing mergers and acquisition activity since 1993: an illustrative example

Between 1993 and 2017, Boeing made 69 acquisitions with most being relatively small. According to *Defense News* (2018), however, six were valued at more than $1 billion. In then-year dollars, the largest was McDonnell-Douglas in 1996 for over $13 billion, followed by Rockwell International Aerospace in 1996 for $3.8 billion. After the 1998 Lockheed-Martin, Northrop-Grumman merger disapproval, Boeing's larger-scale acquisitions were somewhat curtailed. In 2000, Boeing acquired Hughes Electronics Satellite for $2.1 billion and Jeppesen Sanderson for $3.1 billion. Boeing later acquired Aviali Inc. in 2006 for $2.1 billion, and Vought's South Carolina Facility in 2009 for $1 billion. Boeing's commercial divisions motivated some acquisitions such as the Vought facility; while the defense business primarily motivated others, such as McDonnell-Douglas (IMMA 2018). Many benefited both divisions.

More recent Boeing activity includes two rather large transactions, Embraer, a joint commercial venture, and KLX, an acquisition (see Table 2.2). However, Boeing's recent merger and acquisition activity generally consists of relatively small firms offering competencies deemed useful in Boeing's overall business.

Diversification of defense industrial firms

In the 1990s, conventional wisdom held that large defense firms would include more commercial business in their portfolio and the defense base would become more integrated into the industrial base. In particular, Lockheed-Martin would have only 25 percent of its revenue from defense by 2010 (Wayne 1998a). Lockheed-Martin's defense sales percentage of revenue, however, increased from 64 percent in 1998 to 93 percent in 2010 (*Defense News* Top 100, 2018).

If the defense industrial base was becoming more integrated into the general economy, then one would expect that concentration ratios[9] would decrease in the 21st century. Two serious studies of defense market concentration ratios indicate otherwise—one for the U.S. (Greenfield and Brady 2008) and one with an international focus (Dunne and Smith 2016). Greenfield and Brady (2008) consider the U.S., with a concentration ratio data from 1958–2006. Over the period 1990–2006, the top 100 concentration ratio has not changed very much (as the dotted trend line indicates). Dunne and Smith (2016) report similar results.

Source selections

With the main acquisition bureaucracies increasingly focused on the administrative process (Laird 2018), and the need for fielding new capabilities more quickly, the services will likely use special (but not temporary) methods to

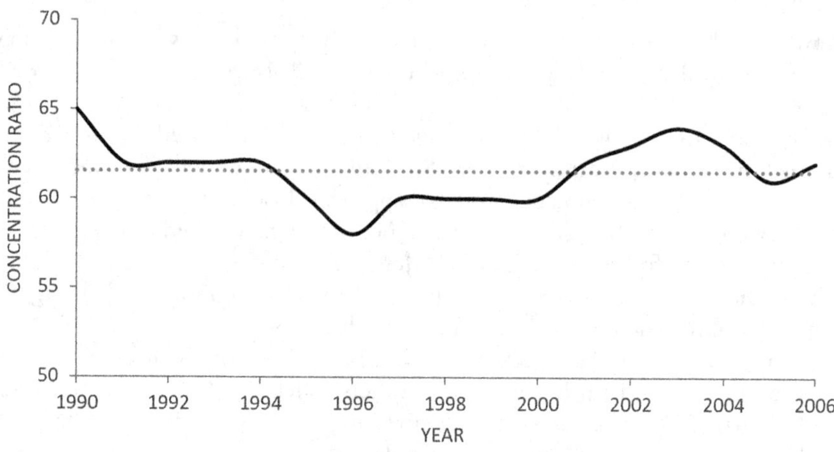

Figure 2.3 U.S. top 100 concentration ratio 1990–2006 (adapted from Greenfield and Brady 2008, esp. Figure 2.4 on p. 56).

answer the need for speed. Some have operated for a long time, such as the U.S. Air Force's Big Safari (1952). Others are relatively new such as the U.S. Air Force Rapid Capabilities Office, a U.S. Army counterpart, and the U.S. Office of the Secretary of Defense's (OSD's) Strategic Capabilities Office.

Needing to respond effectively to serious military threats, but doing it on the cheap, DoD is much less likely to press the technical envelope in new systems. Accordingly, industry can expect more emphasis on Lowest Price Technically Acceptable (LPTA) selection criteria. Among other things, this has involved fixed-cost development contracts and an associated transfer of risk from DoD to the winning bidder.

This was DoD's basic approach to the KC-X selection in 2011, which, among other things, meant greater risk borne by the winning team, Boeing. It is also DoD's approach in its more recent selections such as MQ-25 UAS, T-X trainer aircraft, and the replacement ICBM support helicopter (Insinna 2018b; Kendall 2018; Sanders 2018). LPTA source selections also seem to be more resistant to protests, which can significantly delay acquisition programs.

With industry bearing greater risks, only large, diversified, and solvent defense companies can afford to be primes for major acquisition programs. Boeing, for example, has lost $3.5 billion (and counting) on the KC-46 (Boeing's version of the KC-X) development contract (Insinna 2018b). Boeing, however, is sufficiently large and profitable that it can take such events in its stride. Boeing is about to acquire KLX, which involves more than the KC-

46 overrun, and Boeing states that such events have no major effect on current financial management (Reuters 2018).

Boeing is taking similar risks with its recent victories (MQ-25, T-X and UH-1 replacement) for many reasons. First, being both a civil and military company is deeply embedded in Boeing's corporate ethos. Second, its current leadership believes being in both markets has major advantages for increasing profitability and mitigating uncertainty (Thompson 2018). Third, it can use its lucrative commercial airliner business to cushion defense market risks in defense markets (and conversely). Finally, Boeing accepts significant short-term losses as good long-term investments, the returns being future business opportunities (Cameron 2018). At present, Boeing appears to be an early adapter to this apparently emerging defense market era. Other firms, however, have taken notice and apparently intend to change their corporate strategies accordingly (e.g., Lockheed-Martin; Warner 2018a). As a result, one can expect that the already-formidable barriers to entry into the U.S. markets will only increase. It is worth noting that major European airframe companies, Leonardo and Saab, were partners in successful 2018 Boeing proposals and were not primary players. This will likely continue under the Budget Control Act; major-programs with long-term, high-value, winner-take-all source selections will likely reinforce this tendency.

The U.S. government as a sovereign monopsonist

The U.S. government is essentially the only customer, a sovereign monopsonist, for U.S. defense firms and sales to other customers generally require its consent. Greenfield and Brady (2008, 63–66) nicely summarize the microeconomics of this situation. At the same time, the defense marketplace in the United States is subject to sovereign rules made through various legislation and regulations. The U.S. DoD defines what products are to be sold—through a requirements process and the government pays for product development.

Even though the government is a monopsonist, rule-maker, and product developer, its reign is not absolute.

First, the government is not a unitary whole. It consists of separate and sometimes contentious parts inherent in its separation-of-powers structure. Franck and Udis (2017), for example, concluded that the government sometimes functions more like a "quarrelsome committee" than the monopsonist in standard economic theory. This helps explain DoD's source selection attempts for the KC-X aerial tanker. At times, the rival bidders, Boeing and Airbus Group, exploited the committee's quarrels, which appeared to grant them veto power over the process (Franck, Lewis and Udis 2008, esp. 2, 36).

Second, there has been a long-term decrease in the number of first tier contractors. The consolidations called for in the 1993 "Last Supper" have facilitated this shift. A contemporary observer noted the following, "Power has shifted from the Defense Department to the defense contractors. The Pentagon has less leverage when there are fewer places to go" (Wayne 1998a).

Third, after program source selection, the power relations, referred to as "fundamental transformation" in Transaction Cost Economics literature (e.g., Williamson 1996), change significantly. The winning firm becomes the sole supplier of the product in question for products such as the F-35 and has something of a monopoly position. This results in bilateral monopoly consistent with the model summarized in Greenfield and Brady (2008, 66). The annual bargaining ritual between DoD and Lockheed Martin for F-35 prices serves as an example. As a *sovereign* monopsonist, however, DoD can dictate a price, as in Production Lot 9 (Clark 2016).

A fourth limit to government power is bid protests, which are intended to provide self-interested enforcement of competitive norms through challenges to procurement decisions. Bid protests, or the possibility, can increase defense firms' bargaining power relative to DoD.

Employment in defense industries

Estimating defense industry employment is difficult, if not impossible. Researchers making inquiries into defense employment and particularly those making international comparisons are likely to encounter a number of serious data issues. Most importantly, there is no clear and unambiguous standard definition of what constitutes defense industrial employment. The primary definition, for example, is those working in end-item producers. A secondary definition is suppliers to primary producers, with tertiary being "induced" employment. Hartley (2017, 32) notes varying definitions across nations as to whether it includes suppliers of end-item producers in employment estimates (33) or lower tiers of the supply chain (some are unaware of the connections with a defense firm) (30). Hartley (2017) also comments on the differing U.S. defense industrial employment estimates ranging from a low of 800,000 to a high of 3,500,000 (33). In this section, we consider recent estimates from the Aeronautical Industries Association (AIA), and Deloitte, a global consulting company actively involved in the defense sector.

AIA developed a methodology with IHS Markit, using some proprietary information; data came from sources such as the Census Bureau, Bureau of Labor Statistics, and from the American Association for the Advancement of Science. Table 2.3 depicts the AIA results.

Using Bureau of Labor Statistics data in addition to various corporate reports, Deloitte estimates direct employment for specified North American Industry Classification System (NAICS) codes. The next step is to estimate connections with other codes using the Bureau of Economic Analysis' Regional Input-Output Modeling System (2018). It is unclear how much non-defense employment, however, this particular method captures. Even

Table 2.3 Estimates of defense industry employment (AIA 2018, esp. 1; Deloitte 2016, esp. 5) (all numbers are in thousands)

Data source (year)	*Defense industrial*	*Commercial aerospace*	*Total direct*	*Indirect employment*	*Total employment*
AIA (2016)	355	488	843	1,587	2,430
Deloitte (2014)	845	331	1,233	2,909	4,141

though Deloitte makes a serious effort to do just that, it is questionable whether they obtain precise estimates.

While both AIA and Deloitte methodologies are credible, they involve methods and data not fully disclosed. It, therefore, seems likely that these estimates are impossible to replicate and verify. Furthermore, the reported results vary significantly, which likely results from the variance in the underlying methods.

Domestic and international operating environment

The industrial and regulatory policies of the Federal Government are key to understanding U.S. defense industrial affairs.

Federal Acquisition Regulation (FAR)

Defense industrial policy meets practice in the Federal Acquisition Regulation (FAR), jointly published by the General Services Administration (GSA), DoD, and the National Aeronautics and Space Administration (NASA). Its stated purpose is "use by executive agencies in acquiring goods and services" (GSA 2018). Further guidance includes the Procedures, Guidance and Information (PGI); the Defense Federal Acquisition Regulation Supplement (DFARS); and the services, Army (AFAR), Navy (NFAR), and Air Force, supplements the FAR (GSA 2018).

The entire FAR system seems intended to comprehensively prescribe permissible actions in the federal purchase of goods and services, to include circumstances in which deviations are authorized. The length and complexity of the FAR has resulted in difficulties dealing with commercial firms in the general economy. The summary report of a federal forum on managing the defense supplier base observed, "the challenge of operating in accordance with complex federal acquisition regulations discourage small and innovative businesses from partnering with the government," particularly in sectors such as bio technology (GAO 2006, 7).

Another effect seems to encourage defense acquisition through FAR "workarounds." Initiatives have included the Air Force Rapid Capabilities

Office, DoD's Strategic Capabilities Office (Franck, Hildebrandt and Udis 2016), and using Other Transactional Authorities (OTA). Existing legislation authorizes these for some contracts and provides "the opportunity to craft procurement arrangements specifically targeted to novel ideas and technologies, without having to shoehorn the process into the complex and often arcane world of traditional government contracting" (Radthorne 2008).

Bid protests

The Competition in Contracting Act (CICA) of 1984 is the legislative foundation for the DoD's bid protest system. The stated purpose of bid protests is to lessen the risk of fraud or error in federal government procurement and to increase competition. In addition, bid protests provide a decentralized network of self-interested overseers to ensure that the procurement process operates consistently with competitive norms and allows losing bidders to protest—thus encouraging prospective vendors to compete for defense business (Melese 2018, 669).

There are some reasons to believe the protest system works reasonably well. A recent RAND study (Arena et al. 2018, esp. xvii–xviii) reported that protests have the following characteristics:

- they are generally viewed favorably by contractors and unfavorably by government officials;
- they are relatively uncommon, but increasing in recent years;
- they are unlikely to be filed without having merit;
- they have a declining appeals rate if unsuccessful.

The Report recommended some adjustments to the current system, such as emphasizing the quality of debriefings to unsuccessful bidders.

A U.S. General Accountability Office (GAO) report on protests filed with the agency in FY2017 reported that 17 percent of protests were sustained, generally due to errors or inadequacies in the source selection. GAO also noted the affected agencies undertook corrective actions on their own for reasons they did not report to GAO to settle a significant fraction of protests (GAO 2018, 1–2).

KC-X: an illustrative example

With two mature contenders, Boeing and Northrup Grumman, the U.S. Air Force could have concluded the KC-X source selection quickly and cleanly. Instead, it was a prolonged process starting in 2001 when the first tanker recapitalization initiative, an effort to lease 100 tanker versions of the Boeing 767, began. The U.S. Air Force subsequently awarded a leasing contract for 100 KC-46s in May 2003. The program was subsequently suspended, however, due to misconduct by a major U.S. Air Force official (Cahlink 2004).

The Air Force restarted the KC-X selection process in 2007 with teams from Boeing and Northrup Grumman-EADS (NG-EADS) submitting proposals. On February 29, 2008, the Air Force awarded the contract to the NG- EADS KC-45 entry. Boeing protested the contract award on March 11, and the GAO ruled in favor of the Boeing protest on June 18, citing Air Force failure to follow its own selection rules.

Finally, in 2009, the Air Force released a draft Request for Proposals (RfP) with a fixed-price development contract for 179 aircraft with an emphasis on cost (Air Force Materiel Command 2009) and simplified criteria intended to preclude protests. Among many other things, this episode indicates that contract award protests can have a major delaying effect. (Boeing's KC-46 was finally selected in 2011.)

Other considerations in bid protests

Bid protests have disadvantages. Protests and their resolution can extract transaction costs associated with stop-work orders and delays in programs. Strategic bidders can threaten a protest, with the intent of influencing the competition itself or extracting some advantages from risk-averse or hurried program managers. Melese (2018, 670) called this practice "fedmail."

To avoid the risks of bid protests, program managers have included protest proofing approaches in the bid process. One approach is to simplify the selection criteria, perhaps to something like Lowest Price Technically Acceptable (LPTA), which is relatively easy to defend against a protest. The Air Force structured the final KC-X source selection (in 2011), for example, according to a variation of LPTA, as Figure 2.4 illustrates below. The first phase was an assessment base on 372 pass/fail tests. Bidders needed to pass all of them for technical acceptability. The next step involved Total Proposed Price (TPP) modified with analyses of operational effectiveness, life-cycle fuel expense, and associated construction costs, which lead to a total evaluated price (TEP). If the TEPs were very close (within 1 percent), then the Air Force used a tie-breaker, a scoring of nice-to-have features (Franck, Lewis and Udis 2008).

This resulted in a labor-intensive evaluation process requiring complete and careful documentation of all (372x2) passes competitors needed to be technically acceptable. As Under Secretary of Defense Lynn put it, "We think we've established a clear, a transparent and an open process. We think we've executed on that, and that will not yield grounds for protest" (OASD-[PA] 2011). This approach may well become a major DoD template.

Another possible form of protest-proofing is stating specifications which only one potential bidder can meet. In the case of the Presidential Helicopter program, the Air Force apparently ruled out the airframe that won the original competition in its revised specifications, and received only one bid in the second round.

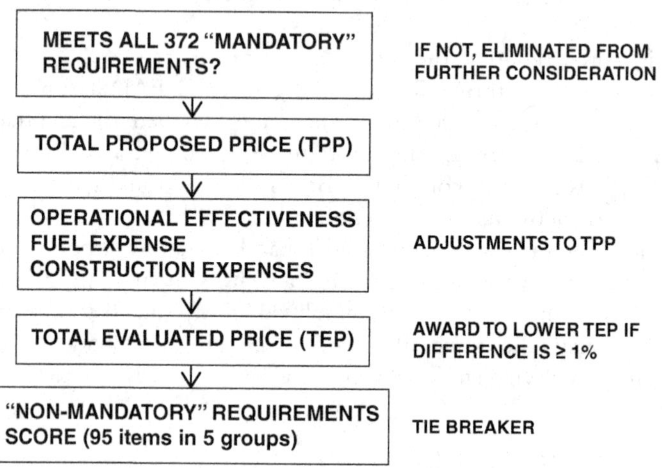

Figure 2.4 Overview of the (2011) KC-X source selection criteria adapted from a 2010 DoD briefing.

All things considered, a mixed picture emerges; Schwartz and Manuel (2015) characterize the major issues very well.

The Committee on Foreign Investment in the United States (CFIUS)

A number of countries, including the United States, are concerned about the national security implications of foreign investment in their economies. Accordingly, they have systems in place to monitor, and possibly forbid, foreign investment with significant national security risks (Masters and McBride 2018).

In 1975, the federal government instituted the Committee on Foreign Investment in the United States (CFIUS). The Committee, charged with vetting foreign firms' investments with national security interest, operates to implement provisions of the Defense Production Act of 1950 (DPA) (Treasury 2018a).

Over time, the CFIUS mission has become increasingly demanding and complicated and the U.S. Government's concerns grew that the overall performance system was insufficient (CFR 2018, 2). Accordingly, the U.S. Government tightened the CFIUS regulatory regime. In 1988, the Exon-Florio Amendment to the DPA "authoriz(ed) the President to suspend or prohibit foreign acquisitions, mergers, or takeovers of U.S. companies when there is credible evidence that a foreign controlling interest might threaten national security."

In 2007, the Foreign Investment & National Security Act of 2007 (FINSA) provided additional legislative guidance to the CFIUS. Among other things, FINSA adds members to the Committee and mandates increased senior-level participation and accountability (Treasury 2018b). In 2018, the United States enacted the Foreign Investment Risk Review Modernization Act motivated, at least in part, by fears of the People's Republic of China's "weaponized investment" (Masters and McBride 2018). While it is too early to gauge the effect of the modernized regime, CFIUS has rejected several investments under FINSA such as the $1.2 billion proposal in early 2018 between MoneyGram of Dallas, Texas and Ant FinancialMoney a Chinese company (Yoon-Hendricks 2018).

Export controls: the International Trade in Arms Regulations (ITAR)

Two examples illustrate impacts of U.S. export controls. First, a French view: "We are at the mercy of the Americans. Is that satisfactory? No. But we don't have any choice" (Florence Parly, French Minister of Defense). Second, a U.K. view: "I would encourage U.K. industry to design around the U.S. International Trafficking in Arms Regulations (ITAR) and produce ITAR-free items." (James Arbuthnot, Chairman of the UK House of Parliament Select Defense Committee).

As noted in the introduction, the United States is a major exporter of defense goods and services. Military sales, however, can have consequences beyond the transaction itself. Accordingly, the U.S. Government considers a variety of national security and other policy goals in controlling military exports (DDTC 2018). The legislative foundations for the export control regime include the Arms Export Control Act (AECA) of 1976 and the Export Administration Act (AEA) of 1979. While the U.S. Government authorizes three federal departments, State, Commerce, and Treasury, to issue export licenses, Defense, Homeland Security, and the Intelligence Community are also involved in operating the controls system. The State Department's ITAR and the Department of Commerce's Export Administration Regulations (EAR) contain the rules for administering the export control regime.

The U.S. Government applies the ITAR system, basically, to "U.S. persons" who wish to sell munitions or other goods and services with national security implications to "non-US persons." All economic entities in the United States which deal in goods and services with national security implications, including technical data, as defined by the U.S. Munitions list must register with the Directorate of Defense Trade Controls (DDTC 2018). Any U.S. entity wishing to sell such goods and services to a non-U.S. entity must obtain export authorizations—which include restrictions on retransfer and re-exports and continue no matter how many times sellers transfer the item. Retransfer authorizations are generally as time-consuming as the original authorization with violations resulting in major criminal or civil penalties. In addition, security concerns result in export restrictions for selling to countries that use a lot of non-nationals in their military, such as Qatar, UAE, and Oman.

Assessing the export control regime

The system of export control itself has a number of benefits. However, they consist mostly of bad outcomes avoided and are difficult to enumerate, much less quantify. There is some anecdotal information. The United States prevented Venezuela's export of F-16 fighter aircraft to Iran, a U.S. adversary (AP 2006). It also prevented sales of air transports to Venezuela in that same year.

For the private sector participants, the direct costs of export controls include processing authorization requests. Boeing, for example, had about 100 fulltime employees dealing with ITAR matters in the *commercial* Boeing 787 program (Gates 2006a).

Some costs associated with the export control system are also difficult to quantify. They include worsened relations with longstanding military allies like the United Kingdom and France as noted in the quotes above. Perhaps the most serious costs are distortions in behavior of both customers and producers. U.S. allies report that they are seriously considering reducing military relations, equipment purchases, and joint production with the United States in order to avoid the ITAR regime (Altmeyer 2018). Boeing resorted to some rather exotic and expensive measures to lessen 787 model exposure to ITAR (Gates 2006b).

Reform of the export control regime

"At some point people need to lift their eyes from their military concerns and look around at how the global market has changed" (Loren Thompson, quoted in Gates 2006a). For some time, some U.S. Government agencies, such as GAO, expressed dissatisfaction with the export control regime (2007 September). In August 2009, during the first term of the Obama Administration, the President directed a comprehensive review of the program. The review concluded that the current system was seriously, if not comprehensively, broken. The overarching recommendation was to refocus the effort to better protect really critical technologies, the "crown jewels" (White House 2010). The recommendations, with President Obama's approval, also focused on moving to a single control list, a single primary enforcement agency, a single licensing agency, and a single IT system.

Implementation measures included two executive orders (White House 2010, 2013). The legislation needed to fully implement the reforms, however, had, as of 2018, not yet appeared on the Congressional agenda. The Trump Administration has continued export reform, albeit with different policy priorities. A new Conventional Arms Transfer (CAT) policy was introduced (per NSPM-10, April 19, 2018). The practical effects have included a significant increase in approved requests for Foreign Military Sales (Mehta 2018a).[10]

The United States is the leading arms exporting nation and is also a major arms importer (17th, by SIPRI TIV metrics).[11] It is, however, difficult for foreign defense firms to enter the U.S. market. EADS' attempt to become a major supplier to DoD serves as an illuatrative example.[12] EADS was a diversified and profitable enterprise, with a robust portfolio of defense business, and a successful line of commercial air transports. In the first decade of this century, it had substantial resources (in many dimensions) to effect an entry to the U.S. defense market.[13]

EADS entered the 21st century with a mixed assessment of future profitability. While the Airbus division was a leading supplier of commercial airliners, European governments'sharing development risks was under increasing pressure. The airline market was also cyclical and not consistently profitable. A Five Forces (Porter 1980) assessment of the threats to EADS profits around 2003 would look something like Table 2.4.

EADS set out to increase its defense business by targeting the U.S. market. There were, however, significant barriers to entry. First were well-established U.S. incumbents with market knowledge, military technology, and political connections. Second was a strong Buy-American sentiment. Finally, U.S.-French relations were less than cordial at the time. There was, however, room for more firms in the market following the U.S. consolidations in the 1990s. Boeing, for example, was the only domestic source for a replacement U.S. Air Force aerial tanker (KC-X) with EADS as the most credible alternative.

To exploit the KC-X opportunity, and others, EADS made serious efforts to resemble a U.S. firm. It built, or acquired, production facilities within U.S. borders. It chose at least some locations to influence Congressional sentiment. EADS hired executives with local knowledge. It also partnered with Northrop-Grumman (NG)—a major aerospace firm with associated market knowledge and customer connections. The NG-EADS public relations campaign portrayed its KC-X proposal as an American system with

Table 2.4 A Five Forces assessment of EADS/Airbus, early 2000s

Force	*Threat to profits*	*Comments*
Internal Rivalry	Moderate to High	Excess capacity at low part of commercial cycle; less diversified than Boeing
Entry Threat	Low	Economies of scale; political relationships.
Substitutes & Complements	Low	Few substitutes for large air transports; many complements.
Supplier Power	Low	Many suppliers; few buyers
Buyer Power	Varies Widely	Buyers drive hard bargains at low points in airliner sales,..

Table 2.5 Assessment of EADS' entry prospects in the U.S. defense market, early 2000s

Market characteristics	*EADS situation*	*Comments*
Own Economies of Scale	Favorable	Large, established defense supplier.
Reputation, brand loyalty, protection of incumbents	Highly unfavorable	Testy US-French relations; strong *Buy-American* sentiment.
Access to distribution channels, raw materials, technology, good locations	Moderately Favorable	Well-established enterprise. Interoperability issues with US systems.
Marketing advantages for incumbents	Highly unfavorable	US firms' much better access to the government.
Expected retaliation	Favorable	Well-protected in Europe.

substantial U.S. content. In short, EADS chose to protect its profitability by diversifying into the U.S. defense market. Taken within the context of the Five Forces model, this can be construed as seeking a new, less risky market niche (Porter 1980, esp. Chapter 16). EADS' entry prospects at the time are summarized in Table 2.5.

EADS' well-conceived entry strategy did not quite succeed. The NG-EADS team won the first KC-X source selection in 2008, but Boeing successfully protested that result, and won the repeated competition in 2011. Currently, Airbus Group (formerly EADS) has only limited sales to the DoD. BAE is the only non-U.S. firm currently among DoD's largest suppliers, ranking 9th (Ausink 2018).

Future trends in the defense industry

DoD is facing multiple challenges in the future including changes in the security and financial environment, the need to accelerate technological innovation, and changes in the defense industrial environment and rising unit costs in real terms. The U.S. position as sole superpower will grow more tenuous as it has decidedly limited resources with which to deal with emerging peers (e.g., USNI Proceedings October Cover 2018) such as China and Russia.

DoD will face serious budget pressures in the 2020s and beyond, driven by competing needs for readiness, modernization, and force size, plus growth of entitlements. In 2028, the U.S. Government expects that entitlement outlays will account for about 15 percent of GDP and that interest on Federal debt will be at three percent. Discretionary expenditures would then be about six percent of GDP, about half of which they estimate for defense (Congressional Budget Office [CBO] 2018, esp. 66, 84).

In addition, spending by DoD on services contracts, ranging from clerical and administrative work to vehicle maintenance to research and development, amounted to just under $200 billion in 2011, more than 50 percent of total DoD contract spending and nearly a third of the entire DoD budget. From 2000 to 2011, DoD services contract spending increased at an average annual growth rate of 7.2 percent and DoD expects growth to continue changing the nature of defense industries the DoD uses. This could potentially curtail the funding available for modernization. Finally, defense firms increasingly depend on global financial markets, which act according to returns on investment, not on national security.

DoD provides financing for contracts through prompt payment of invoices and through a mechanism known as progress payments where firms invoice on work done before the product is delivered. Section 831 of the 2017 National Defense Authorization Act encourages DoD to use performance payments when compensating defense firms. As a result, and as part of a broader set of changes to the acquisition rules and to increase accountability, the Undersecretary of Defense for Acquisition and Sustainment hopes to change how companies receive their cash flow based on performance measurements among other things (Mehta 2018b). Complicating this initiative is that DoD incentives do not currently reflect tradeoffs of schedule, engineering, cost, and performance and do not consistently reward companies who control costs.

The U.S. Third Offset Strategy emphasizes developing asymmetric advantages by harnessing disruptive technologies and operational innovations to capitalize on strengths and exploit weaknesses. The innovations include hypersonic systems, deep augmented reality, quantum computing, learning systems, behavioral learning, human machine collaboration and combat teaming, network enabled cyber systems, big data, and biological sciences, such as biosensors, growing custom organisms, and bio inspired engineering.[14]

As an outreach to the tech community and to encourage the development of disruptive technologies, the Pentagon undertook several initiatives, such as creating an outpost in Silicon Valley, the Defense Innovative Unit-Experimental (DIU-X),[15] charged with accelerating commercial innovation for defense and subsequently replicated in both Boston and Austin; the Defense Digital Service, which allowed technologists into the Pentagon; and the Defense Innovation Board consisting of technology leaders providing independent advice and recommendations on innovative means to address future challenges.

While DoD officials are promoting closer ties to and encouraging cooperation with high tech companies and acquiring goods and services from a national as opposed to a defense industrial base (Wayne 1998a), there are some disincentives that may hinder this ambitious agenda. These include financial factors, such as a limitation on profit margins. As an example, Apple and Google generated margins of around 30 percent in 2014 while Lockheed Martin's profit margins for the F-35 fighter have not yet reached double digits. Another factor involves safeguarding intellectual property with policy trends diluting safeguards for companies' ownership of their intellectual property. In addition, managing the overwhelming regulatory burden and vagrancies of the political system may be off-putting for companies (Thompson

2015). While some companies such as Microsoft and Amazon have declared their willingness to sell technology to and cooperate with DoD, others such as Google have refused due to strong internal staff opposition steaming from moral objections to weaponizing their work (Sanger 2018; Shane, Metz and Wakabayashi 2018). Finally, as technology development continues to be more international, the U.S. export control regime needs to adjust to and recognize the global origin of innovation and the foreign ownership of firms (Berteau 2011).

There are no easy solutions to the future challenges facing the U.S. defense industry, but most importantly, the U.S. DoD can undertake some initiatives to better manage the uncertainty and send clear demand signals to industry. Primarily, the United States needs a better articulation of national security strategy and national military strategy with clearly defined courses of action. This will permit better prioritization of budget and force structure needs and guide reductions including managing the inherent tensions between readiness and modernization. If there is a focus on readiness, then in the case of budget reductions and as modernization programs are cut, all is not lost. DoD needs to ascertain which elements of the industrial base are most vulnerable and find a better way of supporting the base and including that information in budget decisions.

The matter of industrial base vulnerabilities and risks has the US Government's attention (e.g., DoD 2018; GAO 2018; White House 2018b). Key areas of concern include workforce qualifications (human capital), overall decline of the US industrial base, government procurement practices, and policies of defense industrial competitors (especially China). The extent to which these problems can be ameliorated remains to be seen. Among other things, there needs to be a clear articulation of ends so that the technological means have a purpose and are no longer technology for technology's sake.

Notes

1 *Defense News*, a news organization focused on global defense news (www.defensenews.com/), defines defense revenue as sales that support military, intelligence, and homeland security. *Defense News* has multiple sources for the revenue data: companies submit the data; data gleaned from analyst communities; contract data from defense ministries such as the case of Japan.

2 The top 10 defense companies on the *Defense News* list are the same as the top 10 on the SIPRI list. There are, however, some differences in ranking. These are driven by (a) Boeing's forming a "global services" division which includes some activities previously identified with defense work, and (b) technical issues with Almaz-Antey (Russia)—including ruble-dollar conversions and less detailed reporting of defense work.

3 See Tables 6.1 and 6.2. DOD Procurement outlays have risen pretty much in keeping with the Reagan and "other contingencies" increases, the procurement holiday of the 1990s, the post-2001 increases (with an interesting spike in 2008 corresponding to the "surge" in Iraq), and then downturn in procurement corresponding to the Budget Control Act of 2011.

4 The dinner became known as the "Last Supper."

5 For acquisitions, the first firm listed in the left column is acquiring the second firm.
6 Transaction values vary somewhat, depending on source and date. This could reflect the status of ongoing negotiations, but the open literature is not clear on this issue.
7 According to available reports, the joint venture involves Embraer's commercial operations. Those same reports, however, indicate the emerging strategic alliance will likely include manufacture and marketing of the Embraer KC-390 (a military transport-tanker).
8 All top 100 companies are identified with their 2018 *Defense News* ranking.
9 Investopedia (2018) calculates the concentration ratio as the sum of the market share percentage held by the largest specified number of firms in an industry. In this case, we consider the concentration ratio of the top 100 firms (measured in percentage of total defense purchases)
10 Other factors may also be involved, such as increases in international tensions in the MidEast and Pacific Rim.
11 SIPRI's primary unit of measurement is TIV (trend indicator value) in lieu of direct financial value. See www.sipri.org/databases/milex for further explanation.
12 EADS became "Airbus Group" in 2014. This discussion is a much-abridged version from Franck, Lewis and Udis (2008, 106–114) with updates.
13 In 2002, EADS was ranked 7th in revenue among defense firms, due mostly due to its market position in Europe (Defens News, Top 100).
14 This list is a compilation of predictions from various sources to include the popular press (e.g., Burnett 2018).
15 Based on private discussions there is some criticism leveled at DIU-X including its choice of locating in defense space making access difficult for companies and creating an environment that is not conducive to the exchange of ideas. DIU-X has gone through several distinct phases in its growth. It was initially staffed by defense acquisition staff with minimal expertise in a startup environment that needs to promote interactions with startups and innovative companies. DIU-X then went through a period when it recommended that startups must partner with major defense contractors to do business with DoD instead of facilitating direct interactions. Performance metrics were then set up for DIU-X that may nudged DIU-X contacts with industry in the wrong direction. These include measuring the number of engagements set up between DoD and startups and the money spent by DIU-X.

References

Aerospace Technology. 2014. "Boeing Agrees to Acquire ETS Aviation." May 26. www.aerospace-technology.com/news/newsboeing-agrees-to-acquire-ets-aviation-4276964/.

AIA (Aerospace Industries Association). 2018. "Facts and Figures: U.S. Aerospace and Defense." www.aia-aerospace.org/wp-content/uploads/2018/07/2018_-Annual-Report_Web.pdf.

Aitoro, Jill. 2018. "The List is Here: The Largest Defense Companies on the Globe, Revealed." *Defense News*, www.defensenews.com/top-100/2018/08/09/the-list-is-here-the-largest-defense-companies-on-the-globe-revealed/.

Altoro, Jill. 2016. "30 Years: A Norm Augustine Retrospective." *Defense News*, October 25. www.defensenews.com/30th-annivesary/2016/10/25/30-years-a-norm-augustine-retrospective/.

AP (Associated Press). 2006. "Venezuela Defense Minister Backs off Fighter Jet Sale to Iran." Accessed December 11. www.foxnews.com/story/venezuela-defense-minister-backs-off-fighter-jet-sale-to-iran.

Arena, Mark V., Brian Persons, et al. 2018. *Assessing Bid Protests of U.S. Department of Defense Procurements: Identifying Issues, Trends, and Drivers*, RAND Corporation, RR-2356-OSD, DOI: https://doi.org/10.7249/RR2356.

Ausink, Paul. 2018. "America's 15 Biggest Defense Contractors." *24/7 Wall St.*, July 2. https://247wallst.com/special-report/2018/07/02/americas-15-biggest-defense-contractors/.

BAE Systems. 2018, 2017. "Annual Report." www.annualreports.com/HostedData/AnnualReports/PDF/LSE_BA_2017.pdf.

Bartz, Diane. 2018. "U.S. Approves United Tech Purchase of Rockwell Collins." *Reuters*, October 1. www.reuters.com/article/us-utc-m-a-rockwell-collins/us-approves-united-tech-purchase-of-rockwell-collins-idUSKCN1MB3V1.

Baumol, William J., John C. Panzer, and Robert D. Willig. 1988. *Contestable Markets and the Theory of Industry Structure* (revised ed.). Jovanovich: Harcourt Brace.

Bender, Michael C., Gordon. Lubold, Kate. O'Keeffe, and Jeremy. Page. 2018. "U.S. Edges Toward New Cold-War Era with China." *The Wall Street Journal*, October 12. www.wsj.com/articles/u-s-edges-toward-new-cold-war-era-with-china-1539355839.

Berteau, David J. 2011. Creating a 21st Century Defense Industry: Statement Before the House Armed Services Committee Panel on Business Challenges Within the Defense Industry." Center for Strategic & International Studies. November 17. www.csis.org/analysis/creating-21st-century-defense-industry.

Bialos, Jeffrety., Christine E. Fisher, and Stuart L. Koehl. 2009. "Fortresses & Icebergs: The Evolution of the Transatlantic Defense Market and the Implications for U.S. National Security Policy." Washington, D.C.: Center for Transatlantic Relations. https://apps.dtic.mil/dtic/tr/fulltext/u2/a531716.pdf.

Bloomberg. 2013. "Company Overview of CPU Technology, Inc." Accessed December 11. www.bloomberg.com/research/stocks/private/snapshot.asp?privcapId=1475851.

Boeing. 2014a. "Boeing Acquires Government Software Development and Services Firm Ventura Solutions." June 27. http://boeing.mediaroom.com/2014-06-27-Boeing-Acquires-Government-Software-Development-and-Services-Firm-Ventura-Solutions.

Boeing. 2014b. "Boeing Acquiring AerData to Expand Airplane Maintenance and Leasing Records Management Capabilities." May 27. http://boeing.mediaroom.com/2014-05-27-Boeing-Acquiring-AerData-to-Expand-Airplane-Maintenance-and-Leasing-Records-Management-Capabilities.

Boeing. 2015a. "Boeing Acquires 2d3 Sensing to Enhance Imaging and Intelligence Services." April 10. http://boeing.mediaroom.com/2015-04-10-Boeing-Acquires-2d3-Sensing-to-Enhance-Imaging-and-Intelligence-Services.

Boeing. 2015b. "Boeing Acquires Leading Provider of Pilot Training Software." *PR Newswire*, October 12. www.prnewswire.com/news-releases/boeing-acquires-leading-provider-of-pilot-training-software-300157691.html.

Boeing. 2018. "Boeing and Embraer to Establish Strategic Aerospace Partnership to Accelerate Global Aerospace Growth." *PR Newswire*, July 5. www.prnewswire.com/news-releases/boeing-and-embraer-to-establish-strategic-aerospace-partnership-to-accelerate-global-aerospace-growth-300676467.html.

Brandenburger, Adam M., and Barry J. Nalebuff. 1996. *Co-opetition*. New York: Doubleday.

Bureau of Economic Analysis. 2018. *RIMS II: An Essential Tool for Regional Developers and Planners*. Washington, D.C.: BEA. www.bea.gov/sites/default/files/methodologies/RIMSII_User_Guide.pdf.

Burnett, Derek. 2018. *Inventing the Soldier of the Future*, Reader's Digest, September.

Cahlink, George. 2004. "Ex-Pentagon Procurement Executive Gets Jail Time." *Government Executive*, October 1. www.govexec.com/dailyfed/1004/100104g1.htm.

Cameron, Doug. 2018. "Defense Companies Battle Over Price." *The Wall Street Journal*, October 24. www.wsj.com/articles/defense-companies-battle-over-price-1540408079.

CBO (Congressional Budget Office). 2018. *The Budget and Economic Outlook: 2018 to 2028*. Washington, D.C.: CBO. www.cbo.gov/system/files?file=115th-congress-2017-2018/reports/53651-outlook.pdf.

Clark, Colin. 2016. "F-35: DoD Forces Lockheed to Accept Its Price for LRIP 9", *Breaking Defense*, https://breakingdefense.com/2016/11/jpo-to-lockheed-no-more-talkie-heres-lrip-9-deal/.

Corrin, Amber. 2015. "5 Policies that Shaped the Pentagon." *Federal Times*, December 14. www.federaltimes.com/management/2015/12/14/5-policies-that-shaped-the-pentagon/.

Davis, Thomas M. 2017. "Northrop-Orbital: A Sound Merger in Law and Policy." *Breaking Defense*, December 21. https://breakingdefense.com/2017/12/northrop-orbital-a-sound-idea-in-law-and-policy/.

DDTC (Department of State, Directorate of Defense Trade Controls). 2018. "Registration." www.pmddtc.state.gov/.

Defense News Top 100 List. 2018. *Defense News*. Accessed October 20. https://people.defensenews.com/top-100/.

Deloitte. 2016. "US Aerospace and Defense Labor Market Study." February. www2.deloitte.com/content/dam/Deloitte/us/Documents/manufacturing/us-ad-labor-market-study-2016.pdf.

DoD (U.S. Department of Defense). 2008. "Foreign Sources of Supply FY2007 Report." Annualreport of United States Defense Industrial Base Capabilities and Acquisitions of Defense Items and Components outside the United States. www.hsdl.org/?view&did=713562.

DoD 2018, (US Department of Defense), Fiscal Year. 2017. "Annual Industrial Capabilities Office of the Under Secretary of Defense for Acquisition and Sustainment Office of the Deputy Assistant Secretary of Defense for Manufacturing and Industrial Base Policy." www.dsiac.org/sites/default/files/reference-documents/ousd_asd_fy2017_annual_industrial_capabilities_report_20180412.pdf.

DoD Comptroller. 2017. "National Defense Budget Estimates for FY17 ('Green Book')." https://comptroller.defense.gov/Portals/45/Documents/defbudget/fy2017/FY17_Green_Book.pdf.

DoD Comptroller. 2018. "National Defense Budget Estimates for FY18 ('Green Book')." https://comptroller.defense.gov/Portals/45/Documents/defbudget/fy2018/FY18_Green_Book.pdf.

Dunne, Paul J., and Ron P. Smith. 2016. "The Evolution of Concentration in the Arms Market." *The Economics of Peace and Security Journal* 11 (1): 12–17. doi:10.15355/epsj.11.1.12.

Eakin, Britain. 2018. "Merger of United Technologies, Rockwell Collins Gets Go-Ahead." *Court House News*, October 2. www.courthousenews.com/merger-of-united-technologies-rockwell-collins-gets-go-ahead/.

"Economic Report of the President." 2000. Washington, D.C.: Government Publishing Office. www.gpo.gov/fdsys/pkg/ERP-2000/content-detail.html. Table B-1.

"Economic Report of the President." 2003. Washington, D.C.: Government Publishing Office. www.gpo.gov/fdsys/browse/collection.action?collectionCode=ERP&browsePath=2003&isCollapsed=true&leafLevelBrowse=false&isDocumentResults=true&ycord=0. Table B-1.

"Economic Report of the President." 2018. Washington, D.C.: Government Publishing Office. www.gpo.gov/fdsys/pkg/ERP-2018/content-detail.html. Table B-2.

Erwin, Sandra. 2018. "Boeing to Acquire Millennium Space Systems." *Space News*, August 16. https://spacenews.com/boeing-to-acquire-millennium-space-systems/.

Esterline. 2018. "TransDigm to Acquire Esterline Technologies in $4 Billion All Cash Transaction." October 10. www.esterline.com/Newsnbsp;PressCenter/EntryId/6232/TransDigm-to-Acquire-Esterline-Technologies-in-4-Billion-All-Cash-Transaction.aspx.

Etherington, Darrell. 2017. "Boeing to Acquire Aurora Flight Sciences in Bet on Autonomous Flight." *Tech Crunch*, October 5. https://techcrunch.com/2017/10/05/boeing-to-acquire-aurora-flight-sciences-in-bet-on-autonomous-flight/.

Feldman, Noah. 2012. *Cool War: The Future of Global Competition.* New York: Random House.

Fleurant, Aude., Alexandra. Kuimova, Nan. Tian, Pieter D. Wezeman, and Siemon T. Wezeman 2018. "The SIPRI Top 100 Arms-Producing and Military Services Companies, 2017." www.sipri.org/sites/default/files/2018-12/fs_arms_industry_2017_0.pdf.

Franck, Raymond, Gregory Hildebrandt, and Bernard Udis. 2016. *Toward Realistic Schedule Estimates*, Monterey, CA USA: Naval Postgraduate School, Proceedings of the 13th Annual Acquisition Research Symposium, Vol I, 95–116, Naval Postgraduate School.

Franck, Raymond, Ira Lewis, and Bernard Udis. 2008. "Echoes across the Pond: Understanding EU-US Defense Industrial Relationships. Acquisition Research Sponsored Report Series. NPS-AM-08-002." Monterey, CA: Naval Postgraduate School. https://my.nps.edu/documents/105938399/108621172/NPS-AM-08-002.pdf/6f8ad5b6-d617-44b5-b17f-074189c8c3d5.

Franck, Raymond and Bernard Udis. 2017. "Quarrelsome committees in US defense acquisition: the KC-X case", *Defence and Peace Economics*, 28:3, 344–366, DOI: 10.1080/10242694.2015.1073488.

Fuller, Sarah L. 2017. "10 Significant Aviation Investments, Mergers, Acquisitions in 2017." *Aviation Today*, December 19. www.aviationtoday.com/2017/12/19/5-significant-2017-investments-mergers-acquisitions/.

GAO (Government Accountability Office). 2018c. "Implementation of Exon-Florio and Related Amendments. December. GAO/NSIAD 96-12." Washington, D.C.: GAO. www.gao.gov/assets/230/221994.pdf.

GAO (US Governmental Accountability Office). 2018. "Defense Industrial Base: Integrating Existing Supplier Data and Addressing Workforce Challenges Could Improve Risk Analysis, Report to the Chairman of the Committee on Armed Services." House of Representatives, GAO-18-435, www.gao.gov/assets/700/692458.pdf.

GAO (US Government Accountability Office). 2006. "Managing the Supplier Base in the 21st Century: Highlights of a GAO Forum, GAO 533-SP", www.gao.gov/new.items/d06533sp.pdf.

Gartzke, Ulf. 2010. "The Boeing/McDonnell Douglas and EADS Mergers: Ethnocentric vs. Regiocentric Consolidation in the Aerospace and Defence Industry and the Implications for International Relations." London: London School of Economics and Political Science. http://etheses.lse.ac.uk/266/1/Gartzke_Boeing%20-%20McDonnell%20Douglas%20and%20EADS%20Mergers.pdf.

Gates, Dominic. 2006a. "Separation Anxiety: The Wall Between Military and Commercial Technology." *Seattle Times*, January 22. http://old.seattletimes.com/html/businesstechnology/2002754224_boeingitar22.html.

Gates, Dominic. 2006b. "How B-2 Data Wound Up in 787 Program." *Seattle Times*, January 22. http://old.seattletimes.com/html/businesstechnology/2002754229_boeingitarsidebar22.html.

Government Accountability Office (GAO). 2007. "Clarification and More Comprehensive Oversight of Export Exemptions Certified by DoD Are Needed. September. GAO 07-1103." Washington, D.C.: GAO. www.gao.gov/assets/270/268269.pdf.

Greenfield, Victoria., and Ryan R. Brady. 2008. "The Changing Shape of the Defense Industryand Implications for Defense Acquisitions and Policy." Proceedings of the 5th Annual Research Symposium, Monterey, CA: Naval Postgraduate School. www.dtic.mil/dtic/tr/fulltext/u2/a493916.pdf.

Gross, Charles. 2015. "Boeing Acquires 2d3 Sensing for $25M." *Yahoo Finance*, April 10. https://finance.yahoo.com/news/boeing-acquires-2d3-sensing-25m-090401382.html.

GSA (General Services Administration). 2018. Federal Acquisition Regulation (FAR), www.gsa.gov/policy-regulations/regulations/federal-acquisition-regulation-far.

Harrison, Todd., and Seamus P. Daniels. 2018. "Analysis of the FY2019 Defense Budget." Washington, D.C.: Center for Strategic and International Studies. www.csis.org/analysis/analysis-fy-2019-defense-budget.

Heilman, Wayne. 2015. "Merger Creates Third Largest Defense Contractor in Colorado Springs." February 7. https://gazette.com/business/merger-creates-third-largest-defense-contractor-in-colorado-springs/article_c6b0b881-d6f0-5f49-ba59-690d22cba4a7.html.

IMMA (Institute for Mergers and Acquisitions). 2018. "M&A Boeing: Top 10 Deals". https://imaa-institute.org/project/boeing/.

Insinna, Valerie. 2018a. "US Air Force awards $9B Contract to Boeing for Next Training Jet." *Defense News*, September 27. www.defensenews.com/breaking-news/2018/09/27/reuters-air-force-awards-9b-contract-to-boeing-for-next-training-jet/.

Insinna, Valerie. 2018b. "Boeing Adds $179M in Cost Overruns to KC-46 Aircraft as Delivery Draws Near." *Defense News*, October 24. www.defensenews.com/industry/2018/10/24/boeing-adds-another-179m-in-cost-overruns-to-kc-46-as-delivery-draws-near/.

Investopedia. 2018. "Concentration Ratio." October 14. www.investopedia.com/terms/c/concentrationratio.asp.

Jane's HIS. 2018b. "Defense Industry." Accessed October 19. https://ihsmarkit.com/products/janes-world-defense-industry.html.

Jane's IHS. 2018a. "Defense Budgets." Accessed October 19. https://ihsmarkit.com/products/janes-defence-budgets.html.

Kendall, Frank. 2018. "Boeing and the Navy Place A Big, Risky Bet on the MQ-25 Unmanned Air Vehicle." *Forbes*, September 12. www.forbes.com/sites/frankkendall/2018/09/12/boeing-and-the-navy-place-a-big-and-risky-bet-on-the-mq-25-unmanned-air-vehicle/#72abb2024bbd.

Laird, Robbin. 2018. "A Visit to EOS in Australia: A Payload Company Innovates for 21st Century Operations." *Second Line of Defense* (SLDInfo.com), August 20. https://sldinfo.com/2018/08/a-visit-to-eos-in-australia-a-payload-company-innovates-for-21st-century-operations/.

Masters, Jonathan, and James McBride. 2018. *Foreign Investment and U.S. National Security*. Washington, D.C.: Council on Foreign Relations. www.cfr.org/backgrounder/foreign-investment-and-us-national-security.

Mattioli, Dana., Dana. Cimilluca, and Doug. Cameron. 2018a. "Boeing Nears Deal to Buy Aerospace-Parts Specialist KLX." *The Wall Street Journal*, April 27. www.wsj.com/articles/boeing-nears-deal-to-buy-aerospace-parts-specialist-klx-1524850049.

Mattioli, Dana., Dana. Cimilluca, and Doug. Cameron. 2018b. "Harris, L3 Technologies Announce Merger Plan." *The Wall Street Journal*, October 15. www.wsj.com/articles/military-communications-firms-harris-l3-near-deal-to-combine-1539443888.

Mehta, Aaron. 2017. "US Clears Record Totals for Arms Sales in FY12." *Defense News*, September 13. www.defensenews.com/pentagon/2017/09/13/us-clears-record-total-for-arms-sales-in-fy17/.

Mehta, Aaron. 2018a. "State Department Cleared $70 Billion in Foreign Military Sales Requests for FY18." *Defense News*, October 10. www.defensenews.com/global/2018/10/05/state-department-cleared-70-billion-in-foreign-military-sales-requests-for-fy18/.

Mehta, Aaron. 2018b. "Facing Industry Pressures, Pentagon Backs Off Contract Payment Changes." *Defense News*, October 2. www.defensenews.com/pentagon/2018/10/02/facing-industry-pressure-pentagon-backs-off-contract-payment-changes/.

Melese, Francois. 2018. *Cost-Benefit Analysis of Bid Protests: A Representative Bidder Model*, Monterey, CA, USA: Naval Postgraduate School, SYM-AM–18–072.

OASD [PA] (Office of the Assistant Secretary of Defense (Public Affairs). 2011. News briefing with Deputy Secretary Lynn and DOD senior leaders to announce the Air Force KC-46A tanker contract award. www.defense.gov/Transcripts/Transcript.aspx?TranscriptID=4776.

Oden, Michael. 1999. "Cashing In, Cashing Out, and Converting: Restructuring of the Defence Industrial Base in the 1990s." In: *Arming the Future: A Defence Industry for the 21st Century*, edited by Ann R. Markusen, and Sean S. Costigan, 74–105. New York: Council on Foreign Relations Press.

Pendleton, John H. 2018. *Air Force Readiness: Actions Needed to Rebuild Readiness and Prepare for the Future (testimony)*. Government Accountability Office 19-120T. www.gao.gov/assets/700/694923.pdf.

PMA (Department of State, Bureau of Political-Military Affairs). 2018. *U.S. Arms Sales and Defense Trade. Fact Sheet*. www.state.gov/t/pm/rls/fs/2018/280506.htm.

Porter, Michael E. 1980. *Competitive Strategy: Techniques for Analyzing Industries and Competitors*. New York: Free Press.

Radthorne, Daniel. 2008. An Overview of "Other Transaction Authority," Procurement Playbook, www.procurementplaybook.com/2018/02/other-transaction-authority-an-overview/.

Reuters. 2018. "Boeing to Buy Aerospace Parts Maker KLX for About $3.2 Billion in Cash." May 1. www.cnbc.com/2018/05/01/boeing-to-buy-aerospace-parts-maker-klx-for-about-3-point-2-billion-in-cash.html.

Ricks, Thomas E., and Jeff. Cole. 1998. "How Lockheed and Northrop Had Their Merger Shot Down." *The Wall Street Journal*, June 19. www.wsj.com/articles/SB898139629613188500.

Rockwell Collins. 2017. "Rockwell Collins Completes Acquisition of B/E Aerospace." April 13. www.rockwellcollins.com/Data/News/2017-Cal-Yr/RC/FY17RCNR25-BEAV-Close.aspx.

Sanders, Chris. 2018. "Boeing Wins First Leg of $2.4 Billion Helicopter Deal from U.S. Air Force." *Reuters*, September 24. https://uk.reuters.com/article/us-boeing-pentagon/boeing-wins-first-leg-of-2-4-billion-helicopter-deal-from-u-s-air-force-idUKKCN1M42JC.

Sanger, David E. 2018. "Microsoft Says it Will Sell Pentagon Artificial Intelligence and Other Advanced Technology." *The New York Times*, October 26. www.nytimes.com/2018/10/26/us/politics/ai-microsoft-pentagon.html?action=click&module=Top%20Stories&pgtype=Homepage.

Schwartz, Mose and Kate M. Manuel. 2015. *GAO Bid Protests: Trends and Analysis*, Washington, DC: Congressional Research Service, R40227.

Shane, Scott., Cade. Metz, and Daisuke. Wakabayashi, 2018. "How a Pentagon Contract Became an Identity Crisis for Google." www.nytimes.com/2018/05/30/technology/google-project-maven-pentagon.html.

SIPRI (Stockholm International Peace Research Institute). 2018a. "Military Expenditure Database." Accessed October 20. www.sipri.org/databases/milex.

SIPRI (Stockholm International Peace Research Institute). 2018b. "Arms Industry Database." Accessed October 20. www.sipri.org/databases/armsindustry.

Stynes, Tess., and Doug. Cameron. 2016. "Boeing Agrees to Acquire Liquid Robotics." *The Wall Street Journal*, December 6. www.wsj.com/articles/boeing-agrees-to-acquire-liquid-robotics-1481058792.

Thompson, Loren. 2015. "Five Reasons Why Silicon Valley Won't Partner With the Pentagon." *Forbes*, April 27. www.forbes.com/sites/lorenthompson/2015/04/27/five-reasons-why-silicon-valley-wont-partner-with-the-pentagon/#7f626c204de9.

Thompson, Loren. 2018. "Boeing CEO Dennis Muilenburg Has A Strategy That Will Work in Both Good Times and Bad." *Forbes*, April 26. www.forbes.com/sites/lorenthompson/2018/04/26/boeing-ceo-dennis-muilenburg-has-a-strategy-that-will-work-in-both-good-times-and-bad-times/#67232ee74a7b.

Tirpak, John A. 1998. "The Distillation of the Defense Industry." *Air Force Magazine*, July. www.airforcemag.com/MagazineArchive/Pages/1998/July%201998/0798industry.aspx.

Treasury, U.S. Department. 2018a. "The Committee on Foreign Investment in the United States (CFIUS)." Accessed October 19. https://home.treasury.gov/policy-issues/international/the-committee-on-foreign-investment-in-the-united-states-cfius.

Treasury, U.S. Department. 2018b. "CFIUS Reform: The Foreign Investment & National Security Act of 2007 (FINSA, summary)." Accessed October 19. www.treasury.gov/resource-center/international/foreign-investment/Documents/Summary-FINSA.pdf.

Treasury, U.S. Department. 2018c. "Summary of the Foreign Investment Risk Review Modernization Act of 2018." www.treasury.gov/resource-center/international/Documents/Summary-of-FIRRMA.pdf.

Tu, Michael. 2016. *Reexport and Retransfer Controls*. Taipei, Tawian: EXBS STCs Roundtable. www.trade.gov.tw/App_Ashx/File.ashx.

Warner, Ben. 2018a. "Lockheed: DoD Focused on Lowest Price in Recent Competitions; May Affect LM Participation in Future Bids." *USNI News*, October 23. https://news.usni.org/2018/10/23/37506.

Warner, Ben. 2018b. "Boeing Lands Contracts with Upfront R&D Investing." *USNI News*, October 25. https://news.usni.org/2018/10/25/boeing-lands-contracts-with-upfront-rd-investing.

Wayne, Leslie. 1998a. "The Shrinking Military Complex; After the Cold War, the Pentagon Is Just Another Customer." *The New York Times*, February 27. www.nytimes.com/1998/02/27/business/shrinking-military-complex-after-cold-war-pentagon-just-another-customer.html.

Wayne, Leslie. 1998b. "Lockheed Cancels Northrop Merger, Citing U.S. Stand." *The New York Times*, July17. www.nytimes.com/1998/07/17/business/lockheed-cancels-northrop-merger-citing-us-stand.html.

Wayne, Leslie., 2006. "British Arms Merchant with Passport to the Pentagon." *New York Times*, August 16, C1. www.nytimes.com/2006/08/16/business/worldbusiness/16defense.html.

White House. 2010. *Fact Sheet on the President's Export Control Reform Initiative*. April 20. www.whitehouse.gov/the-press-office/fact-sheet-presidentsexport-control-reform-initiative.

White House. 2013. *Executive Order 13637*. Administration of Reformed Export Controls. https://en.wikisource.org/wiki/Executive_Order_13637.

White House. 2018a. "National Security Presidential Memorandum Regarding U.S. Conventional Arms Transfer Policy (NSPM-10)." www.whitehouse.gov/presidential-actions/national-security-presidential-memorandum-regarding-u-s-conventional-arms-transfer-policy/.

White House. 2018b. "Assessing and Strengthening the Manufacturing and Defense Industrial Base and Supply Chain Resiliency of the United States, Report to President Donald J. Trump by the Interagency Task Force in Fulfillment of Executive Order 13806." https://media.defense.gov/2018/Oct/05/2002048904/-1/-1/1/ASSESSING-AND-STRENGTHENING-THE-MANUFACTURING-AND%20DEFENSE-INDUSTRIAL-BASE-AND-SUPPLY-CHAIN-RESILIENCY.PDF.

Williamson, Oliver E. 1996. *The Mechanisms of Governance*. New York: Oxford University Press.

Yoon-Hendricks, Alexandra. 2018. "Congress Stengthens Reviews of Chinese and Other Foreign Investments." *The New York Times*, August 1. www.nytimes.com/2018/08/01/business/foreign-investment-united-states.html.

3 China's defence industry

Sarah Kirchberger and Johannes Mohr

1. Introduction

In the face of toughening strategic competition between the People's Republic of China (PRC) and the United States, Beijing has begun to call for the creation of a world-class military. To achieve this, the Chinese Communist Party (CCP) pursues an aggressive strategy of technological innovation promotion that aims to put China into the top tier of innovative countries worldwide by 2035. By 2049, the centenary of the PRC's founding, China plans to be the world's most technologically advanced country (Nurkin, 2015).

In order to match American military power and defence-industrial innovation capacity, China's defence industry must be able to: a) develop sophisticated weapon systems and subsystems that enable net-centric warfare operations; b) enable the build-up of a complete nuclear triad, including a credible and survivable seaborne deterrent; c) deliver global power-projection capabilities, presumably including several aircraft carrier battle groups; and d) develop and maintain the necessary space and cyber capabilities to enable and support such missions. Efforts to achieve all these capabilities are currently ongoing.

China has already demonstrated technological mastery in some advanced military-technological niche fields, such as ballistic missiles and unmanned systems, and is poised to take a leading role in a few cutting-edge areas such as quantum computing and AI. Deficiencies continue to exist in several critical fields, especially aircraft engines, naval propulsion systems and defence electronics. Furthermore, despite attempts to enhance the level of civil-military integration at least since 2003, China's arms industries overwhelmingly remain state-owned, centrally controlled, and monopolistic, and as a result, the defence sector is characterized by over-bureaucratization, overcapacities, misallocation of resources, cost overruns, quality control problems, and pervasive corruption (Hartley, 2017, 99–100).

1.1 Background statistics on Chinese defence spending (1980–2018)

1.1.1 Chinese defence spending data

There is an ongoing debate on the extent to which defence expenditures are underreported in the official Chinese budget, and various Western research institutions produce diverging estimations of China's actual defence spending (CSIS, 2018). The PRC is often criticized for not including officer pensions, nuclear and strategic missile programme costs, its military police budget and other items such as locally funded security activities in the official budget, but such underreporting is not actually uncommon (cf. Liff and Erickson, 2013, 18–19).[1]

The PRC's official 2016 defence budget totalled to approximately RMB 976 billion (US$144 billion: *China Statistical Yearbook*, 2017), but a SIPRI estimate placed the actual budget in the region of RMB 1.436 trillion (US$228 billion: SIPRI Military Expenditure Database, 2018), while the US Department of Defense's estimate lies between those figures at some RMB 1.240 trillion (US$180 billion: Department of Defense, 2017, 66).

1.1.2 Development of defence spending since 1979

During the first decade of the Reform and Opening Up Era (1979–1989), the modernization of the People's Liberation Army (PLA) was postponed in the face of more pressing priorities (Joffe, 1996, 17). The official defence budget stagnated during this time and rose only slightly from RMB 19.4 billion in 1980 to 21.8 billion in 1988. This changed with the end of the Cold War. In contrast to Western countries that availed themselves of a "peace dividend" in the face of a reduced military threat, China's leaders confronted an intensified threat level due to: a) the collapse of communist states during 1989–1991; b) the adverse Western reaction to the CCP's violent suppression of unarmed protesters in June 1989; c) the 1991 Gulf War against Iraq, which demonstrated the superiority of American precision-guided munition; and d) various "humiliating" experiences, such as the 1995/96 Taiwan Missile Crisis that saw US aircraft carriers operating in the Taiwan Strait, or the 1999 US bombing of the Chinese embassy in Belgrade (cf. Raska, 2014, 32).

Military spending accordingly increased throughout the 1990s. The need for additional funds was exacerbated by inflation that threatened to diminish the buying power of the military, forcing Beijing to contemplate the downsizing of the PLA or the closing or conversion of many defence enterprises (Ding, 1996, 89). Instead, China's rulers opted for a massive injection of cash. Following a period of steady growth, China's official defence spending skyrocketed after 2000 and rose from RMB 120 billion to ca. RMB 908 billion in 2015 (cf. Figure 3.1).

Double-digit growth rates over a course of two decades seem to indicate a massive expansion of military spending, but nominal figures do not

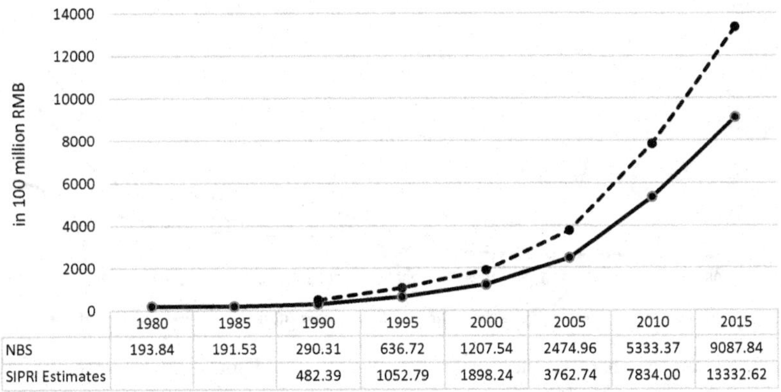

	1980	1985	1990	1995	2000	2005	2010	2015
NBS	193.84	191.53	290.31	636.72	1207.54	2474.96	5333.37	9087.84
SIPRI Estimates			482.39	1052.79	1898.24	3762.74	7834.00	13332.62

Figure 3.1 China's nominal defence budget, 1980–2015: comparison of official figures and SIPRI estimates.

Source: Graph created with data compiled from *China Statistical Yearbook* (various years) and SIPRI Military Expenditure Database.

accurately portray inflation effects. The high nominal growth during the early 1990s (1990: 9%, 1991: 12%, 1992: 14%, 1993: 15%) did not yield any actual increase of the PLA's purchasing power. The factual stagnation of the budget during this time caused the PLA to start its own economic activities in order to bolster the official budget with profits from PLA-run enterprises. Joffe (1996, 17; 20) estimates that PLA-operated companies increased the official budget by about 20%. If inflation-adjusted real figures are used, the defence budget growth rate actually exceeded 10% only during 2000–2009 (Liff and Erickson, 2013, 4–5).

According to the 2008 *China Statistical Yearbook*, data collected before 2007 and afterwards are not comparable due to changes in the way data is collected and analyzed. Note also that until 2007, different expenditures and items were grouped together or split apart.

In comparison with other state expenditures, the PRC's military spending surprisingly does not stand out as a clear priority. The growth rate of other budgetary items such as education or social security has far outpaced the defence budget (cf. Figure 3.2). Furthermore, SIPRI data shows a significant drop of military spending as a percentage of overall government expenditures during that timeframe. While the PRC had devoted about 13.4% of total government expenditures to the military in 1989, and even 17% in 1992, the defence budget's share afterwards decreased to a mere 6.1% of government spending in 2017. Despite high GDP growth rates throughout this period, military spending as a share of total government expenditure has therefore not risen, but instead, it declined sharply in comparison with other Chinese spending priorities.

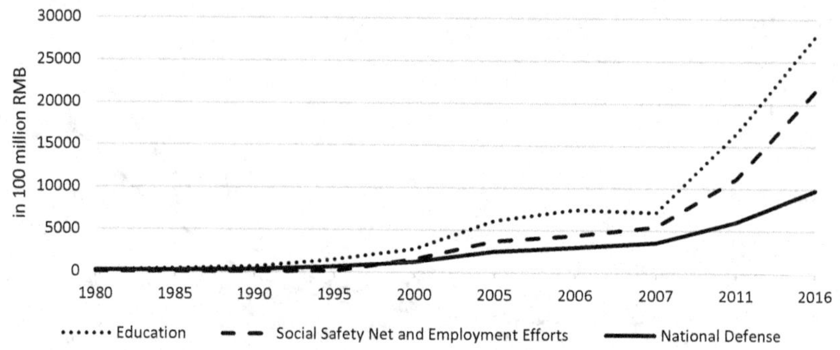

Figure 3.2 Comparison of Chinese defence, education, and social safety net expenditures growth (1980–2006).

Source: Data compiled from *China Statistical Yearbook*, various years.

According to SIPRI estimates, China's defence spending as a GDP percentage has constantly hovered around the 2% mark since 1989, dropping from 2.5% in 1989 to 1.9% in 2017. This spending level corresponds with the 2% of GDP military spending recommendation of NATO to its member countries (McTague, 2014). Due to the vast size of China's national economy, even a smaller GDP share nonetheless yields huge nominal budgets. As of 2018, China's nominal defence budget is second only to the US military expenditure, and far surpasses the aggregate EU, Indian, Russian, and Japanese defence budgets.

1.2 Share of military expenditure spent on equipment

Military spending is an input variable and as such not a useful measure of output in terms of actual military capability (Stålenheim and Surry, 2006, 2). In most countries, between 10 and 30% of the annual budget is available for equipment purchases – most often about 15%. By far the greater part of military expenditures is typically spent on personnel and training costs and for the maintenance of infrastructures and facilities, such as military bases (Hartley, 2017, 6; 24). For China, military commentator A. Pinkov has estimated that the share spent on equipment purchases might be as high as 30% (cf. Ping, 2010, 21). Official Chinese media have reported that about one-third of the defence budget is spent on procurement and defence research and development (R&D) combined (Wolf et al., 2011, 86). This is much more than the some 20% that the European Union (EU) states on average spend on procurement (EDA, 2018).

Bitzinger (2017, 67) estimates that in nominal terms, China spent about US$50 billion on equipment procurement in 2015 (up from about US$3.1 billion in 1997), of which about US$10 billion (or one-fifth) might have been dedicated to R&D. This indicates that China's procurement spending is likely the second highest, and its defence R&D spending the second or third-highest in the world, behind the US. Such large sums allow for the procurement of extremely costly weapon systems that are financially out of reach for most other regional militaries, e.g. nuclear-powered submarines, aircraft carriers, and stealth fighters. They also allow China to invest heavily into new R&D projects of potentially "game-changing" new technologies, such as quantum computing, energy weapons, artificial intelligence, robotics, and unmanned systems and to massively bolster its space and cyber capabilities.

1.3 Defence equipment imports and export figures

1.3.1 Chinese arms imports

Due to the limited ability of domestic defence industries to provide all necessary arms, China has consistently been one of the world's largest importers of military technologies. Since the Western arms embargo of 1989, these imports were chiefly sourced from post-Soviet countries Russia and Ukraine, and until 2005, from Israel (see Chapters 4, 13 and 18).

China was the world's largest arms importer during the early 2000s, but its total imports decreased by 11% during 2012–2016. China fell to fourth place during that timeframe, with Russia its most important supplier (Raska, 2017). *IHS Jane's* estimated in 2011 that the PRC imported defence products worth US$1.5 to 3 billion annually from Russia during 2000–2011, and that Chinese orders accounted for some 20% of all Russian arms exports during 1997–2007 (Anderson, 2011). Ukrainian imports were at a much lower average level of a few hundred million US$ per year, while imports from Israel, another major supplier until US pressure moved Israel to cut arms sales to China in 2005, have in recent years been mostly dual-use items in the AI, cyber security, and unmanned systems fields (Grevatt, 2011a, 2018).

The fact that China's arms imports dropped by about 58% during the period 2007 to 2011, when at the same time it began to become more active in the arms export market seemed to indicate a growing self-sufficiency of Chinese arms industries and a lessening dependence on Russian (and Ukrainian) support (cf. Figure 3.3; Lague and Zhu, 2012).

Whether that trend will be reversed by a recent large Chinese import order of 24 Russian *Su-35* fighter planes and six battalions of the *S-400* air-defence system remains to be seen (Schwartz, 2017).

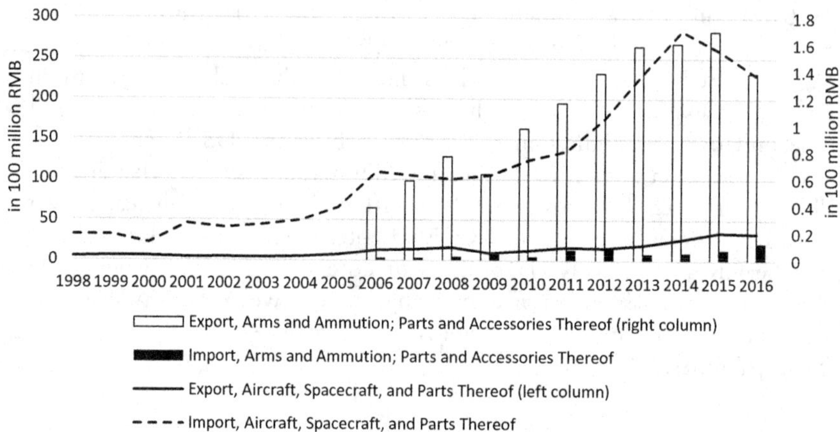

Figure 3.3 Chinese arms exports and imports, 1998–2016 (official Chinese figures).

Source: Data compiled from China Trade and External Economic Statistical Yearbook, various years.

1.3.2 Chinese arms exports

The total volume of Chinese arms exports from the beginning of the Reform Era until the end of the Cold War (1979–1991) was estimated at US$21 billion (Joffe, 1996, 22). The United Nations Register of Conventional Arms database (UNROCA) only contains information supplied by China on its arms exports until the mid-1990s. Between 1996 and 2005, China did not actively report any data. Since 2006, China again began to notify UNROCA of its exports, which then markedly increased (cf. Figure 3.3). According to SIPRI, the volume of Chinese arms exports grew by 211% between 1998 and 2017 (cf. Nouwens and Béraud-Sudreau, 2018). Between 2001 and 2011, Chinese exports increased by 95%, and between 2012 and 2016, by 74% (Lague and Zhu, 2012; Raska, 2017). During the latter timeframe, China's share of global arms exports grew from 3.8 to 6.2%, with China supplying defence products to a total of 44 countries.

UNROCA data shows that until 2000, China mostly exported arms to South and Southeast Asian countries (Pakistan, Sri Lanka, Bangladesh, Thailand, Myanmar, and Laos) and later also to some African countries (Cameroon, Tanzania, Sudan, Chad). The Chinese ordnance conglomerate NORINCO was the largest individual exporter among the Chinese defence groups (Sun, 2018). Pakistan continued to take the lion's share of Chinese exports, and together with Bangladesh and Myanmar accounted for more than 60% of major arms sales, while 22% of Chinese exports went to African countries (Raska, 2017).

2 Definition of the Chinese defence industry

2.1 Historical development of China's arms-industrial base

2.1.1 From Soviet support to Sino-Soviet split (1949–1978)

During the 1950s, the newly founded PRC was almost wholly dependent upon Soviet military aid. China imported weapon systems, blueprints, production facilities, and teaching materials in a wholesale manner, and with the help of many Soviet advisors, effectively transplanted the Soviet Union's military and military-industrial culture to China (Li, 2009, 122–25). Following the Sino-Soviet Split, China resorted to reverse-engineering of previously imported, vintage Soviet systems, and embarked on a road of indigenous innovation in a few strategically important fields such as nuclear weapons and nuclear propulsion systems (Bussert and Elleman, 2011, 5–6; Lewis, 2014, 47–49). Notable breakthroughs during this period included the development of an atomic bomb (1964) and a hydrogen bomb (1967), of an ICBM (1971), as well as of a nuclear submarine propulsion system.

2.1.2 Reform and Opening Up: defence industries take the back seat (1978–mid-1990s)

The effects of Deng Xiaoping's Reform and Opening Up policy from late 1978 brought mixed effects for the defence industries. Despite efforts to improve the management of large state-owned enterprises (SOE), a category that included all defence enterprises, they remained in constant crisis and accumulated losses (Cheung, 2009, 118–19). Defence industries suffered from the misallocation of resources and a drop in equipment orders at a time when economic reconstruction was mainly focused on improving people's living standards rather than strengthening national defence. This left the industry with huge overcapacities. Radical estimates from China claimed that only 15% of the military industrial complex would be needed to satisfy manufacturing demand. By the mid-1990s, much of the defence sector was in "atrophy" (Cheung, 2009, 102). To overcome this situation, PRC authorities adopted policies to facilitate the conversion of military enterprises to civilian production, and by the early 1990s, around 70% of their total production was designed for the civilian market, up from a mere 8% in 1978 (Joffe, 1996, 13). These measures were not a clear success, since potentials were not fully utilized and most of the civilian products were low-tech and low-value items (Ding, 1996a, 87; Frankenstein, 1998, 23). Besides conversion, downsizing of enterprises and layoffs were inevitable (Cheung, 2001, 207; Medeiros, Cliff, Crande and Mulvenon, 2005, 43–44).

The new openness in China's economy and foreign policy also brought about some positive effects for the defence industries. For a few years during the 1980s, against the backdrop of an American strategic interest in containing the Soviet Union, China gained access to some previously unattainable

Western military technologies (Medeiros, Cliff, Crande and Mulvenon, 2005, 138). Chinese arms producers massively benefited from contact with Western advisers, purchased Western arms technologies (including missiles, sonar, propulsion plants, and defence electronics), and even engaged in joint production. The short-lived honeymoon in Chinese-Western arms trade ended abruptly after the June 4, 1989 Tiananmen Massacre, when Western nations and US allies in Asia imposed arms embargos against China.

2.1.3 Defence modernization progress, mid-1990s to the present

Corporate reforms of the state sector introduced during the second half of the 1990s to guide SOEs through market incentives ("marketization") and to free them from politics ("corporatization") were more successful than earlier reforms (Naughton, 2018, 345). The defence enterprises regrouped into new large conglomerates (Bitzinger, 2017, 57). At the same time, the PLA was ordered to relinquish its commercial economic engagement, clarifying its primary function: to deter aggression and to prepare for "winning local wars under high-technology conditions" (1993), later changed into "winning local wars under informationized conditions" (2004) (Zhonggong zhongyang bangongting, 1998; Zhongguo de junshi zhanlüe, 2015). This strategic clarification marked the beginning of a dynamic modernization process that emphasized indigenous innovation supplemented by selected imports, mainly from Russia, Israel, and Ukraine (Bitzinger, 2017, 50; Naughton, 2018, 363).

2.2 *Size of the industry*

2.2.1 Number of enterprises and employees in the defence sector

There are no official statistics openly available that yield detailed information on the exact size of the Chinese defence industrial sector, and most analysts therefore rely on informed estimates. For the year 1985, David Bachman (2001) provides an exact number of 693 large and medium-size enterprises, and in contrast to other sources, also explains his method of accounting.[2] Frankenstein (1998, 7) presented Chinese official figures for 1993, according to which the Chinese military industrial complex was then constituted by approximately 1,000 large-sized enterprises with an average workforce of 3,000 employees each, and more than 200 major research institutes. Other sources speak of 2,000 large enterprises, with hundreds of affiliated research institutes (Joffe, 1996, 13–14).

What seems clear is that the size of the defence sector has not remained static, either in terms of number of enterprises or in terms of total employees, and newer analyses indicate that especially the network of privately or partly privately-owned companies (that are often lower-tier subsidiaries of state-owned enterprises) has been steadily expanding. An *IHS Jane's* estimate in 2013 assumed the entire defence industrial base (including private enterprises) to consist of at least 10,000 large and small state-owned and privately-owned companies with about 2.5 million employees (Grevatt, 2013). Most of these enterprises are affiliated with one of the leading defence conglomerates, such as NORINCO or AVIC. At the same time, several rounds of structural reforms with the aim of enhancing productivity and reducing overcapacities have led to a marked reduction in the total workforce. According to an analysis by Cheung quoted by Bitzinger (2017, 64), between 1990 and 2006, the total number of workers declined from some 3.15 million to 1.67 million, a reduction of nearly 1.5 million jobs.

Figures from 2012 indicate that the military-industrial complex by that time consisted of about 1,000 state-owned companies with some one million employees organized under then 11 fully state-owned holding companies. The size of the entire sector including private companies was estimated at 10,000 firms and 2.5 million workers (Grevatt, 2013; Lague and Zhu, 2012). As of 2018, according to official Chinese figures, the top nine defence conglomerates of the PRC employ about 1.7 million people and have 563 first tier subsidiaries and research affiliations (Figure 3.1). If these figures can be trusted, this would mean that as of this writing there are only 563 first tier entities left of the originally 1,200 large-sized enterprises and research institutes that were once affiliated with China's defence conglomerates in the 1990s.

2.2.2 Annual sales

In 2008, the combined profits of China's defence industries were reported to be about RMB 45 billion (US$6.5 billion), and by 2016, this figure had grown to some RMB 200 billion (about US$28.7 billion), based on sales of about RMB 2.5 trillion (US$359.7 billion) (Grevatt, 2017b). *IHS Jane's* estimated in 2013 that the annual revenues of the then 10 large state-owned defence corporations were on average growing by about 20% per year (Grevatt, 2013). Bitzinger (2017, 64) mentions the following figures for the combined revenues of the 10 leading Chinese defence conglomerates: 2010: RMB 70 bn (US$10.3); 2011: RMB 80 bn (US$12.1 bn); 2017: RMB 43 bn (US$5.5 bn). In 2017, the combined officially declared sales of nine of these ten entities (excluding CSIC, which did not publish a figure) reached a value of RMB 3.066 trillion, or about US$317 billion (Figure 3.1).[3]

2.3 Regional distribution and major locations of the Chinese defence industry

Political decisions made during the early years of the PRC still affect the regional distribution of China's defence enterprises today. During the 1950s, Soviet support led to the construction of military industries mainly in the provinces near Russia. Other industries were located in the central Chinese provinces. After the Sino-Soviet split, Beijing decided to build a so-called "Third Line" by moving defence industries to inland provinces as a precaution against attack (Joffe, 1996, 14). Defence enterprises in coastal areas were forced to open plants in China's interior. The western central

Chinese area of Sichuan Province became China's most important military industrial region and home to major facilities of the electronics, aerospace, and nuclear industries. Other major locations for arms factories were in Shaanxi, Guizhou and Liaoning provinces, while some of the most important nuclear facilities were built in Gansu (Bachman, 2001, 278–279). The government put enormous effort into this undertaking during 1965–1979 and invested more than 40% of the country's total construction budget into building these "Third Line" plants.

During the 1990s, approximately 55% of the military industry was still located in the so-called Third Line areas, but factories in coastal areas began to gain ground (Bitzinger, 2017, 54). Currently, there is (again) a trend of moving towards coastal areas. Inland defence enterprises headquartered in the Sichuan/Chongqing area account for 74% of all newly established subsidiary companies in coastal China by moving parts of their production (or whole enterprises) into cities near the coast, such as Beijing, Nanjing or Jinzhou (Wang and Wan, 2018, 125). The economic benefits of this reorientation are obvious, since the remote and scattered Third Line locations are at a heavy economic and logistic disadvantage.

3 Structure, conduct and performance of the industry

3.1 Structure

Until being commercialized and reorganized as enterprises in the 1980s, the Chinese military-industrial complex was controlled by five "line ministries," such as the Ministry of Ordnance (later transformed into the state-owned enterprise NORINCO) or the Nuclear Ministry, which later became the China National Nuclear Corp. (CNNC: Cheung, 2001, 204). In 1982, the line ministries were transferred to the State Council, China's Central Government, and renamed as follows: Ministry of Machine Building, Ministry of Nuclear Industry, Ministry of Aviation Industry, Ministry of Electronics Industry, Ministry of Ordnance Industry, Ministry of Shipbuilding Industry, and Ministry of Astronautics Industry (Ding, 1996a, 82). During the 1980s and early 1990s, these ministries were reorganized into five large state-owned enterprises, but according to Cheung (2009, 118), this change was purely "cosmetic," as they "continued to function as state bureaucracies rather than independent commercially minded corporations."

In the course of a large-scale 1998–1999 reorganization of the entire state sector under then State Premier Zhu Rongji, the five large defence conglomerates were split in order to introduce a sense of competition into the monopolistic situation of each sector, thereby creating 10 large entities or "group corporations," two in each of the five major fields. The aim was to "establish shareholder relationships within a company to further remove the government from firm operations, to distribute risk, and to increase accountability for profits and losses" (Medeiros, Cliff, Crande and Mulvenon, 2005, 41).

Nonetheless, the pairs of group corporations in each sector tended to focus on different products or regions rather than entering into actual competition. In 2002, an eleventh conglomerate, China Electronics Technology Group Corporation (CETC), was created in the new key sector of defence electronics (Cheung, 2009, 119). The number of conglomerates came down again to nine after the two aviation entities, AVIC 1 and AVIC 2, were fused in 2008 to form AVIC, and in early 2018, the two nuclear industry entities CNNC and CNECC were recombined and henceforth named CNNC (Sun, 2018).

The entire defence-industrial sector thus remains effectively under the control of nine large state-owned group corporations or conglomerates that each hold a vast, tiered network of subsidiaries – both state-owned and partly privatized companies – and research institutes, employing hundreds of thousands of people. As of 2018, two conglomerates are active in each of the major sectors aerospace (CASC and CASIC), shipbuilding (CSSC and CSIC), and ordnance (NORINCO and CSGC), and one each in aviation (AVIC), nuclear technologies (CNNC), and defence electronics (CETC) (IISS, 2018, 234). Between them, these companies represent all defence-industrial sectors and are responsible for nearly all military R&D (Barabanov, Kashin and Makienko, 2012, 1).

3.1.1 Leadings arms firms

The nine (formerly ten) large state-owned conglomerates function as holding companies of many lower-tier subsidiaries and research institutes, among them the major naval shipyards and aviation plants (Table 3.1). These subsidiaries are scattered in various locations, but concentrated mostly in the old landlocked and remote "Third Line" regions and in industrial centres along the coastline, while the large conglomerates themselves are without exception headquartered in Beijing and owned and overseen by SASAC, reflecting a high degree of central state control over the entire system exercised hierarchically from above.

Another noteworthy state-owned company is China Poly Group Corporation, the official trading house responsible for conducting China's arms exports, which curiously enough has sizeable civilian side businesses in the arts trade and real estate fields. It has some 90,000 employees and 11 subsidiaries, and like the nine principal defence conglomerates is headquartered in Beijing and controlled by the State-owned Assets Supervision and Administration Commission (SASAC). Its 2017 business revenue was given on the company website as RMB 250 billion (US$38.4 billion).

Apart from the large SOEs, four large non-state-owned companies active in dual-use sectors (mostly in the new fields of computer and information technology) have become important players in the Chinese defence industry. These are Huawei Technologies, Great Dragon Telecommunications Equipment, ZTE Corporation, and Datang Telecom (Cheung, 2009, 215–21).

Table 3.1 The nine leading Chinese defence conglomerates (as of 2018)

No.	*Company name*	*Date of foundation*	*Segment*	*Notes*
1	China National Nuclear Corporation, Ltd. (CNNC)	Founded in 1988. 1999–2018 split into CNNC and China Nuclear Engineering & Construction Corporation, Ltd. (CNECC)	Nuclear Industry	HQ in Beijing ca. 100.000 employees, about 36.000 are engineers (before takeover of CNECC) About 100 subsidiaries and research institutes (before takeover of CNECC) Business revenue CNNC (2017): 77 billion RMB Business revenue CNECC 2016: 41 billion
2	China Ordnance Industries Group Corporation, Ltd. (NORINCO) a.k.a. China North Industries Group Corporation, Ltd. (CNGC)	Founded in 1980.	Ordnance/ Land Systems	HQ in Beijing ca. 250.000 employees More than 50 subsidiaries and research institutes Business revenue (2017): 432 billion RMB (BFZG 2018)
3	China Ordnance Equipment Group Corporation, Ltd., also knowns as China South Industries Group Corporation, Ltd. (CSGC)	Founded in 1999.	Ordnance/ Land Systems	HQ in Beijing 170.000 employees More than 60 subsidiaries and research institutes Business revenue (2017): 301 billion RMB
4	China State Shipbuilding Corporation, Ltd. (CSSC)	Original CSSC founded in 1982. 1999 split into newly founded CSSC and CSIC.	Shipbuilding (in the East and South of China)	HQ in Beijing. 40 subsidiaries and research institutes Business revenue (2016): 190 billion RMB
5	China Shipbuilding Industry Corporation, Ltd. (CSIC)	Founded in 1999.	Shipbuilding (in the North and West of China)	HQ in Beijing. ca. 170,000 employees 84 subsidiaries and research institutes Business revenue: no data

(*Continued*)

Table 3.1 (Cont.)

No.	*Company name*	*Date of foundation*	*Segment*	*Notes*
				Total asset volume (2017): 440 billion RMB
6	Aviation Industry Corporation of China, Ltd. (AVIC)	Created 1993 out of the old Aviation Ministry. 1999–2008 was split into two units, AVIC 1 and AVIC 2.	Aviation	HQ in Beijing. ca. 450.000 employees More than 100 subsidiaries* and research institutes Business revenue (2017): 403 billion RMB
7	China Aerospace Science & Technology Corporation, Ltd. (CASC)	Founded in 1999.	Aerospace and Missiles	HQ in Beijing 170.000 employees 22 subsidiaries and 8 research institutes Business revenue: 232 billion RMB
8	China Aerospace Science & Industry Corporation, Ltd. (CASIC)	Founded in 1999.	Aerospace and Missiles	HQ in Beijing 150.000 employees 17 subsidiaries and 6 research institutes Business revenue (2017): 227 billion RMB (CASIC Annual Report 2017, 12)
9	China Electronics Technology Company, Ltd. (CETC)	Formed in 2002 through the merger of 47 state-owned research institutes and 26 enterprises.	Defence Electronics	HQ in Beijing. 160.000 employees 48 subsidiaries 18 "national key laboratories" and 10 research institutes Business revenue (2017): 204 billion RMB

* "Subsidiaries" only refers to directly subordinate units of the second tier. These in many cases hold further subsidiaries of their own (third tier) which are not included in the number.
Source: *Official company websites (in English and Chinese versions) and SASAC website; company annual reports; various news sources;* Cheung (2009, *120–22); "Wo guo dayue 3000 jia minqi yi jinru jungong caigou yixian" (2018);* Sun (2018).

3.1.2 Entry conditions

Monopolistic structures continue to be prevalent in the Chinese defence industrial sector. Bitzinger (2017, 65) points out that China's many rounds of structural reforms have "failed to produce much in the way of competition," and consequently there exists "a state monopoly situation in most technology fields" (Hartley, 2017, 99–100). The government has long attempted to remedy the associated negative consequences by introducing a limited amount of competition within sectors (e.g. by creating two large conglomerates per sector in 1999). However, where those have not yet been reintegrated (i.e. in shipbuilding, ordnance, and aerospace), there exists in practice a division of work between them, either regional (as in shipbuilding and ordnance) or in terms of their products. This means that most industry players remain de facto monopolists in their respective fields, and even the companies that are nominally competing within the same sector, such as the two aerospace groups CASC and CASIC, have "practically no overlaps" among their product portfolios. Even in those few areas where a potential for actual competition exists, arms programmes tend to be "spread out evenly among all the major defense firms" rather than having firms actually compete for a contract, as when the fighter jet *J-10* is being built by Chengdu Aircraft Industry Group, while the *J-11B* is produced by Shenyang Aircraft Corp. The only sectors where actual competition does seem to occur (albeit in an oligopolistic fashion) are helicopters, trainer jets, and occasionally naval shipbuilding (Bitzinger, 2017, 65).

According to Cheung (2009, 216), "PLA procurement regulations prohibit the acquisition of sensitive equipment from nongovernment companies." Only if critically important equipment is unavailable elsewhere from domestic sources have private or semi-private companies such as Huawei or ZTE been allowed to circumvent such restrictions.[4] Private companies typically have limited access to arms programmes directly, but are often involved in defence contracts as subcontractors of state-owned entities. In October 2008, The Ministry of Industry and Information Technology even issued "Guidelines on the participation of non-state-owned companies in the development of the defense industry" that stipulate that private companies should be "encouraged and enticed to participate in the development of the defense industry" and "encouraged to bid for defense contracts." According to Barabanov, Kashin and Makienko (2012, 3), they will nonetheless most likely continue to play "second fiddle" to the giant state-owned corporations.

The telecommunications company Huawei is one of the few non-state-owned companies that have been able to become heavily involved in PLA procurement projects – mostly due to the fact that it was founded by former high-ranking military personnel and is therefore a special case. The unusual role enjoyed by Huawei was according to Cheung (2009, 216) even "translated into strong financial backing for the firm from the country's state banking system," with the company reportedly being given access to a US$10 billion credit line from a state-owned bank (cf. Section 3.3.1).

3.1.3 National and global supply chains

The 1989 Western arms embargo against China has so far not been lifted, even though various countries interpret the restrictions differently and allow many types of dual-use exports despite potential military uses of some exported equipment. The US focus lies on restricting access to four especially sensitive areas: missile technology, nuclear technology, intelligence-gathering technology, and anti-submarine warfare technology (Zhang and Hyer, 2001, 104). Mastery of these fields would have massive implications for the PLA's transformation into a world-class military capable of fighting and winning wars under "informationized" conditions. Consequently, technologies that contribute to these areas are the most sought after by Chinese companies (cf. Hannas, Mulvenon and Puglisi, 2013, 205–07).

Apart from slowing down the pace of China's military modernization during much of the 1990s, the embargo had two noted effects: (1) a re-orientation towards post-Soviet arms producers after 1991; and (2) the employment of various ingenious coping strategies. Methods for alleviating technical bottlenecks that are or were used by Chinese arms developers include the exploitation of academic contacts with Western countries; the "capturing" of technology through forced technology transfers in joint ventures; the reverse-engineering of Western and post-Soviet arms (including of wreckages and unexploded shells that were obtained via third countries or collected from war zones); and state-sponsored espionage, including cyber espionage (cf. Hannas, Mulvenon and Puglisi, 2013; Joske, 2018; Parsons, 2011; Stumbaum, 2009, 11). Illegal activities were not limited to Western targets, and have led to friction with Russian arms industries on several occasions (e.g. when China was accused of reverse-engineering the Russian *Su-27* fighter plane, the *Kilo* class submarine, or the *Mineral-ME* fire-control radar system: Cheung, 2011, 6–7; Johnson, 2015a).

China is furthermore determined to exploit dual-use technologies for their potential to create synergies between the civilian and military industrial sectors, not least in order to bring some of the dynamism and innovation potential of civilian enterprises into the defence-industrial sphere. This policy was first proposed under State and Party Leader Jiang Zemin in the mid-1990s and overseen by his son Jiang Mianheng, but more actively pursued since the early 2000s (Cheung, 2009, 6–9; 180ff.). "Civil-military integration" (CMI) has since become one of the major goals proclaimed by the government in its 13th Five-Year Plan (2016–2020), but similar formulae have been used at least since the 10th Five-Year Plan (2001–2005). A so-called "836 Programme" was modelled after the "organizational structure and operational procedures of the Maoist strategic weapons program" to oversee joint civilian-military research & development (R&D), involving nearly 10,000 defence researchers and engineers and more than 1,500 individual research projects. Its sub-programmes with the strongest implications for military development include R&D in the fields of space, laser, optoelectronics, super-large-scale integrated circuits, turbofan engines, and new materials, and reportedly achieved over "one hundred important technological breakthroughs by 2002 in areas such as space technology, computers, and information technology" (Cheung, 2009, 191).

Legal imports of dual-use technologies have been a fruitful field for arms-industrial collaboration between some Western and Chinese entities outside of embargo restrictions. Unclear and at times inconsistent rules that are furthermore applied differently from country to country have allowed China to gain access to a variety of advanced technologies from Western suppliers including helicopters, sonar, marine diesel propulsion, and various space technologies and infrastructures (cf. Stumbaum, 2009). Western, and especially European, space industries have been especially open to cooperation with Chinese "civilian" space researchers and entities, even though all space-related activities in China, including its manned missions, are in fact overseen by the PLA and often intimately connected to the military space programmes (Cheung, 2009, 10–18; 180; Nurkin, 2015).

Mergers and Acquisitions (M&A) have become a further vehicle through which Chinese arms industries have acquired key technologies and valuable business information from abroad, including managerial and procedural knowledge. Especially since the financial crisis of 2008, crisis-ridden Western aerospace and defence as well as electronics companies have become attractive investment targets. *IHS Jane's* has tracked over a dozen acquisitions of Western (including US) commercial aerospace companies by Chinese counterparts during the period of 2009–2014 alone (Nurkin, 2015). Some acquisitions have led to unintended transfers of strategically important technology: The 2008 takeover of British chip maker Dynex Semiconductor by the Chinese SOE Zhuzhou CSR Times Electric is assumed to have given China the ability to manufacture insulated-gate bipolar transistor (IGBT) chips, a critical component for building electromagnetic catapult systems (EMALS) for aircraft carriers.[5] This technology is explicitly defined as subject to EU export controls and was since 2009 listed "on the category III of the UK Strategic Export Control Lists as part of the EU Council Regulation 428/2009," but in 2008, the takeover was not blocked by the then UK government. China's unexpectedly early acquisition of EMALS technology could mean that China will be able to leapfrog over the stage of steam catapults for its future carrier – which according to defence analyst R.D. Fisher is a "tragedy" for the United States who expected to be the sole user of this most advanced catapult technology for a long time (Huang, 2018).

3.2 Conduct

3.2.1 National procurement policy

The highest decision-making authority in all matters of the Chinese defence industry rests with the State Council and the CCP's Central Military

Commission (CMC). In 2016, the procurement process for conventional weapon systems was overhauled, resulting in the creation of the CMC Equipment Development Department in place of the General Armament Department (GAD). This new body focuses on joint development programmes rather than only the ground forces as before. At the same time, a new Science and Technology Commission (STC) was established within the CMC that was reportedly modelled after the US Defense Advanced Research Projects Agency (DARPA), whose focus is on R&D in "strategic, cutting-edge or revolutionary capabilities" and aims to connect more strongly with civilian researchers. It is, however, part of the PLA hierarchy and led by a two-star general (IISS, 2018, 233). The thrust remains on furthering domestic innovation and autarchy, and on civil-military integration (CMI).

According to a recent *IHS Jane's* analysis, the Chinese government continues to prefer sole-source contracts for arms purchases, thereby cementing the decades-long influence of the large state-owned defence enterprises: "The process encompasses negotiation between the armed forces' procurement agencies and specific military contractors, who are identified in a PLA suppliers' database (which is not published), followed by a contract award." According to the same analysis, while this continues to apply for all major and sensitive equipment procurement programmes in areas related to national security, regulations have been somewhat relaxed and modernized in less sensitive areas, such as logistics, training equipment, auxiliary services, and non-military purchases. Procurement programmes in less sensitive areas are since January 2015 conducted through an official military procurement website (www.weain.mil.cn) that was set up in an attempt to "increase transparency and competition" (Grevatt, 2017b).

Reforms of the procurement process are also taking place within the large defence conglomerates themselves. The shipbuilding group CSSC, which controls among others the Jiangnan, Shanghai Waigaoqiao, and Guangzhou Wenchong naval shipyards, on January 5, 2017 issued a statement that it had charged its subsidiary, China Shipbuilding Industry Logistics, with introducing "a centralised procurement system and other related initiatives that will look to streamline the sourcing of Tier 2/3 services and products from domestic suppliers" in order to "centralise purchasing requirements in relation to materials, components, and subsystems" as a result of "a survey across the group about how to improve productivity in 2017" (Grevatt, 2017a).

3.2.2 Price and non-price competition including private and state funded R&D

It is known that the government has a longstanding policy of limiting the maximum profit from military contracts to 5% on costs (Grevatt, 2017b). Given much greater profit margins in many commercial sectors, this policy likely limits competition by making it financially unattractive for private sector companies to bid for defence contracts.

Details of major defence contracts pertaining to national security, including information such as pricing and target cost, are considered state secrets and are not publicly disclosed. There is therefore little to no public accountability regarding procurement and budgetary issues, and very little to no media scrutiny of the PLA's largely autonomous procurement. Calls for the eradication of corruption in the arms procurement system through the establishment of dedicated decision-making committees seem to indicate that procurement decisions can actually be made by individual leaders (Grevatt, 2017b).

As to state-funded defence R&D, China has launched several state-led initiatives, including the National High Technology Programme ("863 Programme") since March 1986 for innovations in critical technology areas (e.g. information technologies, space, lasers, new materials, biotech, and automation). Supported with generous funding by state-owned banks, such initiatives were used to infuse the system with innovative potential that is not easily generated within a rigid, state-controlled, hierarchical system (Bitzinger, 2017, 68). A new reform initiative in 2017 aims at restructuring the ownership of fully state-owned defence-industrial research institutes to allow them to raise capital on the stock market. A batch of 41 research institutes, mostly in the aerospace sector and subordinate to CASC and CASIC, were the first to undergo ownership reform. Another element of the reform included the creation of "system-design innovation centres" as "centralised hubs to drive advanced original R&D in their industrial sectors." Among the first ten such centres, missile, naval, and aviation development featured prominently (IISS, 2018, 234).

3.3 Performance

3.3.1 Defence industry productivity and profitability

It seems clear that China's defence industries have struggled to generate profits during the first two decades of the Reform Era (1979–1999) when defence modernization was not a strong state priority and the defence sector was still plagued by vast over-bureaucratization. Cheung (2009, 118, fn. 56) reports that the nadir in performance was reached in 1998, when official Chinese sources reported that over 60% of all defence enterprises were losing money. Total net losses of the entire defence-industrial base after subtracting profits at that time reportedly amounted to around RMB 2.5 billion (ca. US$300 million).

A major restructuring of the state-owned sector in 1998/99 and official encouragement by China's leaders for the SOEs to raise capital by listing their subsidiaries on the domestic stock markets and by issuing bonds, together with growing defence budgets and official support for indigenous development, finally turned the tide. In 2008, 62 defence enterprises were already listed or in the process of being listed on China's or Hong Kong's stock exchanges. The initial public offering (IPO) of the civilian operations of aerospace conglomerate AVIC 2 at the Hong Kong Stock Exchange in 2003 raised US$248 million, and COSTIND officials expected the combined defence industries to raise between RMB 50 to 60 billion until 2010 (Cheung, 2009, 125). According to IISS (2018, 234), defence companies have raised more than US$30 billion since 2013 from "asset securitization" via IPOs and other financial vehicles, and have mostly reinvested these funds into the development of new products.

China's leaders furthermore utilized their control over the state-owned banking sector to infuse vast amounts of capital into the defence industries via credits. Under the 12th Five-Year Plan for 2011–2016, the government announced the intent to pour a further US$600 billion into strategic sectors. According to 2017 *IHS Jane's* data, since 2007, all publicly announced loan deals by state banks for the state defence sector (mostly aerospace enterprises) amounted to at least RMB 600 billion (US$87 billion) next to an unknown number of non-publicly disclosed deals (Grevatt, 2017b).

De-facto state subsidies of such magnitude that can be used for the financing of a wide variety of mostly undisclosed purposes (e.g. construction projects, R&D in advanced technologies) make it difficult to assess the actual productivity and profitability of China's defence industries. Furthermore, a trend towards cross-shareholding between defence holdings and state-owned banks has been observed in recent years, with defence groups NORINCO and CSSC becoming strategic investors in the China Everbright Bank, and AVIC, CNNC, and CASC becoming key investors in the Agricultural Bank of China. This points to the emergence of a "military-industrial-financial-complex" of enormous proportions (Grevatt, 2011b).

In sum, the combination of all the above named factors has massively improved the financial basis of China's defence enterprises since the mid-2000s. As Bitzinger (2017, 68) points out, alongside technology, "capital is a critical enabler of technology acquisition." It seems clear that China's leaders are mostly pursuing a strategy of injecting large funds into the system, rather than opting for difficult structural reforms – an approach that has arguably had undeniable success so far in terms of production output.

3.3.2 Revenues and profitability of major chinese arms conglomerates

Exact data on sales, revenue, productivity, or the exact share of defence-related revenues of individual Chinese defence conglomerates, is not publicly available for longer periods or across the entire industry. As a 2018 *IISS Military Balance Blog* entry states, "little is actually known about the performance of Chinese defence groups. In particular, there is no measure in the existing international literature of the financial worth of Chinese defence-industry concerns relative to other major defence firms" (Nouwens and Béraud-Sudreau, 2018). For this reason, Chinese companies remain summarily excluded from both the *SIPRI Top 100 Arms-producing and Military Services Companies* database and the *Defense News Top 100* as of 2018.[6]

Table 3.2 Chinese conglomerates among the top 22 defence companies per arms sales in US $bn (2016)

Rank in SIPRI Top 100 (2016)	*Rank IISS**	*Company name*	*Country of company HQ*	*Arms sales (US$ bn, 2016)*
1	1	Lockheed Martin	USA	40.8
2	2	Boeing	USA	29.5
3	3	Raytheon	USA	22.9
4	4	BAE Systems	UK	22.8
-	**5**	**CSGC**	**PRC**	**22.1**
5	6	Northrop Grumman	USA	21.4
-	**7**	**AVIC**	**PRC**	**20.9**
6	8	General Dynamics	USA	19.2
-	**9**	**NORINCO**	**PRC**	**13.2**
7	10	Airbus	NL	12.5
-	**11**	**CASIC**	**PRC**	**9.8**
8	12	L-3 Communications	USA	8.9
9	13	Leonardo	Italy	8.5
-	**14**	**CSIC**	**PRC**	**8.4**
-	**15**	**CETC**	**PRC**	**8.4**
10	16	Thales	F	8.2
11	17	United Technologies	USA	6.9
-	**18**	**CASC**	**PRC**	**6.9**
12	19	Huntington Ingalls Industries	USA	6.7
13	20	United Aircraft	Russia	5.2
14	21	Bechtel	USA	4.9
-	**22**	**CSSC**	**PRC**	**4.8**

* Ranking by Nouwens and Béraud-Sudreau.
Source of Data: Nouwens and Béraud-Sudreau (2018).

In 2018, IISS analysts for the first time attempted to make an informed estimate of the defence-related revenue according to the criteria of the *SIPRI Top 100* and *Defense News Top 100* databases for eight of the eleven major Chinese arms group corporations during 2016.[7] According to their study, three among the eight conglomerates studied – CSGC, AVIC, and NORINCO – had generated defence-related revenues that placed them firmly in the global top 10 arms companies of 2016, and four others were at least located within the global top 20 (cf. Table 3.2). In terms of their output, these companies now "operate at a similar level as the most important defence manufacturers in the world. Only Lockheed Martin and, to a lesser extent, Boeing, remain in a different league" (Nouwens and Béraud-Sudreau, 2018).

The only defence-industrial sector that seems to have been less than profitable during the past few years is, surprisingly, shipbuilding, which was strongly affected by a global downturn in demand for commercial vessels since 2008. According to IISS (2018, 234), following consolidation of the aviation and nuclear conglomerates, the two large shipbuilding group corporations CSSC and CSIC might be next in line for being merged in order to compensate for the losses posted by CSSC, the only conglomerate among the top nine Chinese defence corporations to post losses rather than profits during the past few years. CSSC's bad revenue situation seems surprising given its access to huge credit lines and given that among its subsidiaries are some of the most advanced Chinese naval shipyards, Jiangnan and Hudong-Zhonghua, that currently have full orderbooks. Jiangnan is in the process of building China's second-generation indigenous aircraft carrier, the *Type 002,* a flattop design that is rumoured to feature integrated electric propulsion and EMALS catapults; has contracted at least three of the planned class of eight very large, sophisticated *Type 055* cruiser-sized destroyers, and 18 of the highly advanced "Chinese AEGIS" *Type 052D* destroyers, and has also built all six *Type 052C* destroyers in recent years. Hudong-Zhonghua has built at least 15 of the modern *Type 054A* frigates and at least 18 of the new *Type 056* and *056A* corvettes.[8] Most other naval shipyards in the world can only dream of such abundant orders.

As Admiral Sunil Lanba, the Indian Chief of Naval Staff, remarked in a 2018 interview, the output of China's naval shipyards during the past few years is unusually high in global and historic comparison:

> They are commissioning between 12 and 18 ships a year. In the past four-five years, they have commissioned 80 new ships and submarines. No navy has grown at this pace for more than a hundred years, not counting the two world wars .
>
> (Unnithan, 2018; cf. Childs and Waldwyn, 2018)

Furthermore, the publicly disclosed number of hulls might even understate the true size of fleet enlargement. According to Tate (2018), commercial satellite imagery analyses suggest "that the number of warships launched and commissioned in China in 2018 is significantly greater than has been officially confirmed."

If Chinese shipbuilders are unable to build a profitable business in the face of such extraordinarily large national orders of high-end naval vessels while being given access to vast credit lines, this points either to problems in their productivity or to cost overruns due to first-of-class problems of highly complex prototype development, or general systems integration troubles (cf. Kirchberger, 2015, 127; 194). Corruption could also be part of the problem. It is known that the shipbuilding conglomerate CSIC was recently stricken by at least three high-profile corruption and espionage cases connected to its domestic aircraft carrier programme (Zheng, 2018).

3.3.3 Imports and exports of defence equipment – qualitative trends

In the years leading up to the imposition of the Western arms embargo in 1989, China had received a number of US and European defence technology deliveries in several critical fields including missiles, sonar, propulsion, and defence electronics. These transfers included joint production in avionics, aircraft power plants, and naval gas turbines. Notable individual systems included the French *Exocet* and *Crotale* missiles, *TAVITAC* combat direction system, and *Sea Tiger* air search radar; Italian *Aspide* missiles and sonars, and American naval gas turbines (cf. Friedman, 2006, 516; Shambaugh, 2004, 268). Chinese arms industries also used every opportunity during that timeframe to upgrade their outdated production plants with the help of Western experts (Cheung, 2009: 62). The 1989 embargo caused severe disruption of some ongoing large procurement projects due to a sudden unavailability of key parts and loss of supplier support, which forced China to turn towards post-Soviet countries such as Russia and Ukraine, and until 2005, Israel for further defence technology transfers (cf. Kirchberger, 2015, 143, 193).

Roughly since Putin's return to the office of President and Xi Jinping's takeover as State and Party chief in 2012, Russian-Chinese defence-industrial cooperation intensified again after a period of friction (Sinkkonen, 2018, 3). Shortly thereafter, the Crimea crisis of early 2014 not only resulted in Western sanctions against Russia, but led to the break-up of the formerly intimate arms trade relationship between Russia and Ukraine, causing massive bottlenecks and lost market shares in the Russian and Ukrainian arms industries alike. These developments provided Russia and China with strong incentives to form a closer military-industrial relationship (Kirchberger, 2017; Schwartz, 2017). A new, large-scale arms export deal for the sale of 24 Russian *Su-35* fighter planes, four *Lada* class submarines and six battalions of the *S-400* air defence system was officially confirmed in November 2015.[9] This deal had been under discussion at least since 2008, but resistance within the Russian arms industry over fears of Chinese reverse-engineering had delayed its conclusion.[10] Under the changed geopolitical circumstances following the occupation of Crimea, direct involvement of Putin and Xi seems to have removed those obstacles. The deepening military relations between Russia and China received a further boost though the conclusion of a general plan for bilateral military cooperation for the years 2017–2020 in June 2017 (Sinkkonen, 2018, 2).

Apart from Israel, which mostly ceased its arms exports to China in 2005 due to US pressure, Ukraine has been the second most important supplier of advanced arms technologies to China after Russia. Notwithstanding their relatively smaller monetary value, Ukrainian defence exports yielded some highly strategic technology transfers that enhanced China's indigenous arms production capabilities decisively – notably an unfinished aircraft carrier hull, *Kilo* class submarine maintenance blueprints, phased-array radar technology, and licenced production of naval gas turbines (cf. Kirchberger, 2015, 264, 2017).

Often these transfers involved extensive consultancy services:

> As early as the 1990s, Beijing received help from the Ukraine-based Yuzhnoye Design Office, when the PLA's infant nuclear division was seeking breakthroughs in multi-warhead technology and miniaturization of its nuclear warheads.
>
> (Chen, 2017)

Ukrainian expertise was also a key factor for China's attempts to build offensive power-projection vessels. An unfinished *Adm. Kuznetsov* class aircraft carrier hull, the *Varyag*, was transferred from Ukraine to China in 1998 and finished and outfitted there with the help of Ukrainian experts, including reportedly the *Varyag's* lead designer himself. A Chinese news report of 2017 portrayed then 76 year-old naval architect Valery Babich, who had been intimately involved in the design of all three Soviet-era *Moskva* class helicopter carriers, the three *Kiev* class aircraft carriers, the two *Kuznetsov* class carriers and the unfinished Soviet nuclear-powered and steam-catapult equipped flat-top carrier *Ulyanovsk,* as serving with a Chinese research institute named "Qingdao Chinese-Ukrainian Special Ship Design and Research Institute Co., Lt." reportedly established in September 2014 ("Liaoning jian zong sheji shi fu Hua shoupin" 2017). Ukrainian experts also offered China assistance for carrier pilot training (Johnson and Hardy, 2013). Other examples of key Ukrainian assistance concerned the transfer of a Ukrainian C-band active phased-array radar prototype (including the design package) from the Ukrainian Kvant Design Bureau that reportedly enabled China's Nanjing Research Institute of Electronic Technology to develop its indigenous *Type 346* "Dragon Eye" active phased-array radar (which became the cornerstone of the "Chinese AEGIS" area-defense system first integrated into the *Type 052C* destroyer); and a 1997 licence production agreement for Ukrainian Zorya Mashproekt *GT-25,000* naval gas turbines, which alleviated the naval propulsion bottleneck after the American embargo that had crippled China's destroyer programmes after 1989 (Bussert and Elleman, 2011, 29; Friedman, 2006, 222–23; Wertheim, 2013, 115).

Although China has become much less dependent on foreign arms technologies since, Raska points out that "China remains dependent on imports of key weapons systems and advanced components," especially aero-engines for fighter jets. Accordingly, aircraft engines accounted for 30% of China's total arms imports during 2012–2016, "delivered from Russia (57%), Ukraine (16%), and France (15%)" (Raska, 2017). Similar dependencies continue to exist in the area of naval propulsion, with marine diesels and gas turbines produced in China under licence agreements from German, French, and Ukrainian makers.

China was among the top five exporters of arms to developing countries since the early 1950s, but, as Godement points out, until the mid-1970s,

> almost all of it was made up of support to Third World revolutionary movements and new Communist states; most of it was not sold but donated, and the greatest part of the equipment involved consisted of

> small arms and field communication equipment and other supplies, for which China gained a reputation as a rugged producer.
>
> (Godement, 1996, 95)

Actual arms exports for commercial gain (which are to be differentiated from proliferation, e.g. of nuclear or missile technology) began no sooner than during the 1980s, and when such commercial exports declined, proliferation of problematic items, such as ballistic missiles to Pakistan, took an upturn (Godement, 1996, 104ff.) The UNROCA arms exports database shows that until 2000, China mostly exported arms to South and Southeast Asian countries (Pakistan, Sri Lanka, Bangladesh, Thailand, Myanmar, and Laos) and later also to some African states (Cameroon, Tanzania, Sudan, Chad). In the early phase, China's exports were for the most part low-tech arms, with the ordnance group NORINCO the largest single exporter (Sun, 2018).

Roughly since 2005, as a result of improved domestic production capacities, China evolved into a provider of more complex arms technologies to its long-standing customer Pakistan and a growing number of developing countries in Southeast Asia and on the African continent. During the past few years, China's arms exports have begun to include sophisticated platforms, such as new naval surface combatants (as opposed to transfers of used vessels), submarines, and fighter jets. Chinese exporters have become much better at marketing their products abroad, and are increasingly present in the markets with offers of complex systems such as combat trainers, fighter jets (*J-31*), various missile systems, air defence systems, radars, helicopters, transport aircraft, UAVs, tanks, OPVs, corvettes, frigates, and submarines. New markets that China has been recently able to enter include Algeria, Saudi Arabia, Egypt, Morocco, Venezuela, Ecuador, Peru, Mexico, Nigeria, Kenya, Thailand, Indonesia, and Kazakhstan (Raska, 2017).

In recent years Chinese arms producers also tried to export to Western and NATO countries, e.g. by offering NATO member Turkey its *HQ-9* air defence system, and in 2016 for the first time succeeded in fulfilling a contract for the delivery of such an air-defence system to a post-Soviet country, Turkmenistan. In 2014, China was for the first time included in the group of SIPRI's top five arms exporters (before the UK), and is widely expected to become one of the world's leading arms exporters in the foreseeable future, not least due to its ability to provide "low cost and affordable service and upgrade packages without geopolitical strings" (Johnson, 2013; Raska, 2017).

3.3.4 Cost overruns and delays of major defence projects

Not enough detailed information on China's major arms procurement programmes is openly available to make an informed assessment of cost overrun and delay problems across the arms industries. In fact, not even rather basic data, such as the planned total number of a class of warships, the planned timeframe for their commissioning, or the actual commissioning of a vessel into the fleet, are necessarily publicly announced, with such facts sometimes becoming known only retroactively through satellite imagery and photography analyses (cf. Tate, 2018). Given the PLA's exceptionally large equipment orders during at least the past decade, Chinese arms manufacturers should theoretically be able to utilize significant economy of scale effects. Nonetheless, the exceptionally large credit lines repeatedly extended to China's arms conglomerates via state-owned banks suggest that at least part of these funds may be used to cover for losses incurred.

3.3.5 Technical progress

Bitzinger (2017, 49) points out that despite "sizable economic inputs, access to foreign technologies, and considerable political will, China, up until the late 1990s, experienced only limited success when it came to the local design, development, and manufacture of advanced conventional weapons." This situation has since markedly changed. China's arms industries have across the board achieved remarkable technical progress starting from a technologically backward and financially difficult position in the mid-1990s, while operating under an arms embargo that to this day restricts Chinese exchanges with the world's most advanced Western arms producers.

Access to foreign technology – either captured, obtained via (cyber-)espionage, or legally acquired – and an abundance of funds seems to have had the largest impact. In some instances, the acquisitions of foreign companies, such as the above cited Dynex Semiconductor case that apparently enabled the development of an indigenous Chinese EMALS carrier catapult technology, have resulted in China "leapfrogging" over an entire technical-developmental state – in this case, steam catapults (Huang, 2018). Major accomplishments in terms of output under the Xi Jinping administration have included "moon landing, space docking, supercomputers, … aviation prototypes such as J-20, J-16, helicopters and UAVs" as well as the "ongoing construction of domestic aircraft carriers and record number of commissioned ships such as Type 054A, 056 (corvettes) and 052C (and 055) destroyers" (Raska, 2014, 32).

As of 2018, China is heavily engaged in harnessing civilian and dual-use technologies in cutting-edge fields such as AI, robotics, unmanned systems, and space for potential military uses. Civilian companies engaged in AI development, such as Baidu, Alibaba, Tencent and iFlytek develop dual-use technologies and have founded dedicated research facilities for that purpose – e.g. the National Engineering Laboratory for Deep Learning Technologies and Applications lead by Baidu and the State Key Laboratory of Cognitive Intelligence lead by iFlytek (Kania, 2018, 7). Military applications that combine achievements in autonomous systems technology and AI are evident e.g. in the currently ongoing building of a vast underwater surveillance network for ASW purposes in the South China Sea that was first showcased by shipbuilding conglomerate CSSC in 2016. It consists of passive sensors located up to 3,000 meters below the surface working in conjunction with a wide range of unmanned autonomous subsurface systems

(USVs), such as a torpedo-shaped Semi-Autonomous Robotic Vehicle (SARV) that can also be launched from submarines; dual bodied USVs carrying ASW sensor equipment; conventional underwater gliders for measuring a variety of water conditions; and a 5–10 ton Autonomous Robotic Vehicle (ARV) intended for long endurance missions and hauling larger payloads likely for "surveillance, intelligence collection, mine countermeasure and anti-submarine warfare missions" (Lin and Singer, 2016). Another such field is drone swarms, or unmanned aerial vehicles (UAVs) launched in a swarm configuration operating as an autonomous group that is not controlled from the ground and has no lead vehicle. Rather, the drones "communicate with each other," with "decisions relating to individual UAV positions … made by software exploiting AI-technologies." Defence electronics group CETC in June 2018 claimed a "world record for the number of unmanned aerial vehicles (UAVs) launched in a swarm" of 119 UAVs (Grevatt, 2017c).

In June 2018, Lin Yang, the leader of a classified programme named the "912 Project" to develop new-generation military underwater robots, in a rare press interview confirmed that China is building "large, smart and relatively low-cost unmanned submarines that can roam the world's oceans to perform a wide range of missions, from reconnaissance to mine placement to even suicide attacks against enemy vessels." These autonomous submarines would be deployed by the 2020s and be the same size as ordinary submarines. Furthermore, China has built "the world's largest testing facility for surface drone boats in Zhuhai, Guangdong," and military researchers are also "developing an AI-assisted support system for [human] submarine commanders" (Chen, 2018).

3.3.6 Strengths and weaknesses of the Chinese defence industry

In recent years, restructurings of the defence sector have been partially successful. The large group corporations that structure and dominate the Chinese arms industries have successfully "been slimmed down, allowed to shed heavy debt burdens, and given access to new sources of capital" (Cheung, 2011, 6). Since arms development is heavily dependent upon capital, the abundance of funding – a veritable "avalanche of cash" – provided by the state-owned banks to the defence sector was and is an important factor for this success (Bitzinger, 2017, 68; Lague and Zhu, 2012). In terms of output, China's arms industries seem strongest in land and missile systems, with the naval shipbuilding sector becoming increasingly self-sufficient.

Structural weaknesses of the Chinese defence sector include its still severe bureaucratic fragmentation or "Balkanization," which results in a "widespread duplication" of industrial facilities that are "scattered across the country, especially in its land-locked interior;" engage in rivalry; and receive local protectionism, resulting in little cooperation within the sector (Cheung, 2011, 7). Overlapping planning structures, the Soviet organizational legacy, inefficiencies, corruption, and the absence of any real internal competition are further systemic problems. There are also deficiencies in quality control and process standardization (as evidenced in the field of aircraft engine development) (Raska, 2014, 33), and the sector as a whole still has significant overcapacities despite ongoing consolidation efforts (Bitzinger, 2017, 65).

In terms of output, one key weakness is the fact that some critical components can still not be produced domestically, notably in the propulsion and defence electronics fields (Bitzinger, 2017, 68). The PLA remains so far reliant on imported aero-engines, e.g. Russian engines for the *J-10* and *J-11* fighters, and Ukrainian engines for the *L-15* jet trainer. Technical bottlenecks cited include combustion engineering, hot-section technology and the design of digital control systems (Cheung, 2011, 7; Johnson, 2015b). China likely recently chose to import the 24 Russian *Su-35* fighters largely for their jet engines and AESA radars, due to lack of a domestic alternative. China reportedly ordered an unusual amount of six spare engines per fighter rather than the usual two, likely to integrate that engine into its own *J-20* stealth fighter (Johnson, 2015a; Schwartz, 2017).

Such indications point to a lacking indigenous capacity for cutting-edge "systems of systems" R&D that would be necessary to make the leap from imitator to innovator even in difficult, highly integrated fields. According to Nurkin (2015), "China is still developing its capacity to innovate in more complex, highly engineered, and systems-focused sectors," likely because "China's innovative capacity has long been focused on single technology, rather than systems-focused innovation." This marks China more as a "fast follower" or at most a "niche innovator" in military R&D rather than a true innovator (Bitzinger, 2017, 68). Domestic Chinese R&D deficiencies can also be inferred from documented espionage cases: A 2014 US Department of Justice report listed more than 25 cases of "prosecuted espionage regarding theft of controlled items relevant to China's space and broader aerospace programmes" during January 2008 to March 2014. Technologies sought included "thermal imaging cameras, aerospace-grade carbon fibre, electronics used in military radar and electronic warfare, radiation-hardened materials and gyroscopes, military accelerators, military optics, unmanned systems, rocket/space launch technical data, restricted electronics equipment, source code, and space shuttle and rocket secrets" (Hannas, Mulvenon and Puglisi, 2013, 256–70; Nurkin, 2015).

4 Conclusion

As Raska (2014) warns, projecting the future development of China's arms industries over the mid- and long term is a difficult task that poses grave analytic problems. There is a danger of extrapolating current trends in a linear fashion despite the fact that they are both path-dependent and dynamic, and "shaped by multiple variables and input factors that may produce a wide spectrum of potential trajectories." The lack of hard data in some fields and analysts' inevitable biases pose additional problems.

4.1 Future prospects for China's defence industry

Especially under Xi Jinping's administration since 2012, the defence industries have "flourished," and prospects in the near term look equally positive. Building a strong defence economy is part of Xi's larger plan of making China one of the most innovative countries by 2035, while being a necessity for becoming a military peer to the USA (IISS, 2018, 232–33). Given that China's government has committed itself to the express goal of turning the country into the global science and technology leader by 2050, the arms industries enjoy an extraordinarily high level of political support (Nurkin, 2015). However, according to an analysis by Grevatt (2017b), though the technological gap to Western arms industry leaders will likely narrow, it is unlikely to disappear completely.

The necessary conditions for a continued upward trajectory in the future include: continued high levels of financial investment into the defence-industrial base; continued high-level political support for military modernization; and continued high end-user (PLA) demand (Cheung, 2011, 7). China's future economic development and financial stability, alongside the future development of the PLA's military threat perception, are therefore the key factors to consider. A marked drop in economic growth or a financial crisis would undercut funding, while a reduced threat perception would likely push other government spending priorities to the forefront, to the detriment of defence modernization. If economic and financial development however remain stable, and if military tensions in the Asia-Pacific and a threat perception fuelled by Sino-American rivalry continue to grow, then strong progress in the arms industries' performance, and ultimately further success in the field of military transformation and R&D can be expected.

4.2 What might the future defence firm and industry look like by 2070?

As long as the Leninist party-state system in the PRC continues to exist, it is unlikely that China's CCP-lead government would be willing to cede organizational control over the strategically important defence-industrial sector. Therefore, it is to be expected that the basic structure of large, state-owned defence conglomerates acting as holdings of second- and third-tier entities is going to continue. Nonetheless, further consolidation within each sector, and further efforts at civil-military integration are likely to occur.

It is also probable that parts of the Chinese defence industries will become more oriented towards global arms export markets in the future, entering into joint production agreements with customer countries along the "Belt and Road Initiative" (BRI), given that China is increasingly using "arms exports as an instrument of its foreign policy to project power and influence to create strategic dependencies in areas that are vital to China's interests, for example in Southeast Asia" where such contracts with traditional US allies such as Thailand or the Philippines may even help to undermine the US alliance system (Raska, 2017). The existence of large, dedicated credit lines from state banks to arms conglomerates explicitly for supporting arms export financing points to such a direction (Grevatt, 2018).

4.3 Prospects, problems and challenges for industry conversion

Rather than aspiring to convert military industries to civilian production, it can be expected that the PRC will continue its current attempts to consolidate the defence sector, and to integrate and harness dual-use activities of civilian industries for furthering China's military-industrial goals. Civil-military integration (CMI) is therefore a trend that can be expected to intensify. On the other hand, purely civilian business activities of the defence industries (e.g. in the aerospace and aviation sectors) offer the chance to forge partnerships with foreign industry leaders outside of arms embargo restrictions, thereby bringing in foreign market and procedural knowledge as well as access to key decision-makers and stakeholders in various countries, while also bolstering military R&D funding through commercial gains. Therefore it is likely that civilian activities in high-tech fields will be kept within the large defence industry conglomerates, and that their dual-use R&D might become more heavily integrated with military R&D.

Notes

1 Although China's reporting standards compare unfavourably with the world's industrialized nations, they seem more or less comparable with most ASEAN and BRIC countries (Liff and Erickson, 2013, p. 18).
2 In 1987, the PRC published ten volumes presenting its industrial census (1985). Volume I contained aggregated data for all enterprises. Volume II presented more detail about individual enterprises including addresses. Since 693 enterprises were missing from Volume II, Bachman concluded that they must be related to national defence.
3 Aggregate sum calculated from figures given on the official corporation websites as of September 2018.
4 In the case of Huawei, Cheung (2009, 216) points out that

> offered critical equipment that the PLA needed and that was not available elsewhere domestically. The company was also able to meet stringent military requirements over secrecy and other regulatory matters because of the former military backgrounds of its management. In addition, the company enjoyed the strong backing of senior civilian and military leaders who regularly visited Huawei's headquarters in Shenzhen.

5 IGBT chips can "switch electrical current to the windings of the motor in milliseconds to enable the launching of aircraft from the carrier flight deck" (Huang, 2018).
6 Both databases provide a yearly ranking of the global top 100 arms-producing companies according to their defence-related sales. Regarding its decision to exclude Chinese companies, SIPRI states: "Chinese arms-producing companies are not covered by the SIPRI Top 100 due to the lack of data on which to make

a reasonable or consistent estimate of arms sales dating back to 2002" (Fleurant et al., 2018, 2).

7 They excluded the two (now one) conglomerates active in nuclear technologies, CNNC and CNECC, and also the electronics group CETC.

8 The Chinese-language Wikipedia entries of the various Chinese naval shipbuilding programs give build yards for individual vessels. The above mentioned numbers were taken from there.

9 For a Chinese state news report, see "Zhong E qianding junshou da dan" 2015. For comments on the deal itself, see Johnson (2015a) and Foster (2012).

10 Cf. interviews with Russian defence industry representatives published by *Kanwa*, e.g. "Frictions between Russia & China" (2009, 15) and "Russia and China have a widening difference" (2009, 16).

References

Anderson, Guy. 2011. "Bilateral Military Trade Makes Agenda in China-Russia Talks". *Jane's Defence Weekly* (el. ed.), June 20, 2011.

Bachman, David. 2001. "Defence Industrialization in Guangdong". *The China Quarterly* 166: 273–304.

Barabanov, Mikhail, Vasiliy Kashin and Konstantin Makienko 2012. *Shooting Star: China's Military Machine in the 21st Century*. Transl. Ivan Khokhotva. Minneapolis: East View Press.

Bitzinger, Richard A. 2017. *Arming Asia: Technonationalism and its Impact on Local Defense Industries*. London: Routledge.

Bussert, James C. and Bruce A. Elleman 2011. *People's Liberation Army Navy Combat Systems Technology, 1949-2010*. Annapolis: Naval Institute Press.

Chen, Frank. 2017. "Ukrainian Military Expertise Sought After by the PLA". *Asia Times*, Dec. 28, 2017. www.atimes.com/article/ukrainian-military-expertise-sought-pla/.

Chen, Stephen. 2018. "China Military Develops Robotic Submarines to Launch a New Era of Sea Power". *South China Morning Post*, Updated July 23, 2018. www.scmp.com/news/china/society/article/2156361/china-developing-unmanned-ai-submarines-launch-new-era-sea-power.

Cheung, Tai Ming. 2001. *China's Entrepreneurial Army*. Oxford: Oxford University Press.

Cheung, Tai Ming 2009. *Fortifying China: The Struggle to Build a Modern Defense Economy*. Ithaca, NY: Cornell UP.

Cheung, Tai Ming 2011. *Rejuvenating the Chinese Defense Economy: Present Developments and Future Trends*. UC San Diego: SITC Policy Brief 19. Sept. 1, 2011. https://escholarship.org/uc/item/60z7p0kp.

Childs, Nick and Tom Waldwyn 2018. "China's Naval Shipbuilding: Delivering on its Ambition in a Big Way". *IISS Military Balance Blog*, May 1, 2018. www.iiss.org/blogs/military-balance/2018/05/china-naval-shipbuilding.

China Statistical Yearbook 2017. Beijing: China Statistics Press. www.stats.gov.cn/tjsj/ndsj/2017/indexeh.htm.

China Trade and External Economic Statistical Yearbook. Various years. Beijing: China Statistics Press.

CSIS China Power Project. 2018 [2015]. "What does China Really Spend on Its Military?" China Power Project, CSIS, December 28, 2015. Updated May 30, 2018. Accessed August 2, 2018. https://chinapower.csis.org/military-spending/.

Defense News Top 100 of 2018 Database. https://people.defensenews.com/top-100/.

Department of Defense 2017. *Military and Security Developments Involving the People's Republic of China 2017*. Annual Report to Congress. www.defense.gov/Portals/1/Documents/pubs/2017_China_Military_Power_Report.PDF.

Ding, Arthur S. 1996. "Economic Reform and Defence Industries in China". In *Chinese Economic Reform: The Impact on Security*, ed. by Gerald Segal and Richard H. Yang, 78–91. London and New York: Routledge.

EDA 2018. *Defence Data 2016-2017: Key findings and analysis*. Brussels: European Defence Agency. www.eda.europa.eu/docs/default-source/brochures/eda_defencedata_a4.

Fleurant, Aude., Alexandra Kuimova, Nan Tian, Pieter D. Wezeman, and Siemon T. Wezeman 2018. "The SIPRI Top 100 Arms-Producing and Military Services Companies, 2017." SIPRI Fact Sheet. www.sipri.org/publications/2018/sipri-fact-sheets/sipri-top-100-arms-producing-and-military-services-companies-2017.

Foster, Robert. 2012. "Russia to Sell, Co-produce Lada-class Submarines to China". *Jane's Navy International* (el. ed.), December 21, 2012.

Frankenstein, John. 1998. "China's Defense Industries: A New Course?" Asia Research Centre Copenhagen Business School Working Paper No. 5. www.rand.org/content/dam/rand/pubs/conf_proceedings/CF145/CF145.chap10.pdf.

"Frictions between Russia & China on Imitation of Russian Navy Equipments". 2009. *Kanwa Asian Defence* No. 62, Dec. 2009: 15.

Friedman, Norman. 2006. *The Naval Institute Guide to World Naval Weapon Systems*. 5th ed. Annapolis: Naval Institute Press.

Godement, François. 1996. "China's Arms Sales". In *Chinese Economic Reform: The Impact on Security*, eds. Gerald Segal and Richard H. Yang, 95–110. London and New York: Routledge.

Grevatt, Jon. 2011a. "China and Russia Agree to Expand Defence Relations". *Jane's Defence Weekly* (el. ed.), August 9, 2011.

Grevatt, Jon. 2011b. "China to Double Lending to Strategic Industries". *Jane's Defence Weekly* (el. ed.), March 8, 2011.

Grevatt, Jon. 2013. "Briefing: Closing the Gaps". *Jane's Defence Weekly* (el. ed.), July 5, 2013.

Grevatt, Jon. 2017a. "China State Shipbuilding Makes Plans to Centralise Procurement". *Jane's Defence Weekly* (el. ed.), Jan. 6, 2017.

Grevatt, Jon. 2017b. "A Great Leap Forward". *Jane's Defence Weekly* (el. ed.), May 3, 2017.

Grevatt, Jon. 2017c. "China Aims to be A World Leader in Artificial Intelligence". *Jane's Defence Weekly* (el. ed.), July 25, 2017.

Grevatt, Jon. 2018. "China's CSIC secures 'international credit line' worth USD7.3 billion". *Jane's Defence Weekly* (el. ed.), Dec. 6, 2018.

Hannas, William C., James Mulvenon, and Anna B. Puglisi 2013. *Chinese Industrial Espionage: Technology Acquisition and Military Modernization*. London: Routledge.

Hartley, Keith. 2017. *The Economics of Arms*. Agenda: Newcastle.

Huang, Paul. 2018. "By Snatching Up British Company, China Closes Gap on US Naval Supremacy". *Epoch Times*, Dec. 15, 2017. Updated Feb. 4, 2018. www.theepochtimes.com/by-snatching-up-british-company-china-closes-gap-on-us-naval-supremacy_2389025.html.

IISS 2018. *The Military Balance 2018*. London: Routledge.

Joffe, Ellis. 1996. "The PLA and the Economy: effects of involvement". In *Chinese Economic Reform: The Impact on Security*, ed. by Gerald Segal and Richard H. Yang, 11–34. London and New York: Routledge.

Johnson, Reuben F. 2013. "China's Domination of Global Arms Trade 'Inevitable', say Russian, Ukrainian Industry Insiders." *Janes's Defence Weekly*. https://janes.ihs.com/DefenceWeekly/Display/1555180.

Johnson, Reuben F. 2015a. "Su-35 Deal Signals PLAAF's Lack of Faith in Chinese Defence Sector". *Jane's Defence Weekly* (el. ed.), Nov. 25, 2015.

Johnson, Reuben F. 2015b. "China Continues to Depend on Ukrainian Aero Engines". *Jane's Defence Weekly* (el. ed.) Dec 10, 2015.

Johnson, Reuben F. and James Hardy 2013. "Ukraine Preparing to Offer China Use of NITKA Carrier Training Facility". *Jane's Defence Weekly* (el. ed.), November 14, 2013.

Joske, Alex. 2018. *Picking flowers, making honey: The Chinese military's collaboration with foreign universities*. ASPI International Cyber Policy Center Policy Brief, Report No. 10/2018, Oct. 30, 2018. www.aspi.org.au/report/picking-flowers-making-honey.

Kania, Elsa B. 2018. *Technological Entanglement: Cooperation, competition and the dual-use dilemma in artificial intelligence*. ASPI International Cyber Policy Centre Policy Brief Report No. 7/2018, June 28, 2018. www.aspi.org.au/report/technological-entanglement.

Kirchberger, Sarah. 2015. *Assessing China's Naval Power: Technological Change, Economic Constraints, and Strategic Implications*. Berlin & Heidelberg: Springer.

Kirchberger, Sarah. 2017. "The end of a military-industrial triangle: arms-industrial co-operation between China, Russia and Ukraine after the Crimea crisis". *SIRIUS – Zeitschrift für Strategische Analysen* 1(2) (2017): 1–19. www.degruyter.com/view/j/sirius.2017.1.issue-2/sirius-2017-0053/sirius-2017-0053.xml.

Lague, David and Charlie Zhu 2012. "China Builds Its Own Military-Industrial Complex". *Reuters UK*, September 17, 2012. http://uk.reuters.com/article/2012/09/17/uk-china-defenceidUKBRE88F0G720120917.

Lewis, Jeffrey. 2014. *Paper Tigers: China's Nuclear Posture*. London: IISS and Routledge.

Li, Xiaobing. 2009. *A History of the Modern Chinese Army*. Lexington: The University Press of Kentucky.

Liff, Adam P., and Andrew S. Erickson 2013. "Demystifying China's Defence Spending: Less Mysterious in the Aggregate". *The China Quarterly* 216 (2013): 805–830.

Lin, Jeffrey and P.W. Singer 2016. "The Great Underwater Wall Of Robots: Chinese Exhibit Shows Off Sea Drones". *Popular Science*, June 22, 2016. www.popsci.com/great-underwater-wall-robots-chinese-exhibit-shows-off-sea-drones.

McTague, Tom. 2014. "Time to pay your way: France and Germany told to 'urgently' increase military spending as the price of Nato membership". *Daily Mail* online, September 4, 2014. www.dailymail.co.uk/news/article-2743710/Time-pay-way-France-Germany-told-urgentlyincrease-military-spending-price-Nato-membership.html.

Medeiros, Evan S., Roger Cliff, Keith Crande, and James C. Mulvenon 2005. *A New Direction for China's Defense Industry*. Santa Monica: RAND.

Naughton, Barry. 2018. *The Chinese Economy: Adaption and Growth*. 2nd edition. Cambridge: MIT Press.

Nouwens, Meia and Lucie Béraud-Sudreau 2018. "Global Defence-Industry League: Where is China?" *IISS Military Balance Blog*, Aug. 28, 2018. www.iiss.org/blogs/military-balance/2018/08/china-global-defence-industry-league.

Nurkin, Tate. 2015. "Catching Up: China's Space Programme Marches On." *Jane's Defence Weekly* (el. ed.), July 30, 2015.

Parsons, Ted. 2011. "Analysis: Could China Profit From Bin Laden Helo Wreckage?" *Jane's Defence Weekly* (el. ed.), May 6, 2011.

Ping, Kefu 平可夫 (a.k.a. Pinkov, Andrei) 2010. *Zhongguo zhizao hangkong mujian* (China constructs aircraft carriers). Hong Kong: Kanwa Press.

Raska, Michael. 2014. "The Chinese Defence Industry in 2030". In *The Global Arms Industry in 2030 (and Beyond)*, 31–33. *Event Report*, RSIS, Nov. 10, 2014, www.rsis.edu.sg/wp-content/uploads/2015/01/ER150123_Global_Arms_Industry.pdf. Accessed Dec. 27, 2018.

Raska, Michael. 2017. "Strategic Contours of China's Arms Exports". *RSIS Commentary* No. 165, Sept. 11, 2017. www.rsis.edu.sg/wp-content/uploads/2017/09/CO17165.pdf.

"Russia and China have a Widening Difference on Battleship Maintenance". 2009. *Kanwa Asian Defence Monthly* No. 62, Dec. 2009: 16.

Schwartz, Paul. 2017. "Russia-China Defense Cooperation: New Developments". *Special Forum* 5(1): January–February 2017. www.theasanforum.org/russia-china-defense cooperation-new-developments/.

Shambaugh, David. 2004. *Modernizing China's Military: Progress, Problems, and Prospects.* Paperback ed.. Berkeley: University of California Press.

Sinkkonen, Elina. 2018. "China-Russia Security Cooperation. Geopolitical Signalling with Limits". FIIA Briefing Paper 231, January 2018. www.fiia.fi/en/publication/china-russia-security-cooperation.

SIPRI Military Expenditure Database. 2018. www.sipri.org/databases/milex.

Stålenheim, Petter and Eamon Surry 2006. "Transparency in Military Expenditure and Arms Production." Paper presented at the Xiangshan Forum, 22–24 October 2006. www.sipri.org/research/armaments/production/publications/unpubl_aprod/xiangshan.

Stumbaum, May-Britt U. 2009. "Risky Business? The EU, China and Dual-use Technology." Occasional Paper. Vol. 80. Paris: European Union Institute for Security Studies (EUISS). www.iss.europa.eu/uploads/media/op80.pdf.

Sun, Jiansong 孙剑嵩. 2018. "Guowuyuan pizhun Zhongguo he gongye jituan yu Zhongguo he gongye jianshe jituan chongzu" (State Council approves reorganization of China National Nuclear Corporation and China Nuclear Engineering & Construction Corporation). *Sina.com*, Jan. 31, 2018. http://finance.sina.com.cn/chanjing/gsnews/2018-01-31/doc-ifyrcsrw1226244.shtml.

Tate, Andrew. 2018. "China Quietly Increasing Warship Numbers". *Jane's Defence Weekly* (el. ed.), Sept. 21, 2018.

United Nations Register of Conventional Arms database (UNROCA). www.unroca.org/.

Unnithan, Sandeep. 2018. "We can match China in the Indian Ocean region, says Navy chief Sunil Lanba". *India Today*, Nov. 17, 2018. www.indiatoday.in/magazine/interview/story/20181126-we-can-match-china-in-the-indian-ocean-region-admiral-sunil-lanba-1388904-2018-11-17.

Wang, Yi and Liming Wan 2018. "Sanxian jianshe zhong Si-Yu diqu guofang qiye fazhan yu buju (Study on the Development and Layout of National Defense Industry in Sichaun-Chongqing Region during the Third-line Construction". *Xinan jiaotong daxue xuebao (Southwest Transportation University Journal)* 19(1): 123–28.

Wertheim, Eric. 2013. *The Naval Institute Guide to Combat Fleets of the World.* 16th ed.. Annapolis/Maryland: Naval Institute Press.

"Wo guo dayue 3000 jia minqi yi jinru jungong caigou yixian". 2018. (Around 3000 Civil Corporations Already Joined the Military-Industrial Procurement Line). *Xinhua*, March 14, 2018. http://m.xinhuanet.com/mil/2018-03/14/c_129829001.htm.

Wolf, Charles, Jr., Siddhartha Dalal, Julie DaVanzo, Eric V. Larson, Alisher Akhmedjonov, Harun Dogo, Meilinda Huang and Silvia Montoya 2011. *China and India, 2025: A Comparative Assessment*. Santa Monica: RAND Corporation.

Zhang, Qingmin and Eric Hyer 2001. "US 'Dual Track' Policy: Arms Sales and Technology Transfer to China Mainland and Taiwan". *Journal of Contemporary China* (2001), 10(26): 89–105.

Zheng, William. 2018. "China's Aircraft Carrier Troubles Continue with More Researchers Charged with Corruption". *South China Morning Post*, Dec. 28, 2018. www.scmp.com/news/china/military/article/2179855/chinas-aircraft-carrier-troubles-continue-more-researchers.

Zhonggong zhongyang bangongting, guowuyuan bangongting guanyu jundui wujing budui zhengfa jiguan bu zai congshi jingshang huodong de tongzhi. (*Circular of the CCP Central Committee General Office and the State Council General Office about stopping the engagement of the PLA, the Armed Police and political and judicial institutions in commercial activities*). 1998. News of the Communist Party of China, July 25, 1998. http://cpc.people.com.cn/GB/64162/71380/71382/71384/4848043.html.

Zhongguo de junshi zhanlüe (*China's Military Strategy*). 2015. Published by the State Council Information Office, PRC, in May 2015. www.mod.gov.cn/auth/2015-05/26/content_4586723_3.htm.

4 The Russian defence industry, 1980–2025

Systemic change, policies, performance and prospects

Christopher Mark Davis

1. Introduction

Russia has had one of the world's largest defence industries since 1900, with significant institutional continuities, but it has operated in differing political and economic systems and has experienced both failures (World War I) and successes (World War II: Davis, 1999, 2014). During the Cold War the Soviet defence industry functioned as a high priority branch of a centrally planned economy and produced large quantities of innovative and effective modern weapons (Davis, 2002). The Russian defence-industrial complex (OPK) suffered during the 1990s due to the lowering of its priority and the general economic collapse.[1] However, since 2000 the Russian defence industry has again become one of the most powerful internationally due to the country's economic recovery and its renewed high-priority status.

Due to the complexity of developments in the OPK of Russia over the past forty years, the Chapter is divided into three sub-periods (1980–1991, 1992–1999, and 2000–2019), with each having four sub-sections: (1) defence expenditure and foreign trade in weapons and military equipment; (2) politico-economic system, organisation of the defence sector, priority, and features of the defence industry; (3) structure, conditions, and performance of defence industry enterprises; and (4) military procurement and defence industry conversion.

Acquisition by scholars of official information about the OPK in the USSR and Russia always has proved challenging (e.g. strict Soviet censorship), so Russian official material has been supplemented by assessments and estimates produced by foreign governments, international organisations, and academics. Due to the word limit of this chapter, the references in the Soviet and early transition sections are mainly to the past publications of the author, which contain several hundred citations of sources. Fuller referencing is made in the contemporary section (2000–2019), which should be of greatest interest to readers.

2. USSR and Russia defence expenditure and military foreign trade: 1980–2019

a. USSR 1980–1991

The USSR awarded a high priority to the defence sector and allocated substantial resources to support its operations. It also exported large quantities of weapons and military equipment (WME).

Since the arbitrary prices and misleading budgets in the Soviet command economy did not measure or govern real resource flows, this sub-section is based primarily on Western reconstructions of the USSR's defence expenditure (DE) and military foreign trade.[2]

(1) Defence expenditure 1980–1991

Table 4.1 shows that official Soviet defence budget expenditure rose from 13 billion current rubles in 1965 to 20 billion in 1988. The second row provides a later estimate by Maslyukov and Glubokov (2005), who worked in the Soviet OPK. The more plausible CIA estimated value in row three, based on the "building block method" explained in Firth and Noren (1998), increased from 33 billion rubles to 163 billion. CIA estimated real DE (1982 rubles) rose from 66 billion in 1965 to peak of 125 billion in 1988. Soviet budget statistics implied that the country had a low defence burden (DE/GDP) in the 2.3–2.5% range, but the CIA calculated that in current rubles it rose from 13.2% in 1965 to a peak of 17.8% in 1988, whereas in constant 1982 prices it declined from 16.0% to 15.5% (Davis, 2002).

The acquisition of WME (equivalent to procurement) accounted for the largest share of DE in 1985 at 43%, with military R&D (MRD) second at 21%. Soviet production and acquisition of WME was centrally planned, but in 1985 an experimental State Armaments Programme (*Gosudarstvennaya Programma Vooruzhennii*, or *GPV*) was introduced with the intention (not achieved) of using State Military Orders (*Gosudarstvennyy Oboronyy Zakaz*, or *GOZ*) to link the GPV to purchases by the main customer, the Ministry of Defence (MoD) (Zatsepin, 2012, See Section 3.c.(1)).

(2) Exports and imports of weapons and military equipment, 1980-1991

USSR foreign trade in WME was heavily weighted in favour of exports because of the country's policy of self-sufficiency, Western economic restrictions and the advanced state of the Soviet defence industry. Table 4.2 shows that the value of its exports of WME to countries that were in the Warsaw Pact, socialist Third World (e.g. Vietnam), and the non-aligned group (notably India) increased from $17.0 billion (current dollars)

Table 4.1 USSR defence expenditure, 1965–1991

Indicator		*1965*	*1970*	*1975*	*1980*	*1985*	*1988*	*1989*	*1990*	*1991*
Defence Expenditure										
USSR DE (Official Soviet)	Billion Current Rubles	12.8	17.8	17.4	17.1	19.1	20.2	75.2	69.1	96.6
USSR DE (M&S 2005)	Billion Current Rubles	22.3	29.2		48.9	63.4	76.9	77.3	71.0	
USSR DE (CIA)	Billion Current Rubles	33.0	46.9	68.0	94.0	126.2	163.3	160.1	160.0	250.6
USSR DE (CIA)	Billion 1982 Rubles	66.3	82.2	97.3	105.7	111.9	124.8	116.5	109.7	98.7
USA DE (Conversion)	Billion 1982 Rubles	80.9	101.4	73.2	88.1	127.2	154.1	147.5	140.6	135.5
USSR Defence Procurement (CIA)	Billion 1982 Rubles	32.8	41.5	47.8	49.1	47.9	52.7	46.9	42.5	38.2
USSR Military Construction (CIA)	Billion 1982 Rubles	5.7	4.4	4.8	5.9	5.7	6.1	5.9	6.0	5.4
USSR Military Personnel (CIA)	Billion 1982 Rubles	9.6	11.4	12.5	13.3	13.6	13.8	13.5	12.8	11.6
USSR Military O & M (CIA)	Billion 1982 Rubles	9.3	12.8	16.1	18.1	21.0	24.0	22.0	21.6	19.4
USSR Military RDT&E (CIA)	Billion 1982 Rubles	8.9	12.1	16.1	19.3	23.7	28.2	28.2	26.8	24.1
USSR DE (CIA)	Billion 1988 $	190	222	255	270	284	297	286	264	217
USA DE (CIA)	Billion 1988 $	220	260	192	211	283	299	296	286	252
USSR DE (SIPRI)	Billion 2016 $	NA	NA	NA	NA	NA	243.1	225.4	190.7	NA
Defence Burden										
DE/GDP Current Rubles (CIA)	%	13.2	12.2	13.7	14.8	15.9	17.8	15.6	15.4	12.1
DE/GDP Constant Rubles (CIA)	%	16.0	15.4	15.5	15.3	14.9	15.5	14.3	13.8	13.6

Prepared by C. Davis in 2019.

Sources: Davis (2002), which used Noren (1995), Firth and Noren (1998), and IISS (1980–1990) Military Balance. The table has been supplemented by statistics from Maslyukov and Glubokov (2005) and SIPRI Database.

Table 4.2 USSR weapons and military equipment exports and imports, 1980–1991

Indicator	*Units*	*1980*	*1981*	*1982*	*1983*	*1984*	*1985*	*1986*	*1987*	*1988*	*1989*	*1990*	*1991*
U.S. Arms Control and Disarmament Agency (ACDA)													
USSR Exports WME	$ Current billions	17.0	17.8	18.9	19.4	19.4	17.3	21.5	21.9	21.7	19.8	14.2	6.6
	$ Constant 1991 billions	27.7	26.6	26.6	26.2	25.1	21.6	26.1	25.8	24.6	21.5	14.8	6.6
Total USSR Exports	$ Current billions	76.4	79.4	87.2	91.7	91.5	87.2	97.1	107.7	110.7	109.3	101.0	68.0
	$ Constant 1991 billions	125.1	118.5	122.5	123.8	118.8	108.8	117.9	126.8	125.6	118.6	105.0	68.0
WME Share of Total USSR Exports	%	22.2	22.4	21.7	21.2	21.2	19.8	22.2	20.3	19.6	18.1	14.1	9.7
USSR Share of World WME Exports	%	47.4	39.9	38.4	38.5	34.5	34.1	42.7	37.5	39.9	39.6	37.2	26.0
USSR WME Imports	$ Current billions	1.3	1.0	1.0	1.5	1.4	1.2	1.3	1.3	1.2	0.9	1.0	0.0
	$ Constant 1991 billions	2.1	1.5	1.4	2.0	1.8	1.5	1.6	1.5	1.4	1.0	0.1	0.0
Total USSR Imports	$ Current billions	68.5	73.2	77.9	80.4	80.4	83.3	88.9	96.0	107.3	114.7	139.0	78.0
	$ Constant 1991 billions	112.1	109.3	109.4	108.7	104.0	103.0	108.0	113.0	121.7	124.4	144.6	78.0
USSR WME Imports as Share of Total Imports	%	1.9	1.4	1.3	1.9	1.7	1.4	1.5	1.4	1.1	0.8	0.1	0.0

Prepared by C. Davis in 2019.

Sources: ACDA (1990, 1992) World Military Expenditure and Arms Trade (WMEAT).

in 1980 to a peak of $21.9 billion in 1987. During 1975–85 its deliveries included 15,000 tanks, 5,600 fighter aircraft, and 66 surface warships (DOD 1986).

The Soviet Union did not import major weapons, even from Warsaw Pact allies. Table 4.2 shows that imports of WME fluctuated around an average of $1.2 billion (current) over 1980–1989, but fell to zero following the dissolution of the Warsaw Pact. In order to circumvent Western economic warfare, the USSR developed large and sophisticated programmes of trade diversion (e.g. obtaining restricted machinery for the OPK through third-party countries) and technological espionage (the "special information" (*spetsinformatsiya*) system: CIA 1985 and Section 3.a.(9)).

b. *Russia 1992–1999*

In the 1990s Russia's fragmented and weak political system and the low priority of defence in a malfunctioning economy contributed to declines in both defence spending and WME exports.

(1) Defence expenditure 1992–1999

Table 4.3 shows the official statistics of rising DE in current rubles in a high inflation environment. However, the estimated index of real defence spending (1992 = 100.0) fell to a low of 39.9 in 1998 (Noren, 1995; Gaddy, 1996; Firth and Noren, 1998; Davis, 2002). The official *National Defence* budget covered spending on the armed forces (military and civilian personnel minus pensions), operations and maintenance, procurement of WME, military R&D (MRD), military construction, and the military atomic programme (Zatsepin, 2007). However, total DE was higher by around 30% due to contributions from other budget items: interior and border service troops, road construction and railway troops, civil defence and mobilisation measures in industry.

IISS (1990…2019) estimated that in dollar terms defence spending fell from $146 billion ($1997) in 1992 to $55 billion in 1998, or by 62%. Estimates by SIPRI and NATO of declining dollar expenditures and indexes also are provided in Table 4.3.

The share of DE devoted to personnel and O&M (operations & maintenance) rose to from 30% in 1991 to 52% in 1996, whereas that of procurement of WME dropped from around 40% to 16% (Kuzyk, 1999). The estimated indexes of real expenditure on procurement of WME and MRD in Russia fell from 100 in 1991 to, respectively, 9.5 and 7.5 by 1996. According to official Russian statistics, the defence share of GDP in current rubles declined from 4.5% in 1992 to 2.1% in 1998, whereas the SIPRI measure decreased from 4.4% to 2.7%.

Table 4.3 Russian Federation defence expenditure, 1992–1999

Indicator		*1992*	*1993*	*1994*	*1995*	*1996*	*1997*	*1998*	*1999*
Defence Expenditure in Rubles									
Authorised Defence Budget	Mln Current	901	8327	40,626	59,379	80,185	104,318	92,763	107,083
Defence Budget Outlay	Mln Current	855	7213	28,500	49,600	63,891	79,692	68,004	135,116
Outlay Share of Authorised	%	94.9	86.6	70.2	83.5	79.7	76.4	73.3	126.2
Other Outlay on Defence	Mln Current	427	3607	14,250	25,237	31,011	38,551	32,897	62,102
Total Defence Expenditure	Mln Current	1282	10,819	42,750	74,837	94,902	118,243	100,901	197,218
IISS Defence Budget Outlay	Mln Current	855	7210	28,028	47,800	63,900	79,700	56,700	116,000
GDP	Mln Current	19,006	171,510	610,745	1,540,500	2,145,700	2,521,900	2,684,500	4,476,100
Real GDP Index	1992 = 100	100.0	91.3	79.7	76.4	73.8	74.5	71.1	73.4
Real DE Index	1992 = 100	100.0	86.0	83.3	55.4	48.7	52.1	39.9	46.8
Defence Expenditure in Dollars									
IISS Defence Expend $	Bln $ 1997	146.0	114.0	101.0	86.0	73.0	64.0	55.0	56.0
IISS DE $ 1997 Index	1992 = 100	100.0	78.1	69.2	58.9	50.0	43.8	37.7	38.4
SIPRI Defence Expend $	Bln $ 1995	47.5	41.9	40.5	25.7	23.4	24.9	18.1	22.4
SIPRI Defence Expend $	Bln $ 2017	48.7	42.5	40.2	26.5	25.0	27.3	16.2	18.0
SIPRI $ 1995 Index	1992 = 100	100.0	88.2	85.3	54.1	49.3	52.4	38.1	47.2
SIPRI $ 2017 Index	1992 = 100	100.0	87.3	82.5	54.4	51.3	56.1	33.3	37.0
NATO $ Index	1992 = 100	100.0	76.3	60.5	47.3	42.0	36.8	31.5	34.1
Shares of Defence Budget									
Personnel + O&M	%	55.4	50.0	54.4	53.7	51.3	46.4	54.5	51.9
Procurement	%	20.5	18.3	20.8	17.3	16.5	20.1	20.8	19.4
Military R&D	%	8.3	7.2	6.0	8.3	8.1	11.1	13.2	11.4

Infrastructure	%	13.5	16.5	11.8	10.3	9.5	4.8	4.0	2.9
Pensions	%	5.0	5.5	4.9	8.2	12.3	13.3	13.5	10.9
Nuclear, Other	%	2.3	2.6	2.2	2.2	2.3	4.3	7.5	3.4
Defence Burden									
Defence Share of Budget	%	16.0	16.6	20.9	21.3	18.4	19.7	16.4	18.0
Official DE/GDP	%	4.5	4.8	6.6	3.7	3.8	3.1	2.1	2.6
SIPRI DE/GDP	%	4.4	4.2	4.5	3.8	3.8	4.0	2.7	3.1

Prepared by C. Davis in 2019.
Sources: Davis (2002), based on Firth and Noren (1998), IISS (1990 … 2019) Military Balance, NATO (2000), SIPRI Yearbook (2000 … 2018), SIPRI Database (2019).

Table 4.4 Russian weapons and military equipment exports and imports, 1992–1999

Indicator	*Units*	*1992*	*1993*	*1994*	*1995*	*1996*	*1997*	*1998*	*1999*
Weapons and Military Equipment Exports									
(1) OPK 2016									
WME Exports Total	$ Bln Current	2.3	2.5	1.7	3.0	3.5	2.6	2.6	3.4
(2) ACDA and IISS									
WME Exports (ACDA)	$ Bln Current	2.5	3.5	1.7	3.5	3.0	2.6	2.2	3.1
	$ Bln 1999	2.9	3.9	1.8	3.7	3.1	2.7	2.2	3.1
Total Exports (ACDA)	$ Bln Current	43.0	44.3	67.5	81.1	88.6	88.3	74.9	74.7
	$ Bln Constant 1999	49.1	49.3	73.7	86.6	92.8	90.7	76.0	74.7
WME Share of Total Exports (ACDA)	%	5.8	7.9	2.5	4.3	3.4	2.9	2.9	4.2
WME Exports (IISS)	$ Bln Current	2.5	3.2	1.5	3.7	3.4	2.7	2.4	3.3
	$ Bln 1997	2.8	3.4	2.9	3.7	3.6	2.7	2.9	3.4
Russia Share of World WME Exports (ACDA)	%	5.4	7.2	6.8	7.9	7.0	4.5	5.1	6.6
Weapons and Military Equipment Imports									
(3) ACDA									
WME Imports	$ Mln Current	0.0	0.0	0.0	5.0	40.0	30.0	40.0	470.0
	$ Mln 1999	0.0	0.0	0.0	5.0	42.0	31.0	41.0	470.0
Total Imports	$ Bln Current	37.0	32.8	50.5	61.0	74.9	76.1	63.8	43.6
	$ Bln 1999	42.2	36.5	55.1	65.1	78.4	78.2	64.8	43.6
WME Share of Total Imports	%	0.0	0.0	0.0	0.0	0.1	0.0	0.1	1.1

Prepared by C. Davis in 2019.
Sources: (1) Oboronno-Promyshlennyy (2016); (2) ACDA (1992–2000) WMEAT; ACDA WMEAT = U.S () WMEAT Online Database; IISS (1990 … 2019) Military Balance; (3) ACDA (1992–2000) WMEAT; ACDA Database.

(2) Exports and imports of weapons and military equipment, 1992–1999

Table 4.4 shows that the value of Russia's exports of WME fluctuated in the $1.7–$3.5 billion range over the 1990s (around 4% of the value of total exports: Fel'gengauer, 2010). The average annual quantities of weapons delivered by Russia dropped to less than one-sixth of those shipped by the USSR in 1988. The Asia-Pacific region accounted for 43% of Russian sales (China was the largest customer) and the Middle East 24%.

Many of the NATO restrictions on sales of technologies to Russia were relaxed. This resulted in a growth of Russia's legal defence-related imports, especially electronics, from zero during 1992–1994 to $470 million in 1999 (15% of arms exports). The Russian trade diversion system became inactive and its technological espionage was of a lower intensity (Davis, 2016, 2017).

c. *Russia 2000–2019*

During the 2000s Russia's defence spending in real terms and exports of armaments increased because of the recovery of the economy, renewed high priority of defence and the improved performance of the OPK.

(1) Defence expenditure 2000–2019

The initial row of Table 4.5 shows official defence budget expenditures from the statistical yearbook. The second row presents the estimates by IET (2000-2019) of spending from the formal defence budget, which increased from 191.7 billion current rubles in 2000 to a peak of 3777.6 billion in 2016. Both series contain expenditures in 2016 and 2017 that represent settlements of debts to the defence industry (respectively 790 billion rubles and 187 billion) (IET, 2000-2019; IISS, 1990–2019). The defence budget includes expenditures on the armed forces, mobilisation, nuclear weapons complex, international military obligations, and military R&D. Defence-related expenditures in other budget categories include parts of national security, military construction, social support of the military, and pensions (IET, 2000-2019; Davis, 2002; Oxenstierna and Westerlund, 2013). Total DE increased from 292.2 billion current rubles in 2000 to 4913.0 billion in 2016. The index of real (2017 rubles) total DE tripled from 100.0 in 2000 to a peak of 265.8 in 2016.

The table shows the calculations of IET and IISS of DE in current dollar values. SIPRI has estimated that DE in constant (2017) dollars rose from $24.3 billion in 2000 (index 100) to a peak of $82.6 billion in 2016 (index 340), but then declined to $64.2 billion in 2018 (index 264).

The State Defence Order (GOZ) rose slowly from 71.9 billion current rubles in 2000 to 509.1 billion in 2010, or from 71.9 to 128.6 billion constant 2017 rubles (IET, 2000-2019; Oxenstierna and Westerlund, 2013). It then accelerated due to the implementation of the State Armaments

Table 4.5a Russian Federation defence expenditure, 2000–2018

Indicator		*2000*	*2001*	*2002*	*2003*	*2004*	*2005*	*2006*	*2007*	*2008*	*2009*	*2010*	*2011*	*2012*	*2013*	*2014*	*2015*	*2016*	*2017*	*2018*
Defence Expenditure (DE) in Rubles: Rosstat (RSE and RvT), Institute of the Economy in Transition (IET) and IISS																				
Defence Budget Rosstat	Bln R Current	191.7	247.7	295.4	355.7	430.0	581.8	683.4	834.0	1043.6	1191.2	1279.7	1517.2	1814.1	2105.5	2480.7	3182.7	2982.0	2854.2	2770.0
Defence Budget IET	Bln R Current	191.7	247.7	295.4	355.7	430.0	578.4	686.1	839.1	1031.6	1192.9	1278.0	1537.4	1846.3	2111.7	2470.6	3163.8	3777.6	2854.2	2828.4
Other DE IET	Bln R Current	100.5	53.3	129.4	194.0	148.8	196.8	264.5	299.5	405.1	557.5	600.7	626.8	840.2	888.0	977.2	1129.6	1135.5	1402.6	1397.4
Total Defence IET	Bln R Current	292.2	301.0	424.8	549.7	578.8	778.6	947.8	1133.5	1448.8	1748.7	1880.3	2164.2	2686.5	2999.7	3447.8	4293.4	4913.0	4256.8	4225.8
Defence Budget IISS	Bln R Current	191.7	247.7	295.4	355.7	430.0	581.4	681.8	831.9	1040.9	1188.7	1276.5	1516.0	1812.0	2106.0	2479.0	3181.0	2982.0	2666.0	2830.0
Other DE IISS	Bln R Current	95.9	123.9	147.7	177.9	215.0	290.7	371.2	385.1	529.2	670.6	483.0	513.0	693.0	681.0	745.0	845.0	849.0	1046.0	1105.0
Total DE IISS	Bln R Current	287.6	371.6	443.1	533.6	645.0	872.1	1053.0	1217.0	1570.1	1859.3	1760.0	2029.0	2505.0	2787.0	3224.0	4026.0	3831.0	3712.0	3935.0
Total Defence IET	Bln R 2017	1938.8	1714.5	2092.8	2380.2	2083.6	2349.3	2483.2	2609.4	2827.4	3346.0	3150.9	3099.4	3517.5	3763.5	4044.1	4687.6	5176.4	4256.8	3831.3
Total Defence IET	Index 2000=100 Bln R 2017	100.0	88.4	107.9	122.8	107.5	121.2	128.1	134.6	145.8	172.6	162.5	159.9	181.4	194.1	208.6	240.8	265.8	218.7	197.3

Defence Expenditure Current and Constant Dollars: IET, IISS, SIPRI

Defence Budget IET	$ Bln Current	6.8	8.5	9.4	11.6	14.9	20.6	25.1	32.6	42.0	37.5	42.1	51.6	58.3	66.1	64.6	52.2	56.4	48.9	45.1
Total Defence IET	$ Bln Current	10.4	10.3	13.6	17.9	20.1	27.5	34.9	44.3	58.3	55.1	61.9	73.0	85.4	94.0	90.0	70.7	73.3	72.9	67.4
Defence Budget IISS	$ Bln Current	5.1	7.5	8.4	10.6	14.9	18.7	24.9	32.2	40.5	38.3	41.9	51.6	58.8	66.1	64.5	51.9	46.6	45.7	45.3
Total DE IISS	$ Bln Current	7.7	11.3	12.6	15.9	23.6	25.7	38.8	47.6	63.3	57.2	62.9	77.4	88.2	99.2	84.0	66.1	57.2	63.6	63.1
SIPRI DE $	Bln $ 2016	20.4	22.1	24.4	25.6	26.8	30.4	33.7	36.7	40.3	42.3	43.1	46.0	53.3	55.9	59.9	64.6	69.2	55.3	53.3
SIPRI DE $2016	1992 = 100	100.0	108.3	119.6	125.5	131.4	149.0	165.2	179.9	197.5	207.4	211.3	225.5	261.3	274.0	293.6	316.7	339.2	271.1	261.6

Notes: (1) Total DE in current rubles estimated by IET and IISS includes both expenditures from the official defence budget and defence-related spending from other budget categories. Details are provided in their publications; (2) The series on real DE in 2018 rubles and the related index show that defence spending in real terms rose at modest rates through 2010, but then accelerated to reach a peak in 2016; (3) IET and IISS estimate similar DE in current $; (4) The index of real DE in $2016 rose by more than did that of real spending in 2000 rubles.

Prepared by C. Davis in 2019. Sources: IET (2000–2019); TsAST (2006, 2016); Rosstat (2000–2018) Rossiiskii Statisticheskii Ezhegodnik (RSE); Rosstat (2019) Rossiya v Tsifrakh (RvT); IISS, 1990…2019 Military Balance; SIPRI Database (2019).

Table 4.5b Russian Federation defence expenditure, 2000–2018

Indicator	*Units*	*2000*	*2001*	*2002*	*2003*	*2004*	*2005*	*2006*	*2007*	*2008*	*2009*	*2010*	*2011*	*2012*	*2013*	*2014*	*2015*	*2016*	*2017*	*2018*
Expenditures on State Defence Order (GOZ) for Weapons (VVT), Military R&D (MRD), VVT Repair: IET and Tsentr Analiza Strategii i Tekhnologii (TsAST)																				
GOZ Total IET	Bln R Current	71.9	63.0	82.3	120.0	147.5	227.1	270.8	337.3	420.6	500.2	509.1	707.6	888.4	1,283.0	1,676.1	1,767.1	2,106.0	1,468.6	1,297.4
GOZ Total IET	Bln 2000 R	71.9	54.1	61.1	78.3	80.0	103.3	106.9	117.0	123.7	144.2	128.6	154.2	177.4	243.1	295.4	289.5	333.5	221.3	177.3
GOZ Total IET	% Growth Current	NA	-12.4	30.6	45.8	22.9	54.0	19.2	24.6	24.7	18.9	1.8	39.0	25.5	44.4	30.6	5.4	18.9	-30.1	-11.7
GOZ Share DE IET	% Total DE	24.6	20.9	19.4	21.8	25.5	29.2	28.6	29.8	29.0	28.6	27.1	33.0	33.5	42.9	48.5	41.0	42.8	34.5	30.7
GOZ Total TsAST	Bln R Current	NA	NA	NA	NA	NA	186.6	236.7	302.7	365.0	454.1	490.4	574.6	677.4	894.0	1450.0	1800.0	1600.0	1400.0	1300.0
GOZ VVT TsAST	Bln R Current	NA	NA	NA	NA	NA	112.0	115.5	145.0	200.8	254.3	318.8	367.8	447.1	550.0	942.5	1187.6	1040.0	910.0	845.0
GOZ VVT TsAST	% of GOZ	NA	NA	NA	NA	NA	60.0	48.8	47.9	55.0	56.0	65.0	64.0	66.0	61.5	65.0	66.0	65.0	65.0	65.0
GOZ MRD TsAST	Bln R Current	NA	NA	NA	NA	NA	62.8	72.7	97.7	91.3	122.6	107.9	114.9	122.0	165.4	217.5	252.4	304.0	346.0	312.0
GOZ MRD TsAST	% of GOZ	NA	NA	NA	NA	NA	33.7	30.7	32.3	25.0	27.0	22.0	20.0	18.0	18.5	15.0	14.0	19.0	24.7	24.0
GOZ Repair TsAST	Bln R Current	NA	NA	NA	NA	NA	11.8	48.5	60.0	73.0	77.2	63.7	91.4	108.3	177.9	290.0	360.0	256.0	144.0	143.0
GOZ Repair TsAST	% of GOZ	NA	NA	NA	NA	NA	6.3	20.5	19.8	20.0	17.0	13.0	15.9	16.0	19.9	20.0	20.0	16.0	10.3	11.0

Defence Burden (DE as % GDP): IET and SIPRI																				
DE Total/ GDP IET	%	4.0	3.4	3.9	4.2	3.4	3.6	3.5	3.4	3.5	4.5	4.1	3.6	3.9	4.1	4.4	5.2	5.7	4.6	4.1
DE Total/ Budget IET	%	14.9	12.4	12.4	13.9	12.4	11.4	11.3	10.0	10.2	10.9	10.7	10.7	11.5	11.8	12.5	14.5	15.7	13.1	12.5
DE Total/ GDP SIPRI	%	3.3	3.5	3.8	3.7	3.3	3.3	3.2	3.1	3.1	3.9	3.6	3.4	3.7	3.8	4.1	4.9	5.5	4.2	3.9

Notes: (1) The series on expenditures on State Military Orders (GOZ) take into account outgoings and repayments related to a loan scheme to finance military purchases during 2011–2018. The details are discussed in the annual reports of IET; (2) The shares of VVT, MRD and Repair in GOZ were relatively stable over 2011–2015 so they could be used to project equivalent expenditures through 2018 using the IET aggregate estimate; (3) The IET and SIPRI estimated of the defence burdens are largely similar, despite some methodological differences in making the estimates.

Prepared by C. Davis in 2019. Sources: IET (2000-2019); TsAST (2006, 2016); Frolov (2016a, 2017a , 2018a) Ispolnenie..v 2015 godu, ..v 2016 godu, ..v 2017 godu; SIPRI Database (2019).

Table 4.6 Russia weapons and military equipment (WME) exports and imports, (Federal'naya Sluzhba Gosudarstvennoi Statistiki, 2000-2018)

Indicator	*Unit*	*2000*	*2001*	*2002*	*2003*	*2004*	*2005*	*2006*	*2007*	*2008*	*2009*	*2010*	*2011*	*2012*	*2013*	*2014*	*2015*	*2016*	*2017*	*2018*
(1) OPK and TsAST (Tsentr Analiza Strategii i Tekhnologii)																				
WME Exports Total	$ Bln Current	3.7	3.8	4.8	5.4	5.8	6.2	6.4	7.6	8.4	9.0	10.4	13.2	15.1	15.7	15.0	15.0	15.0	15.0	16.0
of which Rosoboroneksport	$ Bln Current	3.0	3.3	4.0	5.1	5.1	5.2	5.3	6.2	6.7	7.4	8.7	10.9	12.9	13.2	13.0	13.0	13.0	13.0	13.4
	% Total	81	87	83	94	88	84	83	82	80	82	84	83	85	84	87	87	87	87	84
of which Other Exporters	$ Bln Current	0.7	0.5	0.8	0.3	0.7	1.0	1.1	1.4	1.7	1.6	1.7	2.3	2.2	2.5	2.0	2.0	2.0	2.0	2.6
(2) ACDA WMEAT																				
WME Exports	$ Bln Current	4.3	4.6	3.7	4.3	5.7	4.2	6.6	5.4	6.8	5.6	7.2	9.4	10.6	10.8	11.6	10.1	11.9	NA	NA
WME Imports	$ Bln Current	1.2	1.5	2.1	2.9	1.9	1.7	1.3	1.1	1.2	1.2	0.7	0.6	0.6	0.5	0.7	0.2	0.1	NA	NA
WME Share Total Exports	%	3.8	4.1	3.0	2.8	2.8	1.5	2.0	1.4	1.3	1.6	1.6	1.6	1.8	1.8	2.1	2.6	3.6	NA	NA
WME Share Total Imports	%	1.9	2.0	2.5	2.9	1.4	1.0	0.6	0.4	0.3	0.5	0.2	0.1	0.1	0.1	0.2	0.1	0.0	NA	NA

Prepared by C. Davis in 2019.

Sources: (1) 2000–2005: Oboronno (2016); 2006–2010: Tsentr Stratigicheskykh Razrabotok (2017); 2011–2015: TsAST (2016), Frolov (2017b) Itogi; 2016–2018 Frolov (2018b) Itogi (2) 2000–2016: ACDA (2000-2018) WMEAT.

Programme (GPV) for 2011–2020 to a peak of 2106.0 billion rubles in 2016 (IET, 2000-2019; IISS, 1990…2019; SIPRI, 2000…2018). From 2000 to 2014 the GOZ share of total DE rose from 24.6% to 48.5%. The share of total DE of GOZ VVT increased from 14.4% in 2005 to 27.7% in 2015.

IET (2000–2019) calculated that the total ruble defence expenditure share of GDP increased from a low of 3.4% in 2001 to a high of 5.7% in 2016, before declining to 4.1% in 2018. The estimates by SIPRI of defence shares of GDP in dollars exhibited similar trends.

(2) Exports and imports of weapons and military equipment, 2000–2019

Table 4.6 shows that the value of exports of WME by Russia increased from $3.7 billion current dollars in 2000 to a peak of $15.7 billion in 2013. Russia has been the second largest exporter of WME after the USA. China was its major customer during 2000–2006, but India became the leading purchaser in subsequent years. Russia's exports of WME were disrupted after 2013 by economic sanctions. However, since most of Russia's arms trade was with countries not imposing sanctions, its exports recovered and reached around $16 billion by 2018 (Davis, 2016, 2017; DIA, 2017; IISS, 2018, 2019; TsAST 2016; Frolov 2015b, 2016b, 2017b, 2018b, Itogi).

The journal *Eksport Vooruzhenii* predicts that the value of exports of WME in 2019 will be similar to 2018, with aviation and air defence equipment dominating sales (Frolov 2018c, Perspektivy).

Legal imports of WME by Russia remained modest, with their value rising to a peak of $2.9 billion in 2003, but then dropping to $200 million in 2015. Economic sanctions after 2013 severely reduced Russia's military-related imports from Ukraine and NATO countries (see Section 5.a.(9)). In response, Russia engaged more actively in trade diversion operations through third countries and in technological espionage to obtain restricted dual-use technologies from foreign countries.

3. The USSR defence industry during the Cold War: 1980–1991

a. Defence industry organisation and relationships with the economy and political system

(1) Definition of the defence industry

Soviet ideas concerning the relationship between economic and military power were summarised by Pozharov (1981, 116–17):

> In order for economic power to be converted into military strength, it is necessary to provide for the production of armaments, combat technology and other items of a military nature, the correct distribution and timely delivery of them to the troops, and the creation of all the conditions for

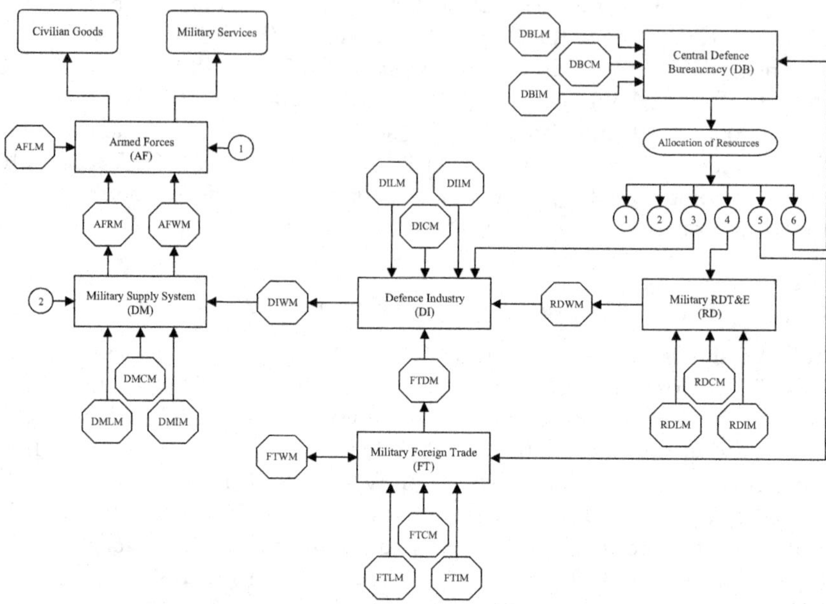

Notes: The defence sector markets, represented by the octagons, show the main flows of goods and services into or out of the defence sector and between the six defence institutions, represented by the rectangles. They do not show payments for supplies or the return flows of tax or profits from institutions to the state. The allocation of resources by the Central Defence Bureaucracy using plans and budgets is represented by the oval and six circles.

AFLM Armed forces labour market
AFRM Armed forces retail market
AFWM Armed forces military commodity market
DMLM Military supply labour market
DMCM Military supply capital market
DMIM Military supply intermediate goods market
DIWM Defence industry military commodity market
DILM Defence industry labour market
DICM Defence industry capital market
DIIM Defence industry intermediate goods market
RDWM Military R&D military technology market
RDLM Military R&D labour market
RDCM Military R&D capital market
RDIM Military R&D intermediate goods market
FTDM Military foreign trade domestic market
FTLM Military foreign trade labour market
FTCM Military foreign trade capital market
FTIM Military foreign trade intermediate goods market
FTWM Military foreign trade world market
DBLM Central defence bureaucracy labour market
DBCM Central defence bureaucracy capital market
DBIM Central defence bureaucracy intermediate goods market

Prepared by C. Davis in 2019.
Source: Based on diagrams in Davis (1990b, 2002).

Figure 4.1 Institutions and markets in the USSR and Russian Federation defence sector.

> their effective utilisation. A special social organism serves these goals – the military economy. The scale and effectiveness of the military economy characterises the military-economic power of the state…

Economic power at the macroeconomic level can be measured by GDP and at the sectoral level by the productive capabilities of branches of civilian economy of relevance to the OPK, such as machine building and steel (Davis, 1990a, 2002, 2017; Knorr, 1957, 1973). Military power is more directly determined by the performance of the six economic institutions of the defence sector, identified in Figure 4.1: armed forces, military supply, defence industry, military R&D, military foreign trade, and central defence bureaucracy. These institutions participate in the markets shown in Figure 4.1.

(2) Defence industry in the USSR politico-economic system and its organisation

Figure 4.2 in Section 5 presents a five-block model of the politico-economic system with linkages to the defence industry that applies to both the Soviet and Russian Federation periods. The CPSU leadership determined national security strategy, military doctrine, state priorities, and defence policies (Block 1: Davis, 1986, 1992b). Central state bodies developed the leaders' decisions into plans and implemented them (Block 2). Coordination was based on compulsory planning and rationing (Block 3). DIEs functioned under ministries that were supervised by central CPSU and state bodies. The vertical relationships of managers of DIEs with ministerial superiors were more important than horizontal ones with suppliers and customers (e.g. the armed forces). The paternalism (lenient control) of ministries ensured that firms had soft budget constraints (Block 4). The high priority status of defence protected it from many of the performance problems of the shortage economy (Block 5: Davis, 1988a, 1990b, 2002, 2014).

The vertical organisation of the Soviet OPK until 1991 in terms of the six institutions is described in Figure 4.2 in Davis (2002). The Defence Council USSR was at the apex of the national security structure (Maslyukov and Glubokov 2005; Voenno-Promyshlennyy Kompleks, 2005). The Military Industrial Commission (MIC) managed the defence industry, which was made up of the enterprises of nine ministries that primarily produced military commodities, three civilian ministries, and the Ministry of Defence (CIA 1986; DOD 1987; Almquist, 1990).

(3) High priority protection of the Soviet defence industry

The Soviet Union had an institutionalised priority system that helped to ensure that important goals of the CPSU leadership would be achieved irrespective of circumstances in the economy. Table 4.7 shows the priority-linked indicators and instruments that were used during plan formulation and implementation. These have been expressed in mathematical-statistical terms and used to evaluate the high-priority Soviet defence industry (Davis, 1988a, 1989; Davis, 1990b, 2002, 2014).

Table 4.7 Priority status of the Russian defence industry and related indicators in three periods: 1980s, 1990s and 2000s

Priority indicator	*High priority in 1980s*	*Low priority in 1990s*	*High priority in 2000s*
During Plan/Budget Formulation			
Defence in Leadership's Objective Function	High Weight/ Lexicographic Ordering	Low Weight/Trade-Offs between Defence and other Objectives	Reasonably High Weight in OF, but Trade-Offs between Defence and Other Objectives
Resource Allocation Responsiveness to Problems	Highly Responsive	Unresponsive	Uusally Responsive
Wage Rates and Labour Conditions	Relatively High	Relatively Low	Relatively High for state-funded sectors, but inferior to successful private sector firms
Adequacy of Financial Norms in Budgets	Generous	Stingy	Generous
During Plan/Budget Implementation			
Outputs	Strong Commitment to Fulfilment of Plans	No State Plans, Minimal Help in Maintaining Output	Reasonably Strong Commitment to Fulfilment of Plans
Budget Constraints	Soft	Relatively Soft	Soft
Supply Plans	Strong Commitment to Fulfilment of Plans	Tolerance of Disruptions	Reasonably Strong Commitment to Fulfilment of Plans
Investment Plans	Ambitious, Strong Commitment to Fulfilment of Plans	Little Investment and Tolerance of Underfulfilment	Ambitious, Moderate Commitment to Fulfilment of Plans
Inventories of Inputs	Large Input Inventories	Depleted Input Inventories	Reasonable Input Inventories
Reserve Production Capacity	Large Mobilization Capacity	Diminished Mobilization Capacity	Revived Mobilization Capacity
Shortage Intensity	Low	High	Low

Prepared by C. Davis in 2019.

Notes and Sources: The conceptual basis of the priority indicators and the evaluation of them in the Soviet command economy and Russian transition economy in the 1990s are presented in Davis (1988a, 1989, 1990b, 1992b, 2002). The assessments of the indicators in the Russian state capitalist economy of the 2000s have been made by the author on the basis of the study of relevant Russian and Western sources.

(4) Soviet industrial policy and the defence industry

Traditional Soviet industrial policy was to promote rapid industrialisation and increases in military power based on high investment in the heavy and defence industries (Davis, 1999, 2014). Special institutional arrangements were developed to support industrial policies, such as the MIC in the defence sector. State-owned industrial firms were designed to be large-scale, monopolistic, vertically integrated, and protected from international competition. These policies enabled the USSR to develop into the world's second largest industrial power, but by the 1980s Soviet industry was characterised by decelerating growth, slow technological progress, low labour productivity, and inefficiencies.

(5) Numbers of enterprises and military R&D institutions

In the mid-1980s the Soviet defence industry consisted of 1,100 enterprises that were controlled by thirteen ministries (CIA, 1986; DOD 1988; Gaddy, 1996; Kuzyk, 2006). Supplies of defence firms came from 3,500 civilian factories that usually did not have high-priority protection. The MRD network contained 920 research institutes and design bureaus.

(6) Outputs and sales of defence industry: military and civilian

The defence industry produced large and increasing volumes of weapons (Table 4.8). This reflected the "quantity drive" that was a characteristic of the shortage economy (Figure 4.2, Table 4.9).

DIEs also manufactured a wide array of civilian consumer goods (e.g. televisions, refrigerators, passenger cars (notably, the Moskvich)), intermediate products (e.g. chemicals, electronic components) and capital equipment (e.g. passenger aircraft, tractors) (Almquist, 1990; CIA, 1986). The civilian share of defence industry output was around 40%. The quality of OPK commodities was higher than equivalents produced by civilian enterprises. The Gorbachev regime's conversion programme raised the civilian share of OPK output to 51% by 1989 (Kuzyk, 2006).

(7) Employment

Military-related employment in the OPK in the mid-1980s consisted of 2.7 million persons in military production, 1.2 million in MRD, and 1.1 million providing social support (e.g. medical care: Gaddy, 1996). It also employed 2.7 million persons in civilian manufacturing and R&D, with 0.9 million in support. An additional 1.4 million were employed in military production in primarily civilian industries. So total USSR employment in military-related production and R&D was 6.4 million (around 5% of the national labour force: Kuzyk, 2006; Maslyukov and Glubokov, 2005).

Table 4.8 USSR defence industry production and weapons of the armed forces, 1965–1991

Indicator	*Units*	*1965*	*1970*	*1975*	*1980*	*1985*	*1990*	*1991*
Defence Industry Production								
ICBMs	Number	100	380	150	200	100	125	100
SLBMs	Number	15	170	175	175	100	65	50
SAMs	Number	5200	25,000	40,000	50,000	50,000	47,000	43,000
Bombers	Number	46	7	20	30	50	40	30
Fighters/Fighter Bombers	Number	850	1000	1200	1300	650	575	250
Helicopters	Number	80	390	630	750	600	175	350
Tanks	Number	2600	3300	2500	3000	3000	1300	850
Armoured Vehicles	Number	1700	3500	4300	5500	3500	4400	3000
SP Artillery	Number	200	600	900	900	1000	400	300
Submarines	Number	14	15	10	13	8	12	6
Major Combatant Ships	Number	12	5	10	11	8	8	3
Inventory of Armed Forces Weapons from Defence Industry								
Tanks	Number	28,000	38,000	42,000	50,000	52,600	54,000	54,400
GF Helicopters	Number	300	800	1550	2000	4300	4500	4500
AF Fighter/Attack Aircraft	Number	2300	2850	3550	5000	5900	4335	4905
ICBMs	Number	281	1472	1469	1338	1371	1378	1006
Total Strategic Warheads	Number	882	2327	3565	7488	9997	11,252	10,164

Prepared by C. Davis in 2019.

Sources: Based on Table IV in Davis (2002), which used material from DOD (1981–1990) Soviet Military Power, IISS (1969–1991) Military Balance (Various Years), and Natural Resources Defense Council (1997).

Soviet DIEs had large labour forces for three reasons: (1) they operated in a shortage economy, so they hoarded labour; (2) firms kept excess workers in connection with war mobilisation requirements; and (3) they were vertically-integrated and supplied social services to their employees.

The high-priority defence industry was able to provide its employees, especially the elite, with generous wages and benefits. However, restrictive conditions of employment related to security concerns increasingly discouraged young high-quality engineers and scientists from accepting OPK positions and prevented workers from earning extra money by engaging in illegal private activities (Davis, 1988ab).

Table 4.9 Characteristics of Russian defence industry enterprises in three periods: 1980s, 1990s and 2000s

Characteristics	*Soviet shortage economy in 1980s*	*Russian transition economy in 1990s*	*Russian state capitalism in 2000s*
Output Side of Defence Industry Enterprises			
Market for Outputs	Sellers' Market, Defence Industry Dominant	Inertia, Sellers' Markets Dominant	DI remains Important as seller, but Gradual Shift to Buyers' Market
Attitude Toward the Quantity of Output	Quantity Drive (striving for continuing increases in output of weapons)	Inertia Initially Maintains Quantity Drive, but Gradual Attempts to Focus on Revenue	Inertia Initially Maintains Quantity Drive, but then a Shift to Revenue Maximization
Attitude Toward the Quality of Output	Relative Neglect of Quality (but military inspectors help maintain agreed standards)	Greater Awareness of Quality Issues but Insufficient Investment to Upgrade Quality	More competitive markets increase pressure to improve quality of products
Stocks of Finished Goods	Minimal Ouput Stocks	Growth of Unsaleable Stocks of Outputs	Low Output Stocks
Production within Defence Industry Enterprises			
Managerial Attitude Toward Risk	Risk Aversion of Managers (but some competition between weapons designers)	Uncertainties of Transition Period Reinforce Risk Aversion of Many Managers	Competition and Increased Financial Rewards Promote More Risk Taking
Technological Innovation	Tech Innovation better in defence industry than in civilian, but slower than in the West	Negligible Technological Innovation due to inadequate investment	Recovery of economy, higher spending and government demands stimulate innovation
Technological Level	Tech Level higher in defence industry than in civilian, but lower than in West	Technological Gaps between Russia and the Developed Countries Increase	Technology level in DI lags behind that in NATO countries, but modest closing of gaps
Stability of Production	Less Forced Substitution and Fewer Production Bottlenecks in defence	Less Pressure for Storming, but Intensification of Production Bottlenecks	High priority helps DI production, but economic disruptions (GFC, sanctions
Inventories of Inputs	Hoarding of Inputs/ Maintenance of large inventories related to mobilization plans	Managers Violate Mobilization Rules and Sell Inventories of Valuable Inputs	Modest mobilization-related stocks, but reliable trade removes need for hoarding
Mobilization Capacity	Large Mobilization Production Capacity	Legal and Illegal Reduction of Mobilization Capacity	Renewed emphasis on mobilization, but below Soviet standards
Input Side of Defence Industry Enterprises			
Budget Constraint	Soft Budget Constraint	Shift to Relatively Hard Budget Constraint	Relatively Soft Budget Constraints

Investment Behaviour	Investment Hunger (constant striving to start new projects and expand capacity)	Unsuccessful efforts to obtain Investment for DI Conversion and Weapons Export Projects	DIE strive to obtain investment from DI budgets and State Armaments Programmes
Conditions in the Market for Inputs	Less Intense Shortages of Inputs in Defence Industry than in Civilian Economy	Acute Shortages of Inputs	New normal state of reliable inputs, but sanctions post-2013 disrupt supplies

Prepared by C. Davis in 2019.

Notes and Sources: The indicators of the of the characteristics of DIEs in the Soviet and Russian economic systems were derived from concepts of the shortage economy presented in Kornai (1980, 1992)) and Davis and Charemza (1989). The assessments of the conditions and behaviours of DIEs in the Soviets and early transition periods are based on past publications of the author (Davis, 1988a, 1989; Davis, 1990b, 2002) and analysis of new material related to the Russian state capitalist economy in the 2000s.

(8) Location

DIEs and MRD institutions in the USSR were distributed unevenly across the fifteen republics and their roughly 150 regions. Important establishments were predominantly located in Slavic republics, with Russia possessing around 80% of DIEs (Gaddy, 1996, 18, 193). The top five territories employing defence industry workers were: Sverdlovsk (350,000), Leningrad (318,000), Moscow City (300,000), Nizhny Novgorod (257,000), and the Moscow Region (225,000). However, for national security reasons numerous DIEs were located in remote regions, which had the highest defence shares of industrial employment: Udmurtia (57%), Kaluga (47%), and Mari-El (46%). Many of the large cities with important DIEs and/or MRD institutions were "closed" (e.g. Perm, Izhevsk).

(9) Foreign economic relations of the USSR defence industry in a period of western economic warfare

The Soviet Union had three main objectives concerning military foreign trade: (1) export WME to support socialist allies and to earn hard currency; (2) minimise legal imports of WME to maintain self-sufficiency; and (3) obtain covertly advanced foreign military technologies. The USSR's state monopoly on foreign trade meant that transactions were centrally planned, used non-market exchange rates and were carried out by government organisations. Although the USSR exported large quantities of WME (Table 4.2), Gaddy (1996, 90–93) estimated that due to barter and subsidies, it actually received only 56% of apparent hard-currency earnings.

All OECD industrialised countries participated in sustained and comprehensive economic warfare directed against the USSR under the direction of NATO's Coordinating Committee (CoCom: Davis, 2016). Supplemental sanctions were introduced in response to unacceptable actions by the USSR (e.g. 1979 invasion of Afghanistan; 1981 martial law in Poland).

The Soviet Union was unable to purchase legally WME from capitalist countries, but it imported military-related commodities from Warsaw Pact members (Davis, 2016). However, the USSR had a large covert trade diversion programme to obtain restricted materials and equipment and a separate *spetsinformatsiya* system that collected foreign military-related technology (CIA 1985, 1986; Hanson, 1987; Kostin and Raynaud, 2011). DOD (1986) estimated that in the 1980s the OPK received annually from its covert collection agencies around 4,000 items of hardware and 20,000 documents.

b. Defence industry enterprises in the command economy: structure, conduct and performance

(1) USSR defence industry enterprises in the command (shortage) economy

Table 4.9 supplements Figure 4.2 by describing the behaviour of DIEs (Davis, 1988a, 2002, 2014). On the output side, firms operated in "sellers' markets" and consistently attempted to expand the volume of production (the "quantity drive"). They were more attentive to the quality of their products (notably weapons) than were civilian enterprises and had low inventories of finished goods due to excess demand. On the input side, their high priority status ensured that they possessed "soft budget constraints", encountered less intense shortages, and demonstrated an "investment hunger". With respect to production, managers tended to be risk averse, technological innovation was slow, technological levels were low by international standards, and war mobilisation requirements meant that DIEs had large inventories of inputs and substantial reserve production capacity.

(2) Structure

In the USSR all OPK DIEs and MRD institutions remained state property and functioned in hierarchies within ministries. Although there was strong vertical control, a characteristic of management was paternalism. Enterprises were monopolistic and vertically integrated to avoid dependence on lower priority civilian suppliers. They maintained social support programmes, mobilisation-related excess production capacity and substantial input inventories. DIEs were large in terms of floor space and employment, partially to simplify planning. The physical size of the Soviet defence industry expanded by 50% in the late Cold War period, according to satellite imagery (DOD, 1988).

Entry into the OPK depended entirely on the decisions of central planners. New production and research facilities usually were established within existing large enterprises. There was little exit because of the focus on production of WME and neglect of efficiency. During the 1980s, the number of major production plants remained stable.

(3) Conduct

DIEs were governed by central plans, operated in sellers' markets for sales of both civilian goods and military commodities and faced negligible competition. Almquist (1990) demonstrated that defence industry managers were able to constrain the demands of the armed forces and MRD scientists, so that the actual requirements for weapons systems were not too ambitious.

DIEs had an "expansion drive" and "investment hunger" due to their quantity drive and soft budget constraints (e.g. no financial risks from failed projects). According to CIA (1986, 3–4) "capital investment in the defense industries has continued at high levels" and "they also have access to the best machinery". However, in the shortage economy not even high priority could fully protect DIEs from delays in completing investment projects.

Intermediate supplies to defence firms were allocated through rationing in DIIM in Figure 4.1. In the 1980s defence industry absorbed the following shares of national outputs: metallurgy 20%; chemicals 17%; and energy 17%. However, most of the 3,500 civilian suppliers to the defence industry had lower priority status, which caused irregular deliveries. According to Almquist (1990, 144):

> On the question of supply, the writings of the defense industry managers suggest that the Soviet defense industry may not enjoy the immunity to problems often assumed; it is certainly clear that the managers are not satisfied with whatever degree of special protection they may have.

(4) Performance

On the whole, DIEs were able to fulfill the targets of state plans due to their high priority status and their quantity drive (see Table 4.9). CIA (1986) argued that "the Soviets have traditionally emphasized numbers rather than sophisticated designs" and have expanded weapons production through "extensive growth".

DIEs had production lines with differing quality standards that were, in descending order: WME for the Soviet armed forces; WME for export; and civilian products. Defence firms emphasised design simplicity and preferred the production of less sophisticated, single-mission weapons (CIA, 1986, 23).

In the defence industry the value indicators of prices, costs and profits were of little significance because the economic system was based on quantity signals and indicators (Kornai, 1980, 1992). Capital and labour productivity remained low throughout the Soviet period.

The USSR OPK produced some excellent WME, such as tanks and fighter aircraft (DOD, 1988). Soviet MRD scientists and engineers generated sophisticated weapons concepts and designs. However, managers of defence industry firms were risk averse with respect to technological innovation. They preferred to make incremental changes to existing production lines because they would be rewarded for fulfilling output plans in quantity terms, but shortages of inputs could delay technological innovation projects and cause under-fulfilment of plans (Almquist, 1990). CIA (1986) found that the Soviet defence industry lagged behind NATO standards in production technologies and maintained obsolete machinery in service.

For most of the Cold War period the Soviet defence industry had stable production conditions because it was protected from the deficiencies of the shortage economy and the effects of Western economic warfare. However, in the 1980s priority protection weakened and the defence industry increasingly experienced erratic supplies, forced substitution of inputs and production bottlenecks (CIA, 1986, 17; Davis, 1988a, 1990b; Almquist, 1990; Gaddy, 1996).

c. *Soviet policies concerning procurement and defence industry conversion*

Soviet government policies concerning the balances in the defence industry between military procurement, civilian production, and defence industry conversion varied over time.

(1) Procurement

The USSR provided armaments to the military on the basis of quantity-oriented plans. This did not constitute "procurement" as in a NATO market economy because value indicators did not influence decisions and the armed forces were not true customers. Defence planning was effective in ensuring that large quantities of modern armaments were produced and distributed to the armed forces.

In 1985 Soviet defence authorities experimented with a medium-term State Armaments Programme (GPV), which specified the deliveries of WME to the armed forces and allocated resources to finance their purchase through the State Defence Order (GOZ), (Maslyukov and Glubokov, 2005; Zatsepin, 2007, 2012). However, these innovations in procedures had negligible beneficial impacts and procurement of WME declined by 8% in 1990 and 25% in 1991 (Gaddy, 1996).

*(2) State-directed defence industry conversion (*konversiya*) to civilian production*

During most of the Cold War period military production was the primary mission of the defence industry. At the start of *perestroika,* the OPK was viewed as a positive model and efforts were made to transfer into the civilian sphere its apparently successful organisational forms and procedures (Davis, 1992a).

After serious disarmament commenced in 1988, a large-scale "State Programme of Conversion of the Defence Industry" was launched (Maslyukov and Glubokov, 2005). A key objective was to increase the civilian share of defence industry output from 40% in 1988 to 60% in 1995. However, this conversion programme was introduced unexpectedly in the middle of the 12th Five Year Plan, when economic circumstances were deteriorating and defence industry mangers were uncertain about the sustainability of the new policy. As a result, little progress was achieved in defence industry conversion through 1991 (Davis, 1992a; Gaddy, 1996).

4. Russian federation defence industry in a collapsing transition economy, 1992–1999

a. Defence industry in the politico-economic system and its organisation

(1) Defence industry in the Russian transition politico-economic system

A hybrid politico-economic system evolved in Russia during 1992–1999.[3] Russian central leadership lowered the priority of the OPK. The state was weakened, but it remained important to DIEs because of its powers to provide budget funds and assistance. There was a shift from "direct bureaucratic control" (e.g. planning) to indirect (e.g. informal signals and hidden subsidies) (Kornai, 1992). In the defence sector markets shown in Figure 4.1 money and prices became only semi-active and quantity processes (notably barter) remained influential. Vertical relations continued to be of greater significance to DIEs than horizontal ones. Sellers' markets and soft budget constraints remained wide-spread. Chronic, intense shortages afflicted all defence institutions.

(2) Developments in defence sector strategy and organisation

The Russian Federation inherited around 80% of the USSR OPK organisations (Fel'gengauer, 2010). Russia's initial national security strategy reflected the beliefs of government reformers that the country was not confronted by serious threats, the OPK was an obstacle, and military power was of

Table 4.10 Russia defence industry production and weapons of the armed forces, 1992–1999

Indicator	*Units*	*1992*	*1993*	*1994*	*1995*	*1996*	*1997*	*1998*	*1999*
Defence Industry Production									
Total DI Output Index	1991 = 100	77.7	62.4	38.4	29.3	21.3	18.5	18.0	23.9
DI Military Output Index	1991 = 100	49.6	32.4	20.9	15.5	11.9	8.8	9.2	12.5
DI Civilian Output Index	1991 = 100	99.7	85.3	52.8	40.3	28.4	28.0	25.8	33.1
ICBMs + SLBMs	Number	55	35	25	10	10	10	10	10
Bombers	Number	20	10	2	2	1	0	0	1
Fighters/ Fighter-Bombers	Number	150	100	50	20	25	35	40	40
Helicopters	Number	175	150	100	95	75	70	40	75
Tanks	Number	500	200	40	30	5	5	15	30
Armoured Vehicles	Number	700	300	380	400	250	350	250	300
Submarines	Number	6	4	4	3	2	2	2	0
Inventory of Armed Forces Weapons from Defence Industry									
Tanks	Number	29,000	25,000	19,500	19,000	16,800	15,500	15,550	15,500
GF Helicopters	Number	3200	3500	2600	2600	2450	2565	2300	2300
Combat Aircraft	Number	5885	5525	2880	2175	2195	2015	2015	1530
ICBMs	Number	950	898	818	771	755	755	755	771
Total Strategic Warheads	Number	9609	8938	8032	7379	7259	6678	6534	6315

Prepared by C. Davis in 2019.

Sources: Based on Table VI in Davis (2002), which used material from Gaddy (1996), IISS, 1990…2019 Military Balance, NATO (2000) and Natural Resources Defense Council (1997).

diminishing importance in international affairs (Allison, 1997). However, during 1994–1999 a centrist consensus evolved that Russia was facing serious military challenges internally (e.g. Islamic separatism) and externally (e.g. NATO expansion) and that the armed forces would play a vital role in deterring and resolving conflicts. Plans were announced for the upgrading of MRD and the introduction of a new GPV with linked GOZ. However, continued poor economic performance undermined efforts to improve conditions in the OPK (Gaddy, 1996; Davis, 2002).

With respect to the vertical organisation of the OPK, the office of the President, supported by the Security Council, was the highest decision-making body. The Military Industrial Commission was abolished. DIEs and MRD institutes were re-organised several times and subordinated to different authorities (Kuzyk 1999; Kuzyk, 2006).[4]

(3) Impacts of low priority on the Russian defence industry

The Russian government maintained a low priority status for the defence sector throughout the 1990s and accepted trade-offs with civilian programmes (Table 4.7). Resource allocations were unresponsive to the problems of the OPK and the real wages and benefits of defence employees deteriorated. The government became indifferent to the attainment of output targets by defence organisations and did not safeguard their supplies. However, the resources from the RMS were used to save defence firms from bankruptcy, so soft budget constraints were continued.

(4) Russian industrial policy and the defence industry

The Russian government had less influence over industry in the transition economy and different goals and instruments (Davis, 1999). The initial key industrial objectives were to privatise most firms (but not the core of defence industry), decentralise decision making and make it responsive to market forces, promote restructuring of enterprises, break up monopolies, expose industry to foreign competition and attract foreign investment. However, after 1993 there were growing commitments to support heavy and defence industry, to encourage the formation of Financial-Industrial Groups and to promote defence industry conversion (see Section 4.c.(2)).

(5) Numbers of enterprises and military R&D institutions

Russia inherited around 900 defence industry enterprises and 800 design bureaus, scientific institutes and experimental factories (Gaddy, 1996). Many of these were merged into Financial-Industrial Groups or other forms of holding companies in attempts to promote resiliency, vertical integration and technological innovation.

(6) Outputs and sales of defence industry

Table 4.10 shows that the index of total output of the defence industry (1991=100) collapsed from 77.7 in 1992 to 18.0 in 1998, or by 77%. The index of military output fell to 9.2 in 1998. Annual production of combat aircraft fell from 150 to a low of 35 and of main battle tanks from 500 to 5. The index of civilian production decreased to 25.8. Civilian demand for both traditional products of defence firms (e.g. televisions) and those generated by conversion was weak because of competition from superior imports. There were equivalent declines in the output of military R&D, which had detrimental impacts on the development of new weapons systems. According to a pessimistic assessment by NATO (2000, 27): "Russia has missed out on a decade of weapons development and may no longer have the human and technical resources to make up lost ground".

However, in 1999 production began to recover in most branches of defence industry. In that year total output was divided between: 20% WME for the armed forces, 34% WME for exports, 26% civilian capital goods, 9% civilian consumer products and 11% exports of civilian goods.

(7) Employment

Employment in the Russian defence industry dropped from 5.4 million in 1988 to 3.0 million in 1995 (Gaddy, 1996, pg. 115). However, the contraction of OPK employment in military production fell more substantially, from 2.7 million to 0.6 million, than did that in civilian production, from 2.7 million to 2.4 million. The number of personnel in military R&D dropped from 1.2 million in 1988 to around 0.4 million by 1999.

There were substantial cuts in the real wages and benefits of OPK employees. By 1996 the monthly wage of defence industry workers was only 60% of the national average for all industry (Kuzyk, 2006). In any event, OPK employees were not paid wages on a regular basis (the phenomenon of "wage arrears"). Employees tolerated the situation because they lived in company housing and continued to have access to social services in their defence firms, but their motivation suffered.

Managers of the DIEs, in desperation, exchanged military and civilian industrial goods from production or inventories for consumer products that could be provided to workers in lieu of wages. The deterioration of work conditions and remuneration resulted in substantial exits from the defence sector labour force, especially by those in early career. The average age of employees in the OPK rose from 39 years in 1990 to 58 years in 2000 (Kuzyk, 2006).

(8) Location

The DIEs and MRD institutions in the OPK were concentrated in Moscow, St. Petersburg and 23 regions (e.g. in the Urals) (Gaddy (1996, 149). The distribution of facilities did not change much during the 1990s due to the severe lack of capital investment and the negligible entry into and exit from the defence industry. However, the regional distribution of defence employment changed significantly due to the decisions of employees to leave their now unattractive jobs in the OPK in remote areas.

(9) Foreign economic relations of the Russian defence industry in a period of reduced economic warfare and sanctions

During the 1990s the primary goal in the foreign trade of the destitute defence industry was to obtain either convertible currency payments or attractive barter goods through exports of WME. Central control of foreign trade in armaments diminished. Since Russian firms were selling weapons that had been produced for the Soviet armed forces, but were no longer needed, they could charge low prices and still make substantial profits. But a significant share of military foreign trade was conducted using barter (Fel'gengauer, 2010). The exports of WME generated three-quarters of the income of the defence industry, but these earnings were insufficient to finance its modernisation (DIA, 2017).

The end of the Cold War resulted in the termination of Western economic warfare directed at Russia (e.g. NATO's CoCom was disestablished in 1994: Davis, 2016). NATO countries maintained less restrictive export controls. In the 1990s Russia was able to legally import directly from NATO countries more machinery and commodities, but actual transactions were limited by the insufficiency of Russian hard currency. Russia's largest defence partner was Ukraine, but transactions between them were transformed from domestic to foreign trade. Over this decade China and India offered Russian firms new supply opportunities because of their rapid industrialisation and the decisions of NATO defence companies in the 1990s to outsource the production of components to low-cost manufacturers in the Third World.

Russia maintained scaled-down programmes of illegal trade diversion and technological espionage (*spetsinformatsiya*). However, the under-resourced Russian defence industry usually could not take advantage of acquired prototypes and technological information.

b. Russian defence industry enterprises in the transition economy: structure, conduct and performance

(1) Russian defence industry enterprises in the hybrid transition economy

Developments in and characteristics of Russian DIEs in the evolving, hybrid economic system of the 1990s are summarised in Table 4.9. Ineffectual reform policies and the poor performance of the economy over the decade had negative impacts on the OPK.

(2) Structure

In the early 1990s government plans called for about 500 out of 900 OPK firms to remain as state entities, while the others were to be privatised (Noren, 1994; Gaddy, 1996; Maslyukov and Glubokov, 2005). However, privatisation proceeded slowly and by 1997 the ownership structure in the OPK was: state enterprises 46.1%, joint-stock companies with state co-ownership 33.6%, and private companies 20.3%. The centralised management of DIEs weakened and they acquired, in theory, greater autonomy. However, in the chaotic economic environment of that time (40% decline in real GDP, inflation over 1,000%), vertical relationships of firms remained of vital importance to enable them to obtain assistance from the paternalistic state.

There was little change in the high concentration and vertical integration of the defence industry due to the severe lack of investment and restrictions on foreign involvement. Defence firms maintained their substantial social support arrangements, although they were poorly funded. The growing destitution of many firms forced them to sell their strategic reserves and mobilisation-related machinery in order to finance their operations and wages (Oxenstierna and Westerlund 2013).

The sizes of Russian firms in terms of floorspace did not change significantly in the 1990s, but they were severely reduced when measured by employment or sales revenue. There was insignificant entry into the OPK and few exits.

(3) Conduct

Compulsory planning of the defence industry was abolished, with the expectation that coordination would be based on the markets shown in Figure 4.1. However, due to the disastrous macroeconomic performance and failures in micro-level reforms, indirect bureaucratic control of the OPK by the government strengthened. Quantity processes, notably barter, became more important for defence industry firms. By 1997, 70% of the transactions of large firms were conducted on the basis of barter (Gaddy and Ickes, 1998).

Horizontal relations in markets for military goods remained dominated by the defence industry, with the armed forces as weak customers. This reflected the fact that, for example, in 1998 the government was able to pay the defence industry only 25% of the sum required by the GOZ. MoD debt to the defence industry rose substantially. There was insignificant competition between DIEs to provide the armed forces with WME. In contrast, the defence industry experienced buyers' markets for the civilian commodities that it produced because of growing imports.

Wholesale and capital markets for the defence industry (DIWM and DICM in Figure 4.1) did not function in the predicted manner. Managers of defence firms and their suppliers, who had been working together for several decades, took decentralised decisions to continue to trade as normal in quantity terms using inter-enterprise credit, with the correct expectation that the debts would be cleared eventually by the government (Noren, 1994). The expansion drive related to capital projects in the defence industry disappeared because investment was reduced by around 90%. Inherited capital stock deteriorated.

The reformers in the central government wanted to impose hard budget constraints on DIEs, which would have caused mass bankruptcies. However, other influential decision makers in central and regional governments ignored them and continued to provide ailing defence firms with hidden subsidies (e.g. tolerance of non-payment of electricity bills), subsidised credit from state-controlled banks and tax relief.

(4) Performance

During the 1990s the main objective of managers of defence industry enterprises was to ensure the survival of their firms. The DIEs initially continued to demonstrate quantity drives by producing Soviet-era WME, which was made possible by decentralised inter-enterprise credit and the availability of capital stock, continuing receipt of current inputs and an experienced labour force.

The quality of the output of DIEs deteriorated due to the severe economic difficulties (Kuzyk, 1999). The failures to shift from sellers' to buyers' markets for WME meant that there was little pressure to raise product quality. In any event, there was no investment available to improve it.

The market-oriented value indicators of costs, prices, interest, and profits were not influential in defence industry. Firms that had WME to export were prepared to receive almost any hard-currency price or attractive barter goods for their products that had been produced at meaningless Soviet-era ruble costs. The capital and labour productivity of defence firms worsened due to the combination of falling sales revenue, obsolete capital stock and demotivated workers.

Technological innovation in the defence industry was impeded by inadequate investment and the risk aversion of managers in an environment that was even more uncertain than that of the Soviet period: investment in military R&D was one-tenth of its former level; 70% of production technologies were obsolete; and more than half of machine tools in defence industry were 100% worn-out. Production conditions within DIEs deteriorated due to the intensifying shortages, bottlenecks and forced substitution.

c. Russian policies concerning procurement and defence industry conversion

The political and economic changes in the 1990s resulted in much lower procurement and repeated efforts to pursue radical defence industry conversion.

(1) Procurement

Although the reformers in government did not achieve their ambitious initial targets to shrink the OPK, the actual outcomes in 1992 were reductions in weapons procurement of 57% and in military production of 38% (Gaddy, 1996). In 1996 the government adopted the *State Programme of Armaments*

(GPV) for 1996–2005 that was based upon a strategy of concentrating scarce resources on the highest priority weapons projects and of guaranteeing sales to defence firms (Korotchenko and Mukhin, 1999; Babakin, 2016). It was supplemented by the *Programme for the Reconstruction and Conversion of Defence Industry During 1998–2000.*

Overall, official procurement plans and programmes had negligible positive influences on developments in the OPK. The GPV 1996–2005 was implemented unsuccessfully due to organisational deficiencies and inadequate funding (only 23% of the announced budget was allocated): (IET 2010; Oxenstierna and Westerlund, 2013; NATO 2015; Babakin, 2016; DIA, 2017). In 1997 28 billion rubles were allocated for the purchase of WME and work by MRD, but only 8 billion rubles were actually provided (Fel'gengauer, 2010). The value of the GOZ for 1998 was approved at 25 billion rubles, but only 3 billion rubles were made available. Over the period 1992 to 1999 the value of procurement in constant 2016 dollars dropped by 65% from \$8.3 billion to \$2.9 billion.

(2) Russian state-directed defence industry conversion in the 1990s

The reformist government pursued a policy of "deep conversion" for the OPK, with the intention of generating a drastic shift away from military production and the transfer of defence firms into the civilian economy. In February 1992 the government passed the law *On Conversion of the Defence Industry* and over the next two years 14 federal and over 1,000 regional, branch or enterprise conversion programmes were established (Gaddy, 1996). In 1997 the government passed a supplemental law on *Reconstruction and Conversion of the Defence Industry in the RF During 1998–2000.*

However, all empirical assessments indicate that little was achieved over the decade, primarily due to lack of funds. Conversion projects received only 18% of the authorised state budget funding in 1995 and 33% in 1996. Another problem was that the growing array of imported consumer commodities in Russia were superior in quality and often cheaper than defence industry offerings (Fel'gengauer, 2010).

5. Russian Federation defence industry during economic revival and international tensions, 2000–2019

a. Defence industry relationships with the economy and political system and changes in organisation

(1) Defence industry in the Russian state capitalist politico-economic system

In the 2000s the Russian politico-economic system acquired the characteristics shown in Figure 4.2. Presidential rule was strengthened under Vladimir Putin (2000–2008, 2012–2024: Block 1). The goals of improving national security and defence programmes were awarded high priority. The state apparatus increased its power and continued to own the majority of OPK establishments (Block 2: Monaghan, 2014). The government continued its indirect bureaucratic control and demonstrated paternalism with respect to the OPK, using the instruments of the Rent Management System (Gaddy and Ickes, 2005: Block 3). Vertical relations dominated horizontal ones, with managers of DIEs bargaining with state officials over GPV-related production targets and soft budget constraints (Block 4). Macroeconomic performance improved, but serious problems remained at the microeconomic level.

(2) Developments in national security strategy and defence industry organisation

The Putin administration adopted modified versions of the *National Security Concept* and *Military Doctrine*, which contained more pessimistic assessments of external threats and called for enhancements of military power (Kontseptsiya 2000; Voennaya Doktrina 2000). The higher priority of defence was reflected in increased military spending (Section 2.c.(1)) and ambitious plans to revive the OPK, which were elaborated in two decrees: in 2000 *About Measures to Promote Concentration and Rationalisation of Military Production in the Russian Federation* and in 2005 *The Main Policies of the Russian Federation in the Field of the Development of the Defence-Industrial Complex in the Period out to 2010 and in a Long-Term Perspective* (Kuzyk, 2006).

In 2012 the government established the *Federal Targeted Programme for the Development of the Defence Industry to 2020.* Over this period Russia adopted three State Armaments Programmes (GPVs) (*to 2005, to 2010,* and to *2015*) that were not effective due to organisational problems and inadequate funding. But the one covering *2011–2020* was better financed and achieved good results (see Section 5. c.(1): (IET, 2010, IISS 2011-2019, Oxenstierna and Westerlund, 2013, DIA, 2017).

In the post-Ukraine crisis period, the Russian leadership approved of new versions of *Military Doctrine* (2014) and the *National Security Concept* (2015), which identified NATO as Russia's most significant threat (President 2014, 2015; DIA, 2017, 15). The government took actions to deal with the challenges posed by Western and Ukrainian economic sanctions (Davis, 2016, 2017). A new *State Armaments Programme to 2018–2027* was adopted in 2018 (Connolly and Boulègue, 2018). However, from 2016 the government gave defence industry and MRD a new mission of accelerating conversion to civilian production (see Section 5. c.(2)).

Figure 4.3 shows the specific organisations of the Russian OPK in 2019 and their vertical relationships, which are linked to the six economic institutions identified in Figure 4.1. The President is the supreme commander. The Military Industrial Commission (MIC) was re-established in 2007 to improve the coordination of defence industry production, procurement, MRD, and military foreign trade (Oboronno, 2015). President Putin became its Chair in 2014. Since 2008 most of the components of the defence industry have been

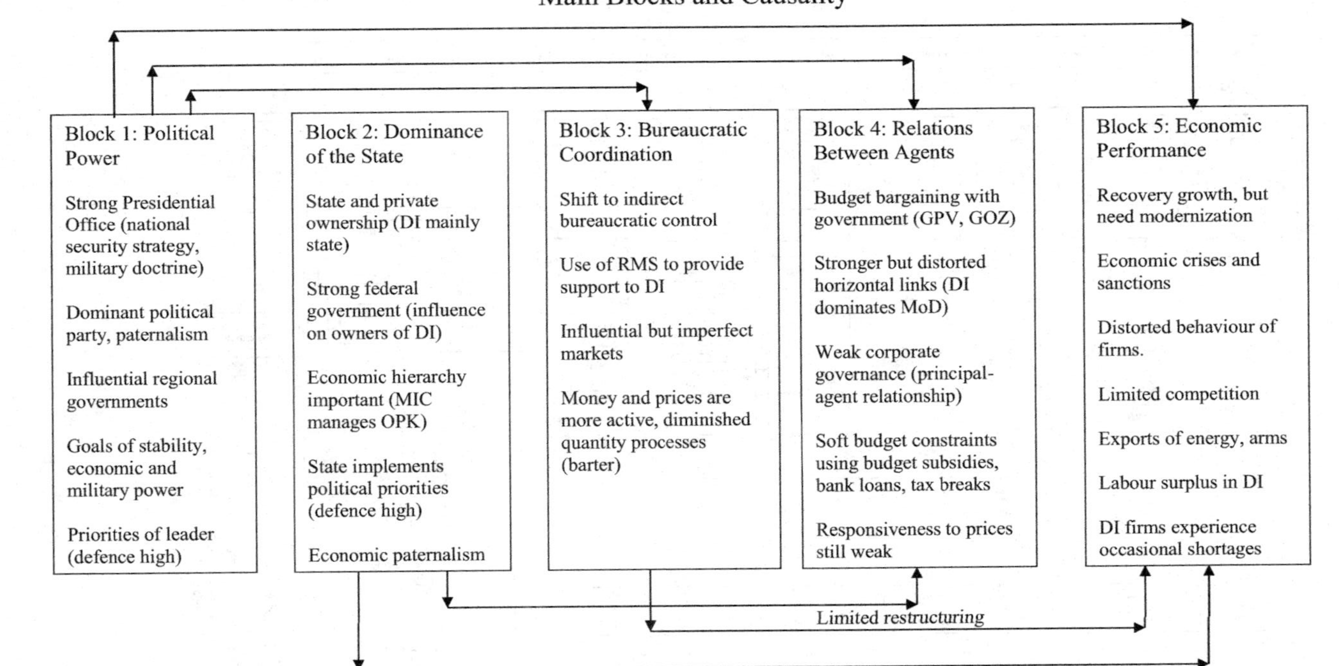

Prepared by C. Davis in 2019.
Source: Adapted to describe the Russia OPK from Figure 15.1 in Kornai (1992), which was used to portray the shortage economyin general.
More information about features and concepts can be found in Davis (1988a, 2002, 2016).Abbreviations: DI = Defence Industry,
MIC = Military-Industrial Commission, OPK = Defence-Industrial Complex, RMS = Rent Management System, GPV = State Armaments Programme,
GOZ = State Defence Orders, MoD = Ministry of Defence.

Figure 4.2 Defence industry in the Russian politico-economic system in 2019.

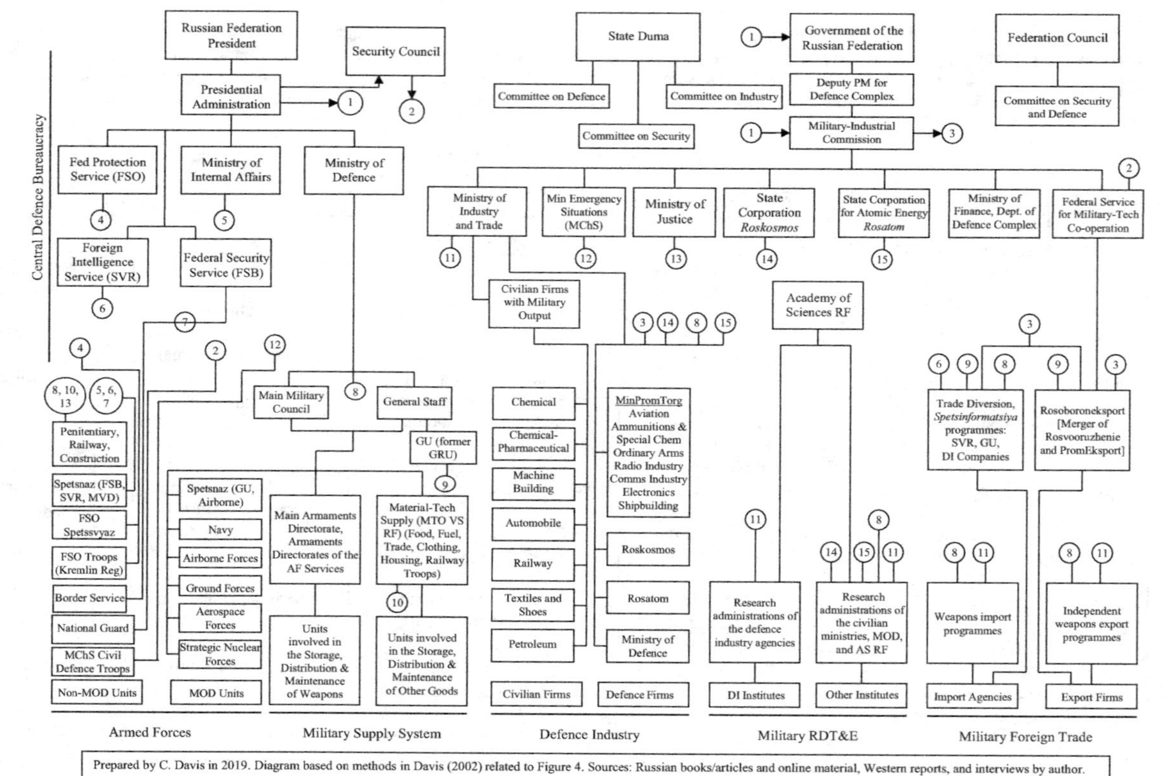

Figure 4.3 Organisation of the Russian Federation defence-industrial complex in 2019.

managed by the Ministry of Industry and Trade (*MinPromTorg*: Kuzyk, 2006). Many DIEs have been merged into vertically integrated state holding companies, with *Rostekhnologii* Public Corporation (or *Rostekh*: established November 2007) being the most important (IET, 2010). The key organisation in military foreign trade has been *Rosoboroneksport* (a subsidiary of *Rostekh*), which controls around 85% of WME exports (Oboronno 2006; DIA, 2017).

4.3 Organisation of the Russian Federation defence-industrial complex in 2019

(3) High priority of the Russian defence sector in the 2000s

Table 4.7 evaluates the high priority of the OPK in the 2000s. Defence budgets have become more important than in the past, but plans (e.g. related to GPVs and modernisation of defence industry) remain significant. During plan/budget formulation the leadership has been willing to accept defence-civilian trade-offs, adequate resources have been allocated to defence to finance adopted programmes, wages in the OPK have been raised and work conditions have been improved, and generous financial norms have been used in defence budgets.

During the implementation phase the government has demonstrated reasonably strong commitments to ensure the fulfilment of defence plans and budgets. Greater emphasis has been placed on the maintenance of inventories and reserve production capacities specified in war mobilisation plans. Budget constraints of defence enterprises and research institutes have been relatively soft and the intensity of the shortages they have experienced has been low.

(4) Russian defence industrial policy 2000-19

Russia has adopted and implemented numerous industrial policies over the period 2000–2019 that have affected defence industry: the Gref *Strategy 2010* (covering 2000–2010); the *Strategy 2020* (2012–2020); the Federal Law No. 488-FZ of 31 December 2014 "About industrial policy in the Russian Federation" (Ryazantsev, 2018); and the Kudrin *Strategy for Russia during 2018–2024* (reflected in the May 2018 Presidential Decree about reforms out to 2024) (see Industry sections of IET, 2000-2019). The invariant objectives have been to diversify the economy away from its dependence on exports of energy and raw materials, accelerate technological innovation, improve the competitiveness of manufacturing and increase exports of industrial goods (Kuzyk, 2006). A post-2013 addition to the list of goals, in response to economic sanctions, has been to promote import substitution (Connolly and Hanson, 2016).

(5) Numbers and sizes

The number of DIEs and MRD institutes listed on the authoritative Ministry of Industry and Trade *Register of Organisations of the Defence-Industrial Complex* has

Table 4.11 Defence industry enterprises and MRD institutes on the OPK registration list in 2014: numbers by branch of Minpromtorg and within other organisations

Organisation			*Numbers by branch*	*Numbers within organisations*
1. Minpromtorg				875
	a	Aviation	189	
	b	Ammunitions and Special Chemicals	94	
	c	Ordinary Armaments	100	
	d	Radio Industry	154	
	e	Communications Industry	102	
	f	Electronics Industry	108	
	g	Shipbuilding Industry	128	
2. Roskosmos				80
3. Rosatom				43
4. Ministry of Defence				169
5. Ministry of Education and Science				14
6. Russian Academy of Sciences				38
7. Interbranch and Other Government				34
8. Civilian Branches of the Economy				86
Total Enterprises and Institutes				1339

Prepared by C. Davis in 2019.

Source: MinPromTorg 2014.

fluctuated from around 1,700 in 1997 to 1,400 in the 2000s due to additions, mergers, bankruptcies and shifts in production from military to civilian goods. Table 4.11 shows the distribution of 1,339 OPK organisations in 2014 (MinPromTorg, 2014; Zatsepin, 2014). Of these, 875 were administratively subordinate to *MinPromTorg* and distributed across its seven branches. Other defence organisations were subordinate to the MoD (169), *RosKosmos* (80) and *RosAtom* (43). There were 86 organisations in the civilian economy. The number of OPK organisations rose to 1,355 in 2018 (Ryazantsev, 2018).

Many of these organisations belonged to large defence holding companies. For example, in 2018 *Rostekhnologii* controlled around 500 companies on the OPK list. Other leading large conglomerates are identified in Table 4.12.

Russian defence industry enterprises have been big in terms of floorspace and employment, but not in sales compared to foreign companies. Only six Russian firms were included in the Top 100 Defense Companies worldwide in 2018 (*Defense News*, 2018). The largest company was Almaz-Antey in 8th position, which represented a rise upward from 11th in 2017 (see Table 4.12).

Table 4.12 Russian firms in the *Defense News* 2018 ranking of the Top 100 defense companies

Rank 2017	*Rank 2016*	*Company*	*2017 defense revenue* (in millions)*	*2016 defense revenue* (in millions)*	*% defense revenue change*	*2017 total revenue* (in millions)*	*% revenue from defense*
8	11	Almaz-Antey	$9,125.02	$6,581.69	39%	$9,125.02	100%
14	14	United Aircraft Corp.	$6,197.25	$5,636.84	10%	$7,746.56	80%
25	32	Tactical Missiles Corporation, JSC	$3,573.95	$2,866.24	25%	3,624.21	99%
36	-	Russian Helicopters	$2,735.16	$2,652.01	3%	4,250.24	64%
46	45	Uralvagonzavod	$1,865.00	$1,584.29	18%	2,626.77	71%
48	50	Concern Radio-Electronic Technologies, JSC	$1,677.48	$1,365.52	23%	1,973.50	85%

Note: Companies were contacted by *Defense News* and completed a survey that reported their total annual revenue and revenue derived from defense, intelligence, homeland security and other national security contracts.
Prepared by C. Davis in 2019.
Source: *Defense News* (2018).

(6) Outputs and sales of defence industry

In 2000 the defence industry production indexes (1991=100) were: total 36.1, military 29.4 and civilian 43.8 (Table 4.13). Over the next decade the average annual growth rates of outputs of the defence industry were high: aggregate 11.6%, military 15.0% and civilian 8.9%. Total output reached the 1991 level in 2011 (index value of 99.4). During 2011–18 the values of state defence orders increased and they were almost fully funded (Oboronno, 2016; Itogi, 2017; Bystrye 2018; MinPromTorg 2018; OPK Rossii, 2018). Although Ukraine-related Western economic sanctions disrupted defense industry production, its aggregate output index climbed from 120.0 in 2013 to 189.7 in 2018 (Postanovlenie 2019). There were significant increases in the production and sales of all categories of weapons, especially from 2011 (Connolly and Sendstad, 2018; See Section 5.c.(1) on Procurement).

Table 4.12 shows that the total sales of the six Russian defence companies included in the *Defense News* Top 100 increased from $20 billion in 2016 to $25 billion in 2017. These values were low relative to USA companies (39 were included in the Top 100), but roughly equal to those of leading European countries.

Table 4.13 Output of the Russian defence industry, 2000–2018

(1) OPK Aggregate, Military and Civilian Annual Growth Rates and Production Indexes: Institute of the Economy in Transition (IET) and Author's Estimates

Indicator		*2000*	*2001*	*2002*	*2003*	*2004*	*2005*	*2006*	*2007*	*2008*	*2009*	*2010*
OPK Agg Output IET	Growth % PY	25.3	7.6	16.5	16.3	3.3	3.8	12.2	15.4	5.1	4.3	17.4
OPK Agg Output IET	Index 1991=100	36.1	38.8	45.2	52.6	54.3	54.4	63.2	73.0	76.7	80.0	93.9
Military Share OPK	%	54.0	55.0	56.0	57.0	58.0	59.0	61.0	63.0	64.0	65.0	66.0
Civil Share OPK	%	46.0	45.0	44.0	43.0	42.0	41.0	39.0	37.0	36.0	35.0	34.0
Published OPK Agg Output Growth	Annual Average Growth in Period	2000–2010: 11.6 %										
Estimated OPK Military Output Growth	Annual Average Growth in Period	2000–2010: 15.0 %										
Estimated OPK Civilian Output	Annual Average Growth in Period	2000–2010: 8.9 %										
Indicator		2011	2012	2013	2014	2015	2016	2017	2018			
OPK Agg Output IET	Growth % PY	5.8	6.4	13.5	15.5	12.9	10.1	5.3	5.2			
OPK Agg Output IET	Index 1991=100	99.4	105.7	120.0	138.6	156.5	171.4	180.4	189.7			
Military Share OPK	%	67.0	70.0	73.0	76.0	79.0	82.0	84.0	83.0			
Civil Share OPK	%	33.0	30.0	27.0	24.0	21.0	18.0	16.0	17.0			
Published OPK Agg Output Growth	Annual Average Growth in Period	2011–2018: 9.3 %										
Estimated OPK Military Output Growth	Annual Average Growth in Period	2011–2018: 13.1 %										
Estimated OPK Civilian Output	Annual Average Growth in Period	2011–2018: 1.1 %										

(2) OPK Branch Aggregate Output Annual Growth Rates and Indexes: Ministry of Industry and Trade (MinPromTorg)

Indicator		2010	2011	2012	2013	2014	2015	2016	2017	2018
OPK Agg Output	Growth % PY	NA	5.8	8.2	13.9	18.8	13.0	10.7	5.3	5.2
	Index 2010=100	100.0	105.8	114.5	130.4	154.9	175.0	193.8	204.1	214.7
Aviation Industry	Growth % PY	NA	9.0	12.3	17.2	18.3	5.2	8.7	11.7	0.3
	Index 2010=100	100.0	109.0	122.4	143.5	169.7	178.5	194.0	216.7	217.4
Missile-Space Industry	Growth % PY	NA	10.6	11.8	15.3	8.6	8.9	99.1	NA	NA
	Index 2010=100	100.0	110.6	123.7	142.6	154.8	168.6	167.1	NA	NA
Conventional Arms Industry	Growth % PY	NA	17.0	7.0	2.8	5.2	97.4	6.7	NA	6.5
	Index 2010=100	100.0	117.0	125.2	128.7	135.4	131.9	140.7	NA	NA
Munitions Industry	Growth % PY	NA	1.7	7.6	9.1	14.0	22.3	14.4	NA	3.0
	Index 2010=100	100.0	101.7	109.4	119.4	136.1	166.5	190.4	NA	NA
Shipbuilding Industry	Growth % PY	NA	-13.2	-7.8	1.4	40.7	14.7	0.6	NA	5.8
	Index 2010=100	100.0	86.8	80.0	81.2	114.2	131.0	131.8	NA	NA
Radio-Electronics Industry	Growth % PY	NA	9.9	17.1	29.5	19.9	33.0	18.5	NA	NA
	Index 2010=100	100.0	109.9	128.7	166.7	199.8	265.8	314.9	NA	NA

Notes: Published statistics on aggregate OPK growth rates were combined with those concerning civilian shares of OPK output at beginnings and ends of periods to calculate average annual growth rates for the 11 years 2000–2010 and the 8 years 2011–2018 (the period of the successful GPV 2011–2020). Civilian growth in the OPK stagnated from 2010 onwards due to market conditions and the squeezing out of production by military orders.

Prepared by C. Davis in 2019.

Sources: (1) OPK Aggregate Output: IET (2000-2019); Civilian Shares of OPK Output: Ryazantsev (2018, 213), supplemented by 1999–2000: Kuzyk (1999) and others, 2010–2011: Zakvasin (2017): President Rossii (2018); (2) MinPromTorg (2014, 2018).

(7) Employment

The total number of employees in the broadly defined defence industry decreased from 2.0 million in 2000 to 1.6 million in 2005 and then rose back up to 2.0 million in 2018 (MinPromTorg 2018). Of these, 1.3 million were engaged in military production and 0.7 million in civilian.

Russian defence companies have high ratios of staffing relative to sales revenue (two to four times higher than those of Western firms) (Oxenstierna and Westerlund, 2013). This is due to inefficiencies, war mobilisation requirements and the in-house provision of social benefits.

In the 2000s wage arrears were eradicated and the real value of salaries increased. From 2010 to 2013 the real monthly salary of OPK industrial workers rose by 8% per annum (IET, 2010, 509). There were improvements in the quality of labour measured by educational standards and in the age profile, although the average age of employees remained high due to the reluctance of younger scientists to commit to careers in the secretive OPK (Fel'gengauer, 2010; Ekonomika i Finansy, 2016; Connolly and Boulègue, 2018).

(8) Location

According to Zatsepin (2014), the regional distribution of the 1,339 organisations on the 2014 *MinPromTorg* OPK register (Table 4.11) showed that the Central Federal District was in first place with 591 units (44.1%), which included Moscow City (306, 22.9%) and Moscow Region (112, 8.4%). The Volga Federal District (238, 17.8%), including the Nizhny-Novgorod Region (55, 4.1%), and the Northwestern Federal District (223, 16.7%), including St. Petersburg (167 or 12.5%), were ranked second and third. The distribution of employment has continued to change with workers and scientists leaving formerly closed cities in remote regions.

(9) Foreign economic relations of the Russian defence industry in a period of intensifying economic sanctions

The organisation of Russian military foreign trade became more centralised and regulated after the establishment of *Rosoboroneksport* in 2000. Table 4.6 shows that Russia had average annual sales of WME of around $14.5 billion over the period 2010–2018, which made it the second largest world exporter of armaments and military equipment (Barabanov and Makienko, 2018).

The dominant source of legal imports of WME during 2000–2013 was Ukraine, which had an OPK that was closely integrated with the Russian one. In 2013 around 200 Russian weapons programmes made use of 3,000 products (e.g. gas turbine engines for ships) made by 160 Ukrainian companies (Connolly and Boulègue, 2018). Russia increased its legal imports of WME from Israel (military drones) and NATO countries. In 2011 Russia signed a contract with France to purchase two Mistral-class amphibious assault ships produced in that country and to build two more under license in Russia. However, NATO (2015, 18) reported that the share of foreign components in Russian military equipment was only about 10% by 2013.

Russia's military foreign trade with Ukraine and NATO countries ceased following the Ukraine politico-military crisis (Davis, 2016). However, the economic sanctions against Russia have been supported by countries responsible for only around 55% of global GDP (Davis, 2016, 2017). Those not participating have included Brazil, China, India, Indonesia, Iran, South Africa, South Korea, and Turkey. Russia has continued legal military foreign trade with these countries. In particular, Russia has been able to take advantage of the accelerating technological capabilities of China and India to obtain defence-related products that in the past could only be acquired from NATO countries. According to the former head of GCHQ (Hannigan, 2018):

> China manufactures an estimated 90 percent of the world's IT hardware, including some three-quarters of all smartphones…it means that the world economy is increasingly sitting on a global IT infrastructure manufactured in China…Over the next 20 years China will emerge as preeminent in numerous areas of technology.

In response to NATO economic sanctions Russia has intensified its programmes of covert trade diversion and technological espionage (*spetsinformatsiya*) to acquire defence-related products and information. Nevertheless, NATO (2015, 18) reported that around 500 Russian defence industrial firms had been adversely affected by sanctions. But they have had only minor impacts on important military programmes.

b. ***Russian defence industry enterprises in the state capitalist economy: structure, conduct and performance***

(1) Russian defence industry enterprises in the state capitalist economy

Table 4.9 supplements Figure 4.2 and section 5.a.(1) by presenting assessments of the characteristics of Russian defence firms with respect to their output side, production, and the input side. The sub-sections below amplify this evaluation.

(2) Structure

The ownership of DIEs has fluctuated in the 2000s, with some additional companies being privatised and others returning to state control. In 2017 the OPK contained 43% state-owned enterprises, 29% joint private-state companies and 28% private companies (Itogi, 2017). The government has prohibited 62% of defence firms from being privatised, but some ownership changes have occurred. For example, in 2013 there was a partial privatisation (49%) of the *Kontsern Kalashnikov* in Izhevsk, which is the country's largest producer of small arms.

Vertical control over defence industry intensified in the 2000s through re-organisations, establishment of powerful state corporations, encouragement of vertical integration, and strengthening of the Military-Industrial Commission. Russian sources have claimed that integrated control has improved management, but Connolly and Boulègue (2018) have argued that the measures have raised costs, encouraged counter-productive competition and increased corruption. Paternalism has remained a strong force in the OPK.

DIEs have continued to maintain comprehensive social support networks for their employees (Oxenstierna and Westerlund, 2013). They also have been put under greater pressure to comply with war mobilisation requirements concerning inventories and production capacity. The combination of vertical integration, social support and mobilisation has increased the overhead costs of defence firms and reduced their profitability.

In the 2000s there have not been significant new entries of defence firms and military R&D institutions into the OPK because start-ups have been authorised primarily in existing organisations. With respect to exit, small numbers of poorly performing defence enterprises not engaged in weapons production either have been forced into bankruptcy or have left the military sphere.

(3) Conduct

Throughout the 2000s Russian government organisations have exerted indirect bureaucratic control over both state and private DIEs through instructions, assignments and inspections, especially if they have been engaged in weapons programmes. Defence sector markets shown in Figure 4.1 have been transformed gradually into more normal ones. However, sellers' markets have survived, in that the defence industry has continued to dominate the armed forces. According to Oxenstierna and Westerlund (2013):

> The industry has a strong position in its negotiations with the MoD due to its monopoly power in many cases. In 2012, the head of *Rosoboronpostavka* admitted that 65 percent of all contracted transactions are made with a single supplier…

Defence firms have operated with low output inventories of WME because of strong demands for products by domestic and foreign customers.

Investment in the defence industry rose substantially from 2005 with the goals of modernising manufacturing (74% of machinery was obsolete in 2000), expanding production of WME and enhancing mobilisation capabilities. Enterprises once again have exhibited expansion drives (investment hunger). However, financial constraints tightened from 2014 and the central government has adopted a priority system to focus the allocation of investment in the defence industry.

During 2005–2013 DIEs did not experience significant shortages, production bottlenecks, instability in manufacturing and delays in investment projects. But Ukraine-related economic sanctions generated supply shocks and disrupted military production, especially that dependent on imports from Ukraine. As a result of precautionary behaviour and the emphasis on mobilisation capabilities, DIEs have built up larger inventories of inputs. They also have received more supplies of microelectronics, machinery, and technological knowledge from Russia's more energetic trade diversion and *spetsinformatsiya* programmes.

Another compensatory action taken by Russia post-2013 to protect its defence industry has been the strengthening of import substitution programmes (Connolly and Hanson, 2016). The government announced a target for the Russian defence industry of manufacturing substitutes for 695 WME items of the 1,070 that had been imported from Ukraine by the end of 2015 (NATO, 2015; Nureev and Busygin, 2017). Later it adopted the ambitious goal of replacing with domestic production 85% of the imports affected by sanctions by 2025 (Connolly and Hanson, 2016; Connolly and Boulègue, 2018). However, the import-substitution programme related to NATO countries has faced substantial technological challenges and by the end of 2018 few successes had been achieved.

An important feature of the environment of the Russian OPK has been the maintenance of soft budget constraints by the government using resources from the RMS. The Russian authorities do not want firms that play significant roles in weapons programmes to become bankrupt.

(4) Performance

During the 2000s the success indicators of defence industry managers shifted from those related to survival to those concerned with satisfying ambitious plans for the production of WME. DIEs have been operating in an environment of high demand for their products due to the military revival, which has enabled many of them to maintain the quantity drive in their production of traditional WME, rather than to shift to profit maximisation with lower volumes of more technologically sophisticated commodities. Managers of DIEs have paid greater attention to product quality due to demands of their superiors, the armed forces engaged in foreign conflicts, more competitive markets for civilian goods and exports of WME and military inspectors (*voenpredy*) in factories.

Value indicators (costs, prices, budgets, interest rates, profit) in defence industry have become moderately more important during the 2000s, but they still do not determine major developments. Prices in DIEs have continued to be measured in a mechanical manner (costs plus 20% normally, but 25% for a unique supplier), which has caused disputes with the armed forces as a customer. Labour, capital and total factor productivity have remained low in the defence industry because firms have maintained excessive labour forces and large stocks of capital.

Technological innovation in the OPK has evolved unevenly in the 2000s (Bat'kovskii et al., 2017). Despite receiving more generous funding, MRD has been impeded by the ageing of the scientific workforce and the lowering of its technical qualifications (Ekonomika i Finansy, 2016). Many managers of defence enterprises have remained risk averse and have pursued incremental changes. However, there have been substantial improvements in military technological innovation since the launch of the *State Armaments Programme 2011–2020*, which was accompanied by high-level monitoring of performance, more investment and improved financial remuneration (Kohkno and Kokhno, 2018).

Production conditions within DIEs improved considerably from 2000 to 2013. Demand for military and civilian outputs increased, barter was eradicated, and the frequencies of shortages, production bottlenecks and forced substitution were reduced. However, the Ukraine-related economic sanctions disrupted production in the relatively small number of Russian DIEs that were dependent on the embargoed products.

c. *Procurement and defence industry conversion in Russia, 2000–2019*

From 2000, the Russian government gradually adopted more ambitious GPVs and supported them with reliable funding from GOZ. This increased procurement, especially from 2011. However, over recent years greater emphasis has been placed on conversion of defence industry to the production of civilian products.

(1) Procurement

The implementation of GPVs has been overseen by the MIC, which used the Russian Defence Supply Agency (*Rosoboronpostavka*) to prepare GOZ contracts and the Russian Defence Order Agency (*Rosoboronzakaz*) to monitor their implementation. These organisations were disbanded in 2015 and their duties were passed on to the Department of State Procurement of the Ministry of Defence and the Federal Antimonopoly Service (it absorbed *Rosoboronzakaz*).

GPV 2001–2010 (adopted in 2000) and *GPV 2007–2015* (2006) had improved records from those in the 1990s, but also were held back by insufficient resources (Kuzyk, 2006; Gorenburg, 2010; Yazbeck, 2010; Zatsepin, 2012; Oxenstierna and Westerlund, 2013). However, *GPV 2011–2020* was allocated almost five times as much as its predecessor (20 trillion rubles), which enabled the armed forces to procure greater quantities of WME from defence industry. Table 4.5 shows that the GOZ share of the increasing total

DE rose from 24.6% in 2000 to 48.5% in 2014. In 2013 the ambitious GOZ for VVT (WME) was fulfilled by 93%.

Some of the main targets for procurement of WME of GPV 2011–2020 and actual procurement over the years 2010–2015 are shown in Table 4.14. According to IET (2016, 467):

> In 2016, the armed forces received 41 intercontinental ballistic missiles, over 3,000 new upgraded samples of weapons and military equipment, including 139 modern aircraft, two submarines, 24 surface ships, crafts and supply vessels, four regiment sets of S-400 surface-to-air missile systems and25 Pantsir-C anti-aircraft missile and gun system combat vehicles.

Within that year the armed forces received 260 unmanned drones, so their overall number amounted to 2,000.

The increased procurement has ensured that progress has been achieved in meeting the goal of 70% of the WME of the armed forces being of modern standards by 2020. The *GPV 2018–2027*, which was adopted in March 2018, has been evaluated in a preliminary manner by Connolly and Boulègue (2018).

Despite the achievements over the past decade, many problems have continued into 2019: (1) the procurement system has had an unstable organisation and flaws in its functioning; (2) the defence industry has remained dominant in sellers' markets for WME; (3) deficiencies in the defence industry and MRD have impeded its ability to develop the armaments requested by the MOD through the GOZ; and (4) arms procurement has been influenced by subjective decision-making and corruption concerning the award of contracts.

(2) State-directed defence industry conversion ("diversification") to civilian production

In 2001 the government introduced the Federal Programme *Reform and Development of the Defence-Industrial Complex (2002–2006)* that had as one objective, out of many, to decrease the number of enterprises in the OPK by converting those not vital to weapons programmes to full civilian production (Fel'gengauer, 2010). Negligible progress was achieved, as in past periods. There were several conversion initiatives over the next fifteen years, but they had low priority in a period dominated by commitments to implement ambitious State Armaments Programmes.

However, from 2016 government began to call attention to the fact that the magnitude of the GOZ would peak in 2020 and then decline. It wanted to keep defence enterprises in the OPK, which meant that they needed to pursue conversion to civilian production (under the new slogan of "diversification") in order to maintain their earning (Fel'gengauer, 2010; DIA, 2017; IET, 2000-2019; Berkutova, 2017; MinPromTorg; 2018, 160–161; Connolly and

Table 4.14 Russia procurement of WME during 2010–2016 and goals of the state armaments programme for 2011–2020

Weapons and military equipment	*2010*	*2011*	*2012*	*2013*	*2014*	*GOZ 2015*	*Total 2011–16*	*Targets for 2020*
ICBMs	27	7	9	15	16	16	91	400+
SLBMs	NA	22	16	16	22	24	113	100+
Iskander Missile Systems	NA	NA	NA	2	2	2	8	10
S-400 Air-Defence Systems	NA	4	3	4	2	6	21	56
Military Satellites	6	8	4	10	NA	NA	60	100+
UAVs	NA	NA	NA	NA	179	NA	860	4000
Fixed-Wing Aircraft	23	28	35	67	96	126	415	850
of which, Combat Aircraft		16	30	45	89	NA	NA	NA
Helicopters	37	82	118	100	135	88	700	1,150
of which, Combat Helicopters	NA	22	35	31	43	NA	170	330
Surface Combat Ships	NA	2	1	5	3	5	18	50
Strategic Nuclear Submarines	0	0	0	3	1	1	4	8
Multi-Role Nuclear Submarines	0	0	0	0	1	0	1	7
Diesel-Electric Submarines	0	0	0	0	2	1	5	7

Prepared by C. Davis in 2019.

Sources: IISS Military Balance: 2013, 207; 2015, 167; 2016, 172; 2017, 195; 2018, 178.

Boulègue, 2018). At a special meeting of defence industrialists in Tula in September 2016 President Putin encouraged defence industry to engage in "diversification" leading to the production of high-tech civilian commodities related to digital technologies, alternative energy and medical equipment. The government announced the objective of increasing the civilian share of OPK output from 16% in 2016 to 18% in 2020 (IISS, 2000-2019). In June 2016 the Fund for Industrial Development created a *Conversion Enterprise*, which was given the mission of promoting civilian products of the OPK.

In January 2018 a large meeting of high-level defence industrialists was held at the Ufa Engine Industrial Association on the topic of diversification (President Rossii, 2018). In his opening speech President Putin outlined the challenges facing OPK enterprises:

> However, the production lines must not stay idle in the future when the volume of state defence spending inevitably declines, once we are past the peak of the Defence Ministry's orders. We need to transition to the

manufacturing of civilian products, while generally ensuring their quality and competitiveness.

Targets were established to increase the civilian share of OPK output to 30% by 2025 and 50% by 2030. Assistance to defence firms in this effort would be provided by the *Conversion Enterprise*, a new special fund to finance diversification projects, the establishment of state orders for OPK civilian products and provision to managers of DIEs of generous financial incentives to engage in diversification. It also was announced that the *Import Substitution Government Commission* would encourage civilian enterprises and government agencies to purchase conversion products of the OPK, rather than importing equivalent foreign goods.

Achievements in conversion through 2019 have occurred to a modest degree due to the long-standing difficulty of state-owned defence firms in identifying civilian goods that would be competitive in domestic markets with foreign alternatives (Anokhin, 2019). IET (2016) provided several examples of conversion products that were reported to be successful, but in reality were not. In sum, the defence industry conversion efforts over 2016–2019 have had many of the failings of those in previous periods.

6. Conclusions

The characteristics and dynamics of the Russian defence industry over the three sub-periods since 1980 can be explained by utilising four instruments of analysis: (1) the five-block model of the defence industry in the politico-economic system (Figure 4.2); (2) the depiction of the horizontal relationships of the six economic institutions of the defence sector and their vertical organisation (Figures 4.1 and 4.3); (3) evaluation of the priority of defence industry during plan/budget formulation and implementation (Table 4.7); and (4.4) the assessment of the behaviour of DIEs concerning outputs, production, and inputs (Table 4.9).

The Soviet Union developed a powerful OPK (Table 4.8) despite its economic shortcomings because it awarded defence high priority status (Table 4.7) and allocated to it substantial resources (Table 4.1). The defence industry expanded its production of modern WME, which were supplied to the armed forces (Table 4.8) and exported (Table 4.2). However, the adverse features of the shortage economy generated difficulties in the OPK (Table 4.9). Defence-related technological gaps between the USSR and NATO countries widened. The reforms of the OPK during *perestroika* were ineffectual.

In the 1990s the OPK had to operate in a malfunctioning hybrid economy with a low priority status (Table 4.7) and reduced defence expenditure (Table 4.3). Defence sector markets (Figure 4.1) remained distorted and inefficient. DIEs received inadequate funding, experienced pervasive shortages and were forced to engage in barter (Table 4.9). The military and civilian outputs of the defence industry collapsed (Table 4.10) and exports of WME declined

(Table 4.4). The large gaps between Russia and NATO countries in defence technologies widened. Reforms of the OPK failed in that decade.

Russia in the 2000s had had stronger political control and a relatively high-growth state-dominated, capitalist economy (Figure 4.2). The OPK has been awarded high priority status (Table 4.7) and has benefited from increased real defence expenditure (Table 4.5). The procurement share of DE has risen to a moderately high level due to ambitious and well-funded state armaments programmes, especially *GPV 2011–2020*. During 2000–2013 the working conditions of DIEs improved (Table 4.9) and the outputs of WME and civilian goods increased substantially (Table 4.13). The annual average value of Russian exports of WME increased from around $5 billion over 2000–2005 to $14 billion during 2010–2016 (Table 4.6). Greater investment in MRD accelerated technological innovation, but Russia's standards of military technology in most areas have remained below those of NATO. Although the Ukraine-related economic sanctions imposed from 2014 have adversely affected segments of the defence industry, Russia has been able to offset some of the negative impacts through the re-arrangement of weapons programmes, import substitution, trade diversion and technological espionage.

Over the period out to 2025 it is likely that the OPK will: retain a high priority status, function in a growing economy (MinEkonRaz 2018), and be allocated sufficient funding to enable it to achieve objectives concerning improvements in capital stock and technological innovation. The anticipated fulfilment of the targets of the *GPV 2018–2027* should enable the defence industry to provide the armed forces with the planned modern WME and to maintain exports at high levels. However, Russia began to reduce real defence spending and to lower its defence burden in 2016 and plans to maintain this downward trend. It has adopted ambitious targets concerning defence industry conversion ("diversification"), including a 30% civilian share of total output of the OPK by 2025. In sum, the defence industry in Russia will continue to produce, in a self-sufficient manner, the armaments required by the armed forces and foreign customers, but the OPK might be able to diversify into civilian production to avoid becoming a detrimental burden on the slowly growing economy.

Notes

1 This chapter follows the current practice in Russia of referring to the defence-industrial complex with the acronym OPK (*Oboronno-Promyshlennyy Kompleks*), instead of the Soviet-era term military-industrial complex with the acronym VPK (*Voenno-Promyshlennyy Kompleks*).

2 This book uses the term *Defence Expenditure* to describe the allocation of resources to support a nation's defence effort, which includes expenditures from the formal defence budget on the armed forces as well as defence-related expenditures from other budget categories. This is consistent with the usage by the CIA (1986), Firth and Noren (1998), DIA (2017), IISS (2000-2019) and NATO (2018). However, other institutions and scholars make use of the term *Military Expenditure*, usually to

cover the same categories: United Nations (2002); Zatsepin (2007); ACDA Database (2018); and SIPRI (2000 … 2018). Please consult the cited sources to understand the differences in terminologies and measurements.

3 The dynamics of the Russian politico-economic system in the 1990s were evaluated insightfully in studies by Gaddy and Ickes (1998, 2005, 2010) using their models of the "Virtual Economy" and the "Rent Management System" (RMS). They revealed how the state obtained "rent" (value) from the energy sector and redistributed it to prop up uncompetitive manufacturing sectors, such as defence industry, which generated negative value added and engaged in barter.

4 The central authorities controlling defence industry were: Ministry of Industry 1991–1992; Russian Committee for Defence Industry 1992–1993; State Committee for Defence Industry 1993–1996; Ministry of Defence Industry 1996–1997; Ministry of the Economy 1997–1998; and jointly the Ministry of the Economy and Ministry of Industry and Science 1999 into the 2000s.

Acknowledgements

I would like to express my appreciation for the support provided to me by three scholars, which has contributed to the preparation of this chapter. First, thanks to Professor Keith Hartley of the University of York for encouraging my research in the field of defence economics over the past twenty years (e.g. Davis, 2002). Second, my research on international security issues has benefited from the scholarship of Professor Roy Allison of the University of Oxford, who has been a congenial partner in teaching a joint course on "Soviet Defence Policy and Arms Control" at the University of Birmingham in the late 1980s, in co-directing a four-year Ford Foundation project on "Soviet/Russian Conventional Arms Control in Europe", and in jointly teaching a Russian and East European Studies core course at the University of Oxford. Third, Professor James Foreman-Peck of Cardiff University (and former colleague at Oxford), an expert on industrial economics, has stimulated and supported my work on Russian industry (e.g. Davis, 1999). Research for this chapter was not financed by a specific grant, but it obtained general assistance from the University of Oxford and more specific help from the Oxford School of Global and Area Studies and the Oxford Institute of Population Ageing.

Abbreviations

ACDA WMEAT = U.S. Arms Control and Disarmament Agency. 1980 ... 2018.
ACDA Database = U.S. Arms Control and Disarmament Agency. 2018.
CIA = U.S. Central Intelligence Agency.
DIA = U.S. Defense Intelligence Agency.
DOD = U.S. Department of Defense.
IISS = International Institute for Strategic Studies.
MinEkonRaz = Ministerstvo Ekonomicheskogo.
MinPromTorg = Ministerstvo Promyshlennosti.
NATO = North Atlantic Treaty Organisation.

Rosstat = Federal'naya Sluzhba.
SIPRI Yearbook = Stockholm International Peace Research Institute, 2000 ... 2018.
SIPRI Database = Stockholm International Peace Research Institute, 2019.
TsAST =Tsentr Analiza Strategii i Tekhnologii.

References

Allison, R., 1997. The Russian armed forces: Structures, roles and policies. *In*: V. Baranovsky, ed., *Russia and Europe: The Emerging Security Agenda*. Oxford: Oxford University Press.

Almquist, P., 1990. *Red Forge: Soviet Military Industry Since 1965*. New York: Columbia University Press.

Anokhin, P., 2019. Diversifikatsiaya po meditsinskim pokozaniyam. *Voenno-Promyshlennyy Kur'er*, 5 February 2019. https://vpk-news.ru/articles/48090 Accessed 18 February 2019.

Babakin, A., 2016. *Tainy Pervoi Gosprogrammy Vooruzheniya 1996-2005 Gody: Spetsialisty, Fakty, Sobytiya*. Moscow, Veche.

Barabanov, M. and Makienko, K., 2018. Otsenka mirovogo rynka vooruzhenii v 2013-2017 godakh. *Eksport Vooruzhenii*, 6 (140), 33–36.

Bat'kovskii, A.M. et al., 2017. *Aktual'nye Problemy Razvitiya Upravleniya Oboronno-Promyshlennym Kompleksom*. Moscow: Ontoprint.

Berkutova, T.A., 2017. *Mekhanizmy Diversifikatsii Predpriyatii Obronno-Promyshlennogo Kompleksa v Usloviayak Voenno-Grazhdanskoi Integratsii*, Izhevsk: OOO Print.

Boulègue, M., 2017. Disentangling the ups & downs of Russia's military-industrial complex. *The National Interest*, 27 June 2017, http://nationalinterest.org/blog/the-buzz/entangling-the-ups-downs-russias-military-industrial-complex-21348.

Bystrye tempy razvitiya oboronno-promyshlennogo kompleksa Rossii v 2017: Ne tol'ko PVO i voennaya aviatsiya. 2018. *Novosti VPK*, 12. 03.2018. https://vpk.name/news/208605 Accessed 18 February 2019.

Connolly, R. and Boulègue, M. 2018. *Russia's New State Armament Programme Implications for the Russian Armed Forces and Military Capabilities to 2027*. London: Chatham House Research Paper: Russia and Eurasia Programme, May.

Connolly, R. and Hanson, P., 2016. Import substitution and economic sovereignty in Russia. *Chatham House Research Paper: Russia and Eurasia Programme*, June 2016.

Connolly, R. and Sendstad, C., 2018. Russian rearmament, *Problems of Post-Communism*, 65 (3), 143–160, DOI: 10.1080/10758216.2016.1236668

Cooper, J., 2006. Appendix 9C. Developments in the Russian arms industry. *In: SIPRI, 2006. SIPRI Yearbook: Armaments, Disarmament and International Security: 2016*. Oxford: Oxford University Press.

Cooper, J. 2016. Russia's state armament programme to 2020: A quantitative assessment of implementation 2011–2015. Stockholm: *FOI (Swedish Defence Research Agency) FOI-R-4239-SE*.

Davis, C., 1986. Economic and political aspects of the military-industrial complex in the USSR. *In*: H.-H. Höhmann, A. Nove, and H. Vogel, eds., *Economics and Politics in the USSR: Problems of Interdependence*. London: Westview Press, 92–124.

Davis, C., 1988a. The high priority defense industry in the Soviet shortage economy. Palo Alto, Hoover-Rand Conference on *The Defense Sector in the Soviet Economy*, Conference Paper, March 1988.

Davis, C., 1988b. *The Second Economy in Disequilibrium and Shortage Models of Centrally Planned Economies*. Durham, NC: *Berkeley-Duke Occasional Papers on the Second Economy in the USSR*, No. 12.

Davis, C., 1989. Priority and the shortage model: The medical system in the socialist economy. *In:* C. Davis and W. Charemza, eds., *Models of Disequilibrium and Shortage in Centrally Planned Economies*. London: Chapman and Hall, 427–459.

Davis, C., 1990a. Economic influences on the decline of the Soviet Union as a great power: Continuity despite change. *Diplomacy and Statecraft*, 1 (3), 81–109.

Davis, C., 1990b. The high-priority military sector in a shortage economy. *In*: H.S. Rowen and C. Wolf Jr., eds., 1990. *The Impoverished Superpower: Perestroika and the Soviet Military Burden*. San Francisco: Institute for Contemporary Studies, 155–184.

Davis, C., 1992a. The defense sector in the Soviet economy during Perestroika: From expansion to disarmament to disintegration. *In:* F.G. Adams, ed., 1992. *The Macroeconomic Dimensions of Arms Reductions*. Oxford: Westview Press, 189–215.

Davis, C., 1992b. The changing priority of the Soviet defense sector: 1985-1990. *In*: C. Wolf Jr. and S.W. Popper, eds., 1992. *Defense and the Soviet: Military Muscle and Economic Weakness*. Santa Monica: RAND Note 3474-USDP, 139–168.

Davis, C., 1999. Russia: A comparative economic systems interpretation. *In*: J. Foreman-Peck and G. Federico, eds., *European industrial policy: The Twentieth-Century Experience*. Oxford: Oxford University Press, 319–397.

Davis, C., 2002. The defence sector in the economy of a declining superpower: Soviet Union and Russia, 1965-2000. *Defence and Peace Economics*, 13 (3), 145–177.

Davis, C., 2011. Russia's military reforms and defense budgets 2011-2013: Goals, assumptions, prospects. *In*: *Proceedings of U.S. Department of State/Department of Defense Conference on Russian Decision Making and Implications for Defense Spending*, 2 March 2011. Arlington: System Planning Corporation, 1–21.

Davis, C., 2014. Industrial performance in the USSR, 1945-1980: Influences of state priorities, economic system, industrial policies, and hidden processes. *In*: A. Nützenadel and C. Grabas, eds., *Industrial Policy in Europe after 1945. Wealth, Power and Economic Development in the Cold War*. London: Palgrave, 337–371.

Davis, C., 2016. The Ukraine conflict, economic-military power balances, and economic sanctions. *Post-Communist Economies*, 28 (2), 167–198. Available Open Access online at:www.tandfonline.com/doi/full/10.1080/14631377.2016.1139301

Davis, C., 2017. Russia's changing economic and military relations with Europe and Asia from Cold War to the Ukraine conflict: The impacts of power balances, partnerships, and economic warfare. *In:* Korea Institute for International Economic Policy, 2017. *Studies in Comprehensive Regional Strategies Collected* Papers *(International Edition) 16–15*. Seoul: KIEP, 195-285. https://papers.ssrn.com/sol3/papers.cfm?abstract_id=2954388##

Davis, C., Charemza, W., eds., 1989. *Models of Disequilibrium and Shortage in Centrally Planned Economies*. London: Chapman and Hall.

Defense News, 2018. 2018 Top 100 Companies. *Defense News*, Rankings available at https://people.defensenews.com/top-100/Data

Ekonomika i Finansy Oboronnogo Kompleksa Rossii: Uchebnoe Sposobie, 2016. Moscow: INFRA-M.

Federal'naya Sluzhba Gosudarstvennoi Statistiki. 2000-2018. *Rossiiskii Statisticheskii Ezhegodnik*. Moscow: Rosstat.

Federal'naya Sluzhba Gosudarstvennoi Statistiki. 2019. *Rossiya v Tsifrakh*. Moscow: Rosstat.

Fel'gengauer, P.E., 2010. Voenno-promyshlennyy kompleks Rossii v 1991-2008. *Istoriya Novoi Rossii*, Online www.ru90.ru/node/1225

Firth, N.E. and Noren, J.H., 1998. *Soviet Defense Spending: A History of CIA Estimates 1950-1990*, College Station, Texas: Texas A & M University Press.

Frolov, A. 2015a, 2016a, 2017a, 2018a. Ispolnenie gosudarstvennogo oboronnogo zakaza Rossii v 2014 godu, … v 2015 godu, … v 2016 godu, … v 2017 godu. *Eksport Vooruzhenii: 2015*, 3(118),26–40; 2016, 3(124),16-27; 2017, 4(132),21-35; 2018, 4(138),10-21.

Frolov, A. 2015b, 2016b, 2017b, 2018b. Itogi voenno-tekhnicheskogo sotrudnichestva Rossii s inostrannami gosudarstvami v 2015 godu, … v 2016 godu, … v 2017 godu, … v 2018 godu. *Eksport Vooruzhenii: 2015*, 6(121),21–31; 2016, 6(127),6-15; 2017, 6(134),19-30; 2018, 6(140),9-17.

Frolov, A. 2015c, 2016c, 2017c, 2018c. Perspektivy rossiiskogo oruzheinogo eksporta na 2016 god. *Eksport Vooruzhenii: 2015*, 6(121),32–34; 2016, 6(127),24-26; 2017, 6-(134),47-49; 2018, 6(140),30-32.

Gaddy, C., 1996. *The Price of the Past: Russia's Struggle with the Legacy of a Militarized Economy*. Washington DC: Brookings Institution Press.

Gaddy, C.G. and Ickes, B.W., 1998. Russia's virtual economy. *Foreign Affairs*, 77 (5), 53–67.

Gaddy, C.G. and Ickes, B.W., 2005. Resource rents and the Russian economy. *Eurasian Geography and Economics*, 46 (8), 559–583.

Gaddy, C.G. and Ickes, B.W. 2010. Russia after the global financial crisis. *Eurasian Geography and Economics*, 51 (3), 281–311.

Gorenburg, D., 2010. *Russia's State Armaments Program 2020: Is the Third Time the Charm for Military Modernization?* Washington DC: CNA Strategic Studies, *PONARS Eurasia Policy Memo No. 125.*

Hannigan, R., 2018. Wake up to the security risks in Chinese tech dominance. *Financial Times*, 27 July 2018.

Hanson, P., 1987. Soviet industrial espionage. Some new information. London: Royal Institute for International Affairs, *RIIA Discussion Paper No. 1.*

IET = Institute for the Economy in Transition (Re-named Gaidar Institute for Economic Policy in 2010).

Institute for the Economy in Transition (Gaidar Institute for Economic Policy). (2000–2019). *Annual Report on the Russian Economy: Trends and Perspectives*, Moscow: Institute of the Economy in Transition (in Russian and English). Sections on: Military Economy and Military Reform in Russia. Authored by Vitaly Tsymbal during 2000–2002, Vitaly Tsymbal and Vasily Zatsepin during 2003-2018, and Vasily Zatsepin in 2019. www.iep.ru/en/publikatcii/category/1419.html

International Institute for Strategic Studies. 1990…2019. *The Military Balance in 1990… 2019.* London: IISS.

Itogi 2017 goda dlya Rossiiskogo oboronno-promyshlennogo kompleksa. *Voennoe Obozrenie*, 22 December 2017.

Knorr, K., 1957. *The Concept of Economic Potential for War.* Washington DC: Industrial College of the Armed Forces, *Publication No. L57-133*, 1–20.

Knorr, K., 1973. *Power and Wealth: The Political Economy of International Power.* New York: Basic Books.

Kohkno, P.A. and Kokhno, A.P., 2018. *Effektivnyy Oboronno-Promyshlennyy Kompleks*, Moscow, Granitsa.

Kontseptsiya National'noi Bezopasnosti. *Nezavisimoe Voennoe Obozrenie*, 14–20 January 2000, 1.

Kornai, J., 1980. *Economics of Shortage.* Amsterdam: North-Holland.

Kornai, J., 1992. *The Socialist System: The Political Economy of Communism*. Oxford: Clarendon Press.

Korotchenko, I. and Mukhin, V., 1999. Vooruzhentsy menyayut prioritety, *Nezavisimoe Voennoe Obozrenie*, 8-14 October 1999: 6.

Kostin, S. and Raynaud, E., 2011. *Farewell: The Greatest Spy Story of the Twentieth Century*. Las Vegas: AmazonCrossing.

Kuzyk, B.N., 1999. *Oboronno-Promyshlennyy Kompleks Rossii: Proryv v XXI Vek*, Moscow: Russkii Biograficheskii Institut.

Kuzyk, B.N., 2006. Oboronno-promyshlennyy kompleks (OPK). *Bol'shaya Rossiiskaya Entsiklopediya*, Online at https://bigenc.ru/text/5045275, Accessed 20 November 2018

Maslyukov, Yu.D. and Glubokov, E.S., 2005. Ekonomika oboronnogo kompleksa. In: *Voenno-Promyshlennyy Kompleks: Entsiklopediya, Tom. I, 2005*. Moscow: Voennyy Parad, 36–67.

Ministerstvo Ekonomicheskogo Razvitiya Rossiiskoi Federatsii, 2018. *Prognoz Sotsial'no-ekonomicheskogo Razvitiya Rossiiskoi Federatsii na Period do 2036 Goda*. Moscow: M, MinEkonRaz, 28 November 2018http://economy.gov.ru/minec/about/structure/depMacro/201828113, Accessed 15 January 2019.

Ministerstvo Promyshlennosti i Torgovli Rossiiskoi Federatsii. 2014. *Perechen' Organizatsii, Vkluchennykh v Svodnyy Reestr Organizatsii Oboronno-Promyshlennogo Kompleksa*. Moscow: Document of MinPromTorg.

Ministerstvo Promyshlennosti i Torgovli Rossiiskoi Federatsii. 2018. *Doklad o Tselyakh i Zadachakh Minpromtorga Rossii na 2018 God i Osnovnykh Resul'tatakh Deyatel'nosti za 2017 God*. Moscow: MinPromTorg, 1–180.

Minyayev, A.V., Kornienko, G.M., Maslyukov, and Yu. D. et. al., 1999. *Sovetskaya Voennaya Moshch': Ot Stalina do Gorbacheva*, Moscow: Voennyy Parad.

Monaghan, A., 2014. *Defibrillating the Vertikal? Putin and the Russian Grand Strategy*. London: *Chatham House Research Paper*, October 2014.

Natural Resources Defense Council, 1997. US and USSR/Russian Strategic Offensive Nuclear Forces, 1945–1996. www.nrdc.org/nrdc/nrdcpro/nudb/dainx.htm

Noren, J., 1994. The Russian military-industrial sector and conversion. *Post-Soviet Geography*, 35 (9), 495–521.

Noren, J., 1995. The controversy over Western measures of Soviet defense expenditures. *Post-Soviet Affairs*, 11 (3), 238–276.

North Atlantic Treaty Organization. 2000. *Defence Economics in Russia, Ukraine, Belarus, Central Asia, Transcaucasus and Moldova*. Brussels: NATO Document AC/127-D/814.

North Atlantic Treaty Organization. 2015. *Russian Military Modernization: General Report*. Brussels: NATO 176 STC 15 E rev.1 fin, October.

North Atlantic Treaty Organization. 2018. Information on defence expenditures. NATO Website: www.nato.int/cps/en/natolive/topics_49198.htm, Accessed 9 March 2019.

Nureev, R. and Busygin, E.G., 2017. The Russian defense industry complex in the conditions of economic sanctions. *The Business and Management Review*, 9 (2), 175–188.

Oboronno-Promyshlennyy Kompleks Rossii v 2012-2015 godakh. 2018. Natsional'naya Oborona, No. 11. www.oborona.ru

OPK (Oboronno-Promyshlennyy Kompleks Rossii: Biograficheskaya Entsiklopediya), 2015. Moscow: Izd. Dom Stolichnaya Entsiklopediya.

OPK (Oboronno-Promyshlennyy Kompleks Rossii: Federal'nyy Spravochnik), 2006 (Vypusk 2), … *2013-2014* (Vypusk 10), … *2017-2018* (Vypusk 14). Moscow: Tsentr Strategicheskikh Program.

OPK (Oboronno-Promyshlennyy Kompleks: Ot Khaosa 90-x k Chetvertnoi Promyshlennoi Revolyutsii), 2016. Moscow: Liga Sodeistviya Oboronnym Predpriyatiyam.

OPK Rossii: Itogi 2017 goda. 2018. Natsional'naya Oborona, 7 July. www.oborona.ru

Oxenstierna, S., Westerlund, F., 2013. Arms procurement and the Russian defense industry: Challenges Up to 2020. *Journal of Slavic Military Studies*, 26 (1), 1–24. www.tandfonline.com/toc/fslv20/26/1

Pozharov, A.I., 1981. *Ekonomicheskie Osnovy Oboronnogo Mogushchestva Sotsialisticheskogo Gosudarstva*. Moscow: Voennoe Izdatelstvo.

Pravitel'stvo Rossiiskoi Federatsii. 2019. Postanovlenie: O Vnesenii Izmenenii v Godudarstvennuyu Programmu Rossiiskoi Federatsii. *"Razvitie Oboronno-Promyshlennogo Kompleksa" ot 6 Fevralya 2019 g. No. 85–86.* http://minpromtorg.gov.ru/docs/#!postanovlenie_pravitelstva_rf_856_ot_06_fevralya_2019_goda

President Rossii. 2014. *Voennaya Doktrina Rossiiskoi Federatsii*. 26 November 2014. http://kremlin.ru/events/president/news/47334, Accessed 20 November 2018.

President Rossii. 2015. *Ukaz Presidenta Rossiiskoi Federatsii ot 31.12.2015 г. № 683: O Strategii Nationalnoi Bezopastnosti Rossii*. 31 December 2015.http://kremlin.ru/acts/bank/40391, Accessed 20 November 2018.

President Rossii. 2018. Meeting on diversifying the production of high-tech civilian products by defence industry organisations at the Ufa Engine Industrial Association, 24 January 2018. http://en.kremlin.ru/events/president/news/56699, Accessed 13 January 2019.

Ryazantsev, O.N. 2018. Ob osnovnykh itogakh razvitiya situatsiya v oboronno-promyshlennom komplekse v 2017 godu I osnovnykh zadachakh na blizhaishuyu perspektivu. *Oboronno-Promyshlennyy Kompleks Rossii 2017-2018* (Vypusk 14). Moscow, ANO Tsentr Stratigicheskikh Programm.

Sandler, T. and Hartley, K., 1995. *The Economics of Defense*. Cambridge: Cambridge University Press.

Stockholm International Peace Research Institute. 2000 … 2018. *SIPRI Yearbook: Armaments, Disarmament and International Security*. Oxford: Oxford University Press. *www.sipri.org/yearbook/*

Stockholm International Peace Research Institute. 2019. *SIPRI Military Expenditure Online Database 1949-2018*. SIPRI Website: https://sipri.org/databases/milex, Accessed 30 April 2019.

Tsentr Analiza Strategii i Tekhnologii, 2006. Rossiiskii Eksport Vooruzhenii i Voennoi Tekhniki. Voennyy Byudzhet, i Godudarstvennyy Oboronnyy Zakaz. Moscow: TsAST.

Tsentr Analiza Strategii i Tekhnologii. 2016. Rossiiskii Eksport Vooruzhenii i Voennoi Tekhniki. Voennyy Byudzhet, i Godudarstvennyy Oboronnyy Zakaz. Moscow: TsAST.

Tsentr Stratigicheskykh Razrabotok., 2017. *Strategiya Rossii na 2018-2024 gg*. Moscow: TsSR. http://csr.ru/, Accessed 3 June 2018.

U.S. Arms Control and Disarmament Agency. 1980 … 2018. *World Military Expenditure and Arms Trade (WMEAT): Annual Report*, Washington D.C.: US ACDA.

U.S. Arms Control and Disarmament Agency. 2018. *World Military Expenditure and Arms Trade (WMEAT) Database.* U.S. State Department Website: www.state.gov/t/avc/rls/rpt/wmeat/c81153.htm, Accessed 30 April 2019.

U.S. Central Intelligence Agency. 1985. *Soviet Acquisition of Militarily Significant Western Technology: An Update.* Washington DC: *CIA ER-81-10085.*

U.S. Central Intelligence Agency. 1986. *The Soviet Weapons Industry. An Overview.* Washington DC: *CIA DI 86-10016.*

U.S. Defence Intelligence Agency. 2017. *Russian Military Power.* Washington DC: DIA. www.dia.mil/Portals/27/Documents/News/Military%20Power%20Publications/Russia%20Military%20Power%20Report%202017.pdf

U.S. Department of Defense. 1981..1990. *Soviet Military Power 1981 … 1990.* Washington DC: U.S. Department of Defense.

United Nations. 2002. *United Nations Standardized Instrument for Reporting Military Expenditures.* New York: UN Department for Disarmament Affairs.

Voennaya Doktrina Rossiskoi Federatsii. 2000. Rossiiskaya Gazeta, 25 April 2000.

Voenno-Promyshlennyy Kompleks: Entsiklopediya Tom 1, 2005. Moscow: Voennyy Parad.

Yazbeck, T. 2010. The Russian economy and resources available for military reform and equipment modernization. Defence R&D Canada, Centre for operational research and analysis, strategic analysis section *DRDC CORA TM 2010-192*, September 2010.

Zakvasin, A. 2017. Oboronka idyot v narod: Zachem Rossiiskii OPK perevodyat na grazhdanskie rel'sy. *RT Na Russkom*, 22 June 2017. https://ru.rt.com/8mbb

Zatsepin, V., 2007. Russian military expenditure: What's behind the curtain? *The Economics of Peace and Security Journal*, 2, 1.

Zatsepin, V., 2012. The economics of Russian defence policy. *In:* R. McDermott, et al., eds., *The Russian Armed Forces in Transition: Economic, Geopolitical and Institutional Uncertainties.* London: Routledge.

Zatsepin, V., 2014. Russia's defence industry complex comes out of shadow. *Russian Economic Developments*, 8.

Zatsepin, V. and Tsymbal, V. 2008 Reforma armii i restrukturizatsiya VPK. *In:* Institut Ekonomiki Perekhodnogo Perioda, 2008. *Ekonomika Perekhodnogo Perioda: Ocherki Ekonomicheskoi Politiki Postkommunisticheskoi Rossii: Ekonomicheskii Rost 2000-2007*, Moscow: Izd. Delo ANKh.

5 The United Kingdom

Keith Hartley

Introduction

The UK has one of the world's major arms industries supplying a comprehensive range of equipment for air, land, sea and nuclear systems. The UK industry supplies its armed forces which have a world military role capable of overseas military operations, together with a submarine-based strategic nuclear deterrent. As a result, the industry is involved in the design, development and manufacture of a range of conventional and nuclear systems. However, not all equipment is supplied by the UK industry and some is imported, mainly from the USA (e.g. missiles for the nuclear deterrent; some large aircraft; helicopters). Nor is the UK the only source of demand for national equipment: foreign government buyers mean that some arms are exported.

The UK arms industry is also involved in post-production work comprising repair, maintenance and modifications. Increasingly, the UK armed forces are outsourcing some of their activities previously undertaken 'in-house' to private contractors. Examples include in-service support, training and the provision of military capabilities such as air tankers for air refuelling. Finally, the industry is also involved in the disposal of surplus military equipment. Disposal of equipment ranges from simple operations such as dismantling and destruction of conventional equipment to the more complex task of disposing of nuclear systems (e.g. nuclear-powered submarines; atomic weapons; the clean-up of nuclear weapons bases and sites).

This chapter reviews what is known and not known about the UK arms industry. It considers definitions of the industry and reviews the available data on the industry, including arms exports and imports. Compared with many other nations, the UK government publishes official data on its arms industry so that some statistics are available to measure the size of the industry. Further data are available from industry trade associations and annual company reports. Structure, conduct and performance are also assessed as well as the economic impacts of government procurement policy. The conclusion reviews the future of the industry.

Definitions

The UK defence industry comprises all UK firms supplying arms, other products and services to the UK armed forces. This is a wide definition of the industry forming the supply-side of the UK defence market. On the demand-side, the UK Ministry of Defence (MoD) is the government Department purchasing equipment for its armed forces. Its equipment purchases range from the cheap and simple to the costly, high technology and complex. Cheap and simple includes paper clips, motor vehicles, housing and cleaning services. Costly and complex includes aircraft carriers, combat aircraft, missiles, submarines, space and nuclear systems. Some of this equipment already exists and is bought 'off-the-shelf' from existing suppliers (e.g. motor vehicles; financial and building services). The costly and complex equipment does not always exist and might have to be developed specifically for the UK government and its armed forces. Such equipment raises complex procurement problems, involving the choice of contractor, the type of contract and its profitability. Alternatively, some equipment might be purchased from overseas suppliers, especially arms which are costly and complex where foreign firms have already developed and produced the equipment (e.g. ballistic missiles; specialist aircraft where the UK requires small numbers). Often, the UK purchases foreign equipment from the USA (part of its 'special relationship').

Ultimately, the MoD has the task of combining its equipment purchases with other factor inputs of labour and capital (e.g. land for military bases) to form its armed forces which provide defence output in the form of peace, protection and security for its citizens. Defence output is difficult to measure and value: there are no data providing a measure of the rate of return for the UK Armed Forces or that of any other country (Hartley, 2017, pp. 6–7).

The UK MoD is not the only buyer of UK arms, other equipment and services. Other buyers include foreign governments and foreign firms. Foreign governments often buy existing UK defence equipment and services which forms UK defence exports. Also, foreign firms might buy UK products to form inputs into their defence equipment and such foreign purchases of UK equipment are measured in UK exports: but unless the equipment is clearly identified as defence it will not appear as a UK defence export. Examples of foreign arms firms purchasing UK products include aircraft engines, avionics, aircraft landing gear, ejector seats, naval propulsion systems and tank tracks.

UK defence numbers

The UK defence effort is reflected in key statistics showing annual spending, defence shares of GDP and numbers of military personnel. UK defence spending at £35.3 billion in 2016–17 was the fifth largest in the world (after USA, China, Russia, Saudi Arabia) and the third largest in NATO (after USA and Greece). Also, in 2016–17, MoD spending made it the fourth highest UK government spending department (after Work and Pensions; Health; and Education). The UK's defence share of GDP at 2.2% in 2016 met the NATO commitment. Its spending on defence R&D was almost £1.7 billion in 2016/17 (about 5% of the defence budget: see Table 5.1) compared with defence R&D real spending of some £3.9 billion in 2000/01 (2017 prices) representing a substantial real terms reduction.[1]

The defence budget purchased inputs of labour and capital. Labour inputs comprised a total of almost 140,000 military personnel allocated between the Army (78,410), the Navy and Marines (29,580) and the Royal Air Force (RAF: 30,850). Expenditure on military personnel represented some 27% of the defence budget in 2016–17 with spending on equipment and support at £15.7 billion or some 34% of the budget (Hartley and Macdonald, 2010; MoD, 2017a).

Table 5.1 shows current and past trends in UK defence spending. Real levels of UK defence spending have fallen substantially since 1985 reflecting the end of the Cold War and major defence reviews (Hartley and Macdonald, 2010). The UK was also involved in conflicts in the Gulf (1990), Afghanistan (2001–14) and Iraq (2003–11) which led to higher defence spending. Overall,

Table 5.1 UK defence

Year	*Defence spending (£mn, constant 2017 prices)*	*Defence share of GDP (%)*	*Total number of military personnel (000s)*	*Number of Army personnel (000s)*	*Number of Navy personnel (000s)*	*Number of Air Force personnel (000s)*
1980	48,083	4.7	320.6	159.0	71.9	89.6
1985	52,035	4.9	326.2	162.4	70.4	93.4
1990	49,056	3.9	305.7	152.8	63.2	89.7
1995	41,057	2.9	233.3	111.7	50.9	70.8
2000	39,516	2.4	207.6	110.1	42.8	54.7
2005	46,761	2.4	188.1	102.4	35.5	40.1
2010	48,142	2.4	177.8	102.2	35.5	40.1
2017	35,300	2.2	138.8	78.4	29.6	30.9

Sources: MoD (2012); MoD (2017a, 2017b); Dunne (2018).

Notes:

i) To the year 1999, the defence budget was on a cash basis. The years 1999 to 2001 were on a transitional basis moving from cash to resource accounting. Since 2001/02, the budget has been on a resource accounting basis.
ii) For spending, years are financial years: for example, 1980 is for 1980/81; 2000 is for 2000/01. All remaining data are for calendar years.
iii) Sales data in constant prices based on RPI data adjusted to 2017 prices.

lower real defence spending was reflected in corresponding reductions in the numbers of military personnel, especially in the RAF. The defence share of GDP showed a long-run decline from almost 5% in 1985 to 2.2% in 2017. The impact of lower defence spending on the size and structure of the UK defence industry are assessed in the next sections.

Industry size

UK defence statistics have been published in a variety of sources and forms. Traditionally, UK defence statistics were published in the annual *Statement on the Defence Estimates Volume 2.* A new publication known as *UK Defence Statistics* was first published in 1992. They were published annually in a single publication with many of the statistics being published for the first time. Explanations were provided of any new statistical series (e.g. resource accounting). After 2012, *UK Defence Statistics* was replaced by a series of statistical bulletins in six series comprising finance and economics; personnel numbers; health of the Armed Forces; equipment; search and rescue; survey of personnel; land holdings; and military family accommodation (MoD, 2012, 2017a). The economic logic of the six series is not at all obvious. For example, what is the contribution of health of the Armed Forces, search and rescue, land holdings and family accommodation to UK defence output?

Originally, *UK Defence Statistics* published annual data on industry and employment. The employment data were comprehensive and comprised numbers of direct and indirect jobs dependent on MoD expenditure divided into equipment and non-equipment spending and employment dependent on defence exports. There were regional data on the annual numbers of regional direct jobs dependent on MoD equipment and non-equipment spending. However, the position changed in 2009 when it was announced that MoD would no longer publish comprehensive national and regional employment estimates claiming that

> …the data do not directly support MoD policy making and operations. The MoD budget has never been allocated or planned on a regional basis and decisions on where contracts with industry are placed are not taken in order to benefit one local economy or industry sector over another.
>
> (MoD, 2009)

This was a strange explanation for withdrawing statistics which added to our understanding of the UK defence industry. By 2017, policy had changed with a new emphasis on the contribution of defence to UK prosperity where numbers of jobs, their skills and location were an important component of such prosperity. It was announced that MoD had resumed the collection of statistical data on its regional expenditure with UK industry and supported employment (MoD, 2017d, p. 18).

Following the 2009 changes, there are expenditure data and some limited employment data providing an indication of the size of the UK defence industry.The MoD publishes annual data on its spending with UK industry which provides one indicator of industry size which totalled £18.7 billion in 2016–17; but this only shows MoD spending with UK industry (Table 5.2). Additional arms spending is reflected in UK defence exports which totalled £9 billion in 2017. There is a further category of defence exports known as security exports which was £4.8 billion in 2017. However, security exports are defined to include a wide variety of activities including border security, policing, counter-terrorism, prison services and cyber security and it is not at all clear whether all these activities should be classed as defence.

Some UK defence industry employment data are published on an occasional basis (Table 5.2; Dunne, 2018). The numbers show a substantial decline in industry employment between 1980 and 2017 reflecting reductions in real defence spending and higher labour productivity.

More details of UK defence industries by both sales to MoD and employment in 2017 are shown in Table 5.3. The highest level of MoD

Table 5.2 UK defence industry size

Year	*Sales by UK industry to MoD (£mn, 2017 prices)*	*UK defence export sales (£mn, 2017 prices)*	*Direct employment (000s)*	*Indirect employment (000s)*	*Total employment (000s)*
1980	21,943	6,455	405	335	740
1985	23,570	5,084	345	280	625
1990	19,709	9,827	295	260	550
1995	18,225	8,596	205	205	410
2000	19,143	6,992	155	145	300
2005	22,602	6,383	165	145	310
2010	24,915	(7,212)	155	145	300
2017	18,653	9,000	140	120	260

Sources: MoD (2012); MoD (2017c); Dunne (2018).

Notes:

i) Years are based on financial year: 1980 is 1980/81; 1985 is 1985/86, etc. Figures are rounded.
ii) Employment for 2010 is based on 2007/08 figures: employment data were not published by MoD after 2009 and published figures in 2009 were for 2007/08. There is a major gap in official employment statistics between 2007/08 and 2017.
iii) Sales by UK Industry are to MoD and exclude UK defence export sales.
iv) Defence exports comprise deliveries of defence equipment and services. From 2009, MoD reported export orders and not annual deliveries. The figure for 2010 is based on 2007 data and the figure for 2017 is based on orders.
v) Data from MoD, UKDS for 1980 to 2010; then from Dunne (2018).

Table 5.3 MoD spending with UK industry and employment, 2017

UK industry	*MoD spending with UK industry (£mn)*	*Number of direct jobs*
Technical, Financial and Other Business Services	4,369	44.500
Shipbuilding and Repair	3,027	19,250
Aerospace	1,850	7,150
Computer Services	1,446	9,500
Weapons and Ammunition	1,147	5,950
Construction	1,201	5,900
Other Manufacturing	924	5,600
Hotels, catering, restaurants	352	6,000
Total	18,653	123,000

Source: MoD (2017c).

Note: Industries ranked by sales. Hotels, etc group shown since it was major employer. Not all industry groups are shown in the total.

spending was with the industry grouping known as Technical, Financial Services and Other Business Services. This group contains a wide range of activities including accounting, legal services, management consultancy, technical testing and analysis, and research and development. Next in terms of levels of MoD spending were shipbuilding and aerospace.

The regional distribution of MoD spending on UK industry and the regional location of defence industry jobs is shown in Table 5.4. In 2017, some 70% of total MoD spending on UK industry and the associated employment was concentrated in the South West and South East, including London, together with the North West. Over the period 1985 to 2017, there were significant regional job gains in the South West, Wales and the East of England; but there were also substantial regional job losses in the remaining UK regions.

Industry structure

The UK defence industry representing the supply-side of the market comprises a small number of large firms often forming domestic monopolies or oligopolies. National monopolies include BAE Systems, Rolls-Royce and Martin Baker. Domestic duopoly exists for sea systems comprising BAE and Babcock, although in 2018 there were MoD plans to extend competition for naval vessels: for example, MoD plans to extend competition through its award of contracts for the new Type 32 frigate. In addition to the small number of large UK prime contractors, there are larger numbers

Table 5.4 Regional analysis, 1985–2017

Region	*2016/17 MoD spending by UK industry (£mn, 2017 prices)*	*2016/17 Numbers of regional direct jobs*	*1985/86 MoD spending by UK industry (£mn, 2017 prices)*	*1985/86 Numbers of regional direct jobs*
South West	5,079	33,500	2,900	22,000
South East	4,862	33,100	9,425	84,000
North West	2,001	12,300	2,030	23,000
Scotland	1,592	10,500	1,160	18,000
London	1,432	7,100	Na	Na
East Midlands	845	6,900	870	8,000
Wales	945	6,300	435	3,000
East of England	918	5,700	290	4,000
West Midlands	544	4,700	725	7,000
Yorkshire and Humberside	232	1,800	580	4,000
North East	100	700	1,160	15,000
Northern Ireland	103	600	290	8,000
Total UK	18,653	123,000	19,865	200,000

Source: MoD (2017c).

Note: Na is not available: the region was not listed in 1985.

of small firms forming the supply chains for the industry. Defence industry supply chains are complex, differing between air, land and sea systems and between prime contractors. Published data are usually unavailable for defence industry supply chains. Obtaining such data is a substantial and costly research exercise requiring prime contractors and supplying firms willing to disclose what they might regard as commercially sensitive information (Hartley, et al., 1997).

In 2016, the UK had eight arms firms in the SIPRI Top 100 (Table 5.5). BAE Systems was the dominant arms firm in both the UK and Europe representing a large firm and national monopoly in some sectors of the UK arms market.

Ownership

The UK MoD is a major buyer of defence equipment and in some cases the only buyer (monopsony: nuclear-powered submarines). Its buying power can be used to determine industry size, ownership, structure, conduct and performance. For example, government contracts determine the size of the industry with rearmament leading to expansion and disarmament leading to contraction, plant closures and job losses. Government can determine

Table 5.5 Major UK arms firms, 2016

Company	*World ranking 2016*	*Arms sales ($mn)*	*Arms sales share of total sales (%)*	*Estimated arms employment*
BAE Systems	4	22,790	95	78,850
Rolls-Royce	16	4,450	24	11,980
Babcock International Group	28	2,950	48	16,800
Cobham	57	1,550	59	6,300
Serco	58	1,500	32	15,040
GKN	68	1,210	10	5,800
Meggitt	80	940	35	3,925
Ultra Electronics	97	720	68	2,720

Source: SIPRI (2016).

Note: (i) Arms employment estimated from arms sales share of total sales applied to total employment. Figures are rounded.

whether to award contracts on a competitive basis or non-competitively and it determines the profitability of non-competitive contracts.

Since 1960, the UK defence industry has experienced periods of both state and private ownership. There was considerable state ownership in the defence research establishments, the Royal Dockyards, the Royal Ordnance factories (RO) and Short Brothers (Belfast). Rolls-Royce was nationalised in 1971 followed by the aircraft and shipbuilding industries in 1977. The nationalisation of shipbuilding resulted in 27 companies involved in shipbuilding, ship repair and marine engineering being merged to create a new public corporation known as British Shipbuilders (BS).

Large-scale privatisations occurred in defence and elsewhere following the 1979 election of the Conservative Government. Privatisation changed ownership and, in some cases, industry structure. Under the Thatcher Government, the first major privatisation of the UK defence industry occurred with the sale of shares in British Aerospace (BAe) in early 1981 and later in May 1985. BAe represented a change from a state to a private domestic monopoly. The privatisation of shipbuilding started with the warship yards after 1983. Initially, these ownership changes meant that a domestic monopoly was replaced by a competitive structure. Later, there were further changes in ownership and industry structure. Vosper Thorneycroft was acquired by Babcock; GEC together with its yards at Barrow and Yarrow, was acquired by BAe and became BAE Systems; and Swan Hunter exited the warship industry.

Rolls-Royce was nationalised in 1971 following its financial collapse resulting from substantial cost overruns on the RB211 aero engine. The state-owned company was privatised in 1987 through a share issue (Parker, 2009,

p. 201). Further privatisations involved the Royal Dockyards and the Royal Ordnance Factories. There were two dockyards at Devonport and Rosyth in Scotland. Critics claimed that the dockyards were inefficient and overmanned, with cost overruns and delays on contracts. The yards were sold separately, resulting in a change from a state-owned monopoly of the dockyards to a privately-owned duopoly. However, this structure changed in 2007 when Babcock acquired both yards creating a private monopoly.

Originally, the Royal Ordnance factories (RO) were a state-owned monopoly producing ammunition, explosives, small arms and fighting vehicles, mostly for the British Army. Continued concerns about the efficiency of RO operations led to debates about whether RO should be sold as one division or as separate entities. RO was privatised in two parts. Its tank business and the Leeds factory were sold to Vickers whilst the remainder of RO was sold to BAe. Privatising RO transferred state-owned assets to the private sector creating private sector monopolies for armaments and tanks. This was contrary to the Government's preferred policy of promoting competition in the UK defence market (Parker, 2009, p. 239).[2]

After privatisation of much of the UK defence industry, there remained the government defence research establishments. In 1995, these were amalgamated into a new agency, the Defence Evaluation and Research Agency (DERA). This agency was dissolved in 2001 and split into two organisations. The larger part was privatised as QinetiQ and the remainder became the state-owned Defence Science and Technology Laboratory (DSTL) responsible for those aspects of defence research best undertaken by government (e.g. nuclear, chemical and biological research).[3]

Industry conduct

Conduct analyses the ways in which buyers and sellers behave and compete in undertaking transactions. Defence markets differ from traditional competitive markets in that they are dominated by a major buyer, namely, the national government rather than the large number of relatively small buyers in competitive markets. As a major buyer, the MoD awards contracts and sets the rules of bidding for its contracts. When buying defence equipment, MoD has at least three procurement choices involving what to buy (choice of equipment), who to buy from (choice of contractor) and how to buy (the form of contract). Equipment choices involve decisions about the performance of equipment (e.g. aircraft speed, range and equipment load). Once the equipment has been determined, a contractor has to be selected where the choice ranges between direct negotiation with a preferred supplier and a non-competitive purchase, or competition either restricted to UK firms or extended to allow foreign firms to bid. The selected contractor is then awarded a contract ranging between the extremes of a firm or fixed price contract or a cost-plus contract with intermediate types of target cost incentive contracts. Each type of contract has different efficiency incentives with firm and fixed price contracts offering maximum efficiency incentives and cost-plus contracts lacking efficiency incentives.

In awarding contracts, MoD has to determine their prices and profitability. With competitive contracts, rivalry between firms determines prices and profitability. In bidding for MoD contracts, especially major high value contracts, firms will use price and non-price variables to achieve success. Whilst competitively determined fixed price contracts appear attractive to government, they have their limitations. Competition can lead to firms offering low prices to win the contract, then finding that unexpected cost overruns lead to losses and a possibility of bankruptcy leading to contractor failure and exit; or a government bail-out to complete the project. Alternatively, a successful contractor can always be acquired by one of the losing firms in a competition. It is also possible that competition in non-price forms will lead to optimistic design proposals and the eventual contractor failure. In bidding for contracts, firms will use a variety of non-price methods to win the contract. Examples include advertising, lobbying and commissioning consultancy reports highlighting the magnitude of the wider economic benefits of the project (e.g. its jobs, technology, export benefits). Examples of such contractor behaviour have arisen in UK defence contracts for nuclear-powered submarines, the Challenger 2 tank and the cancelled Nimrod MR4 maritime patrol aircraft. UK defence exports provide further examples of non-price competition. To obtain export orders, generous government finance might be offered to the buying nation. Allegations have also arisen of firms being involved in bribery and corrupt behaviour to obtain defence export orders.

Non-competitive contracts are even more problematic requiring that both prices and profitability be determined when awarding contracts. The UK has a long history of experience with non-competitive or negotiated defence contracts (e.g. World War II). Controversy has arisen over the allowable costs in such contracts and whether their profitability has been 'excessive' especially for monopoly situations. Cases of 'excessive' profits on non-competitive defence contracts involving Ferranti (1960) and Bristol Siddeley Engines (1959–65) led to the 1968 Profit Agreement and new regulatory arrangements between MoD and industry. The 1968 Agreement aimed to provide defence contractors with a 'fair' return on capital employed defined as equal on average to the return earned by British industry. A Review Board implemented the 1968 Agreement. The Board reviewed specific contracts and advised on the overall profitability of non-competitive UK defence contracts. Criticism of the 1968 Agreement led to new arrangements in 2014. A new Single Source Regulations Office (SSRO) replaced the Review Board. Open book accounting was introduced and recommended profit rates are based on costs (Hartley, 2018a).

UK defence industrial policy

UK defence industrial policy outlines the basis of its procurement policy. This aims to provide the '… Armed Forces with the capabilities they need at best value for money, obtaining this through open competition in the global market wherever possible' (MoD, 2017d, p. 23). But, there are two major constraints on the UK's competitive procurement policy. First, where there are strategic, military and economic benefits to the UK from long-term collaboration with other nations.[4] Second, where competition is neither available nor feasible resulting in single source contracts and long-term partnership arrangements (MoD, 2017d, p. 11). Overall, it is claimed that UK defence procurement is driven by competition and strategic choices and maximising value in single source procurement. However, in 2017, 58% of new MoD contracts by value were placed on a non-competitive basis compared with 36% in 2010 (MoD, 2017d, p. 23).

Where competition at the prime contractor level is not available, MoD aims to promote competition in supply chains focusing on small and medium-sized enterprises. In 2016, MoD made payments to over 16,500 suppliers and at least 5,980 SMEs held direct contracts with MoD (MoD, 2017d, p. 36). MoD aims to make it easier for industry to do business with the Ministry by reducing entry costs for SMEs (e.g. prompt payment by primes: MoD, 2017d, p. 39).

The 2017 UK defence industrial policy refers to defence delivering 'wider economic and international value and national security objectives' (MoD, 2017d, p. 16). It admits that 'value in these areas is often characterised by qualitative assessments which require balanced judgements using the best available evidence' (MoD, 2017d, p. 16). Such a description of policy allows decision-makers opportunities for considerable discretion.

The 2017 policy also required that defence procurement should show how it might contribute to UK prosperity and strengthening productivity, especially at the local level, and to boost exports on a 'sustainable basis' (MoD, 2017d, p. 16). Prosperity impacts from defence spending were defined to include innovation and spin-offs, human capital investments, local economic impacts and long-term impacts on local labour markets. This is an ambitious target and one which needs to include an assessment of opportunity costs in the form of the prosperity impacts from alternative public spending programmes (e.g. infrastructure investments). The concept of prosperity also needs to be subject to critical scrutiny. Questions arise about the definition of prosperity, the economic model and causal relationships which relate defence spending to prosperity, the empirical magnitudes of these relationships and the economic impacts, especially the local impacts of alternative public spending.

UK defence industrial policy has been formulated most clearly for the UK naval shipbuilding industry. The 2017 Shipbuilding Strategy aims to lay the foundation for a modern and efficient sector providing more ships for the Royal Navy with support for more shipyards (MoD, 2017e).[5] The Strategy involves a 30 year Master Plan which specifies the number and types of ships which will be required by MoD over the next 30 years. The Type 26 will be built by BAE Systems on the Clyde (Scotland) which has a single source Target Cost Incentive Fee contract for the first batch of three ships. BAE Systems will remain a key shipbuilder for the Royal Navy. The new Type 31e will focus on exportability The Fleet Solid Support ships will be subject to an international competition.

The 2017 Shipbuilding Strategy states that for reasons of national security, all Royal Navy warships will be built in the UK with competition restricted to the UK. The new Type 31e frigate is the focus for the Strategy with its emphasis on an exportable light frigate and competitive procurement based on encouraging the UK's numerous commercial shipyards to bid for parts of the work. Overall, the MoD will use its contractual powers to determine the size and structure of the UK warship industry.

The 2017 Strategy also admitted that defence will take account of wider factors, including the impact on UK prosperity, when making procurement decisions. Estimates suggest that the Royal Navy's shipbuilding programme supports some 25,000 UK jobs comprising 15,000 direct and 10,000 indirect jobs. Some yards are located in areas of high deprivation and are major employers with defence contributing to these regional economies (BEIS, 2017; MoD, 2017e, pp. 35–36).

Competitive and single source contracting

MoD procurement ranges from competitive to non-competitive contracting. There were peaks in competitive contracting in 1995 and 2015 when typically some 80% of contracts were competitive. In contrast, non-competitive or single source contracting peaked in 1980 and 2010 when single source contracts accounted for over half of all MoD contracts (by value). Usually, competitive contracts are fixed price (including firm price contracts) and non-competitive contracts are target cost incentive contracts (with various types of incentives and sharing arrangements). However, there can be non-competitive fixed price contracts where prices are based on estimated costs and a government-determined profit margin (SSRO, 2018).[6]

There was a further constraint on UK non-competitive contracting, namely, UK membership of the European Union and its Single Market for the procurement of defence equipment (with Brexit planned for 2019). The Single Market rules aim to promote greater competition in defence procurement by opening national defence markets to cross-border competition. Exemptions from the Single Market rules allow member states to protect their national defence industries (Article 346, 2009: MoD, 2018).

Industry performance

There are various indicators for measuring industry performance, including costs, productivity, output, exports, development time-scales for projects, contract performance and profitability. However, data are not always available at the industry level, so firm level data have to be used. Nor is there a single best indicator measuring performance. This section reviews some of the available data for assessing industry performance.

Costs

Cost performance is reflected in various forms: total, unit, money versus real and escalation. Unit costs together with profits determine prices and unit production costs decline with scale and cumulative output which are the features of a decreasing cost industry. Relative unit costs also determine international competitiveness where the US defence industry with its large domestic market has a competitive advantage. For example, the US domestic planned order for its F-35 aircraft totals 2,443 units compared with UK plans for 138 aircraft. Estimated unit costs for the conventional take-off F-35 are almost $90 million per aircraft (2018 prices) and export orders for all types of F-35 have been estimated at some 1,500 units.

UK defence equipment has experienced rising unit costs in real terms. Intergenerational cost escalation varied between 2.8% for submarines and 6.1% per annum for combat aircraft and tanks. Rising unit costs affect all nations leading to fewer new types and smaller production runs for national defence industries and smaller force structures for the Armed Forces. Causes are varied and complex and include the tournament goods nature of defence equipment, project optimism bias, a preference for performance over cost and time and the monopoly nature of defence markets (Hartley and Solomon, 2017). Data on cost escalation are of limited use as performance indicators: for example, they provide targets for new generations of equipment (e.g. beat the typical cost escalation for fighter aircraft). Without similar data for other nations, it is not possible to assess the UK defence industry's performance.

Company data

The lack of data at the industry level means that performance has to be confined to firm level analysis. Here, there are some limited possibilities based on company accounts. Problems arise since most firms publish data for their total business combining military and civil sales. BAE Systems is an exception since it is a defence specialist providing annual data on the sales, employment and profitability of its various divisions (Table 5.6). Divisions with above average Group performance in 2017 were Electronics and Air whereas Cyber and Maritime recorded below average Group performance.

Table 5.6 BAE Systems, 2017

Division	*Sales (£mn)*	*Employment*	*Profits (% on sales)*	*Productivity (sales per employee: £s)*
Electronic Systems	3,635	14,400	13.5	252,431
Cyber and Intelligence	1,820	10,900	2.9	166,972
Platforms and Services (USA)	2,928	11,400	8.3	256,842
Air	8,059	30,100	12.4	267,741
Maritime	3,151	13,800	8.2	228,333
Total	19,626	83,200	10.4	235,890

Source: BAE (2018).

Notes:

i) Platform and Services (USA) includes USA, UK and Sweden with activities in combat vehicles, weapons and munitions.

ii) Air is UK-based air activities.

iii) Maritime is UK-based maritime (warships and submarines) and land activities.

iv) There were organisational changes in January 2018 with the abolition of business segments for Platform and Services (UK) and Platforms and Services (International). The International division included sales to Saudi Arabia, Australia, Oman and its share in MBDA.

v) Profits are percentage rate of return on sales.

vi) Productivity figures calculated by author.

BAE dominates the UK defence industry. In 2018, it was the UKs leading defence supplier to MoD, accounting for some 15% of MoD spending with its top 10 suppliers with 93% of its MoD contracts being non-competitive. Sales to MoD accounted for 18% of BAE sales in 2017. In contrast, some 70% of Lockheed Martin 2017 sales were to the US Government. BAE's overall profits on sales were 10.4% in 2017 compared with an annual return on sales of 10% for Lockheed Martin and 11% for Boeing. BAE's overall performance placed it fourth in the world in 2016.

A consultancy study estimated the economic contribution of BAE to the UK economy in 2016 showing its impacts on output and employment (OE, 2017). The major results are shown in Table 5.7. BAE's contribution to GDP measured by gross value added was £11.1 billion (2016 prices) supporting an aggregate of 130,400 jobs. BAE labour productivity was some 80% higher than the UK average. In 2016, there were some wider impacts through BAE exports (£4.7 billion) and R&D spending (£1 billion).

Rolls-Royce is the UK's second largest defence firm with a world ranking of 16th in 2016. Its annual report provides some data on its defence activities (Table 5.8). Defence Aerospace was its most profitable division in 2017 achieving substantially greater profits (16.4% on sales) than its Civil Aerospace (6.5%). In contrast, the Marine Division incurred a loss and its Nuclear Division had much lower profit rates than the Group average (4.6% compared with 7.8%). Nuclear work is mostly for UK nuclear submarines, with the balance being civil nuclear.[7]

Table 5.7 BAE economic contribution to UK economy, 2016

	Direct	*Indirect*	*Induced*	*Total*
Contribution to GDP (£bn)	4.4	3.6	3.1	11.1
Contribution to Jobs	34,600	59,900	35,900	130,400

Source: OE (2017).

Notes:

i) Direct impacts result directly from BAE.
ii) Indirect results from supply chains.
iii) Induced reflects consumer spending of directs and indirects.
iv) Total is aggregate of direct, indirects and induced.

Table 5.8 Rolls-Royce, 2017

Division	*Sales (£mn)*	*Employment*	*Profit (%)*	*Productivity (sales per employee, £s)*
Civil Aerospace	8,023	24,600	6.5	326,138
Defence Aerospace	2,275	6,100	16.4	372,951
Power Systems	2,923	10,100	11.3	289,406
Nuclear	818	4,400	4.6	185,909
Marine	1,077	4,600	−(2.3)	234,130
Total	15,090	50,000	7.8	301,800

Source: RR (2017).

Notes:

i) Profits are percentage rate of return on sales.
ii) − ( ) shows a loss.
iii) There are some defence activities in other Divisions: Power, Nuclear and Marine.
iv) Nuclear includes civil but military nuclear accounts for 77% of nuclear sales.

Contract performance indicators

Industry performance can also be assessed by contract indicators. The National Audit Office publishes regular reports on the UK's major defence projects giving data on costs, time-scales, cost overruns and delays together with a qualitative statement of actual performance against contract targets. Its 2015 Report based on a sample of 12 projects found relative stability in the cost forecast and additional delays of 60 months. However, this broad overview concealed major cost overruns and delays on specific projects. On four major projects comprising the A400M airlifter, Astute submarines (boats 1–3), two aircraft carriers and the Typhoon combat aircraft, cost overruns ranged from 14% to 75% with delays ranging from 31 to 79 months (NAO, 2015).

International comparisons show that major defence programmes are characterised by significant cost overruns and significant delays. One study showed that for cost overruns, the UK outperformed the USA with an average overrun of 8% compared to 25% but that the US outperformed the UK on delivering projects on time with delays of 25% for the US compared with 32% for the UK. Compared with Australia, the UK delivered projects with a lower average delay but France experienced an average annual delay of 1.5 months compared with six months per year in the UK (Gray, 2009, p. 215). Such international comparisons are problematic requiring identical definitions and allowances for different types of projects.

Exports

Exports can be regarded as the single best indicator of an industry's international competitiveness. But for defence equipment, exports are subject to various factors which affect the reliability of the measure as an indicator of competitiveness. For example, the data are affected by political factors, especially a government's willingness to allow arms exports to some countries and by the availability of government funds for financing exports. There have also been changes in the official data with a shift from annual export *deliveries* to annual export *orders*.

The UK is a major exporter of defence equipment. On a rolling 10 year basis, it was the second largest global defence exporter with defence export orders of £9 billion in 2017 representing a 12% share of the global defence export market. Its largest defence export markets were the Middle East, North America and Europe.[8] Aerospace dominated UK defence exports accounting for 91% of total UK defence exports in 2017 (aircraft, helicopters, engines, equipment and support represented by exports of F-35, Typhoon, Hawk and Rolls-Royce engines). The UK's major rivals in the global defence export market in 2017 were the USA, Russia, France, Germany and Italy (MoD, 2018). The success of UK aerospace reflects its world-class combat air sector which in 2017, directly provided 18,000 jobs and a further 28,000 jobs in the supply chain with MoD aiming to retain first mover advantage in the sector (MoD, 2018).

MoD maintains that defence exports provide economic benefits to both the UK and to MoD. Competitive firms winning export work allows overheads to be spread and scale economies achieved so reducing the costs of equipment and services to MoD. Exports also allow the maintenance of UK industrial capacity during troughs in production work. But exports are not costless (Chalmers, Davies, Hartley and Wilkison, 2002).

Conclusion

The UK publishes considerable official data on its defence industry so that much is known. There are further data from private sources such as

Company Reports and Trade Associations. Nonetheless, some unknowns remain. There is a lack of comprehensive employment data showing labour by skills and location (e.g. scientists; skilled production workers each by region), and data on annual defence export deliveries (compared with orders). Further gaps include a lack of data on the annual import of defence equipment and of data on defence industry supply chains.

What might be the future of the UK defence industry? Its size, structure, conduct and performance will be determined by the Government as a major or monopsony buyer. But the future will be different just as today's industry is different from that of 1945 and 1900: BAE Systems did not exist in 1945 and aircraft did not exist in 1900.

Two variables will dominate the future of the UK industry. First, new technology will continue to revolutionise warfare. Currently, UAVs and drones are replacing manned aircraft, cyber warfare is emerging as a new threat and space might be a future battleground. Second, rising costs of defence equipment will mean fewer new types, shorter production runs and smaller Armed Forces (e.g. a single ship navy and single tank army). The industrial impacts of rising costs will probably mean a smaller number of larger defence firms and more international collaboration offering nations the sharing of R&D costs and opportunities to combine their production orders to achieve economies of learning and scale. International mergers are likely (e.g. with US arms firms) and will create even larger firms and greater challenges of regulating such firms. In the absence of major conflicts, the future UK defence industry is likely to be smaller. Specialist defence firms are likely to diversify their business to reduce their dependence on defence markets.

UK Governments will face major challenges in retaining a national defence industrial capability leading to more specialisation on a smaller range of capabilities (e.g. air systems). But there remains the challenge of retaining industrial capabilities during troughs in development and production work. This is a challenge affecting all nations with a domestic defence industry. Possible solutions include exports, mothballing capabilities, funding the development of technology demonstrators, limited production orders and international alliances and partnering. None of these are costless options and some are only short-term solutions. For example, mothballing appears attractive but there are costs in policing and maintaining industrial plant which is mothballed and there are substantial costs in recreating a skilled labour force. Similarly, technology demonstrators might retain a core of key development staff in the short-term but in the absence of long-term commitments, staff will leave for other work. A more radical alternative is to import defence equipment which will shift the costs of retaining industrial capability to the exporting nation (e.g. USA). Again, the benefits and costs of the importing option need to be estimated and assessed critically.

Notes

1 UK defence R&D spending figures comprise defence research and development spending by MoD. They do not include private R&D spending (e.g. by companies). In 2016/17, MoD defence R&D spending totalled £1,668mn of which £605mn was on defence research (MoD, 2017a).
2 Privatisation raises wider questions about its results: see Parker (2009). Also, see this Chapter's section on industry and firm performance (BAE; Rolls-Royce).
3 Privatisation included the Private Finance Initiative (PFI) where public sector assets were funded by the private sector and then leased to the public sector. PFI included the defence sector. The 2018 Budget announced the end of PFIs.
4 For example, the UK is a Level 1 partner on the F-35 programme with the USA. It is manufacturing 15% of the value of the total programme of some 3,000 aircraft. This is considerably more than if the UK were to build 100% of the 138 aircraft it plans to buy . Similarly, MoD has a long-term agreement with MBDA resulting in MBDA investing in a new manufacturing plant in north-west England creating 500 highly skilled jobs and a similar number in the wider supply chain (MoD, 2017a, p. 29).
5 The strategy is based on a Report by Sir John Parker (Parker, 2016) which identified two problems facing the UK warship industry. First, the Government could not afford the desired number of ships due to rising costs and increased time for procurement leading to falling numbers of ships procured. Second, the UK industry had not been successful in exporting warships. The Report also identified a renaissance of shipbuilding in regional shipbuilding companies (e.g. Cammell Laird; Babcock-Appledore; Ferguson Marine).
6 For an analysis of the regional economic impact of different types of contracts and funding, see Kenney and Mowery (2014).
7 The profitability of UK nuclear submarine work is determined by the SSRO. In 2018/19. The typical profit rate on non-competitive contracts was 7.9% on cost of production (SSRO, 2018).
8 For many years, UK defence statistics published annual data on UK defence export *deliveries*. More recently, published data are based on export *orders* where orders are spread over a number of years and might never materialise (e.g. cancellations). UK defence exports included Typhoon sales to Saudi Arabia and Kuwait; Hawk sales to India and Oman; patrol vessels to Brazil; minehunters to Estonia; and F-35 work to the USA (DIT, 2017).

References

BAE. (2018). Annual Report 2017, BAE Systems, London, March.

BEIS. (2017). *How to Measure the Prosperity Impacts of UK Shipbuilding*, Department for Business, Energy and Industrial Strategy, London, September.

Chalmers, M., Davies, N.V., Hartley, Keith and Wilkison, Chris (2002). The economic costs and benefits of UK defence exports, *Fiscal Studies*, 23, 3, 343–367.

DIT. (2017). *UK Defence and Security Export Statistics in 2017*, Dept for International Trade, London.

Dunne, P. (2018). Growing the contribution of defence to UK prosperity, Ministry of Defence, London, July.

Gray, B. (2009). Review of acquisition for the secretary of state for defence, Ministry of Defence, London.

Hartley, K., Hooper, N., Sweeney, M., Matthews, R., Braddon, D., Dowdall, P. and Bradley, J. (1997). Armoured fighting vehicle supply chain analysis: Vol 1: Report,

Centre for defence economics, University of York, Commercial-in-Confidence, September.

Hartley, K. (2017). *The Economics of Arms*, Agenda, Newcastle.

Hartley, K. (2018a). The economics of European defence industrial policy, in Karampekios, N., Oikonomou, I. and Carayannis, E.G. (eds), *The Emergence of EU Defense Resarch Policy*, Springer, Switzerland.

Hartley, K. (2018b). The profitability of non-competitive defence contracts: The UK experience, *Defence and Peace Economics*, 29, 6, 577–594. November.

Hartley, K. and Macdonald, P. (2010). Country Survey XXI: The United Kingdom, *Defence and Peace Economics*, 21, 1, 43–63.

Hartley, K. and Solomon, B. (eds), (2017). *Defence Inflation: Perspectives and Prospects*, London, Routledge.

Kenney, M. and Mowery, D.C. (eds), (2014). *Public Universities and Regional Growth*, Stanford University Press, Stanford, California.

MoD. (2009). UK defence statistics 2009, Ministry of Defence, TSO, London.

MoD. (2012). UK defence statistics, 1982–2012, Ministry of Defence, London.

MoD. (2017a). Finance and economics annual statistical bulletin 2017, Ministry of Defence, London.

MoD. (2017b). UK defence in numbers in 2017, Ministry of Defence, TSO, September.

MoD. (2017c). Finance and economics annual statistical bulletin: MoD regional expenditure with UK industry and commerce and supported employment 2016/17, Ministry of Defence, London.

MoD. (2017d).Industry for defence and a prosperous Britain: Refreshing defence industrial policy, Ministry of Defence, London.

MoD. (2017e). National shipbuilding strategy: The future of naval shipbuilding in the UK, Ministry of Defence, London.

MoD. (2018). Combat air strategy: An ambitious vision for the future, Ministry of Defence, London.

NAO. (2015). *Major Projects Report 2015 and the Equipment Plan 2015 to 2025*, National Audit Office, HCP 488, London.

OE. (2017). *The Contribution of BAE Systems to the UK Economy*, Oxford Economics Report, BAE Systems, London, November 2017.

Parker, D. (2009). The Official History of Privatisation, Vol. 1, Routledge, London.

Parker, Sir J. (2016). An independent report to inform the National Shipbuilding Strategy, Ministry of Defence, London, November.

RR. (2017). *Annual Report 2017*, Rolls-Royce, London.

SIPRI. (2016). SIPRI Top 100 arms producers, *SIPRI Yearbook 2016*, Stockholm, Sweden.

SSRO. (2018). *Recommendations Factsheet*, Single Source Regulations Office, London.

6 The French defence industry

Jean Belin, Julien Malizard and Hélène Masson

Introduction

As the leading arms producer and exporter in Europe and third in the world behind the United States and Russia,[1] France's defence industry[2] has considerable assets which contribute substantially to national economic activity. According to the latest estimates from the French Ministry for the Armed Forces,[3] the defence industry generates some 200,000 direct and indirect jobs across the country. This sector is structured around a solid core of suppliers, leaders in their respective fields, some of them in a quasi-monopolistic position in the national market, and over 4,000 intermediate-sized companies and SMEs. France's position vis-à-vis the defence industry is set out clearly in the Strategic Review of 2017 and the Military Programming Law 2019–2025.[4] These official texts highlight "the importance of a strong French defence industry, insofar as it is an essential component of France's strategic autonomy and can alone guarantee the security of our supply of equipment to ensure sovereignty and critical weapons systems".[5]

Although historically, this sector may have experienced a certain degree of stability, the situation has changed profoundly in recent years. There have been changes in the acquisition strategies of the State as a customer (opening up to competition, pressure on prices) and of export customers (requirements in terms of technology transfers and partnerships), technological change and the arrival of newcomers from the civilian sector, and the emergence of new competitors on the international stage. All these various factors of change have contributed to an acceleration in movements of consolidation and the internationalization of activity by French companies.

This chapter presents the essential characteristics of a specific industrial sector which is considered as strategic by the national authorities. The first part examines the national defence budget from an historical perspective, and changes that have occurred in equipment expenditure and public funding of defence R&D. The second part describes the history and structure of the French defence technological and industrial base (DTIB) and the change in relations between the State and Industries. In the third part the performance of this industry is analyzed.

An overview of French defence spending

As observed by Fontanel and Hébert (1997), the aim of French defence policy since 1945 has been to achieve strategic autonomy and this has resulted in the development of an autonomous defence industry, an ambiguous position vis-à-vis NATO and the establishment of a nuclear deterrent. This position required significant financial resources.

Trends in the defence budget

Although the proportion of GDP spent on defence has tended to decline since the end of the Second World War (Figure 6.1), it nevertheless remains the third largest budget item, and internationally France is still a major player, especially at the European level.[6]

The SIPRI data shown in Figure 6.1 take a relatively broad definition of the concept of military expenditure, as they include spending on personnel, operations and maintenance, procurement, R&D and infrastructure. Since 1959, France has chosen to present a defence budget with a much narrower definition, including only operating expenses (mainly payroll) and spending on equipment (procurement and R&D), and excluding the Gendarmerie and pensions. Thus, for 2017, the SIPRI data show defence expenditure of 2.3% of GDP against 1.42% in the data from the Ministry for the Armed Forces.

Using the latter set of data as real values (using the GDP deflator published by Eurostat), several major periods emerge in Figure 6.2. In the 1980s, in a continuation of the trend observed previously, defence expenditure moved upwards (+16%), despite a dip from 1983, which corresponds not only to the end of the Euromissile crisis but also to the switch to a policy of "rigor" operated by the French government. The 1990s was a decade of "peace dividends", with a 17% drop in real values. Since the start of the 2000s, expenditure has stabilized at around €30 billion (+5% increase between 2000 and 2018), with a peak observed in 2009 which corresponds to the French

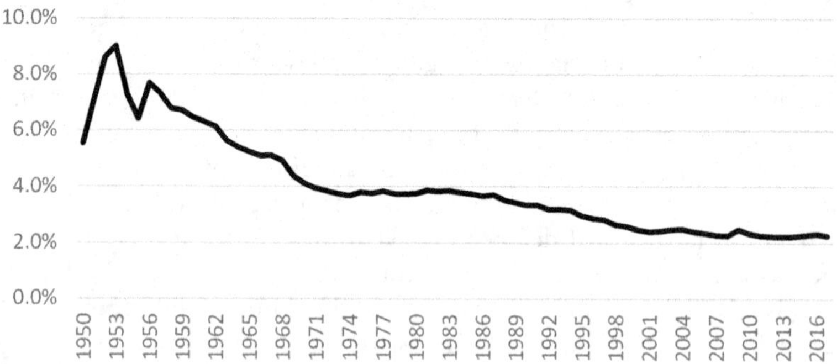

Figure 6.1 Defence spending by France between 1950 and 2017 (% of GDP).

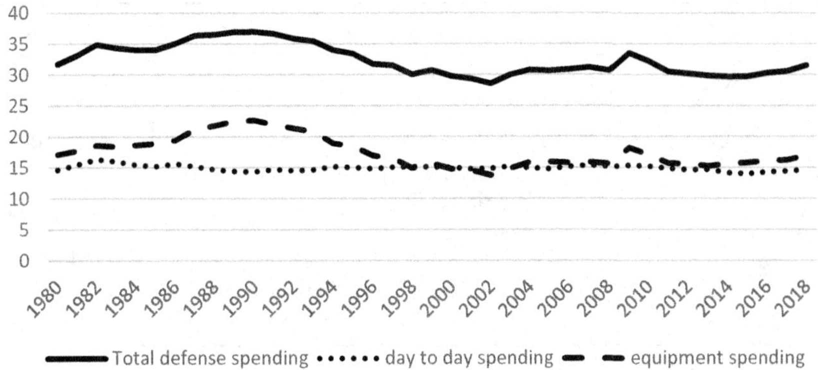

Figure 6.2 Change in total spending, day-to-day spending and equipment spending.

recovery plan. Nevertheless, an upward trend can be seen over the last three years, despite the 2018 budget being less than that for the 1980s.

Day-to-day spending and equipment spending

Figure 6.2 breaks down the defence budget into day-to-day spending and equipment spending (data in 2010 prices). It highlights the way the defence budget is structured: the stability of day-to-day spending and the volatility of equipment spending. The changes in the total defence budget can be explained almost exclusively by changes in equipment spending. In times of economic slowdown, equipment spending is the first to be affected and to a greater extent than day-to-day spending (see Droff and Malizard (2014)).

Defence R&D

A specific feature of France in terms of defence is government support for R&D. According to figures from the Ministry for the Armed Forces, the Ministry spent €4.928 Bn on R&D in 2017.

R&D includes "defence studies" and work on equipment development, including weapons programs that are already underway. Defence studies concern only research and not development. They include, among other things, R&T (research and technology) which measures the upstream budget allocated for weapons programs. This activity draws on studies carried out in the civil sector to acquire the expertise, knowledge and scientific, technological and industrial capabilities needed to define and launch weapons programs. R&T includes upstream studies (contracts signed with industry and innovation grants).

Droff and Malizard (2015) showed that the R&D budget was less affected by budget constraints than the equipment budget. The share of the R&D budget in

Table 6.1 Composition of R&D expenditure 2017

R&D				*€4.928 Bn*
	Of which development			€3.343 Bn
	Of which defence studies			€1.585 Bn
		Of which dual-use Research, CEA, etc.		€734 M
		Of which R&T		€851 M
			Of which upstream studies	€720 M

Source: Ministry for the Armed Forces.

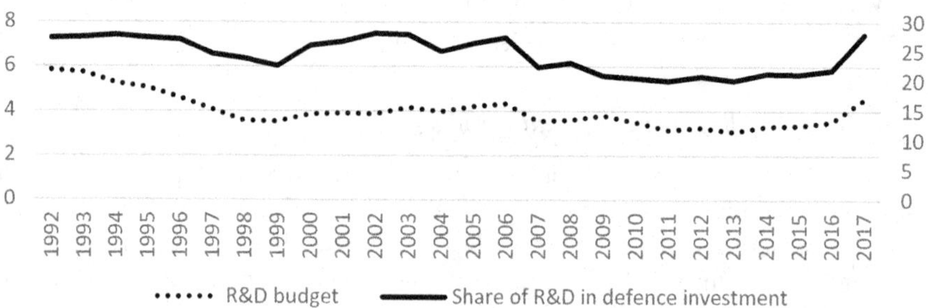

Figure 6.3 Change in Ministry for the Armed Forces R&D budgets and share of operations and equipment in total defence investment.

equipment spending has thus remained stable over time, at around 25% (data in Figure 6.3 in 2010 prices).

European Defence Agency (EDA) data on R&D are available only up to 2014 but they show that France clearly stands out from other European countries in terms of R&D investment. In 2014, France spent 9.1% of the defence budget on R&D, whereas other countries, with the exception of the United Kingdom (7.8%), spent much less (Germany 2.4%, Poland 2.9%, Sweden 2.2%, etc.).

The Military Programming Law (LPM) 2019–2025

The Military Programming Law (LPM) 2019–2025 proposes to take up the challenges set out in the conclusions of the 2017 Strategic Review and increase the defence effort to 2% of GDP (based on a budget excluding pensions) by 2025. For the period 2019–2023, €198 billion will be granted to the Ministry for the Armed Forces, of which €112.5 billion will be allocated to spending on equipment (€172.8 billion up to 2025). This funding will be for major projects: renewal of the Army's motorized capabilities (Scorpion program), vessels for the Navy (FREMM and FTI programs, Barracuda submarines) and aircraft for the Air Force (mainly A400M transport aircraft or MRTT A330 refueling tankers). The launch of research into nuclear-powered ballistic missile submarines (SSBN) or a replacement for the Charles de Gaulle aircraft carrier are also planned.

The national defence industry: history, structure and conduct

The French defence technological and industrial base (DTIB) is structured around a solid core group of suppliers, consisting of eight top class contractors, engine manufacturers and suppliers: Airbus Group, Arquus, Dassault Aviation, MBDA, Naval Group, Nexter, Safran and Thales (see Table 6.2). This situation is the result of government policy decisions dating back to the 1960s and adaptations of industry to its environment.

Historical basis or the Gaullist brand of autonomy and national independence

In France, the desire for national independence is the basis on which the defence industry was founded. In the first post-war decades, government authorities structured the French armament landscape gradually but with a pro-active policy in mind. When General de Gaulle came to power in May 1958 and decided to make France a modern military power, one which was independent and with its own deterrent force, he created the political conditions for a total overhaul of state and industrial structures in the area of weapons design and production. The prime objective then lay in the development and implementation of a strategic nuclear force. In 1961, the newly created Ministerial Delegation for Armaments (DMA, which became the DGA[7] in 1977) was given the task of establishing this independently, while ensuring that conventional weapons programs were maintained to meet the needs of the armed forces (heavy tanks and light armored vehicles, artillery systems, combat aircraft, transport and maritime patrol aircraft, helicopters, tactical missiles).

In a context of radical technological change associated with the development of nuclear power, missiles, electronics and space, scientific research was placed at the heart of this rebuilding. The aim was to bring civil research closer to the Defence bodies and facilitate research in an industrial context (by transferring results and exploratory developments from industry). The creation of a unique body of armaments engineers (1967) would act as an accelerator for this process of scientific, technical and industrial modernization. As a result, this decision not to be dependent on any foreign State for the design, production, implementation, maintenance and modernization of even the most complex weapons systems would also result in the armaments

Table 6.2 Main contractors

Company	*Ownership*	*Sales revenue 2017 K€*	*Defence %*	*Employees*	*Activities*
Airbus Group	-SOGEPA (French State) 11.07% -GZBV (German State) 11.06% -Capital Research & Management Co. (World Investors) 6.17% -SEPI (Spanish State) 4.17%	66,767	15%	129,442	Commercial and military aircraft, commercial and military helicopters, drone systems, civil and military space activities, defence electronics, cybersecurity
Arquus (Renault Truck Defense – RTD)	-Volvo Group Government Sales 100%	~500	100%	~1,500	Wheeled armored vehicles, tactical and logistical vehicles, propulsion systems for armored vehicles, weapon systems (remote weapon systems), maintenance and modernization
Dassault Aviation	-GIMD 62.2% -Airbus 9.9% -Dassault Aviation 0.5%	4,808	39%	11,398	Executive jets, fighter aircraft, unmanned aircraft systems, maritime patrol and surveillance aircraft, pyrotechnics and space activities
MBDA	-Airbus 37.5% -BAE Systems 37.5% -Leonardo 25.0%	3,107	100%	10,500	Air-surface systems, air-to-air missiles, guided missile systems, cruise missiles, anti-ship missiles, anti-tank missile
Naval Group DCNS	-French State 62.25% -Thales 35.00% -FCPE Naval Group Shares 1.80% -Naval Group	3,698	~95%	14,515	Surface vessels, submarines, underwater weapons, combat systems, navigation systems, naval integration of drones, maintenance and associated services for naval bases, marine renewable energies and commercial nuclear energy

(*Continued*)

Table 6.2 (Cont.)

Company	*Ownership*	*Sales revenue 2017 K€*	*Defence %*	*Employees*	*Activities*
	Shareholders 0.95%				
Nexter KMW + NEXTER DEFENSE SYSTEMS (KNDS)	-Giat Industries S.A. 50% -Wegmann & Co. GmbH 50%	2,648	100%	7,329	Wheeled and tracked armored vehicles, weapon systems, artillery systems and ammunition, mechanical and hydraulic equipment, electronic equipment air-land robots, optical and vision systems for armored vehicles, CBRN protection, simulation and training solutions
Safran	-French State 10.81% -Employees 6.80%	16,521	~20%	58,324	Engine manufacturer, systems integrator-equipment supplier, aircraft, space and missile propulsion, aeronautical systems and equipment, optronics, avionics, navigation systems, electronics and critical software, UAS Security (identification, securing, detection)
Thales	-French State 25.71% -Dassault Aviation 24.65% -Employees 2.51% -Thales 0.26%	15,795	~51%	65,118	Aerospace systems and equipment, sensors, systems and communications, weapon systems and ammunition, training and simulation, space

Source: Notebook on International Defence Companies, DGA, 2018.

administration and industrial base being located nationally in terms of spatial organization.[8]

In the 1960s and 1970s, the armament industry experienced a movement of concentration which, with impetus from the State, resulted in the creation of one prime contractor per domain. The public sector was dominant at that time (arsenals, national corporations, public institutions such as the CEA (French Alternative Energies and Atomic Energy Commission) and ONERA (National Office of Aerospace Research)) and worked alongside privately-owned industries, mainly in aeronautics.[9] In this way, until the end of the 1980s, the French weapons production system could be defined, according to Jean-Paul

Hébert (1995), as an "administered system of regulation", founded on the pre-eminence of the role of the State (which was both producer and purchaser) and the priority given to considerations of technological performance and autonomy of production conditions over concerns of competition and price.

With the end of the Cold War and the reduction in military spending, the 1990s became a time when the State's economic role was challenged, signaling its industrial disengagement (separation of industrial activities and State activities in the DGA[10]) and the opening up of the capital of public sector enterprises. Privately-owned companies became the norm, while public bodies were the exception (e.g. the CEA). All the traditional industrial players (Thomson CSF, Alcatel, Sagem, DCN, GIAT, Snecma, Aérospatiale, Matra, Dassault Aviation and SNPE) experienced these moves towards privatization and/or mergers to varying degrees. Economic constraints, the pressure of American competition and national consolidation operations in the United Kingdom, Germany, Spain and Italy, acted as an accelerator. It was time to determine critical size, at national or European level.

In the military aerospace sector, a first form of Europeanisation emerged (creation of co-enterprises and collaborations according to profession), facilitated by the launch of cooperation programs in previous decades (with Germany, Italy and Spain), and culminating in the creation of the Airbus group (formerly EADS) in July 2000 (merger of France's Aérospatiale Matra, Germany's DASA and Spain's CASA) and the missiles producer MBDA[11] in 2001 (whose capital was held by Airbus-37.5%, BAE Systems-37.5% and Finmeccanica-25%: see also Chapter 7). The process of consolidation, on the other hand would happen at national level in the sectors of defence electronics (Thales in 2000), engines and aeronautical equipment (Safran in 2005).

In the military naval sector, the separation of the DGA's industrial and State activities led in 1997 to the creation of a body responsible solely for industrial activity, DCN, which would subsequently be transformed into a department with national authority in 2000, then in 2003 it became a private company with State-owned capital (it was renamed DCNS in 2007, then the Naval Group in 2017).

The land armaments sector followed the same trajectory, culminating in the transformation of the *Groupement industriel des armements terrestres* (GIAT, created in 1971) into a national company with State-owned capital, GIAT Industries SA (1990), and whose core activities were gathered under the Nexter brand from 2006. The manufacturers of light and medium tactical wheeled vehicles, all of which had supplied the Army historically, were then bought in turn by the Swedish group Volvo AB (and incorporated into the Arquus brand): Renault Trucks Defence *via* the takeover of Renault Véhicules Industriels (RVI) in 2001, ACMAT in 2006 and Panhard General Defence in 2012.

These changes resulted in the industrial defence sector becoming even more concentrated in just a few firms, some of which had a dual portfolio of military and civilian activities (Airbus, Dassault Aviation, Thales and Safran), while others specialized in defence (MBDA, Naval Group, Nexter and Arquus). The counterpart to this industrial situation was the growing concentration in public spending too, with these eight companies representing around 70% of government orders (direct orders from the DGA) in 2015 and 75% of the funding of upstream research[12] (with Thales the no.1 beneficiary).

Reconfigurations of capitalism

The privatization process and the opening up of the defence companies' capital, along with the listing of the Airbus, Thales, Safran and Dassault Aviation groups on the stock exchange, were also decisive for the economic and financial situation. As a shareholder, the State would no longer have quite the same degree of flexibility.

Around 2000, the capitalist structure of French companies in the aeronautical and defence sectors was characterized by a high level of public ownership (100% DCNS, 99.9% Nexter, about 30% of the capital of the Thales and Safran groups, and 15% for Airbus), the creation of blocks of shareholders on the basis of cross-holdings between companies, and a limited number of managers for foreign third parties and institutional investors, apart from the national banks. The aim was to stabilize the shareholder base and avoid any unsolicited foreign investment. During the last decade, however, the French State has gradually withdrawn from company capital, while remaining a leading shareholder. The main reasons for this are a desire to facilitate industrial alliances,[13] a response to the expectations of companies hoping to improve their governance, and a context of State deleveraging.

Today, as can be seen in Table 6.2, government participation in the capital of the Thales, Safran and Airbus groups is 25.7%, 10.8% and 11.1%, respectively. The State is still a majority shareholder in the Naval Group, but since 2007 it has been a joint shareholder with Thales (35%). In the framework of the strategic alliance made between the French group Nexter and the German KMW at the end of 2015, a new Dutch incorporated company called "KNDS", has been created. It is equally owned by the State (via the holding company Nexter, GIAT Industries) and the German Bode-Wegmann family (via Wegmann & Co GMBH).[14] However, this shareholding may be adjusted upwards if the protection of the State's strategic interests is at stake. Indeed, in December 2016 the principle of majority ownership was established by the French Government Shareholding Agency (*Agence des participations de l'Etat- APE*) (50.3%) for the capital of AREVA TA[15] (renamed TechnicAtome), a contractor for naval propulsion nuclear reactors, sold by the AREVA group in the context of the restructuring of the French nuclear industry.

The transformation of the shareholder profile of the key industrial players and the introduction of new corporate governance practices have contributed to their distancing themselves from the State. Nevertheless, the State does have two main levers of action, namely, public procurement and the funding of R&D and innovation, with which it can influence companies' strategic directions where necessary and provide support for the transformation of the DTIB.

Since its creation, the Defence Procurement Directorate (DGA), which currently employs 9,600 people on its various sites (which include ten expertise and testing centers), has been given the task of running armaments programs, preparing for the future and promoting arms exports. With €11 Bn in equipment contracts and €820 M in upstream studies for 2017 alone, the amount of investments managed by the DGA puts it in first place among State investors.[16]

Corporate strategies affected as product/services portfolios are adapted and priority given to exports

Armament manufacturers have also adjusted their strategy. In fact, the reduction in equipment spending in France, and in Europe as a whole, combined with the increasingly intense competition in their key markets have resulted in French defence companies adapting their product/services portfolios in the last decade and developing internationally.

As a result, companies have disposed of assets that are unprofitable or too far removed from their core business. At the same time, external growth operations such as takeovers or equity participation have met the need to position themselves in market segments with growth potential, such as cybersecurity, autonomous systems, information and communication systems, service provision, etc. Safran divested itself of all of its "security and identity" operations to refocus on propulsion and aeronautical equipment and concentrate on investment in electrical systems. Faced with American competition from SpaceX and Orbital ATK in the space sector, Safran's propulsion activities (Safran Herakles and Snecma Vernon) were grouped with the launchers of Airbus Group to form the new *Joint Venture* ArianeGroup in 2016. For Airbus Defence & Space, this was their second major operation after the sale of their defence electronics unit to the investment fund KKR.

Thales, meanwhile, acquired several companies between 2015 and 2018 in fields related to connectivity, digital security, cybersecurity and artificial intelligence (cybersecurity activities of Alcatel Lucent, Vormetric, Sysgo, Guavus and Gemalto). In the land armaments sector, the French leader Nexter (now the French branch of KNDS) undertook a consolidation of its Munitions unit (from 20 mm to 155 mm) with the acquisition of the French firm SNPE, the Belgian firm Mecar and the Italian firm Simmel Difesa. It also diversified by developing a range of systems and protection solutions for security forces (adapted armored vehicles, CBRN protection, robotic systems). The Naval Group also initiated a diversification strategy to limit its dependence on defence, by positioning itself in the civilian nuclear sector and marine renewable energies (a new branch called Naval Energies, aims to achieve 20% of turnover by 2025). However, due to a lack of prospects, this strategic direction was reconsidered in 2018 and investment stopped. The Naval Group is focusing on extending its range of military vessels, and has created a Joint Venture (with the French firm Piriou) specializing in low tonnage ships, and hopes to develop its activities in the services and cybersecurity sectors.

The ways and means used to adapt product and services portfolios varied from one company to another, but they were nonetheless clearly similar in that they all saw the need to develop internationally. The French defence industry has a long history of exports,[17] but these have been strengthened in recent times due to national budget constraints and in response to export controls by the Ministry for the Armed Forces. The 2010s have seen a strong move towards exports by the main French platform/integrator and equipment suppliers, not only to the Near East and Middle East (Saudi Arabia, Qatar, Egypt, UAE), a firmly established export zone, but also to Asia (India, China, Japan, South Korea, Malaysia, Singapore), South America (Brazil) and, to a lesser extent, North America and Africa. French order books posted record levels in 2015 and 2016 (€16.9 Bn in 2015 against €5 to €8 Bn per year in previous years), driven by major contracts won in the military aeronautical market (Rafale fighter aircraft selected by India, Egypt and Qatar; helicopters; missiles) and the naval market. In addition, the Naval Group's successful bid in April 2016 for the Australian program to produce their next generation of submarines should certainly strengthen the position of French industry in the Asian market.

However, in view of the increased direct and semi-direct offset requirements of customer States (expressed as technology and skills transfers, coproduction and/or subcontracting contracts, granting licenses, direct investment abroad, staff training and technical assistance), the fundamentals of export have changed. From simple exporting (via a commercial network), the defence industry has shifted to a rationale of internationalizing activities (industrial sites). Offset requirements, the true cornerstone on which arms markets are founded, oblige foreign suppliers to build a really "local footprint" (long-term sites, search for partners, deal with transfers, etc.). These conditions for entering the export markets are imposed on large

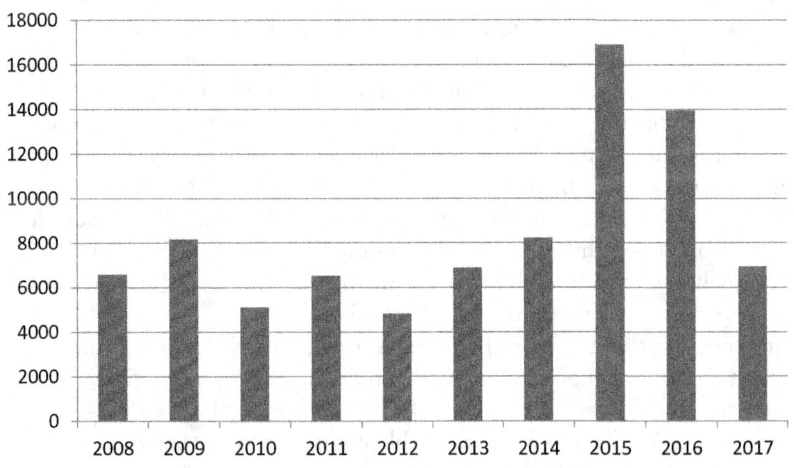

Figure 6.4 French orders for the period 2008–2017 (in €M, current prices).

groups but also on intermediate-sized industries and SMEs (whether they are subcontractors or supplying a complete package), which must then be able to mobilize the human and financial resources needed in order to internationalize their activities in this way. This is a strong trend, which underlies new dynamics for intergovernmental and interindustrial armaments cooperation, as illustrated by the strategic partnerships signed with India, Brazil and more recently Australia. Thus, while export sales by French defence manufacturers have seen substantial growth in recent years (exports often represent over 50% of turnover), they have resulted in many more local subsidiaries being set up and JVs with local partners. The effects that these constraints on accessing the export markets have on the chain of suppliers (companies, jobs and skills) are still to be investigated.

Industry performance

We can look at the performance of these companies from a macro- and micro-economic point of view. To do this we use data produced by the Ministry for the Armed Forces and statistical analyses[18] that we have carried out on companies in the French DTIB. This has enabled us to highlight several features and to analyze their performance.

Macroeconomic performances

At the macro-economic level, we can measure the consequences of the existence of a DTIB on activity, employment, foreign trade, R&D and innovation.

In 2017, the total amount paid by the Ministry of Defence to its suppliers was €19.0 Bn, including €15.6 Bn (82.2% of the total) paid directly to companies based in France and €3.4 Bn to other suppliers (non-resident companies, international organizations, administrations, etc.). In 2017, the major defence companies received the majority (69.4%) of payments from the Ministry of Defence paid to companies resident in France. Intermediate-sized companies received 17.5%, SMEs 9.9% and micro-enterprises 2.8% (Eury, 2018).

Defence companies generate a significant number of jobs. According to the Ministry for the Armed Forces, the defence industry sector probably totals about 200,000 jobs[19] (Ministry for the Armed Forces 2019). The studies that we have been able to carry out (Belin, Guille, Masson 2015) indicate that defence companies differ from other companies in that they have a more highly qualified workforce, composed mainly of executives and intellectually superior professions or intermediate professions.

Estimates by the Defence Economics Observatory (OED; Oudot, 2016) show that defence companies, with their defence and civilian activities, account for a significant percentage of French exports: 19.8% in 2015.

Defence companies also make a sizeable contribution to R&D in France (Serfati, 2014) and play a significant part in structuring and managing research channels.[20] From R&D surveys by the Ministry for Research, we (Belin, Guille,

Lazaric and Mérindol, 2018) have analyzed changes in R&D activity by defence companies since the end of the 1980s. In 1990, defence companies still employed 45% of R&D workers (researchers and technical or administrative support staff) in French companies and accounted for more than half of their R&D expenditure, whereas in 2010, this share had fallen to 24% and 29%, respectively. This relative reduction in the role played by defence companies is the result of a significant increase in R&D spending by non-defence companies, rather than a decrease in the effort put in by defence companies. In fact, R&D expenditure in defence companies remained stable overall during the period covered by the analysis. The defence sector therefore plays a more qualitative role in structuring research networks in France. The DGA is present in most of the competitiveness clusters. Defence companies outsource a large proportion of their research to French companies and this outsourcing is financed in part by public funding.

Microeconomic performances

From the statistical and econometric analyses that we carried out on companies in the French DTIB, we were able to highlight several specific features and analyze their performance (Belin, 2015).

First of all, our comparative analysis of the balance sheets and income statements of defence and non-defence companies revealed greater net borrowing for defence companies. Defence activity requires considerable R&D investment, more highly qualified staff (especially researchers) and a longer production cycle. In addition to investments and wages, companies must also cover the financial requirements of the time-lag between receiving payments from customers and paying their suppliers. Defence companies experience longer delays, although the difference between their situation and the civilian sector is diminishing.

The activity of defence companies can also be more difficult to fund, mainly because of the investment required for R&D and its intangible nature.[21] Defence companies therefore resort more to self-financing or public funding. Because of the strategic nature of these companies, the very specific features of this activity and the historic structuring of this industry, public authorities are also involved in funding defence companies in addition to public procurement. This involvement can be seen in the form of subsidies, R&D tax credits or public funding.

Defence companies perform well, especially in terms of export rates and value added. Thus, we find that defence companies export more than other companies. They also have a higher value added than other companies. However, due to the relatively high level of staff costs and their higher depreciation charges and greater reserves, ultimately their other results (GOS, operating income, pre-tax current income) do not differ significantly from those of non-defence companies.

Conclusion

As a result of its defence spending (amount and structure) France occupies a unique position in Europe. The country's defence industry makes a significant contribution to the national economy (GDP, jobs, innovation, etc.). This is the result of historic developments and adaptation to its environment. Defence is an area that continues to adapt. A series of reforms has been launched, mainly in exports, management of weapons programs and innovation.

The export support system is currently being strengthened. Government authorities have chosen to guarantee the financial equilibrium of the LPM 2014–2019 and 2019–2025 through export contracts. Whereas previously they simply provided additional income, export contracts have now become a pre-condition for the sustainability of industrial activities across a certain number of major sectors. In addition, in the export markets there has been a predominance during this period of schemes such as government-to-government (G-to-G) contracts.

The aim of the latest DGA reform, launched in mid-2018 by the current Minister for the Armed Forces, Florence Parly,[22] was therefore to improve dialogue between the DGA, the armed forces and industry, to simplify and speed up acquisition procedures so that technology can be incorporated into systems more quickly, and to promote international partnerships.

We are also seeing a greater opening up of the field, especially in terms of research and innovation. The Definvest fund and the Defence Innovation Agency have been created. The Ministry and companies alike are strengthening their links with Universities, the CNRS, SMEs and start-ups. The challenge is to create the conditions for the emergence and consolidation of new strategic technological sectors (cybersecurity, robotics, artificial intelligence, biotechnologies, in particular).

The coming decade should see a profound transformation of French DTIB, more internationalized, more open to civil innovation and more deeply rooted in European cooperation.

Notes

1 Over the period 2013–2017. SIPRI, *Trends in International Arms Transfers 2017*, March 2018.
2 A company belongs to the defence technological and industrial base if it is a supplier (direct or indirect) for the Ministry for the Armed Forces or an arms exporter. Dunne's typology (Dunne, 1995) is generally used by the Ministry for the Armed Forces in France (Daffix and Jacquin (2004), Moura (2012)) and by researchers, where three groups of defence companies can be defined: 1) units that compete in the production of weapons systems and lethal equipment (from R&D to maintenance); 2) units that supply non-lethal but strategic products (e.g. fuel); 3) units that supply common products used by the armed forces (e.g. food).
3 Report to Parliament 2018 on French arms exports, Ministry for the Armed Forces, June 2018.
4 Law no. 2018–607 of 13 July 2018 on military programming for 2019 to 2025.
5 Ibid., Annexed report, 3.4.3. Strengthening the DTIB to ensure our strategic autonomy (*Renforcer la BITD pour garantir notre autonomie stratégique*).
6 According to the SIPRI data, which make international comparisons, France has spent more than the United Kingdom since the end of the Cold War, with the exception of the period 2007–2011.
7 *Direction Générale de l'Armement* (Directorate General of Armaments).

8 Comité pour l'histoire de l'armement, *Les origines de la Délégation générale pour l'armement*, CHEAR, Comité pour l'histoire de l'armement, 2002.
9 Especially the company *Société des Avions Marcel Dassault*. See Jacques Weber, *Un demi-siècle d'aéronautique en France*, COMAERO, Etudes et recherches, Tome1, 2008, p. 19.
10 Hence the titles "*maître d'ouvrage*" (owner) and "*maître d'œuvre*" (contractor).
11 Result of the merger of the tactical missile entities of the EADS, BAE Systems and Finmeccanica groups: Matra BAe Dynamics, EADS-Aerospatiale Matra Missiles, Alenia Marconi Systems.
12 DGA Annual Report, 2015.
13 APE, *Rapport d'activités 2015–2016*, p. 28.
14 The two partners are bound by a shareholders' agreement which defines the rules of governance. Strategic assets are protected as the French State holds a specific share and an agreement is in place.
15 Alongside the CEA and Naval Group (20.3% each) and EDF (already holding 9% of capital). See "*L'APE, le CEA et DCNS signent un accord engageant pour acquérir la participation d'AREVA au capital d'AREVA TA, spécialiste français de la propulsion navale*" ("The APE, CEA and DCNS have signed a binding agreement to acquire AREVA's stake in the capital of AREVA TA, a French company specialising in naval propulsion", *APE Press release*, 15 December 2016.
16 DGA key figures (2017).
17 French defence equipment exports increased significantly from the 1970s, peaking in the 1980s before falling sharply in the 1990s.
18 Statistics disseminated on defence expenditure or the DTIB usually cover the entire DTIB, however, we have concentrated specifically on the former group (i.e. arms companies) to highlight their specific features (Belin, Guille and Masson, 2015). These characteristics can be found in all DTIB companies, although they are less pronounced than in arms companies.
19 No breakdown is given of the number of direct and indirect jobs. Direct jobs are those generated directly by orders from the Ministry, i.e. personnel engaged in activities related to defence or armaments in companies receiving orders from the Ministry for the Armed Forces or those exporting armaments. Indirect jobs are employees in other companies working indirectly to fulfil defence or arms orders. These are some of the employees of suppliers, subcontractors and service providers of companies receiving arms orders.
20 See also Bellais and Guichard (2006) or Guillou et al. (2009) for patents policy.
21 The intangible nature of investment in R&D and the financial requirements of the operating cycle mean that defence companies have fewer fixed assets (16% of the balance sheet vs 24.6%), especially tangible fixed assets (8.3% of the balance sheet vs 12.9%) than other companies. These fixed assets are generally used as collateral, which can be a stumbling block when they need to borrow. Defence companies also have a much smaller financial debt than non-defence companies (9.5% of the balance sheet vs 15.8%).
22 Speech by Florence Parly, Minister of the Armed Forces, "Transformation of the DGA (Defence procurement directorate)", Paris, 5 July 2018.

References

APE. 2016. *Rapport d'activités 2015-2016*. Agence des Participations de l'Etat.

Belin J. (2015). Spécificités économiques et financières des entreprises de l'armement, Revue défense nationale, mai.

Belin J., Guille M., Lazaric N. and Mérindol V. 2018. Defence firms within the French system of innovation: Structural changes. *Defence and Peace Economics*, 30(2), 142–158. April.

Belin J., Guille M., Masson H. (2015). Rapport de l'"Observatoire de l'armement", étude pluriannuelle effectuée pour le SGA (Secrétariat Général pour l'Administration - Ministère de la Défense).

Bellais R. and Guichard, R.. 2006. Defense, innovation, technology transfers and public policy in France. *Defence and Peace Economics*, 17(3), 273–286.

Chiffres clés DGA (2017), Ministère des Armées, novembre 2018.

Comité pour l'histoire de l'armement (2002). Les origines de la Délégation générale pour l'armement, CHEAR.

Daffix S., Jacquin Y. (2004). Le périmètre des entreprises liées à la défense, Ecodef, n° 32, DAF/OED,ministère de la Défense.

Droff J. and Malizard J. (2014). Cohérence entre politique budgétaire et budget de défense en France, Revue Défense Nationale, 769, pp. 116–121.

Droff J. and Malizard J. (2015).R&D de défense et politique budgétaire en France, Revue Défense Nationale, no.784, pp. 101–106.

Dunne, J. P. (1995). *The Defense Industrial Base. Chap. 14 in Handbook of Defence Economics*, 399–430. Amsterdam: Elsevier.

Eury M. (2018). Les entreprises fournisseurs de la défense, ECODEF no.111, juin, DAF/OED,ministère de la Défense.

Fontanel, J. and Hébert,J.-P.. 1997. The End of the "French Grandeur Policy". *Defence and Peace Economics*, 8(1), 37–76.

Guillou, S., Lazaric N., Longhi C., and Rochhia S. (2009). The French Defence Industry in the Knowledge Management Era: A Historical Overview and Evidence from Empirical Data. *Research Policy*, 38(1), 170–180.

Hébert J.P. (1995). Production d'armement. Mutation du Système français, *La Documentation française.*

Masson H. (2007). Industries de défense et actionnariat public: une singularité française, Annuaire stratégique et militaire 2006-2007, janvier.

Masson H. (2011). Défense & Armement, des leaders mondiaux sous contrainte, Géoéconomie, no.57, mai.

Masson H. (2017). L'industrie française de défense: dynamiques et défis, Les Cahiers français, septembre.

Ministère des armées (2015), Rapport d'activités de la DGA.

Moura S. (2012). La base industrielle et technologique de défense, Écodef, no.58, Ministère de la Défense.

Notebook on International Defence Companies (2018), DGA.

Oudot J.M. (2016). L'essor des livraisons internationales des entreprises de défense, ECODEF no.79, mai, DAF/OED,ministère de la Défense.

Rapport au Parlement (2018) sur les exportations d'armement de la France, Ministère des armées, juin 2018.

Serfati C. (2014). L'industrie française de défense, Les études de la documentation Française, La documentation française, décembre.

SIPRI (2018). Trends in International Arms Transfers 2017, march.

Weber J. (2008). Un demi-siècle d'aéronautique en France, COMAERO, Etudes et recherches, Tome1.

7 Trans-European arms companies and industries

Keith Hartley

Introduction: the issues

The SIPRI Top 100 arms companies defines trans-European firms as companies whose ownership and control structure are located in more than one European country (SIPRI, 2016).[1] This definition provides a starting point which is developed into a broader definition embracing companies involved in the industrial management of European (trans-national) collaborative projects. The chapter outlines the development and evolution of various types of trans-European arms companies; it considers the role of government and European Union defence industrial policy in providing the framework for the emergence of such companies. Data are presented on the size of Europe's arms industry, its major trans-European companies and various industrial consortia for European collaborative companies.

Two themes emerge. First, the lack of official government data published regularly on the size and structure of the European defence industry. There is a similar absence of data on the industrial management companies for collaborative arms projects. This lack of data is surprising in view of the European Commission's role in formulating policy on the Single Market and European defence industrial policy. Second, governments are central to understanding the size and structure of the European arms industry. Their purchasing power provides funding for domestic firms and new mergers; they can promote or prevent competition in national defence markets; and they can approve or reject mergers (Hartley, 2018a). Given the importance of government, it is surprising that there is a general absence of data on the size and structure of European arms industries (Hartley, 2018b).

What is known

SIPRI listed two trans-European arms firms in its 2016 Top 100, namely, the Airbus Group (previously EADS or European Aeronautics Defence and Space Company) and MBDA. Other firms exist which are not shown in the 2016 Top 100 list, either because they reflect recent restructuring or are not a Top 100 arms firm. Examples include the relatively recent merger to form KNDS and CNH Industrial which was listed in the Top 100 in 2014 but did not reappear.[2] Also some firms are classed as product-specific international consortia based on European collaborative arms projects. These are international firms created solely for the industrial management of the development, production and marketing of specific European collaborative arms projects. Typically, they are aerospace projects embracing combat, trainer, transport, maritime patrol aircraft, helicopters and missiles. Trans-European arms firms are determined by national governments and originally were developed from European collaborative arms projects. Through international mergers, they have contributed to industrial re-structuring resulting in the creation of a smaller number of larger European arms firms more capable of competing with their larger US rivals.

Why trans-European arms companies?

Privately-owned firms pursue profits with mergers and acquisitions resulting from the search for profitable opportunities. Such a search process leads firms to economise on transaction costs by minimising the costs of entering new markets (either new geographical or new product markets) or by reducing costs through economies of scale and learning.

Trans-European arms companies are different. Their arms business means that governments are involved either through the government's role as a major or monopsony buyer of arms and/or through state ownership of arms firms. On this basis, trans-European arms companies are not the result of 'free market forces.' The creation of trans-European arms companies requires government approval and support for the mergers leading to the formation of a trans-European firm. Government approval and support for an international merger to create a new European arms firm is also required where the national arms firms are state-owned. The involvement of Government means that trans-European arms companies will pursue a variety of political and non-economic objectives and not solely profits (e.g. jobs; technology; regional aims).

Trans-European arms companies are not restricted to the SIPRI Top 100 definition which in 2016 comprised two companies, namely, Airbus and MBDA with the recent addition of Newco/KNDS. There is a further group of trans-European arms companies which are single project (product) multi-national firms comprising international companies or consortia created for the development, production and marketing of European collaborative projects. They represent the supply-side and industrial management of European collaborative programmes. The partner governments usually form a similar management group to represent the buyers and their national interests in the project. These international consortia which are included in this chapter are not shown in the SIPRI Top 100.

European defence industrial policy

Trans-European arms companies have been formed in the context of European defence industrial policy. This embraces efforts to create a Single European Market for defence equipment and a European defence industrial base (Hartley, 2018a). This policy developed through various initiatives, including the Western

European Union (WEU), the European Common Security and Defence Policy (CSDP), a commitment to arms co-operation and the creation of a European armaments agency leading to the emergence of OCCAR (Organisation Conjointe de Cooperation en matiere d'Armament or Organisation for Joint Armament Co-operation) and the European Defence Agency (EDA).

The European Commission has a major role in creating a Single Market for defence equipment (EDEM or European Defence Equipment Market). The Single Market aims to promote greater competition between Member States by opening national defence markets to cross-border competition: it allows firms in other Member States to bid for national defence contracts in the EU. The creation of the EDEM requires a legal framework specifying the rules for contract awards. For example, contracts awarded on the basis of the 'most economically advantageous offer.' The legal framework for creating the EDEM is based on a series of defence procurement directives aimed at promoting greater competition by opening national defence markets to cross-border rivalry from other European firms.

There are, however, constraints on the creation of a competitive EDEM reflected in special exemptions from the Single Market rules allowing EU nations to protect their 'essential' security interests when purchasing military equipment (defined as arms, ammunition and war materials, including intelligence services). Initially, the exemptions were based on Article 296 which later was replaced by Article 346. Such departures from the competitive model are predicted by public choice analysis which identifies the role of various interest groups seeking to influence public policy. These groups include vote-maximising politicians, budget-maximising bureaucracies and rent seeking producers. The groups will use their influence to depart from the rules for a competitive EDEM. Examples include the use of discriminatory technical specifications which favour national suppliers, including the application of Article 346 and the interpretation of the most economically advantageous offer in contract bids. Use of Article 346 allows national governments to award non-competitive contracts (Hartley, 2019). Typically, the European Commission responds to anti-competitive behaviour by introducing new legal procurement rules aimed at achieving compliance and 'good' behaviour with the final sanction of references to the European Court of Justice.

Alongside the EDEM initiatives, the EDA is tasked with developing a European Defence and Technology Industrial Base (EDTIB) aimed at reducing the duplication of costly national R&D programmes and small scale national procurement. The fragmentation of European defence equipment markets has resulted in Europe being less competitive than the US defence industry. For example, Europe has 180 different types of equipment compared with 30 for the USA (Hartley, 2018c). Each type of equipment involves a costly R&D programme leading to small national production quantities compared with the scale and learning economies achieved on large-scale US defence procurement. EDA is tasked with creating an EDTIB which is capability-driven, competent and competitive within and outside the EU (known as the 3Cs). However, a new policy initiative was announced in late 2016 known as the European Defence Action Plan (EDAP).[3]

The action plan (EDAP)

The EDAP aims to address the European defence problem of fragmentation in European defence markets, the lack of interoperability, technology gaps, duplication of costly R&D and the failure to achieve scale and learning economies in production to compete with US rivals. In 2013, it was estimated that the annual costs of non-Europe in defence ranged from some Euros 26 billion to Euros 130 billion. Investments in European defence are claimed to be worthwhile with each Euro invested in defence generating a return of 1.6, especially in skilled jobs, research and technology and exports (McKinsey, 2016).

The EDAP has three components: a European Defence Fund (EDF), support for investments in supply chains and regional clusters or centres of excellence and the promotion of an open and competitive Single Market for defence.[4] The EDAP aims to create the conditions for more European defence co-operation (EC, 2016).

The European Defence Fund aims to finance arms co-operation between Member States via research and capability windows. The research window will fund innovative collaborative defence research projects (e.g. electronics; materials; robotics). The capability window will provide funds for the joint development and procurement of defence capabilities. Overall, the EDF will provide funds for European arms co-operation and collaboration for research, development and acquisition (Hartley, 2018c).

The EDAP also has a role for defence SMEs. It supports investment in European defence supply chains, the creation of regional centres of excellence and promoting improved cross-border access by defence SMEs.[5] The Action Plan also aims to support an open and competitive Single Market for defence equipment. Its various initiatives are supported by funding and there is a target for Member States to spend 35% of their equipment expenditure on collaborative projects. The EDAP appears impressive, especially the commitment to provide financial incentives for collaboration. But appearances are deceptive and there remain questions about the sources and size of the EDF, the criteria for spending, the incentives for free riding and the absence of a single decision-making authority at the EU level. For example, within the EU, who can make decisions committing armed forces to conflict and will there be the trust to ensure that in a conflict all Member States will 'turn up'?

Two further policy developments will affect European defence industrial policy. First, Brexit involves the UK departure from membership of the EU with its major defence industry capability and its military forces with a world expeditionary role. Second, the January 2019 Treaty of Aachen between France and Germany which pledge enhanced cooperation between the countries, including foreign policy, security and military cooperation. This Treaty might support more mergers between French and German arms firms.

The European defence industry: size and structure

There are no officially published government data on the size of the European defence industry. Some data are published occasionally by the European Commission[6] but more regular annual data are published by the Aerospace and Defence Industries Association of Europe (ASD). Table 7.1 shows the available data on the size of the European defence industry in 2016. The totals are based m on most Member States of the EU. In terms of sales and number of large companies, the European defence market is dominated by the UK, France, Italy, Germany, Spain and Sweden.

Table 7.1 The European defence industry, 2016

Indicator	*Number*
Defence Sales/Turnover: total	**Euros 96.5bn**
Comprising:	
Military aeronautics	Euros 45bn
Naval	Euros 22bn
Land	Euros 28bn
Military Space	Euros 1bn
Defence Exports	**Euros 42bn**
Comprising:	
Military aeronautics defence exports	Euros 25bn
Land and Naval defence exports	Euros 16bn
Defence R&D expenditure	Euros 10bn
Defence Employment Data	
Comprising:	
Direct employment	445,000
Indirect employment	1,068,000
Total employment	**1,513,000**
Defence Employment Data	
Comprising:	
Military aeronautics	286,580
Land and Naval	137,060
Military space	21,360
Number of SMEs	2,500+
European collaborative defence equipment procurement as share of national defence equipment procurement	20%

Sources: ASD (2017); EC (2018); EDA (2016).

Notes:

i) ASD data are based on 16 EU nations plus Norway, Switzerland and Turkey: hence, they are not an accurate count of totals for the EU defence industry.
ii) Indirect employment was estimated by the author and based on the ratio of direct to indirect for 2014: a ratio of 2.4 indirect to direct employment. In 2014, direct employment data published by the European Commission was 500,000 and indirect employment was up to 1,200,000 employees (EC, 2018).
iii) The data were collected by ASD based on their definitions and methodology.

The European defence industry comprises a few large arms firms together with large numbers of SMEs. Its structure depends on the definition and extent of the market. Within Europe, national defence markets are characterised by domestic monopolies, duopolies and oligopoly for major air, land and sea systems. At the EU level, oligopoly dominates the industry structure. Typically, there is a 'mix' of private and state-ownership with some companies partly or wholly state-owned (e.g. Airbus; Thales; Leonardo). Private ownership is typical in Germany, Sweden and the UK with state-ownership in France, Greece, Italy, Norway, Poland and Spain. There are, however, differences within these broad categories. For example, private ownership embraces private individual national and international investors, family shareholdings and financial institutions and state ownership might include a proportion of private individual shareholders as well as private companies (Belin, Fawaz and Masson, 2019).

European arms firms accounted for 26% of the SIPRI Top 100 arms firms in 2016. Their sales are shown in Table 7.2. Comparisons with US arms firms amongst the Top 26 are revealing. The average size of US arms firm is more than twice the average size of their European equivalent reflecting US mergers in the 1990s. This size difference suggests that if European firms achieved the same average size as the Top 26 US arms firms, the output of the Top 26 European arms firms could be produced by about half their current numbers. On this basis, the European arms industry comprises 'too many relatively small firms' (excess capacity) with considerable opportunities for mergers, acquisitions and exits. Trans-European arms companies might be the solution to industrial re-structuring.

Trans-European arms companies

The SIPRI Top 100 for 2016 identified two trans-European arms firms, namely, Airbus and MBDA, both in the aerospace industry. A third trans-European arms firm in land systems was formed in 2015, known as KNDS (see Table 7.3). Trans-European arms firms are the result of consolidation and mergers in the European defence industry. They have reduced the excessive number of national arms firms creating larger groups capable of competing with US rivals. Brief company profiles follow. They show the changing industry structure and frequent change of names.

Airbus

Airbus was created in 1970 as a consortium known as Airbus Industrie GIE Consortium tasked with managing the development, manufacture, marketing and support of a new jet airliner (A300). As a new entrant, its aim was to compete with the US companies which dominated the world civil large jet airliner market, namely, Boeing, McDonnell Douglas and Lockheed. It was formed in the context of European firms which had built some innovative airliners but with only small production runs. Initially, three Governments

Table 7.2 European arms firms in SIPRI Top 100

Firm	*Arms sales ($ mn, 2016)*	*Rank in Top 100*	*Country*	*Arms dependency (%)*
BAE Systems	22,790	4	UK	95
Airbus Group	12,520	7	Trans-European	17
Leonardo	8,500	9	Italy	64
Thales	8,170	10	France	50
Rolls-Royce	4,450	16	UK	24
DCNS	3,480	23	France	99
MBDA	3,260	25	Trans-European	98
Rheinmetall	3,260	26	Germany	52
Babcock International Group	2,950	28	UK	48
Saab	2,770	30	Sweden	83
Safran	2,600	33	France	14
CEA	2,020	42	France	44
ThyssenKrupp	1,770	47	Germany	4
Fincanteri	1,600	54	Italy	33
Cobham	1,550	57	UK	59
Serco	1,500	58	UK	32
Dassault Aviation Group	1,390	60	France	35
GKN	1,210	68	UK	10
PZG	1,140	75	Poland	90
Krauss-Maffei Wegmann	950	78	Germany	95
Megitt	940	80	UK	35
Nexter	910	82	France	95
RUAG	820	87	Switzerland	43
Kongsberg Gruppen	770	94	Norway	41
Ultra Electronics	720	97	UK	68
Navantia	710	98	Spain	88
Average for all European firms	3,567			46
Average for Top US arms firms	7,795			52

Source: SIPRI (2016)

Notes:

i) Data are for 2016. Ranks are firm ranking in SIPRI Top 100. In 2016, there were 26 European arms firms in SIPRI Top 100.

ii) Arms Dependency is arms sales as percentage share of total company sales. Subsidiaries are excluded.

iii) Average figures for European firms based on 26 firms. Similarly, the Top US arms firms are for the top 26 US arms firms, so using same size samples. Averages for European and US arms dependency are based on medians.

Table 7.3 Airbus size and performance, 2017

Division	*Total sales ($million)*	*Profit rate on sales (%)*	*Employment numbers*	*Defence/sales share (%)*	*Labour productivity ($)*
Airbus	57,583	6.7	74,542	0	77,249
Airbus Helicopters	7,289	5.2	20,108	51	85,981
Airbus Defence and Space	12,209	2.0	32,171	78+	37,950
Total Airbus Group	77,080	5.8	126,821	15	60,779

Source: Airbus (2017).

Notes:
i) Sales in US $ based on Euro-dollar exchange rate in mid-2017.
ii) Labour productivity is sales per employee.

were involved comprising France, West Germany and the UK but the UK withdrew although its Hawker Siddeley company remained as a 'favoured' sub-contractor supplying wings. The founding companies were Aerospatiale and Deutsche Airbus each with 50% shares in the new consortium. In October 1970, CASA of Spain joined with a 4.2% share leaving Aerospatiale and Deutsche Airbus with 47.9% each. Later, in 1979, BAE Systems acquired a 20% share, with Aerospatiale and Deutsche Airbus holding 37.9% shares. Initially, the consortium focused on civil airliners and not defence systems.

The next major development in the consolidation of the European aerospace industry was the creation in 2000 of the European Aeronautics, Defence and Space Company (EADS).[7] EADS included defence activities and comprised the French Aerospatiale and Matra companies, the German company of DASA (which owned MTU, Dornier and MBB) together with the Spanish company, CASA. EADS held an 80% share in Airbus Industries, with BAE Systems holding the remaining 20% (in 2006, the BAE share was sold to EADS). Prior to the formation of EADS, there had been further mergers and joint ventures involving Aerospatiale. These included Aerospatiale and Italy's Aeritalia (later Alenia) forming ATR as a joint venture to develop a regional transport aircraft (1981: ATR 42); Aerospatiale and Deutsche Aerospace merging their helicopter interests to form Eurocopter (1992); and the French government transferring its 45.7% share in Dassault Aviation to Aerospatiale. A further development was the creation of Airbus Military in 1999 which specialised in large military aircraft (e.g. A400M).

In 2017, EADS was re-named Airbus with three Divisions comprising Commercial Aircraft, Defence and Space and Airbus Helicopters. Commercial Aircraft focused on its successful jet airliner series (e.g. A320; A350) with final assembly lines in Toulouse (France), Hamburg (Germany) as well as Tianjin (China) and Alabama (USA). Defence and Space combined Airbus Military, Astrium and Cassidian with involvements in the A400M airlifter (final assembly line in Seville, Spain), A330 MRTT (multi-role tanker transport), the Typhoon combat aircraft, space launch vehicles and launch services and cyber security. EADS Cassidian appeared in the 2013 SIPRI Top 100 as a subsidiary of EADS and was ranked 12th with arms sales of $6,750 million, total employment of 28,850 personnel and a defence share of total sales of 85%. With the change of name from EADS to Airbus Group, Cassidian became Airbus Defence and Space. Similarly, Eurocopter became Airbus Helicopters.

Originally, Eurocopter was jointly-owned by Aerospatiale (France) and MBB (Germany), It was created in 1985 to undertake the development of a new anti-tank helicopter (Tiger) supported by the governments of France and West Germany. Leadership and work were shared equally between the two companies. The Tiger project was criticised because it was costlier than a national project, including the US Apache attack helicopter and would take longer to complete. In 1992, the helicopter divisions of Aerospatiale and DASA were merged to form the Eurocopter company which was a supplier of military and civil helicopters, including the collaborative NH90 helicopter. It was listed in the 2013 SIPRI Top 100 as a subsidiary of EADS and ranked number 31, with arms sales of $3,760 million, total employment of 22,400 employees and a defence share of total sales of 45%. In 2014, Eurocopter became Airbus Helicopters to form one of the world's largest suppliers of military helicopters. All Eurocopter's helicopters were rebranded as Airbus helicopters.

Table 7.3 presents data on the size and performance of the Airbus Group and its divisions. Profit rates as a performance indicator show that sales of civil airliners are the most profitable part of the Airbus business. Similarly, profitability and labour productivity are lowest for the Defence and Space division. These are useful company-provided performance indicators which allow a comparative assessment of Airbus Group's civil and military businesses; but a similar analysis of Airbus Helicopters is not possible since only combined military and civil helicopter sales data are published.

Critics of Airbus have focused on the efficiency of its governance, government interference in decision-making, bribery allegations and controversies between Airbus and Boeing over subsidies. The role of government was illustrated in 2012 when Germany apparently opposed plans for a merger between EADS and BAE Systems: Germany was concerned about its loss of influence in the new merged company. Specific military projects such as the A400M airlifter have experienced cost overruns, delays and performance problems leading to penalties for Airbus. However, the end result is that since its formation as a new entrant in 1970, Airbus is now a duopolist in the world market for large jet airliners, alongside Boeing. Airbus demonstrates that international collaboration in civil jet airliners can be successful; but questions remain about the true costs of Airbus (direct and indirect costs to taxpayers in France and Germany, as well as the UK).

MBDA

MBDA is a European missile specialist and a trans-European company which has contributed to reducing the number of independent national European arms firms. It reduced the number of missile firms in five European nations to one European missile specialist (see Table 7.4).

It started in 1996 with a merger between Matra Dynamics and BAe Dynamics to form Matra BAe Dynamics.[8] MBDA was formed in 2001 with mergers between the French EADS Aerospatiale Matra missiles, Italy's Alenia Marconi Systems and the UK Matra BAe Dynamics. In 2002, MBDA obtained a 40% ownership of the Spanish missile firm, Inmize Sistemas. Later in 2005, Germany's LFK merged with MBDA to form MBDA Germany. The parent companies of MBDA are Airbus (37.5%), BAE Systems (37.5%) and Leonardo (25%) with locations in France, Germany, Italy, Spain and the UK.

KNDS

KNDS, newly created in 2015, forming Europe's largest producer of land systems. It was a merger between the French Nexter company (formerly GIAT Industries) and Germany's Krauss-Maffei Wegman (KMW), each ranked respectively 82nd and 78th in the SIPRI 2016 Top 100 list. The group's sales and employment placed it in the Top 26 of the World's Top 100 arms producers in 2016. The new group reflected the view that the European land system industry contained 'too many' land producers producing 'too many' projects. Initially, the new group was named KNDS (KMW and Nexter Defence Systems) under the KANT Project (K for MW; A for and; N for Nexter; T for Together). KMW is privately-owned by a German family whilst Nexter is French government-owned. KNDS is a 50%/50% joint holding company owned equally by France and Germany with a dual CEO management structure based in The Netherlands. The management structure for KNDS is similar to the original EADS/Airbus Group (it has been called Airbus for tanks). In June 2018, the French and German governments supported the new group by announcing the joint development of a new Main Ground Combat System and a new Common Integrated Fire System.

RheinmettalBAE systems land (RBSL)

In January 2019, BAE sold a majority 55% stake in its Land UK tank and combat vehicle division to its German rival Rheinmettal named Rheinmettal-BAE Systems Land. This new company will be a joint venture to produce the British Army's new infantry vehicles and will compete for other global military vehicles business. It plans to be a European market leader in the military vehicles sector. Both companies are also involved in the international consortium for the Boxer armoured fighting vehicle (see below).

Table 7.4 presents data on the major trans-European arms firms. The data are limited and company-provided with no government data for these companies.

In addition to European trans-national arms firms, there have been related developments involving European arms companies creating project-specific consortia for the sole purpose of the industrial management of collaborative projects. A brief history of such projects places them in context.

European collaborative arms projects: a brief history

Concorde

The first major European collaboration involved the Anglo-French Concorde supersonic airliner project.[9] This was a civil aerospace project but many of its features resembled a military contract (e.g. government finance and support; cost-plus contract; advanced technology). It started with the 1962 France-UK Treaty where both nations agreed to share the costs, work, sales revenue and risks of the project. An international treaty meant that if one nation withdrew it faced heavy cancellation payments. The treaty specified the sharing of air-frame, engine, systems and equipment costs with governments having to agree the sharing arrangements. An international treaty was used rather than

Table 7.4 Trans-European arms firms, 2017

Firm	*Activities*	*Total sales ($mn)*	*Arms sales ($mn)*	*Arms share of total (%)*	*Profit on total sales (%)*	*Profit on arms sales (%)*	*Employment in arms*
Airbus	Airliners; helicopters; Typhoon; military transports; space	78,117	11,679	15	6.4	8.1	22,743
MBDA	All types of missiles	3,600	3,600	100	<1	<1	10,700
KNDS	Land systems: tanks; artillery	2,500	2,500	100	na	na	7,240

Sources: Airbus (2018); MBDA (2017); SIPRI (2016)

Notes:

i) Sales converted from Euros to US dollars at mid-2018 exchange rate.

ii) Airbus profit on sales are for EBIT adjusted on sales. Airbus arms sales are for defence sales only (without space) but profit on arms sales are based on Defence and Space division profits and sales. Airbus arms employment estimated by using ratio of arms sales to total sales applied to total employment: the estimate is a broad order of magnitude.

iii) MBDA profits derived from SIPRI (2016) based on reported profits and arms sales.

iv) Neither KMG nor Nexter published profit figures for 2016: hence not available (na).

a commercial agreement between the two companies (Sud Aviation and BAC): a treaty specified clear rules about the government sharing of costs, risks and sales revenue as well as heavy penalties for cancellation.

Concorde was built by Aerospatiale (formerly Sud Aviation of France) and the British Aircraft Corporation (BAC) who were responsible for the design, development and production of the aircraft with SNECMA (France) and Rolls-Royce (UK: formerly Bristol Siddeley Engines) responsible for supplying the engine. France and the UK shared equally the costs of the project. BAC specialised in the forward fuselage, including the cockpit, and the tail; Sud Aviation (later Aerospatiale) built the centre fuselage; Bristol Siddeley Engines (later Rolls-Royce) and SNECMA supplied the engines.

The management arrangements were distinctive. No special company was formed. Instead, there were special industrial management and Government supervision arrangements. Integrated organisations of airframe and engine firms were created which were responsible for making detailed proposals for the programme, including the award of contracts for suppliers. A Standing Committee of officials from the two nations supervised progress on the project, reported to the Governments and proposed measures for undertaking the project. Inevitably, such committees were the focus of disputes about cost and work sharing and even over the name of Concord(e).

There were numerous disputes and problems. Originally, UK support for the project reflected its desire to join the European Common Market which was not achieved at the start of the project. This also shows the variety of policy objectives pursued by collaborative projects. There were threats to withdraw from the project (UK in 1964/65). The project suffered from cost escalation and delays (c.f. military aerospace projects); it was costly to buy and operate; its sonic boom was a problem; and it received small orders from France and the UK only: a total of 20 aircraft were built (including six non-commercial aircraft and 14 for in-service). The time-scale for the project was lengthy. It started with the Anglo-French Treaty in November 1962, with its first flight in March 1969, service entry in January 1976 and withdrawal from service in October 2003.

Concorde demonstrated that France and the UK were able to collaborate to build an advanced technology and complex civil aircraft. It was the first major co-operative venture between two European countries to design and build a supersonic airliner with the inevitable learning costs arising from 'doing business with strangers' (different languages and management cultures). It was also the basis for future European aerospace collaboration providing an initial benchmark 'model.' Both Britain and France gained valuable information, knowledge and learning from the project: this might be viewed as the era of collaboration by committee providing a model for later collaborations. There followed a series of industrial management firms created for the management of single collaborative arms projects. Significantly, there is an absence of official data on these companies and little data from their parent companies.

SEPECAT: Jaguar

Jaguar was the first joint Anglo-French military aircraft programme. In 1965, both governments signed a Memorandum of Understanding to develop two types of aircraft, a supersonic strike fighter and a trainer. The two governments created an official Jaguar Management Committee. SEPECAT was the industrial equivalent of the government Jaguar Management Committee. It was a joint venture between Breguet (later Dassault-Breguet Aviation) and BAC (later British Aerospace) for the development and production of the airframe. Final assembly was undertaken in each country. To reduce duplication of work, each aircraft component had only one source. Work shares were Breguet building the forward and mid fuselage with BAC building the rear fuselage and wings. There was a separate industrial partnership between Rolls-Royce (UK) and Turbomeca (France) to develop the Ardour engine. Interestingly, the Jaguar eventually emerged as a completely different aircraft from that originally planned: it became a low level strike aircraft rather than a trainer and achieved substantial exports.

EH industries: EH101

EHI was formed in June 1980 by Westland Helicopters and Agusta to undertake the joint development, production and marketing of a new anti-submarine helicopter for the navies of both countries. The project was handled on behalf of both governments by the UK MoD with EHI responsible for the industrial management of the programme. Each company had a 50% interest in EHI and its associated helicopter known as the EH 101. There were to be three versions, namely, naval, commercial transport and utility. Work shares were allocated: Westland the front fuselage and main rotor blade and Agusta the rear fuselage, rotor head and drive system, hydraulic system and part of the electrical system. There was a final assembly line in each country, but single source manufacture of components.

Unlike other collaborative management companies, EHI is an interesting case study leading to a merger and eventual take-over. In 1994, Westland was acquired by GKN and in 2000, Westland and Agusta merged to form AgustaWestland; then in 2004, Westland was acquired by Agusta (Finmeccanica, now Leonardo). Further industrial re-structuring in the European helicopter industry involved Eurocopter and NH Industries.

NH industries: NH90 helicopter

NHI was established in 1992 for the development and production of the NH90 helicopter (NATO helicopter for the 90s). Originally, five nations were involved: France, West Germany; Italy; The Netherlands; and the UK but the UK withdrew in 1987. NHI was established by Eurocopter of France and Germany; Agusta of Italy and Stork-Fokker Aerospace (Netherlands). Work shares were France at 41.6%; Germany at 23.7%; Italy at 28.2%; and

Fokker Aircraft at 6.5%. A contract was agreed with the NATO Helicopter Management Agency (NAHEMA) for the management of the programme. Two variants of the helicopter were planned: a tactical transport and a frigate version with 75% commonality planned. Originally, three final assembly lines were planned for France, West Germany and Italy; but this increased to six final assembly lines with the addition of Australia, Finland and Spain. The NH90 experienced major performance problems with both variants.

Panavia: Tornado

Panavia was formed in March 1969 for the design, development and production of an all-weather, multi-role combat aircraft for Germany, Italy and the UK, later named Tornado. The three parent companies of Panavia were British Aerospace (42.5% share), MBB (Germany: 42.5% share) and Aeritalia (Italy: 15% share). Similarly, a joint company known as Turbo Union was established for the development and manufacture of the jet engine for the Tornado. Turbo Union was jointly-owned by Rolls-Royce (UK), MTU (Germany) and FiatAvio (Italy).

The governments created an international management agency, known as NAMMO (NATO MRCA Management and Production Organisation) with NAMMA as its executive agency. A Tri-national Tornado Training Establishment (TTE) was formed in the UK. Work shares involved British Aerospace building the front and rear fuselage and the tail unit; DASA building the centre fuselage; and Alenia building the outer wings. A total of 992 aircraft were produced with first deliveries in July 1980 and final deliveries in September 1998. Exports to Saudi Arabia totalled 120 aircraft with 872 aircraft bought by the three governments.

Eurofighter: Typhoon

Eurofighter was formed in June 1986 to manage the industrial development and production of the European Fighter Aircraft programme (EFA). It was jointly-owned by Alenia (Italy: now Leonardo), BAe (UK: now BAE Systems), CASA (Spain; now Airbus) and DASA (Germany: now Airbus). Similar jointly-owned companies were created for the engine, known as Eurojet and for the radar, known as the Euroradar consortium. Eurojet was owned by Rolls-Royce (UK), MTU (Germany), Fiat Aviazione (Italy) and ITP (Spain). Euroradar was owned by Marconi (UK), FIAR (Italy), DASA Sensor Systems (Germany) and ENOSA (Spain). Programme management by the participating governments was undertaken by NETMA (NATO Eurofighter and Tornado Management Agency).

Based on planned orders, the initial shareholdings and work shares were 33% each to Germany and the UK, 21% to Italy and 13% to Spain. In 1992, following the end of the Cold War, German demands for cost reductions and a re-examination of the programme led to the relaunch of the programme as

Eurofighter 2000 with delays of three years. A reduction in Germany's planned orders led to re-arranged work shares giving the UK a 37% share, Germany a 30% share with shares of 19% to Italy and 14% to Spain. Further delays arose from technical problems with the flight control system. Originally, the participating nations had a requirement for 765 aircraft but this was later reduced to 620 aircraft followed by a further reduction to 472 aircraft. By 2018, national orders plus exports totalled 623 aircraft (including 151 exports). Work shares were distributed with BAe responsible for the front fuselage, canards, tail fin and rear fuselage, DASA for the centre fuselage, Alenia for the port wing and CASA for the starboard wing. There were similar work share arrangements for the engine, radar and avionics. Development and flight testing was undertaken by each participating nation and each nation had a final assembly line.

Typhoon was subject to cost increases and major delays. Time from formation of the Eurofighter company in 1986 to first service delivery in 2003 was 17 years. Some of the delays reflected a new strategic environment following the end of the Cold War and budget problems for the participating nations, as well as technical problems. Typhoon differed from Tornado in one significant respect. Both were advanced combat aircraft but Typhoon involved the collaboration of four nations compared with three nations for Tornado. More nations in a collaboration involves greater transaction costs, especially where a new member has no previous experience of collaboration. The trend towards more partner nations in collaborative projects moved to the next stage with the A400M airlifter.

Airbus military: A400M Atlas airlifter

The A400M airlifter has experienced a troubled development involving lengthy project formulation, technical problems and contractor losses. It started in 1982 with the establishment of the Future International Military Airlifter group (FIMA) to develop a replacement for the Lockheed C-130 Hercules and Transall C-160. In 1989, Lockheed withdrew from this group to develop its C-130J Hercules. By 1991, the European Future Large Aircraft group had been created (FLA) comprising Aerospatiale, Alenia, British Aerospace, CASA and DASA. Belgian and Turkish industry joined the group. In 1995, the newly created Airbus Military Company acquired industrial responsibility for the FLA and in 1999, it offered the A400M design which was accepted by the participating nations of Belgium, France, Germany, Italy, Spain, Turkey and the UK. In 2003, OCCAR was given responsibility for representing the partner nations on the project. Following the withdrawal of Italy, procurement numbers were reduced to 180 aircraft with one final assembly line (Seville, Spain). An international company was also created to develop and manufacture the TP400 engine for the A400M airlifter. Europrop International consists of four European engine firms, namely, MTU, Safran, Rolls-Royce and ITP Aero.

The project encountered cost overruns, delays, major technical problems and the internal restructuring of Airbus. Technical problems included software, engine problems and the propeller gearbox. Delays meant that the planned first flight due in 2008 was postponed to December 2009 and planned first deliveries were shifted from 2009 to August 2013. Losses on the aircraft led Airbus in 2009 threaten to cancel the project. In 2010, the seven nations agreed a new contract with Airbus given additional financial support but reduced orders from Germany and the UK, resulted in a total order for 170 aircraft. There was an export to Malaysia for four aircraft but South Africa cancelled its export order for eight aircraft due to cost increases.

IJVC: horizon frigates

Aerospace projects have dominated European arms collaboration with relatively few collaborations in sea and land systems. The Horizon frigate is an exception. Its origin was the NATO Frigate Replacement for the 1990s (NFR-90). This NATO project was abandoned in the early 1990s when both the USA and UK withdrew from the project, leading to the Horizon project in 1992. Originally, this was the Common New Generation Frigate involving collaboration between France, Italy and the UK which became known as the Horizon frigate with a joint missile system (the Principal Anti Air Missile System or PAAMS). From the start there were differences in national requirements.

Joint Project Offices represented the national governments for the frigate and missile programmes. In 1995, an Industrial Joint Venture Company (IJVC) was formed for the industrial management of the project comprising the major prime contractors from each nation, namely, DCN (France), GEC-Marconi (UK) and Orizzonte (Italy). In 1999, the UK withdrew from the frigate programme, citing problems with different national operational requirements, work share (choice of prime contractor), delays and rising costs. The UK was particularly dissatisfied with the industrial and management structure for the frigate programme (IJVC). Following its withdrawal, the UK started a national replacement project, namely, the Type 45 destroyer. France and Italy continued with the Horizon frigate project based on DCN (later Naval Group) and Orizzonte (later Leonardo). In terms of performance indicators for the project, both nations planned to buy a total of eight frigates but only four frigates in total were acquired (four being cancelled).

EuroTorp: torpedo

EuroTorp is an industrial consortium of French and Italian companies, formed in 1993 to provide a new lightweight torpedo (MU90). It comprises DCNS and Thales (France) and Whitehead Alenia Sistemi Subacquel (WASS of Finmeccanica: Italy). The torpedo has been sold to the navies of France, Italy, Germany, Denmark, Poland, Egypt, Morocco and Australia.

ARTEC Boxer armoured fighting vehicle

Boxer is a multi-role armoured fighting vehicle designed by ARTEC an international consortium. ARTEC Gmbh is based in Munich and its parent companies are Krauss-Maffei Wegmann, Rheinmettal Military Vehicles and Rheinmettal MAN Military Vehicles Netherlands. Originally, Boxer was a joint venture involving Britain, France and Germany. In 1999, France withdrew from the programme followed by Britain's withdrawal in 2003 with each nation preferring national projects. In 2001, the Netherlands joined the programme which is managed by OCCAR. Later, in 2018, the UK rejoined the Boxer programme with BAE Systems, Thales UK and Pearson Engineering as UK suppliers.

Conclusion

Trans-European arms companies are a relatively unknown part of Europe's arms industries. The SIPRI Top 100 has identified the major firms in this group but with limited data on their size and performance. The lack of data is even more conspicuous for the European collaborative industrial management companies. The financial performance of such consortia is usually concealed within the aggregate accounts of the parent companies. However, all is not lost and some analysis can be undertaken to assess the performance of the European industrial management companies. For example, comparative analysis is possible by comparing the performance of European collaborative projects with similar national programmes. Performance indicators include development time-scales, exports and, if available, unit total and unit production costs together with data on cost overruns and time slippages (Hartley, 2018b, 2014a, chp 13). Further analysis might assess the comparative performance of different types of collaboration, including the number of partner nations (Hartley, 2014b). Examples include comparisons of military and civil collaborative projects and the success of the collaborative Airbus in the large jet airliner market. Comparisons might also be made between the industrial management arrangements for the US F-35 combat aircraft and, say, Eurofighter Typhoon.

The formation of trans-European arms companies cannot ignore the role of governments and their buying power. Government can approve the formation of these companies, they provide funding, they determine the extent of competition within national defence markets and they control ownership. Government can also determine the data provided for such companies, but they have failed to request that such data be provided.

Notes

1 There are broader issues about the nationality of firms embracing the location of company head offices and subsidiaries, the nationality of shareholders and directors and the role of national governments in ownership and control.

2 CNH Industrial was listed as a trans-European arms firm in the SIPRI Top 100 for 2014 but not subsequently. In 2014, it was ranked number 96 with arms sales of $820 million; a defence share of total sales of 2%; and total employment in 2017

of 63,356 personnel. It is a multi-product company with sales of defence vehicles and was created by the integration of Fiat Industrial and CNH Global.

3 A further EU defence initiative is known as PESCO, or permanent structured cooperation (2017). This allows EU defence initiatives without the need for all Member States to agree: it is a treaty-based framework enabling defence cooperation in smaller groups below the threshold of 27 Member States but within the EU framework.

4 Despite frequent public support for improved defence co-operation, there remains a gap between the rhetoric and reality; nor can it be ignored that if arms co-operation is so beneficial, why is it so rare? (Kusters, 2018).

5 The EDF aims to re-structure supply chains. For example, French prime contractors are required to create a consortium with other European SMEs and other leading European companies have to create a consortium with French SMEs.

6 The source for such data is not published but is likely to be obtained from the ASD or Aerospace and Defence Industries Association of Europe, Brussels.

7 Prior to the formation of EADS, in 1998, British Aerospace and Daimler Chrysler agreed a merger; but this was abandoned when BAe purchased GEC Marconi Electronics in January 1999 leading to the formation of BAE Systems.

8 An earlier initiative was Euromissile created in the 1970s by Germany's Daimler Chrysler Aerospace and Aerospatiale of France. The missile work of Euromissile is now part of MBDA.

9 An earlier European aerospace collaboration was the French Breguet Atlantic maritime patrol aircraft. The Atlantic was chosen after a 1958 NATO competition which selected the Breguet design which first flew in 1961. A multinational European consortium known as SECBAT was formed to develop and build the Breguet-designed Atlantic. Unlike Concorde, this consortium built a Breguet design using Rolls-Royce engines and resembled an international production sharing agreement.

References

Airbus. (2017). *2017 Financial Statements*. Amsterdam: Airbus.

Airbus. (2018). *Airbus Company Report: Full Year 2017 Results*. Netherlands: Airbus Group.

ASD. (2017). *Facts and Figures 2017*. Brussels: Aerospace and Defence Industries Association of Europe.

Belin, J., Fawaz, M., & Masson, H. (2019). Shareholder nationality among the major European and American defence contractors: An exploratory data analysis. *Finance Bulletin*. forthcoming.

EC. (2016). *The European Defence Action Plan*. Brussels: European Commission.

EC. (2018). *Defence Industries*. Brussels: European Commission.

EDA. (2016). *Defence Data 2014*. Brussels: European Defence Agency.

Hartley, K. (2014a). *The Political Economy of Aerospace Industries*. Cheltenham: Elgar.

Hartley, K. (2014b). Collaborative projects and the number of partner nations. *Defence and Peace Economics*. *25*(6), 535–548.

Hartley, K. (2018a). *The Economics of Arms*. Agenda: Newcastle-on-Tyne.

Hartley, K. (2018b). Arms Industry data: Knowns and unknowns. *Economics of Peace and Security Journal*. *13*(2), 26–32.

Hartley, K. (2018c). The economics of European defense industrial policy. In Karampekios, N., Oikonomou, I & Carayannis, E. eds., *The Emergence of EU Defense Research Policy*. Switzerland: Springer.

Hartley, K. (2019). The profitability of non-competitive defence contracts: The UK experience. *Defence and Peace Economics*. forthcoming.

Kusters, C. (2018). Defence procurement in the EU. *RUSI Journal*, *163*(2), 52–65. April/May.

MBDA. (2017). *Corporate Social Responsibility Report 2017*. Paris: MBDA.

McKinsey. (2016). *Munich Security Report 2017*. Munich: McKinsey.

SIPRI. (2016). *Arms Industry Database*. Stockholm: Stockholm International Peace Research Institute.

8 The Italian defence industry

Raul Caruso

Introduction

In the realm of international relations, Italy is often described as a middle power. Such a definition is extremely relevant because it highlights the crucial factors beneath the foreign policy and the policies adopted in the realm of military spending and military industrial policy. In addition, Italy is a member of NATO and in fact, during the Cold War Italy had limited scope to elaborate its own foreign policy and independent choices in military spending and procurement. This was true during the Cold War and afterwards. More recently, a rethink of industrial military policy is *de facto* shaping also Italian foreign policy. In fact, the industrial military landscape in Italy is nowadays characterized by the existence of two 'national champions', namely Leonardo (previously known as Finmeccanica) and Fincantieri which are state-owned companies listed among the SIPRI top 100 arms producers. These national champions are surrounded by a plethora of SMEs which are often sub-contractors. In fact, the military industrial sector is small: it employs around 50,000 people only. In spite of its small size, the industrial complex is nowadays evolving much more into an export-led industry so eventually influencing Italian foreign policy. The Italian firms are interlinked with several foreign partners and they also take part in international collaborative projects. These linkages highlight the influence of industrial choices on the country's foreign policy. For example, the linkages of Italian industry with US military companies and agencies (e.g. the benchmark case of the F-35 program) could generate a serious obstacle to further integration with European partners on several issues.

This chapter is organized as follows: the first section presents a brief description of Italian military spending. The second section describes the structure of the industry. The third section presents the national champions. The fourth section outlines the Italian role in the F35 JSF program. The last section summarizes and concludes also highlighting the influence of the industrial military complex in Italian foreign policy.

Military spending

Military spending in Italy and the related industrial policy appear to follow three directions. First, the increasing demand for military expenditures during the Cold War regime; second, a substantial process of spending cuts associated with privatization and concentration in the defence sector; and third, a greater emphasis dictated by export-led industrial policy intertwined with the international commitments of Italy. Military spending in real terms increased until 1989. Since the Cold War a recurring topic with regard to military spending of countries has been the relationship between each country and the leader of the NATO alliance. Caruso and Di Domizio (2016) analyze the relationship between military spending of European countries and US military spending. The association is positive and significant. However, Italy is among the countries which did not exhibit significant coefficients so suggesting that perhaps the mentioned association does not hold. In Caruso and Addesa (2012), the determinants of Italian military spending are highlighted. A negative association with US military expenditure between 1988 and 2008 suggested a free-rider behavior. In the aftermath of the Cold War, military spending decreased until 1995 before re-gaining momentum until 2004. Since then, the trend appears to be negative until 2015. Such a negative trend is explained first in the light of the abolition of military conscription which occurred in 2005. In the period 2009–2015 the decrease can be explained by the severe financial crises in late 2008 which eventually became extremely pervasive in 2011 so imposing further budget cuts on public spending. Figure 8.1 shows a further increase in recent years. In sum, over the period 2006–2017 military spending decreased by 17%. Since 2017, an independent Italian research center (*Osservatorio Milex*[1]) recalculated Italian military spending providing different figures. The authors of this independent report claim that official figures drawn from the balance sheet of the Ministry of Defence have to be considered partly unreliable because the Italian government used to channel some military spending through other ministries. Revealing in this respect is the special case of peacekeeping and international military missions. The budget for these missions is not included in the budget of Ministry of Defence but rather in that of the Ministry of Economy. Therefore, they propose a recalculation of the Italian military expenditure so showing that it increased by 4.8% between 2006 and 2017 in real terms (2010 prices).

Beyond the critics about the calculation, in the very latest years, the increase of military spending appears to be motivated also by commercial reasons. In brief, it seems that the Italian government is to shape its foreign policy and participation in military missions to favor the exports of the national defence industry. In the White Paper for International security and Defence released in 2015 it is clearly stated that

> Exports represent important resources useful in intergovernmental relations important to military cooperation. With these, partnership policies and technology transfer can be developed, focusing on "intergovernmental" agreements. In this perspective, the Defence will continue to provide its support to domestic industry, also in coordination with other competent administrations ....

Such an approach is by no means exempt from critics and complications. At the time this chapter was written, for example, in the public media there had been a debate on a military mission in Niger to counter human trafficking. The mission is regulated by a treaty between the two countries signed in September 2017. The treaty states that there would be military transfers to Niger. That is, the rationale of the military mission appears to be the promotion of the national military industry worldwide.

Since the end of World War II, Italy has been among the world's top exporters. According to SIPRI TIV data,[2] exports of conventional weapons from Italy have been increasing in recent years with aircraft forming the largest share (see Figure 8.2).

The public commitment to the defence industry

Like many other European countries, Italy has always heavily supported its national defence industry. Italy has used the national security exemption to protect its industrial base from European and international competition (Flournoy and Smith (2005), Nones (1996), Pianta and Perani (1991)). In the 2000s, because of the increasing global competition Italy has pursued a strategy of national consolidation intertwined with an explicit support for

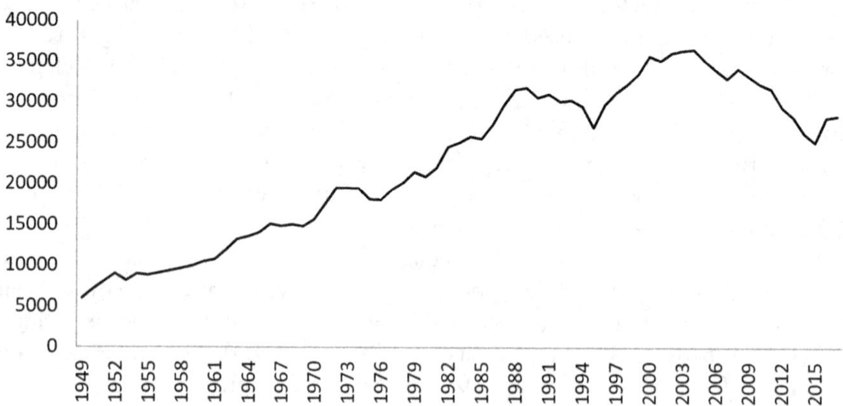

Figure 8.1 Military spending in Italy (1949–2017); data in US$ m., at constant 2016 prices.

Figure 8.2 Arms exports from Italy; source SIPRI, data in TIV US$ million.

exports of defence firms.[3] In 2012, the prime minister issued a decree (DPCM 253/2012) to highlight which sectors and technologies were to be considered vital for the economic growth and the competitiveness of the country. Eventually, in very recent years, this white paper confirmed the commitment of the Italian government in favor of the defence industry.

In sum, Italian policy-makers have favoured a development path for its military industry which can be defined along two strategic lines: (1) gaining access to the North-American market;[4] (2) securing access to emerging markets. The strategy to gain access to the North-American market took shape recently when the Italian champions, namely Leonardo-Finmeccanica and Fincantieri acquired some defence firms in the U.S. Similarly, General Electric acquired a large Italian firm, namely Avio. Above all, the participation in the F35 JSF program led by Lockheed Martin has strengthened such relationships. Someone might infer that such integration with U.S. poses a clear-cut political constraint on the Italian foreign policy and, perhaps, a severe obstacle to further integration with other European Countries in the industrial defence domain.

The structure of Italian defence industry

The Italian defence industry is characterized by a few large companies and a handful of medium-sized and small firms. According to SIPRI, the two Italian state-owned arms producers (Leonardo and Fincantieri) stand among the top 100 arms producers. In particular, Leonardo ranks among the top ten producers whereas Fincantieri stands around the 55th place. However, looking at the employment level, the Italian military industrial sector is rather

Table 8.1 The defence industry in Italy (December 31, 2017)

Name	*Revenue from sales (thousands of EUROS)*	*Employees*
LEONARDO – SOCIETA' PER AZIONI	7,765,899	27,307
FINCANTIERI S.P.A.	2,737,782	7,471
GE AVIO S.R.L.	1,455,168	3,836
ORIZZONTE – SISTEMI NAVALI S.P.A.	634,287	72
IVECO DEFENCE VEHICLES S.P.A.	337,164	861
THALES ALENIA SPACE ITALIA S.P.A.	331,113	2,139
FABBRICA D'ARMI PIETRO BERETTA – S.P.A.	173,460	806
FIOCCHI MUNIZIONI S.P.A.	143,624	646
SUPERJET INTERNATIONAL S.P.A.	134,244	258
VITROCISET – SOCIETA' PER AZIONI	128,823	829
BENELLI ARMI S.P.A.	103,793	273
RHEINMETALL ITALIA S.P.A.	96,429	297
PIAGGIO AERO INDUSTRIES SOCIETA' PER AZIONI*	91,417	1,223
RWM ITALIA S.P.A.	90,483	162
OHB ITALIA S.P.A.	66,134	191
MOREGGIA & C. S.P.A	50,067	83
SIMMEL DIFESA S.P.A.	44,136	162
CHEDDITE ITALY S.R.L.	40,650	50
MAGNAGHI AERONAUTICA S.P.A.	39,396	280
SICAMB – S.P.A.	38,475	333
AEREA S.P.A.	38,308	144
O.M.P.M. – OFFICINA MERIDIONALE DI PRECISIONE MECCANICA – S.R.L.*	35,396	52
COSTRUZIONI AERONAUTICHE TECNAM S.P.A.	35,363	168
CRESSI SUB SOCIETA' PER AZIONI	33,751	50
IAMCO – INTERNATIONAL AEROSPACE MANAGEMENT COMPANY – SOCIETA' CONSORTILE A RESPONSABILITA' LIMITATA	26,860	15
NOBEL SPORT MARTIGNONI S.P.A.	24,170	110
LUCIANO SORLINI S.P.A.	13,831	24
ARMI PERAZZI S.P.A.	13,674	67
MECCANICA DEL SARCA S.P.A.	12,609	122
EUROTECH S.R.L.	11,482	23
EUROPEAN AIR-CRANE S.P.A.	11,322	12
FRATELLI TANFOGLIO DI TANFOGLIO BORTOLO & C. SNC	10,974	54
FIMAC SPA	10,313	79

(*Continued*)

Table 8.1 (Cont.)

Name	*Revenue from sales (thousands of EUROS)*	*Employees*
VINCENZO LA GATTA S.R.L.	10,111	75
M.T.A. S.R.L.	9,288	83
VULCANAIR S.P.A.	8,903	85
CHIAPPA FIREARMS S.R.L.	8,815	61
FABARM-FABBRICA BRESCIANA ARMI S.P.A.	7,733	57
TECNOLOGIE INDUSTRIALI & AERONAUTICHE S.R.L.	5,567	42
AEROSVILUPPI S.R.L.	4,636	55
MECCANICA VADESE S.R.L.	4,226	45
P.R. TRADING S.R.L.	2,788	14
AVIOMEC S.R.L.	2,665	14
WORLD MONTAGES S.R.L.	2,382	79
S.A.B. AEROSPACE – S.R.L.	2,193	19
C E B SRL	2,148	14
AVIONITALY & C. GROUP S.R.L.	1,434	93
INVESTARM S.R.L.	1,416	9
ALISPORT S.R.L.	1,372	11
PROMECC AEROSPACE S.R.L.	1,339	28
SIGHT SYSTEM S.R.L.	1,277	15
METITALIA S.R.L.*	1,119	14
AVIOTEC S.R.L.	1,042	12
ELECTRONICS AEROSPACE S.R.L.	880	14
UNIMEC S.R.L.	779	9
SILMA ARMS SRL	758	11
TECHNOLOGY FOR PROPULSION AND INNOVATION S.R.L.	649	13
F.P. FLY S.R.L.*	496	10

Source: AIDA;
* balance sheet 2016.

small. Downloading the financial data of defence firms from the AIDA databank, one would find that in 2017 only 60 firms were now listed in the defence sector.[5] The number of employees at the end of 2017 was around 50,000 only. The dominant employer is Leonardo which counts for 55% of the employees. The second national champion Fincantieri counts for 15% followed by GE Avio (owned by GE aviation) which counts for 7.7%. Top small arms manufacturers Beretta and Fiocchi Munizioni count respectively for 1.6% and 1.3% only with less than 1,000 people employed in each.

Interestingly, 18 firms out of 60 have less than 25 employees. In fact, many SMEs are sub-contractors of the larger firms. As pointed out in Caruso and Locatelli (2013), only a few years ago the structure was characterized by four big corporations (Finmeccanica, Fincantieri, Avio and Iveco), a set of medium-size companies and a larger set of small firms. The latter were used to work as sub-contractors for services or components to larger firms (Briani, 2009). The evolution and characteristics of aerospace industry in Italy have been analyzed in Graziola et al. (2016) and Graziola e Parazzini (2006) whereas the current structure of the Italian defence industry is well described in Catalano (2016). Interestingly, the structure of the defence industry is confirmed also for innovative programs like the Forza NEC program as explained in De Zan (2016). The latter is a program which is aimed to enhance the operational capabilities of Italian Army through digitization and integration of the different platforms of Italian Armed Forces. In brief, the Italian defence industry confirms what Hartley and Sandler (2004) had envisioned with regard to the future of the defence firm. In the early 2000s they have stated clearly that the future defence firm would have been a large global company focused on prime contracting and buying-in specialist tasks from other firm throughout the world.

The Italian champions: Leonardo-Finmeccanica and Fincantieri

Leonardo – Finmeccanica

The first 'Italian champion' is Leonardo (previously known as Finmeccanica) which is among the top ten arms producers in the world. Founded in 1948, Finmeccanica has been for years a major state-owned company. Until recently, the Finmeccanica group had firms and activities in both the civilian and military sectors.[6] After a process of consolidation and divestments the core-business of Finmeccanica (eventually renamed Leonardo in 2016) turned to be focused almost completely on the military sector. In particular, in the late 1990s, Finmeccanica expanded its activities in the military sector by means of joint-ventures, mergers and acquisition. In 1998, a joint-venture between Finmeccanica and the British GEC Marconi generated Alenia Marconi Systems which had been a major integrated defence electronics company until its dissolution in 2005. In 1999, another joint-venture with Britain's GKN generated the world-leading helicopter producer, namely, Agusta Westland which eventually became totally owned by Finmeccanica in 2004. The European top producer of missiles MBDA, was created in 2001 as joint-venture between Alenia Marconi Systems, EADS and BAE systems. In this expansion path, the most relevant acquisition has been that of American DRG Technologies (now renamed Leonardo DRS). Through that acquisition Finmeccanica secured a major presence in the US defence market. In fact, the acquisition would have not been possible without the agreement of the US Department of Defense and without a plan to mitigate foreign ownership,

Table 8.2 Some performance indicators of Leonardo-Finmeccanica

	2018	*2017*	*2016*	*2015*	*2014*
Revenues*	12,240	11,734	12,002	12,995	12,764
EBITDA*	1534	1602	1907	1866	1569
Group Net Debt*	2351	2579	2845	3278	3962
ROI	16.4%	15.7%	16.9%	15.7%	12.7%
ROE	9.7%	6.7%	12.6%	6.2%	0.4%

Source: Leonardo.
* data in millions €.

control and influence (FOCI).[7] In fact, the governance of Leonardo DRS is firmly in the hands of American top managers and executives. At the time of writing, the CEO of Leonardo DRS was a former US Deputy Secretary of Defense. The acquisition of DRS was extremely controversial because of the huge debt generated. The focus on military production was completed in 2015 when the non-military activities of Ansaldo Breda and Ansaldo STS were sold. In 2016, the consolidation process was finalized when most subsidiaries were incorporated as business divisions. In this development path, the lion's share was taken by aerospace and defence also reflecting the massive R&D expenditures in those sectors. It must be noted that R&D expenditure on aerospace and defence has been favoured heavily by Law 808/1985. In Caruso and Locatelli (2013) the breakdown of R&D expenditure between 1995 and 2007 showed that although in those years the group included both civilian and military activities, a long-term investment has been undertaken only for defence.

Leonardo is currently listed in the Borsa Italiana. The state has to hold a share which cannot be lower than 30% (currently it is 30.2%) whereas the remaining shares constitute a floating stock. Interestingly, the geographical distribution of institutional floating rate does violate the stylized fact of 'home bias' given that almost 90% of the institutional floating stock is held outside Italy. More precisely, 43.5% of floating stock is held in North America. The stock price on January 31, 2008 was 17.94 euros. On January 31, 2019 the stock price was 8.45 euros. Figure 8.3 reports the daily stock price trend between January 2000 and December 2018.[8] It is clear that the long term investors have experienced a severe loss.

Despite decreasing in recent years (see Table 8.2) the net debt is still very high and it represents the major risk faced by the managers. Because of the high debt and uncertainty, the credit ratings are not high. In late 2018, the Moody's short term rating was Ba1 so highlighting a substantial credit risk and in the same vein Fitch'credit rating in late 2017 was BBB-.[9] In fact, Leonardo is a company which is not considered able to repay its obligations in the presence of some unforeseen circumstances.

Figure 8.3 Leonardo-Finmeccanica Stock Price (January 3, 2000 – December 31, 2018).

Fincantieri

Fincantieri is the second Italian 'champion'. It is one of the world's top shipbuilders. In fact, the Fincantieri group is not focused solely on military production but it has also a civil division. Military production increased substantially in recent years. Fincantieri is a state-owned company listed in Milano stock exchange. At December 31, 2017, 71.6% of the Company's share capital was held by Fintecna S.p.A. (100% of the share capital of Fintecna S.p.A. is owned by Cassa depositi e prestiti S.p.A., 82.8% of whose share capital is owned by Italy's Ministry of Economy and Finance) whereas the remainder of the share capital constitutes a floating stock. The stock price on January 2, 2015 was 0.77 euros: at January 3, 2019 the stock price was 0.95 euros. Figure 8.4 reports the daily stock price trend between July 2014 and December 31, 2018. The long-term of stock price trend appears to be increasing. According to SIPRI in 2017 Fincantieri ranked 58th among the top 100 arms producers in the world. The percentage of arms sales in total sales is around 30%. According to the data provided by the company in 2018 the percentage of total revenues from defence shipbuilding is 31%. Only a few years ago Fincantieri used to be a national contractor only. In 2002, all orders were from the Italian navy. Recently, Fincantieri has enlarged its operations worldwide, especially in North America. In 2008 it acquired the marine segment of the Manitowoc Co. Inc. so strengthening its position in the US. In the US, Fincantieri owns Fincantieri Marine Group LLC and Fincantieri Marine Systems North America Inc. (Engines and mechanical products). Besides the Italian Navy, the main customers of Fincantieri are the US

Figure 8.4 Fincantieri Stock Price July 7, 2014–December 31, 2018.

Navy and the US Coast Guard (especially for mid-sized vessels).[10] The company has been expanding into new naval markets, particularly in the Middle East. In 2016 Fincantieri and the Qatari Ministry of Defence signed a contract for the construction of seven surface vessels. This is claimed to be the largest order acquired by Fincantieri over the last 30 years.[11] Overall, Fincantieri appears to have increased dramatically its role in naval supply at the world level. In any case, it must be also noted that the recent positive performance in profitability is due to the increasing trend in the world demand of luxury and cruise vessels generated by the high expectations on global cruise tourism. In fact, it is plausible that the growth in revenues and the stock price has been determined mainly by this.

Participation in the F-35 program

A special focus needs to be made on the participation of both the Italian government and industry in the F-35 Joint Strike fighter program. The F-35 fighter program developed by Lockheed Martin is a multinational collaborative program of an unprecedented size.[12] Italy is a level 2 partner in the program.[13] Different levels of participation are associated with different cost burdens. According to Marrone (2013) and Tosato (2014), besides military and strategic considerations, participation in the F-35 program has also been dictated by industrial reasons. In fact, in line with offset schemes of the military industry,[14] Lockheed Martin awarded the subcontract for producing the wing boxes of the Italian F-35s to Alenia Aermacchi (now absorbed in the aircraft division of Leonardo). Other firms are also involved in the procurement.[15] In particular, in the Piedmont Region (in Cameri) a FACO

(Final assembly and Checkout) plant has been created. In fact, the Cameri FACO is assembling Italian F-35s and 29 Dutch F-35s.

It is widely known that the F-35 program has experienced severe cost increases. The average procurement unit cost has risen to 130.6 in then year million dollars whereas in 2001 the expected figure was 69 in then year million dollars. The goal announced by the American DoD is to target the procurement unit cost at $80 millions. An assessment on the participation of Italy in the F-35 program is not easy. Recently the Italian Court of Auditors released a report which summarizes and analyzes in depth the costs and economic returns of Italian participation in the F-35 program.[16] First, the court of auditors highlighted the opportunity cost of the program. In fact, because of its extremely high financial cost, it largely crowds-out any other possible commitment. It appears to be a kind of 'tied hands' problem. Participation in the F-35 prevents the Italian government commitment to any other similar program. Besides the long-run opportunity cost aspects, the auditors highlight that the economic assessment is complex because of many other factors which also changed since the first agreement. In particular, it has to be considered that there had been a severe cut in the expected orders since the beginning of the program. In fact, in March 2012, because of the severe economic crisis the Italian government reduced its order from 131 to 90 aircraft. The impact of this cut is Janus-faced. On the one hand, it resulted in severe cost-cutting. On the other hand, the cut has determined a reduction of the indirect benefit because of the related reduction in the production volumes of wing boxes. So, when considering the expected figure of labor force employed, the actual outcome is significantly lower. In 2008 the estimated workforce was around 10,000 employees whereas the actual figure in the second semester of 2016 was 1,569 employees. Actually the current workforce estimates in the worst case scenario is 3,586 whereas in the best case scenario it is 6,395 employees.

In brief, what can be maintained is that the F-35 program highlights the very nature of military industry in Italy: namely a big prime contractor interlinked with smaller firms and in particular a plethora of SME for specialist tasks. However, the crucial role of the national government as a monopsonist is confirmed.

It must be also noted that joining the F35 JSF hides the results achieved with the Eurofighter Typhoon. As explained in Hartley (2008) the Typhoon programme – in spite of some inefficiencies – has shown the potential of a collaborative industrial projects.

Conclusion

This brief chapter has analyzed the Italian defence industry by highlighting three fundamental aspects. First, the military industrial sector in Italy is characterized by two national champions. This is not uncommon in the defence sector. In Italy, this is a recent evolution because only few years ago the dominant national champion was only Finmeccanica (eventually renamed Leonardo). Recently, Fincantieri has gained further size and strength. Besides other factors, the existence of national champions prevents efficiency gains. However, it is widely accepted that policies promoting national champions are not to be analyzed in economic-efficiency terms but rather taking into account political-economy considerations. There is no room for efficiency in the presence of national champions. Yet, the two national champions are surrounded by a plethora of SMEs which often play the role of sub-contractors. It must be also noted that the existence of national champions is not only dictated by strategic reasons but also to protect some 'economic sovereignty'. In fact, in the 2015 white paper on Defence, it is clearly stated that some technologies must be retained nationally in order to maintain some key 'sovereign competencies'. The second point to be highlighted is that in spite of the emphasis posed by the Italian government, the military sector is rather small. In 2017 it employed only 50,000 persons. Therefore, beyond strategic considerations, it does not provide the national economy with high returns in terms of employment creation. This is to be taken into account when considering the expected total benefits for the economy.

Third, the military industrial complex poses a substantial constraint in the making of future Italian foreign policy. This is rather likely when considering that nowadays the future relationship between NATO and the EU is to be developed in the light of the common European initiatives on security, in particular the PESCO. In other words, the question is whether the industrial relationships between state-owned Italian and US companies are to prevent Italy from a deeper relationship with other European allies. The case of F35 Joint Strike fighter program is emblematic in this respect. As pointed out above, the F35 is a 'tied hands' program because it is so pervasive to prevent Italy from taking part into any other similar program. In fact, this poses some serious obstacles of cooperation with France and Germany which have announced a joint effort to develop a next-generation fighter aircraft also highlighting that it would be a pillar of a future European common defence. That is, if the common defence in Europe has to be based on industrial cooperation, the current scenario is likely to be changed radically. Moreover, as pointed out in Hartley (2006), a superior efficiency would take shape when a more efficient defence industrial policy within an alliance takes shape.

In sum, what appears likely is that the current structure of the Italian defence industry will be re-shaped in the very near future. Political considerations can be expected to lead this process. However, budget cuts are also likely because of the massive Italian public debt.

Notes

1 See http://milex.org/
2 See the SIPRI page on methodology for information on TIV . www.sipri.org/databases/armstransfers/sources-and-methods
3 It is also worth-mentioning in this context that in the aftermath of the Cold War the government failed to support or design a conversion strategy. Some conversion initiatives have been implemented at regional leval. See on this point Perani (2000) and Perani (1997) and Pianta and Castagnola (1990).

4 On this point see also Marrone and Ungaro (2014).
5 However, when considering the figures provided by AIAD (the Italian association of firms in aereo-space, defence and security industry) the figures appear to be slightly higher. In fact, in 2017 more than one hundred firms were associated with AIAD. Despite See the website http://www.aiad.it/en/homepage.wp
6 To have a complete account of Finmeccanica's history see Zamagni (2009) and Felice (2010).
7 Needless to say, the U.S. Government allows only foreign investment consistent with the national security interest. On FOCI please see https://www.dss.mil/ma/ctp/isia/bams/foci/
8 Source: Datastream
9 Information available on Leonardo's website.
10 See Slocombe (2017) on Fincantieri's Littoral Combat Ships acquired by US Navy.
11 The client portfolio in 2018 also includes the UAE Navy, the Iraqi Navy, Indian Navy, Peruvian Navy, Turkish Coast Guard, Algeria Navy, Bangladesh Coast Guard, Kenya Navy, Armed Forces of Malta and Saudi Arabia Navy. Information available on www.fincantieri.com
12 For a comprehensive analysis of the F-35 Program see among others Von Hlatky and Rice (2018).
13 Italy and Netherlands are level 2 partners; Turkey, Australia, Norway, Denmark and Canada are Level 3 partners. See the GAO (2004) for better details on the participations in the program.
14 On offsets see Brauer and Dunne (2011)
15 Some of the firms involved in the procurement are: Avio, Galileo Avionica, Marconi Selenia Communication, Aerea, Datamat, Gemelli, Logic, Selex communication, Sirio Panel and others.
16 See Corte dei conti (2017).

References

Brauer J., Dunne P. (2011). Arms trade offsets: What do we know?. In Coyne C., Mathers R.eds., *The Handbook on the Political Economy of War.* Cheltenham: Edward Elgar.

Briani V. (2009), L'industria della difesa italiana, in Osservatorio della politica internazionale, 3.

Caruso R., Addesa F. (2012). Country Survey: Military Expenditure and Its Impact on Productivity in Italy, (1988–2008). *Defence and Peace Economics*, vol. 23, n.5, 471–484.

Caruso R., Di Domizio M. (2016). Interdependence Between US and European Military Spending: A Panel Cointegration Analysis (1988-2013). *Applied Economics Letters*, vol. 23, n.4, 302–305.

Caruso R., Locatelli A. (2013). Finmeccanica amid International Market and State Control, a Survey of the Italian Military Industry. *Defence and Peace Economics*, vol. 24, n.1, 89–104.

Catalano C. (2016). *La politica industriale nel settore della difesa.* Roma: Cemiss.

Corte dei conti (2017), Deliberazione n.15/2017, Partecipazione italiana al Programma Joint Strike fighter – F35 – Lightning II, available at the address www.corteconti.it/export/sites/portalecdc/_documenti/controllo/sez_contr_affari_com_internazionali/2017/delibera_15_2017_e_relazione.pdf [last access january 2019].

De Zan T. (2016), *Italy and the Forza NEC Program.* Marrone, Nones and Ungaro. eds. Vol. 3, 101–137.

Felice E. (2010). State Ownership and international competitiveness: The Italian Finmeccanica from Alfa Romeo to Aerospace and Defense (1947-2007). *Enterprise and Society*, vol. 11, n.3, 594–635.

Flournoy M., Smith J. (2005). *European Defense Integration: Bridging the gap between Strategy and Capabilities.* Washington (DC): Center for Strategic and International Studies.

GAO (2004), Joint Striker Fighter Acquisition, Observations on the supplier Base, GAO-04-554, available at www.gao.gov/new.items/d04554.pdf

Graziola G., Cristini A., Sciortino G. (2016). The Italian Space Industry in 2010-2012. Structure, performance and returns from a high tech sector. *L'industria*, vol. 37, n.1, 11–50.

Graziola G., Parazzini S.S. eds. (2006). *L'industria Aereospaziale tra militare e civile all'inizio del terzo millennio.* Milano: Vita e Pensiero.

Hartley K. (2006). Defence Industrial Policy in a Military Alliance. *Journal of Peace Research*, vol. 43, n.4, 473–489.

Hartley K. (2008). Collaboration and European Defence Industrial Policy. *Defence and Peace Economics*, vol. 19, n.4, 303–315.

Hartley K., Sandler T. (2003). The Future of the Defence Firm. *Kyklos*, vol. 56, n.3, 361–380.

Mampaey, L. (2008). La nascita di un sistema industriale-militare di sicurezza europeo. In *L'industria militare e la difesa europea. Rischi e prospettive, a cura di* C. Bonaiuti, D. Dameri E A. Lodovisi. Milano: Jaca Book, 29–73.

Marrone A. (2013). Italy and the F-35, Rationale and Costs. *International Journal*, vol. 68, n.1, 31–48.

Marrone A., Nones M., Ungaro A. (2016). eds. *Technological Innovation and defence: The Forza NEc program in the euro-Atlantic Framework.* Roma: edizioni nuova cultura.

Marrone A., Ungaro A., (2014), Relations Between the United States of America and Italy in the Post-Cold War Period: A Defense Industrial Perspective, Cahiers de la Méditeranée [online], 88, available at https://journals.openedition.org/cdlm/7542.

Ministry of Defence (2015), White Paper for International Security and Defence, available on line at www.difesa.it/Primo_Piano/Documents/2015/07_Luglio/White%20book.pdf

Nones M. (1996), L'Economia della difesa e il nuovo modello di difesa, IAI quaderni 1.

Nones M., Darnis J.P. (2005), Control of Foreign Investments in Aerospace and Defence. *The International Spectator*, vol. 40, n.3, 83–90.

Perani, G. (1997). Conversion experiences and policies in Italy. In *Defense conversion strategies*, edited by R. F. Dundervill, P. F. Gerity, A. K. Hyder, and L. H. Luessen, 407–429. Dordrecht, the Netherlands: Kluwer Academic.

Perani G. (2000). Italian contrasts in Regional Military Industrial Conversion. *International Regional Science Review*, vol. 23, n.1, 91–102.

Pianta, M., A. Castagnola. (1990), *La riconversione dell'industria militare. Firenze*, Italy, Edizioni Cultura della Pace.

Pianta, M., Pierani, G. (1991), *L'industria militare in Italia. Ascesa e declino della produzione di armamenti*,Roma, Edizioni Associate.

Tosato F. (2014). *Il Programma F35 in una prospettiva Italiana.* Roma: CESI.

Von Hlatky S., Rice J. (2018). Striking a Deal on the F-35: Multinational Politics and US Defence Acquisition. *Defence Studies*, vol. 18, n.1, 19–38.

Zamagni, V. (2009). *Finmeccanica. Competenze che vengono da lontano.* Bologna: il Mulino.

9 Germany

Michael Brzoska

Introduction – main features of the German situation

Germany is among the second tier of defence producers in the world. While the portfolio of military technology produced in the country is broad, German companies are particularly strong in naval shipbuilding, tank, artillery, ammunition and small arms production. In other fields, such as aerospace, electronics and IT, production in Germany mostly often occurs in collaboration with companies from other European countries or the US.

The profile of the German defence industry has not changed much from the one of the West German defence industry in the 1970s. From its beginnings in the second half of the 1950s, after a period of Allied limitations following World War II, industry in the Western part of the country developed in a combination of pre-war strength in arms production, for instance with respect to artillery and small arms production, with interaction with technologically advanced civilian capabilities, for instance in the land vehicle and shipbuilding sectors (Albrecht et al. 1978; Brzoska 1983; Creswell and Kollmer 2013). Close integration of civilian and defence industry continues to be a hallmark of German arms production. It was also a characteristic of the East German defence industry which was incorporated into the Warsaw Pact's division of labour in defence production, specialising in optronics and other high-end defence technologies (Diedrich 2015).

After the end of the Cold War, domestic demand for arms substantially fell and exports also plummeted (see Table 9.7). Between the late-1980s and the mid-1990s, sales and employment dropped by about 50%. Most production facilities in East Germany ceased operation as did some West German companies. Many defence companies diversified into civilian sectors, some, such as Daimler-Benz Aerospace (which later became part of EADS and Airbus) with great success (Weingarten et al. 2015). Another company strategy, also supported by the German government, was to enter the growing market for civilian security equipment (BMWi 2016). The mingling of defence and security production became so prominent that an industry association (Bundesverband der deutschen Sicherheits- und Verteidigungsindustrie, BDSV) combining the two sectors was founded by major companies in 2009. It has become a vocal voice of the industry, often more public than the various industry associations with membership from defence companies – aerospace (Bundesverband der Deutschen Luft- und Raumfahrtindustrie), shipbuilding (Verband für Schiffbau und Meerestechnik), electronics (Zentralverband Elektrotechnik- und Elektronikindustrie) – or the Federal German Industry Association (Bundesverband der Deutschen Industrie), which also lobbies for the defence industry. A recent study commissioned by the BDSV claims that turnover and employment for the production of public security goods, by defence companies and others, were substantially higher in the mid-2010s than production of arms and ammunition (Ostwald and Legler 2015).

The German government has not developed clear positions on the German defence industry in recent years, despite officially formulating a defence industrial policy (BMWi 2015) which however combines various, partially contradictory, objectives. The government wants to advance Europeanization of defence production but also has declared its interest in maintaining a strong German defence industry. It wants to promote tough competition in defence markets and opposes subsidies to the industry but also intends to protect core areas of defence production ("Kernkapazitäten"). Obviously, in the balance between competition and protection, the border lines between the two principle approaches to defence industrial policy are of major importance. The German government, however, has been reluctant to consistently define what it considers to be the core capacities it intends to protect (see below). In practice, it has aimed, through a combination of procurement and export policies, to keep occupied most of the existing defence industrial capacities.

Fundamentally, European, regional and sectoral considerations are important factors for defence policy-making. There is a general preference for joint European production in most sectors of the defence industry, but an insistence on *juste retour*, basically requiring that German money spent for procurement leads to employment in Germany. However, where German defence companies are capable to survive on a national scale, as in the shipbuilding industry, there is no pressure from the government to Europeanize. The government has also, at times, prohibited changes in the industrial structure which might have led to the weakening of German defence industry, the most notable case being its opposition to a merger between Franco-German EADS (now Airbus) and British BAE Systems in 2012.

In macroeconomic terms, German defence industry is of minor importance, with less than one percent of industrial employment, value added and exports (Table 9.1). However, it is of major importance for some regions and industrial sectors (Table 9.2).

At least since the 1960s, the German government has claimed to be very restrictive on arms exports. Arms exports are controversial in Germany (compare e.g. GKKE 2018; Krause 2018). While Germany has become one of the

Table 9.1 Recent estimates of value added, turnover and employment in the German defence industry

Source	*Estimate for year*	*Category*	*Units*
VDI TZ 2015	2014	Sales defence industry	20.4 billion €
Ostwald and Legler 2015	2014	Sales defence and security industry	25.3 billion €
Table 9.A1	2016	Sales defence industry	22.1 billion E
Schubert and Knippel 2012	2011	Value added defence and security industry	8.3 billion €
VDI TZ 2015	2014	Value added defence industry	10.5 billion €
Table 9.A1	2016	Value added defence industry	10.2 billion €
Ostwald and Legler 2015	2014	Value added defence and security industry	12.2 billion €
VDI TZ 2015	2014	Direct employment defence industry	65,700
Schubert and Knippel 2012	2011	Direct employment defence and security industry	98,000
VDI TZ 2015	2014	Direct plus indirect employment (civilian industry)	116,000
Weingarten et al. 2015	2014	Direct and indirect employment defence industry	90–100,000
Ostwald and Legler 2015	2014	Direct employment defence and security industry	135,700
VDI TZ 2015	2014	Share of direct employment in defence industry in German manufacturing employment	0.8 %
Table 9.A1 and Statistisches Bundesamt	2017	Share of defence industry sales in	
		• German National Income	0.6%
		• total sales of German manufacturing	1.1 %
		• total German exports	0.7%

largest arms exporters in the world, its share in global arms exports (about 5–6%) is considerably lower than its share in the global export of manufacturing goods (Krause 2018). However, the reliance of German defence producers on arms exports has increased over time (see Table 9.A1) and has been around 50% in the 2010s. While in the past the large majority of exports were to NATO- and EU-member countries, the share of exports to other countries has increased considerably over the last few years, surpassing sales to allied countries (GKKE 2018).

Table 9.2 Relative importance of major sectors of defence production in Germany, 2014

	Direct employment	*Value added*	*Sales*	*Share of direct defence employment in sector*	
Sector	*Share of sector in total (%)*				*In percent of employment in sector*
Aerospace (including space)	24	36	33	Aerospace and space including missiles and UAV	19.0
Vehicles	20	11	19	Vehicles	1.4
Electronics (including electrical)	17	8	14	Electronics (including electrical)	1.3
Naval shipbuilding	14	12	14	Naval Shipbuilding	61.0
Arms and ammunition	12	9	9	n.a.	
Missiles and UAV	7	7	6	n.a.	
Others	6	16	6	Others	0.8
Total	***100***	***100***	***100***	***All industries***	***0.8***

Sources: VDI TZ 2015, p. 16; Statistisches Bundesamt 2018.
Note: n.a. = not available.

Data and definitions

This chapter presents a mixture of official data and estimates coming from a variety of sources, including industry associations, consultants and research institutes. The defence industry is not a category in the national account nor industry statistics. Neither is there an official definitions of its boundaries nor is there official data on value added, turnover or employment.

Estimates from various consultancies and academic researchers (Ostwald and Legler 2015; Schubert and Knippel 2012; VDI TZ 2015; Weingarten et al. 2015) are based on differing definitions, strongly influenced by the availability of data. Those attempting to estimate turnover or employment in the German defence industry have generally relied on combining various types of information, including official procurement and export data, information collected on individual companies as well as official data on industrial production, including input-output tables. Various shapes of a synthetic German defence industry can be composed from the available data. All are problematic because available data have major shortcomings. Official procurement and export data include different types of goods and services in their definitions. Few companies publish information distinguishing production for civilian and military customers. There are no data on arms imports, neither for domestic procurement nor for foreign materials and components used by the German defence industry. Such import data therefore needs to be estimated. There also are no official data on employment. Estimates are either based on collection of information on companies (VDI TZ 2015; Weingarten et al. 2015) or on combining data on the demand with data on labour productivity (VDI TZ 2015, Ostwald and Legler 2015). Because of the data requirements, no long time series are available on details of the German defence industry. While differences among studies are considerable, there is agreement on the rough size of the German defence industry (discussed below (Table 9.1)).

Official data on German defence spending is available in the annual federal government's budget statement (and for recent years also on the website by the German Ministry of Defence). However, as the data are more restrictive than what is internationally agreed (e.g. in the context of NATO) and has fluctuated in respect of what is included and not (certain external deployments of German armed forces have been budgeted in general government accounts), NATO data on defence expenditures are preferable for time series analysis and are used for the data presented in the Table 9.A1 (NATO 2018). For similar reasons, NATO data (NATO 2018) are also used for procurement in the Table 9.A1. German data on procurement contained in the federal budget covers some civilian products in addition to products from the German defence industry and not all purchases of military goods are budgeted as procurement, for instance if they are bought by regional commands rather than through the central federal procurement agency (Bundesamt für Ausrüstung, Informationstechnik und Nutzung der Bundeswehr). Official data on defence research and development (R&D) is available from the German Ministry of Education and Research in its biannual reports on research in Germany as well as on its website (Bundesministerium für Bildung und Forschung, various years).

The German government has published official data on single arms export licences since 1999 (BMWi, various years). The definition of arms exports corresponds to the European Union's definition of military goods. The German government also publishes data on the export of weapons of war, a more narrow category, which has its origin in allied prohibitions on arms production after World War II. As this category is unique for Germany, the broader category of arms exports is preferable for comparison with other countries. It also has a higher degree of correspondence with the definitions of procurement and defence production used in this chapter. However, there are no data on actual arms exports, which may be lower or higher than the value of single licences. Single licences may not actually be used (or not in the year they are authorized) and exports may also be the result of general licences, which authorize the export of arms within the scope of cooperative production projects and are not covered by single licences (Brzoska 2016). For the estimate of German arms exports reported in the Table 9.A1 a correction was made in order to capture the time difference between authorization of licences and actual transfers.

Structure of the German defence industry

The German defence industry is of minor macroeconomic importance. With about 20–25 bn € of sales, 10–12 bn € of value added, about 60–70.000 directly and another 30–50.000 indirectly employed persons it accounts for slightly over one percent of German manufacturing and 0.6% of National Income. Numbers and shares are somewhat higher when sales of security equipment to civilian agencies and private customers are included, whether they come from defence companies or companies which can be considered as part of the German security industry (Table 9.1).

The situation is different, however, for certain regions and specific industries. The regional concentration is high and has increased since the end of the Cold War and the relative importance of sectors, for which arms production is important, such as aerospace and shipbuilding, has grown. Many of the major arms producing companies, however, are diversified, with civilian markets more important than military markets.

Regional structure

Arms production in Germany occurs in both economically highly advanced regions, such as Bavaria, as well as in regions with economic difficulties, such as the federal states of Bremen and Schleswig-Holstein. The largest number of employees works in the area around Munich (VDI TZ estimates 10,800 persons), followed by South-Eastern Baden-Wuerttemberg (VDI TZ estimate: 6000 persons), which includes a concentration of defence companies close to Lake Constance, and Schleswig-Holstein in the North of Germany (VDI TZ estimate: 6000 persons: VDI TZ 2015, pp. 11–13).

As some of these regions are major industrial locations, the regional dependence on arms production differs from what one might expect from the data on employment. The largest shares of defence employment in manufacturing employment can be found, according to the VDI TZ data (p. 13), in Bremen (6.2% of all employment in manufacturing), South Eastern Baden Wuerttemberg (5.9%), Southern Bavaria (3.1%) and Schleswig-Holstein (3.1%). Southern Bavaria and South-Eastern Baden-Wuerttemberg are centers of aerospace and electronics industry, while naval shipbuilding is dominant in Northern Germany. There is very little defence production in Eastern Germany. Shares of defence employment are also comparatively low in the industrial centres of Western and Central Germany.

Economic sectors

Beyond its economic importance for certain regions, defence production is also an important element in certain industrial sectors. Prominent among these are shipbuilding and aerospace and space. In terms of sales, aerospace is the most important branch in German defence production, followed by vehicles, electronics and shipbuilding (see Table 9.2). The ranking is slightly different for value added and employment, with electronics industry, which also includes electrical equipment, having a high share of employment but a rather low share in value added. Major reasons for the differences among sector with respect to the various indicators are, in addition to data problems, differing labour productivities and use of imported materials and components.

There are major differences with respect to the importance of defence production for relevant industrial sectors. Military customers are very important for the German shipbuilding sector, providing in the 2010s more than 50% of sales, followed by aerospace, with military work constituting about one fifth of production activity. In the vehicle industry production for military customers is of comparatively minor importance, even though manufacturing of small and light tanks as well as military-style trucks, is one of the competitive strengths of German defence industry. However, the German automobile industry is very large and arms production small in comparison. In fact, it can be argued that the competitive edge of German producers of tanks and other vehicles largely derives from the large civilian research and development spending and the high engineering quality of the civilian German vehicle industry. While the companies selling vehicles to military customers are generally not the brand names of the German vehicle industry, much of the technology, for instance with respect to engines and moving parts, is shared. In the electrical and electronic goods sector defence production also is of minor importance. This is the weaker sector of German defence industry, and as the data from Table 9.2 indicates, dominated by production requiring fewer skills and thus marked by comparatively low labour productivity.

Looking at the German defence industry from a defence industrial base perspective, Germany is well placed. In general, arms production is marked by a high degree of close integration with civilian production, either within companies, particularly in aerospace and space, or within the industrial sector. This characteristic has not changed much since the beginnings of German defence production post-1945 (Brzoska 1986, Creswell and Kollmer 2013). Only small segments of arms production are separated from relevant civilian production. Defence production in many fields, particularly in shipbuilding and vehicle production, can directly benefit from technological innovations in civilian industry with technology transfer occurring within and between companies. The level of defence research and development (R&D) in Germany (Table 9.A1) is low if compared to other major European arms producers (EDA 2016). It is also not high within the German defence industry, compared with other industries in Germany. Ostwald and Legler conducted, in cooperation with the German industry association Stifterverband der Deutschen Wirtschaft, a survey of the technology intensity of a number of manufacturing sectors. With a share of 7.1% of R&D spending in turnover, the defence and security industry ranks above the vehicle industry (6.4%) but below aerospace (12.1%) and the pharmaceutical industry (12.9%) (Ostwald and Legler 2015, p. 29). Overall the available data indicates that the German defence industry is not exceptional with respect to R&D intensity among German industries (Rammer 2011).

However, because of the close integration of the German defence industry with civilian industry, the data are somewhat misleading. Defence policy decision-makers in government and industry are expecting technology flows from civilian to the defence industry to complement genuine defence research and development. The government therefore has focused the overwhelming majority of defence R&D funding on those aspects of weapon systems which have little innovative potential or are technologically too advanced for civilian markets (Altmann 2000; Heidenkamp 2013).

Major companies and concentration in the defence industry

By far the largest producer of arms in Germany, in terms of turnover and employment, is a multinational company, Airbus, earlier known as EADS (see Table 9.3). It has a diversified production portfolio for military customers ranging from naval electronics to helicopters. Airbus has a high share in German procurement orders and also is a major German arms exporter. Its share in sales of the German defence industry has been around one third in recent years (Table 9.4). Airbus incorporates a great number of production sites in both the North and the South of Germany as a result of earlier mergers and acquisitions of both private and public smaller arms producers.

While considerably smaller in terms of turnover and employment than Airbus, Germany also has additional industrial champions of international reputation. Four of them have been consistently listed among the Global Top100 list produced annually by the Stockholm International Peace Research Institute (SIPRI).

Rheinmetall is a major producer of artillery and large-calibre ammunition both for the German Bundeswehr and foreign military forces. Thyssen-Krupp's Marine Systems divisions is one of the world's leading producers of submarines and is involved in the production of surface vessels. The company also produces small armoured vehicles, such as the PUMA. Krauss Maffei-Wegmann's best known product is the Leopard II main battle tank but the company is also producing smaller armoured vehicles.

Beyond these four companies, others have been among the SIPRI Top 100 in various years, depending on their sales success in domestic and foreign markets (Table 9.3). Some smaller companies also deserve mention because they are important in certain market segments. These include Lürssen, a producer of small naval surface ships as well as the small arms producer Heckler und Koch. These and other companies hold strong competitive positions in smaller market segments of German procurement and are also globally active. In most cases these companies have long histories of international competitiveness. Overall, and considering name changes, there has been rather little change in the listings of major arms producers in Germany between the days of the Cold War and the mid-2010s (cf Table 3 in Brzoska 1983).

Table 9.3 The 10 largest (defence sales) arms producers in Germany, 2015

Company	*Sector*	*Sales in € billion, 2015*	*Share of arms production in total sales*	*Persons employed in arms production*	*Rank in SIPRI Top 100 list, 2015*	*Rank in SIPRI Top 100 list, 2002*
Airbus Group (Germany only)	Aircraft, electronics	6.4	17	15,000	12	14
Rheinmetall	Artillery, ammunition	2.8	50	9,200	30	21
ThyssenKrupp	Warships, armoured vehicles	1.9	4	3,000	47	39
Krauss-Maffei Wegmann	Tanks, armoured vehicles	0.8	95	2,600	88	60
Diehl	Electronics, missiles	0.6	33	3,000		66
ZF Friedrich-shafen	Tank and ship parts	0.8	5	2,000		69
Siemens	Electronics	0.7	1	500		
Rohde und Schwarz	Electronics	0.5	20	1,000		
MDBA (Germany only)	Missiles	0.5	100	1,300		
MTU Aero Systems	Jet engines	0.5	12	1,200		78

Sources: SIPRI 2018, Weingarten et al. 2015; own estimates.

Table 9.4 Concentration rates in German defence industry, 2014

Share in defence in percent	*Sales*	*Employment*
Share of largest company	31	23
Share of top 3 companies	54	41
Share of top 10 companies	76	59

Sources: Table 3, VDI TZ 2015.

The degree of concentration in the German defence industry is fairly similar to that in overall German industry. One often used measure of concentration is the HerfindahlHirschman Index (HHI). It is defined as the sum of the square of the revenue shares (s) of all the suppliers in a market for a year (t), and thus measures the concentration of revenue shares in a market. The HHI ranges between 0 and 10,000, where 10,000 describes a monopoly.

The HHI of the defence industry in Germany is about 1,500, similar to that of the HHI for the average of German manufacturing industry (Monopolkommission 2017, p. 173). A HHI of 1,500 generally is seen as on the border between unproblematic and problematic in terms of competition (Monopokommission 2017, pp. 165–166). Another indicator of concentration in an industry are the shares of the largest companies in total sector activity (Table 9.4). The differences between shares of major companies in sales and employment indicate different degrees of production depth. The larger arms producing companies in Germany tend to farm out larger shares of their orders to smaller companies (and to imports) compared with companies which are not among the largest.

While overall concentration in the German defence industry is not very high, it is a major concern in particular subsectors, such as aerospace and space, with Airbus as the dominant company, and tank production, with Krauss-Maffei Wegmann as by far the largest company. In the past, the German anti-trust authority (Bundeskartellamt) has studied several cases of mergers and acquisitions, coming to different conclusions. In 1988 it stopped the acquisition of the then largest German aerospace company MBB by the automobile company Daimler-Benz because of the dominant position of the new company in various defence markets (Günther 2003). Later the merger went ahead but Daimler-Benz had to shed considerable parts of the company's production portfolio. Also, it permitted the merger between Krauss Maffei Wegmann and Nexter of France. An important factor in its approach is a broader look at relevant markets, with the European, rather than the German, market attaining more importance when analysing any danger to competition.[1]

The general characteristics of close integration of production for civilian production, which has already been mentioned, not only distinguishes most of the major producers in Germany, it is also true for smaller producers. German procurement authorities have been promoting small and medium enterprises for many years (VDI TZ 2015), but success has been limited. In one recent estimate, the share of small and medium enterprises (SME) in final sales of military products to German and other militaries is estimated at slightly over 5%, measured in terms of employment (VDI TZ 2015, p. 11). Another study, looking at the defence and security industry together, estimates a larger share of SMEs, but this may be driven by its broad definition of security industry (Ostwald and Legler, pp. 23–25). The role of SMEs may be larger in the security than the defence industry. In the defence industry, it is typical that final customers predominantly procure from the larger companies, which however are pressured to favour SMEs among potential suppliers. It is well possible that the importance of SMEs is higher than estimated by VDI TZ. For all of German manufacturing, for instance, the share of SMEs is as large as 35% (VDI TZ 2015, p. 11). However, no official data for the involvement of SMEs as suppliers to sellers of military goods is available and estimates are difficult. Few SMEs can or want to rely on military business and most are highly diversified. As a result, it is very difficult, and highly dependent on definitions, to estimate the number of smaller companies involved in defence production in Germany.

Conduct

Industry government relations and key technological capabilities

The German defence industry is heavily dependent on government policy with respect to ownership, export and procurement policies, all of which are contested in several respect (Heidenkamp 2016; Heidenkamp et al. 2013). While the position of most representatives of German defence industry is clear on exports – government policy is seen as overly restrictive- there are differing views on the appropriateness of procurement policies, in particular with respect to a German versus a European perspective.

The German government is committed to support the development of a European defence industry (BMWi 2015). It has supported various initiatives to harmonize demand and increase competitiveness at the European level (Moelling 2015). However, it has also stated, for instance in its 2015 Strategy Paper on the Defence Industry (BMWi 2015), that it is the task of industry to foster integration on the supply side. Furthermore, the government has stated its intention to maintain national key technological capabilities.

The definition of key technological capacities in the 2015 Strategy Paper (which the government elected in 2017 continues to see as the main document on defence industrial policy according to the Coalition Treaty of the ruling parties) is rather vague (BMWi 2015, p. 4). It distinguishes between basic military capabilities on the one hand and domains (land, sea, air, cyber) on the other. Only a few concrete technologies are named: crypto technology, sensors, protection technologies, but also technologies relevant for tanks and submarines.

The definition of key technologies was heavily contested, prior to the formulation of the 2015 Strategy paper, between the ministries in charge of procurement (the Ministry of Defence) and arms export policies (Ministry of Economics). The Ministry of Defence had initiated a major procurement reform effort in 2013 (Heidenkamp 2016, Linnenkamp and Mölling 2014). As an aspect of that reform, it wanted to reduce its responsibility for protecting German defence capacities. It therefore argued for a minimal definition of national key capabilities. The Ministry of Economics, led by a social democratic minister, on the other hand, was concerned about potential job losses in the defence industry on the one hand, and pressure to liberalize arms export policies. It argued for a broad definition of national key technologies whose protection would be the responsibility of the Ministry of Defence through its procurement policy.

There are also different views in the German defence industry on this issue, which could not be resolved in several rounds of talks and negotiations between government and industry representatives. In general, companies, such as Airbus, which see their prospects in more open competition on the European (or even transatlantic) stand against those who fear to lose from a less protective German procurement policy.

Ownership issues

Following a privatisation drive in the 1970s and 1980s, German defence industry has been almost fully in private hands since the early 1990s. A major exception is a minority participation of German public authorities in Airbus. However, the government has considerable influence on the strategic management decisions of major companies.

An important legal instrument is the Foreign Trade Act (Aussenwirtschaftsgesetz §4) which requires foreign companies to register their interest when they intend to attain more than 25% of a defence company (the same requirement exists for companies operating critical infrastructure) with the German government. The Ministry of Economics and Technology than has a maximum of three months to study and, if it so decides, stop the merger or acquisition. While cases of the application of the regulation are rare, the provision also acts as a deterrent. A case in point was the planned merger of BAE Systems and EADS (now Airbus). The German government made it clear to the companies in 2012 that it was opposed to the plan and it was shelved by the companies.

Arms export policy

German arms export policy is shaped by a number of, partially contradictory interests and considerations. A major aspect is the support of, and integration into, NATO and the EU. The governments arms export guidelines sharply distinguish between exports to NATO- and EU member states (and a few states, such as Switzerland and Australia, who are considered to be on equal footing) and "third states". While restrictions for NATO- and EU-member states are to be exceptional, for instance in cases of major human rights violations, exports to "third states" officially need specific justifications in terms of German security and foreign policy interests. Economic interests cannot justify arms exports to third states. Major human rights violations, as well as serious concerns about the appropriateness of the international behaviour of states and the economic capacity to sustain arms imports are reasons for the governments to deny export licences (BMWi 2018).

The official political guidelines for arms exports, last changed in 2019, are, at least for "third states" more restrictive than the EU's Common Position on

Arms Exports controls of 2008. However, there are major questions about the actual implementation of the official policy, for instance with respect to the importance of economic aspects of arms exports (Brzoska 2017; GKKE 2018). In practice, different sectors of the defence industry, as well as different regions of the world, are treated differently. There are, for instance, few records of denials of the export of warships (e.g. to Taiwan in the early 2000s) while battle tanks have only been exported to few countries. Compared to other major European arms suppliers, Germany has been a reluctant supplier to Middle East countries, with the exception of Israel, which has been treated, in practice, similar to a NATO-member state. A case in point was the decision by the incoming government in 2018 to ban exports to Saudi Arabia because of the country's involvement in the war in Yemen, but to exempt the delivery of patrol craft ordered by Saudi Arabia.

One explanation for German export policy is the importance of public opinion. Arms exports are not popular, judging by public opinion surveys (Brzoska 1986, 2017). This may be shaped by German history and a broader sceptical mood about the consequences of strengthening the military in many parts of the world. The importance of public moods makes German arms export policy volatile. Arms export scandals and changes in government regularly lead to political debates about changes in policy, with the left-wing and green parties demanding more restrictiveness and the conservative and liberal parties arguing for maintaining the status-quo. As the level of German arms exports over the years (Table 9.A1) indicates, however, exports have been driven more by changes in demand and long-term supply relationships with customers than by changes in governments.

Procurement policies and European integration

Most major procurement projects are organized in closed bidding procedures with invitations to bid extended to a small number of select companies. Generally these include, in addition to German companies, major suppliers from foreign countries, including the US. Still, the majority of orders goes to German contractors and, in the field of aerospace and space, Airbus subsidiaries (Table 9.5).

The German defence industry exhibits the general patterns of defence industrial integration in Europe. Most of the major products produced in the aerospace industry are co-produced with other European companies. Most of these projects are led, or fully conducted, by Airbus, which as an international company is in a strong position to pursue such projects. In shipbuilding and vehicle production, however, national projects dominate. It remains to be seen whether this will change in the near future, for instance following the agreement in 2015 between Krauss Maffei Wegmann, the largest German tank producer, with French Nexter to coordinate production in the KNDS Holding, and the purchase of various smaller German naval yards as well as the French CMN naval yard by the Privinvest Group from Abu Dhabi (see Chapter 7).

Table 9.5 Major German procurement projects

Program	*Weapon type*	*Main German contractor*	*Program cost (billion €)*	*Start date*	*Contractor states*	*Cost overrun by early 2018, in percent*	*Time Overrun by early 2018 in months*
EUROFIGHTER/ TYPHOON with AESA Radar	Fighter aircraft	Airbus Defence and Space	17.6	1988	UK/G/ I/S	38	149
TIGER	Attack helicopter	Airbus Helicopters	4.2	1995	F/G/S	22	80
NH90 TTH	Transport helicopter	Airbus Helicopters	3.9	2000	F/G/I/ NL	6	134
Schützenpanzer PUMA	Armoured vehicle	Kraus Maffei Wegmann/ Rheinmetall	3.2	2002	G only	38	57
A400M with DIRCM	Transport aircraft	Airbus Defence and Space	9.3	2003	UK/G/ F/S	16	139
CH-53 modernization	Transport helicopter	Airbus Helicopters	0.6	2007	G only	16	45
Class F125	Frigate	Thyssen Krupp Marine Systems/ Lürssen	2.2	2009	G only	41	45
P-3C Orion Modernization	Reconnaissance aircraft	Lockheed	0.5	2015	USA	25	11
NH90 NTH (SEA LION)	Naval helicopter	Airbus Helicopters	1.2	2015	F/G/I/ NL	3	0
TanDEM-X	Radar satellite	Astrium (Airbus)	0.5	2015	G only	-24	-12
Mobile Taktische Kommunikation (MoTaKo)	Tactical communication system	Rohde und Schwarz	0.3	2017	G only	18	0
Class K130 (Batch 2)	Corvette	Lürssen/Tyssen Krupp Marine Systems/German Naval Yards	1.5	2017	G only	0	0

Source: BMVG 2018; author's archive.
Notes: Sorted by program start date (date of authorization of phase of program current in 2018 by German Bundestag), prices in current €
Country codes: France (F), Germany (G). Italy (I), Spain (S), Netherlands (NL), United Kingdom (UK)

The general preference for German companies, at least outside the aerospace sector, has for a long time been criticized as cause of substantial cost and time overruns in many procurement projects (Table 9.5). These are substantial for most of the major projects. Several reforms have been initiated, often in the context of efforts to Europeanize procurement (Heidenkamp 2016). The latest round of procurement reforms, initiated in 2013, however, primarily aims to streamline procedures and increase management control by the federal procurement agency (BMVG 2018).

Performance

Competitiveness by sector

In defence, Germany is a niche producer with enough buying power to have stakes in an almost the complete range of military technology. German defence industry continued to be particularly strong in the production of submarines and surface warships, as well as armoured vehicles and tanks. Strong positions also exist in smaller niches, such as small arms and certain types of artillery.

The specialization of German defence industry is somewhat obscured in statistics of the relative size of sectors (Table 9.2) because of the preference for domestic companies in procurement decisions. It comes out more clearly in the data on arms exports (Table 9.6): Particularly revealing is the comparison of data on production and exports (Table 9.2 with Table 9.6).

It shows that aerospace has a much lower share in exports than in production. As much of production and export is via Airbus, the comparison of the

Table 9.6 German arms exports, shares of major sectors (%)

	Military goods categories	*2001–2005*	*2006–2010*	*2011–2015*	*2016–2017*
Aerospace and space	10	5,2	6,4	9,8	10,3
Vehicles	6	30,3	27,2	31,4	24,5
Electronics	5,11,14,15,20,21	16,0	17,0	18,9	12,6
Naval shipbuilding	9	16,4	18,0	9,2	20,7
Arms and ammunition	1–3,12	13,8	13,6	13,9	14,4
Missiles	4	5,1	5,5	6,7	7,2
Other	7,8,13,16–15,22,23	13,1	12,3	10,2	10,3
Total	**In billion €**	**19,8**	**22,4**	**27,8**	**13,0**

Source: BMWI, various years.
Note: Military goods categories of German arms export reports.

two data sources needs to be understood with the intricacies of intra-company trade in mind, which may not be fully reflected in the statistics. Still the difference is striking. It supports the contention, that German defence aerospace industry in general has not been very competitive on an international scale. The export sales are increasing, suggesting growing competitiveness, but remain small compared to what one would expect from the size of production in Germany.

For vehicles, and to a lesser extent naval shipbuilding the sectoral shares in exports (Table 9.6) are substantially larger than those for value added, sales and employment in production (Table 9.2). This confirms that German companies are particularly strong in these two sectors. Export shares are also higher for arms and ammunition, while for electronics shares in export and production are about the same.

Profitability

Rather little is known about the profitability of German arms producing companies. This is partly due to their ownership structures – a good number, such as Kraus-Maffei Wegmann and Rohde und Schwarz, are family owned with limited publicity requirement. Companies active in both civilian and military markets also rarely publish detailed information on profits from defence sales.

Most contracts with the German procurement authority are cost-plus, guaranteeing either a fixed amount or fixed percentage above production costs. Profit margins vary and are negotiated between companies and the procurement authority. Efforts to move towards fixed-price contracts, which have been repeatedly promoted within the government and by outside actors, such as the Federal Audit Office (Bundesrechnungshof), received a severe blow from the Airbus-led A-400M program (Wörner 2013, S. 39–38; Heidenkamp 2016). The company realised in the late 2000s that it could not produce the aircraft for the amount agreed between the company and the governments involved in the program. Airbus threated to withdraw from the program unless the government agreed to a higher price tag. After intense negotiations the company and governments agreed on a compromise, which, however, according to the company, substantially reduced the overall profitability of Airbus.[2]

Future prospects

The newly elected German government, under heavy pressure from NATO allies and particularly the US, decided in 2018 to increase defence spending from the current level of about 1.3% to 1.5% of national income by 2022. However, the defence ministry in September 2018 presented a modernization plan for the German armed forces up to 2031, which will require additional funding to be realized. Procurement spending may well increase substantially in the next decade, which, in theory, brightens the prospects for German defence companies.

However, there are also some question marks concerning the prospects for the German defence industry. Much will depend on the future of efforts to Europeanize (or even transnationalize within NATO) defence markets. If plans in this direction, which are officially supported by the German government, succeed, this may well benefit only some sectors of German defence industry, such as shipbuilding and vehicles, but lead to losses of production sites and employment in other sectors, such as aerospace and electronics. But even without more open markets in Europe, German defence industry may not reap much benefits from higher procurement spending because of increases in imports from other countries, particularly the US.

The future of the German defence industry is also highly dependent on political decision for export markets, which have become equally important for the industry as domestic procurement (Table 9.A1). Arms exports remain a highly politized topic in Germany, and major changes, both in the direction of more control and a more liberal attitude, are possible.

In view of these uncertainties, major German arms producers continue to be cautious in assessments of their future prospects. The two largest producers, Airbus and Rheinmetall, have announced their intentions to strengthen their civilian sales in order to reduce dependence on volatile arms markets. Even Thyssen Krupp, which holds a strong order book for submarines, is looking for a buyer for most of its defence assets.

Still, the most likely course is continuity, both with respect to government policies and company behaviour, and thus the structure and conduct of the German defence industry. The political framework for arms production in Germany, which is so important for the industry, is shaped by competing interests – national versus European (or transatlantic), economic versus moral, efficient versus preserving – which look fairly constant in the near future.

Notes

1 Bundeskartellamt. 2015. Bundeskartellamt clears merger of French and German tank manufacturers. www.bundeskartellamt.de/SharedDocs/Meldung/DE/Pressemitteilungen/2015/24_08_15_Panzer.html

2 www.produktion.de/nachrichten/unternehmen-maerkte/airbus-debakel-mit-a400m-schmaelert-gewinn-erheblich-127.html

References

Albrecht, U., P. Lock and H. Wulf (1978) *Arbeitsplätze durch Rüstung?* Reinbek: Rowohlt.

Altmann, J. ed. (2000) *Dual-use in der Hochtechnologie – Erfahrungen, Strategien und Perspektiven in Telekommunikation und Luftfahrt.* Baden-Baden: Nomos.

BMVG (Bundesministerium für Verteidigung). Rüstungsbericht März 2018. Berlin, www.bmvg.de/de/aktuelles/ruestungsbericht-maerz-2018-substanzielle-schritte-nach-vorn-22992.

BMWi (Bundesministerium für Wirtschaft und Technologie) (2015) *Strategiepapier der Bundesregierung zur Stärkung der Verteidigungsindustrie in Deutschland.* Berlin, 8 July 2015, www.bmwi.de/Redaktion/DE/Downloads/S-T/sicherheit-verteidigungsstrategie-strategiepapier-vertindustrie.pdf?__blob=publicationFile&v=4.

BMWi (Bundesministerium für Wirtschaft und Technologie) (2016) *Strategiepapier der Bundesregierung zur Stärkung der zivilen Sicherheitsindustrie in Deutschland.*Berlin, 21 December 2016, www.bmwi.de/Redaktion/DE/Downloads/S-T/sicherheit-verteidigungsstrategie-strategiepapier-zivsicherheit.pdf?__blob=publicationFile&v=6.

Brzoska, M. (1983) Federal Republic of Germany. In *The Structure of the Defence Industry. An International Survey*, edited by N. Ball and M. Leitenberg. London: Palgrave Macmillan.

Brzoska, M. (1986) *Rüstungsexportpolitik*. Frankfurt: Haag und Herchen.

Brzoska, M. (2016) Rüstungsherstellung und Rüstungsexport: Gebote, Verbote und Paradoxien. In *Handbuch Friedensethik*, edited by Ines-Jacqueline Werkner and Klaus Ebeling. Wiesbaden: Springer VS 2016.

Brzoska, M. (2017) Rüstungsherstellung und Rüstungsexport: Gebote, Verbote und Paradoxien. In *Handbuch Friedensethik*, edited by I. Werkner and K. Ebeling. Wiesbaden: Springer VS.

Creswell M. H. and D. H. Kollmer (2013) Power, Preferences, or Ideas? Explaining West Germany's Armaments Strategy, 1955–1972. *Journal of Cold War Studies* 15: 55–103.

Diedrich, T. (2015) Zwischen Anspruch und Möglichkeit. Die Rüstungsindustrie der DDR. In *Militärisch-Industrieller Komplex? Rüstung in Europa und Nordamerika nach dem Zweiten Weltkrieg*, edited by D. H. Kollmer. Freiburg: Rombach.

GKKE (Gemeinsame Konferenz der Kirchen für Entwicklungspolitik) (2018) *Rüstungsexportbericht 2017*. Bonn. www3.gkke.org/78.html.

Günther, M. (2003) *Das Prognoseproblem in der Fusionskontrolle: Eine theoretische und empirische Analyse am Beispiel des Falles „Daimler-Benz/MBB"*. Dissertation Technische Universität Dortmund https://eldorado.tu-dortmund.de/bitstream/2003/2897/1/MelanieGuentherunt.pdf.

Heidenkamp, H. (2016) *Deutsche Rüstungspolitik: Ein Politikfeld unter Handlungsdruck.* Opladen: Barbara Budrich.

Heidenkamp, H., J. Louth and T. Taylor (2013) *The Defence Industrial Triptych: Government as a Customer, Sponsor and Regulator.* London: RUSI.

Krause, J. (2018) Deutschlands Rolle im internationalen Handel mit konventionellen Waffen und Rüstungsgütern: Sind wir die „Waffenkammer der Welt"? *Sirius* 2: 137–157.

Linnenkamp, H. and C. Mölling (2014) *Rüstung und Kernfähigkeiten. Alternativen deutscher Rüstungspolitik*. Berlin: Stiftung Wissenschaft und Politik. www.swp-berlin.org/fileadmin/contents/products/aktuell/2014A45_lnk_mlg.pdf

Moelling, C. (2015) *Der europäische Rüstungssektor. Zwischen nationaler Politik und industrieller Globalisierung*. Berlin: Stiftung Wissenschaft und Politik. www.swp-berlin.org/publikation/der-europaeische-ruestungssektor/

Monopolkommission (2017) *Stand und Entwicklung der Unternehmenskonzentration in Deutschland*. Berlin: Monopolkommission. http://monopolkommission.de/images/HG22/HGXXII_Kap2_Unternehmenskonzentration.pdf

NATO (2018). Defence Expenditure of NATO Countries (2011–2018). NATO, Brussels, www.nato.int/cps/en/natohq/news_156770.htm

Ostwald, D. A. and B. Legler (2015) *Der ökonomische Fussabdruck der deutschen Sicherheits- und Verteidigungsindustrie.* Berlin: Bundesverband der deutschen Sicherheits- und Verteidigungsindustrie. www.bdsv.eu/files/downloads/publikationen/2015-11-BDSV_WifOR-Studie.pdf

Rammer, C. (2011) *Bedeutung von Spitzentechnologien, FuE-Intensität und nicht forschungsintensiven Industrien fuer Innovationen und Innovationsförderung in Deutschland.* Mannheim: Zentrum für Europäische Wirtschaftsforschung.

Schubert, S. and J. Knippel (2012) *Quantifizierung der volkswirtschaftlichen Bedeutung der Sicherheits- und Verteidigungsindustrie für den deutschen Wirtschaftsstandort.* Berlin: Bundesverbands der Sicherheits- und Verteidigungsindustrie e.V., Berlin.

VDI TZ (VDI Technologiezentrum) (2015) *Analyse der strukturellen Lage der Verteidigungsindustrie in Deutschland.* Düsseldorf: Bundesministeriums für Wirtschaft und Energie. www.bmwi.de/Redaktion/DE/Downloads/S-T/sicherheit-verteidigungsstrategie-studie.pdf?__blob=publicationFile&v=4

Weingarten, J., P. Wilke and H. Wulf (2015) *Perspektiven der wehrtechnischen Industrie in Deutschland.* Frankfurt: Hans Böckler Stiftung.

Wörner, J. (2013) *Ökonomische Aspekte der Rüstungspolitik in Europa.* Dissertation Helmut-Schmidt-Universität, Universität der Bundeswehr Hamburg http://edoc.sub.uni-hamburg.de/hsu/volltexte/2013/3025/pdf/2013_Worner.pdf.

Data sources

Defence expenditures and procurement: NATO Defence Expenditures, www.nato.int/cps/en/natohq/topics_49198.htm

Defence research and development: Bundesministerium für Forschung (und Bildung), Bundesbericht Forschung und Entwicklung 1990-2018, Datenband (biannual), www.datenportal.bmbf.de/portal/de/tabthemes.html

Arms exports: Bundestagsdrucksachen 10/2858, 10/2174, 11/4587, 11/2120, 12/3884, 12/4794, 13/569018/00439, BMWI (annual since 1999). *Rüstungsexportbericht.* Berlin, www.bmwi.de/Redaktion/DE/Dossier/ruestungsexportkontrolle.html

Data on major arms producers: SIPRI (Stockholm International Peace Research Institute). SIPRI Arms Industry Database, www.sipri.org/databases/armsindustry

Industry data: Statistisches Bundesamt. Industrie, Verarbeitendes Gewerbe, www.destatis.de/DE/ZahlenFakten/Wirtschaftsbereiche/IndustrieVerarbeitendesGewerbe/IndustrieVerarbeitendesGewerbe.html

Table 9.A1 Basic data for German defence industry, 1980–2017 (in billion €, constant prices of 2016)

Year	Defence expenditures	Procurement expenditures	R&D expenditures	Value of arms export licences	Estimate of arms export	Estimate of imports	Estimate of value added	Estimate of total sales	Share exports in sales
	in billion €, constant prices of 2016								
1980	50,9	7,5	3,3	1,8	1,8	2,3	10,3	19,7	14%
1981	51,5	8,9	3,3	2,9	2,3	2,9	11,6	22,8	16%
1982	50,9	8,9	3,4	2,3	2,6	2,8	12,0	23,5	17%
1983	51,3	8,9	3,6	6,4	4,4	3,8	13,0	26,3	26%
1984	50,8	8,4	3,4	5,8	6,1	3,5	14,3	28,8	34%
1985	50,9	7,5	3,0	5,6	5,7	3,3	13,0	26,2	35%
1986	52,3	8,3	3,1	5,6	5,6	3,5	13,6	27,5	33%
1987	53,2	9,1	2,6	5,5	5,6	3,6	13,7	28,3	32%
1988	52,8	10,2	2,7	6,0	5,7	4,0	14,6	30,5	31%
1989	52,6	10,0	2,7	5,0	5,5	3,7	14,5	30,0	30%
1990	55,4	9,8	2,9	4,3	4,6	3,5	13,8	28,3	27%
1991	51,3	8,0	2,6	6,5	5,4	3,6	12,4	25,8	34%
1992	48,8	6,5	2,3	3,9	5,2	2,6	11,4	23,1	37%
1993	43,9	4,9	1,9	3,8	3,9	2,2	8,5	17,3	36%
1994	40,9	4,5	1,8	3,2	3,5	1,9	7,9	15,8	36%
1995	40,2	4,6	2,1	2,7	3,0	1,8	7,8	15,3	31%
1996	39,5	4,4	2,2	3,0	2,8	1,8	7,5	14,8	30%
1997	38,0	4,1	1,9	2,7	2,8	1,7	7,2	14,1	32%

(*Continued*)

Table 9.A1 (Cont.)

Year	Defence expenditures	Procurement expenditures	R&D expenditures	Value of arms export licences	Estimate of arms export	Estimate of imports	Estimate of value added	Estimate of total sales	Share exports in sales
	in billion €, constant prices of 2016								
1998	38,1	4,8	1,7	3,8	3,2	2,2	7,7	15,8	33%
1999	38,9	5,1	1,8	3,8	3,8	2,2	8,5	17,4	36%
2000	38,3	5,2	1,7	3,6	3,7	2,2	8,4	17,2	35%
2001	37,7	5,3	1,4	4,5	4,1	2,5	8,3	17,6	38%
2002	37,8	5,3	1,2	3,9	4,2	2,3	8,5	18,1	39%
2003	37,3	5,1	1,3	5,8	4,9	2,7	8,6	18,6	43%
2004	36,1	5,3	1,2	4,5	5,2	2,5	9,3	19,8	44%
2005	35,6	5,0	1,4	4,9	4,7	2,5	8,7	18,4	42%
2006	34,7	5,2	1,4	4,8	4,8	2,5	9,0	19,0	42%
2007	34,8	5,1	1,5	4,1	4,4	2,3	8,7	18,2	40%
2008	35,8	6,1	1,5	6,3	5,2	3,1	9,7	21,1	41%
2009	37,1	6,5	1,4	5,5	5,9	3,0	10,8	23,2	43%
2010	37,5	6,6	1,4	5,1	5,3	2,9	10,4	22,3	40%
2011	36,4	6,0	1,2	5,7	5,4	2,9	9,7	21,0	43%
2012	37,3	6,1	1,1	4,9	5,3	2,7	9,8	21,2	42%
2013	35,2	4,5	1,3	5,9	5,4	2,6	8,6	18,5	48%
2014	35,0	4,5	1,1	4,0	5,0	2,1	8,5	18,0	47%
2015	36,1	4,3	1,1	7,9	5,9	3,1	8,3	18,5	52%
2016	37,6	4,6	1,1	6,8	7,4	2,9	10,2	22,1	57%
2017	38,9	5,3	1,1	6,1	6,5	2,9	10,1	22,0	50%

Sources and methods: Defence expenditures: NATO, various years Procurement expenditures: NATO, various years R&D expenditures: Bundesministerium für (Bildung und) Forschung, various years Value of arms export licences: Brzoska 1986; Bundestagsdrucksachen 10/2858, 10/2174, 11/4587, 11/2120, 12/3884, 12/4794, 13/569018/00439, BMWI (annual since 1999) Estimate of arms export: Estimated as 50% of licences of current year plus 50% of licences of past year Estimate of imports: estimated at 25% of procurement expenditures and arms exports Estimate of value added: Procurement expenditure plus R&D expenditures plus estimate of arms exports minus estimate of arms imports Estimate of total sales: Doubled procurement and R&D expenditures plus estimate of arms exports minus estimate of arms imports

10 The Spanish defence industry

A long way to go

Antonio Fonfría and Carlos Martí Sempere

Introduction

The objective of this chapter is to analyze the evolution and characteristics of the Spanish defence industry taking into consideration the European context. In this context, the traditional protectionism that countries have maintained in relation to their defense industries seems to be coming to an end. The changing situation in which the sector lives makes it necessary to take decisions that will shape its future and will imply significant modifications in the behaviour of market agents.

The Spanish industry is a middle-size and intermediate-technology sector within European industries. This position is the result of an historical evolution that yields as main output a weak budget and a less than coherent industrial and defense policy. To what extent is this situation a handicap for the industry? To answer this question, both the structure, the behaviour and the aggregate results of the industry need to be analyzed with a long-term perspective. In such analysis, the two most important considerations are related to the new role of EU policies and the foreseeable future that this context will bring to the industry.

The chapter begins by briefly reviewing the history of the Spanish defense industry. Then it considers the basic features of its structure, behavior and performance. Thirdly, some changes that the new European scenario can generate for Spanish industry will be analyzed. The chapter ends with a few conclusions.

A short history

The Spanish defence industry cannot be understood without considering the delayed industrialization and relative backwardness of this economic sector in the 19th and 20th centuries when compared with other EU countries (Carreras and Tafunell, 2010; Trebilcock, 1981). Indeed, the Spanish civil war (1936–1939) showed not very technical armies, whose most advanced weapons were provided by foreign countries (Germany, Italy or the Soviet Union). Furthermore, at the end of the war, due in part to the economic blockade, the official industrial policy was autarky. That policy has had a strong impact on how this sector has evolved.

It is not possible to date the birth of the Spanish defence industry accurately. Since it is constituted by a heterogeneous group of companies belonging to very diverse industrial sectors, it is not feasible to state its moment of origin. However, its formation can be linked to specific companies mainly in the aeronautical, naval, armament, engineering and, later, communications sectors.

In 1923 CASA-Construcciones Aeronáuticas SA was born – the aircraft construction company that was the Spanish flag carrier until 1999. Its growth was marked by very different stages that led it to be a public company, integrated in the National Institute of Industry (INI) in 1971, to a private firm belonging to an international group formed by the German DASA and the French, Aerospatiale-Matra, namely the EADS Group (later Airbus: see Chapter 7). EADS gave the opportunity to create a counterpower to the American hegemony coming from the mergers that took place in the early 1990s in that country (Salas, 1987).

Initially the construction of aircraft was carried out under licenses from other countries such as Germany and Italy, but the production of their own models followed soon. This is the case of the C-207 Azor in the civilian sphere. In the military domain the F-5, combat aircraft began production in 1965 in collaboration with the US Northrop company.[1] The purchase of Mirage III aircraft meant the participation of CASA in its production through an offset agreement signed with the Spanish government. The process was more ambitiously repeated in 1982, with the purchase of the F-18 from the United States.

More recently the famous C-235 and C-295 models were built and exported to a number of countries with great success. Currently one of the star models is the Eurofighter Typhoon which has been developed through an international consortium formed by the United Kingdom, Germany, Italy and Spain.

In the development of the Spanish aeronautical sector, more companies are involved, highlighting the current ITP (*Industria de Turbo Propulsores)*, nowadays owned by Rolls Royce, whose specialization in motors has boosted the sector notably and whose birth dates back to 1989. Finally, there is IINTA (*Aerospace Technology Institute Esteban Terradas)*, a research center founded in 1942 in the field of aeronautics and space owned by the Ministry of Defence.

The naval sector is the second most important segment of this industry. Obviously, its origin is much earlier, but in terms of modernity, its birth could be dated to 1947 when the National Company *Bazán de Construcciones Navales Militares* was created, also under the umbrella of INI based on the former Royal Navy shipyards. During the 1950s and part of the 1960s, its main role was the modernization of warships, many of them from the USA based on the agreement signed with that country in 1953. In the1970s and until the mid-1980s, domestic production expanded, both in relation to surface vessels, basically frigates and submarines (class S-60 – Dolphin – and class 70 – Galerna – with the support of the French DCN).

Special mention must be made of the Prince of Asturias aircraft carrier, based on a North American design, which allowed Bazán to rise in the list of companies capable of building an aircraft carrier, even exporting one to Thailand some years later.

From mid-1980s, along with the industrial reform that characterized the following decade, Bazán suffered a major crisis, due to the problems generated by the fall of orders. This situation demanded measures to boost the sector, both in terms of employment and economic importance in locations like Cádiz, Cartagena and Ferrol, for solving the labour demands of both workers and inhabitants of those zones. As a result, in the second half of the 1990s, it merged with AESA, creating the company Izar. However, shortly afterwards, it was transformed into Navantia, a name that still stands.

Currently, Navantia builds frigates of class F-100 (F-110 under development), aircraft carriers (LHD) and submarines (S 80) which make it a key player in European shipbuilding and an important exporter of surface ships. In addition, it has generated an important industrial complex around it, not only auxiliary companies and suppliers, but smaller competitors that focus on the construction of patrol boats or inflatable boats. However, its size, ownership structure and low profitability seem to be an important burden for its future in the European context.

For the land systems sector, its heterogeneity is the most outstanding characteristic, since it includes the manufacture of vehicles, light and heavy armament, tanks, etc. However, as in the previous cases, it is worth mentioning the core companies of the sector, the *Santa Bárbara National Company*. Although its creation dates from 1959, an important productive activity of armament linked to the Army was already in place. These activities were absorbed by Santa Bárbara and in the 1970s it began to manufacture tanks, such as the AMX-30 with the technical support of France. However, the continuous losses meant that the government in 2001 privatized and later sold the firm to the American company General Dynamics. Its production has focused ultimately on the manufacture of components for the M1 Abrams tank of the USA, the armoured vehicle Pizarro (developed with the Austrian Steyr company) and the Leopard 2E, an indigenous version of the German Leopard.[2]

Other companies and centers not less relevant are the famous CETME (*Center of Technical Studies for Special Materials)* which developed the rifle used by the Spanish Armed Forces. ENASA (National Company of Trucks) better known as Pegaso, developed the BMR vehicles among others with French assistance, being actually a division of the Italian IVECO.

More recently, an increasing number of companies whose developments are more generic have entered the sector due to the evolving needs of Armed Forces based on the development of new technologies. It is particularly the case of the spatial environment, with the use of satellites (both of communications and surveillance), and the increasingly important area of information and communication technologies including cyberspace, which more and more permeates the rest of the areas of traditional equipment. In this area, the firm Indra, which was the result of the merger of INISEL and Ceselsa, can be considered the main supplier.

The arrival of democracy to Spain and its integration in the European Union was accompanied with a promotion of the industry aimed at achieving a qualitative leap into the sophisticated champions league of defence firms. It triggered the involment of the industry in international projects such as the International European Porgramme Group (IEPG) or the Eurofighter. However, the end of the Cold War left the industry in dire conditions due to the reduction of orders and the appearance of new competitors such as Brazil or South Korea in the export market. These problems recurred with the economic crisis of 2008.

In short, the defence industry has played a role in the modernization of the Spanish industry through the absorption, adaptation and generation of new technologies, which, although they were of military origin, nowadays are applicable to the civilian sector such as electronics, aerospace, software or telecommunications.[3] It has also to be said that the quality requirements of defence goods has promoted innovation in subcontractors and the need for highly qualified human capital, capable of being at the frontier of knowledge in many fields, has generated also spillovers in the economy.

Market structure

The structure of the Spanish defence industry is similar to that observed in other EU countries, namely, a single buyer,[4] a few large main contractors, some smaller size first tier providers and a large number of SMEs which supply, often through the value stream of the main contractor, very specialised components and services. According to DGAM (2017), there are 578 firms registered in the Spanish MoD, from which 407 sold products and services in 2016. 247 of them sold their product indirectly through supply chains.[5] The industry is geographically concentrated around Madrid (60%) and the Sevilla-Cadiz axis (around 20%).

Information about the size of the market is shown in Table 10.1. In comparative terms, and according to the "*Asociación Española de Empresas Tecnológicas de Defensa, Aeronáutica y Espacio (TEDAE)*" and the "*Aerospace and Defence Industries Association of Europe (ASD)*" data, the Spanish industry represents only 4.80% of European defence sales and 4.84% of the labour force, resulting in a defence sector relatively small compared with the whole EU and its more advanced countries of the UK, France, Germany or Italy.

Nowadays, there are four main contractors that supply each kind of capital goods used for missions by armed forces. The former *Construcciones Aeronáuticas, S.A.*, now renamed EADS-CASA is a division of the Airbus conglomerate and mainly supplies aerospace equipment. Other firms in this market

Table 10.1 Spanish defence industry's profile

Main indicators	2007	2011	2016	Average year variation rate 2007/16 (%)
Total turnover (mill.€)	124,335	71,166	57,257	-8.3
Defence turnover over total (%)	8.7	8.0	10.3	1.9
Total employment	41,000	21,600	18,840	-8.3
Defence employment over total (%)	8.4	10.9	11.0	3.0
Defence exports (mill. €)	1,160	4,057	4,933	17.4
Defence exports over total defence turnover (%)	41.2	68.3	83.3	8.1

Source: Author's estimate based on General Directorate of Armament and Material. Spanish Ministry of Defence.
Note: Constant prices 2016.

segment are Sener, ITP, Aernnova, Eurocopter España (a subsidiary of Eurocopter) and GMV (e.g. aerospace). Navantia supplies all kind of ships like aircraft carriers, frigates, corvettes, logistic ships and submarines. Rodman Polyships builds patrol boats and other small ships. GDELS Santa Barbara, owned by the U.S. General Dynamics conglomerate, supplies land vehicles, artillery pieces, guns and ammunition. Other firms working in the sector are UROVESA, Servicios y Proyectos Avanzados (SPA), EINSA, Santana Motor, Langa Industrial, EXPAL and SAPA Plasencia. Indra supplies mainly electronic and information and communication systems such as radars, sensors and Command and Control systems. Other important firms in this sector are Amper (since 2014 a subsidiary of Thales Group), Tecnobit, Page, SAES and Astrium CRISA.

The small number of main contractors is due to the high price of equipment and the limited budget of the Ministry of Defence for acquisitions. It means that only a single contractor is feasible due to the small number of units required and the fact that more than one provider will be much more expensive due to reduced scale economies.

Indra and EADS-CASA also operate in the civilian market since their products are more dual-use, whilst Navantia and Santa Barbara play a limited role in this market because their civilian markets are more limited.[6] The four firms operate in the international market because their output cannot be fully absorbed by internal demand, and because their R&D expenditures can only be properly amortized through sales in that market.[7] In 2016 exports represented 83% of defence output according to DGAM (2017). EADS CASA aircraft are sold throughout the world as well as Navantia ships and Indra electronic equipment. Yet, these firms do not have large overseas subsidiaries, having only small sales and representation offices in foreign countries where they perceive chances of selling their goods and services. These offices are located in many countries of South America. Subsidiaries are only built when *joint ventures* are required under offset contracts, where part of the production will be made domestically in the purchasing country. The purchase of PZL Warszawa-Okęcie by EADS CASA in 2001 is probably a special case, justified because they produce very similar airplanes and share a similar market niche.

Whereas these four companies share around 75%[8] of the Spanish defence market, their size is considerably inferior to the size of the largest EU companies like BAE, Thales or Leonardo. Only Navantia remains in position 98 in SIPRI 2016 Top 100 companies, since EADS-CASA and GDELS Santa Barbara are part of EADS (Airbus) and General Dynamics conglomerates, respectively. Despite such position, these companies supply only partially the armed forces needs of equipment, due to the bounded nature of their development and production capabilities, being unable to supply equipment like missiles, satellites, helicopters or avionics.

Whereas prime contractors may sell their products directly to defence, usually first and second tier suppliers sell their product through the supply chain of the main contractor, since the MoD prefers the more reliable primes due to their size. The complexity of this supply chain is proportional to the sophistication of the product, since it will require very different technologies and skills to obtain the functionality and performance demanded for field operations. The main contractor has to accumulate and properly manage such varied industrial assets to develop and produce the system. Sub-contractors often represent a large proportion of the whole equipment added value, reaching in some cases nearly one half of the total value.[9] Foreign companies are often the best option for some equipment in the supply chain as is the case for engines or weapons. This contrasts with the desire for the autonomous supply of the armed forces.[10]

The supply of advanced defence equipment tailored to the armed forces' needs means that a development phase will be needed before starting production. These costs are quite high and may represent a large proportion of the final product cost. They are paid by the government due to the risk and often low reusability of the outcome of such developments in the civilian market. They are usually awarded through a bidding process, where only firms with adequate development and production assets can succeed. Since these capabilities are very specialized and specific, firms able to participate in the complete supply chain are few. Moreover, the arrangement of the value stream supply structure takes times and is costly. The use of markets by participants are restricted to very standardized components whose suppliers are many and are easily substitutable.

Once the development has been made and the product approved by the armed forces, this supply structure becomes unique.[11] This is because forming another alternative supply structure is too expensive for countries like Spain with a very limited defence budget. Therefore, this structure remains, with little variations, as the product supplier for the whole life-cycle sharply reducing competition, because barriers to entry are insurmountable to other potential suppliers.[12] Such successful structure assures an important business, having in mind that the purchase only represents around 20% of the life-cycle costs and modifications and upgrades of the product will be required across such life until retirement. This provides market power to first-movers able to be awarded with a development contract which ends successfully. As Leibenstein (1966) explains such power may favour hoarding, shirking, unneeded investments and the creation of layers of fat. Typically, the cost structure of defence firms is characterized by large investments in development and production equipment requiring highly qualified personnel with the knowledge and skills to supply the products demanded by the armed forces.

Vertical integration in the Spanish defence market has been reduced. Core firm activities tend to be internal, whereas complementary activities and supplies tend to be agreed through consortium agreements or sub-contracting based on product specification. Whereas firms may vary from case to case such relations tend to surpass a single supply and become permanent due to the social capital created which make the substitution of partners in the supply chain expensive and less desirable.

Under such circumstances competition in this market is rather limited since the number of bidders for developing and producing defence equipment is rather small, being often reduced, in the case of Spain, to a single supplier. Yet, the problem extends also to the build-up of the supply chain since the certified suppliers, or suppliers with the desired knowledge and product quality, are scarce. Competition only occurs in the initial stage of a programme, where a new system is planned to be acquired. In such a case, collusion is rather unfeasible. On the contrary, the fact that winners will take all the business, makes that competition, being more than one potential bidder is rather intense (Scherer, 1970, 187). Such intensity may cause optimistic estimates of performance and underestimate of costs which may be a source of problems (Marshall and Meckling, 1962). Yet, only a single firm will be chosen, based on the evaluation of proposals, since it is too expensive to fund more than one development.[13]

In this context, it is no surprise that the defence market is strongly regulated to avoid the abuse by firms of their dominant position.[14] A firm's bidding budget is often made using a cost-plus method where the mark-up over cost is known and controlled by the Public Administration. Such industrial relations are more close to hierarchies than markets, where agent's decisions are much more decentralized. In fact, the bidding process does not use standard bidding where the winner is the one with the best quality/price ratio, it frequently being a negotiated procedure, through which the scope of the development and the final price is bargained. This is mainly a principal-agent relation where the principal cares and works closely with the agent to achieve desired goals and where the agent failure to fulfil the principal quality requirements may mean a loss of confidence and the signing of future contracts. Such relations generate important transactions cost both for controlling the execution and for providing detailed reports about the project's progress, which may even be insufficient for the early discovery of problems. This context also creates strong links between parties that could be expensive to untie, which leads to hold-up problems, since non-cooperative behaviour of one of the parties may unnecessarily generate costs to the other.

Conduct

In this section, the four main features of a firm's conduct in the defence sector are analysed, namely, pricing behaviour, product strategy, research and innovation and advertising/lobbying.

Pricing behaviour is usually based on production cost with a mark-up added by the supplier whose value is only allowed within a certain range. Large scale contracts usually include clauses regarding the review of prices due to inflation and modifications of the supply due to customer needs. In certain contracts, price reductions are mandatory when production is subject to economies of scale and learning curves, since the time and effort for producing a single unit will diminish through time. Costs are usually audited before the awarding and during the contract to verify its value. However, the Administration often works with less information than the firm, which may give rise to abuse when verifying incurred cost is too complex. Public-private partnership contracts have not been used in Spain.

When firms offer their product to foreign countries, through an international open competition, prices are more adjusted to the real production cost with the aim of winning the contract, producing some form of price-discrimination. However, since the sale is normally included within a bunch of additional services like technological support and transfers for local production of some parts of the system, firms have more room to fix the final price in an environment where purchasers enjoy less information than sellers.

Product strategy is mainly driven by armed forces needs which demand that firms supply tailor-made products whose functionality and performance surpasses the ones of potential adversaries. This practice, also known as *gold-plating*, may produce too sophisticated products from the social point of view. Whereas this is mainly due to armed forces preferences, often translated in functional and performance specifications that form part of the contract, such practice is often stimulated by firms in order to isolate their product from competition not being challenged by price, thus creating excessive differentiation from the social point of view. This is clearly seen in the variety of ships, aircraft and other systems in Europe when compared with the United States and when there appears a lack of joint programmes within the North Atlantic Alliance.

When national production is infeasible, another purchasing strategy is required. One is the creation of an international programme where a consortium formed by national companies of the purchasing countries forms the supply as, for example, the Eurofighter and A-400M aircraft (see Chapter 7). In other cases, a collaboration agreement is made for the supply of essential equipment or services needed for the product delivery (e.g. Aegis system with Lockheed Martin – AFCON Consortium), a preference stated for main platforms such as aircraft (C-295), ships (F-110) and land vehicles (VCR 8x8). In other cases, the equipment is purchased directly from a foreign firm through competitive bidding, when reasons of urgency or reduced demand make unaffordable indigenous production. In such a case, a complementary agreement can be signed by the seller with domestic firms for participating in the supply through the assembly of components, the fabrication of subsystems, parts or components or the maintenance and repair of such equipment as has been the case of Sener with the purchase of the General Atomics MQ-9 Reaper, although this arrangement is not necessarily the more efficient solution from the economic point of view.[15]

Product strategy also includes its sale in international markets for countries which lack an industrial and technological base to produce the equipment. This is done through international bidding, where considerations regarding offsets agreements and technology transfers are not uncommon as, for example, in the sale of Spanish frigates to Norway or corvettes to Saudi Arabia. Success in this market, however, is complex since these sales are closely related to foreign policy, where political considerations can play a significant role in the final result[16] and where government institutional support is required. In other cases, where defence demand is insufficient, the products might be developed for other market like security, as in the case of Indra in border protection profiting from its military knowledge in radars, or other civilian products like EADS-CASA transport aircraft. However, this is not easy for products whose dual use is scarce and civilian market are not interested in such high-quality and expensive items. Regarding this question there is a lack of economic information about spin-offs for Spanish defence firms.

The need of research and innovation is quite relevant in defence. In fact, some studies show that defence firms are more innovative than the average industrial firm (Ortega, Gamella, Coomonte, Illescas and Martí, 2010). This is because each equipment generation requires more advanced functionalities and performance which is only achievable through a complex R&D phase. During this phase new technologies are developed or some of them, being sufficiently mature, are integrated in the new product providing higher performance, which requires personnel with qualified skills and abilities (e.g. highly-qualified engineers). The (applied) research is often performed with the support of university departments, as for example, the Superior School of Telecommunications of the Polytechnic University of Madrid which has collaborated with Indra in the development of radar technologies. The effort, cost and time of this phase may be sizable for large platforms and systems and requires decades (e.g. A-400M, S-80, Pizarro) until the product becomes operational. Such development is usually funded by the government and being successful, firms will assured of a long life in this business niche, since they will not find competitors.[17] However, this phase is largely subject to uncertainty and risk and initial estimations may fail so the final cost of the product is much larger than expected, even doubling the value, to the extent that the firm cannot assume such expenditure without risking survival. Such problem triggers a bargaining process between the Administration and the main contractor which also raise transaction costs and may even result in litigation, a case rather frequent in the development of large capital defence goods like aircraft carriers, fighter aircraft or land vehicles in Spain. Even more, failure can be complete, and the programme may be finally cancelled without the contractor receiving the largest premium in the form of a production contract (e.g. Abengoa fuel cell for S-80 submarine).

Due to the budgets limitations in defence R&D most of the innovation activities in Spain have focused on defensive innovation. Such behaviour profits from the successes of the leading/offensive innovators (Freeman, 1986), saving in failed research lines of prime-movers, adapting innovations to their product and adding features that differentiate the product from competitors. Since defensive innovation requires to be a "*fast second*", something difficult in complex defence products, such strategy has not worked well for reaching a competitive market position in some areas (see Figure 10.1).

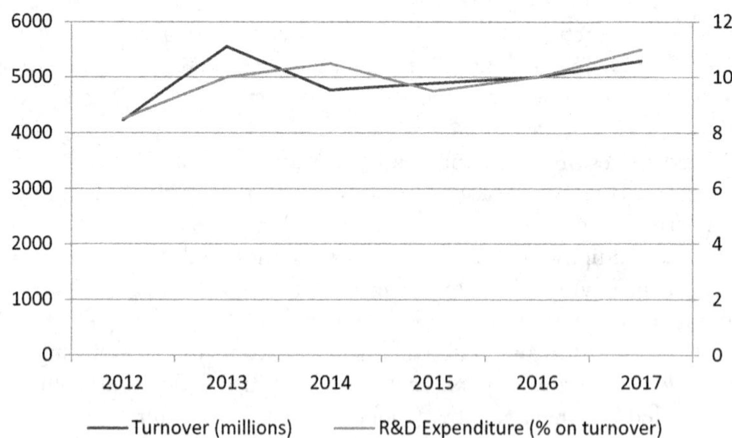

Figure 10.1 Turnover and effort in R&D (in constant 2016 prices).

Innovation in production methods and equipment is rarer in defence, unless it is essential for producing the quality required to support operational requirements. Spanish firms often have profitted from mature methods and technologies commonly used in the civilian markets.[18]

Advertising in defence takes different forms. Whilst specific products are not advertised to the general public, there is a constant pressure through communication media, whether general or defence specific, to highlight the relevance of this economic sector arguing, for example, its strategic role, its support for national sovereignty and autonomy and the spin-off effects on the rest of the economy that benefits the whole nation. Such a role is also strongly supported by trade-unions whose main goal is to preserve the labour force of the sector. These statements, hard to verify objectively, appeal for a close support of the sector, through increasing R&D and acquisition budgets and the large participation of domestic firms in the supply and discrimination against foreign suppliers justified by the preservation of essential national security interests that may be harmed if potential supplier are selected as well as the loss of domestic business if supply contracts are awarded to foreign firms. Much of this lobbying is made with the aid of TEDAE which maintains close links with decision-makers of the Spanish MoD.

Other forms of influence include advertising through mock-up and prototype demonstrations and field tests, marketing expenditures (in the form of seminars, congresses and workshops), unsolicited proposals and the preparation of high quality proposals, which can be an over-expenditure and represent an unnecessary social costs that unduly ricochets on a higher product price, a value that increases when there are many rivals. However, this conduct is hard to correct since the premium for the firm being the winner is too large to restrict such investment to the rational social value.

In sum, it can be said that some form of military-industrial complex can be perceived in Spain. The success of this complex can be observed in an accumulated debt of €30,075 million of the defence special armaments programmes up to 2030.[19]

Performance

Performance analysis will focus on five basic indicators: employment, the evolution of labor productivity, profitability, the exporting capacity of the industry and dynamic performance.

In recent years, the Spanish defense industry generated about 22,000 direct jobs on average. In turn, another 20,000 indirect and some 8,000 induced jobs are generated. Almost half of this employment results from the aeronautical sector and another 20% from the naval sector, which indicates their importance in the industry as a whole. During the economic crisis, employment in this sector has remained rather stable. The reasons that have led to this situation can be found in the difficulty of replacing workers in some jobs with high technological sophistication and the high maturation and production times of the weapons systems, which impose certain rigidities on companies.

An important feature is the high level of education of employees. For the largest companies in the sector between 30% and 45% of employees have university degrees, particularly in engineering, so it is expected that the added value they provide would be high. However, the differences in productivity between large companies and smaller ones are considerable. Thus, in 2016 the large companies achieved a productivity of more than €185,000 per employee, while SMEs stood at €87,000 per employee and micro-enterprises a little over €60,000.

As stated by Duch-Brown *et al.* (2014, 16) for the Spanish defence industry

> The impact of the market structure and conduct variables on performance, i.e., the technical efficiency measure, reveals that market share, which is often associated with profitability, was negatively and significantly related to technical efficiency in general .... On the contrary, in the aerospace sector, we found a positive relationship between market share and efficiency

In relation to the profitability of companies, it is necessary to distinguish what is obtained from activities carried out in the civilian sphere and those linked to the military part of the business. The profitability obtained in the military part has been reduced by almost a quarter in relation to the situation prior to the economic crisis. In 2007, the ratio between profits and turnover was 8.2%, while in 2010 it was reduced to 6.3%.[20]

When comparing the results of companies that work only in the civilian field with those that operate in defense, a difference in profitability is observed in favor of the latter of more than 20%. This may be due to the greater degree of oligopoly in the defense industry than in civil industry. In this sense, companies are able to exploit significant market power and transfer a greater proportion of their costs to the customer, a fact called "cost shifting" by Rogerson (1992).

With regard to exports, as can be seen in Table 10.2, the defense industry shows an important competitive capacity (the data of the export–import ratio is above 100% which means that imports are lower than exports).[21] Something similar happens in the case of the Relative Balance of Trade (RTB) with positive data in all sectors. The evolution of exports has been positive since the beginning of the 2008 crisis doubling the percentage from 40% to more than 80% of total sales. The reasons for this fact are many. The first has to do with the significant drop in the Spanish defense budget that has led companies to seek less dependence on it. The avoidance of such dependence has driven firms to diversification in both civilian products and military foreign markets. Second, companies are convinced that their survival depends on a greater integration in international markets as a way to gain new projects and improve their knowledge, skills and competence. Some of the factors that

Table 10.2 Relative balance of trade and export–import ratio

Sectors	2014		2016	
	RBT	*Export–import ratio*	*RBT*	*Export–import ratio*
Aeronautics	34,0	203,0	20,6	151,8
Naval	73,1	643,9	50,5	304,0
Automotive (Land vehicles)	36,7	215,9	58,2	378,5
Electronics & Computers	56,3	357,9	54,9	343,1
External services	6,8	114,6	73,5	653,5
Space	56,4	358,3	38,2	223,5
Armament & ammunition	-14,3	75,0	70,3	573,1
Missiles	70,4	575,0	85,5	1280,0
TOTAL	37,0	217,3	29,5	183,8

Source: Own estimates based on General Directorate of Armament and Material. Spanish Ministry of Defence.
Note: RBT=(X-M)/(X+M), expressed in percentage, where X means exports and M imports.

demonstrate it are the increasing entry of foreign capital[22] and the high volume of exports.

Some studies show that the intervention through active public policies improves the export performance of companies (Castellaci and Fevolden 2012). In this sense, the policy of export promotion has been an important but not a determining factor. Government-to-government agreements are possibly the most relevant factor to take into consideration. However, for this type of policy to be successful, it is necessary that companies have some type of advantages, among them high productivity. As Duch-Brown et al. (2014) work shows Spanish companies that export on a regular basis have a 50% higher productivity than non-exporters.

Finally, regarding dynamic efficiency (i.e. the ability of industry to produce the goods and services demanded by their customers), it has been commented that the industry has been able to produce such goods and services, despite often having problems regarding their requested functionality and performance, combined with overcost and delivery delays. On this issue, there is a lack of in-depth studies.

The future: the Spanish defence industry in the EU market

The European defence industry is a significant sector in size since it employs more than half a million workers – 1.7% of the EU's industrial employment – and, indirectly, generates more than 1.2 million jobs of European industrial employment. With regard to sales, in 2014 it accounted for almost one trillion euros – 12% of EU industrial sales which includes both large companies and a large group of SMEs. In addition, it makes a significant effort in R & D.

However, the European market has major problems, many of them structural and long-term. One of the most important is the market fragmentation observed both on the supply and demand sides. In terms of supply, each country decides what are its defence needs and tries to cover it through national providers. However, although the EU is a single market in the case of defence, in practice it is far from this situation. Normally all countries tend to favour domestic versus foreign companies, which limits competition between companies. This situation has led to a significant *de facto* protectionism that is contrary to the community spirit, but is tolerated for national security interests (Article 346 of the TFEU).

Industrial collaboration and agreements between countries and firms are essentially due to the needs to be met, the lack of resources at the national level and the economies of scale, scope and learning that characterizes this industry. It has been the case of large international collaboration projects such as the Eurofighter. This type of project can achieve important competitive advantages to the industry as well as better equipment for the armed forces. However, the degree of collaboration within the EU for the acquisition of defence equipment has diminished in recent years at an important pace, so that between 2006 and 2014 the fall was over 14% (EDA figures).

The causes of this situation can be found in the way in which this collaboration is carried out, which imposes very high transaction costs. These costs reduce the usefulness of collaboration both in terms of performance of systems, and the possibility of reducing acquisition costs. Along with this, there is a potential negative effect for industries of medium or small countries as opposed to those with greater industrial capabilities. Obviously the loss of the national market or fewer opportunities for national development programmes reduce the incentive for collaboration.

The current Spanish defence industrial policy was based on a set of guidelines underpinned on two aspects related to the needs of the companies and those of the Ministry of Defence. These needs can be summarized as: sovereignty and industrial and technological independence; the freedom of action of the Armed Forces through the capacities developed by the industry; the operational advantage, which requires a high level of performance of the systems provided by the industry; and security of supply, both in the systems and their spare parts. However, given the structure-conduct-performance paradigm of this market such a goal is infeasible being necessary to modify Spanish industrial defence policy. The development of a new policy is not simple to address and requires an in-depth analysis of the current situation, the objectives to be achieved in the future and the strategies necessary to achieve them.

The current industrial strategy needs to be modified taking into account, at least, two issues. The first one refers to the greater integration that will be needed in the future in the industry, due to the need for companies to increase business size to become competitive and survive. Secondly, the Spanish defence industry is in a position of weakness compared to other European countries. This is due to two reasons: the more advanced industry of large countries which will try to have the largest share in the biggest programmes, giving less room to Spanish industry and, on the opposite side, the less competitive countries will try to enlarge their share through low labour costs in tasks less complex technologically and more labour-intensive. The Spanish industry, even having advantages in certain market niches, cannot easily compete with the large conglomerates of countries such as France or Germany and does not have labour costs as low as some European countries. It could be said that this is the situation of an intermediate country that is at a crossroad.

Conclusions

The historical trajectory followed by the Spanish defence industry has led to a structure very similar to that observed in other countries, although the large Spanish companies are smaller than their French, English or German counterparts. This situation represents a challenge to this industry in the European and international context. This is due to the increasing European integration that involuntarily favours big conglomerates or "national champions", against more modest industrial structures such as the Spanish case.

For this reason, it is necessary to develop long-term policy strategies which combine the needs of the Armed Forces, the industrial needs, the contributions from the scientific and technological fields and the new European scenario of the Permanent Structure Cooperation (PESCO) and the European Defense Acquisition Programme (EDAP). In this scenario, there are many important opportunities for first-movers that used well may leverage the Spanish industry. In this sense, the proven export capabilities of the industry are a good basis, but more internationalization commitments, investment efforts and higher integration with other EU companies seem to be necessary.

Notes

1 See Salas (1983) for a detailed analysis. Willy Messerschmitt developed in the 1950s the "HA-200 Saeta", a training and attack aircraft built by *Hispano Aviación* that had only limited commercial success.

2 See García Alonso (2010).

3 See Molas (1992).

4 The Public Administration comprises the Ministry of Defence or the Ministry of Internal Affairs. Whilst firms may also export their product to foreign countries, this is only when they have supplied the product to the national MoD. In Spain, the largest purchases are centralized in the "Dirección General de Armamento y Material" with the aim of a higher control and the achievement of scale economies when the equipment demand involves more than one service.

5 It may be the case that some firms that supply through the supply chain are not accounted when their products are standard and can be used both in civilian and defence markets.

6 The case of Navantia is due to the disapproval by the European Union of state aids to former Izar, which jointly operated civilian and military production of ships. It forced the creation of the defence firm Navantia for receiving aids supported by article 346 of the Treaty, but establishing strong restrictions to this firm for operating in the civilian ship market, in order to assure fair competition. See "Commission decision of 12 of May 2004 on the State Aid implemented by Spain for further restructuring aid to the public Spanish shipyards. State aid case C 40/00 (Ex NN 61/00)".
7 In this way, the minimum efficiency scale (MES) can be achieved.
8 DGAM (2017).
9 See Bellouard and Fonfría (2018).
10 According to DGAM (2017) Spain imported €2.683 million in 2016, whilst it exported € 4933 which reflects the growing internationalization of supply chains. Main suppliers are France and Germany.
11 On the difficulty of forming such supply chain see for example Demsetz (2018).
12 Exit barriers are also considerable since the sale of assets or the allocation of these assets to other activities will necessarily result in a loss of value. In fact, changes of market structure in Spain have been minimal in the last decade.
13 This has not occurred in the AIP-system of the S-80 where two firms where contracted for the development due to the failure of the first attempt and the high risk of this development.
14 However, the concentration in the Spanish defense industry increased substantially between 2008 and 2016. Thus, 75% of turnover was in the hands of 8% of companies in 2008 while in 2016 that percentage had been reduced to 5% – DGAM, several years.
15 The EU is trying to avoid such kind of agreements, also known as offsets. See on this COM (2013) 542 Final. However, it seems that this practice is still maintained in some way in Spain.
16 Exports have also regulations in Europe as the Common Position 2008/944/ CFSP and Council Regulation (EC) No 428/2009.
17 Since defence R&D budget largely differ between EU Member States, an unlevelled playing field is created in this way, something that difficult the opening of national market more for welfare reasons than sovereignty reasons.
18 See of this Pavitt (1984).
19 See "Defensa pagará 1.824 millones de los 30.075 pendientes por programas de armas" in "La Vanguardia" digital edition (30/03/2017).
20 See Fonfría (2012)
21 This ratio shall be taken with care, since it may be feasible that imports are not properly labelled as defence products.
22 Various reports from the Ministry of Defense show the growing volume of foreign capital in the Spanish defense industry. See DGAM (2015) and (DGAM, 2017), among others.

References

Bellouard, P., and Fonfría, A. (2018). The relationship between prime contractors and SME´s. How to best manage and found Cooperative Programmes. ARES, Policy Paper, 24.

Carreras, A. Y., and Tafunell, X. (2010). Historia económica de la España Contemporánea (1789–2009).

Castellaci, F., and Fevolden, A. (2012). Capable companies or changing markets? NUPI Working Papers, no 795.

Demsetz, H. (1988). The theory of the firm revisited. *Journal of Law, Economics, & Organization, 4*(1), 141–161. Spring.

DGAM. (2015). *La industria de defensa en España. Informe 2014.* Ministerio de Defensa. Dirección General de Armamento y Materia. Subdirección General de Inspección, Regulación y Estrategia Industrial de Defensa.

DGAM. (2017). *La industria de defensa en España. Informe 2016. Versión 2.* Ministerio de Defensa. Dirección General de Armamento y Materia. Subdirección General de Inspección, Regulación y Estrategia Industrial de Defensa.

Duch-Brown, N., Fonfría, A., and Trujillo-Baute, E. (2014). Market structure and technical efficiency of Spanish defense contractors. *Defence and Peace Economics, 5*(1), 23–38.

European Commission. (2013). *A new deal for European defence. Towards a more competitive and efficient defence and security sector.* Brussels.

Fonfría, A. (2012). Estructura, conducta y resultados de la industria de defensa española. In *Cuadernos Aragoneses de Economía.* Vol 22 (1–2), 2ª época, 11–30.

Freeman, Christopher. (1986). *The economics of industrial innovation.* Cambridge, MA: The MIT Press.

García Alonso, J. M. (2010). *La Base Industrial de la Defensa en España.* Madrid: Ministerio de Defensa.

Leibenstein, H. (1966). Allocative Efficiency versus "X-Efficiency". *The American Economic Review, 56*(3), 392–415.

Marshall, A. W., and Meckling, W. H. (1962). *Predictability of the costs, time and success of development.* Santa Monica, CA: The RAND Corporation.

Molas Gallart, J. (1992). *Military production and innovation in Spain.* Reading: Harwood Academic Publishers.

Ortega, V., Gamella, M., Coomonte, R., Illescas, E. Y., Martí, Cs (2010). Investigación, Desarrollo e Innovación en el Sector de Defensa. Análisis de la Situación (1998–2008). Cuadernos Cátedra Isdefe-UPM.

Pavitt, K. (1984). Sectoral patterns of technical change: Towards a taxonomy and a theory. *Research Policy, 13*, 343–373.

Rogerson, William. (1992). Overhead allocation and incentives for cost minimization in defense procurement, *The Accounting Review,* 67(4), 671–690.

Salas, J. (1987). Reseña histórica de la Industria Aeronáutica Española. *Revista De Aeronáutica Y Astronáutica, 563*, 1117–1124.

Scherer, F. M. (1970). *Industrial market structure and economic performance.* Chicago: Rand McNally College Publishing Company.

Trebilcock, C. (1981). *The industrialization of the Continental Powers 1780-1914.* London-New York: Longman.

11 Greece

Christoforos Kalloniatis and Christos Kollias

1 Introduction

Driven by acute national security needs, Greece has invariably ranked among the major recipients of conventional weapons globally. Despite the country's relative economic size – its GDP on average represented 0.4% of global GDP during 1980–2017[1] – Greece is ranked as the eleventh largest arms importer in the world during this period.[2] Most of the military hardware used by the Greek armed forces is imported. For technologically advanced weapons systems, such as fighter planes, rocket systems, main battle tanks, missiles, electronics it relies exclusively on imports from the USA and West European suppliers. Notable exceptions to this general rule are naval vessels such as frigates, submarines, fast attack and patrol boats built by local shipbuilders under license from the original developer and manufacturer. For instance, under license from the German manufacturer HDW,[3] Hellenic Shipyards built locally three[4] out of the four Type 214 conventional submarines operated by the Greek Navy. Similarly, Elefsis Shipyards built locally under license from BAE Systems Surface Ships the five fast attack missile boats of the Roussen class[5] operated by the navy.

A fairly large constellation of mainly small and medium sized enterprises make up the defence industrial base of Greece that also includes some large,[6] mostly publicly-owned industries. For instance, the Hellenic Defence Systems (henceforth EAS)[7] that produce ammunition and light infantry weapons such as assault rifles, light machine guns and pistols and the Hellenic Airspace Industry (henceforth HAI)[8] that apart from advanced stage maintenance, repair and overhaul capabilities also manufactures sub-assemblies for civil and military aircraft. Hence, although by far a net arms importer, Greece possesses a domestic defence industrial base with noteworthy capabilities given the size and general technological development of the economy (Petrakis, 2012). The demand for ammunition, portable infantry weapons, jeeps and trucks, APCs and IFVs, airplane and helicopter maintenance, is largely satisfied by domestic production as also noted in more vintage studies of the Greek defence industry (Bartzokas, 1992; Kollias and Rafailidis, 2003; Matthews, 1999; Mouzakis, 2002). However, such indigenously produced inputs represent only a small proportion of the total demand for military hardware and weapons systems as noted in the *National Defence and Industrial Strategy 2017* document of the General Directorate for Defence Investments and Armaments (henceforth GDAEE) of the Ministry of Defence (MoD).[9]

Currently, the *Hellenic Defence Industries Catalogue*[10] (henceforth HELDIC) published by GDAEE lists 34 companies of various sizes in terms of turnover and employment that produce defence inputs. Total employment for 2016[11] for the companies included in HELDIC 2018 edition, is estimated at around 5200. Their total turnover at just over 800 million Euros, corresponds to 0.46% of GDP for the same year. In practice, the figures are slightly higher[12] given that there are a number of other enterprises that also engage in the production of various defence inputs, but on a less regular base or for various reasons are not included in the MoD defence industry catalogue. Defence companies are organized around two professional associations, namely, the Hellenic Manufacturers of Defence Material Association (SEKPY) and the Hellenic Aerospace Security & Defence Industries Group (HASDIG). The following section presents an overview of defence spending in Greece and then discusses briefly issues in the arms procurement process and arms imports, before moving to a detailed presentation and discussion of the domestic defence industrial base (section three).

2 Defence spending in Greece: a brief overview

A member of both NATO and the EU, having joined them in 1952 and 1981, respectively, Greece annually allocates a comparatively large share of its GDP to defence. During 1980–2017 military spending as a percentage of GDP averaged around 3.5% while the corresponding EU average was around 1.9% for the same period (Table 11.1). As many studies have shown, defence expenditures are determined by a cohort of both external and domestic factors.[13] The former include membership of the NATO Alliance and Turkey that presents by far the predominant threat to Greek national interests (Dokos, 2011; Dokos and Tsakonas, 2003). The latter include mainly the

Table 11.1 Military spending as a share of GDP

	EU	*Greece*
1980–89	2.6%	4.7%
1990–99	2.0%	3.5%
2000–09	1.5%	2.9%
2010–17	1.4%	2.5%
1980–2017	1.9%	3.5%

Source: SIPRI.

state of the economy and the concomitant budgetary constraints as well as the political composition of the incumbent government (Kollias and Paleologou, 2003).

As Kollias et al. (2016) point out, although the Turkish threat features prominently in the Greek national security agenda, what ultimately determines the allocation of resources to national defence is the state of the economy. During periods of relative economic affluence with no pressing fiscal constraints defence spending increases and so does the procurement of military hardware from both external as well domestic suppliers. Figure 11.1 shows that the recent economic crisis and the acute fiscal problems as a result of the sovereign debt crisis that ensued resulted in unprecedented cut-backs in the defence budget. In real terms, defence spending declined by almost 50% between 2009 and 2014. It is only in the past couple of years that this sharp fall seems to have halted and levelled-off (Figure 11.1). The sharp reduction in the defence budget directly affected procurement spending and this had a direct bearing on the domestic defence industrial base given that it is heavily dependent on orders from the Greek armed forces. Not surprisingly, equipment expenditure as a share of the total defence budget has appreciably declined because of the acute fiscal constraints: about 11.4% in 2010–17 compared to 18% and 21.5% in 1980–99 and 1990–99, respectively (Table 11.2).

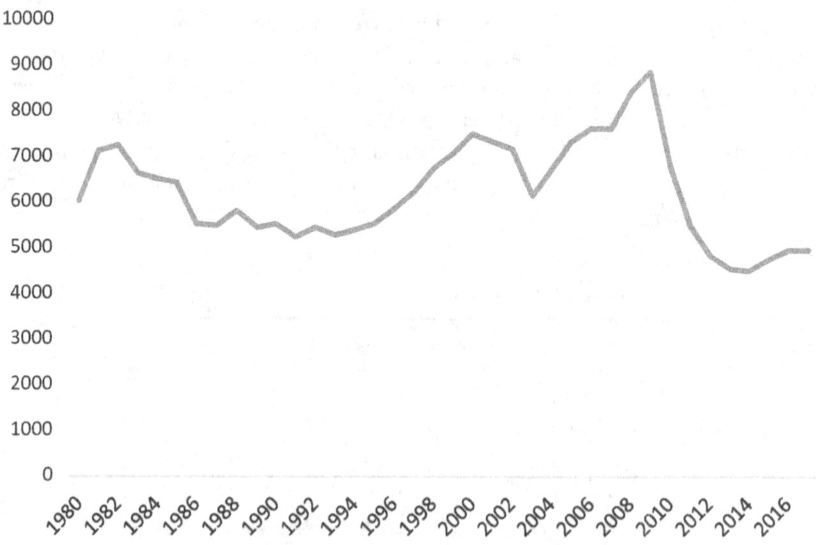

Figure 11.1 Greek defence spending.

Table 11.2 Equipment expenditure as a share of total defence spending (%)

1980–89	*18.0*
1990–99	21.5
2000–09	14.9
2010–17	11.4

Source: NATO.

3 Arms imports and import substitution industrialization: pious hopes and hard realities

Greece is a net arms importer relying almost exclusively on imports for almost all the sophisticated and technologically advanced weapons systems operated by its armed forces. During the period 1980–2017 it ranked as the eleventh largest importer of conventional arms globally although this rank significantly varies depending on the time-window examined. For example, as a result of the recent economic crisis and the concomitant acute fiscal constraints that ensued, procurement spending sharply declined affecting both imports as well as domestic procurement. Specifically, equipment expenditure declined from 2,128 million Euros in 2009 to 322 million Euros in 2014.[14] Between 2010 and 2017 Greece ranked as the 30th largest importer globally from the fourth place during 2000–09 (i.e. the period just before the debt crisis that currently is afflicting Greece and affecting all public spending that has contracted sharply). Figure 11.2 shows the sharp decline in arms imports caused by the Greek debt crisis and official default.[15] This decline echoes the one presented in Figure 11.1. A similar sharp downward trend is the case for both annual defence spending (Figure 11.1) as well as arms imports (Figure 11.2). The similar trend in the value of arms imports observed in the 1980s can also be attributed to the stagnant economy of that period. The reversal in the 1990s coincided with the more vigorous economic performance during most of that decade. As one would expect, the reduction in procurement programs due to the recent acute fiscal constraints has also affected the domestic defence industry that has experienced a decline in terms of turnover as will be shown subsequently.

Greece's main arms suppliers are the USA and its EU partners (Table 11.3). During 1980–2017, the lion's share of imports was of US origin. It accounted for 44.6% of total imports, followed by Germany (25.2%) and France (10.7%). Noteworthy is the share of imports from Russia during the same period.[16] With 4% it is the sixth largest supplier of weapons to Greece. During this period, as noted by Kollias and Rafailidis (2003), weapons

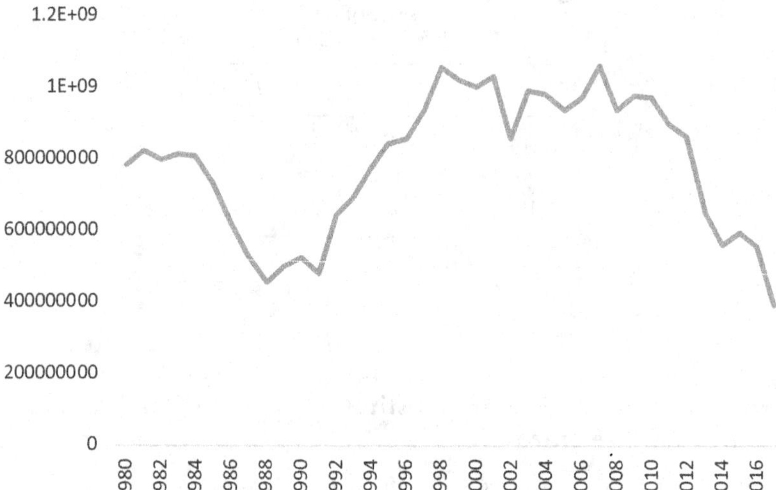

Figure 11.2 Value of arms imports.

Table 11.3 Arms suppliers 1980–2017

USA	*44.6%*
Germany	25.2%
France	10.7%
Netherlands	7.7%
Italy	2.4%
Russia	4.0%
Others	5.5%

Source: SIPRI's Arms Transfers Database.

procurement practices have gradually changed from direct commissioning from foreign suppliers, to international competitive tenders that invariably included stringent contractual requirements for increased domestic participation and domestic value added through the partial production of parts or sub-assemblies by local manufacturers. This practice aimed to support the domestic defence industry and generate economic, industrial and technological benefits for the country's weak industrial sector. It was terminated as a prerequisite for procurement contracts awarded to successful international bidders in 2011.[17]

A number of factors have been cited as the motivating drivers for developing indigenous arms production capabilities in small or developing countries (*inter alia*: Bitzinger, 2009; Brauer, 2007; Dunne, 1995; Hartley, 2017; Mouzakis, 2002). They include both strategic and economic considerations as well as national prestige and pride. The former includes security of supply and relative autarky in military equipment that enhances national security and augments the degrees of freedom in conducting foreign policy. The economic benefits that can accrue from import substituting domestic arms production comprise savings in foreign currency, defence industrialization, increased employment, technological progress that also spills-over to the rest of the economy and hence benefits national economic and technological progress.

Greece has invested in the development of a domestic defence industry for many years. The defence industrialization plan can be traced back to the seven-year military dictatorship (1967–74) that was isolated by most of the international community and faced arms embargoes but not particularly stringent or rigorously observed ones (Kollias and Rafailidis, 2003). Although before that period, indigenous arms producing capabilities were virtually non-existent, small explosives producers[18] catered for some of the needs of the armed forces apart from the mining sector[19]. The main pillar in the efforts to establish a national defence industry was the public sector.

Two public enterprises were founded in the 1970s: the Hellenic Arms Industry (EBO) in 1977 for the licensed production of the Heckler & Koch range of light infantry weapons commissioned by the Armed Forces, and the Hellenic Airspace Industry (HAI)[20] in 1975. In 1979 the Hellenic Industry of Vehicles[21] (ELBO), founded in 1972 as a subsidiary of Steyr-Daimler-Puch, came under state ownership. The majority of the company's shares passed into the public portfolio and it was nationalized. The same was the case in 1982 with PYRKAL an explosives and ammunition producer originally founded in 1874. For many years, and certainly throughout the 1980s and most of the 1990s, these public enterprises along with Hellenic Shipyards[22] formed the backbone of the domestic defence industry (Bartzokas, 1992; Kollias and Rafailidis, 2003; Ploumis, 2017). As in most cases, domestic arms production was seen as a vehicle that through import substitution would assist the country's industrial and technological development, increase employment, generate savings in currency reserves[23] and signal the country's industrial and technological prowess.

Although significant achievements were attained in the process, the original ambitious plans never quite came to full fruition. The public companies that were to act as the steam-engines of defence industrialization were continuously plagued with many managerial and financial problems and invariably used by incumbent governments to serve clientelistic purposes.[24] Efforts for the indigenous design, development and production of weapons systems proved in practice to be projects that siphoned substantial funds without any

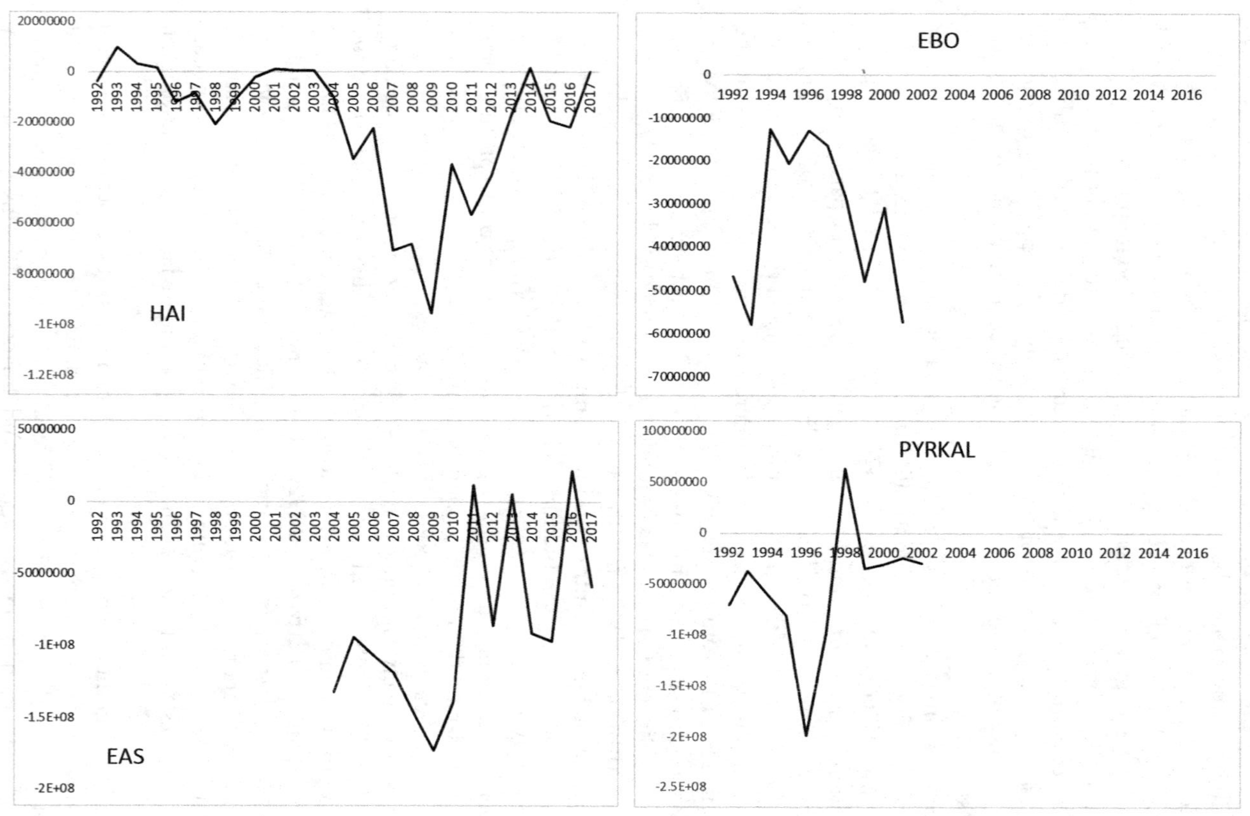

Figure 11.3 Profit/loss of public defence companies.

Note: In Euros, current prices. PYRKAL and EBO were merged in 2004 to form EAS.

tangible benefits[25]. Such failures also contributed to the accumulation of financial losses. The hard reality is that importing advanced weapons is invariably a more cost-effective option for countries that lack the industrial and technological development to undertake the development of sophisticated weapons systems. The size of the local market is another inhibitor for such projects. As a result of all these factors, the public defence industries constantly faced financial problems, invariably recorded annual losses and heavily relied on government subsidies for their operation and survival. In an effort to resolve the accumulated financial problems of the public sector defence companies and to avoid closing them down with the concomitant job losses, two of the firms – EBO and PYRKAL – were merged in 2004 to form a new public entity in the defence industry, namely, the Hellenic Defence Systems (EAS). The aim was to create a financially more viable firm. However, as can be seen in Figure 11.3, EAS is almost consistently a loss-making firm just as were the two firms that were merged to establish EAS (EBO and PYRKAL). The same applies for HAI, perhaps the technological flagship of the public sector defence companies. All have invariably exhibited poor economic performance, with the concomitant need for the government to continuously support and subsidize their operations financially. Similar problems also afflicted the other publicly-owned defence industry, the Hellenic Industry of Vehicles (ELBO).[26] In an effort to resolve its dire financial situation, over 40% of its shares were sold along with the management of ELBO to a private firm in 2000.[27] The effort was not successful, and the firm was sold back to the state in 2011.[28] Compared to the attempts for domestic production of large systems for the army and the air force, indigenous production of large naval units such as frigates, submarines and landing ships proved to be a more successful venture. It seems that the pre-existence of a developed industrial branch (in this case ship construction: i.e. a potential arms production base), is more often than not a prerequisite for success in developing domestic defence industrial capabilities.[29]

4 Domestic defence industrial base: the two faces of Janus

In an earlier survey of the Greek defence industry, Kollias and Rafailidis (2003) observed that it was characterized by a dualism between public and private companies. With few exceptions, the latter generally are small and medium-sized enterprises in terms of employment compared to the publicly-owned ones. Public firms were the main channel through which the rather ambitious aims of the National Defence Industrial Strategy (NDIS) were implemented in the initial stages of the efforts to establish and develop indigenous arms producing capabilities in the late 1970s and early 1980s. Table 11.4 offers a summary picture of all the companies that are included in the HELDIC 2018 edition.[30] As can be seen, with 1385 employees, HAI,[31] one of the two publicly-owned defence manufacturers in the defence producers registry, is by far the larger employer. EAS,[32] the other publicly-owned company, is the third largest employer with 520 employees in 2016.[33] In the second place with 746 employees in 2016[34] is Systems Sunlight S.A., a private company specializing in the development and production of batteries and energy storage systems with a strong export orientation[35] like many of the private defence manufacturers. It should be mentioned, that the two publicly-owned companies (HAI and EAS) included in the catalogue also engage in noteworthy export activity. However, in terms of financial performance they cannot be compared to the private sector manufacturers as will be shown below. Most of the companies included in the HELDIC 2018 list were founded over the past two and a half decades. In particular, only six out of the 34 companies were established before the 1980s, six in the 1980s, 13 in the 1990s and nine in the post-2000 period. As can be seen in Table 11.4, the manufacturing activity of the 34 companies in HELDIC 2018 covers a wide range of defence related products. It includes electronics, communication equipment, sensors, ammunition, light infantry weapons, protective clothing, and platforms for all the branches of the armed forces as well as offering maintenance, repair and overhaul capabilities such as the ones offered by HAI for fighter and transport aircraft and helicopters. Some are products with a high technological content; others less so. Not all of the companies are exclusively defence producers but for many, defence related production constitutes a significant part of their annual turnover.[36]

In terms of turnover and employment, Table 11.4 is obviously a static snapshot. It does not narrate the intertemporal development process of the defence industrial sector in Greece. This is shown in Figure 11.4 where the yearly total turnover of the 34 producers in Table 11.4 is presented. As can be observed, allowing for the inevitable yearly fluctuations, the overall trend is upward up to the mid-2000s. It then exhibits greater annual volatility and on average shows a downward propensity. This latter trend is in all probability the outcome of the sharp reduction in national defence spending[37] caused by the recent sovereign debt crisis. Between 2009 and 2014 defence expenditures declined by around 50%.[38] A similar sharp reduction was also the case in the share of equipment expenditure. It declined from 2,128 million Euros in 2009 (35.3% of the total defence budget) to 322 million Euros by 2014 (8% of the total real spending).[39] Given that for many defence producers the Greek MoD is the main customer, this sharp decline in equipment expenditure, adversely affected their annual turnover. Since acute fiscal constraints will for many years affect government spending, a noteworthy reversal in equipment expenditure cannot be anticipated over the medium term. In this context, domestic defence producers have no alternative but to seek participation in international collaborative arms production projects. Such opportunities for SMEs that are the dominant characteristic of the Greek defence industrial sector are to be found in the recently established European Defence Fund.[40] Stronger links and integration in the unfolding efforts for a more coordinated and comprehensive European defence industrial integration has

Table 11.4 Defence producers included in the HELDIC 2018 catalogue

		Established	*Turnover (mil. Euros)*	*Employment*	*Sector*
1	METKA S.A.	1962	280,6	300	Machinery, Materials & Structures, Ground Vehicles & Related Systems/ Services, Naval Platforms & Related Systems/Services
2	SYSTEMS SUNLIGHT S.A.	1991	168,4	746	Energy & Power Systems
3	HAI S.A.	1975	70,0	1385	Aerospace & Related Systems/ Services, Electronic, Communication & IT Systems/Services
4	IDE S.A.	2001	57,4	406	Ground Vehicles & Related Systems/Services, Naval Platforms & Related Systems/Services, Electronic, Communication & IT Systems/Services, Unmanned Systems/Services, Electronic Components, Assemblies & Harnesses, Energy & Power Systems
5	SPACE HELLAS S.A.	1985	44,9	270	Electronic, Communication & IT Systems/Services
6	EKME S.A.	1973	26,3	230	Machinery, Materials & Structures
7	THEON SENSORS S.A.	1997	23,0	102	EO & RF Sensors
8	COSMOS BUSINESS SYSTEMS S.A.	1988	21,1	78	Electronic, Communication & IT Systems/Services
9	HDVS S.A.	2001	19,2	53	Ground Vehicles & Related Systems/Services, Machinery, Materials & Structures
10	MEVACO S.A.	1993	17,2	157	Machinery, Materials & Structures
11	SIAMIDIS S.A.	1991	11,5	35	CBRN protection & Personal Gear
12	THALES HELLAS S.A.	2000	9,1	40	Electronic, Communication & IT Systems/Services
13	SIELMAN S.A.	1982	8,4	110	Ground Vehicles & Related Systems/Services,

(*Continued*)

Table 11.4 (Cont.)

		Established	*Turnover (mil. Euros)*	*Employment*	*Sector*
					Machinery, Materials & Structures Electronic Components, Assemblies & Harnesses
14	EAS S.A.	2004	8,2	520	Armament, Ammunition, Explosives & Related Services
15	ONEX S.A.	2004	8,0	162	Electronic, Communication & IT Systems/Services
16	NORSAFE HELLAS S.A.	1974	6,5	85	Naval Platforms & Related Systems/Services
17	ISI HELLAS S.A.	1993	4,7	57	Electronic, Communication & IT Systems/Services
18	ELFON LTD	1975	4,3	60	Electronic Components, Assemblies & Harnesses
19	ELMON S.A.	2005	3,2	16	CBRN protection & Personal Gear
20	GLASSART S.A.	1980	3,1	55	Field Infrastructure, Logistics & Services
21	PRISMA ELECTRONICS S.A.	1991	3,0	80	Electronic, Communication & IT Systems/Services, Electronic Components, Assemblies & Harnesses, Naval Platforms & Related Systems/Services,
22	MILTECH HELLAS S.A.	1997	2,9	68	Aerospace & Related Systems/Services, Electronic, Communication & IT Systems/Services, EO & RF Sensors,Electronic Components, Assemblies & Harnesses
23	AKMON S.A.	1988	2,5	40	Electronic Components, Assemblies & Harnesses, Field Infrastructure, Logistics & Services
24	EGNATIA FOUNDRY S.A.	1997	1,7	49	Machinery, Materials & Structures
25	TEMMA S.A.	1961	1,6	25	Machinery, Materials & Structures
26	SSA S.A.	1990	1,5	19	Electronic, Communication & IT Systems/Services
27	VALPAK S.A.	1990	1,3	12	Field Infrastructure, Logistics & Services

(*Continued*)

Table 11.4 (Cont.)

		Established	*Turnover (mil. Euros)*	*Employment*	*Sector*
28	ALTUS LSA S.A.	2011	1,3	16	Unmanned Systems/Services
29	ISD S.A.	1998	1,3	N/A	Electronic, Communication & IT Systems/Services, Electronic Components, Assemblies & Harnesses, Electronic Components, Assemblies & Harnesses
30	BOSA S.A.	1996	1,2	18	Aerospace & Related Systems/ Services, Machinery, Materials & Structures, Electronic Components, Assemblies & Harnesses
31	ALEXMOLDS	1986	0,4	6	Machinery, Materials & Structures
32	FEAC ENGINEERING P.C.	2014	0,1	6	Consulting & Engineering
33	SGL ENGINEERING LTD	2008	N/A	4	Naval Platforms & Related Systems/Services, Consulting & Engineering
34	BARRACUDA	1992	N/A	N/A	Naval Platforms & Related Systems/Services

Source: HELDIC 2018.
Note: Data for 2016. Latest year for which information is available for all variables, for all the companies in the table.

the potential to yield appreciable benefits for the comparatively weak defence industrial base of Greece.[41]

As a next step in the analysis, it was decided to put the defence industry's turnover in perspective vis-à-vis the size of the Greek economy. Figure 11.5 presents the annual turnover of the 34 arms producers in the HELDIC 2018 list as a share of GDP. The broad picture that emerges is one of an increasing share allowing for the inevitable annual fluctuations. On average, during 1995–2016 the annual turnover of the defence companies was around 0.38% of GDP with a maximum value of 0.66% in 2011 and a minimum of 0.22% in 1998. Finally, the broadly upward trend seems to be reversed in recent years.

The second aspect of the dualism mentioned earlier is that, in comparative terms, the private companies engaging in defence production generally are profitable enterprises whereas public firms suffer from chronic weaknesses, bad management and financial problems. We start with a snapshot of the performance of the 34 companies examined here. Table 11.5 lists them hierarchically in terms of

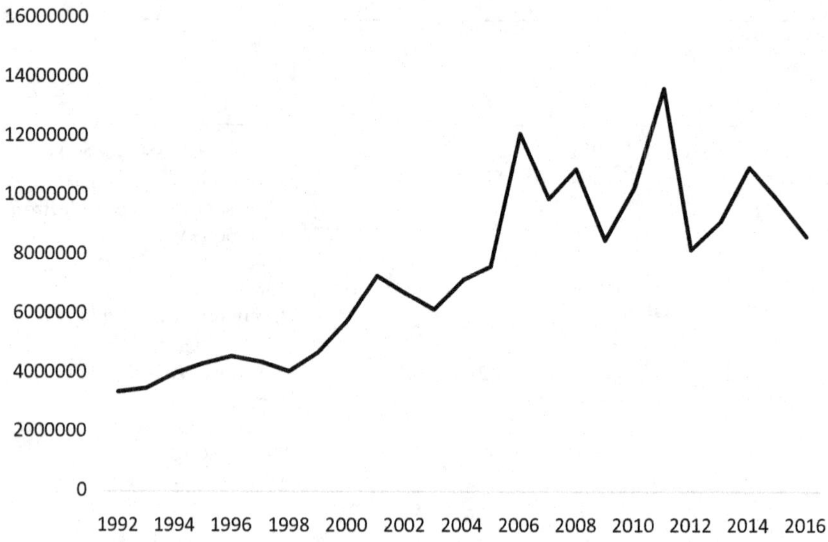

Figure 11.4 Annual turnover (in Euros) of the HELDIC 2018 industries.

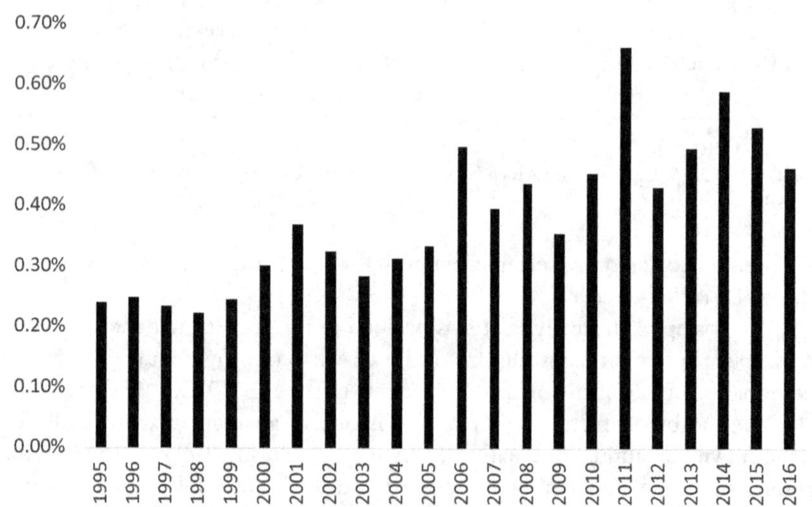

Figure 11.5 Defence industries' annual turnover as a share of GDP.

Note: The figure includes only the 34 HELDIC 2018 companies. Each year is the sum of the turnover of the companies operating in that year for which data are available.

productivity in 2016.[42] As a crude measure of productivity, we use turnover per employee. A noteworthy variation between the various firms is clearly evident using this index of measuring productivity. As a threshold for comparison purposes, for the same year, GDP per person employed was 43,225 Euros. Hence, it

Table 11.5 Turnover per worker in the HELDIC group of companies (Euros)

	Turnover per employee 2016	*Profit/loss per employee 2016*
METKA S.A.	935480	95557
HDVS S.A.	362625	52242
SIAMIDIS S.A.	327772	15150
COSMOS BUSINESS SYSTEMS S.A.	270023	787
THALES HELLAS S.A.	227984	-8288
SYSTEMS SUNLIGHT S.A.	225784	7066
THEON SENSORS S.A.	225282	28704
ELMON S.A.	201472	2393
SPACE HELLAS S.A.	166319	3748
IDE S.A.	141471	3938
EKME S.A.	114496	104
MEVACO S.A.	109746	-2409
VALPAK S.A.	109417	4992
ISI HELLAS S.A.	82456	-
ALTUS LSA S.A.	80231	1598
SSA S.A.	79912	459
NORSAFE HELLAS S.A.	76279	-15366
SIELMAN S.A.	76131	20229
ELFON LTD	71887	11315
BOSA S.A.	69058	17044
AKMON S.A.	63468	1431
TEMMA S.A.	62333	1202
ALEXMOLDS	58333	-
GLASSART S.A.	56323	8324
HAI S.A.	50575	-15621
ONEX S.A.	49675	69
MILTECH HELLAS S.A.	42008	137
PRISMA ELECTRONICS S.A.	36877	-5842
EGNATIA FOUNDRY S.A.	35166	-2880
EAS S.A.	15840	40922
FEAC ENGINEERING P.C.	10013	2153
ISD S.A.	-	-
SGL ENGINEERING LTD	-	-
BARRACUDA	-	-

would appear than the majority of the companies in the defence sector, perform better than the national average as captured by the GDP per person employed index. Both public enterprises included in the group (HAI and EAS) perform worse that the group's average score of 143,046 Euros: 50,575 and 15,840, respectively. As a further insight into company performance Table 11.5 shows the profit or loss per employee. Again, significant variation is the broad picture that emerges. Five of the group record losses for 2016. Among them, one of the two public companies (HAI) also has the highest losses per worker (-15,621 Euros). The other public company, EAS, shows profits of 40,222 Euros. However, this is more of a year specific effect and does not reflect the long-term performance of the public defence enterprises. Operating losses have been the rule rather than the exception for the publicly-owned companies. This was shown in Figure 11.3 where the profit/loss position was presented for the two public companies. Throughout 1992–2017 the two public enterprises of this sector (HAI and EAS) have almost invariably been afflicted by poor economic performance, with the concomitant need for the government to continuously support their operation financially. In contrast, private firms have overall performed better, reaffirming the dualism of the defence industry in Greece.

5 Concluding remarks

A combination of both strategic and economic factors were the driving force behind Greece's defence industrialization strategy. As in most cases of small or medium sized powers, initial ambitious plans fell short in view of the hard realities associated with such a task. The Greek defence industrial base exhibits a dualism. On the one hand, the publicly-owned defence companies with accumulated financial and managerial problems that rely heavily on state subsidies for their operation. Next to these, there exists a number of private enterprises, most of them small and medium sized, that exhibit an appreciably better performance, many engaging in collaborative programs as subcontractors with larger international defence producers. A number of them have a strong export orientation. In view of the size of domestic market and the fiscal constraints that Greece will continue to face in coming years, a viable option for the defence industry of Greece is to seek more actively deeper integration in the evolving joint European defence industrial base (Blauberger and Weiss, 2013; Calcara, 2018; Hartley, 2012). Recent developments point to a stepping up of the speed towards a common European security and defence policy. In the scenarios discussed by Mogherini and Katainen (2017) concerning the future of European defence, particularly strong emphasis is placed in the role of the European defence industrial base as a driver towards the potential formation of a European Defence Union. The establishment of a European Defence Fund offers the opportunity for financing joint R&D programs by European defence firms. The funds that will be made available to this effect are envisaged to reach annually 5.5 billion Euros in the post-2020 period. For Greek defence industry SMEs this opens a window of opportunity through their participation in the evolving European defence industrial division of labour given the small sized national market. Such participation either in joint ventures or as subcontractors in larger R&D defence products can also act as a channel for technological flows to the Greek economy, with potential beneficial spillovers to other sectors.

Notes

1 Data from the Word Bank's World Development Indicators (henceforth WDI) database. Ranked as the 30th largest economy in 1980 and 51st in 2017.
2 Data from SIPRI's Arms Transfers Database.
3 Howaldtswerke-Deutsche Werft.
4 Launched in 2006–07. Commissioned in 2015–16.
5 British designation Super Vita. Build between 2005 and 2015.
6 By Greek industrial standards.
7 Companies' official acronyms used throughout.
8 Published by GDAEE. 2018 Edition. Available at: www.gdaee.mil.gr/en/companies/heldic-catalogue
9 In Greek. Available at: www.gdaee.mil.gr/images/PDF/EABS_2017.pdf
10 See note 8.
11 Latest available figure in the 2018 HELDIC catalogue.
12 For instance, if Elefsis Shipyards (not included in the HELDIC catalogue) employment is added, total employment rises above 6000 persons.
13 For a comprehensive and critical survey of the relevant defence economics literature, see Brauer (2002, 2003).
14 Latest available data from the European Defence Agency. Constant 2010 prices.
15 For a discussion of the issues concerning the Greek sovereign debt crisis, see among others Petrakis (2012), Katsimi and Moutos (2010), Vasilopoulou et al. (2014), Trantidis (2016).
16 For a discussion on the nexus between foreign and defence policy in Greece see Stergiou and Kollias (2018).
17 With law 3978/2011 successful international bidders are no longer required to commit to technology and/or know-how transfers to domestic firms and/or to offer offsets and domestic industrial participation in the production of the hardware procured.
18 Mainly PYRKAL founded in 1874 the main supplier of ammunitions and explosives to the Greek Armed Forces. [17] Efforts for domestically produced defence inputs can also be found in the pre-World War II period. They included the State Factory of Airplanes (KEA), a plant that manufactured British Blackburn Dart planes with the Greek designation *Velos* (see Kollias and Rafailidis, 2003).
19 Ibid.
20 Greek acronym EAB.
21 Produced trucks, light infantry vehicles, armoured personnel carriers (APC) and infantry fighting vehicles (IFV).
22 Also nationalized in 1985. Privatized and initially sold to the British firm Brown & Root and subsequently to the German HDW and then to Thyssen Krupp when HDW was taken over by the latter. Currently Abu Dhabi Mar owes around 75% of the stocks.
23 Before Greece adopted the euro as its currency.
24 For a primer on clientelism in Greece see Papadoulis (2006) and Trantidis (2016).

25 An example of such a project failure is the attempt to domestically design and produce a close-range antiaircraft system, the Artemis-30. Only a few units were produced despite the funds that went into its development.
26 Nationalized in 1979. Current employment estimated at around 345 persons.
27 METKA, a private firm that also engages in defence production (see Table 11.4 in the next section). The largest in terms of turnover in 2016 of the companies in the HELDIC 2018 list.
28 Reportedly for the symbolic price of one Euro.
29 For a discussion on the Potential Capacity for Defence or the Potential Arms Production Base see the seminal contributions by Deger (1986) and Kennedy (1974).
30 As mentioned earlier, a number of other firms also engage in defence related production activities but these, for various reasons unknown to the authors, are not included in the catalogue of the MoD. For instance, the two biggest shipyards, Hellenic and Elefsis, that have built many naval units commissioned by the Greek Navy such as frigates, submarines, fast attack missile boats, patrol boats, landing ships. In most cases, these naval units were built under license from the foreign manufacturer. Local construction involved the hull and superstructures while the weapon systems, electronics, radars, propulsion plants etc were imported and fitted locally.
31 Hellenic Airspace Industry. 3rd in the table.
32 Hellenic Defence Systems. 14th in the table.
33 Latest available year.
34 All data drawn from HELDIC 2018
35 Customers include the MoDs of Egypt, France, Germany, Italy, The Netherlands, Pakistan, Peru, Poland, Portugal, Sweden, S. Africa, Ecuador, Ukraine, Venezuela.
36 Data on what percentage of their annual turnover is defence related, is not available.
37 See Figure 11.1 above
38 Estimated from SIPRI's data
39 Constant 2010 prices. Data drawn from the European Defence Agency. Available at: www.eda.europa.eu/info-hub/defence-data-portal
40 http://europa.eu/rapid/press-release_IP-17-1508_en.htm
41 For a more comprehensive discussion of the issues associated with a European defence industrial policy and cooperation in joint development and production programs as well as procurement see among many others Blauberger and Weiss (2013), Calcara (2018), DeVore (2014), Hartley (2003, 2006, 2012)
42 Latest year for which data are available for almost all the 34 defence producers in the HELDIC 2018 list.

Acknowledgements

The chapter has greatly benefited from insightful comments and suggestions by the Editors of the volume. The usual disclaimer applies.

References

Bartzokas, A. (1992) The Developing Arms Industries in Greece, Portugal and Turkey, in M. Brzoska and P. Lock (Eds.) *Restructuring of Arms Production in Western Europe*. Oxford: Oxford University Press.

Bitzinger, R. A. (Ed.) (2009) *The Modern Defense Industry: Political, Economic, and Technological Issues*, Santa Barbara: Praeger Security International.

Blauberger, M. and M. Weiss (2013) If You Can't Beat Me, Join Me! How the Commission Pushed and Pulled Member States into Legislating Defence Procurement. *Journal of European Public Policy*, 20(8), 1120–1138.

Brauer, J. (2002) Survey and Review of the Defence Economics Literature on Greece and Turkey: What have We Learned? *Defence and Peace Economics*, 13(2), 85–107.

Brauer, J. (2003) Turkey and Greece: A Comprehensive Survey of the Defence Economics literature, in C. Kollias and G. Gunluk-Senesen (Eds.), *Greece and Turkey in the 21st Century. The Political Economy Perspective*, New York: Nova Science Publishers, 193–241.

Brauer, J. (2007) Arms Industries, Arms Trade, and Developing Countries, in T. Sandler and K. Hartley (Eds.), *Handbook of Defence Economics*, Vol. 2, Amsterdam: North- Holland, Elsevier, 973–1011.

Calcara, A. (2018) Cooperation and Conflict in the European Defence-Industrial Field: The Role of Relative Gains. *Defence Studies*. doi:10.1080/14702436.2018.1487766.

Deger, S. (1986) *Military Expenditures in the Third World*. London and Boston: Routledge & Kegan Paul.

DeVore, M. (2014) International Armaments Collaboration and the Limits of Reform. *Defence and Peace Economics*, 25(4), 415–443.

Dokos, T. (2011) Mediterranean 2020. The Future of the Mediterranean Security and Politics. The German Marshall Fund of the United States. www.gmfus.org/publications/mediterranean-2020future-mediterranean-security-and-politics.

Dokos, T. and P. Tsakonas (2003) Greek–Turkish Relations in the post-Cold War Era, in C. Kollias and G. Gunluk-Senesen (Eds.), *Greece and Turkey in the 21st Century. The Political Economy Perspective*. New York: Nova Science Publishers, 9–35.

Dunne, J. Paul, 1995. The Defense Industrial Base. In: Keith Hartley and Todd Sandler (eds.), *Handbook of Defense Economics*, edition 1, volume 1. London: Elsevier.

Hartley, K. (2003) The Future of European Defence Policy: An Economic Perspective. *Defence and Peace Economics*, 14(2), 107–115.

Hartley, K. (2006) Defence Industrial Policy in a Military Alliance. *Journal of Peace Research*, 43(4), 473–489.

Hartley, K. (2012) *White Elephants? The Political Economy of Multi- National Defence Projects*, Brussels: New Direction – The Foundation for European Reform.

Hartley, K. (2017) *The Economics of Arms*, Newcastle upon Tyne: Agenda.

Katsimi, M. and T. Moutos (2010) EMU and the Greek Crisis: The Political Economy Perspective. *European Journal of Political Economy*, 26(3), 568–576.

Kennedy, G. (1974) *The Military in the Third World*, London: Duckworth.

Kollias, C., S-M. Paleologou and A. Stergiou (2016) Military Expenditure in Greece: Security Challenges and Economic Constraints. *The Economics of Peace and Security Journal*, 11, 23–29.

Kollias, C. and A. Rafailidis (2003) A Survey of the Greek Defence Industry. *Defence and Peace Economics*, 14(4), 311–324.

Kollias C. and Paleologou S-M. (2003), Domestic Political and External Security Determinants of the Demand for Greek Military Expenditure, *Defence and Peace Economics*, 14(6), 437–445.

Matthews, R. (1999) Greek Turkish Tensions Fuel Defence Industrialization. *RUSI Journal*, 144(1), 52–58.

Mogherini, F. and J. Katainen (2017) Reflection Paper on the Future of European Defence, https://ec.europa.eu/commission/sites/beta-political/files/reflection-paper-defence_en.pdf

Mouzakis, F. (2002) Domestic Production as An Alternative to Importing Arms, in J. Brauer and P. Dunne (Eds.), *Arming the South. The Economics of Military Expenditure, Arms Production and Arms Trade in Developing Countries*, London: Palgrave.

Papadoulis, K. (2006) Clientelism, Corruption and Patronage in Greece: A Public Administration Approach. *Teaching Public Administration*, 26(1), 13–24.

Petrakis, P. (2012) *The Greek Economy and the Crisis Challenges and Responses*, Heidelberg, Dordrecht, London, New York: Springer.

Ploumis, M. (2017) Hellenic Defence Industrial Base in the Era of Economic Crisis. *South-Eastern Europe Journal of Economics*, 2, 103–125.

Stergiou, A. and C. Kollias (2018) Between Pragmatism and Rhetoric: A Critical Assessment of Greece's Defence and Foreign Policy in the 1980s in Light of New Primary Sources. *Southeast European and Black Sea Studies*. doi:10.1080/14683857.2018.1553603.

Trantidis, A. (2016) *Clientelism and Economic Policy. Greece and the Crisis*, New York: Routledge.

Vasilopoulou, S., D. Halikiopoulou, and Th. Exadaktylos (2014) Greece in Crisis: Austerity, Populism and the Politics of Blame. *Journal of Common Market Studies*, 52(2), 388–402.

12 Polish defence industry

Learning to walk again

Stefan Markowski and Antoni Pieńkos

1. Introduction

Poland, a NATO member since 1999 but also a former satellite of the USSR and a member of the Warsaw Pact, is a relatively modest defence spender with an annual military expenditure (milex) equivalent to about a fifth of that presently spent on defence by France or Germany. Poland hosts a largely obsolete but still sizable defence industry, which is a legacy of its past membership of the Warsaw Pact. In 2017, Poland was estimated to have spent €8.68 billion on defence (in current €), which was equivalent to 1.9% of GDP and 4.5% of all government spending (EDA 2018). This burden of defence is expected to increase in the not-too-distant future as Poland is keen to demonstrate its compliance with the NATO-prescribed defence spending target of at least 2% of GDP. Of Poland's total 2017 milex, 44% was spent on personnel, 24% on the procurement of military equipment (exceeding the NATO-prescribed 20% target), 3% on defence-related R&D, 7% on military infrastructure, and 22% on operations and maintenance. In 2017, the Polish Armed Forces (PAF) numbered nearly 107,000 uniformed personnel (a third in the Army) and about 34,000 defence civilians.

The Polish defence industry is mostly sustained by domestic defence spending as directed by successive governments. Military exports are negligible, although they support some successful pockets of activity. As the sector is mostly state-owned with limited scope for diversifying production into civilian output, the government of the day decides what is to be made in country and what is to be imported and at what cost. In this respect, Poland is not much different from most other countries where governments use their monopsony power to determine the scale, scope and profitability of the domestic defence industry. And, as in most democracies, the legacy of past military investment and procurement commitments tends to weigh heavily on subsequent make or buy sourcing decisions. This is because obsolete but highly specialised production capabilities (e.g., naval shipyards) cannot be easily adapted to other uses and making the military buy what it does not want or need is often the politically most convenient way of protecting jobs in outdated plants and parliamentary seats in vulnerable marginal constituencies.

However, in contrast to many other democracies, Poland has also been struggling with the legacy of being the former Soviet satellite state for some 45 years of its post-WWII history (1944–1989). That is, much of the Polish economy has had to make a radical transformation from the Soviet-style (state-owned and centrally-planned) entity to a largely privately-owned, market driven and open (to trade and foreign direct investment) economic system. Overall, it has been a surprisingly smooth and successful process with the Polish economy growing fast, catching up with its western European neighbours and, following Poland's accession to the European Union in 2004, increasingly absorbed into the European Union's division of labour (OECD 2018). However, unlike the Polish economy at large, the Polish defence industry sector has been a laggard in this process of institutional transformation.

Paradoxically, Poland's defence industry thrived when Poland was a member of the Warsaw Pact as, under the Soviet division of labour, substantial resources had to be allocated to the production of military materiel by every Soviet satellite state. While the centrally planned economy of Poland stagnated and eventually suffered a catastrophic collapse, its military industrial segment prospered under the Moscow-directed division of military labour (see below). However, following the implosion of the communist system in the early 1990s, the arms industry has found it difficult to adapt to the new NATO-centric reality of post-communist defence and, thus, it has been limping along, starved of adequate resources to divest its Soviet inheritance by innovating new products and processes. Consequently, the industry has been poorly placed to compete against materiel imports from foreign, now mostly NATO, suppliers.

More recently, this vulnerability has been compounded by the Polish government's commitment to import US-made military equipment to demonstrate Poland's credentials as a new member of NATO and as a 'keen-to-please' junior ally of the US. These imports are designed in part to induce the Americans to enlarge their military footprint in Poland. Arguably, this is seen as a prudent investment intended to persuade the US to include the eastern flank of NATO under the US-provided military umbrella to deter Russia from expanding west into its former satellite states. To signal its military commitment to the US-led regional defence, Poland wants to be seen buying US-sourced arms supplies (e.g., the order for the Patriot air defence missile systems). However, with a large fraction of the Polish defence procurement budget dedicated to imports (American as well as some smaller European supplies), there is little left for Polish producers even if some local content 'offsets' come their way (RAPORT 2018). There are some bright spots in this gloomy tale, which we describe below, but, overall, it is a tale of an industry in decline weighed down by obsolete capacities, underfunding, resistance to change, political interference and nostalgia about its past export successes.

The aim of the chapter is to: (a) sketch the Soviet past of the Polish defence industry and challenges associated with its transition to the post-communist market economy, which partially explain its present difficulties to adapt to the post-communist reality (Section 2); (b) provide a perspective on its structure, conduct and performance (Section 3); and (c) offer a simple diagnosis of where the adopted restructuring strategy appears to have gone wrong over the past few years (Section 4).

2. Soviet legacy and challenges of post-communist transition

2.1 Warsaw Pact legacy

Following World War II, the Soviet Union assigned all its newly acquired central and southern European satellite states, including Poland, different military tasks under the overarching Soviet division of military labour. This was driven partly by the siege mentality of the 1930s, when the USSR was the sole communist state in the world, and in part by the Marxist aspiration to conquer, if need be by military force, and replace the 'western capitalist order' with the 'inherently superior socialist system' modelled on the centrally-planned economy of the USSR. Thus, while the US and most of its wartime allies chose to reduce their armed forces immediately after the end of WWII hostilities and convert their wartime military production back to peacetime production, the USSR retained the size and readiness of its armed forces at their war-end strength well into the late 1940s.[1] It was also keen to maintain its military industrial effort to allow the Red Army to modernize and replenish its stocks of military materiel. Although the newly acquired Soviet satellite states were not to be trusted as allies – as they were mostly nations that had either been historically hostile to Russia/the Soviet Union (e.g., Poland) or aligned with the Nazi Germany during WWII (e.g., Hungary) – their military and economic resources had to be harnessed to boost the overall military strength of the USSR and enhance its preparedness for the then anticipated military conflict with the US and its NATO allies (Yoder 1993). Poland, as the largest of all Soviet satellite states, was to field a substantial conscript army to fight alongside the Red Army, while its defence industry was to be incorporated in the Soviet division of labour to use its pre- and war-time capabilities as a component maker and an assembler of a wide variety of military equipment.

Under the Soviet division of military labour no satellite country was to become an independent producer of military materiel. Consequently, the PAF was expected to be fully interoperative with the Soviet Army, as well as with all other armed forces of the Soviet bloc, and use standards, equipment, components and consumables designed/approved by the USRR and mass produced at different locations within the Soviet bloc. While the PAF was the main recipient of military materiel produced in-country, the Polish arms industry was also expected to export a large proportion of its intermediate and final products to the USSR and other Soviet satellites. In part, this spatial dispersion of the intra-bloc production capability was intended to sustain the Soviet military domination and prevent the satellites from achieving high levels of military autonomy, which could threaten Soviet military domination. In part, however, it was intended to foster functional specialisation to make good use of limited manufacturing resources available to the Soviet bloc. As a result, this centrally directed and USSR-dominated division of labour facilitated large scale and, by Soviet standards, cost-effective production of military materiel. Soviet bloc production facilities were not only designed for scale- and scope-related efficiencies and potential 'surges' into wartime production but they were also well utilized in peacetime so that these potential efficiencies could actually be harnessed. It also necessitated large scale, intra-bloc trade in components, consumables, and semi- and fully-assembled military equipment.

Over time, as the Soviet 'empire' consolidated and, after the death of Stalin, the puppet communist regimes in central and eastern Europe morphed into more independent junior partners of the USSR, the post-war Soviet division of military labour was also re-fashioned in 1955 into the *Warsaw Pact* – a multinational military alliance part-modelled on NATO.[2] In reality, the Pact was an 'alliance' in name only as no junior member state could either refuse the Soviet invitation to join or easily terminate its membership (although Albania succeeded in the late 1960s). However, in contrast to NATO – where the legacy of old rivalries between European powers such as France and the United Kingdom, tended to impede the consolidation of uni-national defence industries led by national industrial champions into the pan-European defence sector capable of competing against the ever larger US military suppliers – the Warsaw Pact provided a relatively effective means of coordinating the Soviet bloc's military industrial effort. This was because the Pact continued to be totally subordinated to the military command of the USSR and, as in previous years, all military standards, specifications and designs continued to be either developed or approved by the USSR. Non-European communist countries, China in particular, were also included in the Soviet division of labour in that they were given access to various Soviet military technologies and adopted Soviet technical standards in their home manufacture of military materiel. This division of labour and the associated central direction of all military activities of the Pact allowed the Soviet bloc to specialize and, thus, to harness economies of scale, scope and agglomeration to produce large quantities of relatively modern, robust and affordable military equipment (Cooper 2013).

Although the Soviet system struggled to keep up with western market economies to produce consumer and producer goods of acceptable quality in sufficiently large numbers, the efficient production of military materiel and space equipment allowed the Warsaw Pact to punch well above its otherwise mediocre economic weight (ibid.). Arguably, this was the one and only area where the Soviet bloc could claim the superior effectiveness of the central direction of military resource allocation. Intra-bloc trade in military components, fully integrated systems and consumables was an important aspect of this centralized approach even though Soviet bloc currencies were only partially convertible and the associated exchange rates, like all Soviet bloc prices, were mostly arbitrary and divorced from underlying resource scarcities (ibid.). As the Cold War progressed and the Soviet Union adopted a more supportive stance of various 'unaligned' fellow travellers in Asia, Middle East, Africa and Latin America, the bloc's exports of military hardware and consumables grew. That meant that countries such as Poland were allowed to become significant arms exporters, usually to client totalitarian regimes of the Soviet Union in the Middle East (e.g., Syria, Libya, Egypt, Iraq), selected African 'liberation fronts' (Angola, Mozambique), the pro-Soviet Cuba and 'unaligned' powers such as India.

Furthermore, the distinction between the military and civil industrial capabilities was deliberately blurred under the Soviet system. Pockets of military capability were purposely dispersed by central planners throughout the economy to facilitate wartime production surge, seamless conversion of civil capacities into military production, and the broadening of the military-relevant technological knowhow. As civilian consumer needs were mostly subordinated to those of the state, the opportunity cost of investing in and sustaining all these Cold War-related military capabilities was largely immaterial: any trade-offs between 'guns' and 'butter' were invariably resolved in favour of 'guns' for as long as there was enough 'butter' to command the loyalty of the communist *priviligentsia.*

By 1989, when the communist regime in Poland imploded, the country supported a largely conscript-based military force of some 0.5 million soldiers, sailors and airmen, equipped with mostly Soviet-designed but partially home-made weapons systems including the whole spectrum of conventional equipment from the AK-48 assault rifles, through a wide variety of munitions and explosives, main battle tanks, armoured personnel carriers, self-propelled artillery and rocket launchers, warships, radars, to fixed and rotary wing combat aircraft. Thus, the Polish defence industry produced and integrated a plethora of military components and sub-assemblies for home use, export to other Warsaw Pact members, and supply to various third party clients. By the late 1980s, it employed some 250,000 people (Myck et al. 2016: 57) and for most state-owned military enterprises this was the golden era of Polish military production and exports.

Clearly, the most sophisticated and strategically critical weapons systems, in particular nuclear capabilities, strategic delivery systems, telecommunications, space and satellite systems were solely produced in the USSR and their availability was strictly restricted to the Red Army to allow the Soviet Union to retain its military dominance. However, even in this USSR-centric world, the Polish defence industry was also encouraged to develop some indigenous designs such as the military jet trainer *Iskra*, radars, pontoon bridges and heavy logistic support equipment. However, these Polish designs were not mass produced as, albeit with few exceptions, other Soviet bloc armies were only expected to use the USSR-approved standard equipment. All other equipment made by the Soviet satellites was purchased at the discretion of individual states. Systems made in small batches were also less exportable to third parties.[3] This dependence on Soviet designs and standards impeded the post-communist export potential of the Polish defence industry as shipments to Warsaw Pact countries ceased in the early 1990s and there were hardly any Polish-designed and manufactured systems in use elsewhere that could *only* be sustained and/or replaced by Polish arms manufacturers.

2.2 The post-communist transition

By 1991, when the Warsaw Pact was formally dismantled, Poland was left with the legacy of Soviet-style defence industry geared to the production of Soviet-type equipment to be used by large, predominantly land forces expected to roll west alongside the Red Army. This equipment was no longer suitable for the effective defence of a mid-European sovereign country aligned with its former NATO foes. Some of the Soviet era equipment was exportable to the former clients of the USSR in the Middle East and to countries such as India, which have had a long history of using it. Thus, well into the 2000s, Poland continued to produce and partially export weapons that were increasingly obsolete at home. Also, some production of legacy systems had to be sustained to maintain and modify the Soviet-era equipment in service with the PAF.[4] In the 1990s and the early 2000s, there were no funds to invest in the development of new weapons systems or pay for large equipment imports from NATO suppliers.

By 1999, when Poland formally acceded to NATO, it was increasingly obvious that a radical restructuring solution was needed to scale down the much-too-large Polish defence industry, modernize its production technologies and refocus its product lines. This change was also imperative with the PAF moving away from the mass conscription model of the communist era to become a labour-saving, capital-intensive professional fighting force capable of operating at high levels of readiness and interoperable with Poland's NATO allies, particularly the US, in various expeditionary tasks (e.g., Iraq, Afghanistan).

To respond to these restructuring challenges, one, albeit extreme, option was to discontinue much of the domestic arms production by state enterprises, fire sell those segments of the sector that were of potential interest to western arms manufacturers and domestic buyers and close most of the rest. Under this option, Poland would invest in military capabilities at the sharp end of defence value chain but not in the upstream segments of it. This would have been an industrial disinvestment option as, given the modest size of the Polish defence budget and considerable overcapacity in NATO defence industries, there would have been little incentive for western arms manufacturers to acquire large industrial footprints in Poland at the expense of their existing home-based production facilities. Some elements of defence industry would continue to operate in country as Polish manufacturing has successfully attracted foreign direct investors and the

PAF would have to be supported by local maintenance capabilities. Nevertheless, this option would have attracted considerable political opposition in Poland, in part, because it would have led to increased unemployment in politically vulnerable locations, and, in part, because the public at large and much of the media commentariat would have viewed the decline of indigenous defence industry as the *de facto* abandonment of sovereign national defence. The promise of a peace dividend was viewed rather sceptically by Polish voters mindful of the country's traumatic history and aware that Russia's period of military weakness in the 1990s offered only a temporary respite and a window of opportunity for smaller east European countries to acquire EU and NATO membership.

A more politically acceptable option was to consolidate the existing defence industry into a single, state-owned holding entity cum-national champion, which would be progressively restructured and corporatized while some pockets of activity were sold to domestic manufacturers and service providers and/or to foreign defence companies keen to invest in local manufacture and service support. This holding entity could have been modelled on the Swiss RUAG or the Swedish SAAB arrangements. By the 2010s, after some institutional experimentation, the holding concept got enough political traction for the *Polish Armaments Group* (PAG) to be formed in 2013 as an overarching governing entity spanning a cluster of about 60 state-owned, defence-related but often technologically incompatible and independently managed enterprises. An obvious moral hazard of this arrangement was that the formation of a state-owned holding group straddling a myriad of independently managed, state-owned enterprises would open the group's management to capture by political interests keen to reward their supporters with plum managerial positions rather than implement radical restructuring changes. There was also a risk that some successful group members would be held back by those unable or unwilling to change. In this respect, the PAG appears to function as a relic of the Soviet era industrial structure and an outlier in the otherwise dynamic and increasingly market-savvy Polish manufacturing industry.

In contrast to the state sector, where entrepreneurial successes of some companies are often overshadowed by the PAG's overall poor performance (see below), some segments of the Polish defence industry have been acquired by foreign interests (e.g., PZL Mielec by Sikorsky/Lockheed Martin; WSK 'PZL Świdnik' by Augusta Westland; with other aerospace facilities acquired by Pratt & Whitney, Airbus Defence and Space Company, and MTU Aero Engines). These foreign subsidiaries appear to be doing reasonably well, especially as exporters (see below). In addition, a new Polish private company, WB Electronics (later WB Group) was established in 1997 and has quickly grown into the largest private firm in the Polish defence sector.

3. Industry ownership, structure, conduct and performance

3.1 Ownership, output and financial viability of arms producers

In 2014, when the first stage of PAG consolidation was completed, the Group posted its annual turnover of US$1.62 billion (c. €1.49 billion) and was ranked 61st on the SIPRI's list of the world's 100 largest defence companies.[5] But a year later, its turnover declined to US$1.32 billion (c. €1.27 billion), of which 90% were military sales, and the Group was ranked 73rd on the SIPRI list. In 2018, it employed well over 17,000 people and reported turnover of about US$1.3 billion (€1.08 billion).[6] Since 2016, the governmental responsibility for the general oversight of all publicly-owned defence industry, including PAG, was transferred from the Treasury to the Ministry of Defence. This has brought to an end a series of demarcation disputes between the two departments regarding the strategic direction and management of the industry.[7] But, the institutional consolidation of the Group remains a work in progress and much of its central and mid-level management has been stacked with political appointees rather than professional industrial technocrats (RAPORT 2018).

The flagship plant of the PGZ is its *Huta Stalowa Wola* (HSW) steelworks, which is the producer of self-propelled heavy artillery, armoured personnel carriers, combat support vehicles, as well as engineering equipment for the land forces. The plant was built in the late 1930s as a heavy equipment maker for the Polish army and continued in that capacity throughout the communist period. In the 1980s, it diversified into civilian construction equipment, which in the 1990s comprised much of its output. Only in 2008, the Ministry of Defence commissioned HSW to develop new military products, such as the *Krab* 155 mm self-propelled howitzer, and to modernize Poland's self-propelled rocket launchers *Langusta*. In 2012, the company sold its civilian production line to concentrate solely on military products. It also acquired *Jelcz*, a former truck and bus maker (and later another bus company *Autosan*) to diversify into the manufacture of vehicle chasses and heavy trailers for tanks and artillery systems.[8] In addition, HSW made significant investments in new production capabilities (e.g., machinery for the production of 155 mm cannon barrels) to become a vertically integrated maker of complex artillery systems.[9] It is presently the leading domestic arms supplier to the PAF with the contract to deliver 120 *Krab* howitzers (the largest of recent armaments contracts) and a new design for a wheeled howitzer *Kryl*.[10]

Arguably, the most financially successful member of the PAG holding group is *Nitro-Chem*, one of NATO's largest suppliers of explosives, which exports over 80% of its output mostly to the US (Wachowski 2016). It also makes and exports explosives for civilian uses in mining and construction.[11] Other members of the PAG are a mixed bag of hopefuls and dead-end, Soviet era enterprises (RAPORT 2018: 5). For example, *MESKO S.A.* is Poland's largest producer of munitions covering the whole range of products from small arms to tank and heavy artillery munitions. It has recently expanded into the production of laser-based precision munitions for Krab and Kryl artillery made by HSW (Zieliński 2016). While the company is potentially viable, it has been held back by delayed and reduced home demand and limited opportunity to export its products. Another company seen as a potential success story, given its past scale of activity, is the maker of heavy armoured vehicles *ZM Bumar-Łabędy*. It is presently set out to modernize, in partnership with the *German Rheinmetall Landsysteme Gmbh*, 128 Leopard 2A4 tanks and additional Bergepanzer armoured technical recovery and support vehicles. The overall contract is said to be worth €550 million, of which over 60% is to be the local content provided by ZM *Bumar-Łabędy* (Kiński 2016). This has been hailed as an example of a potentially viable way forward for member companies of the PAG as import substitution in component manufacture and equipment maintenance and upgrades offer more scope for financial success than the development and production of new equipment. However, at the time of writing, there appear to be some schedule slippages and it is still unclear whether this old industrial dog can actually learn new tricks as a component maker, maintainer and upgrader.

In 1997, two private entrepreneurs founded *WB Electronics* – initially a producer of electronic systems and software – which has rapidly grown into the largest private defence company in Poland. In 2009, the company was restructured as the *WB Group* and acquired an interest in *Flytronic* (the leading producer of UAV in Poland) and, in 2011, it acquired *Radmor* (a manufacturer of communication equipment).[12] In 2017, the state-owned *Polish Development Fund*, supporting strategic investments in Polish enterprises, acquired 24% of the Group's equity (for about €30 million) to provide funding for new product investments and export expansion.[13] The Group's most important products are *Fonet* systems (digital communication and command systems) and *Topaz* (artillery fire control and battle management systems). It also makes the *FlyEye* system (the first home-made UAV to be acquired by the PAF) and the loitering ammunition *Warmate* (the Group's flagship export product). In 2016, the Group realised about €85 million of sales revenue with pre-tax profits of about €13 million (15%). It currently employs over 800 people of whom more than half are R&D engineers.[14]

Another private company is the *Remontowa Shipbuilding* (a part of *Remontowa Holding* capital group), the largest private shipbuilding company in Poland and, at the time of writing, one of the two in-country naval shipbuilders (the other being PGZ Stocznia Wojenna)" capable of constructing vessels for the Polish Navy (e.g., currently building two *Kormoran* Class minehunters and six tugboats). The shipyard was previously known as the *Northern Shipyard* and in the 1960s it built research vessels and warships for the Polish Navy and for export to the USSR.[15] The group also includes a repair yard, a design office and some component makers.[16] As the privately-owned prime contractor for the *Kormoran* Class minehunters, the *Remontowa Shipbuilding* also leads a consortium of companies including two state-owned entities, which are part of the PAG: *PGZ Stocznia Wojenna* (PGZ Naval Shipyard) and *Ośrodek Badawczo-Rozwojowy Centrum Techniki Morskiej* (the leading naval R&D centre in Poland). This is an unusual business model in the Polish defence industry as normally state-owned firms are selected as prime contractors and consortia leaders. However, in comparison with the large order book and exports of the *Northern Shipyard* in the 1960s, the current level of activity is modest and the company remains vulnerable as its order book depends on capricious and often delayed local procurement.

3.2 Exports

Defence-related industrial exports from Poland are relatively small and most local commentators regard this outcome as highly disappointing (e.g., Łuczak 2017). Poland is compared, for example, with Spain, which in 2016 exported military materiel valued at €3.72 billion while Polish exports, at €383 million, represented about a tenth of the Spanish sales (ibid.). In 2017, Poland was ranked the 42nd in the SIPRI top 50 list of international arms exporters, behind New Zealand and, what the local commentariat finds particularly hard to accept, behind the Czech Republic and Bulgaria (ibid.: 8). In 2006, Poland was ranked 14th (its best post-communist ranking following the sale of 48 tanks to Malaysia and some armoured recovery vehicles to India) and, in 1991, at the outset of the post-communist transformation, it was ranked the 22nd.[17] The present export performance is often nostalgically compared with volumes achieved during the golden period of Polish arms sales when the country was a member of the Warsaw Pact and, in 1976, was ranked the world's 10th largest arms exporter with sales valued at US$406 million (current US$). These were the bygone years when Poland exported warships, aircraft and armoured vehicles to the Soviet bloc and to countries such as India, Iraq and Czechoslovakia.[18]

In contrast to actual exports of military materiel by Polish firms, which have decreased in recent years, the value of export *permits* issued to potential exporters has increased steadily since 2011 (Łuczak 2017)[19]. In 2016, for example, 700 export licenses were issued in Poland, which authorized €1.23 billion worth of potential exports – about three times the value of that year's actual exports. While it is not surprising that the value of actual exports lags behind the value of export licences, it is rather puzzling to observe companies apply for more export permits when their actual export sales decline over time.

The largest (actual) export item in 2016, valued at €152 million and representing 40% of all exports, were aircraft components shipped to the US and Canada from the local subsidiaries of American aerospace (e.g., Sikorsky) and to Spain by the local subsidiary of Airbus (MSZ 2017). Interestingly, the aerospace component shipments to North America have also declined significantly from their peak of €295 million in 2014 (when they comprised 75% of all exports).[20] Excluding these intracompany transfers of aerospace intermediate products, Polish arms exports amounted to €160 million in 2016, of which munitions exported by the state-owned *Nitro-Chem* accounted for

€51 million. The private company *WB Group* is also a significant exporter of products such as electronics and loitering munitions.[21] Other small-scale exports include light weapons and bullet-proofed vests.

Future prospects for Polish arms exports remain uncertain. It is hoped that the expanded production of self-propelled artillery systems, armoured vehicles, radars and loitering and precision munitions may eventually boost Polish export sales (Łuczak 2017). There are also hopes that the increased intra-EU collaboration, under the auspices of the EDA PESCO initiative and part subsidised by the EU European Defence Fund, may assist the Polish industry as an exporter and supplier of import replacement products (Łuczak 2018). The establishment of the Polish Arms Procurement Agency may also help if it uses its modest monopsony power to enhance the local content of imported military materiel.[22]

3.3 Conduct and performance

Most of the Polish defence industry is state-owned and largely dependent on the PAF for its survival. However, PAG and its state-owned member companies have too little market power to twist the government's arm to ensure that procurement orders flow their way at the expense of imports. The overall financial situation of PAG is, thus, very fragile if the government opts to divert its procurement budget to imports of US materiel while orders for home made products are cancelled or delayed. Within the Group, 18 member companies are said to be on the verge of insolvency and another 11 are potentially vulnerable (RAPORT 2018: 5). There is also considerable overemployment in the PAG, where 17,000 people on the current payroll only generate €1,080 million of sales revenue. Using a crude measure of revenue per employee achieved by the privately-owned WB Group in 2016, the state-owned PAG could shed some 6–7,000 jobs to achieve levels of efficiency observed in the private sector. Excluding employees involved in the production of civilian goods and services, we estimate that about 20,000 people have been engaged in arms-related production activities in Poland in 2018. It appears that at least a third of these positions is vulnerable and could be made redundant if the public sector is allowed to rationalize.

4. Way forward

The idea of integrating the bulk of the Polish defence industry into a single holding entity aimed at achieving economies of agglomeration by combining scale- and scope-related efficiencies appears to be a sound one. This could have been modelled on the corporatized Swiss RUAG organisation to make it detached from political interference in management, but not necessarily privatised, as there is no indigenous equity capital capable of running an arms-making national champion to compete against international arms suppliers. To make this model work, successive governments would have to assign preference to import substitution in defence procurement as part of a move towards higher levels of defence industrial self-sufficiency and, if necessary, commit to paying cost premia to enhance the local content of military materiel purchased by the PAF during the early years of the holding organisation. They should also insist on its integration into the European division of labour to make Poland share in and benefit from the joint development and supply of 'European' defence systems.

Instead, the present Polish government appears to have opted for the US military umbrella as a substitute for more European defence. This is a legitimate, albeit controversial, strategy to adopt if one believes that a large physical US military footprint in Poland offers a better long-term prospect for the nation's security than the broad, alliance-based collective defence or the yet-to-be-conceptualized European defence.[23] However, like all resource management choices, the apparent preference for direct imports of US-provided security has its opportunity cost. It mitigates against more resources being made available for in-country arms makers to develop new competitive products and modernize their production facilities to make these products more affordable and exportable. Clearly, some 'offsetting arrangements' will be negotiated under the US-oriented defence arrangements to increase the local content of imported materiel. That said, US supplies are notoriously difficult to subcontract as the US government and large American defence contractors apply stringent ITAR provisions to protect their intellectual property and are usually reluctant to make IT source codes and 'keys' to equipment 'black boxes' available to facilitate deep maintenance and modification of US equipment by third parties (re: the Australian experience: Chapter 22). Thus, the opportunity cost of the increased American footprint in Poland is likely to be the continuing decline of the state-owned Polish arms industry especially if, as a result, it is not only starved of resources to expand but also prevented from meaningful participation in joint European defence initiatives.

Not surprisingly, the PAG as whole resembles a relic of the centrally-planned, Soviet-style economy of the 1980s. It appears to be too-big-to-fail but also politically too complex to shift. In contrast, the private segment of the Polish arms industry has performed reasonably well as it uses its entrepreneurial flair and draws on the available technical talent to innovate product lines and seek orders in areas of activity, where the state-sector is too bureaucratic and too hamstrung by its political masters to operate efficiently.

Notes

1 As WWII came to an end, the USA, the UK and Canada reduced their collective armed force personnel from over 3.7 million in 1945 to about 900,000 in 1946 and converted a large part of their wartime industrial capacity back to civil production. The Soviet Union, however, retained its armed forces at their wartime strength of six million and its military industries continued to operate at full capacity in 1946 (Sandler and Hartley 1999: 25).

2 This was meant to be a delayed response to the earlier formation of NATO as the US-led western military alliance but more specifically a reaction to the admission in 1954 of the then German Federal Republic as a new, 'frontline' NATO member.
3 Rather exceptionally, *Iskra* was imported by India.
4 For example, at the time of writing Poland continues to modernize its fleet of Soviet era helicopters Mi-2 of which 60 remain in service with the PAF. Wroński, P. (2019) 'Błaszczak chwali się modernizacją armii. Jak jest naprawdę?', *Gazeta Wyborcza*, 10/01/2019.
5 SIPRI Arms Industry Database, *Data for the SIPRI Top 100 for 2002–2017*, SIPRI Arms Industry Database, Stockholm: Stockholm International Peace Research Institute, www.sipri.org/databases/armsindustry (accessed 1 Dec 2018).
6 PGZ official website, http://pgzsa.pl/ (accessed 1 Dec 2018).
7 *Polska zbrojeniówka w 2016 roku i perspektywy na rok bieżący*, *Defence24.pl*, www.defence24.pl/polska-zbrojeniowka-w-2016-roku-i-perspektywy-na-rok-biezacy (accessed 1 Dec 2018).
8 See HSW official website www.hsw.pl/p/29,80-lat-hsw-s-a (accessed 5 Dec 2018).
9 'Huta Stalowa Wola znów zbrojeniową potęgą', *Rzeczpospolita*.pl, www.rp.pl/artykul/144029-Huta-Stalowa-Wola-znow-zbrojeniowa-potega.html (accessed 5 Dec 2018).
10 Still awaiting a supply order from the PAF, (re: 'Raki i nowe Kraby idą do wojska', *Defence24*.pl, www.defence24.pl/raki-i-nowe-kraby-ida-do-wojska, accessed 5 Dec 2018).
11 Its export successes are in part attributed to the F-16 offset arrangements negotiated in 2003, which allowed the company to enter the US market.
12 *WB Electronics przejmuje Radmor*, Rzeczpospolita.pl, www.rp.pl/artykul/542239-WB-Electronics-przejmuje-Radmor.html
13 M. Wysocki, '128 mln zł dla WB Electronics – PFR nowym inwestorem', *Wgospodarce.pl*, http://wgospodarce.pl/informacje/42439-128-mln-zl-dla-wb-electronics-pfr-nowym-inwestorem (accessed 1 Dec 2018).
14 *MON kupi od WB Electronics tysiąc zestawów Warmate*, WNP.pl, www.wnp.pl/przemysl-obronny/mon-kupi-od-wb-electronics-tysiac-zestawow-warmate,311201_1_0_0.html.
15 Remontowa Shipbuilding website, www.remontowa-rsb.pl/, accessed 1 Dec 2018.
16 'Remontowa Shipbuilding w Gdańsku buduje dla MON. Stępka pod pierwszy z sześciu holowników dla Marynarki Wojennej', *Dziennik Bałtycki*, https://dziennikbaltycki.pl/remontowa-shipbuilding-w-gdansku-buduje-dla-mon-stepka-pod-pierwszy-z-szesciu-holownikow-dla-marynarki-wojennej-zdjecia/ar/12874276, accessed 1 Dec 2018.
17 *TIV of arms exports from the top 50 largest exporters, 1950–2017*, SIPRI Arms Transfers Database, http://armstrade.sipri.org/armstrade/html/export_toplist.php (accessed 10 Oct 2018).
18 *TIV of arms exports from Poland, 1950–2017*, SIPRI Arms Transfers Database, www.sipri.org/databases/armstransfers (accessed 10 Oct 2018).
19 All intended arms exports from the EU, including Poland, require an application for an export licence.
20 Further, from the declared value of Polish exports in 2016, one should also subtract €30 million, which was the stock of old ammunition donated to Jordan, and the value of 40 wheeled armoured personnel carriers sold to the United Arab Emirates in 2015 but recorded as exports in 2016 (another €40 million).
21 *WB Group z Ożarowa zarabia tyle co państwowy gigant Polska Grupa Zbrojeniowa*, Rzeczpospolita.pl, www.rp.pl/Przemysl-Obronny/309219892-WB-Group-z-Ozarowa-zarabia-tyle-co-panstwowy-gigant-Polska-Grupa-Zbrojeniowa.html (accessed 10 Oct 2018).

22 'Rząd usiłuje uratować wciąż spadający eksport polskiej broni', *Rzeczpospolita.pl*, www.rp.pl/Przemysl-Obronny/309199908-Rzad-usiluje-uratowac-wciaz-spadajacy-eksport-polskiej-broni.html (accessed 10 Oct 2018).
23 At the time of writing, the Polish government is keen to construct in Poland a large garrison facility to house US troops permanently based at the eastern flank of NATO (the so-called Fort Trump) to ensure that this would serve as a trip-wire to American direct involvement in the defence of the eastern Europe and, thus, deter the Russian Federation from future expansion into the region.

References

Cooper, J. (2013) 'From USSR to Russia: The fate of the military economy', in Hare, P. and Turley, G. (eds.) *Handbook of the Economics and Political Economy of Transition*, London and New York: Routledge: 98–107.

EDA. (2018) *EDA Collective and National Defence Data 2005-2017*, Brussels: European Defence Agency, www.eda.europa.eu/info-hub/defence-data-portal (accessed Nov 2018).

Kiński, A. (2016) 'Rheinmetall i Bumar-Łabędy wspólnie zmodernizują Leopardy 2A4', *Wojsko i Technika*, March: 10–14.

Łuczak, W. (2017) 'Konsekwentne oddawanie pola. Eksport specjalny Polski w 2016', *RAPORT Wojsko Technika Obronność*, 09/17: 8–16.

Łuczak, W. (2018) 'Unia na kursie konsolidacji europejskiego przemysłu zbrojeniowego', *RAPORT Wojsko Technika Obronność*, Special edition Raport EDF, May: 5–11.

MSZ. (2017) *Eksport uzbrojenia i sprzętu wojskowego z Polski, Raport za rok 2016*, Warszawa: Ministerstwo Spraw Zagranicznych Rzeczypospolitej Polskiej: 20–32.

Myck, W., Pieńkos, A., Kościuk, L., Głębocki, R., Markowski, S., Pawłuszko, W. and Najs, J. (2016) *Bezpieczeństwo i konkurencyjność: rekomendacje dotyczące strategii przemysłowo-obronnej RP*, Warszawa: Narodowe Centrum Studiów Strategicznych.

OECD. (2018) *Economic Survey of Poland: Towards an Innovative and Inclusive Economy*, Paris: The Organisation for Economic Co-operation and Development. www.oecd.org/eco/surveys/economic-survey-poland.htm (sourced 1 Nov 2018).

RAPORT. (2018) 'Udany Salon w cieniu problemów przemysłu', *RAPORT Wojsko Technika Obronność*, 10/18: 4–37.

Sandler, T. and Hartley, K. (1999) *The Political Economy of NATO: Past, Present and into the 21st Century*, Cambridge: Cambridge University Press.

Wachowski, T. (2016) 'Eksport – filar sukcesu Nitro-Chemu', *Wojsko i Technika*, April: 54–55.

Yoder, A. (1993) *Communism in Transition: The End of the Soviet Empires*, London: Taylor & Francis.

Zieliński, Z. (2016) 'Precyzyjna amunicja z Mesko', *RAPORT Wojsko Technika Obronność*, 09/16: 22–25.

13 Ukraine

Denis Jacqmin

1. Historical background and the turning point of 2014

a. Two messy decades

When Ukraine gained its independence in 1991, it inherited a significant part of the Soviet military industrial complex estimated at 30% of the defence industries and 20% of the defence related research and development capacities.[1] This amounted to 1840 companies employing 2,7 million workers.[2] Military production constituted the main activity for 700 of these companies. Besides those industries, Ukraine inherited massive stocks of weapons and ammunitions that were stored on its territory, mostly small arms and light weapons (Griffiths & Karp, 2008). Those stocks created an unprecedented challenge considering the lack of proper stockpile management and record-keeping which facilitated thefts, diversion and trafficking of these weapons in the 1990s. The existence of those stocks combined with a lack of direct threat to Ukraine's territorial integrity led to an important decrease in funding for the Ukrainian armed forces in the 1990s and 2000s and, as a consequence, for the Ukrainian defence industry. Hence, most of the arms exports of Ukraine were coming from the stocks and were sometimes transferred to grey area markets including countries under UN embargo.

If the period of the Kuchma presidency (1994–2005) has been characterised by competition between Ukraine and Russia in export markets, the Yanukovych presidency era (2010–2014) made the case for a stronger collaboration between the two military-industrial complexes both on the production and maintenance sides.[3]

b. Ukroboronprom: an answer to a specific context

UkrOboronProm was created by the Yanukovych government in December 2011[4] in the framework of a larger administrative reform designed to rationalise and optimise the functioning of the administration. The objectives and tasks given to UkrOboronProm were, among others, to coordinate and regulate the activities of its members mainly in marketing, fundamental research, representation abroad in exhibitions and fairs, to attract foreign investments, to negotiate research and development partnerships with foreign companies, to act as a broker for raw material imports, provide forwarding services, etc. The stress was put on improving the image of Ukrainian companies abroad, rationalising the supply chain, boosting R&D activities between Ukrainian companies as well as with foreign partners and attract investment.[5]

Besides the advantages promised by the rationalisation and the economies of scale, the creation of UkrOboronProm was also a response to a Russian request to identify an interlocutor to the very centralised structure of Rosoboronexport. Indeed, the Ukrainian defence industry was deeply intertwined with the Russian one, providing parts for major systems assembled in Russia, and representatives from the Russian defence industries and government had trouble in identifying who among the Ukrainian Ministry of Defence or the Ministry of Industrial Production was responsible for the defence industry.[6] Moreover, the creation of UkrOboronProm reinforced the presidential grip on the Ukrainian defence industry.

c. *The turning point*

In November 2013, protests against the refusal by president Yanukovych to sign the EU-Ukraine Association Agreement led to what is now called the "revolution of dignity" forcing Yanukovych to flee the country on February 22, 2014 as a new interim president was taking office.

The annexation of Crimea by Russia in March 2014 and the support for the separatists in the East have deeply changed the Ukrainian perception of Russia and quickly rendered industrial cooperation in the defence sector with the "aggressor state" politically impossible. On the 29 March 2014, UkrOboronProm issued a moratorium forbidding its members to export military products and components to Russia. This decision was a risky one as the new Ukrainian government was on a tight political line. Indeed, the majority of major defence plants are located in the South and the East of Ukraine where a part of the population had sympathies for Russian views and distrusted the new institutions in Kyiv. Massive unemployment could have been a direct threat to the new government by increasing the influence of separatists' ideas in Russian-speaking cities.[7] On 16 June, the newly elected president, Petro Poroshenko tightened the moratorium to expressly include dual-use products. This moratorium was reinforced by a resolution of the Ukrainian National Security and Defence Council enacted by president Poroshenko on 28 August forbidding all export for Russian military end-use (Malmlöf, 2016).

The consequences of this brutal severance of industrial ties were important for both countries. To give an idea of the impact of this measure, Ukraine produces the following materials:

- The private company Motor Sich, based in Zaporijia, produces engines for all the helicopters produced by Russian manufacturers (Kamov, Mil), jet engines for the Russian air forces transport aircraft (Ilyushin, Yak, Antonov, Beriev) as well as small jets engines for Russian cruise missiles (Malmlöf, 2016).

- Antonov based in Kyiv, produces strategic transport aircraft including the An-124 and the An-70, that were of particular interest for the Russian MoD, as well as the smaller tactical transport aircraft An-148.
- Zorya-Mashproekt, a company based in Mykolaiv, is specialised in gas turbines engines for civilian and military ships. 31 of the 54 surface combat ships the Russian navy planned to acquire were supposed to be equipped with an engine produced by Zorya-Mashproekt (Kirchberger, 2017).
- Yuzmash, based in Dnipro, produced InterContinental Ballistic Missiles (ICBM) for the Russian Strategic Forces, particularly the R-36 missile (SS-18 Satan) and dealt with the maintenance of these missiles in Russia. Other systems as the RTP-2M Topol (SS-25 Sickle) and UR-100NUTTkh (SS-19 Stiletto) were also impacted due to the fact that their guidance systems were produced by the Khartron Scientific Combine based in Kharkiv.
- Air-to-air missiles like the medium-range R-27 (AA-10 Alamo) and the R-73 (AA-11 Archer) were manufactured by Artem, a Ukrainian company based in Kyiv, although parts were imported from Russia. The infrared seeking system for the R-73 was produced by Arsenal, also based in Kyiv. Those two missiles constitute the bulk of air-to-air missiles deployed on Russian fighter aircraft.
- Sighting devices for aircraft and helicopter-mounted guns and machine guns were also produced by Arsenal and installed on Mig and Sukhoi aircraft as well as Kamov and Mil helicopters.

d. *Aftermaths on Russia and Ukraine*

Even if the trade in military components only amounted to 4.4 % of Russian total imports, it is estimated that 30% of those parts were difficult to replace.[8] This embargo had therefore a tremendous impact on the modernisation plan of the Russian armed forces, especially helicopters and battleships, and forced the Russian industry to either copy the parts, or substitute them with imports from other source, mainly China (although this increased the cost or lowered the performances of the final products). Russia also tried to attract Ukrainian technicians to avoid a disruption of maintenance activities for Ukrainian-made systems or parts[9]. Some Ukrainian companies continued to supply components to the Russian industry using companies based in Belarus or China or even declaring their exports as civilian goods[10]. Moreover, considering the strategic impact of some components, thefts and smuggling of parts, sometimes illegally manufactured, were also identified and prevented by the SBU[11] (Security Services of Ukraine: Kirchberger, 2017).

From the Ukrainian side, the situation was different but equally difficult. The Ukrainian industry is mainly a components industry directed towards export and it develops few complete weapons systems (the T-84 main battle tanks and Antonov airplanes being the exception). Russia absorbed between 40 and 70% of Ukrainian defence exports[12] and 70% of Ukrainian defence companies depended on Russia for their supply of components.[13] According to Roman Romanov, director of UkrOboronProm between July 2014 and February 2018, "Our defence industry has lost UAH 3,3 billions (200 million USD) as a result of the termination of cooperation with Russia. We used to import about 30,000 product items from the Russian Federation."[14]

2. The Ukrainian response

To answer the challenge of the disconnection between the Ukrainian and Russian defence industries, different measures were put in place. First, an increase of state orders to rebuild the Ukrainian army with modern equipment, second the replacement of imports of Russian components by western ones or components manufactured in Ukraine ("Ukraïnisation"), third the search for new export markets mostly towards NATO and emerging players like Turkey and China and finally a reform of UkrOboronProm with a new strategy "Ukrainian shield" to make it more profitable, more attractive for foreign investors and to produce more technology-intensive products.

a. Rebuilding the Ukrainian forces

As the war in the East intensified, the defence industry was mobilised to fulfil the needs of the Ukrainian armed forces. The Ukrainian army had suffered from years of low investment and corruption practices that left it unable to fight (Puglisi, 2015). The initial reaction to the advance of separatist forces had to come from battalions of volunteers, poorly equipped but highly motivated. In July 2014, president Poroshenko appointed Roman Romanov, a former businessman and advisor on the presidential campaign, as head of UkrOboronProm with a clear objective: "Today, Ukrainian production will be loaded with high-precision weapons systems, Ukrainian drones, everything the Ukrainian army needs – from body armour to thermal imagers, billions of people's money will no longer be spent on unnecessary research programs."[15] The production of UkrOboronProm was reoriented from an almost exclusive focus on exports towards the internal needs for the Ukrainian army which included repairing the damaged material or restoring the operational capability of stored equipment. This absolute priority also resulted in the redirecting of equipment produced for export.[16] Nevertheless, it seems that these redirections of material and delays did not lead to cancellation of contracts.[17]

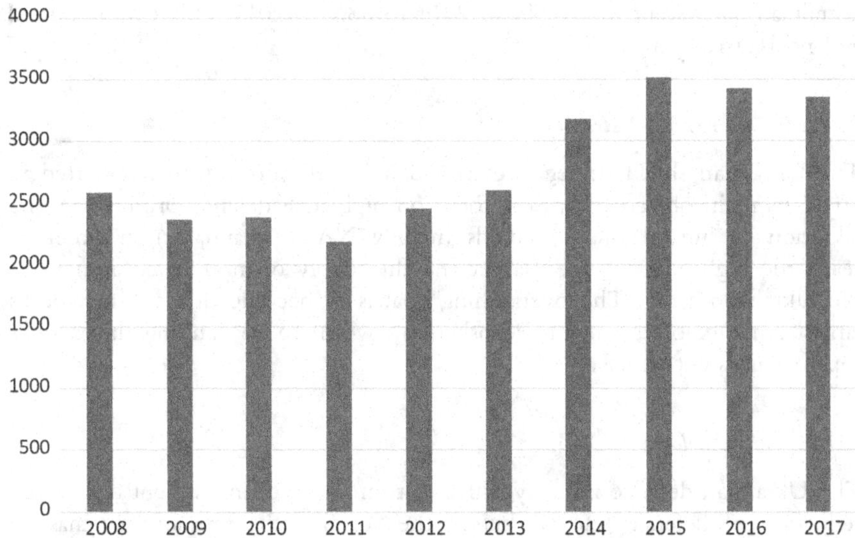

Figure 13.1 Ukrainian military expenditures (2008–2017) constant 2016 USD millions (SIPRI).

Source: SIPRI.

This rebuild of the Ukrainian armed forces also meant a sharp increase in military expenditures (see Figure 13.1). While the figures presented in the graph are in constant USD of 2016, the Ukrainian national currency (Hryvnia) lost two-thirds of its value against the dollar between the end of 2013 and the beginning of 2016.

b. Import substitution policy

With the severing of industrial ties with Russia, UkrOboronProm companies needed to find 30,000 replacement items to compensate the ones supplied by Russian companies.[18] One year after the first moratorium, UkrOboronProm had found alternative sources for one third of those parts, a majority of them from Ukrainian companies, others from European and American suppliers. UkrOboronProm was also granted access to the NATO Item Name Directory search tool which allowed Ukrainian companies to find alternative suppliers. In 2015, UkrOboronProm started a program of import substitution with the regional governments from Ukraine. UkrOboronProm engaged more than 447 companies mainly SMEs to provide spare parts or components that were formerly imported from Russia.[19] As a result of this import substitution policy, UkrOboronProm announced in 2018 that on the BTR-4 armoured vehicle, the proportion of Ukrainian parts went from 45% in 2014 to 88% in 2017 with 12% imported and no Russian parts.

c. "Ukrainian shield" strategy

The Ukrainian shield strategy developed by UkrOboronProm has started in 2016. Its main objectives are the focus on high-tech defence production, the adoption of international standards (mainly NATO standards) in order to reach the high-end defence market and the supply of modern equipment to the Ukrainian army. The overarching goal is to become one of the world's largest arms exporters and in Poroshenko's words to be "among the world's top-five arms exporters".[20]

i. Focus on technology

The Ukrainian defence industry suffered from a lack of investment due to the reduction of defence budgets before the conflict, the presence of massive stockpiles, the difficulty for foreign investors to cooperate with Ukrainian companies and the focus on maintenance and improvement of Soviet-designed equipment. "Ukrainian shield" aims at bringing some change in that respect in order to develop new products that will be technology intensive and therefore more profitable.

A first step to reach that goal is to attract foreign investment and develop industrial cooperation with European and American companies in order to obtain technology transfers. The arguments put forward by UkrOboronProm to attract investment are the experience in arms production in Ukraine, the high qualifications of Ukrainian workers and engineers combined with low labour costs.[21]

Another path to reinforce the technological content of the armament developed by UkrOboronProm is to establish partnerships with universities and research centres in Ukraine.[22] Memorandum of understanding have been signed with these establishments to allow UkrOboronProm to use their research facilities and provide courses for students interested in a defence industry career.

Third, technology can also come from inside of UkrOboronProm by developing a culture favouring innovation and dedicating funds for it. This is why the Ukrainian government recruited Anthony Tether, the former head of DARPA under the G. W. Bush administration, to reorganise the science and technology sector in Ukraine.[23] Tether was also nominated to the supervisory board of UkrOboronProm. The idea was to replicate the American DARPA and create a platform that brings together developers, start-ups, investment funds and the military. The status and responsibilities for this platform, named GARDA (General Advanced Research & Development Agency) are still being negotiated with the State Finance Institution for

Innovations (SFII), which operates under the authority of the Ministry of Economic Development and Trade and could serve as a basis to develop a "Ukrainian DARPA".[24]

ii. Clusters

UkrOboronProm includes more than a hundred companies which is the cause of duplication, internal competition and a lack of coordination. This situation created difficulties in managing the development of complex weapons systems. In order to rationalise their work and improve the production cycle of weapons systems, UkrOboronProm started a politics of "clusterisation".[25] Five sectors were identified: aviation, armoured vehicles, shipbuilding, high-precision weapons as well as radar, communications and electronic warfare. Each cluster will be organised as an ecosystem around one leading company. The first cluster created in May 2016 was Ukrainian Aircraft Corporation (UAC), the aviation cluster organised around Antonov. The creation of this cluster would help in streamlining the production, facilitate the cooperation with private partners, centralising the purchase of raw materials and develop a common marketing and sale strategy.[26] The clusters can also play a role in replacing the supply of spare parts that were coming from Russia.

iii. Adopting international standards

Adopting international standards and especially NATO standards (NATO STANAG) has been a motto of the Ukrainian government since the ties were cut with the Russian industry. President Poroshenko stated several times he wanted a full transition to NATO standards by 2020.[27] Some political reasons might explain this ambitious objective, adhering to NATO has indeed been a foreign policy priority for Ukraine after the outbreak of the conflict. Therefore, the Ukrainian government might want to make sure there is no technical impediment to its adhesion when the political decision will be made. There are also military reasons why the adoption of NATO standards is important. The Ukrainian army receives a lot of help from NATO in terms of training and reform of the security sector. Ukraine armed forces are also increasingly collaborating with NATO countries (for example in the LITPOLUKRBRIG)[28] and this requires equipment that would be compatible with NATO standards.

But there is also an economic incentive to adopt those standards or at least to produce equipment that is compatible with those produced by NATO countries. As Roman Romanov, director of UkrOboronProm between July 2014 and February 2018 explained it, "This [adoption of NATO standards] is a matter of national defence capability, but also a matter of business as we are exploring new markets in Europe, not just in Asia or Africa, as was the case until recently."[29] The economic objective is therefore for

UkrOboronProm to be able to enter the western defence industry supply chain and cooperate on defence projects with NATO countries. In 2017, the NATO Support and Procurement Agency (NSPA) offered to add Ukraine's defence industry enterprises to the list of defence manufacturers which means UkrOboronProm can participate in tenders for the supply of products and services to NATO or NATO members.[30]

One particular issue for the certification of equipment to NATO standards is that there is no accredited centre in Ukraine that can proceed to the testing of the equipment and deliver such certification. Consequently, Ukrainian companies have to carry out this certification process abroad. The issue of a Ukrainian certification centre is important because of the high costs attached to these procedures (between 50,000 Euros for the test of a ballistic protection equipment to 900,000 Euros for an armoured vehicle).[31] The creation of this centre, the assistance for the training of the personnel and the implementation of the certification procedures is part of the agenda of the NATO-Ukraine Commission and more particularly the NATO-Ukraine Joint Working Group on Defence and Technical Cooperation.

3. The challenges of export markets

a. MCO and upgrade of Russian weapon systems

Ukraine defence industry holds a considerable expertise regarding the upgrade and maintenance of soviet equipment, especially aircraft and armoured vehicles. Regarding aircraft, it includes companies like Plant 410 of Civil Aviation (specialised in Antonov transport airplanes), Konotop Aircraft Repair Plant Aviakon (Mi-series helicopters), Mykolaiv Aircraft Repair Plant NARP (Su-24, IL-76), Zaporozhye State Aviation Repair Plant MigRemont and Lviv State Aviation Repair Plant (Sukhoi and Mig aircrafts). Considering the number of aircraft exported worldwide by Antonov, Ilyushin, Mig and Sukhoi, the market for maintenance and modernisation remains important for countries that do not have the means to buy new aircraft[32]. The recent US sanctions against buyers of Russian weapons will also increase the attractiveness of Ukrainian companies for the modernisation of Soviet equipment.

Ukrainian industries are also well-known for their skills in armoured vehicles and main battle tanks. Ukrainian companies propose modernisation kits for BMP tracked armoured vehicle that include upgrade of the engines, fire control systems, armour and reactive armour.[33] Besides modernisation of the vehicles, Ukrainian industries also developed a series of armed turrets[34] that can be adapted on BMP or BTR armoured vehicles to increase their firepower. On the side of the main battle tanks, Ukrainian defence industry offers an entire range of vehicles going from the cheaper T-64-E to the modernised T-64BV. Ukraine still counts numerous Soviet tanks (mainly T-64 and T-72) abandoned in tank graveyards that can be repaired and modernised.[35] These modernisations may include bringing the vehicles to NATO standards. UkrOboronProm collaborated with the Polish company Zakłady Mechaniczne "Bumar-Łabędy" to bring the T-72 MBT to NATO standards which included a 120 mm gun designed by Kharkiv Morozov Machine-Building Design Bureau.[36]

b. Coproduction and the transfer of know-how

The Ukrainian defence industry does not focus only on the overhaul of Soviet designed equipment. It aims to create new designs and acquire new technologies from international partners. Some countries are particularly interested to develop specific products in order to acquire a know-how in a particular field. The best example is the development of the Antonov An-132D transport aircraft with the Saudi companies KACST (King Adbulaziz City for Science and Technology) and Taqnia Aeronautics. The Saudi government already ordered six An-132D, and would be interested in acquiring 80 aircraft in different versions with the rest of the production being assembled in Saudi Arabia. Saudi companies could produce up to 60% of the components of the aircraft.[37] The An-132 has therefore been jointly developed to further the Kingdom's industrial defence aerospace capabilities.[38] Other coproduction agreements could be implemented with countries of the Gulf around antitank missiles.[39]

c. Cooperation with specific countries

i. Poland

The Polish defence industry plays an important role with a strong cooperation between UkrOboronProm and Polska Grupa Zbrojeniowa (PGZ, Polish Armement Group). This cooperation is supported by a common strategic vision between the two countries at the highest political level. Poland supplied military equipment to Ukraine in 2014 when other European countries adopted a rather restrictive export policy.

A defence cooperation agreement was signed in December 2016 by the Polish and Ukrainian defence ministers. The agreement identifies 24 areas of cooperation including industrial cooperation in the field of defence such as joint military research programmes, new weapons systems development and the modernisation of Soviet equipment.

Several specific industrial collaborations are already taking place like the development of the Polish antitank missile Pirat based on the Ukrainian RK-3 Korsar. The Polish electronic company WB Electronics has designed a loitering ammunition in cooperation with the Ukrainian private company JSC "CheZaRa". WB electronics also created a consortium with the Ukrainian company Artem for the supply of R-27 air-to-air missiles for the Polish Air Force. The two companies also developed the ZRN-01 "Stokrotka" multiple rocket launcher system.[40] Other cooperation projects include the supply of Ukrainian power packs for the modernisation of Polish army tanks as well as the supply of electro-optics components from the Polish company

PCO SA to the Ukrainian Zhytomyr armoured Plant.[41] Both countries are interested in the development of a new multipurpose helicopter based on the experience of the MSB-6 Ataman designed by Motor Sich and the W-3 by Sokol.[42] Development of UAS, air defence systems, self-propelled guns, maritime patrol aircraft and precision guided munitions are also among the potential joint development projects.[43]

ii. Turkey

Industrial cooperation in the defence sector between Ukraine and Turkey has gained a new pace over the last few years. The two countries have shared strategic considerations on the equilibrium of power in the Black Sea but also have complementary industrial gaps. Ukraine lost most of its naval assets when Russia annexed Crimea and is very interested in the Turkish know-how on ship-building while Turkey has an interest in the Ukrainian skills in armoured vehicles (main battle tanks mostly) and aeronautic design. Turkey being a NATO country is another reason why Ukraine has a keen interest in industrial cooperation. Additionally, as the Turkish regime start to behave in a more and more authoritarian fashion, European government became reluctant to grant export licences to Turkey therefore reinforcing Ukraine's trading position.[44] Military equipment contracts and defence industrial cooperation project between the two countries are numerous. Turkey recently ordered Ukrainian hard-kill defence systems for its main battle tanks deployed in Syria[45] while Ukraine ordered Aselsan communication equipment with significant technology transfers. A MoU was signed in May 2017 between Turkish Aerospace Industries and Antonov on the development of military drones for the Ukrainian army[46] with a joint venture agreed in July 2018. Simultaneously, another memorandum was signed between Antonov and Aselsan to provide electronic equipment for the transport aircraft An-178.[47] Discussion are under way on the joint development of a new heavy military cargo aircraft, the An-188.[48] Other cooperation areas include ammunition production, ballistic missiles, radar technology and jet engines.[49]

iii. China

China developed a specific relationship with Russia in terms of armaments supplies with Russia as the main provider of Chinese equipment. But this relationship has become strained among Russian concerns over Chinese "reverse engineering" versions of Russian weapon systems which ultimately led to increased competition in external markets for the Russian industry. Since Ukraine's independence, China has used the Ukrainian industry either as a leverage to obtain equipment Russia refused to export or at better prices as an alternative source for cutting-edge technological transfers (Kirchberger, 2017). The loss of the Russian export market for the Ukrainian industry has made China an interesting alternative. Indeed in 2017, China was the first export market for Ukrainian arms, before

Russia while Ukraine was the third supplier of military equipment to China.[50] Chinese industrials have a keen interest in Ukrainian technologies as they have not fully mastered helicopters and jet engines, the heavy strategic airlifter (like the An-225 Mirya),[51] tank engines, naval gas turbines, etc. The relationship with China was recently strained as a Chinese company close to the Chinese regime tried to take control of Motor Sich through an offshore financial arrangement. The transaction was blocked by a Ukrainian court and the Security services of Ukraine raided the company on corruption charges.[52]

4. The need to reinforce quality controls

Reputation is an important asset in the defence industry considering the high budgets spent and the long life-cycle of some weapons systems. UkrOboron-Prom leadership is aware that the Ukrainian industry must change its reputation from the 1990s and 2000s when Ukraine was best known for shady deals and low-quality standards.[53] In this respect, the Ukrainian industry has had a few missed opportunities: two specific contracts will be mentioned here. The first was the order by the Iraqi government for 450 BTR-4 in 2009. This order was the most important military contract since Ukraine independence. The first and second batches of vehicles have been accepted by the Iraqi authorities despite corrosion issues but the third one was refused. Problems of rusted chassis and cracked armoured plates had been detected. Inspectors from Kharkiv Morozov Machine Building Design Bureau (KMDB) inspected the two first batches and found numerous problems. Of the 88 BTR-4 armoured personnel carriers delivered to Iraq and tested by Kharkiv specialists, only 56 were able to be started. Of the 56 vehicles that were able to start, only 34 were able to move. On ten BTR, the starters were faulty (or completely absent).[54]

Another damaging contract was the refurbishment of Croatian Mig-21 fighter jets by Odessa Aviation Plant, part of UkrOboronProm. In 2015, the Croatian government selected UkrSpetsExport to refurbish seven Croatian Mig-21 and buy five used other jets. When the aircraft returned to Croatia, only three jets were operational and there were serious doubts about the origin of the spare parts considering the fact that the technical documentation did not match the serial numbers of the parts. In addition to this, it seems the five jets bought from Ukraine actually belonged to the Yemeni Air Force.[55] Two Croatian Defence ministry employees were since indicted on corruption claims.[56]

5. Attracting investment

a. Corruption and transparency

Corruption is a real threat for Ukrainian society and the defence sector is not spared. Numerous cases of suspicious contracts have been revealed, sometimes with a clear conflict of interest between industry and the authorities.[57] One of the biggest problems that enables corrupt practices is the secrecy around the procurement system for the armed forces. 95% of the armament and military equipment bought by the Ukrainian state are considered as "State secret" which results in single source contracts, higher prices, risks of nepotism and corruption as well as lower quality products.[58] Since, an increasing part of UkrOboronProm profits come from the State Order, it is crucial to bring more transparency on how the acquisition decisions are made by the government.

Corruption has also been a threat inside UkrOboronProm which resulted in failures to fulfil orders and the delivery of sub-quality products. ProZorro, an online e-procurement system designed by civil society was introduced in November 2014 to bring more transparency to UkrOboronProm procurement system and increase competition between suppliers. But if ProZorro can reveal some suspicious deals, the problem lies with law enforcement agencies and courts where the cases often collapse. The corruption problems of the Ukrainian defence industry are therefore part of a larger problem that includes the reform of the judicial system.

b. The transformation of the legal framework

In order to attract investment and cooperate with western industries, UkrOboronProm will need to change from a very opaque and sometimes inefficient public company to a modern consortium able to set up joint ventures and receive technology transfers. When Roman Romanov was appointed director of UkrOboronProm in July 2014, he implemented management changes designed to make UkrOboronProm profitable again. These changes include the introduction of electronic bidding for raw material purchase to cut nepotism and corruption, the dismissal of directors from ineffective companies, the simplification of logistical chains, the publication of activity reports, etc.[59] Romanov also proposed the corporatisation of UkrOboronProm, the creation of a supervisory board and the conduct of an audit by a major auditing firm. The supervisory board's positions have finally been filled in January 2018, the tender for the audit was published in November 2017, but it had not been decided as of September 2018. This financial audit would bring transparency on the real value of UkrOboronProm companies and therefore bring clarity on the opportunity or not for external investors to invest in those companies in order to modernise their production chains. This corporatisation of UkrOboronProm companies and their transformation into joint stock public companies should be completed by the beginning of 2020 if the government emerging from the next elections chooses to continue this process.[60]

The legal framework around the governmental procurement for the needs of the Ukrainian armed forces must also be adapted. Beyond the issue of transparency, the biggest problem is the fixed pricing by the government based on production costs which leaves very little profit margins for the companies to reinvest in the production lines or in R&D.[61] As Pavlo Bukin, Director General of UkrOboronProm, puts it

> One of the issues that need to be solved is the problem of pricing and price control in the state defence order. To date, we have a system of state defence orders, in which the customer – the Ministry of Defence – fully controls the cost of the product, its profitability and wages of employees, established by the regulatory and sectoral directories of the Ministry of Economic Development and Trade.[62]

The pricing policy becomes a further impediment for manufacturers when inflation is strong and there is no automatic mechanism to revise the prices between the order and the delivery.

6. Private industry

With around a hundred companies, UkrOboronProm represents the bulk of the Ukrainian defence industry. But the picture would be incomplete without mentioning the role of private defence companies that are increasingly gaining market shares on UkrOboronProm. If UkrOboronProm used to fulfil 60–70% of the Ukrainian state defence order in 2014–2015, this share is now under 50% due to the rise of private companies. At the end of 2016, private defence companies formed the public association "League of defence companies of Ukraine" in order to defend their interests and establish a level-playing field with the public companies. The "League of defence companies of Ukraine" includes more than 50 companies including Practika (armoured vehicles), Radionix and JSC Holding company, UkrSpetsTechnika (radars and electronic counter measures) and TEMP 3000 (individual ballistic protection). The main claims of "League of defence companies of Ukraine" revolves around specific competences of UkrOboronProm that puts it in a position of conflict of interest. Indeed, while not being a regulatory body, it is responsible for granting import and export licences for strategic goods traded by private companies. Private companies are also required to use the services of special exporters like Ukrinmash or Spetstekhnoeksport that belong to UkrOboronProm and have an exclusive right to negotiate export contracts and fix their prices. These special exporters also take a commission on those transactions making the export contracts from 5 to 20% more expensive.[63] The risk is therefore high that UkrOboronProm could block a direct competitor from concluding an export contract.[64] The legal framework is currently being revised to allow private companies to export directly at their own prices.[65] Besides, the proximity between UkrOboronProm leadership and the decision makers at Ministry level often means their state orders are decided around what UkrOboronProm can produce rather than what the army really needs,[66] putting the private companies at a disadvantage.

7. Conclusion

The Ukrainian defence industry sector which is mainly represented by the public consortium UkrOboronProm is at a crossroad. Having inherited a large part of the Soviet industrial complex, the Ukrainian industry has been neglected during the first years of independence due to low orders for the national defence forces, the presence of massive stocks on its territory and endemic corruption. The creation of UkrOboronProm in 2011 responded to the need to better cooperate with the Russian industry mainly by supplying components for weapon systems assembled in Russia. The Maidan revolution and the conflict with Russia that followed forced the Ukrainian government to put a halt to these transfers and UkrOboronProm had to operate a radical transformation. UkrOboronProm had to redirect its production from the traditional export market towards the supply of modern equipment to the Ukrainian army while finding new suppliers of components to replace the Russian ones. A new strategy was designed according to which UkrOboronProm would focus on technology intensive products, adopt NATO standards, develop industrial clusters and start a process of corporatisation. These reforms are currently halfway waiting for new pieces of legislation from the Ukrainian parliament in order to transform UkrOboronProm from a state-owned company to a joint stock public company. The international audit planned for 2019 will be a milestone and will reveal the real state of UkrOboronProm companies and therefore their attractiveness for international investors. The attraction of private investments and transfers of technologies will be crucial for the future of Ukraine's defence industries as the market of Soviet equipment modernisation, while currently promising, cannot last forever.

Notes

1 Ukrainain Defense Review, January–March 2013, p. 13
2 Idem
3 Kuzio, T, Growing Ukrainian-Russian Arms Export Cooperation, *Eurasia Daily Monitor*, 9: 92, May 15, 2012.
4 Кабинет Министров постановлением №993 «Некоторые вопросы Государственного концерна „Укроборонпром“», August 31, 2011.
5 Idem.
6 Valentyn Badrak, Vasyl' Laptiychuk, Leonid Polyakov, Sergiy Zgurets, Potentials for cooperation between Ukraine and the European Union in the sphere of security, Konrad Adenauer Stiftung, Policy paper 19, May 2011. Oliker, Olga, Lynn E. Davis, Keith Crane, Andrew Radin, Celeste Gventer, Susanne Sondergaard, James T. Quinlivan, Stephan B. Seabrook, Jacopo Bellasio, Bryan Frederick, Andriy Bega, and Jakub P. Hlavka, *Security Sector Reform in Ukraine.* Santa Monica, CA: RAND Corporation, 2016.
7 Los Angeles Times, Ukraine's freeze on military exports to Russia carries risks, November 26, 2014.
8 Sutyagin, I., Clarke, M., Ukraine Military Dispositions. The Military Ticks Up while the Clock Ticks Down, RUSI Brieging paper, April 2014, p. 6
9 Ukrainain Defense Review, April–June 2015, p. 8.

10 Ukrainian Week, Finding the balance, April 28, 2017.
11 See SBU, Kirovohrad region: SBU blocks supply of dual-use goods to Russia, June 23, 2018 and SBU, Kharkiv region: SBU blocks attempt to export dual-use goods to Russia, July 7, 2018
12 Ukrainian Defence Review, April–June 2014, p. 2. Washington Post, Ukraine factories equip Russian military despite support for rebels, August 15, 2014.
13 Foreign Affairs, Close Ranks, May 25, 2014.
14 Ukrainain Defence Review, January–March 2015, p. 10.
15 Kyiv Post, Poroshenko: Ukrainian companies to produce everything Ukrainian army needs, May 25, 2014.
16 For example, T-64BV-1 main battle tanks that had to be delivered to the Congolese army have been redirected to the Ukrainian armed forces. The tanks promised to the DRC have finally been delivered in 2016. The production of T-84 Oplot main battle tanks for Thailand has also been severely delayed.
17 According to Serhiy Pinkas, first Deputy Director General of UkrOboronProm: "To date, our first priority is to meet domestic market requirements. We arranged with our partners, who agreed to postpone deadlines on the completion of several contracts, especially as they know that our equipment is going to go through actual war trials, so they would get it already improved and upgraded. Some 1,000 changes have been made in engineering documentation and manuals for the BTR-3E and BTR-4 vehicles over the past few months alone. Not one single contract has been terminated nor a penny worth of penalty imposed on us. So, we were able to focus on domestic supply orders while retaining our presence on external markets." Ukrainian Defence Review, April–June 2015, p. 9.
18 Ukrainian Defence Review, January–March 2015, p. 10.
19 UkrOboronProm, "Ukroboronprom" in 2017: Import Substitution – 21 Regions and 447 Enterprises, January 15, 2018.
20 UkrOboronProm catalogue 2016–2017, p. 5
21 UkrOboronProm advertises that at 1.20 USD per hour, Ukrainian workers are cheaper than Chinese workers. This competitve advantage is mainly due to the collapse of the Ukrainian national currency in 2014–2015. Kyiv Post, Ukrainian arms exports falling short of lofty goals, October 27, 2016.
22 UkrOboronProm, UkrOboronProm will implement innovations of specialists of the leading university of the country, February 26, 2016.
23 *Defense News*, What is DARPA doing in Ukraine? March 1, 2018.
24 Interfax Ukraine, Zgurovsky: A financial audit of Ukroboronprom will answer the question about the past, a strategic audit – about the future of the concern, 31 juillet 2017.
25 UkrOboronProm, Clustering (http://ukroboronprom.com.ua/en/reforms/reforms-kluster)
26 Forecast International, Antonov Becomes Cornerstone of New Ukrainian Aircraft Corp, August 23, 2016.
27 Radio Free Europe/Radio Liberty, Poroshenko Says Ukraine to Meet NATO Standards By 2020, July 10, 2017.
28 LITPOLUKRBRIG is a trinational brigade grouping forces from Lithuania, Poland and Ukraine that was first estblished to be deployed in peacekeeping missions but is also capable to participate in joint NATO exercices. It is based on the model of the EU battle groups and operates according to NATO standards.
29 Ukrainian Defence Review, January–March 2015, p. 11.
30 Ukroboronprom, NATO opens the door for Ukrainian defense industry, May 29, 2017.

31 The League of Defence Companies of Ukraine, «We do not ask for money from NATO, but we ask for information and methodological help» – Ulia Vysotskaya, director for external relations of the League.
32 Youtube, Interview of Denys Gurak at New Ukraine Investment Conference 2017, July 7, 2017.
33 For example, the BMP-1UMD proposed by Zhytomyr Armored Plant.
34 Like the Shturm, Shkval, Parus or Grom turrets.
35 Kyiv Post, War machines arise from Kyiv's "tank cemetery", October 17, 2015.
36 Ukroboronprom, Tank PT-17 for Poland meeting NATO standard: role for Ukraine and a new level of Ukrainian defense, September 8, 2017.
37 Aviation Week, Taqnia To Build An-132D In Saudi Arabia, January 18, 2017.
38 IHS Jane's Defence Weekly, Antonov's An-132 makes maiden flight, April 3, 2017.
39 UkrOboronProm, Pavlo Bukin: stable loading of production capacities does not depend on export, it depends on the state defence order, May 31, 2018.
40 WeapoNews, "Daisy" – a miracle the Polish-Ukrainian engineering, 1 September 8, 2017.
41 Defence24, MSPO 2017: Polish-Ukrainian Stokrotka Rocket Launch System, September 9, 2017.
42 *Defense News*, Ukraine, Poland to jointly build helicopters, April 26, 2017.
43 Ukrainian Defense Review, July–September 2017, p. 13.
44 In 2017, Austria and Gremany refused to allow the export to Turkey of diesel engines that would have been installed on the Turkish main battle tank project Altay while Ukraine has a real expertise in these engines.
45 Defence Blog, Turkey to equip tanks with a new high-tech protection system, February 28, 2018.
46 Ukroboronprom, Ukroboronprom breakthrough: IDEF-2017 results, May 12, 2017
47 IHS Jane's, IDEF 2017: Aselsan, Antonov team up on aircraft electronics, May 10, 2017.
48 *Defense News*, Turkey, Ukraine advance An-188 co-production talks, July 27, 2018.
49 Kyiv Post, Ukraine, Turkey deepen defense cooperation, 27 Octobre 2017.
50 Kyiv Post, China sees Ukraine as alternative to Russia in arms trade, expert believes, May 14, 2017. SIPRI Fact Sheet, Trends in international arms transfers, 2017, March 2018.
51 Business Insider, China and Ukraine are going to build the largest plane in the world, September 1, 2016.
52 South China Morning Post, Blocked Chinese takeover of Ukrainian aerospace firm no closer to being resolved, June 17, 2018.
53 Youtube, Interview of Denys Gurak at New Ukraine Investment Conference 2017, July 7, 2017.
54 ZN.ua, Из 88 поставленных в Ирак украинских БТР-4 завести удалось лишь 56 машин, May 20, 2017.
55 *Defense News*, Croatia Probes Fighter Jet Deal With Ukraine Amid Corruption Claims, March 29, 2016.
56 Balkan Insight, Croatia Indicts Two for Ukraine Jet Deal Bribery, December 30, 2016.
57 Several examples can be found in Foreign Policy, Ukraine's anti-corruption Agency Alleges Fraud in Arms Industry, December 21, 2017 and Kyiv Post, Corruption Kills, March 16, 2018. BBC, Corruption claims taint Ukraine military, December 7, 2016.

58 Transparency International Defence and Security, Transparency International Ukraine, Six Red Flags: The most Frequent Corruption Risks in Ukraine's Defence Procurement, June 2018.
59 See Slideshare, UkrOboronProm – The year of accomplishments, July 10, 2015.
60 Interfax Ukraine, Zgurovsky: A financial audit of UkrOboronProm will answer the question about the past, a strategic audit – about the future of the concern, July 31, 2018.
61 League of Defence companies of Ukraine, Representatives of the League took part in a seminar on development of the defense industry complex, October 11, 2018.
62 Defense Express, International Conference "Legislative Provision of Parliamentary Control in the Defense Industrial Complex of Ukraine", March 19, 2018
63 Unian, Ukrainian arms export in 2016, August 11, 2017.
64 Kyiv Post, UkrOboronProm breeds conflicts of interest in lucrative foreign arms sales, April 2, 2018.
65 OPK, Ukrainian normative and legal base allowes the enterprises of all forms of property to leave the international market independently – deputy minister of Economic Development and Trade, October 9, 2018.
66 Carnegie, Ukraine's Toughest Fight: The Challenge of Military Reform, February 22, 2018.

References

Hugh Griffiths and Aaron Karp (2008) Ukraine: Coping with Post-Soviet Legacies, *Contemporary Security Policy*, 29:1, 202–228.

Rosaria Puglisi (2015) Heroes or Villains? Volunteer Battalions in Post-Maidan Ukraine, IAI Working Papers, 15:8 www.iai.it/sites/default/files/iaiwp1508.pdf

Sarah Kirchberger (2017) The end of a military-industrial triangle: Arms-industrial co-operation between China, Russia and Ukraine after the Crimea crisis, *SIRIUS – Zeitschrift Für Strategische Analysen*, 1, 1–19.

Tomas Malmlöf (2016) A Case Study of Russo-Ukrainian Defense Industrial Cooperation: Russian Dilemmas, *The Journal of Slavic Military Studies*, 29:1, 1–22.

14 Switzerland

Keith Hartley

Introduction[1]

Swiss defence policy has two distinctive features. First, it is dominated by geography. Second, its neutrality policy. This chapter outlines its defence economy comprising military spending and its defence industry.

Military spending

Switzerland is a land-locked country and a mountainous region. Its mountains form a natural defence barrier to any invading forces. Defence focuses on the protection of the major mountain passes and tunnels. Historically, these were defended with fortresses and the aim was to deter aggression by threatening to impose substantial costs on any invaders. Its policy of neutrality means that its army is not involved in armed conflict in other countries although it has been involved in international peace-keeping missions. Critics question whether an army is needed, especially for a neutral country with no enemies. Also, given its location, Switzerland can 'free ride' on European defence capabilities.

Defence is provided by the Federal Department of Defence, Civil Protection and Sport (the Swiss equivalent of a Ministry of Defence). Switzerland's armed forces comprise an army and air force with a mostly conscript force (military service of 260 days). The army also provides a maritime protection role through a small fleet of patrol boats. Total armed forces personnel number some 160,000 and they are tasked with home defence.

Table 14.1 presents data on defence spending levels. Between 1988 and 2017, real military spending peaked in 1990 and then declined following the end of the Cold War although there was a real increase in 2015 to 2017. The Table also shows Switzerland's defence burden in the form of defence shares of GDP. Over the period 1988 to 2017, defence shares have almost halved falling from 1.6% of GDP in 1988/1990 to 0.7% in 2010/17. Such reductions in defence shares are a simple indicator of the peace dividend for Switzerland.

Table 14.1 Switzerland military spending

Year	*Total Spending (US$ millions, 2016 prices)*	*Defence Share of GDP (%)*
1988	6828	1.6
1990	7383	1.6
1995	6162	1.4
2000	5112	1.0
2005	4496	0.9
2010	4256	0.7
2015	4395	0.7
2017	4630	0.7

Source: SIPRI (2019a).

The defence industry

Limited data are available on the Swiss defence industry, with the main sources being trade association data, company reports and the internet. These provide an indication of the Industry's size and structure.

Industry size

Measured by employment, industry size was over 10,000 employees in 2013. Industry size has fluctuated. Direct employment in arms production was some 9,700 employees in 1990 but fell to 3,700 employees in 2000 (Armada, 2013; GS, 2013). Industry size reflected changes in Swiss defence policy as the country shifted from a policy of independence to interdependence. Reductions in the size of the Swiss army meant major reductions in the size of the domestic arms market with adverse effects on domestic arms producers.

The small size of the Swiss domestic weapons market and the needs of a militia army meant a requirement for large numbers of simple weapons (e.g. rifles) rather than a few costly weapons requiring highly-trained, long-service military personnel. Historically, national autonomy required a domestic weapons industry but independence became 'too costly.' Exports were the industry's response to a declining domestic market. It is claimed that the domestic market is 'too small' for the industry's survival and that exports are 'vital.' But, the Swiss government's neutrality policy is a major constraint on Swiss arms exports and on the size of its defence industry.

Industry structure

The industry comprises a large number of small firms and a few larger companies resembling monopolistic competition. Estimates suggest a total of some

100 companies (Armada, 2013). Firms offer a range of products and services: some are subsidiaries of large multi-national corporations; some are defence specialists; others supply both military and civil goods and services.

Major restructuring of the industry started in the late 1990s, involving downsizing together with changes in ownership and structure. Mowag the military vehicle firm was initially acquired by General Motors, USA and later by General Dynamics, USA. The producer of anti-aircraft systems, Oerlikon Contraves, was acquired by the German company Rheinmetall. In 2000, the small arms business of the Swiss SIG group was sold with the businesses acquired by Swiss Arms and by two entrepreneurs, with subsequent reductions in the size of the Swiss-based facilities of the former SIG Arms group. There were also changes affecting RUAG when in 1999, the federal armaments enterprises were hived-off from the former Defence Procurement Agency and transferred into a limited company and reorganised into a group structure.

The major Swiss arms companies are shown in Table 14.2. RUAG dominates the industry, with other major firms including Rheinmetall Defence (Schweiz, AG), Pilatus, Mowag and Thales. Further Swiss arms companies include Andair (shelters), Atos (IT services), Cassidian (IT and communications), Swisstronics Contract Manufacturing (electronics), Meteolabor (lightning protection), Roschi Rohde and Schwarz AG (communications solutions) and Systems Assembling (military cables; aircraft harnesses: Armada, 2013). There is also a Swiss aerospace cluster representing small and medium-sized Swiss firms in the aviation and space industry, embracing both military and civil businesses. The following section presents brief notes on the major companies.

RUAG

RUAG is the largest Swiss arms company and in 2016, it ranked number 87 in the SIPRI Top 100. RUAG was formed in 1998 and has an international

Table 14.2 Major Swiss arms firms

Company	*Defence business*	*Defence employment*	*Total company employment*
RUAG	Maintenance, repair for Swiss armed forces	2,500	9,000
Rheinmetall	Air defence systems	1,300	11,832
Pilatus Aircraft	Trainer aircraft	875	2,113
GD European Land Systems–Mowag	Armoured vehicles	750	2,200
Thales Suisse	Tactical communications	220	66,000

Sources: Armada (2013); FC (2019); Pilatus (2017).

Note: Employment numbers at 2017.

reputation in aeronautics and defence engineering. It is the industrial partner for upgrading and maintaining weapons and systems for its key customer, namely, the Swiss armed forces. The Swiss Confederation was its major shareholder, but there were major changes in 2019 when decisions were made about its future involving 'unbundling' of its business with plans to develop the company from an armaments enterprise into an aerospace technology group and to privatise the firm in the medium term (DDPS, 2004; FC, 2019). In January 2020, RUAG will become a new holding company with two subsidiaries, namely, MRO Switzerland and RUAG International. MRO Switzerland will be responsible for providing services to the Swiss armed forces, employing about 2,500 personnel. RUAG International employing some 6,500 personnel will be responsible for other areas of the business focusing on aerospace with planned privatisation in the medium term. Privatisation plans include the sale of RUAG Ammotec which is a specialist supplier of small calibre ammunition and the Federal Council does not believe that its sale will affect the security of supply (FC, 2019).

Pilatus Aircraft

Pilatus Aircraft is a privately-owned company and a member of a group producing military trainer aircraft and business aircraft, including business jets. In 2017, Pilatus Aircraft achieved sales of almost $1 billion; its arms sales were 54.4% of total sales; and its profit rate on total sales was 13.7%. Almost half its business was in civil aerospace so it is not a defence-dependent company.

Rheinmetall Defence: RWM Schweiz AG

Rheinmetall Defence Group is a German company specialising in defence technology, security equipment and military vehicles (including the Leopard tank). Its Swiss subsidiaries form one of the country's largest private defence companies. RWM Schweiz was formerly Oerilkon Contraves Pyrotec specialising in the development and manufacture of medium calibre ammunition, including intelligent munitions. The company has plants in Zurich, Altdorf and a test centre in Ochsenboden.

General Dynamics European Land Systems – Mowag

General Dynamics European Land Systems (GDELS) is the European arm of General Dynamics. GDELS acquired the Swiss MOWAG company in 2004 with MOWAG as a world leader in troop carriers. MOWAG was established in 1950 and its Piranha family was a successful wheeled armoured vehicle operated by over 20 armies worldwide. Its Swiss plant is located in Kreuzligen.

Thales Suisse SA

Thales Suisse is contractor for the Swiss Army supplying command, control and information systems, helicopter simulators and systems for other land-based projects. There is also Thales Alenia Space Switzerland which acquired RUAG's opto-electronics business in 2016 with 75 employees.

Industry conduct

Conduct embraces various forms of price and non-price competition. Examples include price discounts, advertising, product differentiation, R&D and political lobbying. Illegal activities include various forms of bribery and corrupt payments in cash and kind. Firms will determine their precise mix of price and non-price competition depending on Swiss public procurement rules and the number of potential rivals for any contract.

Armasuisse is the Swiss procurement agency which has to choose between competitive and non-competitive purchasing. Much will depend on society's preferences for national independence and security of supply, the available number of arms firms both domestically and overseas and acquisition costs. The Government has 'key' industrial partners in Switzerland to provide security of supply. RUAG is the Swiss Army's most important industrial partner and ' ... has an exceptional position with respect to the DDPS' (FC, 2018, p. 5). Where there are rival suppliers in national and/or international markets, procurement can be competitive with Armasuisse buying existing arms 'off-the-shelf.'

Switzerland's 1994 Federal Act of Public Procurement (FAPP) favours competitive tendering with contracts awarded to the most commercially advantageous bid. There are four main award procedures, namely, open (any bidder), selective (based on qualifications criteria), negotiated (with a preferred supplier) and invitation procedures (contracting agency determines suppliers allowed to bid). However, the FAPP does not apply to the procurement of weapons, munitions, war materials nor to the construction of fighting and command infrastructure for overall defence and the army (ICLG, 2019). The Swiss Competition Commission can intervene in defence procurement decisions. For example, in 2005 a helicopter firm applied to the Competition Commission to investigate whether Armasuisse had infringed competition law in a procurement of light transport and training helicopters. The Commission found that whilst Armasuisse was exempt from procurement law, it was not exempt from competition law.

Switzerland's position as a neutral state affects its defence industrial policy. As a neutral state it is not a member of a military alliance nor is it entitled to military support from other countries. Nonetheless, Switzerland has a Security-relevant Technology and Industry Base (STIB) which provides key selected technologies that are vital for national security. These comprise information, communication and sensor technologies. Core industrial capabilities are also needed in Switzerland to support an operational army. The STIB aims to provide essential services so that systems deployed by the army can operate reliably and are sustainable (FC, 2018). State support for the STIB is achieved through domestic procurement, offsets, international cooperation, applied research, promotion of innovation, exchange of information with industry and export controls.

Switzerland acquires its costly, high technology defence equipment from foreign suppliers (e.g. combat aircraft; missiles; tanks). In 2018, Switzerland's procurement agency, Armasuisse, announced plans to acquire a new air defence capability comprising 30 or 40 combat aircraft and a ground-based air defence system. New aircraft under consideration included the Saab Gripen, Dassault Rafale, Eurofighter Typhoon, Boeing F-18 Super Hornet and the Lockheed Martin F-35 aircraft. The short-list for the ground-based air defence system included the Eurosam consortium's SAMP/T system, Raytheon's Patriot system and Israel's Rafael David's Sling missile system. In the event, only Eurosm and Raytheon submitted bids: Rafael failed to submit a bid. The final choices for the aircraft and air defence system will be subject to a referendum vote.

The new air defence capability competition specifies the operational requirements of the systems with procurement based on competition and cost-effectiveness. RUAG is named as the designated centre for maintenance, overhaul and repair for the new combat aircraft and the air defence system (unless the producer of the selected system has a subsidiary in Switzerland. Procurement also requires a 100% offset of the purchase price of the contracts. Offsets will be part of the selection criteria. There are two parts to the offset, namely, 60% for the STIB comprising 20% direct offsets and 40% indirect offsets plus 40% for other industries. The offset also has a regional element requiring 65% of the offset to be allocated to the German speaking region, 30% to the French region and 5% for the Italian region (DDPS, 2018). Cost-benefit analysis over a 30 year life-cycle will be used to evaluate the rival bids.[2]

Industry performance

Arms exports are one indicator of industry competitiveness. In 2018, Switzerland ranked 11th globally with total arms exports of $515 million. Its main export customers were Germany, Denmark, USA, Romania and Italy. Arms and munitions accounted for one-third of Swiss arms exports with other exports including armoured wheeled vehicles and missiles. Major arms exporting firms included RUAG, Rheinmetall, Mowag and Pilatus. In 2018, efforts to liberalise the rules on Swiss arms exports were abandoned by the government following widespread public criticism. Interestingly, in 2014, despite Switzerland's neutrality policy, it ranked as the world's fifth largest arms exporter *per capita*.

Swiss arms exports are shown in Table 14.3. Its arms exports were mostly aircraft, air defence systems, sensors and armoured vehicles. Comparisons can

Table 14.3 Swiss arms exports 2015–18 (all units in US$ millions)

Swiss arms exports: major recipients	*2018*	*2015–18*
Australia	74	123
China	33	195
France	74	74
Indonesia	0	101
Saudi Arabia	0	186
TOTAL	***243***	***1108***
Sweden: Total	***134***	***668***
New Zealand: Total	***6***	***17***

Source: SIPRI (2019b).

Notes:

i) Major recipients defined as receiving over $100mn of Swiss arms exports for the period 2015–18. Not all recipients are shown: hence, totals exceed the numbers shown in the table.

ii) Values are in current prices and are SIPRI Trend Indicator Values (TIVs). TIVs indicate the volume of arms transfers and not their money values.

be made with Sweden which is also a neutral country with mountainous territory and New Zealand which is a small economy where geography in the form of remoteness provides a defence barrier. The SIPRI data on arms exports for 2015–18 ranked Switzerland 14th in the world, compared with rankings of 15th for Sweden and 42nd for New Zealand. On this basis, Switzerland's arms export performance is impressive.

Conclusion

Switzerland is a unique case study where defence and defence industrial policy are determined by its neutrality and geography. Officially-provided data on its defence industry are lacking; but other sources provide sufficient data for an economic evaluation of its arms industry.

The Swiss defence economy in the form of the armed forces and defence industry represent a solution to its neutrality and the need for independence and security of supply. The defence industry provides the arms needed for its armed forces with small arms, ammunition and armoured vehicles for the army supplied from the domestic industry. More costly and complex equipment such as combat aircraft, air defence systems and tanks are imported. Foreign purchases are subject to competition and an offset is usually required. Offsets provide work for the Swiss defence industry.

Whilst offsets appear attractive (e.g. jobs), they have their limitations. Firms providing offsets have incentives to include all their activities as offsets, focusing on total business rather than real net additional work (i.e. work which would not otherwise have been obtained). Nor are offsets costless: they might involve trade diversion rather than trade creation and the resulting work might be temporary rather than permanent (Hartley, 2017). Offsets and support for the national defence industry form part of the price which Switzerland is willing to pay for neutrality.

Notes

1 This chapter was written by Keith Hartley as Co-Editor. It was not possible to obtain a national author willing and able to contribute in the required time-scale. Switzerland was included in the book since it had one company in the SIPRI Top 100 arms companies (RUAG).

2 An earlier effort to purchase a new combat aircraft selected the Saab Gripen E; but this choice was rejected in a referendum vote in 2014.

References

Armada (2013). *Defence Industry of Switzerland*, Armada International, Bangkok, Thailand, edition 2013.

DDPS (2004). *Security and Motion*, Department of Defence, Civil Protection and Sport, Bern.

DDPS (2018). *Specifications for the Procurement of a New Combat Aircraft (NKF) and a New Ground-Based air Defence System (Bodluv)*, Department of Defence, Civil Protection and Sport, Bern, March.

FC (2018). *Principles of the Swiss Federal Council for the Armaments Policy of the DDPS*, Federal Council, Bern, October.

FC (2019). *Federal Council Decides on Future of the RUAG Technology Corporation*, Federal Council, Bern, March.

GS (2013). *Swiss Arms Industry*, Global Security.org.europe.

Hartley, K (2017). *The Economics of Arms*, Agenda, Newcastle.

ICLG (2019). *Switzerland: Public Procurement 2019*, International Comparative Legal Guides, London.

Pilatus Aircraft (2017). *Annual Report 2017*, Stans, Switzerland.

SIPRI (2019a). *Military Expenditure Database*, Stockholm International Peace Research Institute, Stockholm, Sweden.

SIPRI (2019b). *Arms Transfer Database*, Stockholm International Peace Research Institute, Stockholm, Sweden.

15 The Swedish defence industry

Drawn between globalization and the domestic pendulum of doctrine and governance

Martin Lundmark

Introduction

Britz (2004) described how national defence-industrial policies were increasingly becoming integrated into an EU context, including Sweden.[1] Andersson (2007) stated that the Swedish military had become denationalized, its primary role was to contribute to international peace-keeping.[2] Ikegami (2013) argued that the Swedish defence industry was becoming increasingly irrelevant to Swedish defence needs due to its 'over-reliance' on export and that the export to extra-European markets was leading to the erosion of Swedish national security and Swedish defence readiness.[3] DeVore (2015) described how the Swedish defence industry covered many types of defence system until the 1980s and then gradually became specialized as niche actors in successful segments, driven by established products demanding incremental innovation, whereas new products would require radical innovation.[4] As this chapter will show, the Swedish defence industry has experienced several swings in national military doctrine, government defence-industrial governance and strategy for defence acquisition. The national traits of the defence industry have thereby experienced considerable change.

The Swedish parliamentary Defence Commission issued the Defence White Book on May 14, 2019. The White book is issued every five years, and structures the military priorities for the next defence planning period – in this case for the years 2021–2025. The 2019 White Book is highly ambitious and changes the conditions and future of the Swedish defence industry. The White book will be discussed later in the chapter, together with the likely implications for the domestic defence industry.

The development of a Swedish defence industry

During the 17th and 18th centuries, Sweden was a nation highly engaged in warfare. During the early 17th century, Sweden controlled most parts around the Baltic Sea. In order to support the strength of such a warring nation, an armaments-production infrastructure was developed. By the late 19th century, Sweden had two highly developed facilities for armaments production:

Bofors, which produced cannons (established in 1646 as an iron ore plant). Karlskronavarvet (established in 1689) produced naval ships for the Swedish Navy.[5] Sweden's oldest military company Åkers krutbruk[6] was established in 1552, but was closed in 2018.

Sweden was not engaged in the First or Second World Wars. Sweden gradually built up a broader domestic defence industry, during WWII and afterwards. Development and production started with indigenous jet aircraft (Saab), artillery and missiles (Bofors), surface ships and submarines (Karlskronavarvet and Kockums) together with radar and communications systems and several other types of armaments. During the Cold War the Swedish government strongly supported a close interaction between defence industry, industrialists, the procurement organization, the Armed Forces, certain state-owned companies, academia and certain non-military companies. The Wallenberg family have from that time been, and still are, majority owners of Saab and companies involved in this national defence technology complex. During the Cold War, a strongly institutionalized and trust-based 'military-industrial complex' was created. Karlsson (2015) described that during the period 1946–1992 there was a stable political consensus about having a Swedish defence industry. The consensus also held the view that the defence industry should be technically sophisticated, modern and more cost-efficient. Until the late 1960s, there was a highly stable course of development and corporate landscape. At that time, due to changing Swedish development ambitions, the defence industry strived for more export, civil production and more collaboration between companies.[7]

Sweden was at the height of its national defence technology development strength by the mid-1980s. Sweden was by then self-reliant in a broad spectrum of defence technology expertise and arms development. It produced its own fighter aircraft, naval vessels and submarines, armoured vehicles, artillery, radars, ground combat weapons, ammunition and C3I solutions. It had developed the world's most advanced data-link for its Air Force, it was in the global forefront of developing a fly-by-wire fighter aircraft. At the same time, Sweden had for several decades had strong support from the US, which transferred certain advanced technologies especially to the Swedish aircraft industry. Also, since the 1950s, there was a non-disclosed, close security and defence technology collaboration between the US and Sweden. Sweden received advanced aeronautics, avionics and jet propulsion from the US. Sweden was highly self-reliant, but depended on the US for certain missiles and critical technologies for fighter aircraft.

Corporate landscape

Sweden has a large and sophisticated defence industry for its size. The Swedish defence industry employs around 30,000 personnel in direct military development and production.[8] Table 15.1 below presents an overview of the present corporate landscape. The corporate landscape is dominated by the

Saab Group, which accounts for some 75% of the total Swedish production of arms material. Of Saab's turnover, 45% is in Aeronautics, 22% in Land, 14% in Naval, 10% in Civil Security and 8% in Commercial Aeronautics. Saab is organized in five business areas: Aeronautics, Dynamics, Surveillance, Support and Services, and Industrial Products and Services. Saab Kockums (naval vessels and submarines) is organized as a separate business area.[9] Swedish defence procurement is around 70% directed to Saab, and the two highly dominant Swedish product developments – the Gripen fighter and the A26 submarine – are in Saab's product portfolio. Thus, Saab strongly dominates the Swedish defence-industrial landscape.

The military systems and products will be described in more detail below under the heading Products. In Civil Security, Saab's product portfolio primarily offers surveillance and traffic management systems for airports and harbours. Combitech is a Saab Group affiliate, an independent technical consulting company. In Civil Aeronautics, Saab used to produce turboprop aircraft (Saab 340 and 2000), but exited civil aircraft production and transformed in the 1990s into a supplier to Airbus and Boeing.

The second biggest company is BAE Systems Sweden. It consists of the entities BAE Systems Sweden Hägglunds and BAE Systems Sweden Bofors. Hägglunds develops armoured vehicles and related systems, and system integration for armoured vehicles. Bofors develops artillery, naval guns and munition for artillery.[10]

The third biggest company is Nammo, which develops and produces ammunition end energetic material for rocket propulsion. Nammo is a result of a fusion of the state-owned ammunition facilities in Finland, Norway and Sweden in 1998. Initially, it was owned 40% by Norway, 30% by Finland and Sweden 30%. Nammo is now a Norwegian company, 50% owned by the Norwegian state, and 50% by the Finnish company Patria.[11] Other important companies producing defence materiel are, for example, FLIR (US-owned, IR sensors), Eurenco (energetic materials), Aimpoint (rifle red point scopes) and GKN (jet propulsion).

Under these larger companies are a wide diversity of small-and-medium-sized companies. Many of them are primarily suppliers to or consultants at FMV (Swedish Defence Materiel Administration, the military procurement authority), or suppliers to the larger Swedish defence companies. Several of them also sell to foreign customers.

There are also a number of very large, primarily civil-oriented companies that also sell components, systems and platforms to the Swedish military and other militaries. Examples are Volvo Trucks, Scania (trucks) and Trelleborg. The Swedish defence companies presently on average have 17% self-financed R&D. Saab states it has 23%, so the other defence companies thereby have much lower self-financed R&D.

Systems integration concerns 'the capability to combine diverse knowledge bases and physical components into functioning systems'.[13] Responsibilities for system integration have gradually been transferred from the state

Table 15.1 Swedish defence companies[12]

Company	*Foreign owned?*	*Previous name*	*Turnover 2017*	*Work force*
Saab	-		31.4 billion SEK	16,400
BAE Systems Hägglunds	BAE Systems	Hägglunds	3.4 billion SEK	729
BAE Systems Bofors	BAE Systems	Bofors	1.3 billion SEK	281
Nammo	Nammo A/S, Norway		507 million SEK	297
GKN	GKN, UK	Volvo Flygmotor	(8.5 % military)	2,100
Eurenco Bofors AB	GIAT/Nexter, Fra	Part of Bofors	470 million SEK	207

Source: Company homepages and email inquiries to companies.

(especially from FMV) since the 1980s. The state actors' competence for system integration and the functioning of complex defence systems has decreased as a result of the increased complexity of system integration – a complexity magnified by the numerous make-buy decisions in globalized sourcing.[14] This is a development that Sweden shares with several nations (e.g. France). However, in France the defence industry is involved in and performs all system integration up to the highest levels of military sensitivity, whereas in Sweden there are some capabilities defined as 'integrity-critical' where the system integration and software is performed by state actors, without participation of the defence industry. This Swedish approach is taken in order to minimize the number of people that have insight into these capabilities' design and functioning, and also that the companies' foreign industrial and military partners shall not be able to receive insight into sensitive Swedish capabilities.[15]

The ownership of intellectual property from defence technology developed through government financing becomes the property of the state (FMV). FMV thereby receives revenues from exports when state-owned technology is included, and the state can deny export of its technology. There have been issues when foreign owners have demanded to transfer Swedish state-owned technology to the mother company, but the Swedish state has blocked the transfer.[16] Technology defined as military (and certain dual use technologies) developed by the companies' own financing does not have this restriction, but the export still requires state approval.

Products

In Aeronautics, the Gripen fighter is the dominant product. The first version, A/B became operational in 1996, and the C/D version became operational in 2004. The Swedish Air Force is presently flying the second version, the C/D. This version has also been exported to South Africa and Thailand and is being leased to Hungary and the Czech Republic. One C/D has also been sold to the UK, for use in training. The C/D's for South Africa were co-produced with South Africa,[17] the other nations have received surplus C/D's from the Swedish Air Force inventory.[18] The Swedish Air Force ordered a total of 204 C/D, and 40 of these are presently in service in other nations. The Gripen E/F version (also called Gripen NG) is under development, and is co-developed with its first foreign buyer, Brazil. Brazil has ordered 36 aircraft, and the aircraft's development is performed in collaboration between Saab and the Brazilian company Embraer (see Chapter 23). The E/F is almost a new aircraft, with its longer range, stronger engine, extended fuselage and ability to carry a heavier payload. Saab have responded to procurement interests and is presently (June 2019) offering Gripen at various levels of capability to the following nations: the C/D version to Austria, Botswana, Bulgaria, Colombia, Malaysia, Philippines andSlovakia; and the E/F version to Canada, Finland, India and Switzerland.

In October 2018, Boeing and Saab won the US Air Force order for the next US trainer aircraft, the T-X. In its first phase until 2023, the project will produce five T-X, and the program plans to produce 351 T-X aircraft. The system is planned to be fully operational by 2031 with all aircraft delivered. The aircraft is also likely to have very strong export potential, especially for the international F-35 users. Saab's share of the program is around 10%, and its production will be undertaken in the US.

In the Land sector, Saab produces hand-held mortar systems, missiles, radar systems and C3I systems, especially Carl Gustaf armoured rifles and its derivatives, the Giraffe radar systems and derivatives which have been successful export products.

In the Naval sector, for Saab Kockums, the dominant product area is submarine development. The next generation submarine, the A26, is presently under development and is expected to be operational in 2023. Kockums has also produced six Visby frigates for Sweden. Kockums has had limited export success, with Collins submarines to Australia in 1986 and two retrofits of Swedish Navy surplus submarines to Singapore in 2005 and 2009. Saab Kockums has a strategic partnership with Damen Shipyards (NL) for the development of submarines. Saab Kockums acquired the Swedish company Dockstavarvet in 2017, which produces smaller patrol and combat boats. Kockums has developed air-independent submarine propulsion based on the Stirling technology. Japan uses Stirling in its submarines through a licensing agreement. Saab Dynamics develops torpedoes and has a light and medium torpedo in its product portfolio. The torpedoes are wire-guided and only the Swedish navy has them in operational use. Saab also develops unmanned underwater vehicles and underwater sensors.

Saab Dynamics are partners in the consortia for three air-to-air missiles: Meteor, Iris-T and Taurus. Iris-T is presently being developed for Sweden's short-range ground-based air defence. It has further developed two other air defence missiles: RB 70 and Bamse. The RB 70 is also available in a newer version, RB 70 NG, which it has sold to Brazil and the Czech Republic. Furthermore, Saab has the RB 15 sea-to-air system, which it has sold to Germany, Poland and Croatia.

Saab acquired Ericsson Microwave in 2004 and has thereby a series of radar products. The Giraffe and the Sea Giraffe radars, the Erieye/Globaleye Airborne early warning and control system (AEW&C). The Arthur counter-battery artillery radar is also an export success.

Saab Barracuda produces camouflage solutions. The majority of its sales have been to the US, where Barracuda has a production site (Lillington, North Carolina). Saab also produces electronic warfare and countermeasure systems. Saab has been highly successful in the export of its families of ground combat weapons, especially to the US. The products are shoulder-launched and the product portfolio holds NLAW (developed with the UK), AT4, Carl-Gustaf and the Bill anti-tank missile. Furthermore, Saab also develops and produces systems for electronic warfare and countermeasures, as well as C4I systems for decision support, combat management and other C4I solutions.

Hägglunds has families of tracked, armoured combat vehicles, especially the CV90 family which has been sold to many nations. Further vehicles presently on offer are Bv510 Beowulf and the Bv206 and derivatives of it. In 2019 and 2020, Hägglunds delivers the 40 acquired Armoured mortar vehicle 90 to the Swedish Army, based on a CV90 chassi.

Bofors produces the Archer, a self-propelled gun system, based on a 155 mm automated howitzer, a Protector remote controlled weapon station mounted on a Volvo hauler. Its munitions inventory has Fuze and Bonus munitions, together with the Lemur remote control weapon station and three types of naval guns (40 Mk4, 57 Mk3 and Mk110). There is also Excalibur which is a guided artillery shell and is a collaborative effort between Bofors and Raytheon.

Aimpoint develops red dot sights for military use and for hunting. Since the start, it has sold more than 2.5 million sights, including over one million to the US – a large share of them to the US military.

Swedish defence companies have production sites in the US. Saab produces its camouflage equipment and ground combat systems in the US and it acquired the air traffic management company Sensis in 2011. Bofors and Nammo also have production sites in the US.

Government policy

The Swedish system for defence acquisition is that the Armed Forces decides what capabilities it needs. FMV has to find solutions that meet the specifications of the Armed Forces' desired capabilities. FOI performs defence research financed by the Armed Forces.

Until the 1990s, arms development occurred in a combination of state-owned companies, state arsenals and private companies. The state-owned facilities became concentrated in Förenade Fabriksverken (FFV) in 1986, and in 1991 they were reorganized into a more commercial set-up within the conglomerate Celsius. At the time, Celsius produced missiles, naval vessels, submarines, mortar rifles, explosives and ammunition. Since 1999, the Swedish government commenced a highly market liberal governance policy for the domestic defence industry. The state-owned defence company Celsius was divested and state ownership ended. Large parts of Celsius became privatized or acquired by Saab. Foreign ownership had started with Hägglunds being acquired by Alvis plc. (UK) in 1997. The submarine and naval ship company Kockums following the Celsius dismantlement was acquired by HDW[19] (Germany). The artillery and munitions company Bofors was acquired by United Defense (US) in 2001; then BAE Systems acquired Alvis in 2004, and United Defense in 2005. Thereby Bofors and Hägglunds became parts of BAE Systems. BAE Systems also acquired a 35% minority share in Saab in 1999, which was gradually reduced to zero by 2005. Along with this, a few other, smaller companies were acquired from abroad. Sweden was in a European as well as a global perspective very market-liberal, as most European nations had and still have considerable state ownership and several have restrictions on foreign ownership.

The Swedish government has never had an official defence-industrial policy. Swedish defence procurement has, however, always been highly pro-Swedish. In 2007, the Armed Forces and FMV issued a joint materiel acquisition strategy. The strategy stated that the procurement priorities should be firstly, to acquire operational equipment off-the-shelf; secondly, to develop international collaboration; and thirdly, and exceptionally, to develop domestically. In 2009 the government proclaimed its 'Principles for the Armed Forces' materiel acquisition', which resembled the previous strategy but further enforced market orientation. The Principles defined the priorities as firstly, prolong and upgrade the use of existing equipment, preferably with other nations; secondly acquire off-the shelf, preferably with other nations; thirdly develop in collaboration; and fourthly, develop domestically. The EU Defence and Security Procurement Directive (2009/81/EC) was set into national legislation in 2011. Thereby, from 2007 to 2011, radical changes in government policy and legislation were set in place. We will return to their effects.

As stated above, Kockums was acquired by HDW in 1999. HDW was in turn acquired by the US investment fund One Equity Partner in 2002. OEP thereafter divested HDW to ThyssenKrupp (Germany) in 2004. Under ThyssenKrupp, the Swedish defence acquisition and the Armed Forces' demands did not integrate well. ThyssenKrupp was a competitor to Kockums in foreign markets, and acted in order to restrict Kockums competitiveness in foreign markets where both German and Swedish submarines were on offer, as they were in most cases. This strongly limited Kockums' business possibilities as well as its ability to develop the next generation of Swedish submarine, the A26. The relationship between ThyssenKrupp (and concerned German authorities) deteriorated more and more. In 2015, the Swedish government organized together with FMV and Saab a drastic take-over. First, in March, the orders to Kockums were halted motivated by the German owner's unwillingness to cooperate. After this, Saab started to recruit engineers from Kockums. In July 2015, Saab acquired Kockums from ThyssenKrupp at a much lower price than ThyssenKrupp had demanded at the beginning of the year. Thereby, Swedish naval competence and facilities came under Swedish control.[20]

In 2014 and 2015, the Swedish government declared two 'essential security interests': fighter aircraft and underwater capability. This shall be seen in relation to the EU Defence Procurement Directive, where national preference (and thereby non-competitive procurement) must be justified by declared essential national security interests. The two main development projects directly related to these essential security interests – Gripen and A26 – accounted in 2017 for around one third of the development and procurement budget,[21] and with the adjoining supporting systems that are directly needed for the capability; the share is around 50%.[22] In a planning document, a third essential security interest was declared in 2017: 'integrity-critical parts of C4I systems', and more specifically pointing to cyber defence.

After the Cold War, there was a long period of unclear threat perception, and considerable downsizing of the Armed Forces' national bases, equipment, logistics and readiness. From around 2000 to 2014, the main defence priority was participation in international peacekeeping operations. From 2014, the Russian military attacks in Georgia 2008 and Ukraine 2014, paired with massive military build-up and aggressive security rhetoric, changed the Swedish posture and doctrine. The primary military priority became in 2014 declared as operational military capabilities and homeland defence. Thus, after a period of many processes of market liberalization and harmonization, weakening of national defence capability, a clear shift occurred in the Swedish defence posture and priority.

Compared to, for example, France, UK and the US, Sweden's support to and activities for engaging SMEs are very limited. FMV has an obligation from the Ministry of Defence to support increased SME involvement in defence supply chains, but very limited activity is seen from FMV.[23]

Many nations have programs for supporting and enhancing increased use of civil technology in military applications. Sweden has quite limited dual use programs, with the exception of the NFFP program (National Aeronautics Research Programme). NFFP engages civil and military aeronautics companies and academia. NFFP started in 1994, and is now in its seventh round. It is financed 50% by industry and 50% from the state. The primary activity is to finance doctorate students and since the start in 1994, it produced 95 PhDs by 2017.

Internationalization

The largest defence spenders in Europe started armaments collaboration in the 1950s. France, Germany, Italy and the UK engaged in especially missile and aircraft development. These developments gradually deepened its integration and led to joint ventures and finally into industrial conglomerates such as Airbus, MBDA, EADS and EuroTorp in the 1990s and 2000s.[24] Sweden did not really engage in armaments collaboration until the late 1990s. Examples of collaboration starting in the 1990s are Cision, Bonus, Meteor, Archer, Iris-T, NH90 and Excalibur.[25] In recent years, Sweden has engaged in fewer and smaller collaborations. The primary exception is the bilateral development of Gripen E/F with Brazil, where Brazil has acquired 36 Gripen E/F for 38 billion SEK. The development is a development between Saab, Embraer and the Brazilian state. The Swedish state and Saab are also eagerly searching for an international partner for the development of the A26 submarine (see Chapter 7).

The Armed Forces and the government have in recent years clearly prioritised homeland defence due to the worsened security and threat situation. In 2016, three nations were declared as the most important regarding military and security policy: Denmark, Finland and the US. This has resulted in many programs and activities in order to improve interoperability and certain capabilities, logistics and shared security threats. It has not resulted in new major procurements or developments for the defence industry, but companies involved in defence logistics and maintenance have received more orders.

Sweden became a member of the EU in 1995. It has never joined NATO, but has in recent years (without joining) come very close to NATO military planning. There is also substantial coordination and collaboration of procurement and logistics through the NORDEFCO[26] organization (together with Denmark, Finland and Norway). NATO and NORDEFCO more directly relate to Sweden's homeland defence, whereas EU defence activities are seen as more indirectly contributing to Sweden's military capabilities. Due to this, there has been a subtle shift of priorities, favouring NATO and Nordefco activities to EU and EDA[27] activities.[28]

Government funding

NATO recommends its member states to have a defence budget at 2.0% of GDP. Several members have in recent years moved towards this recommended level. Sweden had for a long period decreased its share which in recent years was 1% to 1.1%. From 2017, a slow upward trend started, and there is strong political consensus after an August 2019 political agreement that it shall continue to gradually increase towards a level of around 1.5% of GDP by 2025.

Defence research and technology

The Swedish Armed Forces annually allocates the Research and Technology (R&T) funds primarily to FMV and FOI (Swedish Defence Research Agency). From 2005 to 2011, the R&T funds decreased by 60% to 460 million SEK, primarily due to reallocation of funds in order to finance procurement and operations for the Afghanistan mission (2004–2011). For the years 2020–2021, the R&T funds are shown in Table 15.2.

R&T appropriations for 2018–2021 are presently not finally assigned, and the figures in the table cover more than R&T. In any case, R&T has increased, but moderately. Thus, despite the increased priority on military capabilities and homeland defence from 2014, the defence R&T budget has only been affected marginally, with even a downward trend from 2014 to 2017.

Development and procurement

The Swedish procurement budget for materiel and facilities is shown in Table 15.3.

The Swedish procurement budget has increased by some 40% over the period. In 2018, the distribution of acquisition and development funds is shown in Table 15.4.

Present development projects

Sweden presently has the following major development projects: A26 Submarine (Saab Kockums); Gripen E/F (Saab and Embraer); Lightweight torpedo (Saab Dynamics); NH90 helicopter (Saab); armoured mortar vehicle 90 (Hägglunds); Strategisk Ledning Bataljon (SLB, [Strategic Battalion

Table 15.2 Swedish defence R&T funds 2013–2021

Year	*2013*	*2014*	*2015*	*2016*	*2017*	*2018*	*2019*	*2020*	*2021*
Million SEK	481	483	471	459	452	642	642	642	642

Source: data received over email from the Armed Forces. Current prices.

Table 15.3 Swedish procurement budget for materiel and facilities

Year	*2013*	*2014*	*2015*	*2016*	*2017*	*2018*	*2019*	*2020*	*2021*
Budget, million SEK	8825	10864	9845	9298	10035	10816	12727	13038	12072

Source: data received over email from the Armed Forces. Current prices.

Table 15.4 Distribution of budgeted investments by activity, excluding facilities

Area	*Army*	*Marine*	*Air Force*	*Operative management*	*Logistics*	*Support functions*
Investment (million SEK)	1980	2563	3654	1401	293	1115
% of total	18.0	23.3	33.2	12.7	2.7	10.1

Source: data received over email from the Armed Forces. Current prices.

Command] (Saab)); electronic surveillance monitoring vessel (Saab, but produced in Poland). Presently, there are also the following larger upgrade projects: submarine Gotland class (Saab Kockums) and Main Battle Tank Leopard 122 (Hägglunds and Bofors). The A26 and Gripen projects in total encompass around 50% of the entire development and procurement budget.

Current procurement programs

Table 15.5 shows the major procurement programs under the management of FMV.

The Swedish government ordered four Patriot systems in August 2018 at a cost of SEK 12.1 billion. It is doubtful as to whether it will suffice with SEK 12.1 billion for the Patriot procurement. The life cycle cost will likely amount to around two to three times that cost.

Out of total procurement between 2014 and 2017, the share for Swedish companies was 72.8%, 70.1%, 66.0% and 69.9%, respectively. International armaments collaboration and procurement collaboration constituted 17% of total procurement investments (2016).[31]

The present defence materiel acquisition policy based on the 2007 and 2009 defence acquisition strategies favour off-the-shelf acquisition, and next in priority adaptation of existing materiel, and exceptionally development. A 2016 report[32] shown in Table 15.6, shows the distribution by acquisition type for 2015–2017.

The aforementioned defence acquisition strategy by Armed Forces/FMV in 2007, the 'Principles for the Armed Forces' defence acquisition' by the MoD in 2009 and the EU Defence Procurement Directive implies that Sweden should have moved towards a high share of off-the-shelf acquisition, less dependence on the domestic defence industry and less domestic, preferential supplier selection. However, the figures on the allocation and distribution of the acquisition budget show that some 50% of the sea budget is allocated to domestic development. On average over recent years' 70% of the budget is allocated to Swedish companies, Saab has become very dominant with 75% of the domestic production and the two large essential security interests – fighters and underwater capability –

Table 15.5 Current Swedish procurement programs[29]

Name	*System*	*Lead contractor*	*Swedish company involved*	*Cost*	*Comment*
Patriot	Medium range ground-based air defence	Raytheon (US)	-	SEK 12.1 billion	
Iris-T	Short range ground-based air defence	Diehl (Germany)	Saab Dynamics	SEK 270 million	
Trucks	Thirteen different types of vehicles	Rheinmetall	Skeppsbron	€ 2 billion[30]	Procurement collaboration with Norway
Bridge vehicle	Armoured vehicle-launched bridge	Not decided			
Satellite communication		Not decided			
Trainer aircraft		Not decided			

Source: data received over email from the Armed Forces. Current prices.

Table 15.6 Acquisition type distributed over military domains

	Land	*Sea*	*Air*	*Logistics*
Development	33.3 %	50.9 %	35.7 %	31.8 %
Adaptation	32.2 %	20.0 %	14.3 %	18.2 %
Off-the-shelf	34.5 %	29.1 %	50.0 %	50.0 %

Source: data received over email from the Armed Forces. Current prices.

strongly reside in Saab. This shows that the implemented policy documents and legislation has had limited impact on the Swedish defence materiel acquisition.

Export[33]

Swedish defence companies were at the end of the 1990s primarily producing for Swedish demand, around 70% of production was domestic, and 30% export. The Swedish orders and the rate of new development programs decreased gradually after the Cold War. The Swedish government therefore

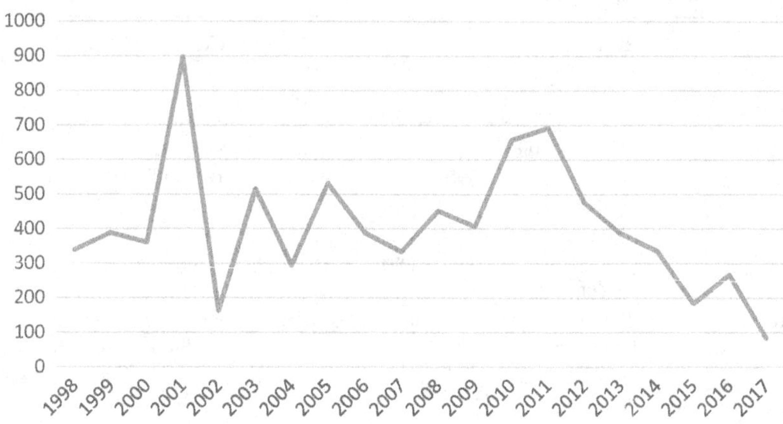

Figure 15.1 Swedish defence exports, 1998–2017, $ million.

around the year 2000 encouraged Swedish companies to engage more in export, and the government started to allocate more resources to export support. The arguments were that Sweden needed a competitive defence industry that could meet Swedish demands, that it represented a large and sophisticated work force, that the export generated revenues to Sweden and thereby financed the investments in defence technology and competence, and also that the defence innovation generated spin-offs to Swedish innovation and industry in general.

In 2001, there was a large increase in exports, followed by a slump in 2002. Then, after a period of an upward trend from 2002 to 2011, exports have experienced a steady downward trend from 2011 to 2017 (Figure 15.1).

Sweden is a large defence exporter, globally one of the highest per capita. Sweden is consistently a net exporter. Aggregated over the period 2008–2017, Sweden was the world's 12th largest defence exporter at total value of $3.94 billion. Sweden was in 2010 the 8th largest exporter ($657 million) but in 2017 the 20th largest ($83 million), so there are substantial variations (see Figures 15.2 and 15.3).[34] Over the period 2008–2017, Sweden exported five times more than it imported.[35] As can be seen in Table 15.2, the export has been steadily declining since 2011.

Sweden's exports during this period were to 46 nations, and the ten biggest buyers are shown in Table 15.7.

What is not shown in the SIPRI data is the Gripen export to Brazil in 2015, which amounted to SEK 38 billion – Sweden's largest export order ever of all categories of industry. This order likely plays out over many years, commencing after 2017.

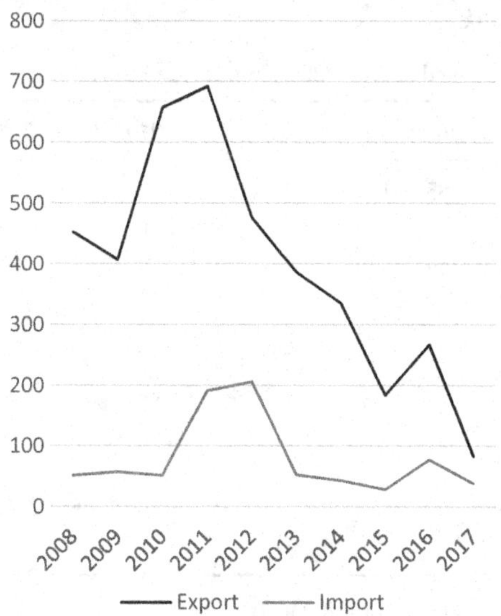

Figure 15.2 Swedish exports and imports, 2008–2017.

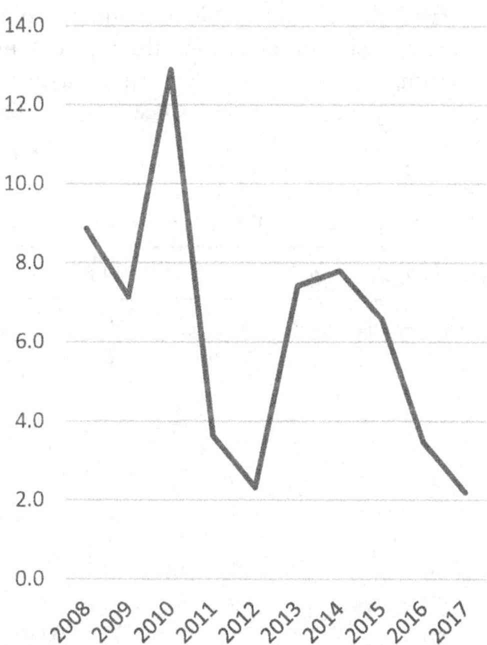

Figure 15.3 Swedish defence export/import ratio, 2008–2017.

Table 15.7 Export from Sweden 2008–2017: ten largest buyers

$ million	*2008*	*2009*	*2010*	*2011*	*2012*	*2013*	*2014*	*2015*	*2016*	*2017*	*Total*
South Africa	132	105	158	184	105						684
Thailand			27	158	36	171	8	13	13	4	428
Pakistan	11	84	244	4	4	4	4	4	4	4	367
UAE	1	1	40	47		72	57	65	17	5	305
Netherlands	54	54	63	63	61						295
Singapore				119	114	15					248
United Kingdom	16	25	46	40	55	23					203
Saudi Arabia			3	3			160		1		167
Denmark	74	64	4		3		5				149
Greece	120										120

Source: SIPRI Arms Transfers Data Base. SIPRI TIV values.

Table 15.8 shows Swedish defence exports over different armaments categories. Aircraft dominate with 41% of the total, followed by sensors with 18%. This table only partly reflects actual exports. Bilateral agreements government-to-government may not be reflected. What is especially missing is the substantial export to the US of shoulder-mounted combat weapons. In the table, the US should likely also be among the top ten buyers, due to such government-to-government sales. These government-to-government arms exports are not covered in the SIPRI data since they are based on delivered

Table 15.8 Swedish defence export 2008–2017 by armaments category

$ million	*2008*	*2009*	*2010*	*2011*	*2012*	*2013*	*2014*	*2015*	*2016*	*2017*	*Total*
Aircraft	139	193	464	382	129	158	160		11	0	1636
Armoured vehicles	115	106	72	77	71	1	0	16	14	27	499
Artillery			0								0
Engines	5	13	14	13	16	13	4	10	17	12	116
Missiles	12	37	65	69	93	39	16	26	120	18	492
Naval weapons	5		5	8	5		8	18	10	15	73
Sensors	142	35	36	47	63	118	91	58	95	12	695
Ships	36	24		99	99	57	57	57			430
Total	452	407	657	692	476	386	335	184	267	83	3940

Source: SIPRI Arms Transfers Data Base. SIPRI TIV values.

exports reported by the companies, and government-to-government sales have the Swedish state in the form of FMV as the seller.

According to the government authority ISP,[36] Swedish defence exports in 2017 were SEK 11.3 billion. Compared to the SIPRI figure of $83 million, this is a difference by a factor of around 12.[37] ISP also states that exports increased by 2% from 2016 to 2017, whereas SIPRI's data show a decrease by 69%. Another striking difference between SIPRI's data and ISP's data is that ISP states that the largest recipient in 2017 was Brazil (Gripen E/F program) with India second (antitank rifles and munition). In SIPRI's data, neither Brazil nor India appear among the top ten recipients. So why are there such striking differences between SIPRI's and ISP's data? One explanation is that SIPRI's definitions of what constitutes 'defence export' is different to ISP's (e.g. that consultancy, technology transfer, services etc. are not included in SIPRI's data). A second explanation is that follow-on deliveries and government-to government (FMS) deliveries likely are not be covered by SIPRI's data.[38] A third explanation is that SIPRI's data solely covers '*major* arms transfers' and are expressed in their own metrics: 'TIV' values. Still, the order of difference casts doubts on the significance of SIPRI's data in this regard.

Table 15.9 shows the biggest arms sellers to Sweden. Also in this case, there are government-to-government acquisitions that are not fully covered in the data.

A reform of Swedish arms export regulations was initiated in 2011 through the government's KEX directive. One of the objectives of this directive was to introduce a 'democracy criterion' that aims to restrict defence export to nations with 'weak democratic structures'. A reformed arms export regulation was passed by the Parliament in April 2018 – including a democracy criterion. The effect of this criterion on defence export is unclear, but the case-by-case interpretation of the criterion will gradually form a pattern and a practice. What is clear is that it will have some decreasing impact on exports to certain nations, especially to the Gulf nations. Nations such as Saudi Arabia and the United Arab Emirates have been large buyers, so the reform could have sizeable effects on Swedish defence exports.

The 2019 Defence White Book[39]

The Defence Commission issues a Defence White Book every five years, defining priorities for capabilities and acquisition for the next defence planning period – in this case the White Book presented on May 14, 2019 covers the years 2021–2025. The Defence Commission is a parliamentary group that includes members from all parties in the Parliament. The Defence Commission's White Book by tradition becomes the outline for how the next defence planning period; the defence ministry will implement it. The ministries can due to unforeseen budgetary or security events amend the plan, but only marginally. Thus, the White Book is the Master plan.

Table 15.9 Imports to Sweden, 2008–2017: ten largest sellers

	2008	*2009*	*2010*	*2011*	*2012*	*2013*	*2014*	*2015*	*2016*	*2017*	*Total*
United States	9	2		150	185	16	1	2	9	5	379
Germany (FRG)	1	40	40	8	8				44	29	168
France				28		7	21	23	20		99
Finland						13	20				33
South Africa	12				7	14					33
Italy	17	6									22
United Kingdom		2	6	6	6						20
Norway			5			2	1	3	5	4	19
Canada	10										10
Israel	2	7									9
Denmark	1										1
Total	51	57	51	191	206	52	43	28	77	38	792

Source: SIPRI Arms Transfers Data Base. SIPRI TIV values.

The 2019 Defence White Book describes a deteriorated security situation since the previous 2014 White book that requires fundamental reinforcements of capabilities and equipment. The Armed Forces will until 2025 increase from 60,000 to 90,000 personnel. Regarding acquisition, sustainment and issues directly related to the Swedish defence industry, the following issues stand out:

- The defence budget shall gradually be increased up to 1.5% of GDP by 2025, up to a level of SEK 84 billion.
- The Gripen C/D will not be phased out by 2027, it will serve until 2038. Thereby Saab will have around ten more years of supporting the C/D. The C/D will serve as a capability complement to the E/F, and also as an advanced trainer. Two more Air Force divisions will be added, increasing the number to eight.
- Acquisition of a new trainer for basic pilot training.
- The logistics function and readiness will be profoundly reinforced, where 'considerable quantities of equipment will be acquired'; lorries; special vehicles; command control and signals equipment; munitions and special equipment.
- The 'entire stock of armoured fighting vehicles and main battle tanks' will be upgraded.
- A new artillery system for the mechanised brigades.
- Acquisition of a 'simple, man-portable' anti-aircraft missile system.

- Upgrading of the Navy's existing ships with anti-aircraft missiles and new anti-ship missiles for all five Visby class corvettes. Two new surface combatant vessels acquired after 2025.
- Upgrading of present three Gotland class submarines, and acquisition of replacement acquisition should be commenced no later than in 2025. The number of operative submarines will be increased from four to five.
- Strengthening of mine-laying capabilities.
- Air defence capabilities will be strengthened through the acquisition of air-launched cruise missiles and additional air-to-air missiles.
- Upgrading of the sensor chain for air surveillance.
- Defence R&D shall be 'assigned further resources'.

In sum, these statements bring very good news to the Swedish defence industry. Saab Aeronautics and Saab Kockums (especially) can foresee strongly reinforced order streams from the Armed Forces. BAE Systems Hägglunds and BAE Systems Bofors (especially) will have much more impressive order books, thereby making them stronger in the eyes of prospective foreign buyers. The missile producer Saab Dynamics has experienced a weak long-term order backlog, but will now likely receive several more assignments and orders. Admittedly, not all of the above acquisition plans will materialize into orders to domestic defence companies, but the aggregate of orders will to a sizeable share likely benefit Swedish companies.

The White Book also more strongly than in previous white books and defence bills underlines the strategic importance of the domestic defence industry and its importance for security of supply. It suggests that a defence-industrial strategy as well as a new defence acquisition strategy should be set in place.

Challenges

There are challenges facing the Swedish defence industry, its competitiveness and its future sales. Saab Kockums has developed the innovative Visby corvette, but has not succeeded in exporting it. Saab Kockums also develops the A26 submarine, where Sweden has ordered two, with an option for a third. There are presently no foreign customers that could help to co-finance the development costs of A26. Poland is at present the most promising prospective buyer, followed by the Netherlands.

Swedish defence acquisition is highly dependent on Saab. This can be seen as a strength: that there is a large and broad domestic company, which is successful in several product segments. A disadvantage is that Saab has a very strong bargaining position vis-à-vis the state, coupled with the Swedish low appropriations for defence R&T. For Saab, a low domestic defence R&T level could signal doubts to foreign prospective buyers about its long-term competence and credibility.

The breadth and ambition level of Swedish defence technology development is not matched by sufficient defence R&T funding, and there are not many new development projects financed by the Swedish development budget. One could say that the Swedish defence technology complex is living off old investments. On the other hand, this situation has been present for a long time, and Saab is developing new generations of missiles, radars and ground combat weapons – partly financed by its self-generated R&D and by foreign customers. Thereby, Saab has a business model which functions under these conditions.

The persistently low defence R&T appropriations (at least related to the innovation ambitions in many areas) and FMV over a long time gradually having been transformed from a technology development authority to becoming more focused on managing procurement by the book – this has weakened the role and influence of the state. The defence companies have become much more export-oriented, depending more on themselves attracting R&D financing, some of them being foreign-owned and there is not a formal defence-industrial policy. This should, according to many critics, result in a gradual attenuation of the Swedish defence companies' competitiveness and attractiveness as partners. The trend of decreasing defence exports from 2011 onwards points to this. Such a trend is more marked in armoured vehicles and artillery. Saab appears to steadily receive Gripen contracts, and compared to its European competitors (Rafale and Eurofighter) is doing quite well. Saab and the Swedish state declared in July 2019 that they had joined as partners in the FCAS (Future Combat Air Systems) fighter development program together with the United Kingdom and Italy. This highly ambitious project (paralleled by the SCAF project (*Système de Combat Aérien Future*), with France, Germany and Spain as partners) will likely be highly influential for future military aeronautics in Europe. It is, however, too early to judge how this will play out.

A final challenge, or perhaps uncertainty, is how the Swedish defence budget will develop in the next five to ten years. The 2018 acquisition of Patriot swallows a large chunk of the acquisition budget.

Methodological challenges

The published data on defence export and import does not truly reflect what Swedish defence companies sell and to whom, and what Sweden imports. SIPRI data for Sweden should be higher in certain armament categories and concerning certain nations. As discussed above, the government's arms export authority ISP in some cases presents very different data to SIPRI's – ISP presents much higher defence exports.

Some companies are foreign owned, and this makes it much more difficult to retrieve data on turnover, strategy, foreign sales etc. This is especially the case with BAE Systems' two Swedish affiliates Bofors and Hägglunds. Data on these two companies is therefore not satisfying for this study. Saab publishes much more detailed information in its annual report and on its homepage.

Conclusions

Over a longer time, the Swedish defence industry has experienced dramatic changes in its domestic conditions compared to most other nations:

- Ownership: state ownership has ceased and there is extensive foreign ownership. The degree of foreign ownership has, however, decreased through BAE Systems' exit from its 35% minority share in Saab and through the 'repatriation' of Kockums from ThyssenKrupp.
- State governance: The Swedish government through the above ownership changes has a defence-industrial strategy similar to the UK. By international defence-industrial standards, Sweden has a highly market-liberal governance system.
- Doctrine swings: Since the end of the Cold War, the priorities in military doctrine have shifted dramatically, which has fundamentally affected the conditions for defence innovation, procurement and development, and thereby the conditions for the domestic defence industry.
- Export focus: The increased dependence on defence exports is not unique to Sweden. Several other nations have shifted in this way (e.g. France and the UK), but this has fundamentally changed the business models and priorities of the Swedish defence companies: they cannot primarily survive from Swedish orders.

The Chapter started with four statements. First, Britz's (2004) statement that national defence industry policies were being integrated into an EU context. Second, Andersson's (2007) statement that the Swedish defence industry had become denationalized. Third, Ikegami's (2013) statement that the Swedish defence industry due to globalization had lost national relevance for the Swedish military. Fourth, DeVore's (2015) statement that Swedish defence industry after covering many defense system categories until the 1980s had gradually become specialized as niche actors in successful segments, driven by established products demanding incremental innovation, whereas new products would require radical innovation. Changes in military doctrine and security policy priorities in 2014 have swung the pendulum to a state where Sweden defined essential security interests in 2014, 2015 and 2017 (fighters; underwater capability; integrity-critical parts of C4I) and that the required competence for these capabilities shall be Swedish. This constitutes an affirmation of the national importance of certain parts of the defence industry. Companies, competences and technologies that do not fall under the essential security interests are not as fortunate. Decreases in R&T and development appropriations are at historically low levels, large parts of the defence industry must survive on their own competitiveness, and a liberal acquisition procurement practice – all this has led to weaker links and bonds between the state and parts of the research community and certain parts of the defence industry. Thus, the Swedish defence industry is in parts highly national, and in other parts, cogs in a globalized defence market.

The 2019 Defence White Book brings substantial momentum to the Swedish defence industry. However, it still remains to be seen how the plans play out – this written four months after the release of the White Book.

Notes

1 Britz, Malena (2004), *The Europeanization of Defence Industry Policy*, diss. Stockholm University.
2 Andersson, J.J. (2007), 'A New Swedish Defence for a Brave New World', in: Matlary & Österud (eds), *Denationalisation of Defence – Convergence and Diversity*, Ashgate, pp. 135–156.
3 Ikegami, Masako (2013), 'The End of a "National" Defence Industry? – Impacts of Globalization on the Swedish defence Industry', in: *Scandinavian Journal of History*, Vol. 38, No.4, pp. 436–457 (Routledge).
4 DeVore, Marc (2015), 'Defying Convergence: Globalisation and Varieties of Defence-Industrial Capitalism', in: *New Political Economy*, Vol. 20, No.4, pp. 569–593 (Routledge).
5 Karlskronavarvet was incorporated into Kockums in 1989.
6 Krutbruk = powder mill. Åkers krutbruk was acquired by Ibd Deisenroth Engineering GmBH (Germany) in 2002, and was renamed Åkers Krutbruk Protection AB. In the last decades, Åkers Krutbruk Protection AB worked with ballistic protection and signature management for armoured vehicles.
7 Karlsson, Birgit (2015), *Svensk försvarsindustri 1945–1992* [Swedish defence industry 1945–1992], Försvaret och det kalla kriget, Karlskrona.
8 www.soff.se. SOFF is the Swedish defence industry's branch organization.
9 www.saabgroup.com
10 Hägglunds was acquired by Alvis plc. (UK) in 1997; United Defense (USA) acquired Bofors in 2001; BAE Systems (UK) acquired Alvis in 2003; BAE Systems acquired United Defense in 2005.
11 The Norwegian state owns 63.2 % of Kongsberg. In 2016, Kongsberg acquired 49.9 % of Patria and the Finnish state owns the remaining 50.1 % of Patria.
12 Some of the figures are from 2016 and some from 2017.
13 Davies, A. Brady, T., Prencipe, A. Hobday, M. (2011), 'Innovation in Complex Products and Systems Implications for Project Based Organizing', in: Cattani, G., Ferriani, S., Frederiksen, L., Taube, F., Silverman, B (eds), *Project-Based Organizing and Strategic Management*, Emerald Publishing, Ltd, Bingley, UK, pp. 3–26.
14 Gholz, E., James, A., Speller, T. (2018), 'The Second Face of Systems Integration: An Empirical Analysis of Supply Chains to Complex Product Systems', in: *Research Policy*, Vol. 47, pp. 1478–1494.
15 Lundmark, M. (forthcoming), *Quest for Autonomy and Excellence – The National Defense Innovation Systems of France and Sweden*, book chapter, University of California San Diego.
16 For example from Hägglunds to BAE Systems, and from Kockums to ThyssenKrupp.
17 The South African company Denel produced parts of the rear fuselage.
18 The Swedish Air Force ordered a total of 204 Gripen C/Ds, but later declared that it needed 100. Thereby a pool of surplus C/Ds became available for export.
19 Saab was offered to acquire Kockums, but declined.
20 Lundmark, M. (2014), 'Kockums – the Repatriation of the Swedish Underwater Crown Jewel', in: *Défense & Industries (2014),* Fondation pour la Recherche Stratégique, No. 1, Juin 2014, pp. 7–11.
21 Gripen 29 % and A26 5 %.
22 Estimation based on discussions with experts at FOI and the Ministry of Defence.
23 Lundmark, Martin (2016), *CMTC Policy Renewal*, FOI-R – 4263 – SE, FOI, Stockholm.
24 Schmitt, B. 2001.

25 *Bonus*: Bofors-Giat (Fra), guided munition, start 1993; *Iris-T*: Saab-companies from five partner nations (Germany, Greece, Italy, Norway, Spain (replaced by Canada during the development)), infra-red air-to-air missile, 1995; *Cision*: Kockums and DCN (Fra), submarines, 1998; *Meteor*: Saab-MBDA (France, Germany, Italy, Spain, UK), beyond visual range air-to-air missile, 1998; *Excalibur*: Bofors-Raytheon (US), guided artillery shell, 2002; *NH90*: Saab-NHI industries (together with Finland, France, Germany, the Netherlands, Norway, Sweden), helicopters, 2004.

26 NORDEFCO: Nordic Defence Cooperation.

27 EDA: European Defence Agency.

28 Lundmark, Martin and Oxenstierna, Susanne (2016), *Koordinering och prioritering av internationella samarbeten inom materiel- och logistikområdet* [Coordination and prioritization of international cooperation in the defence acquisition and logistics domains], FOI-R – 4388 – SE, FOI, Stockholm.

29 The total costs of these procurements will be higher as other modifications will be needed, and other systems must be coordinated.

30 Norway and Sweden combined, including maintenance specifications. Deliveries until 2026.

31 Nordlund, Peter, Olsson, Per, Jonsson, Ulf and Bäckström, Peter (2016), *Effektiv materielförsörjning – Utveckla, anpassa eller köpa från hyllan?* [Efficient materiel acquisition – develop, adapt or buy off-the-shelf?], FOI-R – 4265 – SE, FOI, Stockholm.

32 Ibid.

33 All import and export figures are from the SIPRI Arms Transfer Database, at www.sipri.se, unless otherwise noted. TIV values.

34 According to Sipri's data. A discussion is presented below in the text regarding the marked discrepancy between Sipri's arms transfer data compared to the government's official data.

35 A statement that has been put forward by proponents of the Swedish defence export and its contribution to Swedish industry and innovation, is that it tripled from the ten-year period from 2002–2011. This is true, but it represents a choice of years for comparison that maximizes such an argument, but does not reflect the longer-term time series. If we make the same comparison over the period 2008–2017, the export has decreased by 82 %. That is, based on Sipri data.

36 ISP: Inspektionen för strategiska produkter [The Inspectorate for strategic products].

37 Depending on the exchange rate between US dollars and Swedish crowns.

38 This shortcoming, or even inadequacy, of SIPRI's data deserves a more thorough study in itself. How this discrepancy plays out for other nations deserves a study as well.

39 Swedish Government, *Värnkraft* [Resilience], Ds 2019:8. Presently (June, 2019), only in Swedish: www.regeringen.se/rattsliga-dokument/departementsserien-och-promemorior/2019/05/ds-20198/. Summary in English: www.regeringen.se/49a295/globalassets/regeringen/dokument/forsvarsdepartementet/forsvarsberedningen/slutrapport-14-maj/defence-commissions-white-book-english-summary.pdf.

16 The Norwegian defence industry

Kjetil Hatlebakk Hove and Jon Olav Pedersen[1]

Introduction

By international standards, the Norwegian defence market and the Norwegian defence industry are small, too small to rely on domestic production of all types of defence equipment. The defence industry is therefore targeting niche markets by emphasizing high quality and performance rather than competing on cost. Size, structure and trade have traditionally been determined by government policy, as the government has acted as customer, owner, and regulator.

When it comes to defence procurement, the guiding principle is that all procurements are to be based on principles of competition, non-discrimination and equal treatment of suppliers. However, national security interests are important in many defence procurements, allowing for exemptions to this rule. The Norwegian defence industry is dominated by two large firms who, within their areas of business, hold near-monopolies in the domestic market (Kongsberg; Nammo). However, domestic production only constitutes a fraction of the market. Norway therefore relies heavily on imports of most of its military equipment. In this sense, parts of the market could also be seen as a monopsony, although when considering market power, it is important to keep in mind the fact that the Norwegian Armed Forces are not a large customer by international standards.

In recent years, the Norwegian defence industry has expanded abroad by establishing offices and subsidiaries, or by mergers and acquisitions. This has been done to create proximity to the markets, to invite collaborating partners, and to provide access to new knowledge and resources, but also to circumvent protectionist and competitive barriers. In 2017, close to 30 per cent of revenue came from overseas operations.

This chapter reviews some key figures related to defence spending, investment, imports and exports. That the Norwegian defence industry is small makes official statistics hard to come by, and it also makes comparison across time difficult. The industry is heterogeneous, so that changes in the defence structure that would hardly be noticeable in other countries can have a major impact on the structure of the industry.

We then proceed to describe the structure and history of the defence industry, before we discuss industry conduct. Here, the national industrial strategy is of vital importance, due to the many roles played by the government. Thus, industry structure is clearly influenced by industry conduct. The performance of the industry, which we then proceed to describe, is also influenced by the industrial strategy. The conclusion outlines some possible future prospects for the industry.

An overview of Norwegian defence spending

As a background to the discussion of the Norwegian defence industry, it is instructive to consider total domestic defence spending.[2] Since 1980, aggregate real Norwegian defence spending has seen three major phases (Figure 16.1). First, significant increases towards the end of the Cold War; second, a "peace dividend" decline during the 1990s; and third, since 2006, a period of new increases. Since 2015, the acquisition of the F-35 has been a significant cost driver.

Within total spending (Figure 16.1), procurement spending displays a downwards, though fluctuating, trend (Figure 16.2 showing shares of total defence spending). In the last few years of the Cold War, investments were high. Cold War levels were not reached until recently, caused by the F-35 acquisition. The major annual fluctuations are influenced by major procurement projects, such as F-16 and submarine purchases in the 1980s, the Nansen-class frigates in the early 2000s, and the F-35 fighters from 2015. Since 1980, the average investment share of defence spending has been

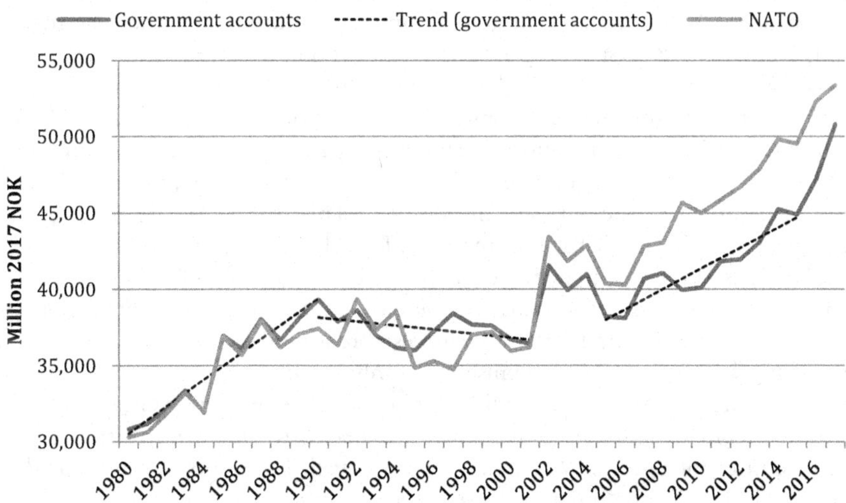

Figure 16.1 Norwegian defence spending 1980–2017 with trends 1980–1990, 1990–2001 and 2006–2014.

Source: Historical defence spending as obtained from government spending data and NATO.[3] Some adjustments made for accounting standards.[4]

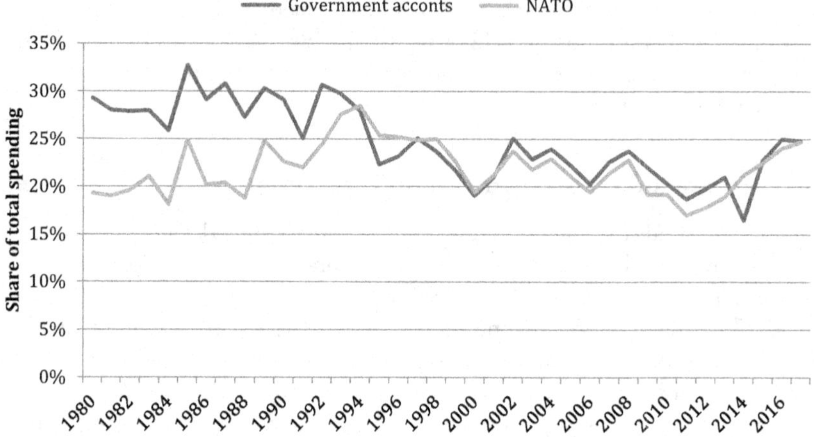

Figure 16.2 Defence procurement spending 1980–2017.

Source: Historical defence spending as obtained from government spending data and NATO.[5]

around 25 per cent. See Johnson et al. (2017) for a more detailed overview of Norwegian defence spending.

Official defence research and development (R&D) figures are unfortunately not readily available. Statistics Norway (SSB) maintain a time series as part of the national accounts, but due to changing definitions and the fact that it only contains R&D spending by the Armed Forces themselves, and not the defence industry, it is more misleading than informative in this context.

A consistent time series for imports and exports is available from 1988. The time series are maintained by Statistics Norway (SSB)[6] and are illustrated in Figure 16.3, along with two other time series with later points of departure, maintained by the Ministry of Foreign Affairs (MFA) and by the Norwegian Defence Research Establishment (FFI). SSB statistics are based on export declarations. Equipment delivered abroad as a result of military agreements, and thus not customs declared, are therefore not included, neither is equipment meant for use by Norwegian forces abroad. MFA statistics are based on reporting by the exporters themselves. Only exports requiring a licence are included in their time series. Different goods categories as well as errors in exports declarations explain the difference between the two statistical series. FFI statistics include non-licensed exports as well. For imports, only SSB data are available. As the numbers are based on import declarations only, the reported numbers should again be too low.[7] Unfortunately, no better data series for weapons imports are publicly available. The major increase in exports from 2014 is not grounded in a particular weapon system, but is due to increased sales in the USA, the Netherlands, Poland and Oman (Ministry

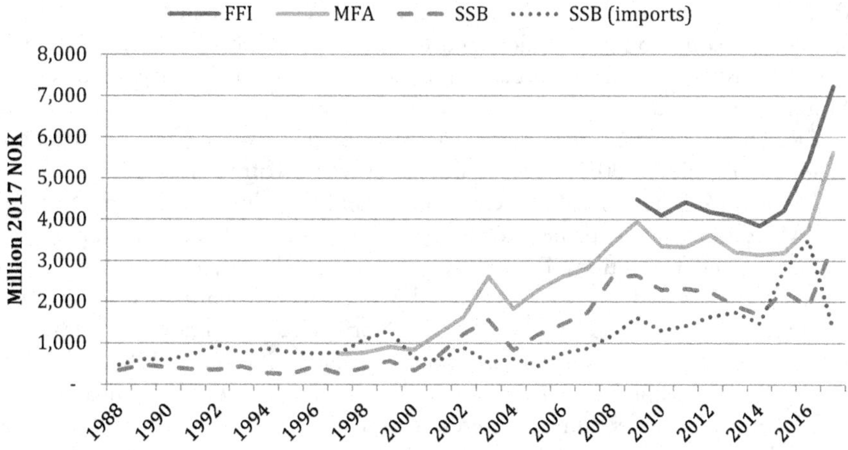

Figure 16.3 Exports of defence equipment.

Sources: SSB: Statistics Norway (2018a); MFA: Ministry of Foreign Affairs (2002, 2005, 2008, 2018b); FFI: Pedersen (2015, 2016, 2017, 2018), Tvetbråten (2011, 2012, 2013, 2014) and Tvetbråten and Fevolden (2011).

of Foreign Affairs 2018b). The temporary increase in imports in 2014 and 2015 is mainly caused by imports related to upgrades and renewals of the CV90 infantry fighting vehicles.

From 2011, FFI has conducted annual surveys of the defence industry. The year 2011 therefore constitutes a watershed with regards to statistics. Before this, information is scarce and scattered, while it improves greatly with the new data series.

The national defence industry and its historical structure

We define the defence industry as companies who produce and deliver products or services that have an impact on national security. This includes companies that deliver directly to the Armed Forces, or companies that are sub-contractors on a larger production, but where the Armed Forces are the end-user. The products or services should have an impact on national security in the sense that they can be categorized within the national strategic areas of priority, as defined in the white paper on the national strategy for the defence industry (Ministry of Defence 2015). We address these areas when we describe industry conduct.

Figure 16.4 shows the number of companies categorized as large (more than 250 full-time equivalents – FTEs), medium (50–249 FTEs), small (10–49 FTEs) and micro (less than 10 FTEs) in 2011–2017. Table 16.1 provides additional information on the four large Norwegian defence companies, their owners, earnings before interest, taxes, depreciation and amortization

(EBITDA) and the number of FTEs. Kongsberg and Nammo have been dominant throughout the history of the Norwegian defence industry. The number of large companies increased from two to three in 2012, when AIM was established, and from three to four in 2016, when the growth of NFM Holding exceeded 250 FTEs.

After the four large companies, the remaining six of the top 10 defence-related companies in 2017 were Thales Norway AS, Kitron AS, Airbus Defence and Space AS, Rheinmetall AS, Comrod AS and Flir Unmanned Aerial Systems AS. Many of these companies are hard to trace historically, due to a long history of mergers and acquisitions. For example, Vinghøg AS was a family-owned company established in 1950. It was acquired by Simrad in 2005, which in turn was acquired by Rheinmetall in 2007. Thales Norway AS was known as Thomson CSF AS until 2000. Thomson CSF bought Alcatel SKF AS in 1989, which in turn had acquired Standard Telefon og Kabelfabrik AS in 1987. Comparisons of single companies across time are therefore difficult.

In the 1980s, more and more privately-owned companies entered the market, particularly companies within electronics, communication solutions, and computing. There is little information describing this development in exact numbers, but at least nine privately-owned companies operated in the defence market in the early 1980s: Simrad; Nera; Elektrisk Bureau; Standard Telefon og Kabelfabrik; Norsk Data; Vinghøg; Nordisk Aluminium; Gustav A. Ring and Norcem Plast (Erlandsen 1983; Wicken 1992).

The 1990s was a decade of industrial consolidation. For example, Norsk Forsvarsteknologi AS (NFT) was partly privatized in 1993, but the government maintained a majority stake. In 1995, NFT changed its name to Kongsberg Gruppen. The defence section, Kongsberg Defence and Aerospace (KDA), was

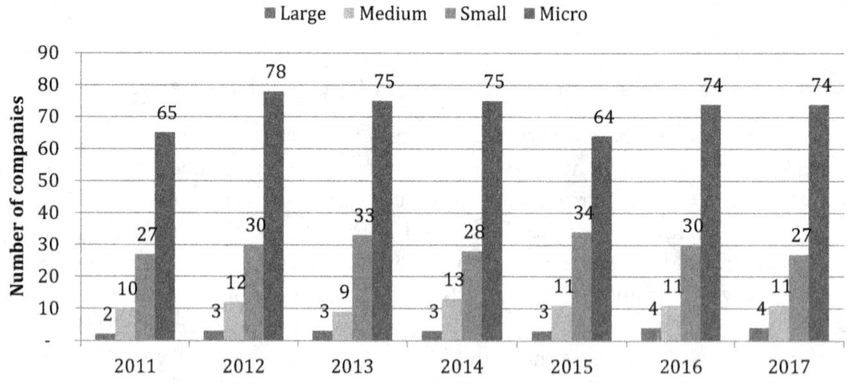

Figure 16.4 Large, medium, small and micro companies 2011–2017.
Source: (Pedersen 2018).

Table 16.1 The four large defence companies in Norway, their ownership, revenue and number of employees

Company	*Ownership*	*Sales revenue 2017*	*Employees*
Kongsberg Defence and Aerospace AS (KDA)	Kongsberg Gruppen ASA, owned 50.001 per cent by the Norwegian government	6.3 billion NOK EBITDA: 0.7 billion NOK	2,400 FTEs
Nammo Group (Nammo)	Norwegian government 50 per cent, Patria 50 per cent[8]	4.5 billion NOK EBITDA: 0.3 billion NOK	2,200 FTEs
Aerospace Industrial Maintenance (AIM) Norway AS	Kongsberg Defence and Aerospace (50.1 per cent) and Patria (49.9 per cent)	1.2 billion NOK	440 FTEs
NFM Holding AS	Privately held	0.7 billion NOK	550 FTEs

Source: Annual Company Reports.

established as its own business area in 1997. Raufoss ASA was also reorganized throughout the 1990s, and merged with Patria (Finland) and Celsius (Sweden) to form the Nammo Group AS in 1998. Kitron bought parts of Elektrisk Bureau in 1996 and was listed on the stock exchange in 1997.

More and more privately-owned companies established a position where they were able to sell to the Armed Forces, but they were also sub-contracting for KDA and Nammo. In addition, foreign subsidiaries of larger companies like IBM, Siemens and Airbus entered the market. By the end of the 1990s, around 11 companies had the defence market as their primary market, while additional 35–40 companies also delivered products and services of significance for national security (Halvorssen & Vamraak 2000). By 2008, the number of companies had doubled to about 100 (deduced from Fevolden et al. 2008; Halvorssen & Vamraak 2000).

Today, the defence industry consists of approximately 115 companies, of which 35 have the Armed Forces and the defence industry as their primary market. Since 2010, an average of 4,500 FTEs have been employed in the defence industry. Of these, around 90 per cent are located in south-eastern Norway and in the proximity of Oslo (Pedersen 2018). Data on the number of employees before 2010 is not available.

Norway has always been dependent on imports of defence equipment and it has never been a political ambition to become self-reliant (Wicken 1992). Instead, it has been a political desire to facilitate a competitive defence industry to secure sufficient domestic supply to maintain national security and to secure continuous improvement of the national procurement competence

(Ministry of Defence 2015). In 2017, imports constituted as much as 74 per cent of defence spending, slightly more than the average over the last few years (see Figure 16.5). The percentage varies from year to year, but from 1995 until 2002, the average annual import was 61 per cent, while it has been 62 per cent since 2010 (see Figure 16.5: Halvorssen & Vamraak 2004; Pedersen 2018). The Norwegian defence industry alone imports approximately 55–60 per cent of goods used in production (Hove 2018). As far as we know, the international supply chain dependencies for the Norwegian defence industry have not been studied.

From the levels of import, it follows that there are not a lot of funds left to maintain a national defence industry.[9] Thus, the Norwegian defence industry has always been dependent on exports in order to maintain necessary production capacities, ensure economies of scale, compensate for fluctuations in demand, and to maintain and develop technological competence in order to remain competitive (Ali et al. 2007). Exports can in this sense be seen as an indicator of the international competitiveness of the Norwegian defence industry.

In the 1980s and 1990s, both the dominating companies had substantial export. For example, about 60 per cent of the total revenue to Raufoss Ammunisjonsfabrikk (now Nammo) during the 1980s came from exports, while it was as much as 80 per cent in 1994 (Wang 1996). To compensate for the decline in defence spending, the companies also diversified their product portfolio and entered various civilian markets (Wicken 1992). In 1996, as much as 81 per cent of the revenue of Raufoss ASA came from civilian products (Ministry of Trade and Industry 2000), which made the companies vulnerable to fluctuations in the civilian market. In 1986, this vulnerability led

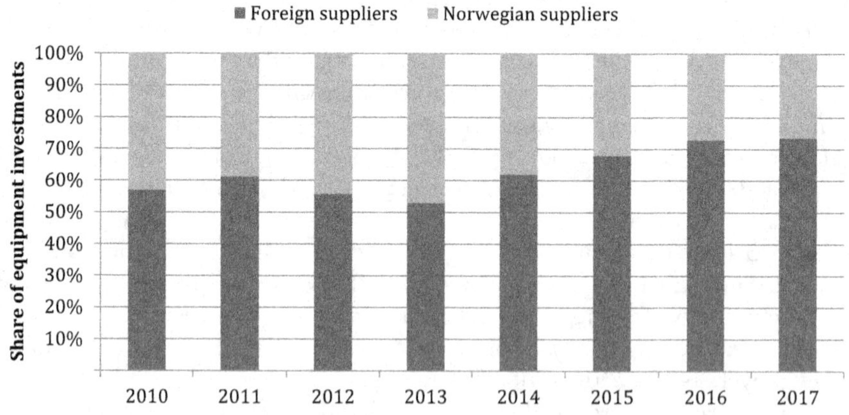

Figure 16.5 Total defence equipment investments from foreign and Norwegian suppliers. Source: Pedersen (2018).

the government to intervene to save Kongsberg Våpenfabrikk (now KDA) from bankruptcy. This was due to the Organization of the Petroleum Exporting Countries (OPEC) crisis and the resulting decline in the civilian market. Raufoss ASA experienced a similar crisis in the early 1990s. This was resolved by selling off the civilian part, and some years later merging the defence part into the Nammo Group (Ministry of Trade and Industry 2000). Nevertheless, the two companies did have substantial defence related exports during the 1980s and 1990s. On average, it came to 1.8 billion NOK annually (Ministry of Trade and Industry 2000; Øyangen 2014; Petersen & Sogner 2014; Wang 1996).

From 2000 to 2009, according to annual reporting by the Ministry of Foreign Affairs[10], defence related exports doubled, as did the number of exporting companies. On average, 48 companies exported for a total of 3.8 billion NOK annually. A part of the explanation for this growth can be traced back to the Spanish companies that needed to fulfil their offset[11] agreements related to the procurement of new frigates. It can also be traced back to KDA, which had an enormous export success to the US market with the Norwegian Advanced Surface-to-Air Missile System (NASAMS) and Protector remote weapon station (RWS). This success absorbed all production capacity in the KDA (Castellacci & Fevolden 2015). In order to fulfil their offset obligations, the Spanish companies thus needed to engage in collaboration with other companies than KDA. Another explanation for the increased number of firms is that the number of importing countries increased from 36 in 1999 to 65 in 2009 (Ministry of Foreign Affairs 2009, 2010).

Despite its growth, the Norwegian defence industry is a small industry by most standards. It specializes in targeting niche markets that emphasize high quality and performance rather than cost competition (Kristiansen 1991). Historically, its size, structure and trade have all been determined by government policy, as the government has not only been the main customer, but also the owner of the dominating companies and the regulator of exports (Ulsrud 2012). Although many state-owned companies have been at least partly privatized, the market is still dominated by the same two companies, and the defence industry is still supported by the government in various ways.

The dominating companies do not face domestic competition within their product portfolios, and are also obvious sub-contractors in large import procurements and partners in offset agreements with foreign suppliers (Halvorssen & Vamraak 2004; Skogstad & Warberg 2005). Thus, the market may be seen as a near-monopoly with regard to at least some specific products and technologies. However, apart from the defined strategic areas of competence, the Norwegian defence market relies upon imports and a competitive foreign market to provide everything else. In this sense, the market may also be characterized as a monopsony. Despite the guiding principles of competition, non-discrimination and equal treatment of suppliers, there are barriers to entry. For example, it is only natural that a proven track-record and a successful long-term collaboration is important in forming and institutionalizing the needs and preferences of the Armed Forces, as well as strengthening the strategic areas of competence necessary for upholding the national security interests. In this sense, it may be difficult for new entrants to establish themselves. In addition, the Armed Forces also have a long organizational memory, so any inability to provide capable products or the inability to collaborate in the past, may also be barriers to re-entry.

Industry conduct

Industry conduct is to a large extent a result of government policy, both in the domestic and the international market. The major companies claim that offset agreements and cost-share/work-share agreements have been important for market access and product development abroad (Castellacci et al. 2014). The defence industry itself describes the Norwegian industrial policy regime as crucial for its survival, and Kongsberg and Nammo have described offset as an important door opener to the international market. Small and medium-sized companies claim to have been less dependent on the industrial policy regime. For these companies, offsets can be important in securing a role as sub-contractors.

A study by Castellacci and Fevolden (2014) points to four major success factors for Norwegian exporting firms. First, the participation in offset agreements; second, the ability to focus on their core competencies; third, their R&D activities and their interactions with the public science and technology system; and fourth, demand opportunities and user-producer relationships.

Castellacci and Fevolden (2014) identify two trajectories for these firms. In the first trajectory, *superstar exporters*, they find that few large oligopolistic enterprises (e.g. Kongsberg and Nammo) have been able to maintain their dominant position for a long time. They have been positioning themselves as internationally competitive system integrators and global firms in a number of different areas. The second trajectory, *specialized suppliers*, contains many small and medium-sized businesses (SMBs) that, despite their smaller size and more narrow competence and product portfolio, have achieved their international position by providing specialized equipment to large overseas defence manufacturers.

Due to factors such as topography, climate and geography, which require much from weapons and sensors, there has been a broad political consensus on the importance of securing the existence of a competitive national defence industry. In the 1980s, this was secured through a direct ownership of the dominant defence companies. As part of the structural changes of the industry in the 1990s, a procurement and industrial policy for the Armed Forces emerged (Ministry of Defence 1995). This policy explicitly stated that the authorities wanted to make arrangements for the Norwegian defence industry to compete for parts of defence procurements (Ministry of Defence 1995). Three years later, this strategy was further elaborated through the national strategy for Norwegian defence and defence-related industry. In their white paper, the Ministry of Defence emphasized the desire to support the industry through (1) procurement policies for the Armed Forces, (2) claim for offset agreements (both civil and military), (3) continued public ownership and control in the defence industry, as well as (4) international cooperation (Ministry of Defence 1998). This policy has been further developed through the two latest defence industrial strategies (Ministry of Defence 2007, 2015).

The 2015 strategy sets two priorities for national defence acquisitions: long-term national security interests and the more short-term needs of the Armed Forces. In times of war or emergency, foreign suppliers might give priority to their national needs before supplying foreign customers. Therefore, the strategy claims that it is necessary to secure a sufficient domestic supply to maintain national security in critical areas. The eight critical areas listed in the white paper are (1) command, control and information, decision support and combat systems, including radar systems, (2) system integration, (3) autonomous systems, (4) missile technology, (5) underwater technology, (6) ammunition, aiming devices, remotely controlled weapon stations, and military explosives, (7) technology specially developed and/or adapted for military use, and (8) life cycle support for military land, air and sea systems. Although semantics have changed, these critical areas have been relatively consistent since the mid-1990s. This consistency has in turn had a significant impact on the procurement practice by the Ministry of Defence and thus the structure and conduct of the defence industry (Skogstad & Warberg 2005).

All public procurements in Norway are governed by the Public Procurement Act (LOA) and associated regulations, including the regulations on defence and security procurement (FOSA, see Warberg 2007) and the procurement regulation for the defence sector (ARF). According to LOA and ARF and as a ground rule, all procurements are made according to the principle of competition. If it is necessary to depart from the principle of competition due to national security, Article 123 of the European Economic Area (EEA) Agreement can be activated.[12] A recent case where this clause was activated was in the government budget for 2017, when it was announced that new coast guard vessels were to be built in Norway (Ministry of Defence 2016). National security was cited as the main reason behind this decision.

Assessment of imports is a balance between national security interests, the needs of the Armed Forces, and costs. Other factors are also assessed and valued. For example, a proven track-record of the supplier and a successful long-term collaboration is important in forming and institutionalizing the needs and preferences of the Armed Forces, as well as strengthening the strategic areas of competence necessary for upholding national security interests. According to Salvesen (2013), exports also "functions as a political and economic tool, which manifests itself as a currency for foreign policy", and it is used for reducing protectionist and political entry barriers for the Norwegian defence industry in foreign markets (Ali et al. 2007; Ministry of Defence 2012). Offset agreements are in this regard an instrument that actively has been used to promote the Norwegian defence industry. In the 1980s, 34 offset agreements with a combined value of 14 billion NOK and a compensation percentage of 60 per cent were signed (Wicken 1992). In the 1990s, offsets became even more systematically used to open foreign markets for the national defence industry (Ministry of Defence 1998). The result was an increase in the average annual value of realized offset agreements to 2.5 billion current NOK, and expected annual offsets of 2.4 billion current NOK for the period 1999–2010 (Halvorssen & Vamraak 2000). This is also consistent with Bendiksen (2018) who outline the average values of annual offset to 2.5 billion NOK for the period from 2006 to 2010.

The two dominating companies, KDA and Nammo, have traditionally benefited greatly from offset agreements. For example, in the 1980s, they received as much as 85 per cent of the offset agreements related to the F-16 procurement (Wicken 1992). This was also the case in the 1990s, but in the period from 2006 to 2010 they have on average received less than 15 per cent each (Bendiksen 2018). In other words, during the last 10 years the conduct of offset has changed, with the result that other companies have benefited.

The outlook with regards to importing has also influenced political restrictions on exports (Wicken 1992). Norway has had strict rules for the export of defence equipment since the late 1800s. Parliament first further intensified such restrictions in 1935, the first official domestic policy on export controls (Enlarged Committee on Foreign Affairs and Constitutional Affairs 1935). This occurred after a series of unfortunate incidents, including sales of arms and munitions for the Bolivian war in Paraguay (Hoel 2017). Later, restrictions were strengthened in 1946, 1959, 1967, 1974, 1977 and 1980 (Wicken 1992). Since 1987, all regulations concerning exports of strategic goods, services and technology have been governed by the Ministry of Foreign Affairs through the 1987 Export Control Act. Norway has also been a signatory to various international agreements on export control.[13] Despite these strong restrictions, questions have been raised as to whether the restrictions are strong enough (see, for example, Hoel 2017, for a criticism). For example, weapons exports to Saudi-Arabia continue, and only in November 2018 did the government announce that no new export licences would be granted (Ministry of Foreign Affairs 2018a).

The government also influences conduct by financing and co-financing research and development projects (Ali et al. 2007). There is an historical close relationship between the Norwegian defence industry, the Norwegian Defence Research Establishment (FFI), and the Armed Forces. This triple-helix model is known as the triangular collaboration, and is often co-financed by the Ministry of Defence as a risk-reduction measure for the industry. FFI and the defence industry cooperate on product development, the industry and the Armed Forces work together on setting requirements, while the Armed Forces and FFI cooperate on evaluation and developing operational concepts (Hove 2018; Ministry of Defence 2015). This collaboration has been in place since the 1950s, when the anti-submarine missile Terne was developed. Among later development projects have been the autonomous underwater vehicle HUGIN and the Naval Strike Missile (FFI 2015), as well as the air defence system NASAMS, the remote weapon control system Protector RWS and the Joint Strike Missile.

Defence industrial policies in other countries also affect the Norwegian defence industry (Hove 2018; Ministry of Defence 2015). The US market is by far the most important and several Norwegian companies have succeeded in establishing local manufacturing capacities and long-term collaboration partnerships with the large US defence firms (Ministry of Defence 2015). Norway's membership in NATO and the European Defense Agency (EDA), and generally the relationship with the EU through the EEA, is also of great importance to the Norwegian defence industry. Although the industry in the past has only had success with specific bilateral and multilateral agreements (Ministry of Defence 2018), the establishment of the European Defense Fund (EDF: see Chapter 7) can be of major importance for a consolidation of the European defence industry and thus also affecting the Norwegian defence industry. Also, Asia has for long been important, but as opposed to the EU and US markets, the Asian markets have been regarded as more open and thus easier to access through competition.

Industry performance

There are few historical data related to the Norwegian defence industry, particularly data on profitability, R&D and employment are difficult to trace back to the 1980s.

We have made an effort to provide an indicator for the levels of revenue. From 1998, the data are based on the four largest companies today and their financial statements. More than 80 per cent of the revenue in all of these companies stems from the defence market. Before 1998, our data are based on the annual statements from Kongsberg Defence and Aerospace and the Nammo Group, since the remaining two of the big four did not exist, or were in the start-up phase. Additional data from other companies are not consistent or available. Most of the data are collected from the financial statement as reported in the anniversary books for the two companies (Øyangen 2014; Petersen & Sogner 2014; Wang 1996). For the Nammo Group, data are also collected from Ministry of Trade and Industry (2000) to cover the period between 1996 and 1998.[14]

From 1980 to 1990, the companies recorded average annual sales of 3.4 billion NOK. As Figure 16.6 indicates, there was a distinct decline in 1987 which was the year when it became known that Kongsberg Våpenfabrikk in collaboration with Toshiba had broken the COCOM rules, the predecessor to the Wassenaar Arrangement. As a result, the company was blacklisted on the US defence market, and thus experienced a decline in revenue (Erlandsen 1987; Wicken 1988). The decline was dealt with by establishing a new company, which took over everything of value and production from the old company. Kongsberg Våpenfabrikk became Norsk Forsvarsteknologi AS, until the company in 1995 changed the name to Kongsberg Gruppen, and the defence production became a separate business area under the name of Kongsberg Defence and Aerospace AS (Petersen & Sogner 2014).

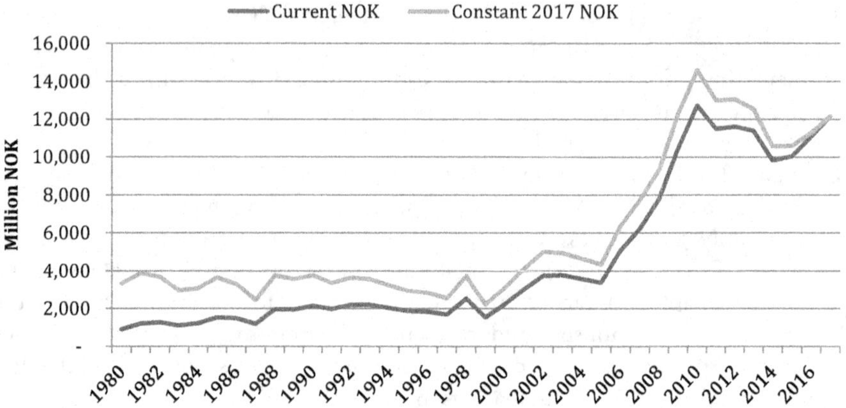

Figure 16.6 Defence related sales revenue of the four largest defence companies.

Sales in the 1990s were clearly affected by the dissolution of the Soviet Union in 1991 and the general decline in most nations' equipment expenditures. From 1990 to 2000, the average annual sales were 3.2 billion NOK. As shown in Figure 16.6, there was a temporary peak in 1998, which was related to the increased sale of NASAMS due to an offset agreement with Raytheon. The decline in sales in 1999 was mainly due to the establishment of the Nammo Group. In 1998, Raufoss ASA had merged with Swedish Celsius AS and Finnish Patria Industries Oyj to form the Nammo Group. The Norwegian part of the Nammo Group needed some time to adjust and experienced a substantial, albeit temporary, decline in sale.

In short, the increase in sales revenue since 2000 can be linked to exports. For example, the increase between 2000 and 2003 is largely due to increased export of the NASAMS. Part of the increase can also be traced to the offset agreements connected to the Norwegian purchase of frigates from Spain (Ministry of Foreign Affairs 2004). The increase between 2006 and 2012 is also due to the export of a specific system – the Protector remote weapon station (RWS). The picture is of course more nuanced – a few weapons systems did not determine all changes. However, such examples serve to show how sensitive performance figures for such a small industry are to one or two major successes or failures.

Since 2008, there has also been another development that has influenced turnover figures: More and more companies have established themselves abroad, either with an office or through subsidiaries, acquisitions or mergers. Establishment abroad is done mainly for three reasons: first, to create proximity to the market and collaborating partners; second, to provide access to new knowledge and resources; and third, to circumvent protectionist and competitive barriers (Aakre 2012). The latter includes both barriers to competing in the market where the business is established, and to be able to circumvent home market barriers, like taxes and export controls. In 2017, 16 per cent of the companies had established activities abroad and 28 per cent of the total defence related revenue came from foreign majority-owned subsidiaries (Pedersen 2018).

The 2018 figures for the Norwegian defence industry show a 5 per cent increase in revenue from 2016 (Pedersen 2018). In total, the defence industry accounted for 16.3 billion NOK in defence-related revenue in 2017, of which:

- 70 per cent can be related to the four largest companies, while an additional 10 percentage points includes the top 10 companies.
- 44 per cent was exports, which was accounted for by 47 per cent of the companies.
- 22 per cent was direct sales to the Armed Forces, of which close to half of inputs were procured by Norwegian SMBs.
- 6 per cent of the total revenue came from subcontracts, of which KDA and Nammo spent approximately one third of their turnover buying from Norwegian SMBs.

The average operating margin for the defence industry was 4.5 per cent, and the EBITDA was about 0.7 billion NOK in 2017. In 2017, the Norwegian companies invested 1.4 billion NOK in research and development (R&D), of which:

- 25 per cent were supported by the Ministry of Defence.
- 40 per cent of the companies invested in R&D in 2017.
- 50 per cent were invested by the four large companies.
- R&D accounted on average for 8.4 per cent of defence related revenue.

The Norwegian defence industry employed 4,400 full-time equivalents (FTEs) in Norway, of which 62 per cent was employed by the four large companies. An additional 2,300 FTEs was employed in foreign subsidiaries in 2017.

The defence industry is marginal compared to the civilian industry in Norway. Based on Statistics Norway (2018a) and Pedersen (2018), it accounts for:

- 0.28 per cent of the FTEs employed in private sector in Norway.
- 0.3 per cent of the sales revenue in private sector.
- 0.7 per cent of the total export.
- 3.5 per cent of the total R&D invested by Norwegian companies.

The production revenue in the defence industry (produced in Norway by Norwegian FTEs) was 1,367 NOK per working hour in 2017 (Pedersen 2018). In comparison, the average for the oil and gas industry was 4,613 NOK, while the Norwegian manufacturing and service industry as a whole (including oil and gas) was 520 NOK per working hour (Statistics Norway 2018b).

Future prospects for the Norwegian defence industry

The military has always been relatively conservative, and the development of weapons systems has involved extremely long development and lead times. Norway has already chosen the F-35 fighter, the P-8 Poseidon surveillance aircraft and Germany as a strategic partner in procuring submarines. These three major procurements will have an impact on the defence industry, not only for the procurement and offset period of the next 15 years, but also for the mid-life update and an additional 15–20 years. Norwegian subcontractors are already engaged in the F-35 program, and the offset agreements for the P-8 and submarines are developing. These purchases further continue an historical preference and at the same time also consolidate an already long-term collaboration for the national defence industry.

With the increased number of actors in the national defence market, we have also seen a greater degree of industrial fragmentation. Put differently, the civilian suppliers are increasingly engaged in delivering subcomponents and specialized products. Generally, Norway has a high degree of high-tech competence, which has at least in part been driven by demanding supplies to the offshore and maritime industry. Offshore will still be a technology driver for oil and gas for many years to come, but also for other industries like the defence industry. Norway is, for example, far ahead in the development of automation technology in the offshore and maritime industry. This has already had a transfer value to the defence market, but may also in the future have a significant impact on the Norwegian defence industry.

Technologies like artificial intelligence, quantum computing, handling of big data, and mini-satellites are all technologies whose consequences are not yet grasped, but it is believed that they will change the nature of demand and perhaps even disrupt the very defence concept. Norway has over time established a triple helix model for innovation. The short decision lines, the frequent interaction, the focus on end-users, and the bond of trust that have been built between research, users, and the Ministry of Defence as a major source of finance, has in the past proven vital to ensure innovation. The model has also proven vital in building and securing the competitiveness of the Norwegian defence industry. As long as there is political will to secure a national defence industry, the triple helix model for collaboration in innovation will also be maintained. It could be present in different forms, with different actors, across national borders, and with a stronger linkage to civilian innovation, but efforts will be made to maintain the strengths of the model.

The defence industry is to a large extent influenced by political processes, due in part to the role of government ownership in the two dominating firms. This ownership has on a regular basis been up for political debate, but there is no indication that there is political will to reduce this ownership. The export-control regime is also another area in which the defence industry is politically influenced. Historically, Norway have promptly ratified and followed up on international agreements, which probably will also be the case in the future.

A future uncertainty is defence spending. Norway is currently spending 1.61 per cent of its gross domestic product (GDP) on defence (NATO 2018), and has through the 2014 Wales Summit Declaration committed to the aim of spending 2 per cent of GDP on defence. The current long-term plan does not account for such an increase. Also, there is political disagreement regarding the realism of the 2 per cent goal, the definition and methods for calculating defence spending, and whether or not oil and gas for this purpose are to be excluded in calculating GDP. Changes in spending will nevertheless be dependent on the spending of other countries, the national security threat, international operations, other political priorities, development of GDP and fluctuations in oil-prices. This should also be seen in the context of the many processes implemented in the European Defence Agency and the EU to coordinate, develop and strengthen the defence capabilities of the European member states (see Chapter 7). Even in the short term this may lead to a long overdue consolidation of the European defence industry, which in turn may increase the level of competition in the specialist and niche markets. However, "the only thing we know about the future is that it is going to be different" (Drucker 1973).

Notes

1 The authors would like to thank Åge Skøelv and Sigurd Iversen for commenting on drafts of this chapter, and to Ålov Runde for proofreading.

2 All numbers are converted to 2017 Norwegian Kroner (NOK) by the consumer price index (CPI) of Statistics Norway (SSB). In late 2018, 1 Euro = 9.5 NOK and 1 USD = 8.3 NOK.

3 Full sources: Defence spending as obtained from government spending data are stated in each government budget for the following year. NATO numbers are from NATO (1980, 1984, 1988, 1992, 1996, 2000, 2003, 2006, 2012, 2018).

4 Adjustments made to correct for changes in accounting standards since 2002: (1) search and rescue helicopters were included in the Armed Forces' spending data from 2009, but are excluded here, (2) costs for buildings and property are counted as a cost both for the branches and The Norwegian Defence Estates Agency, but are only counted once here, and (3) value added tax is not included in the government spending data from 2015, but are added here. The increasing gap in from 2009 between government spending data and NATO is due to changes in the method for calculating pensions (NATO 2012). Currently, the main difference between the two time series is that pensions for retirees are not included in government spending data. An approximation of such costs is added before numbers are reported to NATO. Since 2017, pension provisions for the future pensions of current employees are included in government spending data.

5 Full sources: Annual historical defence spending data as stated in each government budget for the following NATO (1980, 1984, 1988, 1992, 1996, 2000, 2003, 2006, 2012, 2018).

6 Statistics Norway (2018a), SITC commodity group 891. Warships and fighter aircraft are not included in this commodity group, but exports of warships and fighter aircraft from Norway are negligible.

7 In addition, as for exports, warships and fighter aircraft are not included.

8 Patria is a Finnish company owned 50.1 per cent by the Finnish government and the rest by Kongsberg.

9 In the section reviewing industry conduct, we discuss defence procurement policy, which to a large extent determine the level of imports.

10 Ministry of Foreign Affairs (2001, 2002, 2003, 2004, 2005, 2006, 2007, 2008, 2009, 2010).

11 There are a number of terms for the more generic term "offset". Norway is currently using the term "industrial cooperation".

12 Article 123 is similar to Article 346 of The Lisbon Treaty, allowing countries to take necessary measures to protect their security interests. The differences between Article 123 and Article 346 are described in Hove (2018).

13 For example the Brussel Conference Act of 1890, the agreement of St. Germain in 1919 (Wicken 1992), the Co-ordinating Committee for Multilateral Export Controls (CoCom) from 1947, and the Australia Group since 1986 (Kristiansen 1991), the Nuclear Suppliers Group and the Missile Technology Control Regime since 1990, and the Wassenaar Arrangement on Export Controls for Conventional Arms and Dual-Use Goods and Technologies since 1996.

14 We have not been able to find sales figures for 1995 for Raufoss ASA (nor Raufoss Technology AS), thus the figures are calculated as averages of 1994 and 1996.

References

Aakre, M. (2012). Norsk forsvarsindustri i lys av globaliseringen. En analyse av forsvarsvirksomheten i Kongsberg, 1980–2010 [The Norwegian defence industry in the light of globalization. An analysis of the defence division of Kongsberg, 1980–2010] (Master's thesis). Universitetet i Oslo. Retrieved from www.duo.uio.no/handle/10852/13445.

Ali, S., Skogstad, A. K., Skøelv, Å., Warberg, E. N., & Willassen, E. (2007). Næringspolitiske aspekter ved Forsvarets anskaffelser [Defence industrial aspects of Norwegian Armed Forces procurements] (FFI-rapport No. 2007/00915). Kjeller: Norwegian Defence Research Establishment (FFI). Retrieved from www.ffi.no/no/Rapporter/07-00915.pdf.

Bendiksen, S. (2018). Gjenkjøp – Et bidrag til forsvarsevnen?: En analyse av gjenkjøpsordningen i forsvarssektoren [Offsets – A contribution to defence capability? An analysis of offset arrangements in the defence sector] (Master's thesis). Forsvarets høgskole, Oslo. Retrieved from https://brage.bibsys.no/xmlui/handle/11250/2505616.

Castellacci, F., & Fevolden, A. (2014). Capable companies or changing markets? Explaining the export performance of firms in the defence industry. *Defence and Peace Economics*, 25(6), 549–575. 10.1080/10242694.2013.857451.

Castellacci, F., & Fevolden, A. (2015). *Innovation and Liberalization in the European Defence Sector: A Small Country Perspective.* Cheltenham: Edward Elgar Publishing.

Castellacci, F., Fevolden, A. M., & Lundmark, M. (2014). How are defence companies responding to EU defence and security market liberalization? A comparative study of Norway and Sweden. *Journal of European Public Policy*, 21(8), 1218–1235. 10.1080/13501763.2014.916338.

Drucker, P. F. (1973). *Management: Tasks, Responsibilities, Practices.* New York: Harper & Row.

Enlarged Committee on Foreign Affairs and Constitutional Affairs. (1935). Innst. S nr 80: Innstilling fra den forsterkede utenriks- og konstitusjonskomite om forbud mot utførsel av våben og ammunisjon og annet krigsmateriell til Bolivia og Paraguay samt om eksport av våpben og ammunisjon fra de militære fabrikker i sin alminnelighet [Recommendation from the Enlarged Committee on Foreign Affairs and Constitutional Affairs on prohibiting the exports of arms and munitions to Bolivia and Paraguay, and on exports of weapons and munitions from the military factories in general]. Retrieved from www.stortinget.no/no/Saker-og-publikasjoner/Stortingsforhandlinger/Lesevisning/?p=1935&paid=6&wid=a&psid=DIVL1395&pgid=a_0193&s=True.

Erlandsen, H. C. (1983). *Århundrets våpensalg [Weapon sales of this century]*. Oslo: Bedriftsøkonomens forlag.

Erlandsen, H. C. (1987). *TOSHIBA/KV saken [The TOSHIBA/Kongsberg Våpenfabrikk case]*. Oslo: Bedriftsøkonomens forlag.

Export Control Act. (1987). Lov om kontroll med eksport av strategiske varer, tjenester og teknologi m.v. [Act of 18 December 1987 relating to control of the export of strategic goods, services, technology, etc.]. Retrieved from https://lovdata.no/dokument/NL/lov/1987-12-18-93.

Fevolden, A., Karlsen, E. N., & Ringdal, E. (2008). Virkemiddelapparatet og forsvarsindustrien i Norge [Policy instruments and the defence industry in Norway] (FFI-rapport No. 2008/02066). Kjeller: Norwegian Defence Research Establishment (FFI). Retrieved from www.ffi.no/no/Rapporter/08-02066.pdf.

FFI. (2015). FFI FACTS: Triaxial collaboration. Retrieved from www.ffi.no/no/Publikasjoner/Documents/FFIFakta_Triaxial%20collaboration_interactive.pdf.

Halvorssen, T. L., & Vamraak, T. (2000). Effekten av gjenkjøpsordningen på norsk forsvarsindustri 1990–1999 [The effects of offset arrangements on the Norwegian defence industry 1999–1999] (FFI-rapport No. 2000/05788). Kjeller: Norwegian Defence Research Establishment (FFI). Retrieved from http://rapporter.ffi.no/rapporter/2000/05788.pdf.

Halvorssen, T. L., & Vamraak, T. (2004). Materiellinvestering i Forsvaret – Norsk forsvarsindustris rolle [Equipment investments in the Norwegian Armed Forces – The role of the Norwegian Defence Industry] (FFI-rapport No. 2004/01219). Kjeller: Norwegian Defence Research Establishment (FFI). Retrieved from www.ffi.no/no/Rapporter/04-01219.pdf.

Hoel, D. (2017). *Fred er ei det beste. Fra innsiden av den norske ammunisjonsindustrien [Peace is not the best. From the inside of the Norwegian ammunitions industry]*. Oslo: Spartacus.

Hove, K. (2018). Defence industrial policy in Norway. Drivers and influence. Ares Policy Paper 25. Armament Industry European Research Group. Retrieved from www.iris-france.org/wp-content/uploads/2018/02/Ares-25-Policy-Paper-f%C3%A9vrier-2018.pdf.

Johnson, A. U., Hove, K., & Lillekvelland, T. (2017). Country survey: Military expenditure and defence policy in Norway 1970–2013. *Defence and Peace Economics*, 28(6), 669–685. 10.1080/10242694.2015.1101896.

Kristiansen, R. (1991). Norsk forsvarsindustri ved en skillevei? [The Norwegian defence industry at a crossroads?] (IFS Info No. 6/1991). Oslo: Institutt for forsvarsstudier. Retrieved from http://forsvaret.no/ifs/IFS-Info-61991-Norsk-forsvarsindustri.

Ministry of Defence. (1995). St.prp. nr. 48 (1994–95) Forsvarets materiell-, bygg- og anleggsinvesteringer [The investments of the Armed Forces]. Retrieved from www.regjeringen.no/no/dokumenter/stprp-nr-59-1997-98-/id201869/.

Ministry of Defence. (1998). St.prp. nr. 59 (1997–98). Om Forsvarets materiell-, bygg- og anleggsinvesteringer [On the investments of the Armed Forces]. Retrieved from www.regjeringen.no/no/dokumenter/stprp-nr-59-1997-98-/id201869/.

Ministry of Defence. (2007). St.meld. nr. 38 (2006–2007) Forsvaret og industrien – strategiske partnere. Strategi for de næringspolitiske aspekter ved Forsvarets anskaffelser [The Armed Forces and industry – Strategic partners. Strategy for industry political aspects of the Armed Forces' procurement]. Retrieved from www.regjeringen.no/contentassets/beb855ddfb054197a6f55107c65efbd9/no/pdfs/stm200620070038000dddpdfs.pdf.

Ministry of Defence. (2012). Industrielt samarbeid [Industrial cooperation]. Retrieved 13 November 2018, from www.regjeringen.no/no/tema/forsvar/forsvarsindustri/industrielt-samarbeid/id528526/.

Ministry of Defence. (2015). Meld. St. 9 (2015–2016) Nasjonal forsvarsindustriell strategi [National Defence Industrial Strategy]. Retrieved from www.regjeringen.no/contentassets/e7bfdb49872449f3bd1eed10812aa4b0/no/pdfs/stm201520160009000dddpdfs.pdf.

Ministry of Defence. (2016). Prop. 1 S (2016–2017) [The 2017 government budget for the Armed Forces]. Retrieved from www.regjeringen.no/contentassets/186c695600eb4db085dfcf2ca6825e49/no/pdfs/prp201620170001_fddddpdfs.pdf.

Ministry of Defence. (2018). Prop. 1 S (2018–2019) [The 2019 government budget for the Armed Forces]. Retrieved from www.regjeringen.no/contentassets/0d9a279e01a94aa395e95018718ab2b7/no/pdfs/prp201820190001_fddddpdfs.pdf.

Ministry of Foreign Affairs. (2001). St.meld. nr. 45 (2000–2001). Eksport av forsvarsmateriell fra Norge i 2000, eksportkontroll og internasjonalt ikke-spredningssamarbeid [Exports of defence materiel from Norway in 2000, export control and international non-proliferation cooperation]. Oslo: Ministry of Foreign Affairs. Retrieved from www.regjeringen.no/no/dokumenter/stmeld-nr-45-2000-2001-/id194979/.

Ministry of Foreign Affairs. (2002). St.meld. nr. 29 (2001–2002). Eksport av forsvarsmateriell fra Norge i 2001, eksportkontroll og internasjonalt ikke-spredningssamarbeid [Exports of defence materiel from Norway in 2001, export control and international non-proliferation cooperation]. Oslo: Ministry of Foreign Affairs. Retrieved from www.regjeringen.no/no/dokumenter/stmeld-nr-29-2001-2002-/id196204/.

Ministry of Foreign Affairs. (2003). St.meld. nr. 35 (2002–2003). Eksport av forsvarsmateriell fra Norge i 2002, eksportkontroll og internasjonalt ikke-spredningssamarbeid [Exports of defence materiel from Norway in 2002, export control and international non-proliferation cooperation]. Oslo: Ministry of Foreign Affairs. Retrieved from www.regjeringen.no/no/dokumenter/stmeld-nr-35-2002-2003-/id196979/.

Ministry of Foreign Affairs. (2004). St.meld. nr. 41 (2003–2004). Eksport av forsvarsmateriell fra Norge i 2003, eksportkontroll og internasjonalt ikke-spredningssamarbeid [Exports of defence materiel from Norway in 2003, export control and international non-proliferation cooperation]. Oslo: Ministry of Foreign Affairs. Retrieved from www.regjeringen.no/no/dokumenter/stmeld-nr-41-2003-2004-/id198268/.

Ministry of Foreign Affairs. (2005). St.meld. nr. 36 (2004–2005). Eksport av forsvarsmateriell frå Noreg i 2004, eksportkontroll og internasjonalt ikkje-spreiingssamarbeid [Exports of defence materiel from Norway in 2004, export control and international non-proliferation cooperation]. Oslo: Ministry of Foreign Affairs. Retrieved from www.regjeringen.no/nn/dokumenter/stmeld-nr-36-2004-2005-/id407762/.

Ministry of Foreign Affairs. (2006). St.meld. nr. 19 (2005–2006). Eksport av forsvarsmateriell fra Norge i 2005, eksportkontroll og internasjonalt ikke-spredningssamarbeid [Exports of defence materiel from Norway in 2005, export control and international non-proliferation cooperation]. Oslo: Ministry of Foreign Affairs. Retrieved from www.regjeringen.no/no/dokumenter/stmeld-nr-19-2005-2006-/id200515/.

Ministry of Foreign Affairs. (2007). St.meld. nr. 33 (2006–2007). Eksport av forsvarsmateriell frå Noreg i 2006, eksportkontroll og internasjonalt ikkje-spreiingssamarbeid

[Exports of defence materiel from Norway in 2006, export control and international non-proliferation cooperation]. Oslo: Ministry of Foreign Affairs. Retrieved from www.regjeringen.no/no/dokumenter/Stmeld-nr-33-2006-2007-/id472302/.

Ministry of Foreign Affairs. (2008). St.meld. nr. 29 (2007–2008). Eksport av forsvarsmateriell frå Noreg i 2007, eksportkontroll og internasjonalt ikkje-spreiingssamarbeid [Exports of defence materiel from Norway in 2007, export control and international non-proliferation cooperation]. Oslo: Ministry of Foreign Affairs. Retrieved from www.regjeringen.no/nn/dokumenter/stmeld-nr-29-2007-2008-/id515314/.

Ministry of Foreign Affairs. (2009). St.meld. nr. 42 (2008–2009). Eksport av forsvarsmateriell fra Norge i 2008, eksportkontroll og internasjonalt ikke-spredningssamarbeid [Exports of defence materiel from Norway in 2008, export control and international non-proliferation cooperation]. Oslo: Ministry of Foreign Affairs. Retrieved from www.regjeringen.no/no/dokumenter/stmeld-nr-42-2008-2009-/id564541/.

Ministry of Foreign Affairs. (2010). Meld. St. 21 (2009–2010). Eksport av forsvarsmateriell fra Norge i 2019, eksportkontroll og internasjonalt ikke-spredningssamarbeid [Exports of defence materiel from Norway in 2019, export control and international non-proliferation cooperation]. Oslo: Ministry of Foreign Affairs. Retrieved from www.regjeringen.no/no/dokumenter/Meld-St-21-2009–2010/id608556/.

Ministry of Foreign Affairs. (2018a). Export licences to Saudi Arabia [Press release]. Retrieved 18 November 2018, from www.regjeringen.no/en/aktuelt/eksportlisenser-til-saudi-arabia/id2618605/.

Ministry of Foreign Affairs. (2018b). Meld. St. 5 (2017–2018). Eksport av forsvarsmateriell fra Norge i 2017, eksportkontroll og internasjonalt ikke-spredningssamarbeid [Exports of defence materiel from Norway in 2017, export control and international non-proliferation cooperation]. Oslo: Ministry of Foreign Affairs. Retrieved from www.regjeringen.no/no/dokumenter/meld.-st.-5-20172018/id2576728/.

Ministry of Trade and Industry. (2000). St.prp. nr. 41 (1999-2000). Statens engasjement i Raufoss ASA og Nammo AS [Government Commitment in Raufoss ASA and Nammo AS]. Retrieved from www.regjeringen.no/no/dokumenter/stprp-nr-41-1999-2000-/id202925/.

NATO. (1980). Financial and Economic Data Relating to NATO Defence – Defence Expenditures of NATO Countries (1949–1980). Retrieved 29 November 2018, from www.nato.int/cps/en/natohq/news_65894.htm.

NATO. (1984). Financial and Economic Data Relating to NATO Defence – Defence Expenditures of NATO Countries (1970–1984). Retrieved 29 November 2018, from www.nato.int/cps/en/natohq/news_65888.htm.

NATO. (1988). Financial and Economic Data Relating to NATO Defence – Defence Expenditures of NATO Countries (1970–1988). Retrieved 29 November 2018, from www.nato.int/cps/en/natohq/news_65880.htm.

NATO. (1992). Financial and economic data relating to NATO Defence – Defence expenditures of NATO countries (1970–1992). Retrieved 29 November 2018, from www.nato.int/cps/en/natohq/news_23969.htm.

NATO. (1996). Financial and Economic Data Relating to NATO Defence – Defence Expenditures of NATO Countries (1975–1996). Retrieved 29 November 2018, from www.nato.int/cps/en/natohq/news_25050.htm.

NATO. (2000). Financial and economic data relating to NATO defence – Defence expenditures of NATO countries (1980–2000). Retrieved 29 November 2018, from www.nato.int/cps/en/natohq/news_18156.htm.

NATO. (2003). Financial and Economic Data relating to NATO Defence – Defence Expenditures of NATO Countries (1980–2003). Retrieved 29 November 2018, from www.nato.int/cps/en/natohq/news_20270.htm.

NATO. (2006). NATO-Russia Compendium of Financial and Economic Data Relating to Defence - Defence Expenditures of NRC Countries (1985–2006). Retrieved 29 November 2018, from www.nato.int/cps/en/natohq/news_57094.htm.

NATO. (2012). Financial and Economic Data Relating to NATO Defence – Defence expenditures of NATO Countries (1990–2011) (Rev1). Retrieved 29 November 2018, from www.nato.int/cps/en/natohq/news_85966.htm.

NATO. (2018). Defence Expenditure of NATO Countries (2011–2018). Retrieved 13 November 2018, from www.nato.int/cps/en/natohq/news_156770.htm.

Øyangen, K. (2014). Moderniseringslokomotivet. Kongsberg Våpenfabrikks historie 1945–1987 [The Engine of Modernization. The history of Kongsberg Våpenfabrikk 1947–1987]. Oslo: Pax.

Pedersen, J. O. (2015). Forsvarsindustrien i Norge – Statistikk 2014 [The Defence Industry in Norway – 2014 Statistics] (FFI-rapport No. 2015/01798). Kjeller: Forsvarets forskningsinstitutt. Retrieved from www.ffi.no/no/Rapporter/15-01798.pdf.

Pedersen, J. O. (2016). Forsvarsindustrien i Norge. Statistikk 2015 [The Defence Industry in Norway. 2015 Statistics] (FFI-rapport No. 16/02041). Kjeller: Norwegian Defence Research Establishment (FFI). Retrieved from www.ffi.no/no/Rapporter/16-02041.pdf.

Pedersen, J. O. (2017). Forsvarsindustrien i Norge. Statistikk 2016 [The Defence Industry in Norway. 2016 Statistics] (FFI-rapport No. 17/16353). Kjeller: Norwegian Defence Research Establishment (FFI). Retrieved from www.ffi.no/no/Rapporter/17-16353.pdf.

Pedersen, J. O. (2018). Forsvarsindustrien i Norge. Statistikk 2017 [The Defence Industry in Norway. 2017 Statistics] (FFI-rapport No. 18/01675). Kjeller: Norwegian Defence Research Establishment (FFI). Retrieved from www.ffi.no/no/Rapporter/18-01675.pdf.

Petersen, T., & Sogner, K. (2014). Strategiske samspill. Kongsberg Gruppens historie 1987–2014 [Strategic interplay. The history of Kongsberg Gruppen 1987–2014]. Oslo: Pax.

Salvesen, B. B. (2013). Forsvars- eller krigsindustri? Tolkningsrammer om norsk våpenindustri [Defence or war industry? Interpretations of the Norwegian defence industry] (Master's thesis). University of Oslo, Oslo. Retrieved from www.duo.uio.no/handle/10852/38792.

Skogstad, A. K., & Warberg, E. N. (2005). Revisjon av de teknologiske kompetanse- og satsningsområdene for Forsvaret og norsk forsvarsindustri [Revision of the technological areas of competence for the Armed Forces and the Norwegian defence industry] (FFI-rapport No. 2005/01678). Kjeller: Forsvarets forskningsinstitutt. Retrieved from http://rapporter.ffi.no/rapporter/2005/01678.pdf.

Statistics Norway. (2018a). Fakta om norsk næringsliv [Norwegian business facts]. Retrieved 9 November 2018, from www.ssb.no/nasjonalregnskap-og-konjunkturer/faktaside/norsk-naeringsliv.

Statistics Norway. (2018b). Table 08819: External trade in goods, by commodity group (three digit SITC) (NOK 1 000) 1988–2017. Retrieved 22 June 2018, from www.ssb.no/en/statbanken/statbank/table/08819/.

Tvetbråten, K. (2011). Forsvarsindustrien i Norge – Statistikk 2010 [The Defence Industry in Norway – 2010 Statistics] (FFI-rapport No. 2011/02264). Kjeller: Forsvarets forskningsinstitutt. Retrieved from www.ffi.no/no/Rapporter/11-02264.pdf.

Tvetbråten, K. (2012). Forsvarsindustrien i Norge – Statistikk 2011 [The Defence Industry in Norway – 2011 Statistics] (FFI-rapport No. 2011/02433). Kjeller: Forsvarets forskningsinstitutt. Retrieved from www.ffi.no/no/Rapporter/12-02433.pdf.

Tvetbråten, K. (2013). Forsvarsindustrien i Norge – Statistikk 2012 [The Defence Industry in Norway – 2012 Statistics] (FFI-rapport No. 2013/02681). Kjeller: Forsvarets forskningsinstitutt. Retrieved from www.ffi.no/no/Rapporter/13-02681.pdf.

Tvetbråten, K. (2014). Forsvarsindustrien i Norge – Statistikk 2013 [The Defence Industry in Norway – 2013 Statistics] (FFI-rapport No. 2014/02199). Kjeller: Forsvarets forskningsinstitutt. Retrieved from www.ffi.no/no/Rapporter/14-02199.pdf.

Tvetbråten, K., & Fevolden, A. M. (2011). Forsvarsindustrien i Norge – Statistikk 2009 [The Defence Industry in Norway – 2009 Statistics] (FFI-rapport No. 2011/00608). Kjeller: Forsvarets forskningsinstitutt. Retrieved from www.ffi.no/no/Rapporter/11-00608.pdf.

Ulsrud, O. A. (2012). Forsvaret og industrien et strategisk samarbeid? En analyse av den næringspolitiske policyen for Forsvaret anskaffelser. [The Armed Forces and the industry in a strategic cooperation? An analysis of industrial strategy for procurements]. Oslo: University of Oslo. Retrieved from www.duo.uio.no/bitstream/handle/10852/13396/MasteroppgavexLevertxMaix2012.xOlexAndersxUlsrud.pdf.

Wang, T. (1996). *RA i skuddlinja. Industriutvikling og strategiske veivalg gjennom 100 år [Raufoss Ammunisjonsfabrikk in the line of fire. Industrial development and strategic choices through 100 years]*. Raufoss: Gjøvik Grafiske.

Warberg, E. N. (2007). Kontrahering i prosjekters tidligfase; Forsvarets anskaffelser [Acquisitions in early phases of projects; Defence procurement] (Concept-rapport No. 16). Trondheim: Concept-programmet. Retrieved from https://brage.bibsys.no/xmlui/handle/11250/228085.

Wicken, O. (1988). Stille propell i storpolitisk storm: KV/Toshiba-saken og dens bakgrunn [Quiet propeller in a political storm: The Kongsberg Våpenfabrikk/Toshiba case and its background] (Forsvarsstudier No. 1/1988). Oslo: Institutt for forsvarsstudier. Retrieved from https://brage.bibsys.no/xmlui/handle/11250/99511.

Wicken, O. (1992). Moralens vokter eller våpenkremmer? Regulering av norsk våpeneksport 1935–1992 [A moral guardian or peddler of weapons? Regulation of Norwegian military export 1935–1992] (Forsvarsstudier No. 3/1992). Oslo: Institutt for forsvarsstudier.

17 Turkey

Selami Sezgin and Sennur Sezgin

Introduction

Turkey is an important country and is the mid-point of Europe, Asia and Africa with a population of over 80 million. Turkey is located on the border of the western bloc during the Cold War and was an important country for NATO. Following the end of the post-cold war in the early 1990s, the geo-political importance of Turkey was expected to decrease but strategic importance of Turkey's continued because Turkey is located in the middle of biggest energy buyers and energy suppliers. Considering that most of the conflicts in the world are energy-related, defense and security in such a geographical area are becoming increasingly important.

Turkey has always been important throughout history because it is a country founded on the legacy of the Ottoman Empire. After the First World War, the Republic of Turkey was founded in 1923 and despite being Muslim country, it has worked to integrate with the Christian western world. After the First World War there were significant developments in the Turkish defense industry. After the Second World War, Turkey became a NATO member in 1949. After this membership, Turkey abandoned its defense industry and relied on US defense aids. After the intervention in Cyprus in 1974, the US military imposed sanctions on Turkey. After military sanctions, Turkey saw the need for a domestic defense industry and has made significant progress indeveloping its defense industry. In this study, Turkey's defense industry trend and developments, defense procurement policy and future plans will be analyzed together with world developments.

Turkish defence expenditure

Between 2005 and 2015, Turkish defence expenditure was 1.9% of GDP (WMEAT, 2017). This figure was 1.48% in 2017 according to NATO data. Turkish armed forces numbered 355,200 active duty personnel in 2016 (Military Balance, 2017). which makes Turkey the 12th largest in the world and the 2nd biggest in NATO. Before 2000, Turkey allocated a considerably high percentage of its GDP to defence. After 2000 the share declined dramatically. Defense spending, which had the largest share in the budget from 1923 to 2004, fell to second place after 2004 and the share of education expenditures increased. Since the establishment of NATO, Greece and Turkey have had the highest defense burden. But since 2000, this defense burden began to fall in Turkey, However, internal and external threats to Turkey have increased. The main threats are the problem of the continental shelf with Greece, the Cyprus issue, the Syrian civil war and migration, the conflict in Iraq, the Armenian issue and terrorist groups (FETO, DHKPC, PKK and ISIS). There are no countries in the world struggling with such threats at the same time.

The Turkish armed forces are claimed to be the best organized, the best discipled and the largest security establishment in the country (Sezgin, 1997). Although Turkey had one of the world's largest armed forces, but now the number of soldiers has decreased but its military strength and technology have increased. In 2016, an attempted coup took place in Turkey and a significant number of ranking soldiers were removed from the army. Especially during the coup period, most of the combat pilots were removed from the air force due to FETO terror connections. Despite this, the military capabilities of the Turkish army have not decreased. Major military operations were carried out in Syria during this period.

Table 17.1 Share of defence spending in GDP (%)

	2012	*2013*	*2014*	*2015*	*2016*	*2017*
Turkey	1.59	1.52	1.45	1.39	1.46	1.48
Greece	2.29	2.21	2.20	2.31	2.41	2.36
USA	4.42	4.38	3.77	3.56	5.56	3.57
UK	2.17	2.27	2.17	2.06	2.15	2.12
NATO Europe	1.52	1.49	1.44	1.42	1.44	1.46
NATO	2.81	2.64	2.48	2.39	2.40	2.42

Source: NATO, Information on Defence Expenditure.

Table 17.2 Military personnel in NATO and Turkey (000s)

	2012	*2013*	*2014*	*2015*	*2016*	*2017*
Turkey	495	427	427	385	359	416
Greece	110	110	107	104	106	106
USA	1,400	1,382	1,338	1,314	1,301	1,308
NATO Europe	1,956	1,862	1,825	1,740	1,718	1,774
NATO	3,423	3,312	3,229	3,125	3,090	3,153

Source: NATO, Information on Defence Expenditure.

Turkey is one of the leading regional powers in the Middle East and also the most promising of the emerging powers. There have been an arms race with Greece and Turkey. Turkey has terminated its informal alliance with Israel (Wiśniewski, 2015). Turkey needs a strong defense because of its geographic location and relations with other countries.

Procurement policy in Turkey

The procurement system in Turkey comprises units of the Ministry of National Defence (MND) and the Undersecretariat for Defense Industries. Agencies responsible of defence procurement in Turkey are legally subordinated to the Ministry of National Defense. The main policy directive for the procurement methods to be used is given in the Turkish Defense Industry Policy Strategy (TDIPS). Politics did not play primary role in procurement decisions but it affects procurement decision (Kizmaz, 2007).

After joining NATO in 1949, Turkey fully integrated its national security and defense mechanisms to the alliance. The primary threat was the Soviet Union and the Warsaw Pact and therefore the military posture was entirely built to meet this threat, with the doctrine, planning, training, procurement, and sustainment procedures heavily depending on NATO and particularly the United States (Mevlutoglu, 2017).

Until recent years in Turkey, defense procurement policies have been established by the military authorities rather than civilian authorities. In the mid-1980s in Turkey, the Undersecretary for Defense Industries was established due to the insignificance of political authority in procurement policy. In order to make the civilian authority the decision maker in defense policies, the Undersecretariat for Defense Industries was established and military personnel were given as little space as possible in the management of this structure. This situation created a dual structure. Two different procurement systems in Turkey were dominant until recent years. The dual structure between the Undersecretariat for Defense Industries and the Ministry of National Defense has led to a serious problem. In general, the Undersecretariat for Defense Industries was

Table 17.3 The procurement system in Turkey

<table>
<tr><td colspan="2">National Security Council Turkish</td></tr>
<tr><td colspan="2">National Military Strategy</td></tr>
<tr><td colspan="2">Requirements</td></tr>
<tr><td colspan="2">Commander of Forces</td></tr>
<tr><td>-Operation Neccesity Study</td><td>-Plan Capability Target</td></tr>
<tr><td colspan="2">Turkish General Staff</td></tr>
<tr><td colspan="2">Ten Years Procurement Plan (TYPP-OYTEP)</td></tr>
</table>

Source: Kizmaz 2007.

in charge of supplying long-term defence systems and subsystem projects, while other procurements were carried out by the Ministry of National Defense. However, over time, the Undersecretariat for Defense Industries has been considered as the second undersecretary of the Ministry of National Defense. The Undersecretariat for Defense Industries and the Ministry of National Defense have started to implement technology transfer, offset, domestic production and long-term procurement at the same time. Practices such as the Undersecretariat for Defense Industries starting direct procurement programs have led to problems that reduce efficiency in resource allocation.

Although the Ministry of Defense was responsible for procurement policy in Turkey, the armed forces (land forces, air forces, naval forces) were independent of the national defense ministry. Defence procurement policies were mostly determined by the military authorities. Very recently, the General Staff was attached to the Ministry of National Defense, and the Ministry of National Defense became important and decisive in the defense procurement policy. Today, the dual structure in the defence procurement policy has been eliminated. The military structure is subject to civilian authority.

Institutions in the Turkish Defense Industry consist of the Military Factories affiliated to the Turkish Armed Forces, the Machinery and Chemical Industry Corporation of the Ministry of National Defense, the Turkish Armed Forces Foundation companies, and private companies. In the general framework of the defense industry companies are divided into public and private companies, and in the sub-framework, it is possible to differentiate between military factories, state-owned enterprises/Turkish armed forces foundation companies, private companies and foreign partners (Sezgin, 2017).

The Ministry of National Defense has primarily aimed at reducing foreign dependency as a procurement policy and in order to assist the development of the national defense industry, procurement from the domestic market is preferred. Priority in procurement activities; are domestic procurement, procurement by means of joint R&D or production activities with other countries, procurement through domestic common production and overseas procurement.

In the period 1985–1990, procurement policies for foreign purchasing were dominant. From 2006 to the present, domestic procurement models are supported. In particular, between 2006 and 2010, a three-stage procurement strategy was followed in the Presidency of Defence Industries (SSB): they aimed to implement the original development model in priority areas, thus developing the product portfolio of the Turkish defense industry. In cases where the development for the Turkish market is not cost-effective, joint production or consortia are used as a method of partnership. Thus, it aimed to develop the capacity of a design and risk partner. In case where these priorities cannot be provided, procurement is made through direct procurement. When the direct procurement method is selected, job opportunities are provided to Turkish industry through common production and off-set. It is observed that the defense firms have developed further as the procurement methods have been transformed into domestic development over the years.

SSB, which is the procurement authority, works with the defense industry on the basis of projects as the main contractor.

In Turkey, the biggest share of defense expenditure is personnel, with equipment as the second largest expenditure item. The share of personnel expenditures in the majority of NATO countries is higher than in Turkey. The share of infrastructure expenditures has changed little over the years. Turkey has followed a downward trend over the years as the number of military personnel has declined; but no significant drop was observed in personnel expenditures indicating an increase in spending per soldier (Table 17.4).

Table 17.5 shows the arms trade in Turkey. One of the two organizations that regularly and continuously publish data on the arms trade is the US World Military Expenditure and Arms Transfers (WMEAT) and the other is SIPRI. The data of the two institutions may vary. According to WMEAT data, there is no significant improvement in Turkey's share of arms exports: WMEAT does not follow closely the export data of Turkey. Turkey's share in world arms exports is well below 1%. The share of Turkey's arms imports, compared with arms exports, is high. However, over the years the share of

Table 17.4 Distribution of Turkish defence expenditure (%)

	Personnel	*Equipment*	*Infrastructure*	*Other*
1990–1994	50.1	23.7	3.0	22.5
2000–2004	46.1	32.6	4.8	15.7
2005–2009	50.8	28.1	2.9	17.7
2014	56.8	25.0	2.8	15.2
2015	56.8	25.1	2.6	15.5
2016	57.6	25.5	2.4	14.4
2017	51.0	30.6	2.9	15.4

NATO, Information on Defence Expenditure.

Table 17.5 Arms trade in Turkey

Years	*Arms exports*	*Arms imports*	*World share (arms exports %)*	*World share (arms imports %)*
1999	131	3,798	0.14	4.32
2000	128	3,586	0.14	3.80
2005	114	2,402	0.10	2.25
2010	416	3,850	0.26	2.40
2013	393	4,619	0.21	2.54
2014	386	4,919	0.21	2.66
2015	382	3,245	0.21	1.77

Source: WMEAT (2012, 2017) in billions of 2012 constant US dollars.

Turkey's arms imports has fallen. The share, which was over 4% in 1999, fell below 2% in 2015 (WMEAT, 2012; SIPRI, 2018). SIPRI data on arms exports are more reliable. Developments in Turkey's arms exports since 2001 are shown in Figure 17.1 where it can be seen that the export of arms shows regular increases. Turkey arms exports reached nearly two billion dollars over the last three years. Turkey's arms sales increased by 145% with a doubling of arms sales to the Middle East.

Figure 17.2 shows the share of the Turkish armed forces needs provided from domestic resources. In 2003, 25% of the Turkish Armed Forces' needs were provided from domestic sources and this rate increased steadily over the years reaching 65% in 2017. These data indicate increasing support for the

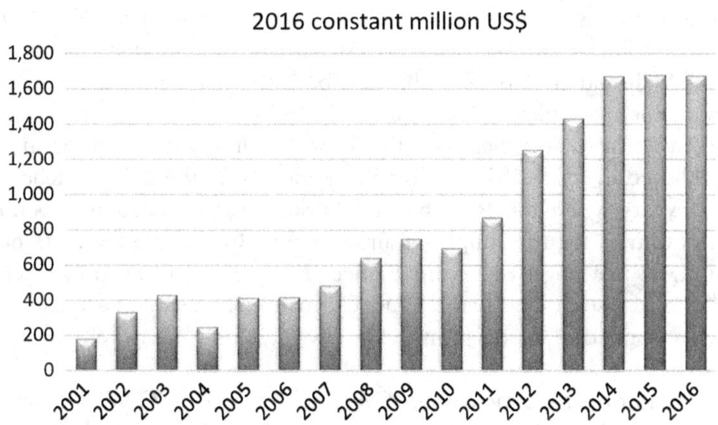

Figure 17.1 Arms exports of Turkey.

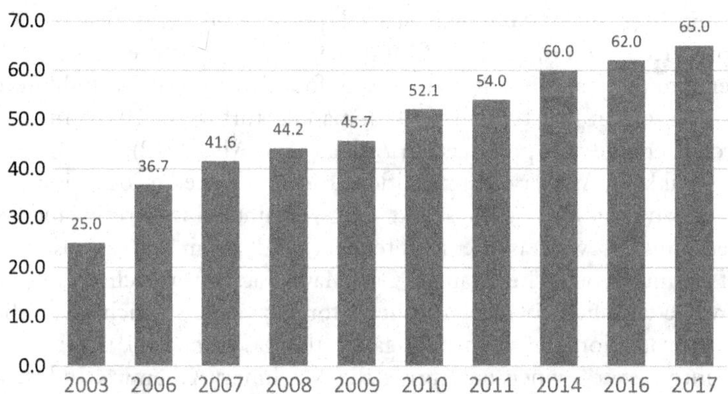

Figure 17.2 Domestic supply rate of Turkish armed force needs (%).

national defense industry. Turkey has carried out military operations for a long time Iraq, Syria and against the terrorist group PKK using more domestically manufactured arms and weapons. Technological progress in the Turkish defence industry is helping Turkey to become a major arms exporter in the region.

Turkish defence industry

History

Turkey inherited its defence industry from the Ottoman Empire. Following the conquest of Istanbul by Fatih Sultan Mehmed, Tophane-i Amire was established in the Tophane district and is one of the first defense industry organizations. Tersane-i Amire has formed the Haliç Shipyard, Taşkızak Shipyard. Baruthane-i Amire (powder mills) construction was completed in 1700. Dolmabahçe pistol cartridge factory was established as a modern factory in the period of Mahmud II. Taşkızak Shipyard built the first battleship in 1828. The shipyard, which completed its armored frigate in 1884 and the first submarine in 1886, was closed together with the World War I. Ankara Weapon Factory was established in 1920–1921 to do rifle repair during the Independence War.

In the years when the Republic of Turkey was founded it depended on foreign countries for the supply of air weapons. In this context. the needs of the country were purchased from France (Breciet and Candron), Czechoslovakia (Smolik system land planes) and Germany (Junkers and sea planes). The Turkish Aeronautical Association (THK) was established in February 1925 to produce air vehicles.

In the field of aeronautics, Kayseri Aircraft Factory, (TOMTAS) was established in Kayseri in 1925 with the partnership agreement with the German Junkers company. The Eskişehir Aircraft Repair Factory was established in 1926 as a TOMTAŞ initiative for the maintenance, repair and renovation of existing aircraft (Kurt, 2018). In 1936, an aircraft factory was founded by Nuri Demirdağ in Istanbul and started production with the Nu.37 type. They produced 24 Nu.37 aircraft and many gliders before closing in 1943. Another attmpt at an aircraft factory was founded by the Turkish Aeronautical Association in 1941which started manufacturing in 1944. In 1948 the first aircraft engine was produced in Ankara (SASAD, 2012).

The Kırıkkale Artillery Ammunition Factory started production in 1929 producing ammunition, bullets and plugs, maintaining Krupp and Nielsen Winther guns, as well as the maintenance and repair of various types and sizes of ammunition. The Mamak Gas Mask Factory, which was opened in 1935, was established to meet the need for gas masks, which were the only means of protection for the army against the gas gun. In 1950 it was transformed into a state-owned enterprise, the Machinery Chemical Industry Corporation (MKEK). Today, MKEK is among the 100 biggest defense companies in the world.

The Turkish republic started the domestic production of various weapons and equipment including aeronautics. After WWII Turkey received an increasing flow of military aid (Sezgin, 1997). Following the Cyprus Peace Operation in 1974, USA imposed an arms embargo on Turkey so Turkey decided to produce its own military equipment.

The Cyprus crisis provided a stimulus for independence policies to form a modern and self-sufficient Turkish defense industry. Within this context, Air Forces (1970), Naval Forces (1972) and Land Forces (1974) Reinforcement Trusts were founded. In 1987, these three trusts were gathered into the Turkish Armed Forces Reinforcement Trust. Until the establishment of the under secretariat for Defense Industries in 1985 the government supported the national defense industry. Turkish people made significant donations to Air, Marine and Land Forces Reinforcement Trusts. In a short time these Trusts set up foundations like Aselsan (1975), Isbir (1979), Aspilsan (1981) and Havelsan (1982) which carried out investments for the national defense industry. Today, these defense industry foundations still have important places in the sector (SASAD, 2017).

Table 17.6 shows the defense firms which were active until 2000. Almost all defense firms were established after 1970 except for the Golcuk shipyard, Taşkızak shipyard and MKEK. In 1975, the US implemented weapon restrictions on Turkey leading to problems in defense procurement: hence, the creation of a national defense industry became Turkey's priority.

Structure and performance

Data on the current defense companies came from the Istanbul Chamber which details the 500 largest industrial companies in Turkey. The defense industry firms and their economic size are shown in Table 17.7. Aselsan and TAI take the first two places in production and also in the number of employees. TAI and TEI take the first place in the Turkish defense industry institutions with the highest export volume. Defense industry companies which have the highest export potential have also been TAI and TEI.

When we compare Turkish defense companies with the world's top 100 defense companies, we find four Turkish defense firms in the world top 100 companies. Although Aselsan and TAI have been on this list for a long time, Roketsan and STM have only entered this list recently.

The turnover, export, R&D and employment figures of defense and aerospace companies are shown in Table 17.9. Significant increases were observed in the total turnover of the defense industry, its R&D spending and in employment.

Looking at the total amount of R&D expenditures of the Turkish defense industry companies, the company that undertakes the highest R&D spending is Aselsan with US$412 million and its share of R&D in total turnover is 33%: this share is quite high. The number employed in R&D is half of the total number of employees. Table 17.10 shows the highest number of defense industry firms engaged in R&D spending. In the second column of the table, the numbers for the company name indicate the ranking among the defense

Table 17.6 Major defense industry organizations in Turkey

Company	*Establishment year*	*Ownership*	*Activity area*
Aselsan	1976	Armed Forces	Military communication, F-16 electronic components
Asil Çelik	1974	Public	Barrel and bullet steel
Coşkunöz	1973	Private	Structural parts production
FMC-Nurol	1992	Joint venture	Armored vehicle
İŞBİR	1977	Armed Forces	Military generator
MARCONİ	1988	Ort.Gir.	HF-SSB radio communication
Mercedes	1967	Ort.Gir.	Tactical Vehicle
MKEK	1950	Public	Small gun, cannon, rocket ramp ammunition, machine gun,
MKEK-pistol cartridge	1930	Public	Ammunition
MKEK-Barutsan	1989	Public	Gunpowder, explosives
Nurol	1982	Joint venture	Weapon Systems
Otokar	1963	Joint venture	Diesel engines
Petlas	1976	Private	Tire
Roketsan	1989	Joint venture	Rocket engines
SGS-Profilo	1988	Joint venture	Mobile phone
STFA_Savoronik	1986	Joint venture	Fire control and security systems
Tusaş TAI	1984	Joint venture	F-16 fighter jet
Tusaş TEI	1985	Joint venture	F-16 engines
Manas	1976	Joint venture	Heavy duty military vehicles
Taşkızak Shipyard	1941	Naval Forces	Shipbuilding
Golcuk Shipyard	1924	Naval Forces	Shipbuilding

Source: Sezgin (1997).

companies in the top 250 firms that spend the most on R&D. Aselsan ranks first among the top 250 R&D spending companies (Acan, 2016). TAI takes second place in R&D spending. Among the top 250 R&D spending companies, there are three defense companies in the top ten and eight in the top 50.

Table 17.7 Defence firms in Turkey (in Top 500 industrial enterprises in Turkey)

Turkey rank 2017	*Turkey rank 2016*	*Firms*	*Production sales (000 TL)*	*Production sales (000 $)*	*Employment (number of person)*	*Export (000 $)*
20	20	Aselsan Electronics	4.484.421	1.685.872	5.735	179.953
28	29	TUSAŞ-TAI	3.608.591	1.356.613	5.721	509.149
75	89	ROKETSAN	1.661.391	624.583	2.326	43.314
79	137	BMC Automotive Industry	1.612.177	606.081	1.419	44.320
87	71	Otokar Automotive and Defense Industry	1.482.404	557.295	2.214	138.801
129	117	TUSAŞ TEI	1.029.814	387.148	NA	261.124
131	121	MKEK – Mechanical and Chemical Industry Company	1.026.255	385.810	5.466	50.724
273	293	HAVELSAN	579.733	217.945	1.397	1.852
350	-	Nurol Machinery and Industry and Trade Co.	443.980	166.910	459	35.038
368	-	FNSS Defense Systems	176.839	66.481	NA	48.450
479	497	Alp Aviation Industry and Trade Co.	328.936	123.660	756	90.173
		STM Defense Technologies Engineering and Trade Co.	984.094	3.699.600	600	NA

Istanbul Sanayi Odası (2018) www.iso500.org.tr/(25.11.2018).

Table 17.8 Turkish defence firms in the world top 100 defence firms for 2018

World Ranking		*Company*	*2017 defense revenue**	*2016 defense revenue**	*% Defense revenue change*	*2017 Total revenue (in millions)*	*Revenue from defense*
2018	*2017*						
55	57	Aselsan	1,425	1,195	19%	1.470	97%
64	61	Turkish Aerospace Industries	1,090	1,084	1%	1.422	77%
96	98	Roketsan	376	364	3%	376	100%
97	-	STM Defense Technologies Co.	370	343	8%	414	89%

Source: *Defense News* (2018) https://people.defensenews.com/top-100/(25.11.2018).

* Sales figures in million US$ and calculated using average market conversion rates over each firm's fiscal year.

Table 17.9 Main indicators of defense and aviation industry

	2012	*2013*	*2014*	*2015*	*2.016*	*2017*
Turnover (million US$)	5.085	5.285	5.212	4.962	5.968	6.568
Export (million US$)	1.722	1.634	18.962	1.950	1.953	1.790
Received orders (million US$)	NA	8.329	11.239	7.770	11.913	7.905
R&D (million US$)	819	964	906	914	1.254	1.214
Employment (personel)	33.491	32.368	31.242	31.375	35.502	44.740

Source: SASAD (2012–2017) www.sasad.org.tr/savunma-ve-havacilik-sanayii-performans-raporu-2017 (25.11.2018) 2016 US$ Constant prices.

Table 17.10 R&D spending in Turkey (2016)

			R&D spending (million $)	*R&D expense to turnover (%)*	*Number of R&D staff*
1	1	Aselsan Co.	411.47	33.00	2,658
2	2	TUSAS Turkish Aircraft Industries Corporation (TAI)	238.69	28.30	1,584
3	5	Roketsan	131.69	32.00	772
4	9	Havelsan	40.07	28.00	834
5	15	FNSS Defence Systems	24.28	16.00	240
6	18	TUSAS Engine Industries Inc. (TEI)	19.36	6.00	332
7	21	MKEK Mechanical and Chemical Industry Company	15.49	4,10	160
8	31	BMC Automotive Industry & Trade Inc.	9.47	3.52	181
9	67	67 Alp Aviation	3.79	4.65	95

Source: Acan (2016).

Structure and features of major defense industry companies

Aselsan

Aselsan was established by the Turkish Armed Forces Foundation (TAAF). After the Cyprus intervention in 1974. Turkey aimed to produce its own communications systems. Aselsan produced tactical radios and defence electronic systems for the Turkish Army. Aselsan expanded its product and customer spectrum. Aselsan's main business sectors are communications and information technologies; microelectronics, guidance and electro-optics; radar and electronic warfare systems; defence systems technologies; and, transportation, security, energy and automation. It has affiliates abroad in Azerbaijan, Kazakhstan, Jordan, the UAE and South Africa and employs more than 4,600 personnel. The company is working to reduce Turkey's dependence on foreign defence equipment. Aselan formed a joint venture based in Saudi Arabia in November 2015, with Taqnia Defense and Security Technologies (Fitch Ratings, 2018).

MKEK

The Mechanical and Chemical Industry Corporation (MKEK) is a key state-owned manufacturing enterprise in Turkey. MKEK was founded in 1832 and is the oldest Turkish land platforms company. It provides the Turkish Armed forces with ammunition, rockets, weapons explosives, chemical and pyrotechnics products. MKEK has 12 factories with over 7000 employees and exports to over 40 countries (Fitch Ratings, 2018). MKEK was established in 1950 as state-owned enterprise within the framework of restructuring of the General Directorate of Military Factories in order to develop the defense industry and meet the needs of a modern army and to work efficiently and profitably (Kurt, 2018)

There are many factories under the structure of MKEK. There are Materials Factories (Kırıkkale Steel Factory and Kırıkkale Brass Alloy Factory), Machinery Factories (Kırıkkale Rifle Factory, Ankara Weapon Factory) Chemical Factories (Elmadağ Barut Factory, Kırıkkale Gunpowder Factory, Silahtarağa Av and Fişek Factory) and Ammunition Factories (Kırıkkale Ammunition Factory, Ankara Fisek Factory: Kurt, 2018).

MKEK, which produces more than one thousand items for military and civil purposes, is focused on meeting the needs of Turkish Armed Forces for weapons and ammunition. MKEK is involved in various projects in land systems. The National Infantry Rifle (MPT-76) produces and supplies the TSK. MKEK participated in the Altay Project, which is the first Turkish Main Battle Tank It has an important place in the Turkish Defense Industry in cooperation with companies such as ASELSAN and Otokar in the T-155 and Panther projects (Kurt, 2018). Also, MKEK was placed at number 121 in 2017 and 131 in 2016 in Turkey's Top 500 Industrial Enterprises list (Istanbul Sanayi Odası, 2017).

Havelsan

Havelsan's main shareholder is the Turkish Armed Forces Foundation (TAFF). Havelsan's fields of activity are information technologies and information management, avionics, simulation, electronic warfare, naval combat systems, land defence systems and security. The main projects of the Turkish Air Force were undertaken by Havelsan. It implemented Lockheed Martin F-16 avionics depot-level maintenance, flight simulator maintenance, as well as repair and overhaul services. The company is controlled by the Turkish Air Force's electronics warfare programme simulation centre, together with the establishment and an operation of the electronics warfare test and training area. The Turkish airborne early warning and control programmes are also maintained by Havelsan. In March 2016, Havelsan opened another Cyber Defence Technology Center, which will focus on the production of 'local solutions' for deterring cyber attacks. This strengthens the organization's digital security activities in Turkey. In April 2016, Havelsan signed a cooperation deal with Ukraine's UkrOboronProm to jointly develop and manufacture radar equipment. (Fitch Ratings, 2018; Chapter 13).

Tübitak sage

Tübitak is the Scientific and Technological Research Council of Turkey. It has multiple branches specialising in electronics and cryptology, chemical, health and environmental research and defence industries. Tübitak – Sage was established in 1972 and its mission is to carry out research, design and development activities for defence systems. Its main products are missiles and bombs. Examples include stand off missile (SOM), precision guidance kit (HGK), penetrator bomb (NEB), wing assisted guidance kits (KGK) and thermal batteries (Fitch Ratings, 2018).

Turkish Aerospace Industries (TAI)

Turkish Aerospace Industries (TAI) is an important aerospace company aiming to reduce the country's dependency on foreign imports. With the decision of meeting the combat aircraft requirement of Turkish Air Force with F-16s, TAI Aerospace Industries, was established by Turkish and US partners in 1984 for a period of 25 years with the aim to realize the manufacture, systems integration and flight tests of F-16. TAI was restructured in 2005, with the acquisition of foreign shares by Turkish shareholders. Along with this restructuring, Turkish Aircraft Industries and TAI have merged under the roof of Turkish Aerospace Industries, Inc. (TAI) (Sezgin, 2017). It is now owned by the SSB (45.45%), the Turkish Armed Forces Foundation (54.49%) and the Turkish Aeronautical Association (0.06%). Its main strategic areas are: aerostructures, aircraft, helicopters, UAS and space systems. TAI-TUSAS will be the main contractor on a programme to manufacture 109 T-70 Black Hawk helicopters (designed by Sikorsky for the Turkish armed forces). The T-70 helicopter is Turkey's version of the S-70 Black Hawk International. Products of TAI include aerostructures (e.g.A400M, JSF/F-35, Bombardier C series), aircraft (e.g.jet trainer, fighter aircraft), helicopters (e.g. T129 attack helicopter) and space systems (TAI, 2018).

Otokar automotive

Otokar was founded in 1963 and is engaged in the production of military vehicles including land vehicles such as personnel carriers, anti-tank carriers, ambulances and fire vehicles (Kurt, 2018). In addition to the production for the automotive sector, it produces wheeled armored and tracked armored vehicles such as Akrep and Cobra for the defence industry. With the experience of licensed production of Land Rovers, Otokar began to turn to original designs in the early 1990s. The first domestic design product Akrep was exported to many countries. Akrep has been used in the armies of Morocco, Iraq, TRNC and Pakistan. The Cobra was put into inventory of 20 countries, including Azerbaijan, Bahrain, Bangladesh, UAE, Algeria, Georgia, Iraq, Maldives, Nigeria and Slovenia (Kurt, 2018). The Modern Tank Production Project (Altay) signed between Otokar and the Undersecretariat of Defense Industries in 2008 and the system qualification and acceptance tests were successfully completed in February 2017 (Otokar, 2017).

BMC industry and trade inc.

BMC started to produce military vehicles in 1999, although it was established already in the civilian automotive sector. BMC started to produce 1859 wheeled armored vehicles and tactical wheeled vehicles in 2008 as part of the tactical wheeled vehicle project carried out by the Undersecretariat for Defense Industries (Kurt, 2018). Its multi-purpose armored vehicles are Kirpi (Hedgehog) and Amazon MRAP (Mine Resistant Ambush Protected). Turkey's Presidency of Defence Industries (SSB) decided in March 2018 to start contract negotiations with BMC for the production of 250 Altay main battle tanks (MBTs) as well as the development of its powerpack (Jane's Defence Weekly, 2018)

Pendik Shipyard and Istanbul Shipyard

Pendik Shipyard performs maintenance and repair activities, ship design and construction for the operational needs of the Turkish naval forces. After 1999, it built 21 military ships including attack boats, mine hunting ships, coast guard vessels, corvettes and auxiliary class vessels.

The Istanbul Shipyard completed the Modernization Project of the SAR-35 Boats in the inventory of the Coast Guard Command. In 2011, a contract was signed between SSB and the Istanbul Shipyard for the construction of a submarine rescue mother ship (MOSHIP) and two rescue and backupsShips (KURYED). Within the scope of MOSHIP and KURYED contracts Technology Achievement Obligation Projects, R&D work has been started with MİLPER (Kurt, 2018).

Baykar makine

Baykar Machinery entered the aviation industry with its R&D activities in unmanned aerial vehicle technology. Baykar contributes to the technical infrastructure of the Turkish defense industry by producing leading systems and sub-systems in the field of unmanned aerial vehicle systems. The first unmanned aerial system of Baykar, designed and developed by Baykar, was included in the inventory of the Turkish Armed Forces in 2007. Bayraktar Mini UAV is also the first national UAV to be exported. As a result of its R&D activities, Baykar has put the TBF tactical class UAV system into production. This system reaches an altitude of 27,030 ft and a 24 hour 34 minute duration: it achieved two national aviation records for the highest altitude and longest flight time recorded in its class (Baykar, 2018)

FNSS

FMC – NUROL Defense Industry Inc. (FNSS) was established in 1987 with 51% of the shares owned by Nurol Holding and 49% by BAE Systems. A large number of armored combat vehicles in various forms were delivered to TSK. The vehicles produced have been bought by the UAE and Malaysia. Currently, FNSS continues its production activities in two overseas countries. An output of over 4,000 armored combat vehicles make it one of the world's leading organizations with more than 200 domestic subcontractors located all over the world (FNSS, 2018).

Roketsan

Roketsan was established in 1988 in order to meet the rocket and missile needs of the Turkish Armed Forces. The other purpose of establishing the company is to produce some part of the Stinger missile systems in Turkey. Roketsan designed and developed the TR-107 Rocket with a design range of 11 km and a TR-122 Rocket with 40 km range and the T-122 Sakarya Multi-Barrel Rocket Launcher (ACR) Weapon System. The first originally designed missile system – the Cirit missile – was delivered to the Turkish armed forces inventory in 2012. In 2014, Roketsan signed an agreement with Roketsan Lockheed Martin for a new generation of precision guided missile. Roketsan's main products are UMTAS (anti-tank missile system), OMTAS (Medium Range Anti-Tank Weapon System), TEBER Laser Guidance Kit, Hisar missiles etc (Roketsan, 2018)

Defense technologies engineering and trade inc. (STM)

STM, which has become one of the most important companies of the Turkish Defense Industry, provides system engineering, technical support, project management, technology transfer, logistic support services, software technologies and software development and maintenance of national computer centers for the Turkish Armed Forces and the Undersecretariat for Defense Industries. STM was established with the decision of the Defense Industry Executive Committee. STM, which has a 34% stake in SSB. It provides engineering services in areas such as project management, design activities, R&D activities in the fields of marine and air platforms, as well as activities in the fields of technology such as cyber security, command control systems, task systems and simulation (SSB, 2018).

Alp aviation

Alp Aviation was founded in 1998 and has a 20% share of Turkey's aviation exports and the company is Turkey's third largest exporter of aviation products. Alp Aviation produces flight critical/rotating components, assemblies and sub-systems belonging to Aerospace Industries. Alp Aviation exports its products to such companies as Lockheed Martin, Pratt & Whitney, Honeywell and Boeing, Pratt & Whitney Canada, Sikorsky and UTC Aerospace Systems. In addition, Alp Aviation makes an important contribution to the air platform and engine programs of companies like Black Hawk, Seahawk, Boeing and Airbus (Kurt, 2018).

Coşkunoz defense and aviation

Coşkunoz Defense and Aviation operates in Eskisehir and produces aircraft and helicopter bodies. Coşkunoz started production in 2006 with an output of more than 1,500 units. The company performs welding, assembly, integration, design and engineering services. In March 2015, it NATO and national security grade facility security certificates. By April 2015, the company produced aircraft and helicopter body and engine parts using precision machining method (Coşkunoz, 2018)

Recent developments and the future of the Turkish defence industry

Turkey has shown significant improvements in its defense industry capability after 2000 and this development continues at an increasing speed. The majority of conflicts in the world are very close to Turkey. This situation creates very high security threats for Turey. For this reason Turkey feels an obligation to ensure security of supply of defense. Therefore, it has made long-term plans for its defense industry. At the same time, Turkey also aims to increase the export of defense equipment in the future. Pakistan emerged as the largest importer of Turkish defense equipment during the period. Artillery accounted for the major defense exports during 2009–2013. Turkey's defense imports are expected to decrease in the near future. The US was the primary supplier of arms to Turkey. Aircraft were the major imported military hardware during 2009–2013. Turkey defense expenditure is expected to grow steadily in the future.

Turkey depends on the US for the supply of fighter aircraft but is having problems with the US. Therefore, it aimed to produce its own fighter aircraft. For this purpose, the British firm BAE Systems and Turkish Aerospace Industries (TAI) signed an agreement in January 2017 to collaborate on the development of a locally-produced fifth generation fighter jet for the Air Force. The multi-role Turkish Fighter aircraft will replace the F-16s of the Turkish Air Force, which will be taken out of service by 2030. Owing to procurement problems for air defense systems with NATO and US supply, Turkey plans to buy air defense system outside NATO countries. It negotiated with China about its air defense system, then decided to take the system from Russia. Turkey in the long terms plans to produce its own air defense system. In 2017, the European firm Eurosam signed an agreement with domestic companies Roketsan and Aselsan to develop long-range air and missile defence systems. In 2017, Turkey and Russia signed a US$2.5bn agreement to purchase Russia's most sophisticated anti-aircraft missile-defence system. Under this agreement, Turkey will receive two batteries of the system within a year, while two more will be produced domestically. Delivery of the S-400 missile defence system is facing rising opposition from the US, which could constrain the delivery of US manufactured defence equipment. Currently, delivery is planned for mid-2019.

The Turkish armed forces received its first F-35 fighters in June 2018 from US Lockheed Martin. However, further sales may be constrained by deteriorating relations with the US. The SSB started to work on the development of a new combat helicopter, the ATAK-2 which is expected to contain only locally-developed systems.

Turkey has some military agreements with Pakistan, Turkmenistan, Qatar, Indonesia, Algeria and Azerbaijan and Somalia. The Pakistan agreement includes air force pilot training exchange agreement and Aeronautical Complex (PAC) Kamrafor the procurement of 52 primary trainers, which will replace T-41D Mescalero and SF-260D trainers. Turkmenistan is reinforcing its maritime border forces with technical assistance from Turkey. The Qatar agreement includes the exchange of operational expertise and training, the development of military industries, the potential for the redeployment of joint troops in both countries when necessary and conducting joint military exercises. In 2016, Turkey and Qatar announced that they would open a joint military base in the Emirate. The Indonesian agreement on defence industry cooperation aimed at expanding defence trade and related industrial collaboration between the two countries. The Algeria agreement involves cooperation in research and development in the defence industry, production of military equipment and technical assistance in modernising those equipments. The agreement with Azerbaijan consists of a strategic partnership and mutual support. Both countries agree to support each other 'using all possibilities' in the case of a military attack against either of the countries. The agreement also includes upgrade of hardware for joint military operations, cooperation in military-technical areas, joint military exercises and training sessions.The Somalia agreement covers military training cooperation (Fitch Ratings, 2018).

In the sectoral strategy document of the defense industry of SSB covering the years 2018–2022, the objectives of SSB's Turkish defense industry companies are as follows: (i) establishing financing models to increase competitiveness in international markets; (ii) establishing a strategic perspective with an integrated approach in international cooperation; (iii) conducting studies to ensure maximum utilization of the incentives in the financing of marketing and (iv) support the defense industry's overseas promotion, business development and cooperation activities.

Some important development programmes of Turkish defence industry are the HGK inertial guidance kit with Aselsan, the ANKA medium-altitude, long-endurance unmanned aerial vehicle (UAV), the Bora-2 long-range missile, 20 mm high-explosive tracer tank gun ammunition with MKEK.the Gokdogan and Bozdogan air-to-air missiles, the Akinci armed unmanned aerial vehicle (UAV), the Hürkus-B turboprop trainer aircraft,a long-range air and missile defence system with domestic firms Aselsan and Roketsan SSB and French-Italian Eurosam. The Turkish-fighter project is a multi-role fighter aircraft being developed by TAI, with the support of BAE Systems, to replace the F-16s of the Turkish Air Force (out of service 2030) together with the development of the Atmaca anti-ship guided missile.

Concluding remarks

This Chapter has reviewed defense expenditures, defense procurement policies, the history of the Turkish defense industry and defense production structures. Turkey could not use the capability of its past defense industry. especially after the Second World War when there was a decline in the defense industry due to US military assistance. Although there were developments in the defense industry in the post-1980 period, the major leap was experienced in the post-2000 period. In this period, significant developments were observed in both industrial production and defense exports. First, developments in the aviation defense industry have emerged. The Turkish defense sector, which achieved a breakthrough in the post-2000 period, should also take some measures to ensure its sustainability. Despite the fact that many projects matured, the sector did not provide a mature platform in export markets. Major arms exporters in developed countries may block Turkey's arms exports in the defense and aviation sectors. The R&D and innovation capacity of the sector is mainly based on the requirements of the local market. When combined with import substitution policies in the sector, it can be considered as a weakness in terms of competitiveness in the global market. (Mevlutoglu, 2017). The lack of coordination and communication between the military and civil bureaucracy has recently disappeared. The potential of the Turkish defense industry depends on the development of a long-term and robust industrial policy and technology management strategy. The sector has a stable growth trend in terms of both local market and export sales. Turkey will develop in the near future as a new force in the defense industry.

References

Acan, Handan (2016) ARGE250, Türkiye'nin Ar-Ge Harcamaları En Yüksek 250 Şirketi [Turkey's R&D Expenditures, Top 250 Company]. www.turkishtimedergi.com/wp-content/uploads/2017/11/AR-GE-250-_-2016.pdf (Accessed 3 November 2018).

Baykar (2018) http://baykarmakina.com/hakkimizda/firma-profili/ (Accessed 3 November 2018).

Coskunoz (2018) www.coskunozholding.com/tr/sirketler/coskunoz-savunma-ve-hava cilik.html (Accessed 3 November 2018).

Defense News (2018) Top 100 for 2018. https://people.defensenews.com/top-100/ (Accessed 5 November 2018).

Fitch Ratings (2018) Turkey Defence & Security Report | 2018. fitchsolutions.com 10 Country Date Agreement.

FNSS (2018) www.nurol.com.tr/fnss-savunma-sistemleri-a-s (Accessed 3 November 2018).

Herschelman, Kerry (2018) Jane's Defence Weekly. www.janes.com/article/79595/turkey-selects-bmc-for-altay-mbt-and-engine-production 26 April 2018 (Accessed 3 November 2018).

International Institute for Strategic Studies (2017) The Military Balance. Institute for Strategic Studies.

Istanbul Sanayi Odası (2017) Türkiye'nin 500 Büyük Sanayi Kuruluşu [Istanbul Chamber of Industry, Turkey Top 500 Industrial Enterprises]. www.iso500.org.tr/500-buyuk-sanayi-kurulusu/2017/ (Accessed 3 November 2018).

Istanbul Sanayi Odası (2018), Türkiye'nin 500 Büyük Sanayi Kuruluşu [Istanbul Chamber of Industry, Turkey Top 500 Industrial Enterprises]. www.iso500.org.tr/500-buyuk-sanayi-kurulusu/2018/ (Accessed 3 November 2018).

Kizmaz, Efsun (2007) Turkish Defense Industry and Undersecretariat for Defense Industries. Department of International Relations Bilkent University unpublished MA thesis.

Kurt, Enes (2018) Türk Savunma Sanayii Tarihine Mikro Yaklaşım: Savunma Sanayii İşletmelerine Dair Bir Envanter ve Dönemselleştirme Çalışması (1836–2018), [Micro Approach to the Turkish Defense Industry: An Inventory and Periodızation Study in Defense Industry Enterprises (1836–2018)]. Yıldız Teknik Üniversitesi Sosyal Bilimler Enstitüsüunpublished MA thesis.

Mevlutoglu, Arda (2017) Commentary on Assessing the Turkish Defense Industry: Structural Issues and Major Challenges. *Defence Studies*, 17(3), 282–294.

NATO (2018) Information on Defence Expenditure. www.nato.int/cps/em/natohq/news_152830.htm (Accessed 3 November 2018).

Otokar (2017) Otokar Annual Report. www.otokar.com/en-us/investorrelations/financial results/AnnualReports/otokar_annualreport_2016.pdf (Accessed 3 November 2018).

Presidency of Defence Industries, SSB (2017) Yıllık Faaliyet Raporu 2017 [Annual Report 2017]. www.ssb.gov.tr/Images/Uploads/MyContents/V_20180301150913377290.pdf.

Presidency of Defence Industries, SSB (2018) Our Defence Industry. www.ssb.gov.tr/WebSite/contentlist.aspx?PageID=47&LangID=2 (Accessed 3 November 2018).

Roketsan (2018) Urun Katalogu [Product Catalog]. www.roketsan.com.tr/wp-content/uploads/2018/05/ProductCatalog-2018.pdf (Accessed 3 November 2018).

SASAD Performance Report (2017) Defence And Aerospace Industry Manufacturers Association Ankara – Türkiye www.sasad.org.tr/uploaded/Sasad-Performans-Raporu-2017.pdf (Accessed 3 November 2018).

SASAD Performance Report (2012) Defence and Aerospace Industry Manufacturers Asso-ciation Ankara www.sasad.org.tr/uploaded/Defense-and-Aviation-Industry-Performance-Report-2012.pdf (Accessed 3 November 2018).

Sezgin, Selami (1997) Country Survey X: Defence Spending in Turkey. *Defence and Peace Economics*, 8(4), 381–409.

Sezgin, Şennur (2017) Hava Savunma Sanayinin Ekonomik Analizi: Türkiye ve İngiltere Karşılaştırılması, [Economic Analysis of Aviation Industry: Comparing Turkey and the UK Nisan Kitabevi]. Ankara 1. Baskı 138 sayfa ISBN: 9786059393256.

SIPRI (Stockholm International Peace Research Institute) (2018) The SIPRI Military Expenditure Database. www.sipri.org/databases (Accessed 3 November 2018).

Turkish Aircraft Industries Corporation (TAI) (2018) Aircraft Indigenous Development. www.tai.com.tr/en/corporate/about-us (Accessed 3 November 2018).

Wiśniewski, Rafal (2015) Military-Industrial Aspects of Turkish Defence Policy. *Rocznik Integracji Europejskiej*, (9), 215–228.

World Military Expenditures and Arms Transfers WMEAT (2012) Arms Transfer Deliveries, 2005–2015. www.state.gov/t/avc/rls/rpt/wmeat/2012/index.htm (Accessed 3 November 2018).

World Military Expenditures and Arms Transfers WMEAT (2017) Arms Transfer Deliveries, 2005–2015. www.state.gov/t/avc/rls/rpt/wmeat/2017/index.htm (Accessed 3 November 2018).

18 The Israeli defense industry

Gil Pinchas and Asher Tishler

Introduction

The development of Israel's defense industry is closly related to Israel's security needs in the last century. Israel, established in 1948, a parliamentary democracy with a population of about 8.8 million in 2018, consisting of 75% Jews and 25% various minorities, of which 21% are Arabs.[1] Today, Israel is a developed country with an economy based mainly on technology industry, light industry, and various services. Israel's 2017 annual GDP and GDP per capita were $348 billion USD and $40,000 USD, respectively.[2] Its annual military expenditure in 2017 was about $20 billion USD (including about $4 billion US military aid), which amounts to about 5.7% of its GDP and about 12% of its government spending.[3] Since about 1985, Israel's government policy has been to increase the share of civilian services and gradually reduce the share of military expenditure in its GDP and government spending (Figure 18.1).[4] Despite this policy, Israel's share of defense expenditures in GDP is currently one of the highest in the world, due to Israel's specific geopolitical situation and, particularly, the on-going Arab-Israeli conflict.[5] The Arab side of the Arab-Israeli conflict includes, on and off, about three to ten Arab countries and several non-country entities, mostly terror organizations. This conflict, started when Israel was created in 1948, consists of endless political frictions and open hostilities, which have, thus far, included five major wars (in 1948, 1956, 1967, 1973, 1982), three major Israeli operations in Gaza, two major Palestinian uprisings (1987–1991, 2000–2005)[6] and numerous terror activities. The pattern of the Arab-Israeli conflict has shifted over the years, from a large-scale regional conflict between states to proxy warfare. One of the most dynamic characteristics of the conflict is the composition of the coalitions formed among Israel's military rivals. For example, Egypt, Jordan, Syria and Iraq took part in the 1967 Six Day War against Israel. Only Syria and Egypt fought against Israel in the 1973 Yom Kippur War. Only Hezbollah, with the active support of Iran and Syria, fought against Israel in the Second Lebanon War in 2006.

The nature of the Israeli-Arab conflict has undergone several major changes over the last seven decades. Egypt and Syria were Israel's main military rivals

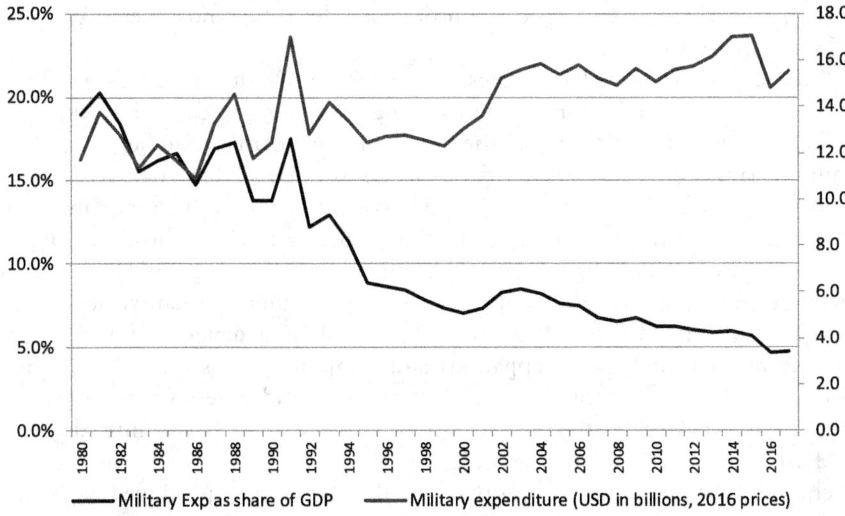

Figure 18.1 Israel's military expenditure (in 2016 USD) and its share of Israel's GDP, 1980–2017.

during 1948–1978. The 1978 Camp David accords shifted the state of hostility between Israel and Egypt into a "cold peace" between the two rivals, leaving Syria, which maintains a noticeably smaller military apparatus than Egypt, as Israel's main rival until about 2000.[7] At the beginning of the first decade of the 21st century, Syria maintained its position as Israel's main rival, due to a substantial increase in its military capablities at that time and its intensive support and use of its Lebanese proxy, Hezbolla.[8] In the last ten years, Iran and its proxies (Hezbolla and Hamas) have become Israel's principal rivals. The main drivers of the current conflict between Iran and Israel are the Iranian military nuclear program and the Syrian civil war, which have forced the Israeli government to allocate considerable financial and human resources to counter these threats.

Trends in Israel's defense expenditures and procurement

More than 55% of Israel's current defense budget is dedicated to expenditure on personnel (including wages, pension payments, rehabilitation of war veterans and payments to families of war casualties); about 8% of this budget is used for research and development (R&D) activities, and the rest is dedicated to procurement and maintenance.[9] Israel buys most of its defense goods from its local defense firms (including various types of vehicles, UAVs, missiles, communication equipment, integrative weapon systems, intelligence systems, etc.), while very expensive sophisticated platforms, such as fighter jets, submarines, small battle ships, and some cutting-edge missile systems, are purchased from highly developed countries like the USA and several Western European countries.

Like other developed countries, Israel's government is very attentive to its citizens' demands for ever-increasing security needs.[10] In addition, being a very small country at the heart of the volatile Middle East, with military rivals on all of its borders, means that Israel has to react within minutes to terror activities and land-based attacks, and instantaneously respond, often within seconds from the identification of a hostile activity, to all types of aircraft, mortar and missile attacks originating from its neighboring rivals. Consequently, to support a suitable security level and adequate quality of life for its citizens, Israel has to develop and maintain an exceptional intelligence apparatus and weapon systems that are effective for its particular security situation (very fast and effective response to numerous types of hostile activities). To achieve that, Israel must develop and maintain its own defense industry, since almost all of its intelligence technology, systems and procedures are developed and produced in-house (see Pecht and Tishler, 2015), and the unique weapon systems that it requires are unavailable elsewhere.

The Israeli government encourages cooperation among its defense firms in order to expand their sales worldwide and, at the same time, decrease commercial tensions among them. For example, the Iron Dome (a weapon system that defends against mortar and non-ballistic missiles) was developed by Rafael and Israel Aerospace Industries (IAI). Furthermore, the government encourages reciprocal procurement transactions by Israel's defense firms in foreign countries, such as the F-35 Helmet Mounted Display (HMD), supplied by RCEVS, a joint venture between Elbit Systems and Rockwell Collins. Note, however, that the government strictly regulates military exports through SIBAT, the Defense Export and Cooperation Division of Israel's Ministry of Defense (MOD), which actively promotes and controls Israel's defense and homeland security exports.

Israel places major emphasis on maintaining independent defense R&D capabilities. Its defense R&D is conducted by a triangle whose vertices are: the Directorate of R&D in the MOD (Mafaat), the technology as well as combat units of the Israeli defense forces (IDF), and Israel's defense firms. High-quality human capital and, consequently, high-quality R&D programs and the development of uniqe and exceptional weapon systems, are Israel's main advantages over its rivals (Kagan, Setter, Shefi and Tishler, 2010; Bar-El, Pecht and Tishler, 2018). The IDF's budget share on R&D activities has remained steady over time, at about 8% (see defense budget books published by the Israel Ministry of Defense, 2009–2012, Ben-Israel, 2001; Nevo and Shur-Shmueli, 2004). About 2% of the IDF's budget is allocated to basic and applied research activities.[11] Although Israel is a very small country, its defense R&D community has succeeded in developing exceptional state of the art weapon systems. According to Kagan et al. (2010), there are several reasons for this success. First, most of

Israel's citizens have some military background (through mandatory military service) and, due to the small number of Israel's engineering and computer science schools, the relationships between the IDF and Israel's defense firms are very close (Mintz, 1985; Dvir and Tishler, 2000). Second, most of the weapon systems development by Israel's defense firms is undertaken in close cooperation with the IDF, even when the IDF is not necessarily commited to purchase these systems. Third, it may be optimal for a small country with high-quality and commited human capital to develop very sophisticated and advanced military capabilities, which outperform the less risky conventional weapon systems (Setter and Tishler, 2006).

Finally, Lavie (2000) lists several characteristics of Israel's public procurement of (military and other) equipment and services: (1) it is very bureaucratic; (2) unless there is only one exclusive supplier that can produce the required product for Israel's Ministry of Defense (MOD), suppliers, including government-owned defense firms, must take part in a public tender in order to sell equipment and/or services to the Israeli government;[12] (3) the large share of defense in Israel's government budget has enabled the government to use it in support of non-defense objectives by directing, for example, some of the IDF's procurement to suppliers located in the periphery or in officially designated "developments zones" (more than $0.6 billion USD in 2016).[13] Clearly, this policy often conflicts with the policy of "least-cost sourcing" of Israel's defense budget.

Figure 18.2 describes Israel's defense budget outlays over the last 20 years.[14] The steady increase in the share of expenditure on personnel in the defense budget during the last decade, from 44% to 53%, was accompanied by a large decline in the budget share allocated to the procurement of defense goods, from 47% to 39% (including procurement from the USA and Western European countries). The budget share of military R&D has remained steady over time. This trend changed in 2016, when the IDF announced its Gideon Plan, a new multi-year operative and budget plan for 2016–2020. The Gideon Plan focuses on the implementation of structural reforms within the IDF, improved efficiency, and resource allocation changes (reducing personnel costs over the years, up to 2040, and increasing procurement and maintenance for IDF force buildup).[15] The Gideon Plan accounts for the new memorandum of understanding (MOU) between the USA and Israel, signed in 2016.[16] Under the new MOU, the US foreign military aid to Israel during 2019–2028 will be $3.3 billion USD per annum, plus an additional commitment of $0.5 billion USD per annum for missile defense assistance. The USA and Israel agreed, in the new MOU, to gradually discontinue by the end of 2027 Israel's Off Shore Procurement (OSP), an arrangement which has allowed Israel to spend 26.3% of its annual US military aid within Israel on non-US products.

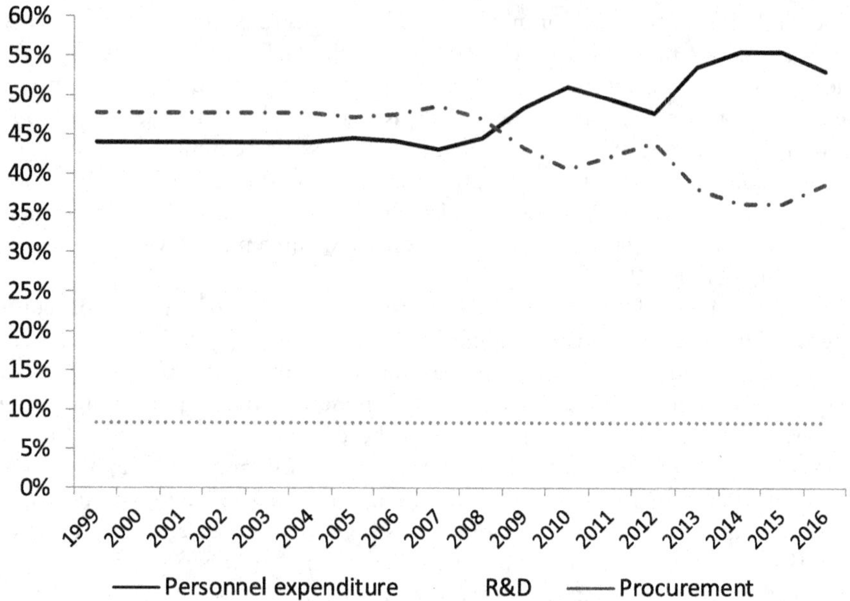

Figure 18.2 Israel's defense budget components (share in total defense budget), 1999–2016.

The Israeli defense industry

Background[17]

The Israeli defense industry was launched in the early 1920s. Its initial activities were focused on the production of weapons and ammunition to defend the small Jewish community from Arab attacks in pre-state Palestine. In 1933, the first industrial defense enterprise, the Israeli Military Industries (IMI), was established. It manufactured rifles, mortars, hand grenades and various types of ammunition.

Following Israel's War of Independence, the country's defense industry started to develop more rapidly due to the creation of new organizations, most of them government-owned:

- 1952: An R&D division was set up within the Ministry of Defense (MOD).
- 1953: Bedek was established for the purpose of maintaining and refurbishing aircraft. Later, it became the Israel Aircraft Industry (IAI).
- 1958: The Ministry of Defense's R&D division was reorganized as a separate entity, Rafael (the Armament Development Authority), which, over the years, evolved to become the country's main defense development organization.

- Several refurbishing and maintenance centers were established within the army for the purpose of maintaining armored and support vehicles. At a later stage, these centers specialized in the reconstruction and improvement of tanks and armored vehicles.

A few privately-owned defense firms were also founded in Israel during the 1950s:

- Soltam, specializing in manufacturing mortars and cannons, was established as a joint venture of Koor (a private firm) and a Finnish consortium.
- Tadiran was formed by the merger of two small privately-owned factories producing batteries and light bulbs.

The rapid growth of the Israeli economy that followed the 1967 Six Day War and the ensuing French embargo on arms sales to Israel at the end of the Six Day War (Sharaby, 2002; New York Times, 2010) had an enormous influence on the subsequent continuous growth of Israel's defense industry over the next two decades. In fact, the French embargo was the main reason for Israel's decision to develop its own arms industry. Rapid growth in the internal demand for weapon systems, particularly after the 1973 Yom Kippur War, and a tenfold increase in Israel's defense exports, sustained this growth. The number of employees in the Israeli defense industry tripled between 1967 and 1975, and increased by a further 50% between 1975 and 1985 (Lifshitz, 2011).

The slow-down in the growth of Israel's defense industry, which started in the mid-1980s, following the termination of IAI's program to develop the Lavi fighter jet,[18] turned into a severe crisis at the beginning of the 1990s, following the end of the Cold War and the signing of the peace treaties between Israel and several of its Arab neighbors. The reduction (in real terms) of the Israeli defense budget during the first decade of the 21st century also harmed the country's defense firms. However, the sales of Israel's defense firms have shown a steady, sometimes rapid, growth over the last decade, due to the rise in the world's military expenditure since 2002 (see the financial reports of Israel's main defense firms: IAI, Rafael, Elbit Systems, and IMI).

The scarcity of reliable macro and micro data on a country's defense industry is one of the main limitations in the assessment of its military capabilities and characteristics, in general, and arms races and defense industries, in particular. This phenomenon is clearly evident in countries involved in active arms conflicts like Israel, Syria, Egypt and Iran. The financial data of (public and private) defense firms is also scarce or unavailable, particularly for state-owned firms and/or defense firms that are not traded on the stock market. Defense firms that publish some data on their financial performance do not provide the breakdown of the data into specific items, such as sales to various countries, R&D projects, average wages, etc.

For the sake of consistency and transparency, we used various sources to obtain the data required for the evaluation of the trends and data in assessing

Israel's defense industry. However, only small amount of reliable data on Israel's defense industry is publicly available, and only for the past 10–20 years.

Overview

While most of the world's large defense firms are privately-owned, several major Israeli defense firms, such as Israel Aircraft Industry (IAI), Israel Military Industries (IMI) and Rafael (Israel), are fully or partially government-owned. The Israeli government is intimately involved in the country's defense industry, both as a major customer of weapon systems and military platforms, and as the owner of the three large defense firms. Procurement by the IDF (or, in some cases, by another government security agency) is (almost) a necessary condition for successfuly exporting an Israeli weapon system or military component. Clearly, the reputation of the Israeli defense apparatus is the main engine of Israel's defense industry exports of weapons systems and defense goods and services. Over the years, the close relationship between the IDF and Israel's defense industry facilitated the development of high-quality, effective and exclusive weapon systems, customized to the IDF's particular needs, and enhanced arms production processes by reducing development time and costs (Mintz, 1985; Swed and Butler, 2015).

The technological development path along which the Israeli defense industry has progressed is similar to that of other developed countries. It develops and utilizes a vast array of technologies, from computers and electronics to electro-optics, aeronautics, mechanical design and metal works, chemical engineering, software engineering and more. It has developed and produced various modern and sophisticated weapon systems and military platforms, like various types of unmanned airborne vehicles (UAVs), battle tanks (Merkava IV), armored personnel carriers (Namer, Eitan), air defense systems (Iron Dome, Arrow), space systems and satellites, missile boats, various types of air-to-air, air-to-ground and ground-to-ground missiles, communication and information systems, armored vehicles, autonomous vehicles, various types of sensors, cyberweapons and homeland security systems.[19]

Data and structure of Israel's defense industry

Currently, Israel's defense industry consists of about 600 firms (including small subcontractors which are part of the supply chain of large defense firms and various civilian firms), employing more than 45,000 employees. Israel's defense firms' overall sales were approximately $10.3 billion in 2017, 90% of which were for military equipment and services. About 95% of these sales belong to to the Big 4 defense firms – Elbit Systems, IAI, Rafael and IMI. Israel's defense firms' total sales during 2008–2017 are shown in Figure 18.3 below.[20]

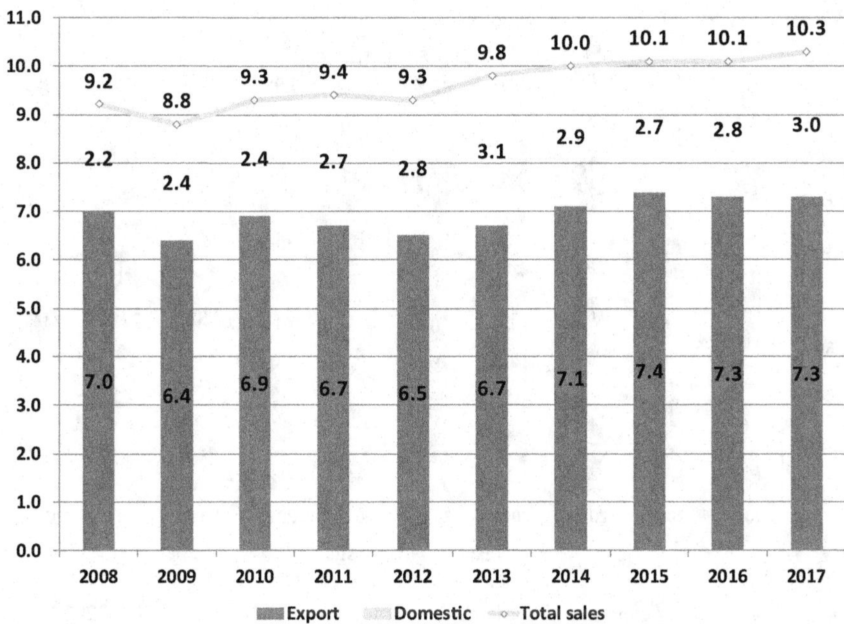

Figure 18.3 Total sales of Israel's defense industry: 2008–2017(US$ billion, 2015 prices).

Source: SIPRI yearbooks, 2009–2017, the Israeli defense firms' financial reports and websites, Pinchas (2018), and various newspaper publications.

Israel's defense industry exports more than 70% of its weapon system production, as shown in Figure 18.4. This phenomenon is unique to Israel, and is the consequence of the country's small size and its need for very high-quality and particular security needs. A considerably lower share of exports out of the total production of the defense goods is exhibited by the US, European and Russian defense industries (24%, 68% and 55%, respectively).

Israel's defense industry can be divided into three distinct groups of firms. The first group includes the three large government defense organizations: Israel Aerospace Industries (IAI), Rafael, and Israel Military Industries (IMI, which was further divided two years ago into two divisions: IMI Systems, which was sold to Elbit Sytems (see Reuters, 2018) and Tomer, which remains a government-owned firm, ensuring that some necessary and irreplaceable vital security interests of Israel remain in Israeli hands). The second group consists of Elbit Systems, a large, privately-owned defense firm, concentrating on the development and production of (almost exclusively) defense products and services. The third group consists of a large number of medium- and small-size privately-owned firms, most of which produce some defense products and services, in addition to civilian products. In addition, the IDF operates several

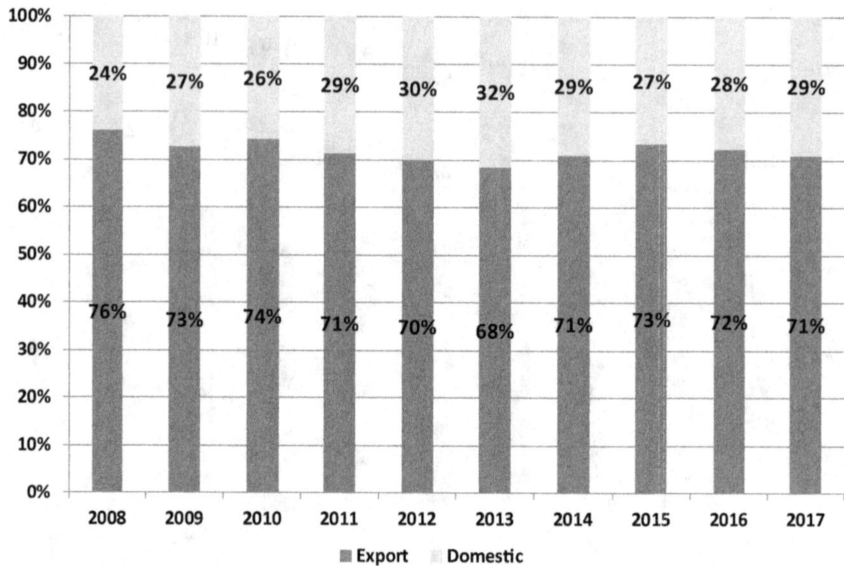

Figure 18.4 Shares of exports and domestic sales of Israel's defense industry: 2008–2017.

Source: SIPRI yearbooks, 2009–2017, the Israeli defense firms' financial reports and websites, Pinchas (2018), and various newspaper publications.

large refurbishment and maintenance centers that are part of its Division of Technology and Logistics. These centers maintain, develop and produce tanks, armored vehicles, aircraft, communication equipment and other support systems for the military. One large refurbishment center is dedicated to the production and assembling of Israel's Merkava battle tank and the Namer armored personnel carrier. The four major Israeli defense firms are among the largest industrial firms in Israel and appear among the 100 largest defense firms in the world (SIPRI Yearbook, various issues).

Israel's defense industry develops and utilizes a vast array of technologies and products. Table 18.1 presents the total sales, military sales, profits, share of exports in total sales, number of employees and main products and areas of expertise of Israel's major defense firms at the end of 2017. The lists of the main products of Israel's main defense firms show that a considerable share of their core production and R&D activities is similar, concentrating on the IDF's key needs in electronics, telecommunications, missiles, etc.

Although the major Israeli defense firms account for less than 3% of the worldwide arms sales in 2017, they are fiercely competitive with each other. This is a very sensitive issue, especially in relation to weapon systems development and orders to the IDF and abroad, since these firms are competing on prices among themselves (Shefi and Tishler, 2005). Thus, the Israeli

Table 18.1 Characterization of Israel's main defense firms in 2017

Firm	*Employees*	*Total sales ($ million)*	*Military sales ($ million)*	*Profits ($ million)*	*Exports ($ million)*	*Exports as % of total sales*	*Gross profits ($ million)*	*Marketing and selling expenses ($ million)*	*R&D ($ million)*	*Main products and areas of expertise*
Elbit Systems	12,781	3,378	3,262	241	2,635	78%	998	280	265	Military aircraft and helicopter systems, helmet mounted systems, commercial aviation, aero structures, unmanned aircraft systems (UAS), communication systems, C4I systems, land vehicle systems and upgrades, electro-optics systems, intelligence, surveillance and reconnaissance, homeland security systems, training & simulation, naval systems, electronic warfare and sigint, cyber systems
IAI	14,857	3,520	2,536	81	2,851	81%	538	90	182	Business jets, unmanned air systems (UAS), radars, mission aircraft and AEW aircraft, elint/esm, sigint and comint, anti-tactical ballistic missiles (ATBM), missiles and smart weapons, satellites, ground stations and space launchers, upgrading of military aircraft and helicopters, maintenance and conversion of commercial aircraft, including conversion to aerial refueling, navigation systems, EO payloads, communications
Rafael	7,624	2,258	2,258	124	1,073	48%	499	90	182	Air defense systems, air to air missiles, air to surface missiles, electronic warfare, C4ISR, tactical precision guided weapons, fuel-air explosive (FAE) minefield clearing, active (soft- and hard-kill) protection solutions, remote control weapon stations, acoustic and electro-optical firearms detection and passive and reactive armor, missile technologies, related to air-to-air, air-to-surface, surface-to-air, naval and anti-tank /multi-purpose missile, cyber systems

(*Continued*)

Table 18.1 (Cont.)

Firm	*Employees*	*Total sales ($ million)*	*Military sales ($ million)*	*Profits ($ million)*	*Exports ($ million)*	*Exports as % of total sales*	*Gross profits ($ million)*	*Marketing and selling expenses ($ million)*	*R&D ($ million)*	*Main products and areas of expertise*
IMI (since 2014)	2,900	500	500		270	54%				Artillery and tank ammunition, air-to-ground ammunition, small caliber ammunition, infantry systems and munitions, homeland security, rocket systems, ballistic armor, armored vehicle protection suits, active protection systems, remote controlled weapon stations, tank guns, inbore subcaliber training devices, bridging
Total of Big 4	**38,162**	**9,656**	**8,556**	**446**	**6,829**	**71%**				
Other firms	2,500	600	600		450	75%				
Total	**40,662**	**10,256**	**9,156**	**446**	**7,279**	**71%**				

Source: SIPRI yearbooks, 2009–2017, financial reports of the firms, December 31, 2017; Websites of the firms; various newspaper publications (subjects: IAI, IMI, Rafael, Elbit Systems, IWI, Magal, Palsan Sasa, Rabintex, Aeronautics, FMS).

MOD and Ministry of Finance (MOF) have been intent on regulating the competition among Israel's defense firms. For example, in 2013, the Israeli MOD froze a major defense contract bidding process in Poland for the sale of UAVs, due to a widely publicized dispute between two Israeli firms (Haaretz, 2015). In 2015, the head of Rafael was suspended from his job (Haaretz, 2015), following several incidents that involved intensive competition among Israeli defense firms over foreign contracts. Another aspect of the competition among these firms became apparent at the end of 2017 when during renewed talks to sell IMI to Elbit Systems, the managements of IAI and Rafael expressed concerns that the acquisition of IMI by Elbit Systems would give Elbit Systems too much power and control over Israel's defense industry.

The fierce competition among Israeli defense firms is likely to intensify during the next decade, due to the new memorandum of understanding (MOU) between the USA and Israel that was signed in 2016.[21] The OSP arrangement under the new MOU is likely to increase Israel's dependence on US defense goods, since it will drive Israel's larger defense firms to establish new partnerships with US firms in order to exploit the US aid to Israel, and expand their exports to compensate for lost sales to the IDF. Thus, although the new OSP arrangement is likely to intensify the competition among Israel's defense firms, as Pinchas (2018) shows it will not change Israel's welfare relative to that under the existing MOU due to the trade-off between the expanding exports and the lost sales. Nevertheless, the new OSP agreement may harm small- and moderate-size Israeli defense firms, as well as firms that are part of Israel's supply chain of its major defense firms, which rely on production and sales of the large Israeli defense firms.

Performance of Israel's major defense firms

As Israel's defense firms were built to serve a small country and, hence, a small military apparatus relative to those of the USA, UK, France and Russia, their R&D, production, and marketing activities are designed to export a large share of their products, in addition to serving the particular needs of the IDF.

To better understand the performance, strengths and weaknesses of Israels defense industry, we start by assessing several key characteristics of the Big 4 (Elbit Systems, IAI, Rafael and IMI).[22] Figures 18.5 and 18.6, depicting the sales of the Big 4 during 1990–2017, exhibit a steady increase in the sales of three out of the four main defense firms (IMI is the exception) through the first decade of the 21st century (during the operations of the USA and its allies in Iraq and Afghanistan), and the relative stability of these sales throughout the last decade (following the end of the operations of the USA and its allies in Iraq and Afghanistan and the withdrawal of most of their troops from these countries). More specifically, there is a dramatic increase in Elbit Systems' sales between 1996 and 2009, a steady increase in the sales of Rafael since 2005, and a steady decline in the sales of IMI, which is focusing on

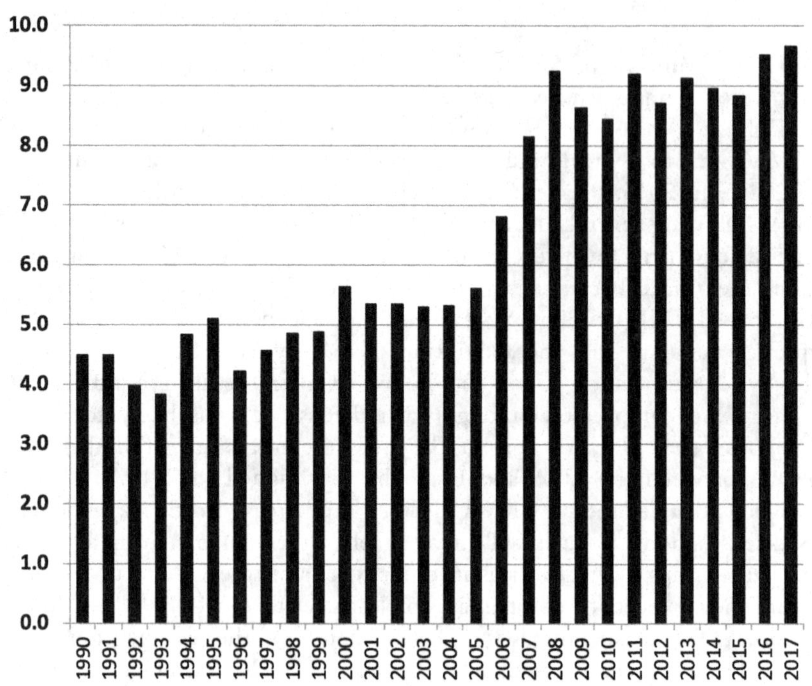

Figure 18.5 Aggregate annual sales of Israel's Big 4 (million US$, 2014 prices).

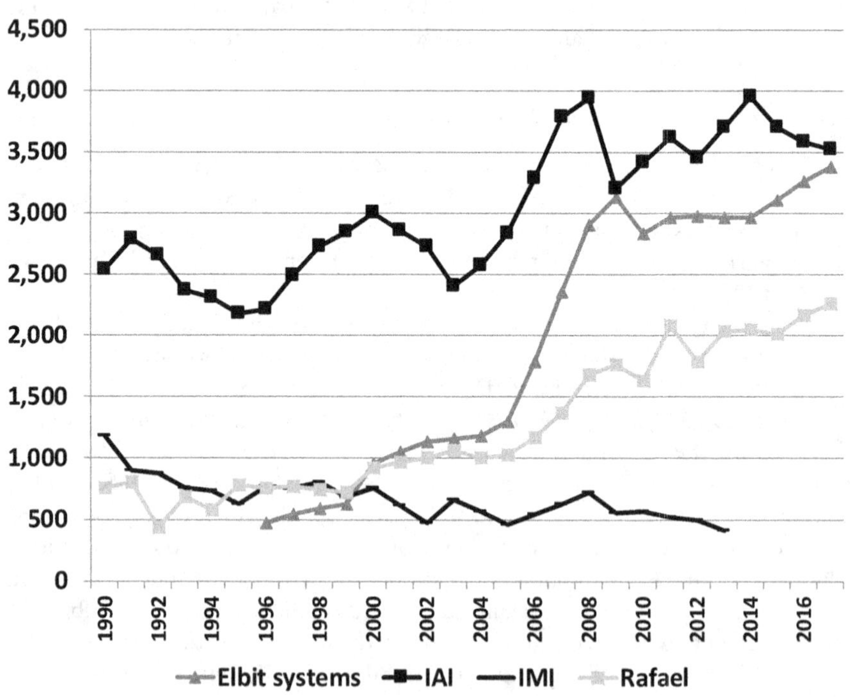

Figure 18.6 Annual sales of each of Israel's Big 4 (million US$, 2014 prices).

more traditional weapon systems, compared to those of Rafael, IAI and Elbit. The Big 4 profits during 1990–2017 are presented in Figure 18.7. Rafael and Elbit were profitable throughout most of the last two decades, while IAI exhibited a dramtic decline in its profits during the last decade, and IMI shows a continuous trend of losses throughout 1990–2017.

The financial data of IAI, Rafael and Elbit, for 2008–2017, summarized in Table 18.2, highlight some of the main differences between government-owned and privately-owned defense firms. The data on gross profits, R&D, and marketing and selling expenses during 2008–2017 demonstrate that the privately-owned Elbit Systems is more profitable (by a factor of 1.5–2) and spends more on marketing (by a factor of 2–3) than the government-owned IAI and Rafael. Elbit Systems' shares of R&D and marketing and selling expenses in sales are similar to those of large defense firms in developed countries (e.g., in 2016, BAE Systems spent 7.4% of its revenues on R&D activities; see BAE Systems 2017 Annual Report). It is interesting to observe that the privately-owned Elbit Systems spends a higher share of its sales on R&D than the government-owned IAI, while Rafael, also a government-owned firm, and Elbit Systems spend a similar share of their sales on R&D. This can be explained by the particular role of Rafael in Israel's security system. Originally established as a research and development authority, Rafael continues to play the role of an R&D center (laboratory) in addition to that

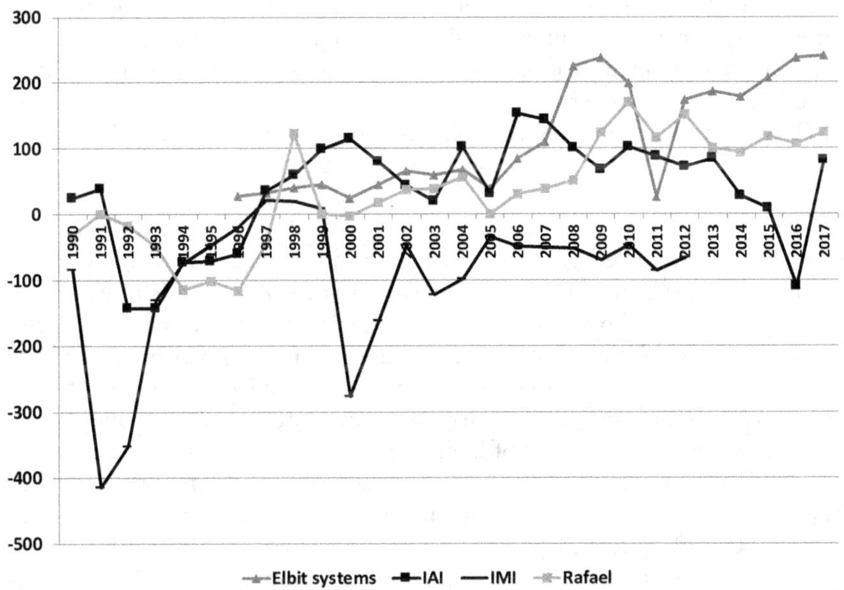

Figure 18.7 Profits of each of Israel's Big 4 (million US$, 2014 prices).

Table 18.2 Gross profits, R&D and marketing and selling expenses of Elbit Systems, IAI, and Rafael (percent of sales)

Year	*Gross profit*			*Marketing and selling expenses*			*Research and development*		
	Elbit Systems	*IAI*	*Rafael*	*Elbit Systems*	*IAI*	*Rafael*	*Elbit Systems*	*IAI*	*Rafael*
2008	29.1%	14.2%	20.8%	7.5%	2.0%	4.3%	7.0%	3.5%	6.6%
2009	30.0%	15.1%	21.9%	8.9%	2.4%	3.8%	7.7%	4.2%	7.3%
2010	29.9%	14.5%	20.2%	8.6%	2.3%	4.3%	8.8%	4.4%	7.8%
2011	26.0%	15.1%	21.7%	8.4%	2.3%	4.7%	8.6%	4.5%	7.0%
2012	28.2%	15.2%	22.8%	8.4%	2.7%	5.2%	8.1%	4.7%	7.7%
2013	28.2%	14.3%	20.0%	8.1%	2.4%	4.0%	7.5%	4.9%	7.6%
2014	27.9%	14.9%	22.7%	7.3%	2.6%	4.1%	7.7%	4.3%	7.4%
2015	28.9%	13.3%	21.4%	7.7%	2.6%	3.7%	7.8%	4.8%	7.0%
2016	29.4%	13.3%	20.9%	8.3%	2.7%	3.9%	7.8%	4.6%	7.2%
2017	29.5%	15.3%	22.1%	8.3%	2.6%	4.0%	7.8%	5.2%	8.1%
Avarage	**28.7%**	**14.5%**	**21.4%**	**8.1%**	**2.4%**	**4.2%**	**7.9%**	**4.5%**	**7.4%**

Source: SIPRI yearbooks, 2009–2017, Israel Government Companies Authority (2018), IAI, Rafael, and Elbit Systems financial reports (2008–2017) and websites.

of an arms producer. Attempting to maximize profits, or market value, privately-owned defense firms seem to have a greater incentive than government-owned defense firms to produce goods and services in the quantity and variety which consumers prefer (Bishop, Kay and Mayer, 1994) and, thus, are more export-oriented than government-owned defense firms and rely on a wide range of customers.

The following section describes and assesses each of Israel's Big 4 firms.

Elbit systems[23]

Elbit Systems, the largest privately-owned defense firm in Israel, has exhibited a dramatic increase in its sales over the last 15 years. About 75% of its sales are exported. The data show that Elbit's share of sales to the IDF was 22% in 2017 and its shares of sales to North America and Asia Pacific, which are the firm's leading markets, are similar to those of the IDF. The wide distribution of Elbit's revenues across the world markets makes it immune to regional demand shocks.

Most of Elbit's sales consist of high-technology products in the areas of airbone systems (in the late 1990s and the beginning of the first decade of the 21st century Elbit invested heavily in developing various types of airborne systems), C4ISR systems, and land systems. The share of Elbit's sales of electro-optic sytems has been declining since 2013. Among its well known products are: the Hermes 900/450/90 UAVs, helmet mounted systems for aircraft, and the Dominator suite (an integrated warrior combat suite).[24]

The increase in Elbit's sales during the last several years has been accompanied by a slight reduction in its labor force (about 4% from 2011 to 2015). Elbit's sales per employee have been increasing since 2010, which is a good indicator of the production efficiency of the firm. Its revenues have been steady or increasing over time, particularly during the last five years, following its acquisition of several small Israeli defense firms. In 2018, Elbit finalized the acquisition of IMI, merging IMI's activities with those of Elbit. Increasing the efficiency of the merged production lines and supply chain, and improving the R&D process and marketing cost structure of the former IMI divisions are the major challenges that Elbit Systems will face over the next several years.

Israel Aerospace Industries (IAI)[25]

The largest government-owned defense firm in Israel, IAI's sales consist of defense and commercial products and services in the areas of air, space, land, sea, cybersecurity, and homeland security. Its sales of commercial airbone products and services have been declining in the last several years. Some of IAI's well known products are the AMOS communication satellites, the Heron UAVs, the Arrow 3 missile systems, and the Naval Barak 8 missile system.[26]

Following the several crises that it experienced in the early 1990s, due to the worldwide decline in defense budgets, IAI initiated a re-organization process to improve its profitability once the world demand for weapon systems started to rise at the end of the 1990s. This resulted in positive, but volatile, profitability at the beginning of the first decade of the 21st century, followed by a sharp decline that culminated in a painfull loss in 2016. The current downward trend in IAI's profits has been a cause for concern and, in response, the firm initiated another re-organization process in 2017 to improve its efficiency by reducing its labor force (*inter alia*, by increasing the number of its retirees).

About 81% of IAI's revenues come from exports and, in contrast to the other major Israeli defense firms, some of its products ae sold to civilian markets.[27] However, during the last five years the share of civilian sales in its total sales declined to about 13%. At the same time, IAI has increased its volume of sales in electronics (radar systems, electronic warfare products, and communications systems), space products, and various missile categories, which accounted for more than 50% of IAI's sales in 2015.

IAI's military sales have been steadily increasing since 2002, reaching about $3 billion in 2017, and together with its declining labor force (from 17,200 employees in 2007 to about 14,850 in 2017) it has succeeded in increasing its sales per employee to about $230,000 during the last three years. Nevertheless, to stabilize (or increase) its revenues and increase its profits to a reasonable level in the next decade, when the new MOU between Israel and USA becomes effective (2019–2028), IAI will have to expand its exports markets and improve its production efficiency by reinforcing and improving its R&D activities, streamlining its labor force and further reducing its labor and other costs.

Rafael[28]

The decline in the worldwide defense budgets during the 1990s is the main reason for Rafael's negative profits during that period. However, its profits have been positive and on the rise since 2000. The three main reasons for this change are: (1) the increase in military expenditure worldwide since 2002; (2) the 2002 incorporation of Rafael (from a division in the MOD) into a government firm; (3) the growing demand for air defense systems and Rafael's successful development of the Iron Dome system following the Second Lebanon War in 2006.[29] Rafael's sales consist of a diversified array of innovative air systems, missiles, naval systems, ground and underwater weapon systems, and various space systems.

In contrast to Elbit Systems and IAI, a major share of Rafael's sales derives from the domestic market (about 52% in 2017). This trend is expected to continue in light of Israel's growing demand for the Iron Dome and other types of missile interceptors, an area in which Rafael excels. The steady increase of Rafael's sales during the last several years has been accompanied by a substantial increase in the number of its employees – an increase of about 30% from 2008 to 2017. Yet, Rafael's sales per employee have increased by about 14% since 2008 to about $296,000 in 2017.

It is very likely that Rafael will further increase its production, sales, exports and profits in the next decade, due to its unparalleled success in developing and producing several types of missile defense systems (see Pecht, Tishler and Weingold, 2013, on the Iron Dome and David's Sling). It should be noted also that Rafael is excelling in developing, producing and selling various other defense systems for the IDF and several foreign countries such as the USA, Romania, and Poland.[30] Other well known Rafael products are the Trophy system (active protection for tanks and armored vehicles) and the Python 5 (air to air missile).[31] Due to its success in various R&D projects during the last 10–15 years, it is also likely that Rafael will continue to receive sizeable grants from the Israeli MOD to further its R&D efforts in the areas of electronics, missiles and air defense systems. Nevertheless, like IAI, the major challenge for Rafael is to expand its export sales in the coming decade in order to maintain stability in its revenues and profits, particularly when the new agreement on OSP between USA and Israel becomes effective.

IMI[32]

IMI, which focuses on traditional, but modern, weapon systems, has experienced enormous losses during the last two decades. In fact, it did not succeed in modifying most of its products and services or adapt to the dramatic changes in the technologies and uses of today's weapon systems. IMI is the sole producer of some weapon systems and munitions that are essential to the IDF's operations, but cannot, for various reasons, be exported and, consequently, are the main reason for its losses. To guarantee its continued existence, the government has been subsidizing IMI and the firm has dramatically reduced the number of its employees during the last 20 years.

IMI specializes in artillery and tank ammunition, air-to-ground ammunition, rocket systems, ballistic armor and active protection systems. Well known products that it produces are EXTRA (extended range artillery rocket systems), 105/120 mm tank shells, LYNX (an autonomous multi-purpose rocket and missile launching system).[33]

The lack of breakthrough innovation and the absence of new product lines and new markets abroad are the main reasons for IMI's dramatic reduction in sales and exports during the last 20 years, which have driven it to the brink of bankruptsy. The government's options for improving IMI's finances have been as follows: (1) privatization, which includes safeguarding the nation's interests (by establishing procedures to ensure that foreign ownership of several of IMI's privatized production lines do not compromise Israel's security); (2) merging the financially weaker divisions of IMI into Rafael, IAI or Elbit; (3) reorganization of the entire Israeli defense industry, including major cuts in the number of the industry's employees.

In January 2012, the Israeli government decided to study and assess a possible privatization of IMI that would include processes to safeguard the country's security interests. Disagreements between IMI's labor union and Israel's Ministries of Defense and Finance prevented the completion of this initiative. An attempt to merge IMI into Rafael was negotiated in 2010 (Globes, 2010), but failed to materialize. In 2014, the Israeli government decided to divide IMI into two divisions, one (IMI Systems) to be sold to Israeli defense firms and the second (Tomer) to continue to operate as an independent government-owned firm, ensuring that several production lines, although losing money, would continue to produce vital supplies of munitions for the IDF. In 2018, after several years of unsuccessful attempts to arrive at a satisfactory arrangement, and following the approval of Israel's antitrust agency (Reuters, 2018), the Israeli government sold IMI Systems to Elbit Systems for $523 million (Globes, 2017). As noted, the merger of IMI's activities into Elbit Systems is a major challenge for Elbit.

The future challenges for Israel's defense industry

Preserving a high level of national security is one of the most important goals of Israel's government. The increasingly volatile nature of the Middle East, the autocratic regimes in the Moslem world, and the inherent difficulties in moving forward with a peace process between Israel and the Palestinians suggests that Israel will have to rely on a strong, innovative and viable military apparatus for at least several decades. Consequently, Israel's defense industry will likely remain large, modern, and, most of all, very innovative, with an emphasis on high-quality human capital and breakthrough innovation. This is ever truer in the light of the current development of the Iranian nuclear program and the establishment of the coalition among Iranian, Syrian and Hezbollah forces on Syrian territory in 2014–2018, which has increased the tensions and accelerated the arms race between Israel and its current military rivals.

The main challenges for Israel's defense industry in the next 10–50 years are as follows.

1. **The new MOU between the USA and Israel.** The gradual elimination of OSP (which will end in 2027) will require Israel's defense firms and their supply chain (firms that sell components to Israel's defense firms) to channel more resources into marketing and market-developing activities in order to expand their exports and find new markets for their products. To efficiently use the US financial aid to Israel, Israel's defense firms will have to establish partnerships and open new production lines in the USA and/or move existing production lines from Israel to the USA. Both of these processes are likely to lead to layoffs of Israeli employees, particularly in small- and medium-size defense firms.
2. **Maintaining technological leadership.** The Israeli defense industry is characterized by the production of high-quality, modern and sophisticated products in the following areas: missiles, missile defense systems (Iron Dome, David's Sling, the Arrow weapon system, Trophy, and more), unmanned aircraft systems, radar systems, electro-optic systems, precision guided munitions, integrative and command and control systems, electronic warfare and more. To be able to maintain their leadership role in these areas and successfully compete with the world's giant defense firms (i.e., with the expanding activities of American and European firms in the world markets), Israel's defense firms must continue to reinforce their R&D investments, recruit and maintain high-quality human capital, and further improve their close connections with Israel's military apparatus.
3. **Increasing cooperation among Israel's defense firms.** As mentioned above, there is intense competition among the three major Israeli defense firms on foreign as well as local defense contracts. In view of the globalization of the arms industry, the fast-increasing costs of production and technology development, it is essential for Israel's defense firms to cooperate, rather than compete, with each other on defense contracts for the IDF and abroad.
4. **Deciding on the optimal structure of Israel's defense industry.** Israel's defense firms compete with many much larger defense firms in the USA and Europe in most markets around the world, as well as in Israel. The intense competition in the world market raises questions about the appropriate structure of Israel's defense industry. Should it be totally privatized or not? Should the number of major Israeli defense firms be three, like today, or should this number be reduced to one or two, or increased to four or five. Finding the right answers to these questions is vital to Israel's security.

We conclude this study with an assessment of the most advantageous structure of Israel's defense industry. Pinchas (2018) developed and applied several (game theoretic) models that describe how Israel's social welfare and national security are affected by the country's economic characteristics and its defense industry's main features (ownership type, size and structure). In evaluating these models he considered four types of interactions: (1) among arms-producing countries; (2) among the world's main defense firms; (3) between two (and possibly more) countries, which are involved in an arms race; and (4) between two types of weapon systems (platforms, and all other). Pinchas applies these models to the Israeli-Syrian/Iranian arms race.

First, Pinchas (2018) shows that a government ownership of the defense industry would lead to somewhat higher levels of social welfare, civilian expenditures and security than private ownership. In addition, Israel's defense firms will have to increase their exports over the next several years in order to maintain the effectiveness of their production, as well as their revenues and profits. Since Israel's privately-owned defense firm is more export- and marketing-oriented, and is more cost efficient relative to the government-owned defense firms, it seems that Israel's defense industry will likely gain higher profits in the future under a regime of wholly privately-owned defense firms. Overall, from the viewpoint of the government and the defense industry, it seems that a privately-owned industry will lead to higher, albeit only by a small amount, level of overall benefits to Israel than a government-owned defense industry.

Second, the small size of Israel's defense firms relative to their main competitors in the USA and Europe has profound effects on their production and marketing cost structure. In addition, the fact that Israel is a small country with a military apparatus that is small relative to those of the USA, UK, France and Russia, forces Israel's defense firms to export about 70% of their production (in contrast to the 20–25% of most of their giant rivals). Hence, private Israeli defense firms which are likely to be more efficient and use more cost-effective production and marketing procedures than government-owned defense firms have some though not much of an advantage in this comparison.

Finally, the results of Pinchas (2018), like those of Golde and Tishler (2004) and Shefi and Tishler (2005), support the claim that a lower level of concentration of Israel's defense industry will likely lead to higher aggregate profits by Israel's defense industry.[34]

Notes

1 Israel Central Bureau of Statistics (2018a).
2 OECD online database, 2018, The World Bank: online database, 2017.
3 SIPRI military expenditure online database (2018).
4 SIPRI military expenditure online database (2018). Israel Central Bureau of Statistics (2018b), Israel's Ministry of Finance budget online database (2018).
5 SIPRI military expenditure online database (2018), The Military Balance Reports, 1998–2015.
6 See Laqueur and Schueftan (2016), Harms and Ferry (2017), Rabinovich (2011) and the timeline of the Israeli-Palestinian conflict in Wikipedia.
7 See Rabinovich (2011).

8 The Military Balance Report (1998–2015).
9 Israel Ministry of Defense: Israel defense budget, 2009–2018 (unclassified books) and Israel Ministry of Finance budget online database, 2018.
10 On this issue see, for example, The Marker (2018) and Shabtay and Tishler (2014). Note that Israel's GDP per capita in 2017 (about $40,000) is on par with that of the UK and France, and higher than those of Japan and Italy.
11 Israel Ministry of Defense: The committee for reviewing the defense budget, priorities and streamlining (2012).
12 In recent years, public criticism of single supplier procurement has increased dramatically, forcing the MOD to be more transparent and bureaucratic than in the past. See, for example, the criticism on the procurement process of the IDF's new ground force cannon, which was awarded to Israel's Elbit Systems via the channel of a single supplier with no international tender (Haaretz, 2017a), Haaretz (2017b).
13 Israel Ministry of Defense (2012a). www.mod.gov.il/Society_Economy/Pages/economic_support.aspx
14 The data were obtained from the Israeli Ministry of Finance budget database and the defense budget publications of the Israeli Ministry of Defense. There are no public data on Israel's defense budget components before 1999. The latest year with official data on Israel's defense budget outlays is 2016.
15 Israel Ministry of Defense: Israel defense budget, 2016–2018 (unclassified publications).
16 MOU (2016).
17 This section is based on the PhD thesis of Gil Pinchas (2018).
18 Clarke and Cohen (1986).
19 Details are available in SIPRI Yearbook (2013), Dvir and Tishler (2000), Haaretz (2018) and the financial reports of IAI, Rafael and Elbit Systems.
20 Data sources are SIPRI yearbooks, 1990–2017, SIPRI arms industry online database, the Israeli defense firms' financial reports and websites, Pinchas (2018), and various newspaper publications. Public data on the sales of Israel's defense industry are unavailable.
21 MOU (2016).
22 Data sources for these assessments include: SIPRI yearbooks, 1990–2017, SIPRI arms industry online database, Israel Government Companies Authority (2018), the financial reports and websites of the firms.
23 Data sources for this assessment are: SIPRI yearbooks, 1990–2017, SIPRI arms industry online database, Elbit Systems' financial reports.
24 See Janes (2018), JPOST (2016), ISRAELDEFENSE (2018).
25 Data sources for this assessment are: SIPRI yearbooks, 1990–2017, SIPRI arms industry online database, Israel Government Companies Authority (2018), and IAI's financial reports.
26 Globes (2018a), Globes (2018b), Ynet (2018a).
27 IAI's sales to civilian markets include business jets, primary aerostructures and landing gear, servo control and actuator systems. In addition, IAI supplies helicopter and fixed wing crashworthy seats to manufacturers around the world.
28 The sources of data in this assessment include: SIPRI yearbooks, 1990–2017, SIPRI arms industry online database, Israel Government Companies Authority (2018), and Rafael's financial reports.
29 Iron Dome is a mobile all-weather air defense system. It is designed to intercept and destroy short-range rockets, mortar and other artillery shells fired from distances of 4 to 80 kilometers, with trajectories that would take them into populated areas. The Iron Dome was declared operational and initially deployed on March 27, 2011. By November 2012, it had successfully intercepted more than 400 rockets.
30 Calcalist (2018), Ynet (2018b), Globes (2018c).
31 Shapir (2013), Calcalist (2018).

32 Data sources for this section are: SIPRI yearbooks, 2009–2017, Israel Government Companies Authority (2018), IMI financial reports, IMI website, and various newspaper publications on IMI.

33 Ynet (2017), Globes (2002).

34 Note, however, that Shefi and Tishler (2005) show that Israel's net defense costs (its government expenditures on defense minus the profits of its defense industry) are minimal when it has only one or two defense firms. Thus, Israel is likely to gain from a consolidation of its defense industry, similarly to the consolidation that took place in the USA and Western Europe during the 1990s.

References

Bar-El, R., Pecht, E. and Tishler, A. (2018). "Human capital and national security", *Defence and Peace Economics*. DOI: 10.1080/10242694.2018.1485088.

Ben-Israel, I. (2001). "Security, technology and the future battlefield". In H. Golan (ed.), *Israel's Security Web*. Tel Aviv: Ma'aracot.

Bishop, M., Kay, J. and Mayer, C. (1994). "Introduction: Privatization in performance". In M. Bishop, J. Kay and C. Mayer (eds.), *Privatization and Economic Performance* (pp. 1–14). Oxford: Oxford University Press.

Calcalist (2018). www.calcalistech.com/ctech/articles/0,7340,L-3741173,00.html

Clarke, D. L. and Cohen, A. S. (1986). "The United States, Israel and the Lavi fighter", *Middle East Journal*, 40(1), 16.

Dvir, D. and Tishler, A. (2000). "The changing role of the defense industry in Israel's industrial and technological development", *Defevse Analysis*, 16(1), 33–52.

Financial reports of Israeli defense firms (2008–2017). "Websites of the defense firms".

Globes (2002). https://en.globes.co.il/en/article-627630.

Globes (2010). www.globes.co.il/en/article-1000611229

Globes (2017). www.globes.co.il/en/article-comptroller-to-deliver-damning-report-on-imi-privatization-1001219853.

Globes (2018a). https://en.globes.co.il/en/article-iai-to-build-amos-8-satellite-1001252365.

Globes (2018b). https://en.globes.co.il/en/article-israel-aerospace-takes-delivery-of-first-arrow-3-canister-1001252654.

Globes (2018c). https://en.globes.co.il/en/article-rafael-set-for-iron-dome-sale-to-romania-1001236817.

Golde, S. and Tishler, A. (2004). "Security needs, arms exports, and the structure of the defense industry", *Journal of Conflict Resolution*, 48(5), 672–698.

Haaretz (2015). www.haaretz.com/.premium-ya-alon-forces-rafael-boss-to-suspend-him self-1.5367951?=&ts=_15174142.

Haaretz (2017a). www.haaretz.com/israel-news/business/arms-makers-anxious-as-imi-pri vatization-is-revived-1.5466859.

Haaretz (2017b). www.haaretz.com/israel-news/.premium-israeli-army-buying-local-can nons-to-sidestep-ban-on-cluster-bombs-1.5441009.

Haaretz (2018). www.haaretz.com/news/diplomacy-defense/israel-is-world-s-largest-exporter-of-drones-study-finds.premium-1.524771.

Harms, G. and Ferry, T. (2017). *The Palestine-Israel Conflict: A Basic Introduction*, 4th edition. Pluto Press. www.jstor.org/stable/j.ctt1s475dd.

Israel Central Bureau of Statistics (2018a).www.cbs.gov.il/reader/newhodaot/hodaa_template.html?hodaa=201811104.

Israel Central Bureau of Statistics (2018b). www.cbs.gov.il/publications17/1680/pdf/t04.pdf.

Israel Government Companies Authority (2018). https://mof.gov.il/GCA.

Israel Ministry of Defense (2012a).www.mod.gov.il/Society_Economy/Pages/economic_support.aspx.

Israel Ministry of Defense (2012b). "The committee for 'reviewing the defense budget, priorities and streamlining'." www.mod.gov.il/Documents/%D7%93%D7%95%D7%97%20%D7%95%D7%A2%D7%93%D7%AA%20%D7%98%D7%99%D7%A9%D7%9C%D7%A8.pdf.

"Israel Ministry of Defense: Israel defense budget, 2009–2018". (unclassified books).

Israel Ministry of Finance budget online database (2018). www.mof.gov.il/en/PolicyAndBudget/BudgetExecution/Pages/BudgetExecutionReportsFiles.aspx.

ISRAELDEFENSE (2018). www.israeldefense.com/en/node/33799

Janes (2018). www.janes.com/article/79686/azerbaijan-shows-hermes-900

JPOST (2016). www.jpost.com/Israel-News/Politics-And-Diplomacy/Troops-can-see-through-armored-vehicles-with-Israeli-firms-new-helmet-456258.

Kagan, K., Setter, O., Shefi, A. and Tishler, A. (2010). "Defence structure, procurement and industry: The case of Israel". In S. Markowski, P. Hall and R. Wylie (eds.), *Defence Procurement and Industry Policy* 228–254). London and New York: Routledge, Taylor & Francis Group.

Laqueur, W. and Schueftan, D. (2016). *The Israel-Arab Reader*, 8th edition. New York: Penguin Random House LLC.

Lavie, Z. (2000). *Procurement Management – From Theory to Practice*. Tel Aviv: Ministry of Defence.

Lifshitz, Y. (2011). *Strategic and Economic Roles of Defense Industries in Israel*. Bar-Ilan University, Israel: The Begin-Sadat Center for Strategic Studies.

The Marker (2018). translate.google.co.il/translate?hl=en&sl=iw&u=www.themarker.com/news/1.6076885&prev=search.

"The Military balance reports, 1998–2015". Routledge. www.tandfonline.com/loi/tmib20www.dni.gov/files/documents/Newsroom/Press%20Releases/2007%20Press%20Releases/20071203_release.pdf.

Mintz, A. (1985). "Military-industrial linkages in Israel," *Armed Forces & Society*, 12, 9–27.

MOU (2016). "Memorandum of understanding between USA and the state of Israel 2019–2028". www.obamawhitehouse.archives.gov/the-press-office/2016/09/14/fact-sheet-memorandum-understanding-reached-israel.

Nevo, B. and Shur-Shmueli, Y. (2004). "The Israel defence forces and the national economy of Israel". In S. Feldman and Y. S. Shapir (eds.), *The Middle East Strategic Military*. Jerusalem: The Israeli Democracy Institute (in Hebrew).

New York Times (2010). "When Israel and France broke up". www.nytimes.com/2010/04/01/opinion/01bass.html.

OECD (2018). Online database. https://data.oecd.org/.

Pecht, E. and Tishler, A. (2015). "The value of military intelligence", *Defence and Peace Economics*, 26(2), 179–211.

Pecht, E., Tishler, A. and Weingold, N. (2013). "On the choice of multi-task R&D defense projects: A case study of the Israeli missile defense system", *Defence and Peace Economics*, 24(5), 429–448.

Pinchas, G (2018). "On the optimal ownership type, size and structure of Israel's defense industry", Ph.D Thesis draft, Tel Aviv University.

Rabinovich, I. (2011). "Peace, normalization and finality", *The American Interest*, 7(3), December 1.

Reuters (2018). www.reuters.com/article/elbit-systems-ma-imi/israel-regulator-okays-defence-firm-elbits-bid-to-buy-imi-idUSL8N1VA07F.

Setter, O. and Tishler, A. (2006). "A brave leap or a gradual climb? The dynamics of investment in R&D of integrative technologies", *Defense and Peace Economics*, 17(3), 201–222.

Shabtay, H. and Tishler, A. (2014). "Budget allocation under uncertainty and the costs of war and insecurity", *Defense and Peace Economics*, 25(5), 461–480.

Shapir, Y. S. (2013). "Lessons from the Iron Dome", *Military and Strategic Affairs*, *5*(1), 81–94.

Sharaby, L. (2002). "Israel's economic growth: Success without security", *Middle East Review of International Affairs*, 6(3), 25–41.

Shefi, Y. and Tishler, A. (2005). "'The effects of the world defense industry and US military aid to Israel on the Israeli defense industry: A differentiated products model", *Defence and Peace Economics*, 16(6), 427–448.

SIPRI Arms Industry online database. retrieved December 2017. www.sipri.org/databases/armsindustry.

"SIPRI Military Expenditure online database, 2018". www.sipri.org/databases/milex.

SIPRI Yearbook (2016). "Armaments, disarmament and international security". www.sipri.org/yearbook/2016

SIPRI Yearbooks, 1991–2017. "Lists of the 100 largest arms-producing companies". www.sipri.org/yearbook/archive.

Swed, O. and Butler, J. (2015). "Military capital in the Israeli hi-tech industry", *Armed Forces & Society*, 41(1), 123–141. www.academia.edu/4720761/Military_Captial_in_the_Israeli_Hi-Tech_Industry.

"The World Bank: online database". (2017). www.elibrary.worldbank.org/page/wb-regions-data.

Ynet (2017). www.ynetnews.com/articles/0,7340,L-4963629,00.html.

Ynet (2018a). www.ynetnews.com/articles/0,7340,L-5245726,00.html.

Ynet (2018b). www.ynetnews.com/articles/0,7340,L-5225153,00.html.

19 The defense industry of the Republic of Korea

Richard A. Bitzinger

Introduction

The Republic of Korea (ROK, or South Korea) has aggressively pursued a "domestic weapons first" policy going back to the early 1970s and the implementation of the first Yulgok Project, an ambitious program of defense industrialization that was intended to lay down "a basic foundation for a self-defense capability for the 21st century."[1] This indigenization process was initially propelled by the threat from North Korea, and the belief that achieving self-sufficiency in defense procurement was essential to maintaining an adequate defense capability. At the same time, domestic arms production was more than merely achieving "security of supply"; very powerful technonationalist impulses can be detected in South Korea's defense-industrialization activities over the past several decades. In case of the ROK, defense-industrial policy had three core objectives. First, to strengthen its national political independence by reducing dependency upon foreign sources of arms. Second, to aid domestic economic development overall by pursuing armaments production as an import-substitution strategy and as a driver of technology-intensive industrialization. Third and perhaps the most important all, to enhance the nation's military-political status and raising its profile as an important geopolitical player in Asia.

Defense spending trends in South Korea

The South Korean defense industrial base has benefitted considerably from consistent and significant increases in ROK military expenditures. According to data provided by the Stockholm International Peace Research Institute (SIPRI), from 2000 to 2017, the South Korean defense budget has grown from US$20.4 billion to US$37.6 billion (as measured in constant 2016 dollars). This translates into 5 percent real growth per annum over this period.

Data put out by the ROK Ministry of National Defense (MND) corroborates the SIPRI numbers. The MND's *2016 Defense White Paper* states that South Korean defense spending 2017 would reach 40.3 trillion won (US$36 billion), equal to about 2.4 percent of the country's gross domestic product (GDP).[2] Of this, 12.2 trillion won (US$11 billion), or around 30 percent of the overall defense budget, was allocated to "force improvement." This category was further broken down into US$2.3 billion for research and development (R&D), and US$8.7 billion for the procurement of equipment.[3] Moreover, the MND's current Mid-Term Defense Program for 2017–2021 projects to spend 73.4 trillion won (US$66 billion) on force improvement over this five-year period, for an average annual increase of 7.3 percent.[4]

The South Korean defense industry: a brief overview

Around one hundred South Korean companies are engaged in some kind of defense contracting, supported by 300 or so subcontractors, employing an estimated 25,000 workers.[5] According to SIPRI, total output of the South Korean defense sector was valued at US$8.4 billion in 2016 (the last year for which data are available); this was a 20.6 percent increase over 2015 revenues. In 2016, the ROK arms industry accounted for 2.2 percent of all sales listed in SIPRI's global "top 100" arms-producing firms.[6]

South Korean arms manufacturing began modestly the early 1970s, when the ROK was permitted a license to produce the US-designed M16 rifle. This was subsequently followed up by licenses to assemble other weapon systems, including the F-5 fighter jet, the MD-500 and UH-60 helicopters, M101, M114, and M109 howitzers, and the PSMM-5 fast attack boat.

Starting in the late 1980s and early 1990s, the ROK began to undertake more sophisticated types of licensed production. Seoul negotiated sizable "offsets" – i.e., coproduction rights – for several of its foreign arms acquisitions. For example, when South Korea decided to purchase 40 F-16 fighters from the United States in the mid-1980s, it demanded and received the right to produce several of the plane's key subsystems, including center fuselage section, cockpit side panels, and ventral fins.[7] This program was followed up by an agreement for an additional 140 F-16s that included the establishment of a complete turnkey manufacturing facility in South Korea in order to build the jet locally. Similar coproduction arrangements were made for Hawk trainer jets acquired from the United Kingdom, for Type-6614 wheeled armored personnel carriers from Italy, and for Bv-206 all-terrain tracked carriers from Sweden. During the same period, Seoul secured an agreement with Germany to construct nine Type-209 submarines (designated the KSS-I by the Koreans), which was subsequently followed up by a similar contract for the manufacture of nine more advanced Type-214 (KSS-II) submarines.

Beginning in the 1990s, the process of indigenous development and design, as well as the local manufacture of weapon systems, began to take on additional momentum, and gradually the ROK armed forces began to phase out foreign equipment and replace them with locally designed and produced systems. South Korea manufactured its own assault rifle, the K2, as well the K200 Korean Infantry Fighting Vehicle (KIFV). By the mid-1990s, the ROK was producing the indigenously designed K1/K1A1 main battle tank, which was subsequently replaced by the more advanced K2 Black Panther tank. Other homegrown weapons systems include the *Chunma* (Pegasus) surface-to-air missile, the *Hyunmoo* family of cruise missiles, the K21 infantry fighting vehicle, and the K9 Thunder 155mm self-propelled howitzer. In addition, the ROK constructs warships of its own design.[8]

Some of the most noteworthy progress toward self-sufficiency has taken place in the domestic aerospace industry. Originally an assembler of foreign systems, the ROK aircraft sector has gradually emerged to become a center of combat aircraft design and development. The ROK aerospace industry's first indigenous product was the KT-1 *Woongbi*, a turboprop basic trainer/light-attack aircraft, initiated in the late 1980s. The KT-1 was followed by the T-50 Golden Eagle, an even more ambitious program to design and manufacture a supersonic advanced trainer/light attack jet. The T-50 is Korea's first indigenous jet aircraft, intended to replace T-38, A-37, and F-5 fighters in the Republic of Korea Air Force (ROKAF), as well as export sales. Launched in the mid-1990s, the plane was originally a joint venture between Samsung Aerospace (later Korea Aerospace Industries) and Lockheed Martin, with the US company supplying critical technologies relating the aircraft's wing, computerized flight-control system, and avionics suite. The T-50 first flew in August 2002 and the aircraft entered service with the ROKAF in 2005. Later versions include the TA-50, a lead-in fighter/trainer/attack plane, and the FA-50, a dedicated fighter aircraft outfitted with more advanced avionics and capable of employing a broader suite of weapons.

Consequently, by the second decade of the 21st century, the ROK has become largely self-reliant in most major weapons systems. The local arms industry is particularly broad-based in scope, aided by sizable investments in the aerospace, land ordnance systems, and shipbuilding sectors. Nearly 80 percent of South Korea's arms are procured domestically, including combat aircraft, main battle tanks, armored vehicles, warships, and submarines, and it is becoming increasingly self-reliant in missile systems.[9]

Korea continues to have ambitious plans for its indigenous defense industrial base. Like other countries in the Asia-Pacific region, the modernization of its armed forces is a high priority, and the ROK military has plans to procure several types of advanced weapon systems over the next several decades, including airborne early warning and signals-intelligence aircraft, standoff munitions, unmanned aerial vehicles, night-vision goggles, and a ballistic missile defense system.[10] In particular, Seoul wants its domestic aerospace industry to design and manufacture a "4++ generation" fighter jet, designated the KF-X (Korea Fighter Experimental). Finally, South Korea has recently launched the first of a planned fleet of nine 3,000-ton indigenous KSS-III class diesel-electric submarines; boats in this class will be equipped with a locally developed lithium-ion battery and a vertical launch system capable of firing indigenously developed ballistic or cruise missiles. Overall, therefore, as Seoul seeks to procure more cutting-edge weaponry, it will place greater demands on its domestic arms industry.

Structure of the South Korean defense industry

Seoul has traditionally relied upon the private sector, rather than state-owned enterprises, in order to carry out national arms production. Most of the country's arms manufacturing is concentrated in just a handful of large industrial conglomerates, or *chaebol*. *Chaebols* are generally highly centralized corporations, usually controlled by a single (founding) family, and are characterized by a complex system of interlocking ownership; they also tend to predominant in one particular part of the country (Hyundai Group, for example, operates mainly in southeastern Korea, around Ulsan).

At present, the most important South Korean *chaebols* engaged in armaments production are: Korea Aerospace Industries (KAI); Hyundai Motor Group; Hyundai Heavy Industries Group (HHI); LG Corporation (formerly Lucky GoldStar); Daewoo Shipbuilding and Marine Engineering (DSME); and Hanwha Group. Hyundai Rotem, a division of the Hyundai Motor Group, manufactures the K1 and K2 main battle tanks. Kia Motors, also a subsidiary of Hyundai Motor, builds heavy trucks for the military. LIG Nex1 (a subsidiary of LG Corporation) produces missile systems and electronics; while DSME and HHI construct submarines and warships. Hanwha Aerospace (formerly Samsung) manufactures jet engines, Hanwha Land Systems produces artillery systems (such as the K9 Thunder self-propelled howitzer), and Hanwha Defense Systems (formerly Daewoo, and later Doosan) builds the K21 infantry fight vehicle, the *Chunma* surface-to-air missile, and the *Chunmoo* multiple rocket launcher.[11] Most arms factories are located in South Korea's southern coastal belt.

Korea Aerospace Industries, the country's leading aircraft manufacturer, is particularly noteworthy. KAI was created in 1999 by the forced merger of three money-losing aircraft companies: Samsung Aerospace (now Hanwha), Daewoo Heavy Industries Aerospace Division, and Hyundai Space and Aircraft Company; the new company is headquartered in Sacheon. KAI produces all of the country's military aircraft, particularly the T-50 Golden Eagle advanced trainer/lightweight fighter jet, the KT-1 turboprop trainer, and the *Surion* utility-lift helicopter. Other KAI products include unmanned aerial vehicles (UAVs), space launch vehicles (e.g., the KSLV-II), and satellites; KAI also performs aircraft upgrades and MRO (maintenance, repair, and overhaul) for the ROKAF.

In a move that is crucial for the future of KAI, the company was recently selected to be the lead contractor to build the KF-X (Korean Fighter Experimental), the ROKAF's next next-generation indigenous combat aircraft. The KF-X fighter is a twin-engine stealthy fighter jet, and it will feature an AESA (active electronically scanned array) radar and other advanced avionics.[12] It has been deemed a "4++ generation" combat aircraft, ostensibly an improvement over standard 4th generation fighters like the F-16, but not as advanced as the F-22 or F-35 (so-called 5th generation fighters). This puts the KF-X in roughly the same class as the Eurofighter *Typhoon*, the Swedish *Gripen*, or the Russian Su-35.

The KF-X is being jointly developed by KAI and US aerospace giant Lockheed Martin, as part of a deal in which the ROKAF purchased 40 F-35 fighters from the United States. The KF-X is expected to achieve first flight by 2022, with deliveries to the ROKAF starting in 2024. The ROKAF plans to procure as many as 120 KF-X fighters, which will replace the air force's aging fleet of F-4 Phantoms and F-5s. Seoul has also succeeded in signing up Indonesia as a partner in the KF-X program, and Jakarta could acquire as many as 50 fighters to meet its own "IFX" requirements. Moreover, Korea expects to export up to 600 KF-X fighters to other countries. Under the terms of the project contract, the KAI-Lockheed team will underwrite 20 percent of incurred development costs, with the ROKAF and Indonesia will cover 60 percent and 20 percent of the costs, respectively. Overall, the KF-X could be worth as much as 8.6 trillion won (US $7.8 billion).[13]

Korea Aerospace Industries is the embodiment of the country's hopes and dreams for its defense industry. The ROK continues to nurture the ambition of becoming a world-class and globally competitive airframe designer and manufacturer. KAI aims to be among the world's top-five aerospace-producing companies by 2030, with sales of 20 trillion won (US$17.7 billion), a tenfold increase over 2017 revenues.[14] In particular, the company expects to become a major arms exporter. KAI has sold the KT-1 trainer aircraft and T-50 fighter jet to several overseas customers (see below). Seoul has had especially high (and probably unrealistic) expectations for its T-50 advanced trainer/lightweight fighter jet, at one point projecting that it would export 800 to 1,000 T-50s over the next several decades and capture one-quarter of the world's market for this kind of aircraft.[15]

In addition to KAI, the Korean Air Lines Co. (KAL) – which manufactured the F-5 fighter and the MD-500 and UH-60s helicopter back in the 1970s and 1980s – continues to run extensive depot maintenance and upgrade services for the ROKAF, as well as producing drones and unmanned systems. Rounding out this list of leading domestic arms manufacturers are Poongsan, which produces ammunition; S&T Dynamics, which manufacturers the K2 assault rifle, machine guns, and 20mm cannon; Hanjin Heavy Industries, which is constructing the *Dokdo*-class amphibious assault ship for the ROK Navy; and STX Offshore and Shipbuilding Corporation, which builds the *Inchon*-class frigate.

While most arms manufacturing is undertaken by private commercial firms, most of these companies function as noncompetitive, sole-source contractors in many segments of the defense industry, such as main battle tanks (Hyundai Rotem), armored vehicles (Hanwha Defense Systems), artillery systems (Hanwha Land Systems), and combat aircraft (KAI). About the only real competition in defense supply appears to be found in the naval shipbuilding sector: DSME and HHI have shared construction of KDX destroyers and production of the KSS-II (Type-214) submarine, while HHI and STX Offshore and Shipbuilding are both building the *Inchon*-class/FFX frigate for the ROK Navy.

Some *chaebol*, such as Samsung and Daewoo, have totally exited the defense business (Daewoo went bankrupt in 1999 and its assets scattered), while others, such as Hanwha, have become new players in arms manufacturing. In general, however, the overall structure and functioning of the Korean defense industry has changed little over the past 20 years. If anything, competition within the Korean defense industry has *decreased*, particularly in the aerospace industry. During the 1990s, three *chaebol* (Samsung, Daewoo, and Hyundai) competed for aerospace contracts with the ROKAF. This led to overcapacity and inefficiencies in the domestic aircraft sector, which was only partially solved with the creation of KAI. The government has pledged that KAI will be granted exclusive rights (to the detriment of KAL) to future ROK military aircraft contracts, particularly the new KF-X fighter jet program.[16]

Conduct of the South Korean defense industry

South Korea's approach to indigenous armaments production can be traced back to the regime of Park Chung Hee (1961–1979) and his policy of "Self-Reliant National Defense." Reducing the country's dependencies on foreign armaments is a critical national security objective, but for reasons that go far beyond national defense. In the first place, South Korea is committed to a strategy of "cooperative self-reliant defense,"[17] an approach that embraces the US-ROK alliance (as embodied in the 1953 Mutual Defense Treaty), but which also seeks to strengthen the country's national defense capabilities[18]– that is, "acquiring the ability to independently develop primary weapon systems for core force capability."[19] This serves as least two military functions. First, having an indigenous defense industry permitted South Korea to tailor weapons systems especially suited for its unique national defense requirements and to take advantage of technological breakthroughs in its own domestic R&D base. Second, local armaments manufacturing can be used as a bargaining chip in joint ventures with foreign arms producers, that is, a means by which to extract industrial or technological concessions, such as technology transfers or production offsets, when it comes to arms imports; this further advances South Korea's efforts to wean itself off its defense-industrial dependencies on larger powers, particularly the United States.

At the same time, defense industrialization was also viewed as at least partially driving the expansion and technological modernization of the overall national economy. Armaments production was a means by which to stimulate the development of new industrial sectors and to underwrite research and development when it came to new technologies, such as in the area of aerospace and electronics. Advanced military technologies were particularly seen as contributing to the growth of import-substituting industries. These military-industrial developments, in turn, could realize important commercial gains. In some cases, these "spin-off" benefits were direct – such as heavy trucks or the MD-500 helicopter, which were produced in both military and civilian versions; in other cases, they could be indirect, such as using military aerospace production as the basis for establishing and nurturing a commercial aircraft industry.[20] Either way, military industrialization went hand-in-hand in South Korea's overall development strategies.

Finally, South Korea's striving for self-reliance in armaments has been as much about expanding the country's autonomy and freedom of action in foreign affairs and regional politics. Possessing an independent defense industrial capability feeds directly into their concepts of national power – not only by creating military power but also by demonstrating the country's industrial and technological prowess, and thereby confirming its status as a regional great power.[21]

Consequently, the South Korean government has been heavily involved in the arms production process, by providing direct and indirect subsidies to manufacturers, by underwriting defense research and development planning, and by designating firms as sole-source suppliers of critical military equipment.[22] In the first place, the central government has underwritten the Korean defense industry by virtue of it (that is, the ROK military) being the prime consumer of locally produced arms. It guarantees procurement and therefore profitability; it has also created "monopolistic or oligopolistic positions with the defense sector, as each individual contractor has been directed to specialize in a certain area of production."[23] In addition, Seoul has encouraged firms to enter into domestic arms production through a variety of incentives – such as tax breaks, low-interest loans, and direct financial support – as well as coercive measures, such as tying defense contracting to state support for engaging in other types of commercial production.[24]

Overall, the defense industry is a highly protected sector of the ROK economy. Particular emphasis has been put on supporting local defense industries and armaments programs, promoting the export of Korean weaponry, and protecting homegrown defense technologies. Foreign investment in local arms or aerospace companies is actively discouraged, to the point that the central government has preferred to take stakes in these firms. State-run financial institutions such as the Korea Development Bank (KDB) and the Financial Services Commission, hold considerable shares in some arms-producing companies, such as KAI (27 percent) and DSME (50.4 percent).

The ROK government has also traditionally assumed most of the risk when it comes weapons development. While most armaments production in Korean is undertaken by the private sector, defense R&D is managed by the government-run Agency for Defense Development (ADD). The ADD operates at the center of the national defense R&D process in South Korea. It has primary responsibility for the research and development of indigenous weapons systems and core technologies, manages the development of dual-use and core technologies, and carries out operational testing and evaluation of developmental systems. The ADD works directly with the local defense industry on prototyping and production of ADD-developed weapons systems, as well as with industry think tanks, universities, and research institutes on basic and applied research and on core technology development.

The ADD is directly responsible to the Ministry of National Defense's Defense Acquisition Program Administration (DAPA). DAPA used to be solely responsible for determining requirements, overseeing mid-term defense planning and procurement, approving indigenous R&D projects, and assessing testing and evaluation results. Following 2014 reforms, the ROK Joint Chiefs of Staff now oversee requirements, while the MND has assumed authority for mid-term planning. DAPA is now focused primarily on drawing up budgets for force improvement programs, managing these programs, and executing contracts.[25]

Performance of the South Korean defense industry

It is difficult, if not impossible, to provide accurate or plausible data regarding the productivity and profitability of leading firms within the South Korean defense industrial base, or details as to cost overruns and delays regarding specific defense programs. Since armaments production is often embedded within much larger conglomerates, economic data as to revenues and profits specific to a firm's arms manufacturing activities is typically unavailable. Some companies, like Hanwha, DSME, HHI, and Hyundai Motor Group, simply do not break out data as to their defense-related activities, and SIPRI data (see Table 19.1) shows that, in the case of many of these companies, military production is a negligible percentage of their overall business. Moreover, so many South Korean defense industries have either changed hands or reorganized several times so much over the past 20 years, that consistent and comparable economic data are unattainable.

Table 19.1 Leading South Korea defense firms, 2016

Company	*SIPRI Top-100 ranking*	*Arms sales ($mn)*	*Total sales ($mn)*	*Arms sales as a % of total sales*	*Total employment*
Korea Aerospace Industries	48	1760	2671	66	4150
LIG Nex1	55	1600	1603	100	3120
Hanwha Corp.	70	1190	40593	3	–
Hanwha Techwin	71	1190	2265	53	3040
DSME	73	1190	9808	12	11260
Hanwha Group	95	740	55430	1	–
Hanwha Systems	95	740	742	100	2060
Poongsan Corp.	100	700	1753	40	3580

Sources: SIPRI, *Factsheet: SIPRI Top 100 Arms-Producing and Military Services Companies 2016* (December 2017); Korea Aerospace Industries website (accessed 4 October 2018).

Further mudding these financial waters is a recent scandal involving KAI. In 2017, nine current and former executives at the company, including the former CEO, were arrested on charges of fraud, bribery, and embezzlement. In particular, KAI executives were accused of inflating corporate sales by 536 billion won (US$472.1 million) and net profits by 46.5 billion won between 2013 and 2017. The most recent data (2017) shows KAI operating in the red.[26]

Overall, arms manufacturing constitutes a small fraction of the South Korean economy. The Hyundai Motor Group, for example, earned revenues of US$84 billion in 2016, while Samsung had sales of over US$300 billion. In comparison, the total output of the entire South Korean defense sector was less than US$8.5 billon.[27]

Information as to South Korean arms exports is more readily available. Initially, the ROK produced military equipment to meet domestic needs (i.e., as an import-substitution strategy) and not as an instrument of export-led growth. However, since the turn of the century at least, both the South Korea government and the local arms industry have aggressively pursued overseas arms sales as an invaluable additional source of revenue. Despite its best efforts, however, for a long time the ROK experienced only modest and sporadic success when it came to overseas arms sales. Exports often consisted mostly of low-tech items, such as uniforms and other general military equipment, small arms and ammunition, trucks, and small patrol boats. It scored one or two sizable deals, such as an agreement with Malaysia for 110 K200 infantry fighting vehicles, but there was nothing sustainable in the form of follow-on sales. Indeed, throughout the 1990s, South Korean arms exports never exceeded US$75 million per year, according to the Stockholm International Peace Research Institute.[28] Even by the ROK government's own statistics, overseas arms sales remained weak until the middle of the first decade of the 21st century.

A key impediment to Korean arms exports were the restrictions placed by Washington on the re-export of ROK military equipment that contained US subsystems or components. This encouraged South Korean arms manufacturers to increase the degree of indigenization in their products. Indeed, starting around the middle of the last decade, the ROK began to experience sustained success when it came to arms exports. According to official MND statistics, South Korean overseas arms sales increased from US$253 million in 2006 to US$3.54 billion in 2015 (see Figure 19.1: values in current prices). The number of countries acquiring South Korean armaments grew from 47 countries in 2006 to 90 countries in 2015, while the number of South Korean firms exporting arms over the same period went from 47 to 156. Approximately one-third of South Korean arms exports were to Southeast Asia, South Asia, and Australia, while 28 percent were to the Middle East.[29]

Major recent export agreements include the sale of KT-1 primary trainer planes to Indonesia, Peru, Senegal, and Turkey; K9 self-propelled guns to

Estonia, Finland, India, Norway, Turkey, and Poland; three Improved *Changbogo*-class (Type-209) submarines to Indonesia; *Makassar*-class landing platform dock (LDP) amphibious warfare ships to Indonesia, Peru, and the Philippines; and one stealthy, multirole frigate to Thailand. In addition, Turkey will coproduce a variant of the K2 Black Panther tank, based on a major technology-sharing agreement with South Korea.[30] In particular, South Korea has broken into the highly competitive global fighter market by concluding export agreements with Indonesia, Iraq, the Philippines, and Thailand for the sale of the T-50 supersonic trainer/light attack jets; altogether, these four countries are buying 72 various versions of the T-50.[31]

In more recent years, the ROK Ministry of National Defense (MND) has also encouraged the private sector to become more active in conducting military-related R&D (including investing their own monies), and to get the South Korean industry to specialize in a particular area of military production, in the hope of increasing and focusing South Korean military-technical activities at the industry level.[32] In 2014, the MND created the Institute of Civilian-Military Technology Cooperation within the Agency for Development; at the same time, it has budgeted 67.7 billion won (US$61 million) to promote civil-military technology cooperation.[33] In particular, the MND's *2016 Defense White Paper* noted three examples of civilian-to-military spin-on: an auxiliary power unit fitted in the *Surion* helicopter; a mid-sized waterjet system used in ROKN high-speed boats; and carbon composites used in the brake discs of the F-16 fighter.[34]

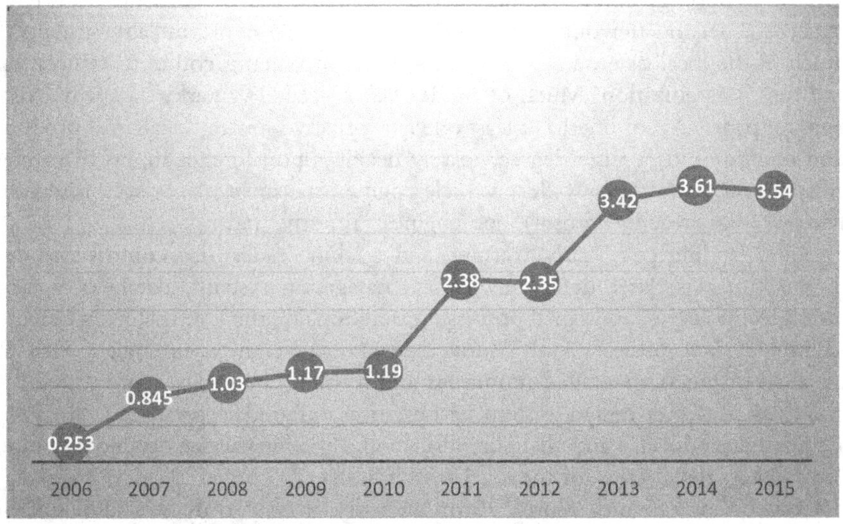

Figure 19.1 ROK arms exports (US$ billions).

ROK military planners are also encouraging private firms such as KAI to engage in high-tech civil programs such as commercial passenger jets, in the hope that such projects will not only make KAI stronger in the global aerospace market, but also help develop advanced civilian technologies that could be applied to military production. As such, KAI is expanding its commercial aviation activities. It has become a major subcontractor to Boeing and Airbus, for example, supplying parts and components for the Boeing 787 and the Airbus A350XWB, as well as other civil airliner programs. More ambitiously, KAI still hopes to develop and produce its own commercial aircraft. In at least one instance, the company was in talks with Bombardier of Canada to collaborate on a 90-seat turboprop passenger plane.[35]

Prospects for the future of the South Korean defense industry

South Korea has achieved an undeniably high degree of success in indigenizing arms procurement. The ROK has, in a matter of decades, built up a domestic defense industrial base capable of producing a broad range of weapon systems, and, as such, approximately 80 percent of its arms are procured indigenously. In many cases, the capabilities and quality of these homegrown arms are said to be as high as could be found in the West (as also evidenced by South Korea's recent success in securing considerable overseas arms sales).[36] As a result, it could be reasonably argued that the ROK has attained most of its goals for autarkic military acquisition.

Nevertheless, even after more than 40 years of significant public and private inputs in infrastructure and technology, South Korea still possesses only limited capacities for self-reliant armaments production. Overall, while the country's defense technology and industrial base has "elevated from a third-tier arms producer to a second-tier one" by virtue of considerable effort and investments,[37] much of the local defense sector remains deficient when it comes to innovation and true indigenization. Much of the ROK's so-called "autarky" actually exists only on paper. According to at least one authoritative source, local arms production continues, to a large degree, to rely heavily upon foreign inputs in several critical areas, such as heavy-duty vehicle engines, transmissions, active protection systems (e.g., reactive armor), jet engines, airborne radar systems and other avionics, landing gear, early warning and tracking radar, fire control systems, thermal imagers, laser detection sensors, navigation systems, datalinks, sensor fusion technologies, and signal processing; additionally, the South Korean defense technology base possesses only "limited structural design technologies," that in the field of precision-guided munitions and missile systems, its "core technologies (such as seeker design, system optimization, infrared sensors, etc.) remain at a rudimentary level," and that surveillance and reconnaissance technologies are "completely new" areas for the local arms industry.[38]

Consequently, South Korea's arms industry is only truly self-sufficient in a few areas, such as small arms, ammunition, and light armored vehicles; in most other cases, a considerable proportion of the value of "indigenous production" is still foreign in origin. For example, several critical components found in the original K1 main battle tank, such as the engine, transmission, gun, and sight, were originally sourced in the United States and Western Europe (although the follow-on K1A1 tank eventually achieved a "localization rate" of nearly 83 percent). The *Chunma* surface-to-air missile is comprised of 43 percent of foreign systems by value, mostly French. While local shipyards are constructing the hulls for the KDX destroyer program, foreign firms continue to supply the bulk of its key weapons systems and electronics, particularly its command and fire control systems. The KDX-III destroyer, for example, incorporates the U.S. *Aegis* air-defense radar and Standard surface-to-air missile; overall, only 54 percent of the KDX-III is localized production. Indigenous aircraft programs are particularly dependent on foreign technologies and systems. The KT-1 trainer plane has a localization rate of only 44 percent, while the localization rate for the country's much-vaunted T-50 advanced trainer/light attack jet is only 61 percent.[39] Lockheed Martin partnered with South Korea on the design of the T-50, and as such was responsible for the development of some of the most critical elements of this plane, including the wing, computerized flight-control system, and avionics suite.

Moreover, even after decades of significant public and private investments in infrastructure and technology, much of South Korea's defense technology base remains weak. While the ROK has proven to be very adept at licensed manufacturing and at the indigenous production of such "low-tech" items as small arms and ordnance, it has had a tougher time developing and designing more demanding types of weapon systems. The K1 tank, for example, was, initially, deemed to be a mediocre performer, with poor ergonomics, as well as being a systems integration nightmare, due to its diverse collection of US and European components and subsystems; it took several years to work out the bugs.[40] The ROK's follow-on indigenous tank, the K2 Black Panther, has experienced similar teething problems, in particularly when it came to its locally developed powerpack (engine and transmission); this led to a temporary suspension of the production of the K2, and eventually a German-made powerpack was substituted.[41] Other domestic weapons systems have suffered similar glitches. The K9 howitzer has experienced problems with software bugs and barrel corrosion; in one instance, when North Korean forces shelled Yeonpyeong Island in November 2010, the ROK Army response was enfeebled, as four of six available K9s were inoperable. In addition, on two occasions, an ROK Army K21 IFV sank twice during use, killing one soldier; subsequent investigations found critical flaws in the vehicle, including a lack of buoyancy and malfunctioning wave plates and drain pumps.[42]

As in many emerging arms-producing countries, "technology overreach" has been the South Korean arms industry's Achilles heel. Early successes with local arms production only bred greater ambitions, which in turn spurred it to pursue programs that increasingly taxed the nation's indigenous technological capabilities to fulfill. While South Korea's defense industry proved to be very adept at licensed manufacturing and at the indigenous production of relatively low-tech items such as small arms and ordnance, it has experienced much less success when it came to developing and designing major weapon systems. At the same time, the predilection on the part of the central government for high-technology "prestige projects," such as combat aircraft and missile systems, and an overconfidence in the abilities of local industry to quickly move such programs into production, tended to result in unexpected development problems, delays, cost overruns, and failure.[43]

Moreover, attempting to undertake such an ambitious range of armaments manufacturing on such a small scale often resulted in highly inefficient and uneconomical structural operations, involving small production runs, high unit costs, and considerable overcapacity in manufacturing. For example, Seoul's insistence on locally assembling the US F-16 fighter added about 20 percent more to the total cost of acquisition than if the ROKAF had procured the aircraft directly from the United States. Earlier efforts to license-produce the F-5 fighter and MD-500 helicopter resulted in similar cost increases.[44]

Heavy investments in armaments production, especially during its initial stages of defense industrialization, resulted considerable excess capacity in the domestic military-industrial complex. From the 1970s through the 1990s, South Korea greatly expanded its arms-manufacturing capacities in response to existing or projected needs, only to later find itself saddled with overlapping and duplicative capacity and underutilized, high-overhead facilities. Around the turn of the century, for instance, capacity utilization of the overall defense sector was estimated to be at around 60 percent – and only 36 percent in the case of the ordnance and ammunition sectors.[45] Even today it is estimated that, in general, the Korean defense industry operates at just 57 percent of capacity.[46] These diseconomies of scale have greatly undermined the efficiency of local defense firms and have constituted a serious drain on indigenous arms development and procurement.

Overall, therefore, the South Korean arms industries appear to be at a "technology plateau," stuck somewhere in the middle of the military production food chain.[47] The ROK has certainly demonstrated its ability to build very good low- or medium-tech weaponry, such as small arms, artillery systems, light armored vehicles, and ship hulls. It has also proven to be a capable performer when it comes to license-producing foreign weapon systems, such as jet fighters or submarines, and a reliable and tech-savvy partner when it comes to joint development programs, such as the T-50 (and most likely the KF-X program). Nevertheless, weapons manufacturing does not necessarily get any easier the more one strives to develop and manufacture increasingly advanced weapons systems – just the opposite, in fact. Moving on to the next level of armaments production – that is, the indigenous development and production of highly advanced and sophisticated weapons – appears to be exponentially more challenging. If anything, the materiel demands of autarkic advanced arms production – money, R&D efforts, personnel, etc. – may be more than South Korea is presently willing to commit, particularly when such sophisticated weapons can be just as easily purchased from abroad. Even with this commitment, enduring structural challenges such as overcapacity, excess competition, and diseconomies of scale and means that success is not assured.

To put it bluntly, the domestic defense market is simply too small to maintain an economically viable and technologically competitive defense industry, and nowhere is this "technonationalist overreach" and plateauing more apparent than in the South Korean aerospace sector. ROKAF procurement is going to be too small to support a national fighter jet program. To be profitable, KAI must sell hundreds of these combat aircraft; yet even with Indonesia chipping in and buying possibly 50 KF-Xs (and Indonesian purchases are as yet not assured), Korea and KAI will have to find other customers for the bulk of its KF-X sales. That said, the South Koreans are finding that breaking into the international fighter jet business is incredibly difficult. The barriers to entry are high, and the market is already saturated with a number of highly capable competing products. Moreover, US, Russian, and European aerospace companies have spent decades cultivating their customer base, and it is hard to win them away. As of 2018, KAI has sold only 72 T-50s to just four countries, while losing bids to Israel, Poland, and Singapore, among others. The biggest blow to T-50 export sales came in late 2018, with its loss in the US$9.2 billion US T-X competition to supply the US Air Force with 350 supersonic trainer jets.[48] Despite limited successes in the global arms market, South Korean arms exports are likely to remain limited in products and number.

Conclusions

The ROK defense industry is an excellent example of how a mid-level arms-producing country can make significant progress in designing, developing, and manufacturing weapons systems. The central government has, consistently and over the long term, devoted significant funds to military R&D, nurtured the development of domestic defense firms, and supported these through a concerted policy of indigenous procurement. It has taken an evolutionary or gradualist approach to armaments production, beginning with the licensed assembly of technologically modest weapons systems (small arms, light armored vehicles), progressing deliberately and cautiously up the "ladder of production" to engage in locally developed but technologically "doable" projects, such as the KT-1 light military aircraft and the K9 Thunder artillery system. At the same time, the ROK also undertook the licensed-production of more advanced Western-designed systems, such as the F-16 combat aircraft and the Type-209 submarine.

Local armaments production also got a significant boost by the buy-in from the country's large and technologically expanding private sector. Many *chaebol*, for reasons of both patriotism and profit, willingly entered the defense business. One particularly noticeable benefit of private sector enlistment into armaments manufacturing was the ability of ROK naval shipbuilding projects (like the first-generation Ulsan-class frigate and the KDX destroyer program) to piggyback on the strengths of the South Korean shipbuilding industry, one of the largest and most advanced in the world.

Problems began, starting in the 1990s, when the ROK government, military, and industry attempted to move into much more ambitious and technologically demanding armaments projects, such as supersonic jets, submarines, and missile systems – and to attempt to undertake such programs by relying on indigenously developed technologies. As it often turns out, the requirements of indigenously developing more ambitious, state-of-the-art defense technologies often tend to become correspondingly more expensive – not only in absolute terms, but also relative to the nation's overall resource and technological capacities. In other words, South Korea bit off more than it could chew, and the results were project delays, cost overruns, and, in particular, the need to return constantly to the well of foreign (and particularly Western) technology when it came to such critical components as jet engines, avionics, radar, and the like.

To be sure, South Korea has made significant progress when it comes to certain classes of indigenously developed weapons systems: these include cruise missiles (the Hyunmoo-3), the KSS-III submarine, and the K9 howitzer. Some of these are quite technologically advanced and show the prowess and potential of the ROK defense industrial base overall. However, given that program costs are rarely disclosed, it is unknowable whether some of these programs are economically defensible, compared to simply importing off-the-shelf. One notable exception might be South Korea's growing inventory of domestically sourced ballistic, antiship, and land-attack cruise missiles, as, until recently, the United States limited the range of such missiles systems sold to the ROK; in this instance, an indigenous system might have been militarily necessary, whatever the expense.[49]

Moreover, in many cases, these new, more technologically advanced – and therefore much more expensive – weapons systems require considerable economies of scale in production in order to recoup their sizeable development and manufacturing costs, and that usually means large overseas sales. This creates one of the gravest challenges to the future of the South Korea defense industrial base: it depends on exports to underwrite local armaments production, and yet such projections are almost certainly unrealistic (even more so, given KAI's loss in the T-X contest).[50] However, if additional sales cannot be found, then the local arms industry could become a major drain on the ROK economy.

The future of the South Korean defense industry is clearly an uphill battle. Its ambitions to become a supplier of advanced, locally developed arms – running the gamut from small arms to fighter aircraft – have not diminished. Enthusiasm alone, however, will not resolve the financial and technological challenges of advanced armaments production.

Notes

1 Jong Chul Choi, "South Korea," in Ravinder Pal Singh, ed., *Arms Procurement Decision Making, Volume I: China, India, Israel, Japan, South Korea and Thailand* (Oxford: Oxford University Press, 1998), p. 183. For more on the ROK defense industry, see Janne E. Nolan, *Military Industry in Taiwan and South Korea* (London: Macmillan, 1986); Janne E. Nolan, "South Korea: Ambitious Client of the United States," in Michael Brzoska and Thomas Ohlson, eds., *Arms Production in the Third World 1971–1985* (Oxford: Oxford University Press, 1987); Kwang-il Baek and Chung-in Moon, "Technological Dependence, Supplier Control and Strategies for Recipient Autonomy: The Case of South Korea," in Kwang-il Baek, Ronald D. McLaurin, and Chung-in Moon, eds., *The Dilemma of Third World Defense Industries* (Boulder, CO: Westview Press, 1989); Ralph Sanders, *Arms Industries: New Suppliers and Regional Security* (Washington, DC: NDU Press, 1990), pp. 77–88; Richard A. Bitzinger, "South Korea's Defense Industry at the Crossroads," *Korean Journal of Defense Analysis*, Vol. 7, No. 1 (Summer, 1995); Dean Cheng and Michael W. Chinworth, "The Teeth of the Little Tigers: Offsets, Defense Production and Economic Development in South Korea and Taiwan," in Stephen Martin, ed., *The Economics of Offsets: Defense Procurement and Countertrade* (London: Harwood, 1996); Kongdan Oh, "U.S.-Korea Aerospace Collaboration and the Korean Fighter Project," in Pia Christina Wood and David S. Sorenson, eds., *International Military Aerospace Collaboration: Case Studies in Domestic and International Politics* (Aldershot: Ashgate, 1999); Myeong-chin Cho, *Restructuring of Korea's Defense Aerospace Industry: Challenges and Opportunities?* (Bonn: Bonn International Center for Conversion, 2003); Richard A. Bitzinger and Mikyoung Kim, "Why Do Small States Produce Arms? The Case of South Korea," *Korean Journal of Defense Analysis*, Vol. 17, No. 2 (Fall, 2005); Chung-in Moon and Jin-young Lee, "The Revolution in Military Affairs and the Defense Industry in South Korea," *Security Challenges*, Vol. 4, No. 4 (Summer, 2008), pp. 117–134; Kaan Korkmaz and John Rydqvist, *The Republic of Korea: A Defense and Security Primer* (Stockholm: Swedish Defense Research Agency, 2012).

2 Ministry of National Defense (MND), *2016 Defense White Paper* (Seoul: Ministry of National Defense, 2016), p. 125.

3 MND, *2016 Defense White Paper*, p. 127.

4 MND, *2016 Defense White Paper*, p. 129.

5 Tae-jung Kang, "South Korea: Asia's New Powerhouse Arms Exporter," *The Diplomat*, May 25, 2014; Jon Grevatt, "Peninsular Procurement," *Jane's Defense Weekly*, October 17, 2013.

6 Aude Fleurant, et al., *Factsheet: SIPRI Top 100 Arms-Producing and Military Services Companies 2016* (Stockholm: SIPRI, December 2017), p. 1, 2, 8.

7 Wesley Spreen, *International Cooperation in the Aerospace Industry* (Kuala Lumpur: ADPR Consult, 1998), p. 118.

8 "South Korea to Order 5 More U-214 AIP Submarines to Bridge to Indigenous Boats," *Defense Industry Daily*, May 08, 2015 (www.defenseindustrydaily.com/KSS-II-South-Korea-Orders-6-More-U-214-AIP-Submarines-05242); Jung Sung-ki, "S. Korea Unveils Cruise, Ballistic Missiles," *Defense News*, April 23, 2014.

9 Grevatt, "Peninsular Procurement"; Choi, "South Korea," p. 185.

10 Jung Sung-ki, "S. Korea Aims to Build Indigenous Missile Shield," *Defense News*, March 26, 2012.

11 Jung Sung-Ki, "Hanwha Emerges as South Korea's Defense Giant," *Defense News*, July 29, 2015.

12 Jeff Jeong, "South Korea Unveils First Images of KF-X Design with European Missiles," *Defense News*, June 29, 2018.

13 Dan Darling, "To Little Surprise, South Korea Selects KAI-Lockheed Team to Develop Its KF-X Indigenous Fighter," *Forecast International*, March 31, 2015.
14 Korea Aerospace Industries (KAI) website, accessed October 4, 2018.
15 Ju-ming Park, "South Korea Targets Growing Global Defense Market," *Reuters*, August 25, 2013; Joo-hee Lee, "KAI Aims to Export 800 Aircraft by 2030," *Korea Herald*, November 25, 2002.
16 KAI website (www.koreaaero.com/english/pr_center/cpr_view.asp). Nevertheless, Korea Air (KAL) has tried to compete with KAI in military aircraft production, at one point teaming up with Airbus Industries in (an ultimately unsuccessful) contest to win away the KF-X program from KAI. "For New Jet, It's a Dogfight between KAI and KAL," *Korea Joongang Daily*, February 6, 2015.
17 Hoon Noh, *South Korea's "Cooperative Self-Reliant Defense": Goals and Directions*, KIDA Paper No. 10 (Seoul: Korea Institute for Defense Analyses, April 2005), p. 5.
18 Lee Jong-sup, "The ROK-US Alliance and Self-Reliant Defense in the ROK," in Alexandre Y. Mansourov, ed., *A Turning Point: Democratic Consolidation in the ROK and Strategic Readjustment in the US-ROK Alliance* (Honolulu, HI: Asia-Pacific Center for Security Studies, 2005), pp. 246–266; Han Yong-sup, "Analyzing South Korea's Defense Reform 2020," *Korean Journal of Defense Analysis*, Vol. 18, No. 1 (Spring, 2008), pp. 129–132; Mikyoung Kim, "The US Military Transformation and its Implications for the ROK-US Alliance," *IFANS Review*, Vol. 13, No. 1 (July 2005), pp. 21–22.
19 ROK Ministry of National Defense, *Defense White Paper 1999: Republic of Korea* (Seoul: Korea Institute for Defense Analyses, 1999), p. 145.
20 Choi, "South Korea," p. 185.
21 For a fuller explanation of this "technonationalist impulse," see Richard J. Samuels, *Rich Nation, Strong Army: National Security and the Technological Transformation of Japan* (Ithica: Cornel University Press, 1994); Christopher W. Hughes, "The Slow Death of Japanese Techno-Nationalism?" *Journal of Strategic Studies*, Vol. 34, No. 3 (June 2011). Although these studies address the Japanese case, South Korean defense industrialization has run along very similar lines. See Richard A. Bitzinger, *Arming Asia: Technonationalism and its Impact on Local Defense Industries* (London: Routledge, 2017), Chapter 5.
22 Cheng and Chinworth, "The Teeth of the Little Tigers," p. 249; Choi, "South Korea," p. 199; Robert Karniol, "South Korean Industry: Learning Curve," *Jane's Defense Weekly*, October 22, 2003.
23 Korkmaz and Rydqvist, *The Republic of Korea: A Defense and Security Primer*, p. 77.
24 Baek and Moon, "Technological Dependence, Supplier Control," pp. 158–159; US Congress, Office of Technology Assessment (OTA), *Global Arms Trade: Commerce in Advanced Military Technology and Weapons* (Washington, DC: Government Printing Office, June 1991), p. 131.
25 MND, *2016 Defense White Paper*, pp. 114–115.
26 Kim Jaewon, "Korea Aerospace Ex-Chief Indicted for Fraud, Embezzlement," *Nikkei Asian Review*, October 11, 2017.
27 Fleurant, et al., *Factsheet: SIPRI Top 100 Arms-Producing and Military Services Companies 2016*, p. 1.
28 SIPRI Arms Trade Database.
29 MND, *2016 Defense White Paper*, pp. 121–122.
30 Jung Sung-ki, "S. Korean Arms Industry Emerges as Global Power," *Defense News*, July 16, 2007.
31 KAI website (www.koreaaero.com/english/pr_center/cpr_view.asp).
32 Korkmaz and Rydqvist, *The Republic of Korea: A Defense and Security Primer*, pp. 74–75.

33 MND, *2016 Defense White Paper*, p. 118.
34 MND, *2016 Defense White Paper*, p. 118.
35 Kyong-ae Choi, "South Korea in Talks to Develop Passenger Plane," *Wall Street Journal*, October 8, 2012.
36 Baek and Moon, "Technological Dependence, Supplier Control," pp. 164–165.
37 Chung-in Moon and Jae-Ok Paek, *Defense Innovation and Industrialization in South Korea – Assessments, Institutional Arrangements, and Comparative Implications*, paper produced for the "Conference on China's Defense and Dual-Use Science, Technology, and Industrial Base," sponsored by the Institute on Global Conflict and Cooperation, University of California, San Diego (1–2 July 2010), p. 1.
38 Moon and Paek, *Defense Innovation and Industrialization in South Korea*, p. 8, 12, 14.
39 Moon and Paek, *Defense Innovation and Industrialization in South Korea*, p. 6.
40 Steve Glain, "Seoul Dallies under US Umbrella," *Asian Wall Street Journal*, April 19, 1994.
41 Jung Sung-ki, "S. Korean Vehicles Suffer Gliches, Budget Cuts," *Defense News*, July 18, 2011; Lee Tae-hoon, "Korea to Buy German Engines for K2," *The Korea Times*, April 2, 2012.
42 Jung, "S. Korean Vehicles Suffer Gliches."
43 Nolan, "South Korea: Ambitious Client of the United States," p. 64; Cheng and Chinworth, "The Teeth of the Little Tigers," p. 276.
44 Dong Joon Hwang, *Economic Interdependence and its Impact on National Security: Defense Industry Cooperation and Technology Transfer*, paper presented to the "National Defense University Pacific Symposium," February 27–28, 1992, Washington, DC, pp. 12–14.
45 See Cheng and Chinworth, "The Teeth of the Little Tigers," p. 250; Choi, "South Korea," p. 201.
46 Jung, "S. Korean Arms Industry Emerges as Global Power."
47 Keith Krause, *Arms and the State: Patterns of Military Production and Trade* (Cambridge: Cambridge University Press, 1992), p. 172.
48 Bryan Harris, "South Korean Defense Sector in Disarray after $16bn US Tender Fails," *Financial Times*, October 4, 2018; Jeff Jeong, "T-X Loss Casts Shadow South Korean Arms Exports," *Defense News*, October 4, 2018.
49 "Missiles of South Korea," *Missile Threat – CSIS Missile Defense Project* website, accessed October 8, 2018.
50 For example, KAI has intentions of exporting the vast majority of its T-50 and KF-X aircraft production – at least 800 T-50s and up to 600 KF-Xs – to other countries.

20 Japan's defence industry

From indigenisation to exploring internationalisation

Christopher W. Hughes

Introduction

Japan's policy-makers, in line with the first modernisation efforts of the Meiji Period (1868–1912) and famous maxim of 'rich nation, strong army', have long viewed an indigenous defence production capability as integral to grand strategy and a means to maintain national security autonomy.[1] Japan thereafter by the early twentieth century built itself into one of the great imperial powers and most advanced producers of warships and airframes. But Japan's catastrophic defeat in 1945, immediate post-war demilitarisation, and subsequent minimalist defensive stance, reinforced by a range of anti-militaristic principles, necessarily limited the type and quantity of military production—most strikingly through eschewing possession of capabilities that form 'war potential'. In turn, Japan's utilisation of defence production and arms transfers for security ends was limited by the self-imposed 1967 and 1976 bans on the export of arms and military technology.[2]

Nevertheless, even as Japan's defence production stance has been constrained in comparison to other major powers in the post-war era it has remained a central element of Japanese security and international strategy.[3] Japanese policy-makers and industry have worked to build an indigenous defence production base (*kokusanka*), with distinctive organisational structures, and that has proved relatively effective for the past several decades in preserving the Japan Self Defence Forces' (JSDF) access to advanced military technology, the potential to step change into more ambitious weapons systems if necessary, and a degree of international leverage for Japan.

In more recent years, however, Japan's model of defence production has come under stress due to a combination of the changing domestic political economy, restructuring of the global defence industry, and pressures of the regional security environment. Japan's policy-makers and defence manufacturers have thus now sought to adapt their production model—retaining many features of the post-war system and domestic production whilst also beginning to embark on new international collaborations.

Japan's post-war security constraints and defence production model

Japan's total defeat in World War II and the ensuing economic devastation, loss of independence under the US-dominated Allied Occupation (1945–1951), and undergoing of the process of the disbandment of the Imperial Armed Forces and demilitarisation embodied in the acceptance of Article 9 of the so-called 'peace constitution' of 1946, imposed a series of particular—if perhaps unique for a major industrialised state and eventually major military power—constraints on Japan's security policy for the entire post-war period.

Anti-militaristic prohibitions and principles shaping defence production

Article 9 of the constitution in its first paragraph renounced war as a sovereign right and the use of force for settling international disputes, and in its second paragraph the maintenance of land, sea and air forces for accomplishing the aims of the first paragraph were prohibited, along with the non-recognition of the right of the belligerency of the state. Although the Occupation authorities originally envisaged Japan's absolute and permanent demilitarisation, and the main opposition Japan Socialist Party viewed Article 9 as prohibiting the maintenance of any armed forces, conservative politicians—eventually to emerge into the long-governing Liberal Democratic Party (LDP)—held to the interpretation that armed forces could be maintained for 'exclusively defence-oriented defence' purposes.

Consequently, as the Cold War took hold in East Asia, the US 'reverse course' meant that it encouraged Japan to function as a partner to contain communism and to reestablish its armed forces, the US-Japan security treaty was signed in 1951 under which Japan provided bases for the US for the defence of the Far East, and the JSDF was founded in 1954. But even as Japan gradually remilitarised in the post-war period, the legacy of wartime defeat and the influence of Article 9 continued to place strong constraints on its doctrines for the procurement and use of military capabilities.

Japan's constraints have included the interpretation since the early 1950s of Article 9 to allow only the exercise of the right of individual self-defence and prohibition on the exercise of the right of collective self-defence, meaning in essence that it could only defend itself and not come to the assistance of its US security treaty partner. Japan was not to reinterpret and lift this ban on the exercise of collective self-defence until 2015.[4] In addition, a series of anti-militaristic principles were enunciated (Table 20.1), derived from the spirit of Article 9 but not constitutionally binding.

Japan has progressively eroded or abandoned these anti-militaristic principles during the course of the post-war era (Table 20.1). Japan has felt obliged to stretch and reinterpret constitutional constraints due to the need to respond to the evolving security environment in the East Asia region and

Table 20.1 Japan's anti-militaristic principles derived from the Constitution

Japan not to become a great military power	
• Japan provides no strict definition of the criteria for this, but stresses that it will not acquire military capabilities above the minimum necessary or that can threaten other states • This has included non-procurement of power projection capabilities such aircraft carriers, long-range missiles and bomber aircraft.	• Japan has indicated since 2018 that it is studying the conversion of *Izumo*-class helicopter carrying destroyers to deploy fixed-wing F-35B fighters and thus acquire 'defensive' aircraft carriers • Japan in 2018 budgeted for the procurement of long-range cruise missiles
Three non-nuclear principles	
• Prime Minister Satō Eisaku introduced the three non-nuclear principles in 1967. • Japan is not to produce, possess, or introduce nuclear weapons. • Japan is to rely instead on the US nuclear umbrella, although it does not regard the possession of its own nuclear deterrent as necessarily unconstitutional if used for the purposes of self-defence. • The first two principles were strengthened by Japan's entry into the Non-Proliferation (NPT) in 1976.	• The third principle has been breached by the introduction into or transit through Japanese ports of nuclear weapons on US naval vessels. • Japanese policy-makers in the past have studied the possible procurement of nuclear weapons • Japan now possesses many of the components of a 'recessed' nuclear deterrent, including solid-fuelled rockets as delivery vehicles, satellites, a QZSS system for GPS and targeting, and re-entry vehicles
Peaceful use of space	
• In May 1969, the Diet imposed a resolution stating that Japanese activities in space should be limited to peaceful purposes, interpreted as meaning 'non-military' activities.	• Japan's development of spy satellites and a BMD system since the 1990s has challenged this principle. • Japan eventually overturned this principle with the Basic Space Law in 2008 allowing the 'defensive' use of space.

Restrictions on the exports of arms and military technology

- In 1967, Prime Minister Satō' Eisaku's administration first enunciated restrictions on arms exports to communist states, countries under UN sanctions, and parties to international disputes.
- In 1976, Prime Minister Miki Takeo's administration ordered restraint in the case of all states, and prohibited the export of weapon-related technology.
- Restrictions have largely held, even though Japan has exported certain dual-use technologies with civilian and military applications

- Prime Minister Nakasone Yasuhiro partially breached this principle by signing an Exchange of Technology Agreement Between Japan and the United States in November 1983.
- Prime Minister Noda Yoshiki in December 2011 issued a 'Statement on Guidelines for Overseas Transfer of Defence Equipment', allowing Japan's overseas transfers of defence equipment to enable a more proactive contribution to international security, to improve the performance of defence equipment, and to strengthen the alliance with the US and with other security cooperation partners.
- Prime Minister Abe Shinzo in April 2014 instituted the new Three Principles of Defence Equipment Transfers, preventing export to states considered to impede international peace and security, such as those transgressing international treaties or under UN sanctions, but allowing export to states contributing to international peace or Japan's security such as the US, NATO countries, and those engaged in UN PKO, and that could prove the controls in place to prevent re-export to third countries.

One percent of GNP limit on defence expenditure

- In 1976, Prime Minister Miki established the principle that defence expenditure should be limited to 1% of GNP.

- Prime Minister Nakasone Yasuhirō in effect breached this principle by pushing defence spending just above 1% in 1986.
- Successive administrations have kept Japanese defence spending at around the 1% level.
- Prime Minister Abe announced in the National Diet in March 2017 that his administration had no intention of suppressing defense expenditure below 1% of GDP and that in fact no such budgetary policy ceiling existed

globally, and increased expectations from its US security partner for a Japanese international security contribution. During the second phase of the Cold War, Japan's prime concern was the expansion of the USSR's influence in East Asia, and in the post-Cold War period Japan has faced North Korea's nuclear and ballistic missile programmes and most significantly China's rise and military modernisation. The consequence was that the JSDF underwent a major quantitative and qualitative expansion in the early and mid-1980s focussed on the build-up of Ground Self Defence Force (GSDF) heavy tanks and artillery, Maritime Self Defence Force (MSDF) destroyers and anti-submarine warfare capabilities, and Air Self Defence Force (ASDF) interceptors to prevent a Soviet invasion of northern Japan and to provide a defensive shield for US power projection from Japan. Since the start of the new millennium, the JSDF has emphasised the shift to a 'joint dynamic defence force', with more mobile and technologically advanced capabilities, ballistic missile defences (BMD), and deployments southwards to respond to North Korean threats and China's maritime activities and incursions into Japan's outlying island territories in the East China Sea. Throughout these periods, Japan has gradually deepened the security relationship with the US, to the point that by 1980 it became referred to as the US-Japan 'alliance'; that by the early 2000s Japan was prepared to despatch the MSDF and ASDF in non-combat roles to the Indian Ocean and southern Iraq to support US operations; and that by the middle of this decade the National Diet passed extensive legislation to enable JSDF collective self-defence in support of the US in a variety of scenarios.[5]

Japan by the contemporary period has thus evolved gradually once again into a significant military power and become a key US ally, deploying highly advanced capabilities. Nonetheless, Japan's development of its post-war security policy and choice of military capabilities has involved a constant navigation between the tensions of constitutional and anti-militaristic constraints and emerging external security drivers. In turn, Japan's development of its defence production model has also been very much entwined within this context and has had to constantly adapt to internal and external constraints.

Japan's rebuilding of an indigenous defence production model in the Cold War period

In the immediate post-war period, and following the logic of demilitarisation, Japan's defence industry faced the genuine possibility of extinction. The Occupation authorities banned all defence production and began to break up the main private industrial conglomerates deemed responsible for encouraging pre-war militarism—including Mitsubishi Heavy Industries (MHI), Mitsubishi Electric Company (MELCO), Ishikawajima Harima Heavy Industries (IHI), Nakajima Aircraft (today Fuji Heavy Industries [FHI]), Kawasaki Heavy Industries (KHI), Hitachi, Sumitomo, Mitsui, and Nippon Kōgyō Sangyō (today Nissan)—into smaller companies, many retooling for civilian production such as automobiles and scooters.

However, the reverse course, outbreak of the Korean War, and US demand for military vehicles and spares, helped to revive Japanese defence production and recoalesce the industrial conglomerates, and more generally stimulate growth for the rest of the devastated economy. Moreover, Japan's policy-makers—the Japan Defence Agency (JDA, Ministry of Defense [JMOD] since 2007), Ministry of Economy and Industry (METI), Ministry of Foreign Affairs (MOFA), and Defense Production Committee (DPC) of the Japan Business Federation (Nippon Keidanren) as the umbrella organisation for a variety of defense producer associations and individual enterprises—never abandoned their belief in the importance of indigenous military technology to help preserve national autonomy and thus have sought to rebuild the defense industrial base.

Japan's policy-makers and industrial actors have articulated a series of objectives for building the defence production base. First, Japan should develop a defense production system capable of maintaining JSDF national deterrent capabilities. Military technology should meet Japan's 'unique' defensive needs, and especially its policy of 'exclusively defense-oriented defense' and geographical particularities of long coast lines and deep surrounding sea space. Second, Japan's defense production should provide a technological base to augment negotiating leverage in the broader international community, but especially technology to bring into the context of alliance cooperation with the US. Third, Japan should ensure self-sufficiency and stable supplies of defense equipment and retain the necessary highly-skilled workers in a market environment of relatively low order numbers to the sole customer of the JSDF, whilst at the same time being able to ramp up production in a time of national emergency. METI and the DPC, in particular, have promoted Japan's limited in scale but technologically advanced defense production base as part of industrial policy and as a means to generate 'dual-use' technology for the civilian sector.

Japan's policy-makers and industrialists have maintained a rough consensus that an indigenous production base would not be redeveloped through a strategy of autarky and large-scale defence spending; this was simply not practical given the initial post-war state of the Japanese economy and history of interconnection with militarism. Instead, Japan would keep defence expenditure to a minimum, and nurture indigenous production in part through the government's direct and indirect subsidisation of the defense industry, but more importantly through embedding it in the larger civilian-oriented sector, and subordinating defence production to the government's civilian developmental priorities. Japan's civilian sector would draw technological 'spin-off' from the military sector, and where necessary the smaller military sector would derive 'spin-on' technology from the civilian sector. In Japan, there was to be nothing akin to the so-called 'military-industrial complex' characterised by large-scale and predominantly defence-oriented corporations with close ties to the military establishment.

Japan would pursue a degree of international cooperation with the US in order to provide foreign military sales (FMS) to supply relatively fast, low-cost, and low-risk technology for the JSDF's immediate needs, and licensed production for learning and innovating upon already tested defence technology to help rebuild indigenous technological capabilities, and to then enable greater national autonomy over the longer term. But Japan's policy-makers have always been wary that reliance on the US for FMS and licensed production may mean restrictions on being able to access and produce the very latest foreign weapons systems, and that the opportunities for learning technologically are necessarily limited. Instead, Japan's traditional preference has been for pure indigenous production and autonomous technology, offering as it does the maximum contribution to the defence production base and maintaining of employment, even if also presenting high technological development risks and high procurement costs.

Japan's defence production structure: budgets, scale, participants

Defence expenditure trends and industry scale

As Japan's 'economic miracle' and period of rapid growth took hold from the 1960s to 1980s, and as JSDF obligations and capabilities increased significantly in the 1980s, so the national defence budget rose steeply. By the mid-2000s, Japan's defence expenditure in nominal dollar terms reached US$40-$45 billion, and received international attention as it ranked amongst the top five globally. The relative size of Japan's defence expenditure was inflated, though, by the strength at that time of the yen against the US dollar. If Japan's defence budget is calculated throughout in nominal yen it can be seen to have stagnated and actually fallen from the late 1990s, with around US$40 billion or ¥5 trillion accepted as a practical accepted ceiling on expenditure (Table 20.2, Figure 20.1).

Japan's defence budget did not experience the large scale growth of the US in the post-9/11 period or of a rising China since the 1990s. The Japanese economic downturn since the early 1990s and heavy government pump-priming expenditure and debt (government gross public debt reaching 200 percent of GDP by 2013; the highest in the industrialised world) has constrained the room for the expansion of defence spending. Japan's government has generally kept defence budget increases at less than 1 percent annually and generally maintained its 1 percent of GNP limit on defence expenditure (Table 20.2). Defence expenditure as a proportion of annual government expenditure has remained constant at around 5 to 6 percent (Table 20.2). Significantly for defence production, the proportion of the defence budget available for equipment procurement has fallen from around 28 percent in 1988 to around 17 percent by 2018, with increasing proportions of the budget earmarked instead for personnel costs and pensions (Table 20.3, Figure 20.2). Research and development (R&D) allocations have fluctuated at around 2 to 3 percent of the defence budget in this period (Table 20.4). Furthermore, defence expenditure has declined relatively as a government priority, staying steady at around 5 percent, in comparison to the increasing proportion of expenditure, at around 40 percent devoted to social security and public works in the last decade.[6] Japan only began to reverse these trends with the ascension to power of Prime Minister Abe Shinzō in 2012 and his administration's implementing of annual

Table 20.2 Japan's defence expenditure in nominal yen, as percentage of GNP, and percentage of total government expenditure, 1975–2018

	Expenditure (¥100 million)	*Percentage of GNP*	*Percentage of total government expenditure*
1975	13,273	0.84	6.23
1976	15,124	0.90	6.22
1977	16,906	0.88	5.93
1978	19,010	0.90	5.54
1979	20,945	0.90	5.43
1980	22,302	0.90	5.24
1981	24,000	0.91	5.24
1982	25,861	0.93	5.21
1983	27,542	0.98	5.47
1984	29,346	0.99	5.80
1985	31,371	1.00	5.98
1986	33,435	0.93	6.18
1987	35,174	1.00	6.50
1988	37,003	1.01	6.53
1989	39,198	1.01	6.49
1990	41,593	1.00	6.28
1991	43,860	0.95	6.23
1992	45,518	0.94	6.30
1993	46,406	0.94	6.41
1994	46,835	0.96	6.41
1995	47,236	0.96	6.65
1996	48,455	0.98	6.45
1997	49,414	0.96	6.39
1998	49,420	0.95	6.35
1999	49,201	0.99	6.01
2000	49,218	0.99	5.79
2001	49,388	0.95	5.98
2002	49,395	1.00	6.08
2003	49,265	0.99	6.02
2004	48,764	0.98	5.94
2005	48,301	0.94	5.88
2006	47,906	0.93	6.01
2007	47,818	0.92	5.80
2008	47,426	0.90	5.71
2009	47,028	0.92	5.30
2010	46,826	0.96	5.10
2011	46,625	0.96	5.00

(*Continued*)

Table 20.2 (Cont.)

	Expenditure (¥100 million)	*Percentage of GNP*	*Percentage of total government expenditure*
2012	46,453	0.97	5.10
2013	46,804	0.96	5.05
2014	47,838	0.96	4.99
2015	48,221	0.96	5.01
2016	48,607	0.94	5.03
2017	48,996	0.86	5.03
2018	49,338	0.87	5.05

Source: Asagumo Shimbunsha, *Bōei Handobukku,* various years.

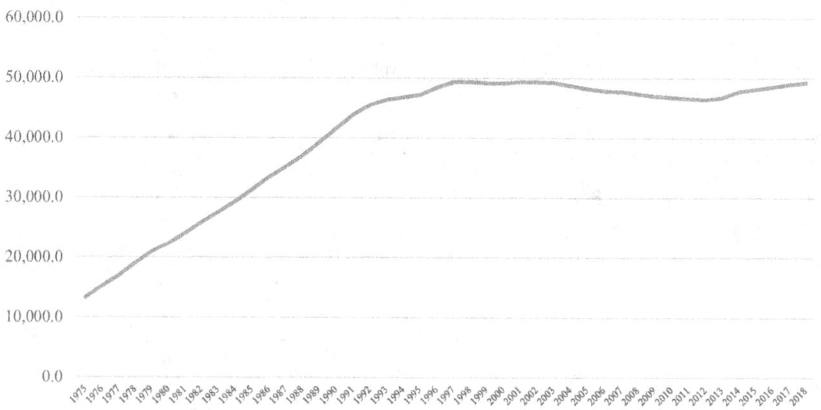

Figure 20.1 Japan's defence expenditure 1975–2018 (¥100 million).

defence increases between 1 and 2 percent from 2013 to 2018. Indeed, the JMOD under the Abe administration in 2018 placed a request for a 2.1 increase to the defence budget for 2019/2020 to create Japan's largest defence budget in the post-war period.[7]

Japan's defense industry in relation to overall national economic size is highly moderate in scale, accounting since the 1980s for less than 1 percent of total industrial production.[8] Additionally, defense production since the early 1980s can be seen to account for only a small proportion of total national production in a number of key industrial sectors; for instance, registering less than 1 percent in electronics communications and vehicles. Ammunition and aircraft (although even military aircraft production has declined as a proportion of national production from over 80 percent in the 1980s to around 30 percent in 2015), and to some extent shipbuilding, are exceptions with much higher percentages (Figure 20.3).

Table 20.3 Defence equipment procurement as a percentage of overall Japanese defence expenditure (%)

1988	28.1
1989	28.0
1990	27.4
1991	27.7
1992	25.1
1993	23.3
1994	21.3
1995	18.4
1996	18.9
1997	18.9
1998	19.2
1999	19.6
2000	18.6
2001	18.6
2002	18.6
2003	18.3
2004	18.1
2005	18.6
2006	17.9
2007	18.1
2008	17.1
2009	17.5
2010	16.5
2011	16.7
2012	16.3
2013	15.9
2014	16.6
2015	15.4
2016	15.8
2017	17.2
2018	16.6

Source: Asagumo Shimbunsha, *Bōei Handobukku*, various years.

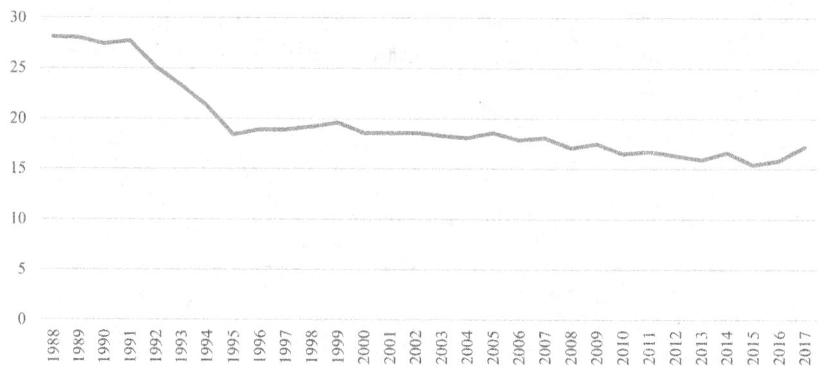

Figure 20.2 Defence equipment procurement as a percentage of overall Japanese defence expenditure, 1988–2017.

Table 20.4 Japan's defence R&D budget, 1988–2018 (Unit: ¥100 million; %)

Year	*Defence budget*	*R&D budget*	*% increase over previous year*	*R&D ratio to defence budget*
1988	37,003	733	–	2.0
1989	39,198	828	12.96	2.1
1990	41,593	929	12.20	2.2
1991	43,860	1,029	10.76	2.3
1992	45,518	1,148	11.56	2.5
1993	46,406	1,238	7.84	2.7
1994	46,835	1,255	1.37	2.7
1995	47,236	1,401	11.63	3.0
1996	48,455	1,496	6.78	3.1
1997	49,414	1,605	7.29	3.2
1998	49,290	1,277	-20.44	2.6
1999	49,201	1,307	2.35	2.7
2000	49,218	1,205	-7.80	2.4
2001	49,388	1,353	12.28	2.7
2002	49,395	1,277	-5.62	2.6
2003	49,265	1,470	15.11	3.0
2004	48,764	1,707	16.12	3.5
2005	48,301	1,316	-22.91	2.7
2006	47,906	1,714	30.24	3.6

(*Continued*)

Table 20.4 (Cont.)

Year	*Defence budget*	*R&D budget*	*% increase over previous year*	*R&D ratio to defence budget*
2007	47,818	1,445	-15.69	3.0
2008	47,426	1,728	19.6	3.6
2009	47,028	1,198	30.7	2.5
2010	46,826	1,588	32.6	3.4
2011	46,625	851	46.4	1.8
2012	46,453	944	10.9	2.0
2013	46,804	1,541	63.3	3.3
2014	47,838	1,477	-4.2	3.1
2015	48,221	1,411	-4.5	2.9
2016	48,607	1,055	-25.3	2.2
2017	48,996	1,217	15.4	2.5
2018	49,388	1,034	-15.0	2.1

Source: *Bōei Hakusho 2006*; *Bōei Handobukku* 1997, 1998, 2007, 2017.

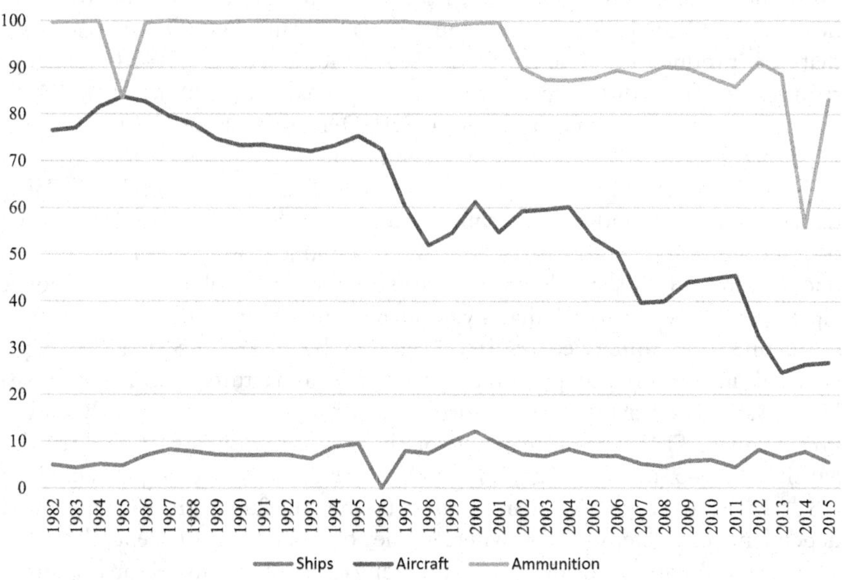

Figure 20.3 Defence production sectors as a percentage of overall industrial production in Japan, 1982–2015.

Defence contractors

In accordance with Japan's techno-nationalist strategy, defense production has been concentrated within a relatively small number of conglomerates largely focused on civilian production. MHI has remained the leading defense contractor over the last two decades (only once losing its top spot to KHI in 2015) in terms of sales and numbers of contracts, and generally securing up to 25 percent of all contracts.[9] (Table 20.5) The top 20 contracts have been dominated by the 'heavies' of KHI, FHI, Sumitomo Heavy Industries (SHI), Toshiba, IHI, MELCO, NEC and Komatsu, and with trading companies such as Itōchū and Sumitomo involved in the importation of defense equipment. These enterprises operate a near oligopoly in Japanese defense procurement with over 75 percent of total contracts, but defense tends to be a small share of their overall business. MHI, despite taking nearly a quarter of defense contracts, typically derives only around 10 percent of its total sales from this sector. The story is similar for KHI, and for others the share is less still at below 4 percent. Globally, Japanese defense contractors are also relatively small in scale, with MHI, from a high of 11th in the list of the world's largest defence contractors by sales in 2000, declining to 43rd by 2018.[10]

However, outside the top 20 defense contractors there exists a range of small and medium enterprise (SME) primary and second subcontractors more heavily vested in defense production. The DPC and JMOD have calculated that the production of a Maritime Self Defense Force (MSDF) destroyer requires up to 72 direct contractors, 1,378 primary subcontractors and 1,073 secondary subcontractors; a Ground Self Defense Force (GSDF) Type-90 main battle tank (MBT) 52 direct contractors, 842 primary subcontractors and 568 secondary contractors; an Air Self Defense Force (ASDF) F-15J 13 direct contractors, 530 primary subcontractors and 593 secondary subcontractors; and an ASDF *Patriot* SAM four direct contractors, 125 primary subcontractors, and 1,093 secondary contractors.[11] The Shipbuilders' Association of Japan (SAJ) has estimated that over 80 percent of the work for destroyers, submarines and minesweepers is carried out by SMEs.[12] SMEs are in part engaged in metal-bashing and component manufacture, but many possess highly-skilled specialist manufacturing capabilities for certain technologies. For instance, SMEs produce many of the key components of the Standard Missile (SM)-3 missile upgrades jointly developed between Japan and the US.[13] Many of these SMEs, in contrast to the top 20 contractors, are highly dependent on defense. For whereas the overall level of dependency on defense of all companies that have some engagement in this sector is approximately 4 percent, there are a considerable number of companies with an annual total turnover of less than ¥500 million (approximately US$5million) which are between 50–90 percent dependent on the defense business.[14]

Table 20.5 Japan's top 20 defence production companies, 1997–2016 (Unit: ¥100 million)

1997					*1998*					*1999*				
Position	*Company*	*No. of contracts*	*Amount*	*Percentage of annual procurements*	*Position*	*Company*	*No. of contracts*	*Amount*	*Percentage of annual procurements*	*Position*	*Company*	*No. of contracts*	*Amount*	*Percentage of annual procurements*
1	MHI	235	2,719	20.6	**1**	MHI	222	3,234	26.7	**1**	MHI	208	2,797	22.1
2	KHI	117	1,468	11.1	**2**	MELCO	188	1,030	8.3	**2**	KHI	97	1,322	10.5
3	MELCO	197	1,287	9.7	**3**	KHI	93	872	7.0	**3**	MELCO	200	1,121	8.9
4	NEC	306	746	5.6	**4**	IHI	78	644	5.2	**4**	Toshiba	116	538	4.3
5	IHI	82	662	5.0	**5**	NEC	207	446	3.6	**5**	IHI	72	535	4.2
6	Toshiba	130	486	3.7	**6**	Toshiba	127	377	3.0	**6**	NEC	293	426	3.4
7	Marine United	4	377	2.9	**7**	Komatsu	47	353	2.8	**7**	Komatsu	44	371	2.9
8	Komatsu	44	344	2.6	**8**	Mitsui Zosen	6	277	2.2	**8**	Hitachi	37	344	2.7
9	Nissan Motors	60	253	1.9	**9**	Nissan Motors	63	267	2.2	**9**	Nissan Motors	61	273	2.2
10	NEC Business Machines	220	252	1.9	**10**	Marine United	1	267	2.1	**10**	NEC Business Machines	233	255	2.0
11	Hitachi	70	238	1.8	**11**	NEC Business Machines	231	262	2.1	**11**	Marine United	1	247	2.0
12	Daikin Industries	67	179	1.4	**12**	Hitachi	53	219	1.8	**12**	Hitachi	55	218	1.7
13	FHI	49	171	1.3	**13**	Mitsubishi Corporation	19	157	1.3	**13**	Fujitsu	129	166	1.3

(Continued)

Table 20.5 (Cont.)

1997					*1998*					*1999*				
Position	*Company*	*No. of contracts*	*Amount*	*Percentage of annual procurements*	*Position*	*Company*	*No. of contracts*	*Amount*	*Percentage of annual procurements*	*Position*	*Company*	*No. of contracts*	*Amount*	*Percentage of annual procurements*
14	Oki Electric Industry	62	164	1.2	**14**	Oki Electric Industry	68	150	1.2	**14**	Yamada Corporation	39	160	1.3
15	Itochu Aviation	48	157	1.2	**15**	Daikin Industries	49	148	1.2	**15**	Daikin Industries	53	134	1.1
16	Shinmaywa Industries	9	148	1.1	**16**	Fujitsu	115	147	1.2	**16**	JSW	21	127	1.0
17	Kanematsu	12	130	1.0	**17**	Itochu Aviation	23	136	1.1	**17**	Itochu Aviation	32	120	1.0
18	NKK Steel	19	114	0.9	**18**	FHI	35	133	1.1	**18**	FHI	25	112	0.9
19	Fujitsu	137	112	0.8	**19**	JSW	16	130	1.0	**19**	Shinmaywa Industries	8	107	0.8
20	Isuzu Motors	62	100	0.8	**20**	Kanematsu	5	111	0.9	**20**	Oki Electric Industry	64	104	0.8
Total		1,930	10,106	76.6		Total	1,646	9.457	76.1		Total	1,788	9	75

2000					2001					2002				
Position	*Company*	*No. of contracts*	*Amount*	*Percentage of annual procurements*	*Position*	*Company*	*No. of contracts*	*Amount*	*Percentage of annual procurements*	*Position*	*Company*	*No. of contracts*	*Amount*	*Percentage of annual procurements*
1	MHI	222	3,074	24.4	**1**	MHI	226	2,755	21.7	**1**	MHI	205	3,481	27.2
2	MELCO	205	1,208	9.6	**2**	KHI	114	1,213	9.6	**2**	KHI	102	1,102	8.6
3	KHI	112	987	7.8	**3**	MELCO	185	1,010	8	**3**	MELCO	178	735	5.7
4	IHI	72	540	4.3	**4**	NEC	328	577	4.5	**4**	IHI	48	527	4.1
5	NEC	336	465	3.7	**5**	IHI	45	545	4.3	**5**	Toshiba	123	498	3.9
6	Toshiba	128	430	3.4	**6**	Toshiba	126	452	3.6	**6**	NEC	312	485	3.8
7	Mitsui Zosen	5	363	2.9	**7**	Hitachi Zosen	33	398	3.1	**7**	Komatsu	43	357	2.8
8	Komatsu	47	354	2.8	**8**	Komatsu	55	372	2.9	**8**	Itochu	5	232	1.8
9	Shinmaywa Industries	11	323	2.6	**9**	IHI Aerospace	53	273	2.2	**9**	Shinmaywa Industries	13	229	1.8
10	NEC Business Machines	234	277	2.2	**10**	NEC Business Machines	179	256	2	**10**	Fujitsu	166	223	1.7
11	IHI Aerospace	46	261	2.1	**11**	Hitachi	78	251	2	**11**	FHI	38	216	1.7
12	Hitachi	78	183	1.5	**12**	Shinmaywa Industries	10	250	2	**12**	NEC Business Machines	164	187	1.5
13	Yamada Corporation	47	159	1.3	**13**	Marine United	2	250	2	**13**	Daikin Industries	57	179	1.4

(*Continued*)

(Cont.)

2000					*2001*					*2002*				
Position	*Company*	*No. of contracts*	*Amount*	*Percentage of annual procurements*	*Position*	*Company*	*No. of contracts*	*Amount*	*Percentage of annual procurements*	*Position*	*Company*	*No. of contracts*	*Amount*	*Percentage of annual procurements*
14	FHI	42	149	1.2	**14**	FHI	28	180	1.4	**14**	IHI Aerospace	42	159	1.2
15	Daikin Industries	53	146	1.2	**15**	Fujitsu	144	160	1.3	**15**	Nippon Kokan	22	143	1.1
16	Fujitsu	143	146	1.2	**16**	Daikin Industries	57	160	1.3	**16**	Hitachi	69	142	1.1
17	Mitsubishi Corporation	23	144	1.1	**17**	JSW	19	120	1	**17**	Mitsubishi Corporation	17	109	0.8
18	JSW	18	143	1.1	**18**	Nippon Kokan	2	111	0.9	**18**	Isuzu Motors	61	94	0.7
19	Itochu Aviation	23	112	0.9	**19**	Isuzu Motors	62	109	0.9	**19**	Universal Shipbuilding Corporation	26	82	0.6
20	Oki Electric Industry	72	98	0.8	**20**	Oki Electric Industry	60	102	0.8	**20**	Itochu Aviation	33	81	0.6
	Total	1,917	9.563	75.9		Total	1,806	9,544	75.2		Total	1,724	9,261	72.4

2003					*2004*					*2005*				
Position	*Company*	*No. of contracts*	*Amount*	*Percentage of annual procurements*	*Position*	*Company*	*No. of contracts*	*Amount*	*Percentage of annual procurements*	*Position*	*Company*	*No. of contracts*	*Amount*	*Percentage of annual procurements*
1	MHI	213	2,817	22.1	**1**	MHI	164	2,706	20.7	**1**	MHI	192	2,417	17.6
2	KHI	97	1,588	12.5	**2**	KHI	97	1,429	10.9	**2**	KHI	83	1,297	9.4
3	MELCO	170	949	7.5	**3**	MELCO	169	1,032	7.9	**3**	MELCO	165	1,142	8.3
4	NEC	306	563	4.4	**4**	NEC	270	906	6.9	**4**	NEC	314	10,078	7.8
5	Toshiba	107	389	3.1	**5**	IHI	40	493	3.8	**5**	Toshiba	96	495	3.6
6	Komatsu	56	376	2.9	**6**	IHI Marine United	5	480	3.7	**6**	Universal Shipbuilding Corporation	27	397	2.9
7	IHI	39	361	2.8	**7**	Toshiba	74	415	3.2	**7**	Kawasaki Zosen	5	353	2.6
8	FHI	35	288	2.3	**8**	Komatsu	50	347	2.7	**8**	IHI	47	348	2.5
9	Kawasaki Zosen	4	257	2	**9**	FHI	36	240	1.8	**9**	Komatsu	45	338	2.5
10	Itochu	3	219	1.7	**10**	Itochu	2	228	1.7	**10**	Fujitsu	185	313	2.3
11	Fujitsu	164	210	12.6	**11**	Fujitsu	161	218	1.7	**11**	FHI	41	291	2.1
12	Hitachi	78	210	1.6	**12**	IHI Aerospace	35	157	1.2	**12**	Itochu	7	274	2.0
13	IHI Aerospace	38	169	1.3	**13**	Hitachi	76	145	1.1	**13**	Hitachi	88	210	1.5
14	Nippon Kokan	22	151	1.2	**14**	Nakagawa Bussan	135	142	1.1	**14**	Nakagawa Bussan	174	207	1.5

(Continued)

(Cont.)

2003					*2004*					*2005*				
Position	*Company*	*No. of contracts*	*Amount*	*Percentage of annual procurements*	*Position*	*Company*	*No. of contracts*	*Amount*	*Percentage of annual procurements*	*Position*	*Company*	*No. of contracts*	*Amount*	*Percentage of annual procurements*
15	Daikin Industries	60	142	1.1	**15**	Daikin Industries	53	136	1.0	**15**	Nippon Oil	88	127	0.9
16	NEC Business Machines	131	130	1	**16**	Universal Shipbuilding Corporation	25	111	0.9	**16**	Daikin Industries	52	122	0.9
17	Mitsubishi Corporation	16	88	0.7	**17**	Nippon Oil	94	107	0.8	**17**	Cosmo Oil	103	121	0.9
18	Isuzu Motors	58	86	0.7	**18**	JSW	18	104	0.8	**18**	MCC	2	116	0.8
19	Oki Electric Industry	43	84	0.7	**19**	NEC Business Machines	84	101	0.8	**19**	Shinmaywa Industries	11	105	0.8
20	Sumitomo Trading	42	77	0.6	**20**	Cosmo Oil	118	94	0.7	**20**	IHI Aerospace	39	103	0.7
	Total	1,682	9.155	71.9		Total	1,706	9,590	73.4		Total	1,764	9,854	71.6

2006					*2007*					*2008*				
Position	*Company*	*No. of contracts*	*Amount*	*Percentage of annual procurements*	*Position*	*Company*	*No. of contracts*	*Amount*	*Percentage of annual procurements*	*Position*	*Company*	*No. of contracts*	*Amount*	*Percentage of annual procurements*
1	MHI	190	2,776	21	**1**	MHI	174	3,275	25.1	**1**	MHI	198	3,140	22.7
2	KHI	103	1,306	9.9	**2**	MELCO	162	961	7.4	**2**	MELCO	178	1,556	11.3
3	MELCO	166	1,177	8.9	**3**	NEC	287	717	5.5	**3**	KHI	96	1,530	11.1
4	NEC	304	831	6.3	**4**	KHI	93	668	5.1	**4**	NEC	306	982	7.1
5	IHI Marine United	1.0	446	3.4	**5**	Toshiba	78	570	4.4	**5**	Fujitsu	165	443	3.2
6	Fujitsu	185	441	3.3	**6**	Fujitsu	172	442	3.4	**6**	IHI	37	383	2.8
7	Toshiba	79	423	3.2	**7**	FHI	49	374	2.9	**7**	Komatsu	44	365	2.6
8	IHI	48	365	2.8	**8**	Komatsu	40	334	2.6	**8**	Toshiba	93	315	2.3
9	Komatsu	40	363	2.7	**9**	IHI	31	320	2.5	**9**	Nakagawa Bussan	316	216	1.6
10	FHI	34	199	1.5	**10**	Kawasaki Shipbuilding Corporation	6	314	2.4	**10**	Nippon Oil	114	193	1.4
11	Hitachi	78	194	1.5	**11**	Nakagawa Bussan	190	216	1.7	**11**	Hitachi	75	182	1.3
12	Nakagawa Bussan	210	148	1.1	**12**	Hitachi	69	198	1.5	**12**	Cosmo Oil	105	164	1.2
13	Nippon Oil	106	143	1.1	**13**	Nippon Oil	101	162	1.2	**13**	Daikin Industries	54	144	1.0
14	Daikin Industries	62	133	1.0	**14**	Cosmo Oil	101	148	1.1	**14**	Itochu Aviation	135	138	1.0

(Continued)

(Cont.)

2006					*2007*					*2008*				
Position	*Company*	*No. of contracts*	*Amount*	*Percentage of annual procurements*	*Position*	*Company*	*No. of contracts*	*Amount*	*Percentage of annual procurements*	*Position*	*Company*	*No. of contracts*	*Amount*	*Percentage of annual procurements*
15	Cosmo Oil	95	131	1.0	**15**	JSW	18	139	1.1	**15**	FHI	35	137	1.0
16	Showa Shell	95	120	0.9	**16**	Daikin Industries	47	138	1.1	**16**	Showa Shell	91	136	1.0
17	Oki Electric Industry	55	118	0.9	**17**	Oki Electric Industry	47	129	1.0	**17**	Universal Shipbuilding Corporation	23	129	0.9
18	IHI Aerospace	32	111	0.8	**18**	IHI Aerospace	31	118	0.9	**18**	IHI Aerospace	37	120	0.9
19	JSW	19	107	0.8	**19**	Itochu Aviation	95	113	0.9	**19**	JSW	18	116	0.8
20	Kamei	395	92	0.7	**20**	MCC Foods	4	112	0.9	**20**	Oki Electric Industry	54	114	0.8
	Total	2,297	9,624	72.8		Total	1,795	9,448	72.7		Total	2,174	10,503	76.0

2009					*2010*					*2011*				
Position	*Company*	*No. of contracts*	*Amount*	*Percentage of annual procurements*	*Position*	*Company*	*No. of contracts*	*Amount*	*Percentage of annual procurements*	*Position*	*Company*	*No. of contracts*	*Amount*	*Percentage of annual procurements*
1	MHI	212	2,629	20.8	**1**	MHI	215	2,600	22.2	**1**	MHI	233	2,888	19.6
2	MELCO	150	1,827	14.5	**2**	MELCO	159	1,016	8.7	**2**	KHI	140	2,099	14.3
3	KHI	102	1,043	8.3	**3**	KHI	106	892	7.6	**3**	MELCO	121	1,153	7.8
4	NEC	287	722	5.7	**4**	NEC	271	863	7.4	**4**	NEC	301	1,151	7.8
5	Fujitsu	158	495	3.9	**5**	IHI Marine United	2	785	6.7	**5**	Fujitsu	169	529	3.6
6	Komatsu	45	343	2.7	**6**	Fujitsu	137	431	3.7	**6**	Toshiba	73	504	3.4
7		2	297	2.4	**7**	Komatsu	40	334	2.8	**7**	IHI	37	354	2.4
8	Hitachi	85	197	1.6	**8**	Kawasaki Shipbuidling Corporation	1	310	2.6	**8**	Komatsu	58	334	2.3
9	Toshiba	66	168	1.3	**9**	IHI	39	280	2.4	**9**	JX Energy	143	272	1.8
10	Mitsui Zosen	17	164	1.3	**10**	JX Energy	129	191	1.6	**10**	Hitachi	88	255	1.7
11	Nakagawa Bussan	194	150	1.2	**11**	Toshiba	63	183	1.6	**11**	Cosmo Oil	158	178	1.2
12	JSW	16	147	1.2	**12**	Hitachi	82	181	1.5	**12**	Daikin Industries	37	158	1.1
13	Nippon Oil	95	146	1.2	**13**	Cosmo Oil	95	165	1.4	**13**	Nakagawa Bussan	180	151	1.0
14	IHI	32	144	1.1	**14**	Daikin Industries	40	140	1.2	**14**	Sumitomo Corporation	20	147	1.0

(*Continued*)

(Cont.)

2009					*2010*					*2011*				
Position	*Company*	*No. of contracts*	*Amount*	*Percentage of annual procurements*	*Position*	*Company*	*No. of contracts*	*Amount*	*Percentage of annual procurements*	*Position*	*Company*	*No. of contracts*	*Amount*	*Percentage of annual procurements*
15	Cosmo Oil	85	140	1.1	**15**	JSW	18	129	1.1	**15**	Oki Electric Industry	49	140	1.0
16	Daikin Industries	46	134	1.1	**16**	IHI Aerospace	25	102	0.9	**16**	Showa Shell	99	130	0.9
17	Isuzu Motors	77	123	1.0	**17**	Nakagawa Bussan	177	100	0.9	**17**	Isuzu Motors	73	125	0.8
18	Oki Elec-tric Industry	47	119	0.9	**18**	FHI	25	96	0.8	**18**	FHI	34	122	0.8
19	IHI Aerospace	27	119	0.9	**19**	Kamei	239	93	0.8	**19**	Sumitomo Corporation	151	111	0.8
20	FHI	27	105	0.8	**20**	Oki Electric Industry	47	91	0.8	**20**	Hanwa Kogyo	141	100	0.7
	Total	1,770	9,212	73.0		Total	1,910	8,982	76.7		Total	2,305	10,901	74.0

2012					*2013*					*2014*				
Position	*Company*	*No. of contracts*	*Amount*	*Percentage of annual procurements*	*Position*	*Company*	*No. of contracts*	*Amount*	*Percentage of annual procurements*	*Position*	*Company*	*No. of contracts*	*Amount*	*Percentage of annual procurements*
1	MHI	225	2,403	15.7	**1**	MHI	195	3,165	24.9	**1**	MHI	213	2,632	16.7
2	NEC	246	1,632	10.7	**2**	MELCO	124	1,040	8.2	**2**	KHI	156	1,913	12.2
3	KHI	120	1,480	9.7	**3**	KHI	128	948	7.5	**3**	NEC	287	1,013	6.4
4	MELCO	115	1,240	8.1	**4**	NEC	256	799	6.3	**4**	ANA Holdings	1	928	5.9
5	DSN	2	1,221	8.0	**5**	IHI	31	483	3.8	**5**	MELCO	118	862	5.5
6	Japan Marine United	3	740	4.8	**6**	Fujitsu	114	401	3.2	**6**	IHI	20	619	3.9
7	Toshiba	73	503	3.3	**7**	Komatsu	27	294	2.3	**7**	Fujitsu	128	527	3.4
8	Fujitsu	111	300	2.0	**8**	Toshiba	54	284	2.3	**8**	Toshiba	70	467	3.0
9	IHI	31	277	1.8	**9**	JX Energy	153	271	2.1	**9**	Komatsu	34	339	2.2
10	Komatsu	31	267	1.7	**10**	Hitachi	64	242	1.9	**10**	Mitusi Zosen	8	319	2.0
11	JX Energy	129	244	1.6	**11**	Cosmo Oil	119	188	1.5	**11**	Itochu Aviation	37	287	1.8
12	Hitachi	64	219	1.6	**12**	Daikin Industries	33	149	1.2	**12**	JX Energy	140	261	1.7
13	Cosmo Oil	125	177	1.2	**13**	Showa Shell	107	146	1.2	**13**	Hitachi	63	219	1.4

(*Continued*)

(Cont.)

2012					2013					2014				
Position	*Company*	*No. of contracts*	*Amount*	*Percentage of annual procurements*	*Position*	*Company*	*No. of contracts*	*Amount*	*Percentage of annual procurements*	*Position*	*Company*	*No. of contracts*	*Amount*	*Percentage of annual procurements*
14	Daikin Industries	39	145	0.9	**14**	Oki Electric Industry	44	135	1.1	**14**	Cosmo Oil	113	207	1.3
15	IHI Aerospace	32	136	0.9	**15**	JSW	20	132	1.0	**15**	Oki Electric Industry	43	162	1.0
16	Oki Electric Industry	34	126	0.8	**16**	FHI	19	119	0.9	**16**	Itochu Aviation	122	160	1.0
17	Nakagawa Bussan	95	120	0.8	**17**	Japan Marine United	2	116	0.9	**17**	Daikin Industries	41	138	0.9
18	FHI	30	119	0.8	**18**	ShinMaywa Industries	11	112	0.9	**18**	Showa Shell	92	123	0.8
19	Showa Shell	92	110	0.7	**19**	Itochu Enex	54	101	0.8	**19**	JSW	21	107	0.7
20	Isuzu Motors	72	100	0.7	**20**	IHI Aerospace	25	92	0.7	**20**	Japan Marine United	3	102	0.6
	Total	1,669	11,559	75.6		Total	1,580	9,217	72.6		Total	1,710	11,385	72.4

		2015					2016		
Position	*Company*	*No. of contracts*	*Amount*	*Percentage of annual procurements*	*Position*	*Company*	*No. of contracts*	*Amount*	*Percentage of annual procurements*
1	KHI	118	2,778	15.3	**1**	MHI	217	4,532	24.6
2	MHI	178	1,998	11.0	**2**	KHI	116	994	5.4
3	IHJ	37	1,147	6.3	**3**	NEC	261	905	4.9
4	MELCO	94	1,083	6.0	**4**	Fujitsu	138	783	4.3
5	NEC	233	739	4.1	**5**	MELCO	119	767	4.2
6	Toshiba	63	573	3.2	**6**	Japan Marine United	2	410	2.2
7	Japan Marine United	3	389	2.1	**7**	IHI	35	355	1.9
8	Fujitsu	98	364	2.0	**8**	Toshiba	35	288	2.3
9	Komatsu	29	291	1.6	**9**	Komatsu	30	317	1.7
10	Sumitomo Shoji	15	261	1.4	**10**	FHI	3	219	1.7
11	Kosoku Marine Transport	1	250	1.4	**11**	Oki Electric Industry	51	348	1.1
12	JX Energy	134	184	1.0	**12**	Nippon Kokan	28	176	1.0
13	Daikin Industries	35	156	0.9	**13**	Hitachi	51	157	0.9
14	JSW	17	152	0.8	**14**	Cosmo Oil Marketing	163	149	0.8
15	GS Yuasa Technology	19	145	0.8	**15**	Daikin Industries	34	130	0.7
16	Hitachi	64	143	0.8	**16**	JSW	19	128	0.7
17	Cosmo Oil	60	126	0.7	**17**	Sumi-Sho Aerosystems Corporation	46	119	0.6
18	Shinmaywa Industries	8	123	0.7	**18**	Shinmaywa Industries	7	114	0.6
19	Nakagawa Bussan	80	121	0.7	**19**	JX Energy	97	113	0.6
20	Fujitsu	25	116	0.6	**20**	Sumitomo Trading	3	110	0.6
	Total	1,311	11,138	61.4		Total	1,400	11,004	59.8

Source: *Bōei Nenkan*, various years.

Table 20.6 Method of procurement contracts, 1993–2016 (Unit: ¥100 million; number in parentheses are percentages)

Financial year	*Amount*	*Competitive bidding*	*Limited competition*	*Non-competitive awards*	*Total*
1993	No. contracts	957 (9.85)	4,954 (51.00)	3803 (39.15)	9,714
	Monetary value	95 (0.69)	1,899 (13.84)	11,724 (85.46)	13,718
1994	No. contracts	1,287 (12.38)	5205 (50.06)	3905 (37.56)	10,397
	Monetary value	138 (1.02)	1,759 (12.99)	11,640 (85.99)	13,536
1995	No. contracts	1,581 (14.56)	5,248 (48.32)	4,032 (37.12)	10,861
	Monetary value	209 (1.57)	2,004 (15.00)	11,141 (83.43)	13,353
1996	No. contracts	2,058 (19.98)	4,645 (45.10)	3,595 (34.90)	10,298
	Monetary value	356 (2.62)	1,588 (11.72)	11,611 (85.66)	13,555
1997	No. contracts	2,771 (28.04)	3,659 (37.03)	3,450 (34.92)	9,880
	Monetary value	493 (3.73)	1,430 (10.83)	11,277 (85.43)	13,200
1998	No. contracts	3,247 (33.80)	3,223 (34.50)	3,046 (31.70)	9,616
	Monetary value	565 (4.60)	1,146 (9.20)	10,720 (86.20)	12,431
1999	No. contracts	5,297 (51.74)	2,124 (20.75)	2,817 (27.52)	10,238
	Monetary value	953 (7.54)	1,580 (12.50)	10,106 (79.97)	12,639
2000	No. contracts	5,872 (60.77)	912 (9.44)	2,879 (29.86)	9,663
	Monetary value	1,063 (8.44)	1,604 (12.74)	9,928 (78.82)	12,595
2001	No. contracts	6,021 (61.43)	847 (8.64)	2,934 (29.93)	9802
	Monetary value	1,000 (7.88)	1,495 (11.78)	10,192 (80.33)	12,687
2002	No. contracts	5,432 (61.12)	674 (7.58)	2,782 (31.30)	8,888
	Monetary value	973 (7.61)	1,324 (10.35)	10,495 (82.04)	12,792
2003	No. contracts	5,045 (59.22)	681 (7.99)	2,793 (3.28)	8,519
	Monetary value	893 (7.01)	770 (6.05)	11,069 (86.94)	12,732
2004	No. contracts	4,586 (56.30)	678 (8.30)	2,878 (35.30)	8,142
	Monetary value	840 (6.40)	1,242 (9.50)	10,979 (84.10)	13,062
2005	No. contracts	4,839 (56.0)	676 (7.8)	3,127 (36.1)	8642
	Monetary value	1,099 (8.0)	901 (6.6)	11,738 (85.4)	13,738

(Continued)

Table 20.6 (Cont.)

Financial year	*Amount*	*Competitive bidding*	*Limited competition*	*Non-competitive awards*	*Total*
2006	No. contracts	6,555 (76.2)	260 (3.0)	1,791 (20.8)	8,606
	Monetary value	3,356 (26.7)	279 (2.1)	9,411 (71.2)	13,226
2007	No. contracts	5,961 (77.2)	177(2.3)	1,583 (20.5)	7,721
	Monetary value	3,698 (28.4)	252 (1.9)	9,085 (69.7)	13,034
2008	No. contracts	6,565 (83.3)	38 (0.5)	1,282 (16.3)	7,885
	Monetary value	5,021 (36.3)	390 (2.8)	8,409 (60.8)	13,820
2009	No. contracts	6,845	17 (17)	873	7,903
	Monetary value	5,957	661	5,434	12,627
2010	No. contracts	5,928	4	795	6,875
	Monetary value	4,652		836	8,704
2011	No. contracts	7,698		836	8,704
	Monetary value	6,915		7,254	14,716
2012	No. contracts	5,906		767	6,833
	Monetary value	6,750		7,205	15,287
2013	No. contracts	5,869	5	828	6,901
	Monetary value	5,005	331	6,288	12,693
2014	No. contracts	5,726	2	994	6,925
	Monetary value	5,284	289	8,338	15,717
2015	No. contracts	5,486	10	930	6,693
	Monetary value	4,992	395	8,333	18,126
2016	No. contracts	5,643	9	919	6,767
	Monetary value	4,549	426	8,628 (46.9)	18,397

Source: *Bōei Nenkan*, various years.

Market operation and incentives

For many Japanese corporations, therefore, defence contracting functions are something of a sideline compared to more substantial and profitable civilian operations. Moreover, Japanese corporations have been cautious about levels of participation in the defence market for reputational reasons, given the legacy of the image of corporations' involvement in pre-war militarism, and concerns about the Japanese public's antimilitarism perception of defence contractors as 'merchants of death'.[15]

Nevertheless, Japanese corporations have engaged in defense for a number of reasons. Firstly, the government has been prepared to nurture and protect the industry. JMOD has offered an increasing number of competitive procurement bids since the early 1990s, but the actual monetary value percentage of competitive bids was below 10 percent for much of this period, although began to rise to the 50 percent level by 2018 (Table 20.6). Japanese defense manufacturers have become accustomed to the award of contracts largely free from major domestic or foreign competition, and that even if they fail to secure the lead contract they are certain—through a process known as *sumiwake*—to receive a share of subcontracting work. JMOD and METI have used the contracting system to build national champions in the defense sector, with MHI emerging as the leader in fighter aircraft, KHI and IHI in transport aircraft, and IHI in aircraft engines. The Japanese government in the past has also provided *de facto* subsidies for R&D of key weapons systems, even though it has preferred private companies to bear these costs if possible. These national *kokusanka* projects in the past have included the YS-11 commercial airliner with eventual military applications in the 1950s; the T-1 fighter trainer in the 1960s; the C-1 transport in the 1960s and 1970s; the F-1 fighter in the 1970s; and attempted indigenous production of the FSX support fighter in the 1980s.

Secondly, defence production has in the past provided, if not spectacular, then steady profits. An element of risk is involved as JMOD does not provide an order down-payment, or even full payment with the first deliveries of defense equipment, preferring instead deferred payments over a number of years to increase budget flexibility. All the same, defense contractors have operated with a strong sense of security. JMOD has been a dependable customer, always paying on time, and until recently there were no incidents of the government backing out of a contract.

Thirdly, Japanese corporations have been confident that the embedding of smaller scale defense production within their large civilian operations enables them to maximise R&D and manufacturing benefits for spin-on and spin-off.

Fourthly, as noted earlier, the Japanese defence market has been relatively protected from direct foreign competition. Japan has continued inward transfers of foreign technology, importing US weapons systems through FMS, such as the *Aegis* radar system, as they offer relatively low-risk, if not always low-cost, provision for the JSDF. More preferable still has been licensed production of systems such as the F-4J and F-15J fighters and engines, and P-3C patrol aircraft, to enable the learning and innovation of technologies. Japan has also in the past begun to utilise co-production with the US as in the development of the F-2 fighter, and the first tentative steps towards the transfer of military technologies through exemptions made in the arms export ban for thirteen different bilateral cooperation projects with the US.

Overall, though, the Japanese defence market has been dominated by domestic procurement, with levels of around 90 percent from the 1950s all the way through to the early part of this decade. Japan's defence market has only experienced significant foreign penetration coinciding with the advent of the Abe administration, levels of domestic procurement falling to 77 percent in 2016 (Table 20.7). Japan has started to acquire highly expensive weapons systems from the US, including the F-35A and *Osprey* V-22, and looks set to procure more, including the *Aegis Ashore* system, as President Donald Trump's administration presses its ally to increase purchases of equipment as a *quid pro quo* for the US contribution to Japan's security.

Industry performance

Japanese successes in indigenisation

Japan has made significant headway in the post-war period in developing a model of autonomous 'techno-nationalism' and civilian-military integration. The government through national *kokusanka* projects, but more importantly through the careful nurturing of a select group of private defense contractors, has created a capable defense R&D and production base whereby much of the initial cost and technological risk of weapons development is offloaded to the private sector. The system's provision of a strong physical civilian-military infrastructure for defense production is demonstrated by the fact that it was estimated in the early 1990s that 90 percent of MHI's capital equipment for military production was available simultaneously for civilian use. MHI famously utilises the same workers to assemble military and civilian aircraft in the same facilities, and its M-90 MBT is built in the same final assembly area as forklift trucks and bulldozers.[16] This mechanism of civilian plants sustaining military production has further enabled the maintenance of 'hotbed' facilities for the rapid expansion of MBT production from normal low annual production runs to higher levels in national emergencies. Japanese corporations have benefitted from significant inter-diffusion of civilian and military technologies: semi-conductors developed for civilian industry finding their way through 'spin-on' into Japanese missiles and radars; and composites for fighter aircraft finding 'spin-on' into use for civilian airliners, and milling techniques for mobile artillery adopted in electricity turbine manufacture.[17]

Japan has achieved notable successes in *kokusanka* and closed the gap in certain technological areas with other larger developed economies and military powers. Japan demonstrated that it was capable of building advanced destroyers; although it has remained dependent on licensed production of engines and FMS for *Aegis* air radar.[18] Japan succeeded in rebuilding its aircraft defense production in the post-war period, using a mix of licensed and indigenous production for the F-86F, F-104J, F-4EJ and F-15J fighters, T-1,

Table 20.7 Changes in equipment procurement methods and sources (Unit: ¥100 million)

Fiscal year	*Domestic procurement*	*Commercial imports*	*Ratio (%)*	*Foreign Military Sales*	*Ratio (%)*	*Domestic procurement ratio (%)*
1950–1961	5,907	266	4.2	253	3.9	91.9
1962	975	76	7.0	41	3.7	89.3
1963	931	70	6.0	162	13.9	80.1
1964	1,120	70	5.6	60	4.8	89.6
1965	1,359	82	5.4	65	4.3	90.3
1966	1,396	126	8.0	55	3.4	88.6
1967	1,859	131	6.4	62	3.0	90.6
1968	2,425	124	4.5	194	7.1	88.4
1969	2,703	128	4.4	53	1.9	93.9
1970	2,308	158	6.2	51	2.0	91.8
1971	3,534	124	3.3	116	3.1	93.6
1972	3,477	358	9.0	117	3.0	88.0
1973	3,697	164	4.1	182	4.5	91.4
1974	4,372	152	3.3	89	1.9	94.8
1975	4,845	160	3.1	107	2.1	94.8
1976	5,197	166	3.0	122	2.2	94.7
1977	5,846	222	3.5	194	3.1	93.4
1978	7,126	209	2.5	1,014	12.1	85.4
1979	7,373	394	4.5	884	10.2	85.2
1980	10,506	567	4.8	801	6.7	88.5
1981	8,158	604	6.0	1,368	13.5	80.5
1982	12,425	618	4.4	978	7.0	88.6
1983	12,673	598	4.3	758	5.4	90.3
1984	12,791	787	5.6	528	3.7	90.7
1985	13,417	636	4.3	707	4.8	90.9
1986	14,075	748	4.8	682	4.4	90.8
1987	14,788	787	4.8	670	4.1	91.0
1988	16,209	502	2.8	1,035	5.8	91.3
1989	17,497	928	4.8	923	4.8	90.4
1990	18,103	834	4.1	1,376	6.8	89.1
1991	17,010	869	4.6	1,023	5.4	90.0
1992	17,676	1,011	5.3	474	2.5	92.2
1993	16,408	1,356	7.0	1,574	8.1	84.8
1994	17,349	1,195	6.1	1,056	5.4	88.5
1995	18,131	914	4.7	598	3.0	92.3
1996	18,725	938	4.6	541	2.7	92.7
1997	18,479	1,173	5.9	376	1.9	92.3

(*Continued*)

Table 20.7 (Cont.)

Fiscal year	*Domestic procurement*	*Commercial imports*	*Ratio (%)*	*Foreign Military Sales*	*Ratio (%)*	*Domestic procurement ratio (%)*
1998	17,344	1,127	6.0	348	1.8	92.2
1999	17,704	1,185	6.1	390	2.0	91.8
2000	17,685	1,249	6.5	439	2.3	91.3
2001	17,971	1,156	5.9	489	2.5	91.6
2002	17,218	1,326	6.8	1,101	5.6	87.6
2003	17,598	1,292	6.5	1,006	5.1	88.4
2004	18,233	1,334	6.5	979	4.8	88.7
2005	18,917	1,525	7.1	937	4.4	88.5
2006	18,818	1,158	5.5	1,047	5.0	89.5
2007	18,649	1,327	6.8	856	4.1	89/5
2008	19,382	1,153	5.4	642	3.0	91.5
2009	18,219	1,290	6.4	620	3.1	90.5
2010	17,611	1,023	5.3	551	2.9	91.8
2011	21,746	1,471	6.2	589	2.5	91.3
2012	20,672	1,216	5.2	1,372	5.9	88.9
2013	18,512	1,204	5.8	1,118	5.4	88.9
2014	19,431	2,245	9.5	1,874	8.0	82.5
2015	19,264	1,631	6.4	4,473	17.6	75.9
2016	21,195	1,515	5.5	4,770	17.4	77.1

Source: *Bōei Nenkan*, various years.

T-2, and the T-4 trainer aircraft, and the C-1 transport. Japan displayed considerable success in missile programs, first purchasing direct or employing licensed production and then substituting with indigenous production.

Japan's policy of *kokusanka* has clearly not been without past problems, including the sheer cost that have raised questions about the sustainability of the defense production model. Much of the equipment produced has not always reached the highest international military performance standard. The F-1 most prominently becoming obsolete almost as soon as it went into production. Japan has also been frustrated in attempts to indigenise systems by pressure from its US ally. Japan in the end refrained from production of its own PXL patrol aircraft and settled for licensed production of the P-3C; and had to settle for co-development of the F-2 with the US. But despite Japan's failure to produce completely indigenous or internationally competitive major weapons platforms, it has scored important successes in an overall strategic industrial sense, in that it has managed to indigenise the most important component technologies of these platforms. Japan, in spite of its relatively small defense production base, has at least kept in step with international competition, and had the latent potential to move into producing fully independent weapons systems in the future.

New challenges: budget pressures, procurement inefficiencies, corruption, international collaboration

However, in the last two decades, serious deficiencies and concerns over sustainability have begun to emerge in Japan's defence production model. The initial challenge is one of resourcing limitations, given the stagnant or declining defence budgets for much of the period since the late 1990s and declining proportion for equipment procurement. Japan's budgetary strains have been compounded by the procurement practices and high costs endemic to its production model. Japan's nurturing of an indigenous defense production base amongst a few manufacturers and the absence of meaningful competition has inflated equipment prices. For example, it is thought that *kokusanka* has resulted in the F-2 costing three times the equivalent of an off-the-shelf equivalent such as the F-16C; and the M-90 was viewed as the most expensive MBT in the world due its low production runs.

The close relationship between defense producers and the JSDF as the sole customer has added further costs. The infamous practice of *amakudari* (literally 'descent from heaven'), or the placing of retired bureaucrats and uniformed officers on the boards of defense contractors, has meant that this interchangeable network of policy-makers and industrialists has lacked incentives to negotiate competitive prices. JMOD revealed in 2008 that over the previous five years there had been around 500 cases of retired JSDF personnel requiring permission under the JSDF Law to take up positions with commercial enterprises, including close to 200 former officers of colonel/captain rank and above, and that companies involved in JMOD recruitment were the most popular destinations, with MHI, NEC and MELCO top ranking.[19] The JDA in 2006 revealed in the National Diet that in 2004 there had been a total of 718 retired JSDF personnel working in firms with JDA contracts, again mostly concentrated in MHI affiliates.[20]

Moreover, these practices are thought not only to increase unit costs but also to give rise to structural corruption. The JDA's Central Procurement Office Defense and then its Defense Facilities Administration Agency (DFAA) were hit by corruption scandals in the late 1990s and 2000s relating to officials encouraging defense contractors to 'pad out' (*mizumashi*) procurement contracts. JMOD's most serious scandal came in 2008 when former Administrative Vice-Minister Moriya Takemasa, the ministry's top official, was convicted and jailed for receiving bribes to steer procurement contracts to trading companies.[21]

In addition, Japan's defence production base is challenged by reliance on techno-nationalist policies that risk leaving its defence industry behind in the development of internationally competitive technologies. Japan's emphasis on the indigenisation of technologies has run into the obstacle of the increasing reluctance of the US and other states to provide FMS or licensed production of advanced weapons systems. Japanese industry estimates that the domestic content under licensed production of U.S. systems has progressively decreased, from 85 percent of the F-104, to 90 percent of the F-4EJ, and 70 percent of the F-15J, with a high black-boxed content for the F-15J, and 60 percent for the F-2.[22] The National Institute of Defence Studies (NIDS), JMOD's academic research arm, produced a report in 2006 which questioned the degree to which the US can be relied on to allow Japan to maintain autonomous technology even in the case of co-development and co-production, arguing that the F-35 project demonstrates the US's disinclination to share technology fully with even its supposedly closest allies and partners.[23] Japan was further frustrated by the US's refusal to transfer the full or even a 'dumbed-down' less-capable version of the F-22 to its ally despite intense lobbying. Japan's highly limited international cooperation to date, especially in terms of co-development and co-production, due to its arms export ban, thus raised concerns of a 'Galapagos effect' due to Japan's isolation from the evolution of international defence production.[24] Hence, as other states have been perceived as forging ahead with consolidation of their defence companies domestically and internationally, and to initiate new multilateral weapons platforms to share technologies and costs through economies of scale, Japan has risked being left as a bystander and surpassed technologically, and over-dependent on its US ally.[25]

Erosion of the defence industrial base

Japan's formerly close government-industry relationship has come under increasing stress. The Japanese government due to the budgetary squeeze cancelled for the first time in the contemporary period a procurement order for a total of 62 AH64D Apache Longbow helicopters after only ten were delivered, leading FHI to sue the government for ¥40 billion in licensing fees already paid to Boeing.[26] A number of Japanese companies are now beginning to exit the defense market altogether.[27] Since 2003, 20 subcontracting firms for fighter production have abandoned military procurements; for tank production, 35 have withdrawn from subcontracting and thirteen have gone bankrupt.[28] JMOD reported in 2010 that since 2005 another 56 subcontracting firms had exited fighter and tank production.[29] The DPC's membership shrunk from 84 members in 1997 to 66 in 2002.[30]

Japan has even experienced the exit of large corporations from the defense market seeking improved prospects in civilian sectors. Japanese corporations have increasingly eyed the benefits of civilian aerospace, with military production as a share of total aircraft production dropping from over 80 percent of total aircraft in the 1980s to around 30 percent in this decade MHI, KHI and FHI, the national defense aerospace champions, are now becoming more vested in the civilian aerospace market to compensate for the shrinking military market—the commercial market offering no barriers to international tie-ups and greater economies of scale, and allowing them to use technologies originally developed for military use, such as composites, to focus instead on civilian airliners.[31]

JMOD has encouraged defense industry consolidation to realise economies of scale. Nissan Motors after its purchase by Renault exited the defense industry by transferring its aerospace division to IHI in July 2000, and Tōyō Tsūshinki transferred its defense electronics division to NEC in May 2004.[32] In October 2000 IHI and SHI moved their military shipbuilding activities into IHI Marine United; in September 2001 IHI, KHI and Mitsui Zōsen formed a work share agreement; in October 2002 NKK and Hitachi integrated their military shipbuilding into Universal Shipbuilding; and in October 2002 KHI formed Kawasaki Zōsen, a new shipbuilding subsidiary.[33] However, JMOD's consolidation policy has been frustrated by the fact that the most manufacturers are civilian production-oriented, that their dual-use spin-on spin-off model cannot easily separate civilian from military production facilities, and thus have no incentive to rationalise their business to suit defence production imperatives.

Industry prospects: domestic reforms and international cooperation

New national projects and procurement practices

Japanese administrations have looked to address these existential challenges for the defence industrial base by supporting new *kokusanka* projects such as the P-1 patrol aircraft, C-2 transport aircraft (with hopes even that the C-2 might be convertible to a version for the civilian market) and Advanced Technology Demonstration-X (ATD-X), or now F-3, stealth fighter prototype. Japan has also built through dual-use technology a very effective space programme with military applications that forms an additional route to develop new technologies.[34] Nevertheless, Japan's procurement of frontline platforms of main-battle tanks, destroyers and fighter aircraft has continued to decline.

Japan has further attempted to stretch the resources available for the defence industry with more efficient systems and competitive tenders for procurement domestically and internationally, following a series of corruption scandals in the mid-1990s, and in 2015 established an Acquisition, Technology and Logistics Agency (ATLA) in an attempt to integrate and manage procurement more efficiently.[35] However, these reforms are in their early stages and appear to have yet yielded few gains, and will be further complicated by Japan's increasing imports of highly-expensive US weapons systems. For instance, Japan's indigenous C-2 transport unit cost was revealed in June 2018 as running 40 percent over estimates; similarly, the FMS unit cost for F35As has inflated by 50 percent; and the FMS *Aegis Ashore* system cost has doubled to US$3.6 billion.[36]

International cooperation and ending the arms export ban

Japanese policy-makers although still intent that the maintenance of a domestic defence production base is an essential component for national autonomy have begun to accept that *kokusanka* alone is not a viable approach. Instead, policy-makers have moved to try to revitalise the defence production base through exploring enhanced international cooperation with the US and now other international partners in line with its overall broadening of security policy.[37]

Japan's primary impulse has inevitably been to strengthen defence production ties with the US as in the joint development and production of the SM-3 Block II-A interceptor missile for BMD and the procurement the F-35A fighter, with some off-the-shelf procurement but also Final Assembly and Checkout (FACO) and development of elements of the fighter's engine parts, radar, and electro-optical distributed aperture systems (EODAS), and participation in Autonomic Logistics Global Sustainment (ALGS) system.[38] ALGS creates under the unitary direction of the US and prime contractor Lockheed Martin a global supply chain for the mutual provision of parts amongst countries deploying the F-35 Joint Strike Fighter platform (potentially incorporating the US itself, the UK, Italy and the Netherlands, Australia, Canada, Denmark, Norway and Turkey as Tier 1, 2 and 3 partners; and Singapore and Israel as Security Cooperative Partners).

However, Japan's breach on its self-imposed ban on arms exports since 2014 has opened the way to explore additional partners for joint development, production and export of weapons technologies. Japan and the UK signed a Defence Equipment Cooperation Framework in 2013, and indicated in July 2014 the intention to work on the joint development of the *Meteor* air-to-air missile. Japan was also rumoured to have attempted to pitch sales of the P-1 to the UK, although the UK in 2015 chose to procure the Boeing P-8 *Poseidon* maritime patrol aircraft.[39] In March 2017, the JMOD announced that it would conduct a joint study with the UK MOD on a future combat fighter system.[40] Japan has been exploring similar defence and military technology cooperation with France since 2012 on unmanned submarine technology.[41] Japan and Germany have started to discuss the exchange of technologies for armoured vehicles.[42] Japan signed a defence technology sharing agreement with Italy in May 2017 concentrating on naval capabilities in naval guns, radar and patrol aircraft.[43] The JMOD is reported to be interested in a similar agreement with Sweden focused on submarine technologies.[44]

Japan has been engaged in discussions with India for the transfer of Shin Maywa's US-2 search and rescue seaplane currently utilised by the MSDF. The two countries established a Joint Working Group (JWG) to explore export or licensed production of the US-2. The Japan-India Summit in September 2014 resulted in a Memorandum of Cooperation and Exchanges in the Field of Defence and directed the JWG to accelerate progress on a 'road map' for the transfer of the aircraft and its technology. The December 2015 summit signed off an 'Agreement on the Transfer of Defence Equipment and Technology' and further inched forward talks on the US-2.

Japan's principal political and commercial efforts for the transfer of arms technology, outside the US-Japan alliance, and representing the best opportunity for transferring an entire platform have been focussed on ties with Australia. Japan and Australia as part of their 'Strategic Partnership' signed in July 2014 concluded 'Agreement Concerning the Transfer of Defence Equipment and Technology'.[45] Japan subsequently entered the competition for Australia's tender to replace its six *Collins*-class submarines with up to 12 new boats by 2030 and worth up to A$50 billion. MHI and Kawasaki Shipbuilding Corporation sought, with strong encouragement from the Abe administration, to export their *Sōryū*-class advanced air-independent propulsion submarine technology.

Japan's attempt to export submarines ended, though, in failure in April 2016, losing the contract to France's DCNS. Japan's failure resulted from a number of factors, including: questions over the appropriateness of the *Sōryū* technology for Australia's defence needs given that a longer range vessel may have been required; the evaporation of Australian domestic political support with the fall of the highly pro-Japan Tony Abbott government in September 2015; and, crucially, the lack of experience of Japanese defence contractors in competing in international markets manifested in limited bidding skills, lack of an offset strategy, wariness to agree to licensed production and reluctance to share advanced technologies.[46]

Conclusion: future scenarios for Japan's defence industry

Japan's defence industry yet again stands at an important juncture for its continued vitality and even existence. Japanese policy-makers and defence producers have demonstrated impressive resilience in the post-war period in rebuilding and sustaining the domestic defence production model and a high degree of indigenisation. However, there is a growing awareness amongst the policy and industrial community that the existing model of 'technonationalism' risks death by a thousand cuts as the national resources and ability to keep pace with international technological developments are simply beyond Japan's national reach, and thus there is a need to find a new way to strike a balance between maintaining domestic production and seeking international collaboration in order to attempt to preserve a measure of strategic autonomy and leverage in the US-Japan alliance and broader strategic contexts. Japanese domestic reforms of procurement processes may deliver more bang for the yen and international co-development and growth of exports are seen as the routes to sustain the existing model, although it is early days as yet for Japan down this path and to judge its efficacy.

Longer term, the evolution of Japan's defence production policy could yet move in more radical directions largely dependent on the external security environment and the strategic choices it poses for Japan. The most likely strategic direction for Japan to follow is to continue the current one: strengthening the alliance with the US and increase its contribution, including defence production, within this structure. This may mean some additional defence expenditure to satisfy US requests for 'burden sharing' that may enable Japan to support its indigenous defence industry as in the past. But it might also mean deeper integration of Japan's defence industry with that of the US on a range of joint projects, and perhaps even the near capture or demise of Japan's autonomous production base by the US if it is obliged more and more to purchase highly expensive off-the-shelf platforms from US contractors.

Another likely complementary, but possibly also alternative path, for Japan is to develop a range of bilateral and multilateral defence production partnerships outside the framework of the US-Japan alliance. Japanese exploration of this option has already been seen in efforts to develop collaborative ties with key European states, Australia and India. These may provide the shared techonology and funding necessary to maintain or further elevate Japan as a truly internationally competitive defence producer and boost its leverage vis-à-vis its US ally and other states. However, this option will certainly be hard going given how nascent the defence relationships are, Japan's relative inexperience of international security cooperation outside the alliance, the US's overwhelming strategic-political leverage over Japan due to the US-Japan security treaty, and the fact that the most significant weapons platforms available for co-development for Japan are US in origin such as the advanced fighters and BMD.

The other and currently least likely option for Japan, and essentially dependent on a seismic shift in its security environment, is to try to truly go it alone in defence production at a much more ambitious scale. If Japan were to be in effect abandoned by the US as a security guarantor in the future, perhaps in the case of US recognition of North Korea as a nuclear power or reaching a strategic accommodation with China that does not take account of Japan's security interests, then there might be witnessed attempts by Japan to convert itself into a fully-fledged military great power. This would open the way for larger scale procurement of new types of systems for greater deterrent power, including deterrence by punishment. Hence, the scenario might be of Japan significantly expanding its defence budget and developing its own next generation of fighter planes, overt fixed-wing aircraft carriers, long-range missiles, cyber capabilities, and most significantly of all a nuclear weapons capability. Clearly, this would be transformational for Japan's defence industry and test fully the proposition that it has developed a latent set of technologies to enable it to leapfrog into becoming a military power capable of fully defending itself. Nevertheless, as noted above, such a scenario remains highly unlikely and the likely trajectory for now is for Japan to attempt to preserve the existing model with more cooperation with the US and other powers but still looking to keep its long-term options open.

Notes

1 Richard J. Samuels, *Rich Nation, Strong Army: National Security and the Technological Transformation of Japan*, Ithaca, New York: Cornell University Press, 1994.

2 Prime Minister Satō Eisaku's administration first enunciated restrictions in 1967 on arms exports to communist states, countries under UN sanctions, and parties to international disputes. In 1976, Prime Minister Miki Takeo's administration ordered restraint in the case of all states, and prohibited the export of weapon-related technology.
3 Christopher W. Hughes, 'Japan's emerging arms transfer strategy: diversifying to re-centre on the US-Japan alliance', *The Pacific Review*, vol. 31, no.4, 2017, pp. 424–440.
4 Christopher W. Hughes, 'Japan's security trajectory and collective self-defence: essential continuity or radical change', *Journal of Japanese Studies*, vol. 43, no. 1, Winter 2017, pp. 93–126.
5 Christopher W. Hughes, *Japan's Re-Emergence as a 'Normal' Military Power*, Oxford: Oxford University Press, 2004, pp. 24–31, 41–48; Christopher W. Hughes, *Japan's Foreign and Security Policy Under the 'Abe Doctrine': New Dynamism or New Dead End?* New York: Palgrave, 2015, pp. 29–36.
6 Asagumo Shimbunsha, *Bōei Handobukku*, Tokyo: Asagumo Shimbunsha, 2018, p. 281.
7 'Japan's Defense Ministry eyes record defense budget amid North Korean and Chinese threat', *The Japan Times*, 31 August 2018, www.japantimes.co.jp/news/2018/08/31/national/politics-diplomacy/japan-eyes-record-defense-budget-amid-north-korean-chinese-threats/#.W40JJy-ZNsM.
8 Bōei Nenkan Kankōkaihen, *Bōei Nenkan 2018*, Tokyo: DMC, 2018, p. 455.
9 Bōei Nenkan Kankōkaihen, *Bōei Nenkan 2018*, Tokyo: DMC, 2018, pp. 456–459.
10 'Defense News top 100', *Defense News*, http://people.defensenews.com/top-100/.
11 Bōeishō, *Bōei Seisan, Gijutsu Kiban*, April 2010, www.kantei.go.jp/jp/singi/shin-ampobouei2010/dai5/siryou1.pdf, p. 5.
13 Asahi Shimbun Jieitai 50nen Shuzaiha, *Jieitai Shirarezaru Henyō*, Tokyo: Asahi Shimbunsha, 2005, p. 263.
14 Bōeishō, *Bōei Seisan, Gijutsu Kiban*, April 2010, www.kantei.go.jp/jp/singi/shin-ampobouei2010/dai5/siryou1.pdf, p. 4.
15 Anzen Hoshō to Bōeiryokyu ni Kansuru Kondankai, *Anzen Hoshō to Bōeiryokyu ni Kansuru Kondankai ni Okeru Kore Made no Giron to Gaiyō 2004*, www.kantei.go.jp/jp/singi/ampobouei/dai7/7siryou1.pdf, p. 5.
16 Richard J. Samuels, *Rich Nation, Strong Army, National Security and the Technological Transformation of Japan*, Ithaca, New York: Cornell University Press, 1994, pp. 294–297.
17 Bōeishō, *Bōei Seisan, Gijutsu Kiban*, April 2010, www.kantei.go.jp/jp/singi/shin-ampobouei2010/dai5/siryou1.pdf, p. 10; Keizai Sangyōshō, *Bōei Sangyō ni Tsuite*, April 2010, www.kantei.go.jp/jp/singi/shin-ampobouei2010/dai5/siryou2.pdf, p. 9.
18 Arthur Alexander, *Of Tanks and Toyotas: An Assessment of the Japan's Defense Industry*, Santa Monica, CA: RAND, 2003, pp. 44–48.
19 Bōeishō, *Bōeishō Kaikaku Kaigi Dai4kai Setsumei Shiryō*, 1 February 2008, www.kantei.go.jp/jp/singi/bouei/dai4/pdf/siryou2.pdf; Bōeishō, *Dai4kai Bōeishō Kaikaku Kaigi Sankō Shiryō*, 1 February 2008, www.kantei.go.jp/jp/singi/bouei/dai4/pdf/siryou2.pdf.
20 'Bōeichō amakudari ōi kigyō juchū mo mashi', *Shimbun Akahata*, 12 April 2006, p. 15; Shūkan Kinyōbihen, *Mitsubishi Jūkō no Seitai: Kokusaku Bōei Kigyō*, Tokyo: Kinyōbi, 2008, pp. 26–32; Bōeichōhen, *Bōei Hakusho 2006*, Tokyo: Ōkurashō Insatsukyoku, 2006, pp. 276–280; Nakatani Gen, *Daremo Kakenakatta Bōeishō no Shinjistu*, Tokyo: Gentōsha, 2008.
21 For a full analysis of Japan's defense industry scandals, see Christopher W. Hughes, *Japan's Remilitarisation*, London: Routledge, 2009, pp. 67–72.

22 Michael E. Chinworth, *Inside Japan's Defense: Technology, Economics and Strategy*, Washington: Brassey's US, 1992, pp. 127, 137.
23 Bōei Kenkyūjo, *Waga Kuni no Bōei Gijutsu Kiban ga Sōbihin Shutoku ni oyabosu Kōka ni kansuru Chōsa Kenkyū*: Tokyo: Bōei Kenkyūjo, 2006, p. 34.
24 Kiyotani Shinichi, *Bōei Hatan: 'Garapagosuka Suru Jieitai Sōbi'*, Tokyo: Chūō Shinsho Rakure, 2010, pp. 185–188.
25 Satō Heigo, 'Japan's arms export and defense production policy', *CSIS Strategic Japan Working Papers*, 2015, http://csis.org/files/publication/150331_Sato_JapanArmsExport.pdf, pp. 1–13.
26 'Fujijū ga Bōeishō teisō heri hacchū chūshi de 350okuen motomeru', *Asahi Shimbun*, 15 January 2010, http://asahi.com/politics/update/0115/TKY201001150358.html.
27 Asahi Shimbun Jieitai 50nen Shuzaiha, *Jieitai Shirarezaru Henyō*, Tokyo: Asahi Shimbunsha, 2005, pp. 269–270.
28 Bōei sangyō, 'tettai aitsugu yosan sakugen de sōbihin no hacchūgen', *Asahi Shimbun*, 24 August 2009, http://asahi.com/politics/update/0820/TKY2000908200165.html.
29 Bōeishō, *Bōei Seisan, Gijutsu Kiban*, April 2010, www.kantei.go.jp/jp/singi/shinampobouei2010/dai5/siryou1.pdf, p. 7.
30 Richard J. Samuels, *Securing Japan: Tokyo's Grand Strategy and the Future of East Asia*, Ithaca, New York: Cornell University Press, 2007, p. 148.
31 '"un-kokusan" kōkūki, ōsora e', *Asahi Shimbun*, 12 May 2007, p. 13; Seishi Kimura, *The Challenges of Late Industrialization: The Global Economy and the Japanese Commercial Aircraft Industry*, Basingstoke: Palgrave Macmillan, 2007, pp. 134–171.
32 Nihon Keizai Dantai Rengōkai, *Teigen 'Kongo no Bōeiryoku Seibi no Arikata ni tsuite': Shiryō*, 20 July 2004, p. 8.
33 Nihon Keizai Dantai Rengōkai Bōei Seisan Iinkai, *Waga Kuni Bōei Sangyō no Genjō Nado ni Tsuite*, p. 33.
34 Paul Kallender and Christopher W. Hughes, 'Hiding in plain sight? Japan's militarization of space and challenges to the Yoshida doctrine', *Asian Security*, 2018.
35 Bōei Nenkan Kankōkaihen, *Bōei Nenkan 2016*, Tokyo: DMC, 2018, pp. 8–43; Tamura Shigenobu, *Bōei Sōbicho to Sōbi Seisaku no Kaisetsu*, Tokyo: Naigai Shuppan, 2016.
36 'C2 yusōki 1ki 700okuzō 2011dohi buhin kōtō santei ni kadai', *Asahi Shimbun*, 22 June 2018, p. 3; 'Kūji F35A junji haibi sōtei yori kagaku jōshō, zaisei no futan ni', *Asahi Shimbun*, 24 February 2018, p. 2.
37 Japan Ministry of Defence, 'Strategy on defense production and technological bases: toward strengthening the bases to support defense forces and "proactive contribution to peace"', June 2014, www.mod.go.jp/j/approach/others/equipment/pdf/2606_e_honbun.pdf, pp. 7–8, 15; Nishiyama Jun 'Nihon no bōei to gijutsu kaihatsu', in Morimoto Satoshi (ed.) *Kiro ni Tatsu Nihon no Anzen: Anzen Hoshō, Kikikanri Seisaku no Jissai to Tenbō*, Tokyo: Hokuseidō, 2008, p. 353.
38 Bōeishōhen, *Bōei Hakusho 2015*, Tokyo: Zaimushō Insatsukyoku, 2015, pp. 266–267.
39 *Japan Times*, 'Japan wants UK to buy sub-hunter jet', 8 January 2014, www.japantimes.co.jp/news/2015/01/08/national/japan-wants-u-k-buy-sub-hunter-jet/#.VK7BQRaqzFI.
40 Bōei Sōbichō, 'Shōrai Sentōki ni okeru Eikoku to no kyōryoku no kanōsei ni kakawaru Niichiei kyōdō sutadei ni kansuru torikime no teiketsu ni tsuite', 16 March 2017, www.mod.go.jp/atla/pinup/pinup290316.pdf.
41 Bōeishōhen, *Bōei Hakusho 2015*, Tokyo: Zaimushō Insatsukyoku, 2015, p. 268.
42 *Asahi Shimbun*, 'Japan quietly inks deal with Germany on defense sharing', *Asahi Shimbun*, 19 July 2017, www.asahi.com/ajw/articles/AJ201707190028.html.

43 Ministry of Foreign Affairs Japan, 'Agreement between the Government of Japan and the Government of the Italian Republic concerning the transfer of defence equipment and technology', 22 May 2017, www.mofa.go.jp/mofaj/files/000262376.pdf.

44 *Nikkei Asian Review*, 'Japan bolsters defense-technology cooperation with Europe', 11 May 2017, https://asia.nikkei.com/Politics-Economy/International-Relations/Japan-bolsters-defense-technology-cooperation-with-Europe.

45 Ministry of Foreign Affairs Japan, 'Agreement Between the Government of Japan and the Government of Australia Considering the Transfer of Defence Equipment and Technology', 8 July 2014, www.mofa.go.jp/files/000044447.pdf.

46 Franz-Stefan Gady, 'Why Japan lost Aussie sub bid', *The Japan Times*, 29 April 2016, www.japantimes.co.jp/opinion/2016/04/29/commentary/japan-commentary/japan-lost-aussie-sub-bid/#.WFvnilfPz-Y; Mochizuki Isoko, *Buki Yushutsu Nihon Kigyō*, Tokyo: Kakugawa Shinsho, 2016, pp. 72–94

21 Canadian defence industrial base

Binyam Solomon and Christopher E. Penney

1. Introduction

On October 19, 2018, the Canadian government announced that a consortium led by Lockheed Martin had been selected as the preferred designer for Canada's next generation of warships. The program, known as the Canadian Surface Combatant project, is the most complex and largest (about C$60 billion or US $45 billion[1]) ever military procurement undertaken by the government. Less than two weeks later on November 2, 2018 the government announced the purchase of a sixth Arctic and Offshore Patrol Ship (AOPS) reversing the earlier commitment to limit the procurement project to a total of five ships. This reversal was made to "maximizing stable employment" for Irving Shipbuilding while providing equipment to the navy.[2]

These announcements are the first major developments in Canadian defence policy since the release of Strong, Secure and Engaged (SSE), the new governmental policy designed to guide the Department of National Defence and the Canadian Armed Forces well into the next decade. In addition to promising stable, predictable funding, the policy announced funding increases of over 70% for the next 10 years. SSE includes a virtually unprecedented increase in capital expenditure aimed at renewing and replacing aging military platforms, most notably the acquisition of a 5th generation fighter aircraft fleet and the procurement of naval surface combatants.

These announcements could indicate a brighter future for the Department of National Defence (DND) the Canadian Armed Forces (CAF) and the defence industrial base. However, Canadian media and think tanks were quick to point out that the last defence policy also promised major capital procurement and a long-term stable funding commitment only to be revised two years later (Perry, 2013). There are also concerns that the procurement system is too cumbersome for acquiring multiple complex military projects.[3]

In the absence of imminent and direct threats and the presence of a powerful ally on its southern border, successive Canadian governments have naturally diverted resources away from the military in times of relative peace. As shown in Figure 21.1, DND has shouldered a disproportionate share of government

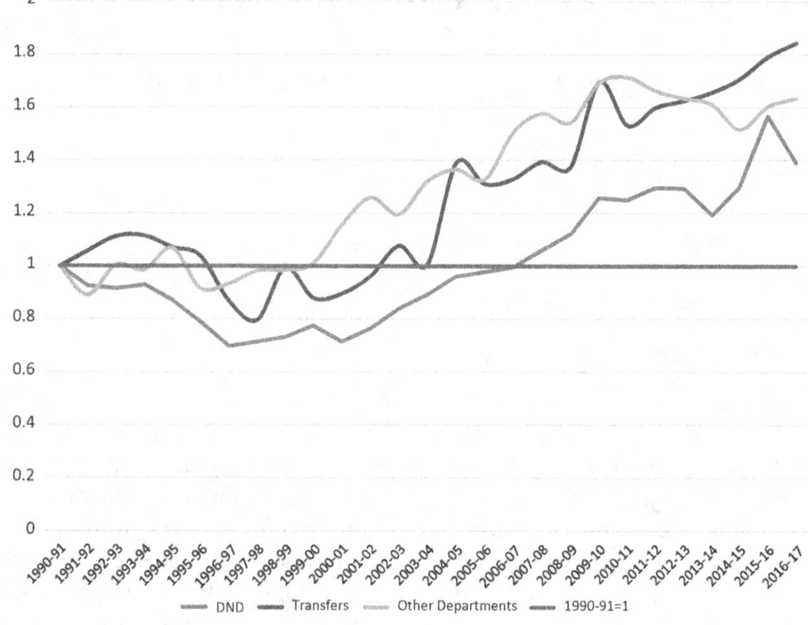

Figure 21.1 Competing demands and choice.

budget cuts during periods of austerity such as the recessions of early 1990s and the 2008 financial crisis and modest increases during periods of economic growth. For example, DND absorbed cuts of 30% in real terms during the early 1990s, compared with cuts of only 11% for other federal departments. Concerns about DND's ability to spend its capital funding are equally valid. Solomon and Stone (2013) show that during the period 2007–2011 DND under-spent between 27 and 46% of its capital budget.

While the above discussion highlights the challenges ahead for government funding, it has a material effect on the supply side and the Canadian Defence Industrial Base (CDIB). In the next section, we evaluate the demand side formally to examine the likely effects on the CDIB and consider such questions as to whether the CDIB is well-positioned to satisfy the new demands given by SSE and whether it is diversified and flexible enough to weather changes in domestic demand over time. In Section 3 we utilize recent survey statistics on the CDIB to examine its dependence on domestic procurement, international profile and overall profitability. In Section 4 we assess the industrial and economic development policies supporting the CDIB and their overall efficacy. We conclude the chapter by re-examining the latest defence policy and its implications for the future of the CDIB.

2. Background

In 2018 Canada's defence spending is forecasted at US$21.6 billion according to the 2018 North Atlantic Treaty Organization (NATO) official statistics. Of this amount, military equipment expenditures account for 18%. The estimated defence spending amount is approximately 1.2% of Gross Domestic Product (GDP).[4]

Table 21.1 provides historical data on the Canadian defence burden measure (i.e., military expenditures as a percentage of GDP) and government budget allocations on defence equipment and research and development (R&D). These measures are important indicators for the demand side of defence production. The main data sources for the data presented in Table 21.1 are the Organization of Economic Co-operation and Development (OECD) and the Stockholm International Peace Research Institute (SIPRI). These sources use common definitions, such as the NATO definition for defence expenditures, to facilitate inter-country comparisons.[5]

Between 1981 and 2017, real (inflation-adjusted) Canadian defence equipment expenditures grew by about 10%, or a compound annual growth rate of just 0.3%. There are pockets of accelerated growth in equipment spending during the period reflecting a significant boom-bust cycle in defence procurement. For example, between 1980 and 1988, spending increased by 80%. In the first decade of the Post-Cold War period (1990–1999), meanwhile, defence equipment spending decreased by 68%.

The proportion of defence spending to GDP does not necessarily reveal anything useful about a nation's military capabilities. However, it is an important indicator of military burden and relative comparator within the context of NATO or other military alliances. Similarly, the proportion of defence-related R&D outlays by a government is better understood when contextualized relative to comparable nations. Figure 21.2 displays defence burden measures for selected years for NATO member counties. The seven largest NATO members (in terms of GDP) reduced their defence burden after the Cold War with varying rates of decline. For example, Canada and the United Kingdom reduced their defence burden by about 40% during the period 1991 and 2001 while Italy's burden declined by a modest 10%. Following the commencement of the global war on terror in 2001, the United States' defence burden increased by 27% while Italy's declined by 13%. Canada is the only other country that increased its relative burden (7%) during the period 2001–2011.

From the perspective of R&D spending, Canada's defence share is compared to a select group of countries in Figure 21.3. Here the choice of nations reflects Canada's security partners in NATO and the Five-Eyes community (particularly Australia).[6] Over the period 1981 to 2015, the defence share of government R&D spending declined substantially for the top five NATO countries. Germany and France, for example, show declines of more than 60% while the United Kingdom and Canada decreased R&D spending

Table 21.1 Canadian defence data 1981–2017

Year	*Defence burden*	*Defence R&D share*	*Procurement constant 2018 US dollars*
1981	1.7%	5.5%	2,034
1982	1.9%	5.8%	2,361
1983	2.0%	5.8%	2,975
1984	2.1%	6.4%	3,203
1985	2.0%	6.8%	2,899
1986	2.1%	6.9%	3,041
1987	2.0%	7.8%	3,461
1988	2.0%	8.3%	3,648
1989	1.9%	6.7%	3,487
1990	1.9%	6.4%	3,300
1991	1.9%	5.1%	3,198
1992	1.8%	5.3%	3,153
1993	1.8%	4.8%	3,075
1994	1.7%	4.8%	2,649
1995	1.5%	4.7%	2,534
1996	1.4%	4.8%	2,094
1997	1.2%	5.7%	1,588
1998	1.2%	5.3%	1,311
1999	1.2%	5.4%	1,058
2000	1.1%	4.8%	1,307
2001	1.1%	4.2%	1,306
2002	1.1%	3.7%	1,511
2003	1.1%	3.8%	1,777
2004	1.1%	3.7%	1,959
2005	1.1%	4.1%	1,953
2006	1.1%	4.0%	2,087
2007	1.2%	3.2%	2,828
2008	1.2%	3.2%	2,891
2009	1.4%	2.7%	2,767
2010	1.2%	3.2%	2,893
2011	1.2%	3.0%	2,451
2012	1.1%	3.4%	1,871
2013	1.0%	3.0%	2,014
2014	1.0%	2.9%	2,290
2015	1.2%	2.6%	2,052
2016	1.2%	NA	1,961
2017	1.2%	NA	2,245

Source: OECD (2018), NATO (2018) and authors' calculation.

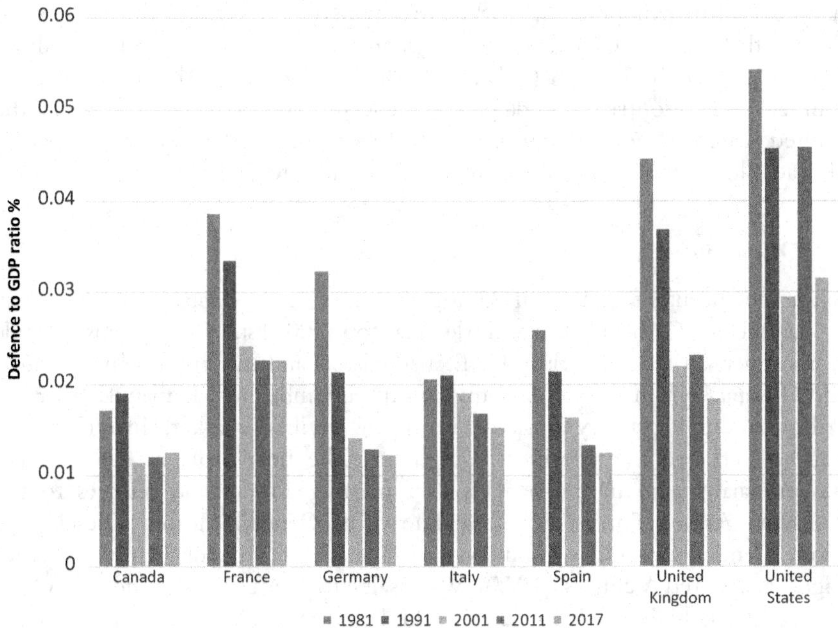

Figure 21.2 Defence burdens for selected NATO members.

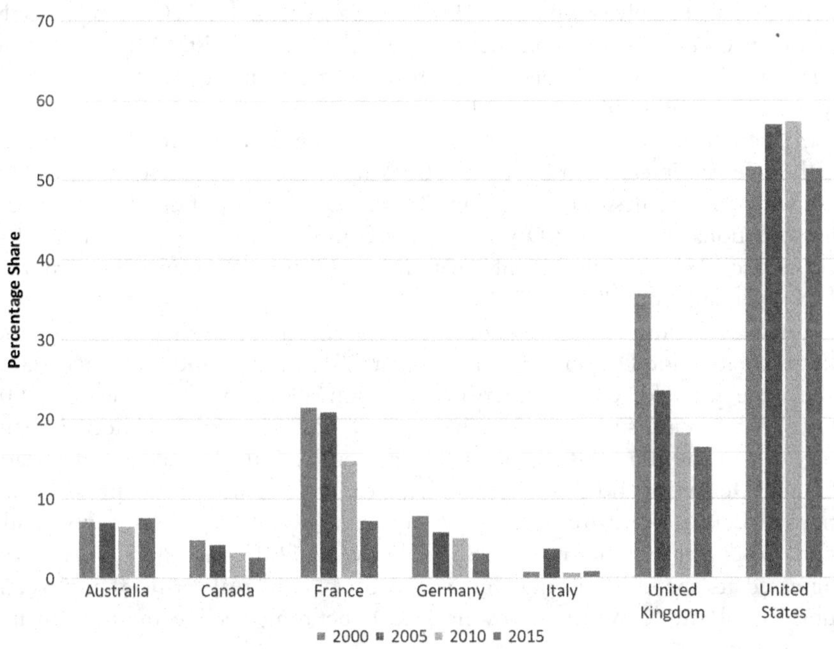

Figure 21.3 Defence share of R&D spending (select NATO and Five Eyes nations).

by 54% and 46%, respectively. The United States' and Australia are the only nations in this grouping that either maintained or increased the proportion during this period. Canada's defence share of government R&D, at about 3%, ranks near the bottom (Italy's at 0.8% is the lowest). About half of government R&D outlays are defence-related in the United States while the United Kingdom devotes approximately 16% to defence. France and Australia allocate close to 7% of government R&D funding to defence.

2.1 Defence industry

Since the inception of the SIPRI top 100 arms firms database in 1990, only a handful of Canadian firms made the top 100 list. These firms include Bombardier, an aerospace firm, CAE, a simulators and training systems provider, and General Dynamics Land Systems Canada, a combat vehicle manufacturer.

Bombardier's primary business is in the civilian market, manufacturing regional jets and transportation equipment. The firm's role in defence sales has primarily been in the provision of training aircraft and services to the Canadian Armed Forces. Formerly known as General Motors' Diesel Division, General Dynamics Land Systems Canada is a major manufacturer of Light Armoured Vehicles (LAV). With sales to NATO allies and the US it has ranked as high as 43rd in the SIPRI 100 (see Table 21.2). The company recently signed a contract for the provision and maintenance of armoured vehicles to Saudi Arabia worth about C$15 billion.

General Dynamics Mission Systems acquired another Canadian firm in the Top 100 list, namely, Computing Devices Canada, in 1998. CAE is the only Canadian-owned firm to consistently make the top 100 list. Despite this, the share of defence to total sales for the firm decreased from about 61% to 38% between 2004 and 2016 (Table 21.2).

In Section 3, we outline survey-based data from 2016 to provide a snapshot of the research intensity in the sector. Looking at the broader research spending trends by the business sector in Canada, we note a few industrial sectors with disproportionately high R&D profiles. We consulted data from Research Infosource Inc.[7] which included information on the top 100 Canadian corporate R&D spenders from 2001 to 2018.

Table 21.3 outlines the top defence and aerospace firms on the list and the associated R&D spending in constant 2018 dollars and exchange rates. The table includes only three firms that consistently rank in the top 100. Note that foreign subsidiaries such as L3, WESCAM and Lockheed Martin show up in the top 100 list, albeit intermittently. Canadian space firm Macdonald, Dettwiler and Associates also appear on the list a few times during the mid-2000s. Bombardier has become the largest R&D spender in Canada with expenditures growing by 853% between 2001 and 2017. CAE also increased its spending during this period by 11% in real terms. The foreign subsidiary Pratt & Whitney saw its R&D spending decline by 15% during this period.

Table 21.2 Canadian firms within SIPRI's top 100 arms industry database (1990–2017)

Year	*Rank*	*Company*	*Arms sales (current year)*	*Arms sales (constant prices 2018)*	*Arms sales as a % of total sales*	*Total employment (current year)*
1996	90	Bombardier	340	506	6	41,150
1996	93	General Motors Canada (GM USA)	320	476	2	–
2002	43	General Motors Canada (GM USA)	900	1,237	–	–
2002	82	CAE	390	536	54	
2003	84	CAE	450	601	58	5,000
2004	89	CAE	460	599	61	4,800
2006	61	General Dynamics Land Systems Canada (General Dynamics Land Systems)	820	1001	--	1,700
2006	100	CAE	500	611	45	5,000
2007	92	CAE	570	677	43	6,000
2008	89	CAE	680	780	44	7,000
2009	96	CAE	710	797	53	7,000
2010	81	CAE	840	949	53	7,500
2011	84	CAE	900	992	49	8,000
2012	91	CAE	840	898	40	7,670
2013	100	CAE	800	845	39	8,000
2015	96	CAE	760	780	39	8,000
2016	89	CAE	780	805	38	8,500

Source: SIPRI Arms Industry Database (accessed November 8, 2018) and authors' calculations for converting to 2018 constant dollars.

The corporate 100 R&D spenders database also highlights three key Canadian statistics. First, the top 100 list tends to be consistently dominated by one or two large firms. During the period 2001–2008, for example, Nortel Networks, a communication company, dominated the rankings. From 2009–2011 another telecommunications giant, Blackberry (Research in Motion) led the rankings. These firms are no longer competitive in their respective sectors (Nortel filed for bankruptcy in 2009). Over the last six years, the aerospace firm Bombardier has dominated the rankings. Second, large foreign subsidiaries account for the bulk of R&D performed in Canada. Aside from Bombardier and CAE, most aerospace firms are foreign subsidiaries. Third, as will be discussed in detail in the next section, most defence firms in Canada are small and medium sized. As noted in Choi and Lee (2018), small and mid-sized firms tend to spend less on R&D than their larger counterparts.

Table 21.3 Top Canadian R&D spenders various years

Pratt & Whitney Canada Corp. (fs)				*Bombardier Inc.*			*CAE*		
Year	Rank	R&D $ 2018	R&D Intensity	Rank	R&D $ 2018	R&D Intensity	Rank	R&D $ 2018	R&D Intensity
2001		$463			$130			128.50	
2002	3	$441	18%	8	$241	1%	20	120.59	10%
2006		$441			$180			87.97	
2007	4	$394	14%	14	$132	1%	21	78.92	7%
2011		$390			$1,103			96.57	
2012	5	$428		1	$1,545	11%	19	116.93	8%
2014		$428			$1,596			117.60	
2015	6	$409		1	$1,812	10%	22	109.73	6%
2016		$400			$1,542			117.49	
2017	5	$395		1	$1,234	8%	19	143.13	7%

Source: www.researchinfosource.com/top-100-corporate-rd-spenders/2018/list (various years) and authors' calculation.

3. Industry structure and characteristics

3.1 Overview

The most recent survey of Canada's defence industry is the Canadian Defence, Aerospace and Marine Industry Survey (CDAMIS) conducted by Statistics Canada on behalf of Innovation, Science and Economic Development (ISED) Canada for 2016.[8,9] Firms with sales in any products or services related to military platforms, sub-systems, in-service support, training, etc. are included in CDAMIS and can be considered *the* definition of defence industries in the Canadian context. Note also that this is consistent with definitions used in prior defence industrial base studies in Canada such as Treddenick (1987), Berkok (2010) and Solomon (2009).

These latest survey results show that Canada's defence industry consisted of 664 firms[10] with a total of approximately C$10.4 billion[11] in industry sales (US$7.6 billion), with direct employment of 27,000 persons. In comparison, Lockheed Martin's arms sales in 2016 totaled US$40.8 billion and employed 97,000 personnel. Using an input-output modelling approach, ISED estimated a C$6.4 billion contribution to Canadian GDP, with a total of 59,800 full-time equivalents generated directly and indirectly. Of the 6.4 billion economic impact, 3.1 billion came directly from the defence industry, while 1.55 billion was associated with consumer spending by employed personnel and 1.75 billion was associated with suppliers of intermediate inputs (Figure 21.4).

The clear majority of the 664 firms in Canada's defence industry are of the small-or-medium enterprise variety; only 32 of the 664 firms have more than 500 employees. These large enterprises, however, account for upwards of 60% of defence industry sales, exports and employment, and 75% of total industry research and development. This confirms the Choi and Lee (2018) findings discussed earlier.

3.2 Distribution of domestic and foreign ownership of Canadian defence firms

Most of Canada's defence firms (550) are either Canadian-owned or owned by a parent company based in Canada, while 68 firms are based in the United States, with the remaining 46 belonging to other countries such as the United Kingdom. Interestingly, Canadian-owned firms accounted for less than half of total industry sales – approximately C$4.58 billion – compared with the 4.65 billion accruing to American-owned firms and over 1.18 billion accruing to firms with other foreign ownership (Figure 21.5).

3.3 Performance

3.3.1 Export intensity and destinations

Canada's defence industry is export-intensive, with C$6.0 billion of the total C$10.4 billion (about 57.5%) in sales destined for foreign trading partners.

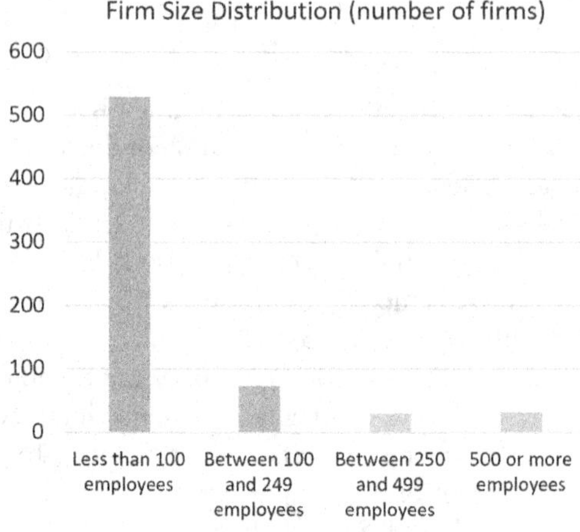

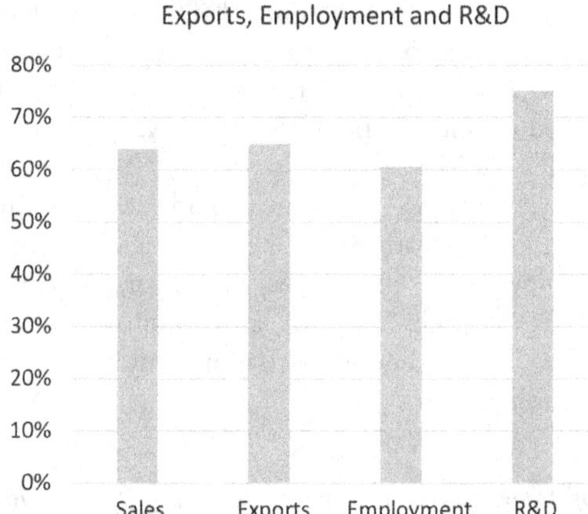

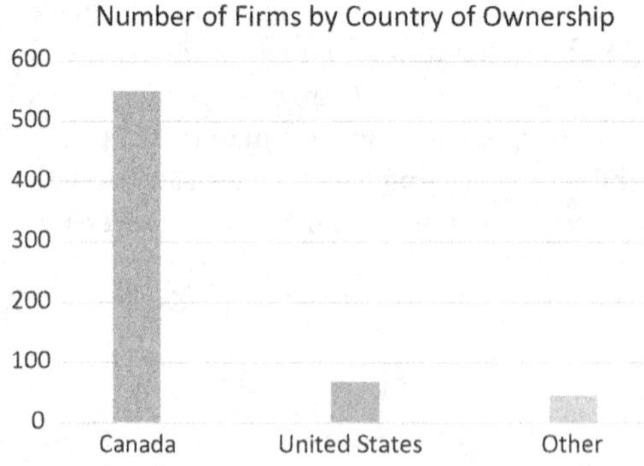

Figure 21.4 Firm structure and characteristics.

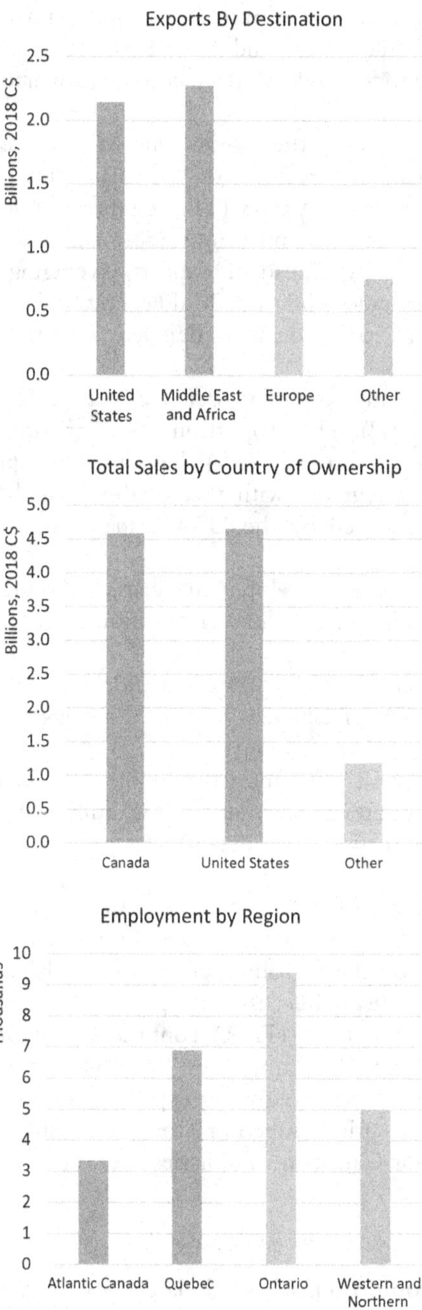

Figure 21.5 Firm ownership and regional characteristics.

The United States is naturally the single largest export destination for Canadian-manufactured defence goods, accounting for approximately C$2.14 billion in total export sales. Middle Eastern and African countries import C$2.27 billion in Canadian defence goods, while Europe accounts for about C$830 million of total exports.

As shown in Figure 21.6, the US and the Middle East and North African countries are the main destinations for Canadian arms exports. This is based on SIPRI's Trend Indicator Values (TIV: essentially trade volume measures). TIV is a useful measure for comparing trading partnership trends. The US is the main destination for Canadian exports, averaging about 26% (during 1981–2017) of total trade while the Middle East and North Africa (MENA) accounted for 20% of Canadian defence exports during the period (Figure 21.6).

Canada imports about 70% of its defence materiel from the United States on average (Figure 21.7). The proportion of imports from the US was higher during the Cold War (excess of 85%) than any other period. The Canadian economy is closely integrated with that of the United States, and this relationship is further codified by the US-Canada Defence Production Sharing arrangement (DPSA).

Through the Defence Development Sharing Arrangement (DDSA) and DPSA, Canada can enter US military acquisition in two ways:[12]

a Through contracts issued to Canadian industries by the US Department of Defense (DoD), facilitated by the Canadian Commercial Corporation (CCC).
b Through commercial sub-contracts negotiated by Canadian firms and the US. These sub-contracts account for the bulk of the trade between US and Canada (see Section 2 for details).

This important access to the largest defence market in the world is punctuated by occasional disputes on both sides. Some US firms believe that the liability assumption by the Canadian government (through CCC) puts them at a disadvantage.[13] Meanwhile, the change in 1999 to the US International Traffic in Arms Regulations (ITAR) continues to worry Canadian defence firms. Specifically, the Department of State regulatory changes imply an increase the number of items requiring export licenses to Canada. This affects the tightly-integrated prime subcontractor relationship that exists with US parent firms and their Canadian subsidiaries and associated supply chains.

3.3.2 Defence industry production and diversification

In terms of production, Canada's single largest category is the manufacture of (land-based) Combat Vehicles and Components; this includes the General Dynamics Land Systems-manufactured LAV III, which is also currently in service in the United States, Colombia, and New Zealand, with Saudi Arabia

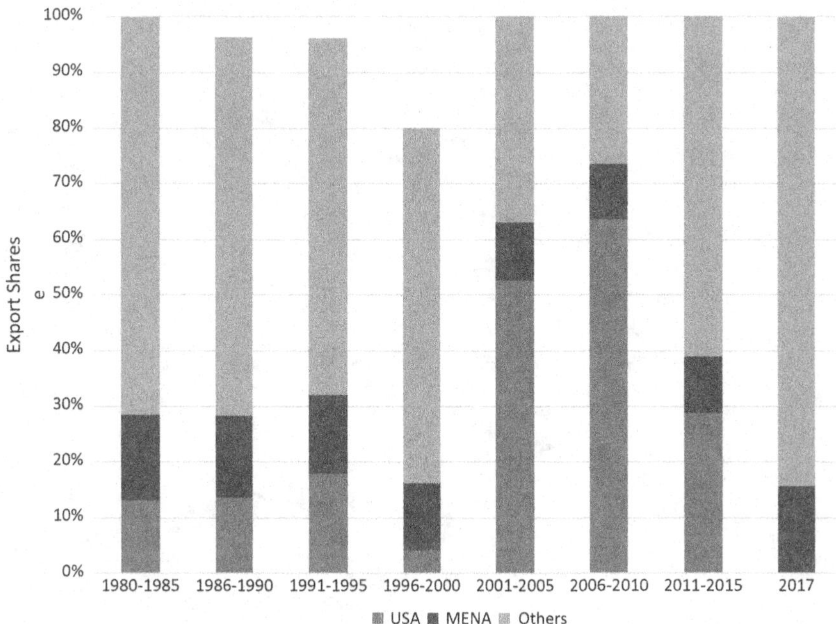

Figure 21.6 Canadian exports based on SIPRI trend indicator values.

soon to become another export destination. In total, the Combat Vehicles and components category accounts for C$2.43 billion of the C$5.1 billion in sales in the Land and Other Defence manufacturing sector.

The Aerospace and Marine Defence industries account for C$3.35 billion and $C1.98 billion of the C$10.41 billion in total Defence industry sales, respectively. Within these industries, Maintenance, Repair and Overhaul (MRO) are the largest categories; in Aerospace, the second largest category in terms of sales is the Electronics, Software and Related Components category[14] which totals approximately C$1.1 billion in sales. With regards to the manufacture of military platforms in the Aerospace and Marine industries, the fabrication of Aircraft Structures and Components accounts for C$0.74 billion in sales, while Shipbuilding and Naval Conversion accounts for roughly C$0.65 billion.

3.4 Regional distribution of Canada's defence industry

The CDAMIS survey includes a regional breakdown of employment in the defence industry and lists major manufacturing activities taking place in each region. Of the 27,000 total persons directly employed in the defence industry, Ontario and Quebec – Canada's most populous provinces – accounted for

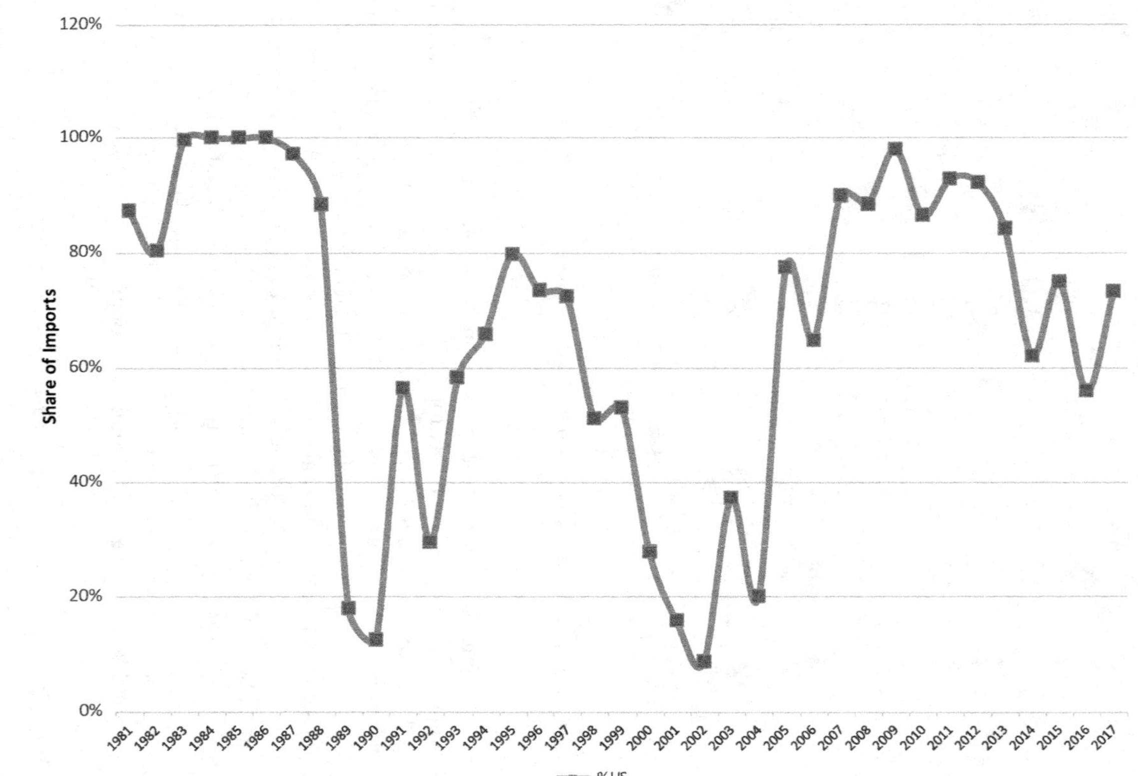

Figure 21.7 US share of total Canadian defence imports based on SIPRI trend indicator values.

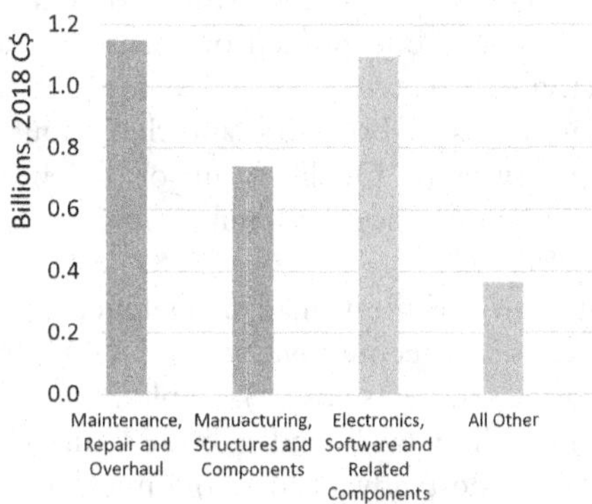

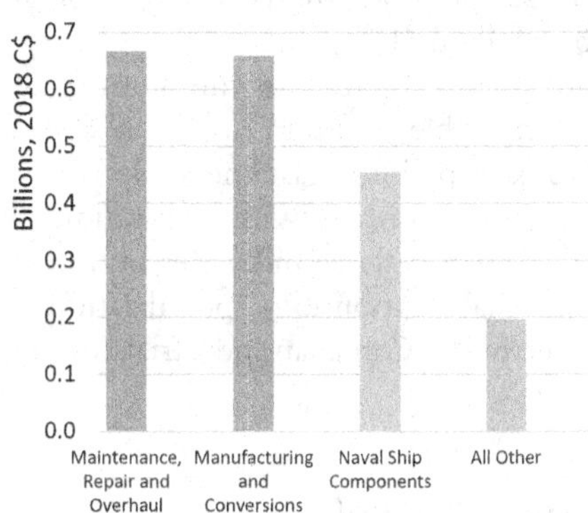

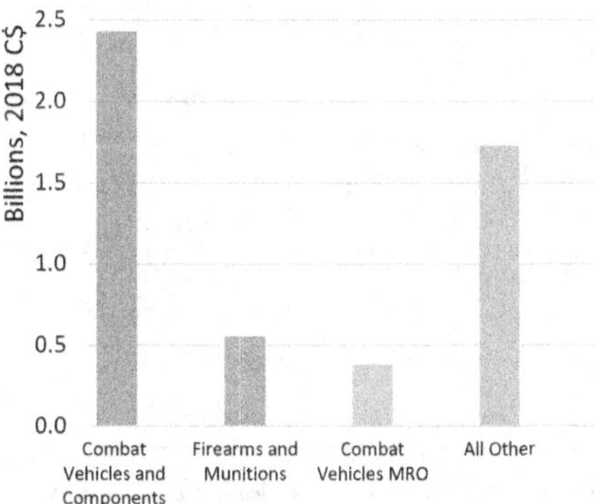

Figure 21.8 Products and services.

over 60% of total employment, while Western and Northern Canada and Atlantic Canada respectively account for 19 and 12%.[15]

Of the major manufacturing activities, Shipbuilding, Naval Conversion, and Naval MRO is naturally concentrated on Canada's East and West coasts. Ontario's largest activities in terms of sales include land-based Combat Vehicle manufacturing, aircraft fabrication, and the manufacture of electronics in support of defence systems. Quebec's major defence industry activities include the production of munitions, aircraft simulation systems and airborne electronics (Figure 21.8).

To contextualize the size of the Canadian Defence Industrial Base (CDIB) within the broader Canadian economy, we use GDP by industry data for 2016 (the same year as the survey statistics). Table 21.4 shows GDP by industry in basic prices (excluding taxes and subsidies on products) for selected aggregates. Canada, like most advanced economies, is primarily a service-based economy: services account for approximately 71% of total industrial output. In contrast, manufacturing with C$198 billion represents 10% of the economy. The public sector is almost twice as large as the manufacturing sector with over C$365 billion (18%).

The CDIB estimate of direct GDP in the amount of C$3.2 billion (this figure is not directly comparable as it is in market as opposed to basic prices) is about 0.2%. By way of comparison, gasoline stations alone contribute C$6.3 billion. These findings are consistent with past studies including the initial pioneering work on Canadian defence industries by Rosenbluth (1967) which identified the same regional distribution, specialization in niche market and relatively minor presence in the Canadian industrial landscape.[16]

Table 21.4 GDP shares of selected sectors (Canada)

Industry aggregate	*$Billion 2018 basic prices*	*Proportion*
All industries	1,903,030	100%
Service-producing industries	1,344,098	70.6%
Public Sector	365,039	19.2%
Mining, quarrying, and oil and gas extraction	141,046	7.4%
Manufacturing	198,033	10.4%
Finance and insurance	126,874	6.7%
Real estate and rental and leasing	243,973	12.8%
Defence services	12,318	0.6%
Gasoline Stations	6,299	0.3%
CDIB*	3,218	0.2%

Source: Statistics Canada Table 36-10-0434-03 Gross domestic product (GDP) at basic prices, by industry, annual average (x 1,000,000) Authors' calculation (conversion to 2018 reference year).

* CDIB figure converted to 2018 constant prices. The conversion biases CDIB's share as the original figure is in market as opposed to basic prices.

This relative consistency is remarkable considering several government-driven industrial initiatives aimed at growing the defence sector, such as major domestic development and procurement (post–World War II), restructuring of the defence bureaucracy (in the 1960s), trade offset and related strategies (since the 1970s) and the recent comprehensive defence industrial strategy (launched in 2014). Each of these policies is briefly described in the next section.

4. Conduct and policy

4.1 Conduct

Taylor (2011) documents several government initiatives to build up military capabilities in Canada. These early attempts adopted a cost-plus arrangement with a profit margin of up to 5% (on cost: Taylor, 2011). The CF-100 project (the Canuck aircraft), the development of the CF 105 (Arrow) and the associated Iroquois jet engine are early examples. However, changing geostrategic relations and cost overruns ended the experiment with cost-plus and domestic development.

Competitive bids such as the infantry carrier (Bobcat and the Bonaventure refit) in the 1950s show that continuous design changes and contract amendments failed to control costs. As noted by Arseneault (1989) and Boileau (2004) competitive bids can be hijacked by "low-balling" and "buy in". Firms gain monopoly advantages after low balling initial costs and subsequently raising prices for spares and modifications. Similarly, the agent in the form of the military will get "buy in" from the principal (government) via small commitments for a project until sufficient investment and "sunk cost fallacy" convinces the government to continue funding at a higher cost.

For more recent examples we utilize a public dataset on government procurement. Specifically, Table 21.5 shows summary statistics on all government contracts between the period 2009 and the early 2018.[17] For the period considered, the dataset shows a total contract value of C$139 billion. Of this amount DND accounts for about C$52 billion or 37%. Sole-source contracting represents about 22% of total contracts. However, DND accounts for half of these sole-source contracts.

Major Crown Projects (MCPs) or government procurement contracts valued at over C$100 million tend to be linked to defence industrial development policies; we focus on these contracts next. MCPs represented about 47% of all government contracts for the period 2009–2018. DND alone represented 41% of all MCPs. Importantly, sole source contracts represented 46% of all MCPs. Of these, DND and related procurement accounted for 78%.

While most government contracts conform to stated goals of competitive bids, MCPs and military capabilities tend to be sole sourced. The new National Shipbuilding Strategy (NSS) also signals the return to costplus

Table 21.5 Government contracting strategy 2009–2017

Contracts 2009–2018	*Amount constant 2018 C$*	*Proportion*
Total Contract Value	$143,718,742,760	
Total Contract DND	$53,397,458,309	37%
Competitive Tender	$112,766,156,642	
Sole Source	$30,952,586,118	22%
Total Sole Source DND	$15,151,107,263	
Total MCP	$67,425,149,178	47%
Total MCP DND	$27,715,702,800	41%
Total MCP Sole Source	$14,310,963,510	46%
Total MCP Sole Source DND	$6,583,798,196	
incl. CCC*	$11,131,162,507	78%

Source: Canada: Public Service and Procurement Canada https://open.canada.ca/en/open-data (accessed October 31, 2018) Authors' calculations.
*Canadian Commercial Corporation (facilitates exports of defence systems).

pricing. This strategy is about consolidating shipyards and minimizing the boom-bust cycles inherent in shipbuilding business. The strategy introduces some performance incentives, but the selected shipyards are expecting profits of up to 14.5% (on costs). Irving shipbuilding and Seaspan are the prefeed shipyards to build up to 28 vessels for DND and the Canadian Coast Guard. The cost of the program is estimated at C$38 billion[18]

4.2 Defence industrial policies

Having abandoned domestic development of military capabilities, Canada now relies on trade offsets and related policy instruments (Berkok, 2010; Solomon, 2009). Other related policies include the Industrial and Regional Benefits (IRB) and, more recently, the Industrial and Technological Benefits (ITB) programs. These programs are also a logical response to declining defence budgets and overall domestic demand.

The industrial offsets strategy is not unique to Canada. Non-Canadian studies on offsets include Martin and Hartley (1996) and Berkok et al. (2012) Industrial offsets are ostensibly about "offsetting" the loss of jobs and other economic benefits because of external procurement. From an economics perspective, it is a poor policy response due to a basic misunderstanding of international trade. If a nation has comparative advantage in producing defence goods and services, then other nations ought to import from it. In a 1985 review of the offsets program Nielsen (1985) concludes that the policy benefits were only marginal. Specifically, the Neilson report claims that 57% of the benefits reported by one major contractor (McDonnell-Douglas) would have occurred without the awarding of the contract.

The IRB policy is the post-Neilson report "improvement" by explicitly articulating a long-term industrial benefits provision. However, the mechanism on how this was to be achieved remains vague and unenforceable (Solomon, 2009). The policy's goal of redistributing defence production to under developed regions has been equally ambiguous. Solomon (2009) shows that some provinces in Canada managed to increase defence industrial sales without the benefits of the IRB policy. The 2016 survey outlined in the previous section confirms that despite such industrial and regional development initiatives, Ontario and Quebec remain the primary industrial regions in Canada.

Using the principal-agent-monitor framework, Taylor (2011) argues that IRBs provided governments a means to ameliorate voters' concern that foreign purchases are detrimental to local industries while the Department of National Defence (DND) officials obtained new military capabilities by adjusting scope to fit the IRB requirements. This exchange between the principal (Government) and the agent (DND) is Pareto efficient in the procurement game but as Taylor (2011) notes, the outcome is not socially optimal. The monitor (Office of the Auditor General) with its mandate of value for money evaluations frequently noted the inefficiencies inherent in these national industrial policies (Taylor, 2011).

Another unique Canadian perspective on industrial policy is its approach to managing its munitions production. Canada's Munitions Supply Program (MSP), existing in several forms since 1978, consists of government-supported franchise monopolies issued to suppliers for different types of munitions. These markets are not subjected to competition, and function largely on a cost-plus contracting basis: that is, the government requests munitions from the suppliers and guarantees them a full compensation of production costs plus an agreed-upon profit percentage. In return, firms are often required to make certain assurances to the government, particularly around "security of supply" and surge requirements. The former concerns the need for the Canadian Armed Forces (CAF) to be supplied munitions in times of conflict and increased demand for munitions; the latter reflects the possibility that large quantities of munitions may be needed on a short turnaround, as was the case at the height of Canada's combat role in Afghanistan.[19] In sum, the munitions industry in Canada is a significant proportion of its defence industrial base, accounting for C$1.6 billion in sales in 2011.

Perspectives on whether the MSP is successful in its stated goal of the provision of security of supply are mixed. A 2007 Chief of Review Services report noted that at time the Canadian military was still largely dependent on offshore sources for critical munitions such as those for naval platforms and aircraft. More recently, Penney (2016) estimated the import content of CAF munitions at approximately 50%.

4.3 Defence industrial strategy

Canada's current Defence Procurement Policy (established in 2014) identified three objectives: "Deliver the right equipment to the Canadian Armed Forces

(CAF) and the Canadian Coast Guard in a timely manner; leverage our purchases of defence equipment to create jobs and economic growth in Canada; and streamline defence procurement processes."[20] The strategy also recognized the fact that defence firms face uncertainties about investments in R&D and capital acquisitions. The strategy makes explicit statements about early industry engagement and stable funding for defence procurement, among others, to reduce uncertainties. This policy is noteworthy in its explicit acknowledgement of the risks and potential hold-up due to uncertain defence funding and requirement environment. The explicit long-term funding in the last two defence policies and the public announcement of the defence investment plan are useful steps in reducing these uncertainties.

However, the three objectives identified above may be mutually exclusive. The encouragement of domestic development of defence industrial capabilities is at odds with the timely and cost-effective delivery of complex military capabilities. As illustrated amply in previous sections, Canada does not have prime contractors or integrators for complex military capabilities. Similarly, streamlining the procurement process requires changes to governance and other government initiatives. For example, the current government procurement process involves three separate government departments, each with its own mandate, focus and incentives. The Department of National Defence wants to acquire capabilities that maximize military effects; ISED is tasked with promoting domestic industrial and technological development; and Public Services and Procurement Canada manages the contractual process. Navigating the procurement process is costly for any new firm contemplating entry into the defence market or to any small or medium enterprise.

There are also issues with the optimal allocation of a limited supply of skilled labour in complex project management. Stone (2015) suggests a partial solution through a separate procurement agency to leverage the limited number of individuals that can understand and shepherd complex military acquisitions.

Canada's Defence Procurement Strategy also introduced a new iteration of the IRB policy, now rebranded as the Industrial and Technological Benefits (ITB) policy. Central to this new policy is the rating and evaluation of offset proposals through a "value proposition" approach. This requires potential trading partners to describe their proposals in terms of several dimensions, notably in terms of "Key Industrial Capabilities" (KICs). The government weights each of the KICs according to their overall desirability; as the name of the new policy suggests, these weights place an emphasis on the technological transfer portion of trade offsets to motivate investments in domestic R&D activity. Other pillars of the policy include domestic economic activity, supplier development, skills development and the development of Canada's export capability.

Beyond technology transfer, the identification and sustenance of the KICs are also about improving Canada's chronic underperformance in productivity and innovation. However, private sector business behavior may explain the productivity puzzle according to Drummond (2011) and the Council of Canadian Academies (2013). As the Council notes "Canadian firms have been as innovative as they have needed to be."[21] If the solution to the productivity puzzle is a microeconomic assessment of business incentives then government intervention may be futile.

Even if we accept that government intervention is required to support KICs, the administering and monitoring of the program needs to be transparent. Currently we do not have visibility on the assessment metrics, expected benchmarks and possible penalties for missing expected results.

5. Future prospects for Canada's defence industry

Canada's defence industrial base, in its current state, can be perhaps best described as a government-supported industry dominated by a handful of foreign subsidiaries. The few Canadian giants in the defence industry such as CAE and Bombardier generally provide inputs into finished systems or support services; shipbuilders such as Irving and Seaspan focus primarily on assembly rather than the manufacture of the high technology components of naval platforms. The Canadian government has historically favoured the use of the defence industry as a means to distribute wealth and economic activity; this is evidenced through policies such as the MSP and ISED's "designated regions of Canada" policy (ISED, 2018). This governmental focus on domestic economic benefits and protectionism has come at the expense of cost and efficiency. Despite these drawbacks, the Canadian defence industry continues to be competitive internationally, with a majority of production in most defence sectors being destined for exports to foreign trading partners.

Looking forward, the 2017 Strong, Secure and Engaged (SSE) defence policy, if fully executed, promises the single largest peacetime investment in defence capital in Canadian history over the next 15 years. As discussed within this chapter, major procurements of high-profile defence platforms including a new line of naval frigates and next-generation fighter aircraft are planned during this period. The associated impacts of these and other major procurement projects on Canadian industry could indeed be quite large, especially if Canadian industry manages to enshrine itself as part of the global supply chain of these advanced defence systems. However, much remains uncertain as Canada's Department of National Defence has historically had difficulty in both the timing and overall execution of major defence procurements; one needs only to look at the chequered past of the ongoing Future Fighter Capability Program, which had begun in earnest in 1997 with the proposed acquisition of Lockheed Martin's F-35 fighter aircraft and, after several iterations, has yet to produce an approved way forward for the procurement of a true next-generation fighter aircraft.

In this vein, Figure 21.9 displays historical and projected defence capital expenditures over the period of 2007–2008 to 2026–2027 as well as the reported lapses in spending according to Canada's Public Accounts data. Over this period, the average rate of lapse was approximately 20%; with SSE's ambitious spending plan, even modest lapses proportional to the proposed spending could result in lapses of several billions of Canadian dollars each year. The projection below assumes a lapse rate of 20%, consistent with DND's historical lapsing behaviour. With this degree of lapsed funding, DND could encounter difficulties delivering

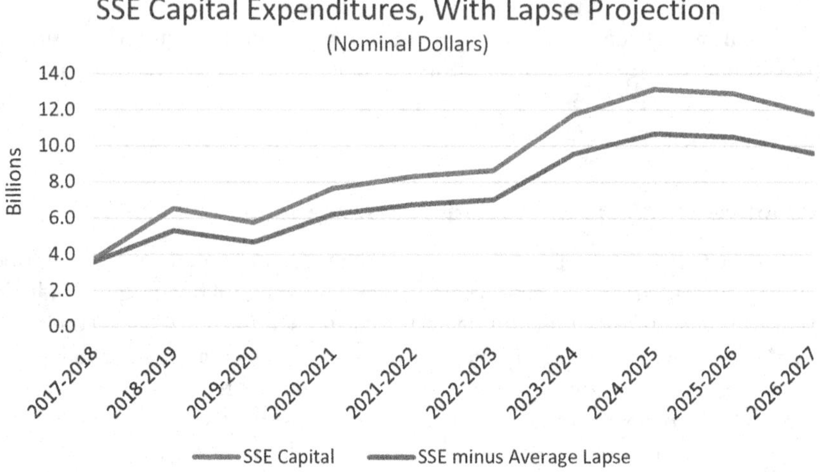

Figure 21.9 Strong, secure engaged future trends.
Source: PSPC, Perry (2018) and authors' extrapolation.

on its promised modernization of important defence platforms due to bureaucratic inertia, changing governments, and budget reallocations.

The long-term outlook on Canada's defence industry is difficult to predict. If history is to be any guide, the Canadian government will continue to support its domestic industry as it ensures its policy goals of economic benefits, regional specialization and technological spillovers are met. This leaves the question of whether Canada will develop a comparative advantage that does not arise from government subsidy. At present, the data suggests Canada's comparative advantage in the defence industry is in intermediate inputs into high-end defence platforms – electronics, software and other support systems. Arguably, we may add the production of light armoured vehicles to this category, with the LAV III continuing to be a platform in demand from other nations. Whether these advantages are artificial and dependent on Canadian subsidies and protectionism is an ongoing question.

Notes

1 The views expressed in this chapter are the views of the authors and do not necessarily reflect those of the Department of National Defence or the Parliamentary Budget Officer. Unless otherwise specified all financial data are in Canadian dollars (C$). For inter-chapter comparisons US$1 buys C$1.183 in 2018.
2 As quoted in the Ottawa Citizen https://ottawacitizen.com/news/national/defence-watch/irving-to-build-sixth-arctic-and-offshore-patrol-ship. Accessed November 8, 2018.
3 Editorials include Craig Stone, "Strong Secure Engaged: A Positive New Opportunity for Defence or Another Meaningless Defence Policy Statement." *Inside Policy*

(Ottawa; McDonald-Laurier Institute, June 8, 2017); available at www.macdonaldlaurier.ca/strong-secure-and-engaged-a-positive-new-opportunity-or-another-meaningless-defence-statement-craig-stone-for-inside-policy/; R. Fetterly, Implementing Strong, Secure, Engaged: The Challenges ahead www.cgai.ca/implementing_strong_secure_engaged_the_challenges_ahead Accessed November 8, 2018.

4 www.nato.int/cps/em/natohq/news_156770.htm Accessed October 31, 2018. The PDF version includes discussion on definitions (page 13). www.nato.int/nato_static_fl2014/assets/pdf/pdf_2017_06/20170629_170629-pr2017-111-en.pdf.

5 For R&D statistics the internationally recognized method is known as the Frascati manual. For details see www.oecd.org/sti/inno/frascati-manual.htm Accessed November 2, 2018

6 The five-eyes is an intelligence alliance consisting of NATO members Canada, United Kingdom and United States and including Australia and New Zealand.

7 https://researchinfosource.com/news/2018 Accessed November 12, 2018

8 Statistics Canada, Canadian Defence, Aerospace and Marine Industries Survey (CDAMIS), 2016. Available at www.23.statcan.gc.ca/imdb/p2SV.pl?Function=getSurvey&SDDS=2933&lang=en&db=imdb&adm=8&dis=2 Accessed November 6, 2018.

9 Innovation, Science and Economic Development Canada, Government of Canada, *State of Canada's Defence Industry, 2018 Report*. Available at www.ic.gc.ca/eic/site/ad-ad.nsf/eng/h_ad03978.html Accessed November 6, 2018.

10 The survey defines a "defence firm" rather broadly, consisting of firms that recorded *any* sales of defence goods and services within the 2016 calendar year.

11 All figures are in 2018 constant dollars.

12 Innovation, Science and Economic Development www.ic.gc.ca/eic/site/ad-ad.nsf/eng/ad00271.html see also the original agreement here: www.ccc.ca/en/canadian-exporters/~/media/9513A3BD3C1448FE8970C22641DD337C.ashx?la=en Accessed November 12, 2018

13 Redesigning Defense: Planning the Transition to the Future US Defense Industrial Base, Appendix A, The North American Defense Industrial Base: Canadian and Mexican Contributions. Congress of the United States, Office of Technological Assessment, 1991

14 This category represents an aggregation of two electronics categories in the CDAMIS survey; these are the "primarily airborne communications and navigation systems, and other information systems, software, electronics and components" category and the "primarily airborne electro-optical, radar, sonar and other sensor/information collection systems, fire control, warning and countermeasures systems and related components" category.

15 A further 9% of total employment is listed as "breakdown not specified"; totals may not sum to 100% due to rounding.

16 Note that these earlier studies utilize input-output based models to generate the economic and employment impacts of the sector.

17 Source Public Service and Procurement Canada (PSPC) https://open.canada.ca/data/en/dataset/53753f06-8b28-42d7-89f7-04cd014323b0 Accessed November 12, 2018.

18 A recent study indicates that 15 of the 28 vessels may cost more than $60 Billion (Story, 2017).

19 A full treatment of Canada's Munitions Supply Program is available in Berkok and Penney (2014) while an assessment of the surge capacity of the MSP is available in Van Bavel (2015).

20 Public Works and Government Services Canada, *Leveraging Defence Procurement to Create Jobs and Benefit the Economy* Press Release February 5, 2014. Ottawa; PWGSC, 2014; available at http://news.gc.ca/web/article-en.do?mthd=tp&crtr.page=1&nid=813789&crtr.tp1D=1 Accessed November 6, 2018

21 Council of Canadian Academies (2013). Paradox Lost, p. 11.

References

Arseneault, J. (1989). "The DDH 280 Program: A Case Study of Government Expenditure Decision-Making." in *Canada's Defence Industrial Base*, edited by David G. Haglund, 118–136. Kingston, Ontario: Ronald P. Frye and Company.

Berkok, U. (2010). "Canadian Defence Procurement". in *Defence Procurement and Industry Policy: A Small Country Perspective*. Edited by Robert Wylie and Stefan Markowski. New York: Routledge.

Berkok, Ugurhan and Christopher Penney (2014). *The Political Economy of the Munitions Supply Program, Defence R&D Canada, Contract Report*. DRDC-RDDC-2014-C92.

Berkok, Ugurhan, Christopher Penney and Karl Skogstad (2012). *Defense Industrial Policy Approaches and Instruments, Aerospace Review*. www.econ.queensu.ca/files/other/Defence%20Industrial%20Policy%20Approaches%20and%20Instruments.pdf accessed 15 November 2018.

Boileau, J. (2004). *Fastest in the World: The Saga of Canada's Revolutionary Hydrofoils*. Halifax, Nova Scotia: Formac Publishing Company.

Canada (Various years). Receiver General of Canada. Public Accounts of Canada Volumes 1–3, Ottawa: PSPC.

Canada, Department of National Defence (2017). *Strong, Secure, Engaged: Canada's Defence Policy*. Ottawa: Department of National Defence.

Canada, Department of National Defence, Chief of Review Services (2007). *Evaluation of the Munitions Supply Program*, 1258-101-4 (CRS).

Choi J. and J. Lee. (2018). Firm size and Compositions of R&D Expenditures: Evidence from a Panel of R&D Performing Manufacturing Firms. *Industry and Innovation* 25(5) 459–481.

Council of Canadian Academies (2013). *PARADOX LOST: Explaining Canada's Research Strength and Innovation Weakness*. Ottawa (ON): Advisory Group, Council of Canadian Academies.

Drummond, D. (2011). Confessions of a Serial Productivity Researcher. *International Productivity Monitor* Number 22 (Fall) 3–10.

Fetterly, R. (2018). *Implementing Strong, Secure, Engaged: The Challenges Ahead* www.cgai.ca/implementing_strong_secure_engaged_the_challenges_ahead accessed November 15th 2018.

Innovation, Science and Economic Development Canada (ISED) (2018). Industrial and Technological Benefits Policy: Value Proposition Guide. www.ic.gc.ca/eic/site/086.nsf/eng/00006.html accessed 30 Nov 2018.

Innovation, Science and Economic Development Canada (ISED) (2018). State of Canada's Aerospace Industry 2016 Report Ottawa; ISED and AIAC, 2016 www.ic.gc.ca/eic/site/ad-ad.nsf/eng/h_ad03964.html accessed November 15th 2018.

Martin, S. and Keith Hartley. (1996). UK Firms Experience and Perceptions of Defence Offsets: Survey Results. *Defence and Peace Economics* 6(2) 123–139.

Nielsen, Erik. (1985). *Management of Government: Procurement*. Canada: Minister of Supply and Services.

North Atlantic Treaty Organization (NATO) Information on Defence Expenditures www.nato.int/nato_static_fl2014/assets/pdf/pdf_2017_06/20170629_170629-pr2017-111-en.pdf accessed October 31st 2018.

Organization for Economic Development and Co-operation (OECD) Main Science and Technology Indicators www.oecd.org/sti/inno/researchanddevelopmentstatisticsrds.htm accessed November 20th 2018.

Penney, C.E. (2016). *A Brief Assessment of the Import Content of CAF Munitions*, DRDC-RDDC 2016-L222.

Perry, D. (2013). A Return to Realism: Canadian Defence Policy after the Great Recession. *Defence Studies* 13(3) 338–360.

Perry, D. (2018). *Strong, Secure, Engaged So Far, Policy Update*. Canadian Global Affairs Institute.

Research Infosource Inc. (2018). Canada's Top 100 Corporate R&D Spender List www.oecd.org/sti/inno/researchanddevelopmentstatisticsrds.htm accessed November 13th 2018.

Rosenbluth, Gideon. (1967). *The Canadian Economy and Disarmament*. Toronto: Macmillan of Canada.

Solomon, B. (2009). "The Defence Industrial Base in Canada." Chapter 6 in *The Public Management of Defence in Canada*, edited by Craig Stone, 111–139. Toronto: Breakout Educational Network.

Solomon, B. and Stone, C. (2013). "Accrual Budgeting and Defence Funding: Theory and Simulations", *Defence and Peace Economics*, 24:3, 211–227.

Statistics Canada Table 36-10-0434-06 Gross Domestic Product (GDP) at Basic prices, by Industry, Annual Average, Industry Detail (x 1,000,000) www.150.statcan.gc.ca/t1/tbl1/en/tv.action?pid=3610043406.

Stockholm International Peace Research institute (SIPRI) Arms Industry Database www.sipri.org/databases/armsindustry;www.sipri.org/databases/armstransfers/sources-and-methods accessed October 3rd 2018.

Stockholm International Peace Research institute (SIPRI) Arms Transfers Database www.sipri.org/databases/armstransfers accessed October 3rd 2018.

Stone, Craig. (2017). *Strong Secure Engaged: A Positive New Opportunity for Defence or Another Meaningless Defence Policy Statement*. Inside Policy. Ottawa: McDonald-Laurier Institute, 8 June 2017 www.macdonaldlaurier.ca/strong-secure-and-engaged-a-positive-new-opportunity-or-another-meaningless-defence-statement-craig-stone-for-inside-policy/ accessed November 21st 2018.

Stone, J.C. (2015). *Improving the Acquisition process* in Canada School of Public Policy Research papers 8 (16) University of Calgary www.policyschool.ca/wp-content/uploads/2016/03/improving-acquisition-process-stone.pdf accessed November 21st 2018.

Story, R. (2017). *The Cost of Canada's Surface Combatants*. Ottawa: Parliamentary Budget Officer.

Taylor, Ivan (2011). *Cost Estimation and Performance Measurement in Canadian Defence: A Principal-Agent-Monitor Perspective*. Ph D Dissertation Order No. NR81550. Canada: Carleton University, 151. http://search.proquest.com/docview/917457503?accountid=9867 accessed November 2nd 2018.

Treddenick, J.M. (1987). *The Economic Significance of the Canadian Defence Industrial Base*, CSDRM, No. 5, Ontario: Kingston.

Van Bavel, G. (2015). *The Munitions Supply Program during Canada's Participation in the NATO International Security Assistance Force in Afghanistan. A look at the effect of a surge in demand on selected calibres* DRDC-RDDC 2015-L316.

22 Defence industry in Australia

Stefan Markowski, Rob Bourke and Robert Wylie

1. Introduction

The Australian defence industry is a product of what Australian governments spend on the acquisition and sustainment of materiel for Australian the Defence Force (ADF) and, to a large extent, what they deem to be the militarily essential to source from in-country suppliers. In FY 2018–19, Australian defence expenditure[1] is budgeted at A$36.4 billion, equivalent to 1.91 percent of the nation's GDP and to 6.4 percent of Australian Government's total budgeted expenditure.

Defence routinely spends about one third of its annual budget on the acquisition and sustainment of ADF *materiel.* Of this over half is allocated to the acquisition of platforms and systems from both local and overseas suppliers ($A7.6 billion budgeted in 2018–19). The balance is allocated to sustainment (predominantly repair, maintenance and adaptation of those platforms and systems – an estimated $A6.3 billion in 2018–19: Hellyer 2018, Table 5.1: 63). Of the total expenditure on the *acquisition* of platforms and systems, over one third is to be spent in Australia. The corresponding figure for *sustainment* is 71 percent.

The total in-country spending by Defence on acquisition and sustainment accounts for at most 0.2 percent of GDP. The proportion of the Australian manufacturing workforce employed in its defence industry is commensurately small – some 2.9 percent. In 2017, the top 40 defence suppliers employed 20,343 people with some of them engaged only in non-defence production (ibid., Table 5.5: 70). Looking ahead, however, the impact of local defence industry on economic activity may increase as major domestic shipbuilding and military vehicle assembly projects gather momentum.

As discussed in greater detail below, the Australian defence industry is predominantly foreign owned: of the top 40 Australian-domiciled defence contractors (including both materiel suppliers and service providers), 27 are overseas-owned, 11 are Australian-owned and one is an Australian government business enterprise (Hinze 2018). Nine of the top ten materiel suppliers are wholly foreign-owned (the government-owned Australian Submarine Corporation, ASC, being the only exception).

Against this background, Section 2 of the Chapter examines the evolution of Australian defence policy since the mid-1970s with particular reference to the nexus between procurement of materiel, supply security/self-reliance and defence industry development. Section 3 discusses the present structure, conduct and performance of the industry and Section 4 considers the industry's future prospects.

2. Evolution of Australian defence industry: policy and procurement

The present structure, conduct and performance of Australian defence industry is a product of shifting Australian defence policies, related defence procurement and commercial investments. Since the 1980s these trends can be viewed as a sequence of overlapping but essentially consecutive phases comprising, respectively, the commercialisation of the defence industry, a quest for industrial self-reliance, emphasis on efficient and effective defence procurement; and – most recently – an initial focus on priority industry capabilities which was overtaken by a broader concept of industrial sovereignty.

2.1 The commercialisation of defence industry

In the mid-1970s the Australian Government responded to the withdrawal of, respectively, the US from South-East Asia and Britain from east of Suez by reforming defence administration and announcing a more self-reliant defence policy (Killen 1976). The reforms were driven by demand for better alignment between defence capability development (including procurement of capital equipment) and government-endorsed strategic and financial guidance (Tange 1973: 47–49; Andrews 2001: 193–211). Defence self-reliance focussed on the military capabilities required to defend the nation against credible threats independent of combat assistance from other nations (Brabin-Smith 2005). In relation to the indigenous defence industry, this policy did not imply defence self-sufficiency: rather, it prioritised local industry capacity to maintain, repair, update and upgrade the ADF's capital equipment "utilising for the provision of equipment and materiel, a combination of local industry, selective stockholding and reliable overseas sources of supply" (Killen 1976: 51).

Australia entered the 1980s with ownership of its local defence industry distributed between government and private interests. As a legacy of two world wars, the Commonwealth government owned three naval dockyards employing over 5,400 naval and civilian personnel and some 15 other government factories employing an additional 7,200 civilian staff and manufacturing, for example, munitions and military clothing or assembling overseas-designed combat aircraft. However, private companies occupied significant niches. For example, Hawker de Havilland not only maintained military aircraft engines and avionics but also manufactured F/A-18 airframe components as part of the then defence offsets program. Local companies – mostly subsidiaries of overseas telecommunications suppliers – met bourgeoning military demand for electronics-based radar, underwater sensors and communications systems. In doing so, however, they had little incentive to undertake independent research and development and looked to Australian government agencies or overseas primes for the requisite intellectual property.

The shift to defence self-reliance and the associated administrative reforms was a contested process that delayed procurement (Andrews 2001: 217–221). Excess capacity in the government factories and dockyards was exacerbated by weak management and chronic industrial disputes, especially in shipbuilding and repair (Coulthard-Clark 1999: 59–60; Holland 2014: 259–260). Commercial-style management of publicly-owned industry assets and their subsequent privatisation were increasingly seen as a potential solution to the inherent problems of rent-seeking, adverse selection of workforce and moral hazards of local sourcing.

Defence-related research and development was concentrated in the Defence Science and Technology Organisation (DSTO) which went beyond high risk/high return research into Australia-specific requirements like sonar technology to develop technology demonstrators and prototypes to meet niche ADF requirements (e.g. Nulka anti-ship missile defence system). DSTO also brokered access to overseas (especially US and UK) military technological innovation. Such access was critical to local development of, for example, the JINDALEE over-the-horizon radar network for surveillance of Australia's northern maritime approaches (JORN). It was clearly recognised that, given Australia's small population and manufacturing base, technological know-how was both very scarce and highly critical for the development of local solutions to the country's military requirements. Economies of scope in knowledge building and sustainment were best achieved by concentrating much of the available expertise in a single defence technology hub with spokes extending into local industry and academia to harness network-based efficiencies.

By 1987 privatisation was generally considered the key to reform of the government factories and dockyards. This ten year process began with the sale of Williamstown Naval Dockyard to a private consortium in January 1988. A contract to complete the two guided missile frigates (FFGs) then under construction provided cash flow and underpinned initial reform of work practices and management. The consortium then embarked on more ambitious reforms with the support of the Government and the wider trade union movement, with an eye to the forthcoming competition – which it won – for a 15 year contract to build ten German-designed ANZAC Class frigates for the Australian and New Zealand navies (Holland 2014: 258).

Thus encouraged, the Government established Australian Defence Industries (ADI) as a government-owned company with a mandate to rationalise the munitions factories and other naval dockyards. It corporatized the government aircraft factories and then sold them to, respectively, Hawker de Havilland (itself subsequently acquired by BAE Systems) and to Rockwell (later taken over by Boeing Defence Systems (Hill 1998: 238–239). In 1996, the

Government awarded ADI a long-term contract to supply ADF ammunition and in 1998, shortlisted it for a billion dollar contract to upgrade the Navy's FFG frigates. In 1999, the Government sold ADI to a French-Australian consortium and in 2006 agreed to the French partner, Thales, assuming full control (Parliament 1999). Such transactions marked a wave of Australian Government-sanctioned take-overs of Australian defence companies by major overseas suppliers. Within a decade, four of the top five Australian defence suppliers – Thales, BAE Systems, Raytheon and Boeing – were foreign-owned (Hall and Wylie 2008).

Once privatisation of the government factors and dockyards was well advanced, policy attention shifted to ADF support. Market testing for the provision of services by Army, Navy and Air Force workshops and warehouses proceeded under the auspices of the Commercial Support Program (Ray 1994: 118–119). The program culminated in comprehensive outsourcing of ADF support capabilities and the reassignment of the military personnel involved (McIntosh et al. 1997: 29–37). By the early 2000s commercial support was critical to ADF preparedness with, for example, Boeing Australia operating ADF fixed communications systems and SERCO providing garrison support services (Wylie 2006: 50–63).

2.2 *The pursuit of defence industrial self-reliance*

The active use of defence procurement to implement defence industry policy began in 1983 with the election of a new Government. In 1984, the new Government promulgated its *Defence Policy Principles for Australian Industry* (Commonwealth 1985) in order to guide local industry involvement in the major re-equipment of a more self-reliant ADF then envisaged. The 1984 principles were subsequently refined and amplified in a wide ranging review of Australia's defence capabilities commissioned by the then Minister for Defence and published in 1986 (see Dibb 1986: 112–113). The nexus between defence self-reliance, defence industry policy and defence capital equipment procurement was formalised in the 1987 Defence White Paper (Beazley 1987: 75–89). More nuance was provided in subsequent strategic reviews (see, for example, Ray 1993: 69–73). The 1994 Defence White Paper broke new ground in stipulating priority local industry capabilities including combat systems software and support; data management and signal processing, command, control and communication systems; systems integration and repair and maintenance of major weapons and surveillance platforms (Ray 1994: 115–116).

Several themes characterise this policy cycle. Firstly, successive Governments expressly recognised that local industry involvement in supply and support of ADF often involved cost premiums. Defence was to determine the acceptability of such penalties on a case-by-case basis having regard to the balance between, on one hand, the defence value of the resulting support capacity and, on the other hand, associated penalties in terms of extra cost, diminished capability or reduced availability.

Secondly, however, contemporary policy statements also reflected muted but persistent concern about the reliability of overseas support. The US had declined Australian requests for access to the software required to adapt the electronic warfare and other sensor systems embedded in the F/A-18 aircraft acquired in 1984 (Hall and Wylie 2010). The 1986 review of Australia's defence capabilities advocated limiting Australia's dependence on overseas sources of repair and maintenance support, especially in electronics and the software needed to support modern weapons systems. It also reaffirmed DSTO's role in fostering the limited range of indigenous design skills Australia needed to meet Australia-specific requirements and to facilitate the selection and adaptation of overseas equipment (Dibb 1986: 112–113). The Government subsequently called for high levels of Australian ownership and control of companies involved in supply and support of selected, strategically sensitive technologies pioneered by DSTO including over-the-horizon radar and the NULKA anti-ship missile defence system (Beazley 1987: 82–83).

Finally, calls for high levels of Australian industry involvement in the procurement of defence capital equipment were constrained by concerns to manage the associated risk of non-defence interests capturing the business, leading the Government to state that

> unless there are compelling reasons to the contrary, defence work will be allocated on a competitive basis using fixed price (as opposed to cost-plus) contracts, with payments against milestones (rather than elapsed time) and with other incentives for improved performance where appropriate.
>
> (Ibid.: 82; see also Chapter 5)

In hindsight, however, Australian defence policy-makers obviously underestimated the challenges inherent in reconciling this hands-off approach to procurement with self-reliance induced demand for high levels of local content in complex and innovative development projects like the COLLINS Class submarines and JINDALEE over-the-horizon radar system. These and similar developmental projects encountered widely publicised and highly politicised difficulties that undermined confidence by government and parliament in the ability of Defence and local industry to manage the nexus between defence procurement and defence industry policy – thereby ushering in the next phase of Australian defence industry development.

2.3 Efficient and effective defence procurement

In the early 2000s, the Government commissioned prominent Australian businessmen to investigate defence procurement policies and procedures and accepted their recommendations that it adopts a more commercial approach to the conduct of defence business. To that end, it established a more autonomous Defence Material Organisation (DMO) operating at arm's length from the Defence customer via a series of project-and task-specific purchaser-provider arrangements (Kinnaird et al. 2003). Capability planners and procurers were required to justify "Australianisation" of equipment having regard to the potential risks and costs involved (ibid.: 19), noting that off-the-shelf purchases would enable Australia to take advantage of larger economies of scale and avoid the considerable risks to cost and schedule inherent in developing new weapons systems (Mortimer 2008: 17). Such commercial logic did not preclude local industry involvement in supply and support of ADF materiel. For example, in 2007, the Australian Submarine Corporation (ASC), Defence and Raytheon Australia formed an alliance to build three Spanish-designed air warfare destroyers in South Australia, with ASC being responsible for integrating the hull modules built in several local shipyards and Raytheon being responsible for the integration of systems (including the AEGIS missile defence system). However, the more rigorous approach to Australianisation precluded local industry involvement in the supply of relatively mature aircraft like the EA-18G "Growler" electronic warfare aircraft and the C-17A Globemaster aircraft which were procured on a Military-Off-The-Shelf (MOTS) basis with local industry involvement confined to in-country support (for which Boeing Defence Australia is prime contractor).

During this phase Australia continued to procure developmental solutions to its requirements for military capability but with greatly reduced appetite for the risk inherent in local industry involvement. For example, the DMO contracted Boeing to design and build the Wedgetail airborne early warning and control aircraft to Australian specifications in Seattle, where Boeing assumed most cost, schedule and technical risk. In 2013, Boeing Defence Australia was awarded the first of several contracts for support of the Wedgetail aircraft in RAAF service. By the end of the 2010s, this new business model resulted in foreign-controlled suppliers accounting for over 80 percent of the defence materiel produced in Australia (DMO 2008). Overseas prime contractors not only established local subsidiaries but also expanded their footprint in Australia through local mergers and acquisitions. This was led by BAE Systems Australia, whose antecedents provided contractor support for British weapons testing at Woomera, doubling its footprint in the defence electronics sector by acquiring AWA Defence Industries and Siemens Plessy in the mid-1990s, branching out into the provision of basic flying training services for the ADF under the auspices of the Commercial Support Program, then diversifying into shipbuilding through acquisition of Tenix Defence Systems (formerly Transfield) in 2008.

In 2007, the US and Australian governments concluded the *Australia-United States Treaty on Defense Trade Cooperation* to facilitate local support for the US-origin platforms and systems being acquired for the ADF. This Treaty – like its UK counterpart – is intended to expedite licensing by the US State Department of US exports of military and military-related technology to Australia. However, the Treaty does not cover key US technologies such as stealth, sensor fusion, electronic warfare and satellites. These remain subject to case-by case licensing by the US State Department, as do software source codes specific to virtually all militarily-significant platforms and systems of US origin (Wylie 2008: 123–127).

2.4 From priority industry capabilities to sovereign industrial capabilities

In 2007, the then Minister for Defence instructed Defence to identify those priority industry capabilities (PICs) that would confer an essential national security and strategic advantage by being resident in-country (Nelson 2007: 10). Defence was also required to monitor the health and sustainability of identified PICs and, where necessary, to take procurement-related action to remedy capability shortfalls. Those actions could include rescheduling defence demand, bundling projects and restricting tenders (Wylie 2007). Defence procurement officials initially declined to promulgate PICs publicly, ostensibly on the moral hazard grounds that doing so would enable those companies hosting PICs to exert unmanageable pressure for government preferment.

In 2010, a new Government set aside these scruples and released an unclassified (and carefully worded) list of PICs, in order to signal its defence industry priorities to local suppliers as clearly as practicable (Combet 2010: 38–39). In this early iteration, PICs focussed on the ability to sustain and upgrade mission-critical elements of ADF materiel and included, *inter alia*, local industry capacity to reprogram the flight safety software on the Army's helicopters, the capacity to continue modifying and upgrading JORN and the production of selected munitions (including small arms). This iteration of PICs covered an estimated 20 percent of local defence industry capacity (Bourke 2019). A particularly instructive inclusion in the 2007 PIC list was active phased array technology developed locally by two ex-Naval officers at their commercial risk. Critical to these entrepreneurs' ability to overcome the prevailing defence scepticism about indigenous innovations was Navy support in-principle for use of active phased array radar to enhance the ANZAC ships' anti-ship missile defence capability (Macklin 2017).

In 2013, Defence published a high level survey of PIC health which indicated that, with the notable exception of the JORN-related PIC, the companies involved had sufficient defence business to obviate the need for a significant level of Defence intervention in the short term. In JORN's case, Defence intervened by placing – and being seen to place – contracts with the companies involved to enable them to retain their highly specialised workforce (Wylie 2013: 116). Thereafter, however, the PIC initiative stalled, hampered by Defence's failure to sustain the requisite administrative and financial resources and eclipsed by yet another Government policy initiative namely the formal designation of Australian defence industry as a *Fundamental Input to Capability* (FIC) and the introduction of the concept of "industrial sovereignty" as the basis for deciding which equipment to build in Australia rather than overseas (Payne 2016: 108–111). The notion of "industrial sovereignty" is not limited to military-strategic necessity and may include considerations of broader economic benefits for Australia. This was followed two years later by the concept of *Sovereign Industrial Capability Priorities* (see below).

With local defence industry accorded FIC status, companies bidding for defence capital equipment procurement worth A$20 million or more were obliged to provide project-specific *plans* for Australian industry capability development, including how the company intended to support the transfer of technology and foster innovation within Australian defence industry. Defence was obliged to evaluate such plans having regard to the quality of the proposals and the benefit to Australian defence industry. And, once in contract, Defence was to enforce the contracted Australian Industry Capability Plan to ensure the benefits are realised (DoD 2016: 49).

According local defence industry FIC status prepared the way for a substantial dilution of the nexus between defence strategy, defence industry policy and defence procurement. In the run-up to the 2016 federal election the then Australia's prime minister announced that the COLLINS Class submarines would be replaced by 12 new French-designed conventional submarines to be built in South Australia. This A$50 billion, two-decade project was not only intended to meet Australian defence requirements but also to reinvigorate Australian manufacturing. Not surprisingly, the announcement included reference to the creation of 2800 new high tech Australian jobs, mainly in South Australia which had borne the brunt of the collapse of the local automobile industry (Turnbull 2016).

Announcing local construction of new submarines was merely the opening salvo in the Government's ambitious and avowedly interventionist naval shipbuilding plan released in 2017. Underpinning the plan was "the greatest recapitalisation of the Royal Australian Navy since the Second World War" encompassing three continuous naval building programs for, respectively, new submarines, major surface combatants, and minor naval vessels, with the work being distributed between the Osborne Naval Shipyard in South Australia and the Henderson Maritime Precinct in Western Australia (Turnbull and Pyne 2017: 11–21).

In 2018, the government released its Defence Industrial Capability Plan aimed at achieving, over the next two decades, an Australian defence industry with the capability, posture and resilience needed to help meet Australia's defence needs (Pyne and Payne 2018: 14). The plan hinges on developing and maintaining *Sovereign Industrial Capability Priorities* (SICP). The latter subsume the old PICs but go wider to include local industry capacity considered essential to achievement of the integrated program of capital investment over the short to medium term or that needs "more dedicated monitoring, management and support due to their industrial complexity, Government priority or requirements across multiple capability programs" (ibid.: 19) including non-defence considerations.

The shift from priority to sovereign industry capabilities moved Australia well beyond a long-standing focus on self-reliance based around the capacity to maintain, repair, modify and adapt defence equipment to the Australian environment. Whereas the earlier PICs covered some 20 percent of Australian defence industry output, the new SICPs cover some 80 percent of production. This suggests a fundamental shift from the thinking that prevailed in the 1980s and early 1990s with in-country construction of a much higher proportion of the ADF's materiel needs now envisaged and commensurately less sensitivity to the extra costs involved.

Pursuit of defence industrial sovereignty on this scale prompted the Productivity Commission (2016: 37) to observe that:

> Paying more for local builds, without sufficient strategic defence and spill-over benefits to offset the additional cost, diverts productive resources (labour, capital and land) away from relatively more efficient (less assisted) uses. It can also create a permanent expectation of more such high-cost work, as the recent heavily promoted 'valley of death' in naval shipbuilding exemplifies. Such distortion detracts from Australia's capacity to maximise economic and social wellbeing from the community's resources. The recent decision to build the new submarines locally at a reported 30 percent cost premium, and a preference for using local steel, provides an illustrative example of how a local cost premium can deliver a very high rate of effective assistance for the defence contractor and the firms providing the major steel inputs.

In this context a key concern is that Defence has stopped collecting price premium data at the tender stage of its recent major acquisition projects – including offshore patrol vessels (A$3 billion to A$4 billion), future frigates (over A$35 billion) and combat reconnaissance vehicles (A$5 billion). If data on premiums are not collected at the tender stage of projects it is unlikely that it would, or even could, be compiled later in the procurement process. As things stand, Defence will now only assemble data on the economic benefits of larger capital equipment projects and will make no attempt to gauge the projects' economic costs, including their price premiums. Under current policy settings, given prevailing governance arrangements, the lack of transparency that characterises sovereign industrial capabilities renders defence procurement vulnerable to capture by related commercial, industrial and political interests and, as a consequence, to loss of public confidence in the integrity of the procurement process.

3. Structure, conduct and performance of the Australian defence industry

Relatively little quantitative information is available on the Australian defence industry's structure, conduct and performance. The main official sources of publicly available data are once-off surveys conducted by the Industry Commission in 1994 and the Department of Defence in 2008. These sparse official sources are usefully augmented by annual reviews of Australia's top 40 defence contractors conducted by the *Australian Defence Magazine* (see, for example, Hinze 2018). Periodic reports published by the Australian National Audit Office constitute the best source of quantitative information about specific defence projects and programs but translating this project-specific data into reliable information about the performance of the industry as a whole poses insurmountable difficulties.

That said, the defence industry sector has a number of readily identifiable features, which coincide with what one would expect to find in a small open economy with a defence policy based on industrial self-reliance, preference for the sourcing of military materiel from the private sector, and the acceptance of foreign ownership of key areas of domestic defence industry. These features include:

- high levels of supplier concentration;
- a maritime-oriented defence industry;
- a highly skilled workforce;
- high levels of foreign ownership;
- low levels of indigenous industrial R&D;
- low levels of exports;
- a geographic clustering of industrial activity, recently focussing on South Australia; and
- relatively high levels of profitability.

Each of these features is addressed in the following discussion.

3.1 Supplier concentration

In 2008, the simple average four firm concentration ratio for Australian defence industry was an estimated 60 percent. The comparable ratio for manufacturing as a whole was around nine percent and around 30 percent for a sub-set of the sectors' defence-related industries (DMO 2008). This relatively high concentration can be attributed to the small scale of Defence's domestic demand and to Defence's preference for doing business with a relatively small number of large prime contractors. The top ten defence suppliers sold directly to DMO 84 percent of the total value of domestically and overseas produced defence materiel sourced through Australia-based companies (ibid.: 2).

Approximately 70 percent of Defence's expenditure on domestically produced materiel is sourced initially through the defence industry's largest ten companies who then channel at least some defence spending through to sub-contractors, many of whom are small-medium sized enterprises with 200 employees or less. Such second and third tier suppliers ultimately receive around 50 percent of what Defence spends in-country, 30 percent direct from Defence and another 20 percent through larger companies. This reflects the fact that Australia has largely eschewed high levels of vertical integration within the industry in favour of a more loosely bound vertical ties through largely foreign-owned military prime contractors combined with policy driven requirement for significant local content in military materiel. Thus, Australia-domiciled prime contractors seem to prefer to focus on system assembly, integration and overall project management and leave a significant proportion of specialised component and service provision to smaller domestic players. Tier One suppliers (contracted directly by

DMO) delivered 77 percent of total sales to DMO and Tier Two suppliers (subcontracted by Tier One companies) 23 percent (ibid.: 2).

It appears that that defence supply chains tend to be relatively concentrated with a small number of prime contractors and OEMs controlling the delivery processes and offsetting some of the ADO monopsony power in niche areas of technologically complex, large projects dominated by bilateral monopolies. Given the relatively large number of prime contractors operating in-country, there appears to be reasonable competition *for* the market at Tier 1 level of supply but much less scope for contestability *in* the market once prime contracts are let (limited opportunities for switching suppliers at that level). Defence is thus compelled to rely on one or very few upstream domestic sources of supply and to use the threat of direct imports to secure value for money.

In the absence of direct import competition, Defence is forced to price regulate a substantial proportion of the industry to achieve economically efficient outcomes. Effective regulation has proven to be a challenging task and survey data relating to the industry's profitability suggest that it may not have been entirely successful. Although the industry might face higher levels of risk than many other areas of manufacturing due to a combination of intermittent Defence demand and technical complexity of defence-specific production, it still appears to enjoy relatively high levels of profitability.

3.2 Sectoral composition of defence materiel

In 2008, electronics accounted for 33 percent of total value of defence materiel produced in Australia for DMO, maritime products for 25 percent, aerospace for 23 percent, "land products" (e.g., vehicles but also clothing) for 15 percent, and weapons and munitions for four percent. Put another way, DMO acquisitions in 2008 comprised nearly 63 percent of all domestic shipbuilding and maritime repair, 31 percent of all aircraft manufacture and repair (aerospace), over four percent of electronics and computing, and 1.4 percent of all "land products" (ibid.: 3). It can be argued that the more Defence dominates a given sector, the less it can rely on other parts of the economy to offer support if necessary and the more careful it must be in managing its expenditure with an eye to the industry's development. This suggests that naval shipbuilding is the most vulnerable segment of the Australian defence industry, not least because highly skilled human resources may easily be competed away to other sectors or overseas. Moreover, in-country maritime platform building creates relative few jobs, at high cost per job and does not appear to offer much strategic military advantage (Davies et al. 2012). In contrast, Defence only accounts for a very small proportion of local sales and production in electronics and computing (although it may dominate particular niches). This suggests that in contingencies, mobile resources may be attracted from the civil sector to improvise creative solutions to the emergent problems.

3.3 Skilled workforce

In 2008, the largest ten companies employed over 12,000 people on DMO projects while the 50 largest suppliers deployed nearly 15,000 (DMO 2008). That workforce is also relatively well skilled and educated: employees with tertiary or trades qualifications averaged around 85 percent for the Top 10 suppliers in 2008, about 80 percent for the next Top 11–50 contractors, and nearly 85 percent for the Top 50 suppliers. This compares with the average of 70 percent for defence-related areas of Australian manufacturing and less than 60 percent for all Australian manufacturing (ibid.: 4). These figures suggest that Australian defence industry must meet at least some of its demand for highly qualified workers by competing them away from other parts of the national economy (Davies et al. 2012) – a scenario that would qualify the more extravagant claims of economic benefit generated by local construction of naval ships and other platforms.

3.4 Foreign ownership

In 2008, 82 percent of defence materiel produced in Australia for DMO by the Top 50 suppliers was subject to foreign control (DMO 2008). Of the ten largest suppliers to DMO, nine were foreign owned and/or controlled. The corresponding figure for the next 41–50 defence suppliers was over 50 percent and for the Australian manufacturing as a whole nearly 60 percent. Thus, while the ten largest companies are mostly foreign-owned and controlled by overseas prime contractors (e.g., BAE Systems, Thales, or Boeing), the ownership/control of Tier Two in-country Defence suppliers is broadly similar to that of the manufacturing sector as a whole. Australian defence industry's dependence on inflows of foreign-capital and associated expertise – especially post-privatisation – accords with that of the Australian economy as a whole. A common perception is that although nearly all the primes are foreign-owned, the companies beneath them are not. This is clearly not so for the second tier of suppliers, although there are some notable exceptions. As a result, Australia's dependence on foreign direct investment is considerably higher in this sector than first impressions suggest. Generally, acceding to calls for enhanced Australianisation of local defence industry would compromise defence industrial self-reliance.

3.5 Industrial research and development

Australian defence industry historically undertakes relatively little R&D. This could be attributed primarily to Defence's long standing practice of funding R&D in-house via DSTO rather than encouraging local private sector participation. However, the consequences of this practice are exacerbated by DSTO's role as in-house technology adviser, which precludes it from partnering with companies competing for local defence development contracts.

Other factors include Australia's relatively small domestic market, its need to concentrate on new technologies unique to its physical environment but not applicable to the environment of other countries. Finally, all else equal, foreign-owned companies are more likely to import proprietary technologies from their overseas parent rather than engage in indigenous innovation (see Section 4 for evidence on spin-offs).

3.6 Exports

In 2008, six percent of all defence materiel produced in Australia by the Top 50 defence suppliers was exported. By value, exports accounted for 6.5 percent of sales of the ten largest DMO suppliers, 5.7 percent of the next 41–50 companies, and 6.4 percent of the Top 50 suppliers. In comparison, Defence-related areas of Australian manufacturing exported over 28 percent of their production and for Australian manufacturing as a whole the share was 22.5 percent (ibid.: 4). Modest defence exports can be attributed to the high barriers to trade applying in overseas defence markets, the limits to international competitiveness that come with limited domestic demand, unwillingness of foreign prime contractors to substitute Australian sub-contractors for overseas lower tier suppliers, and, arguably, Defence's relatively strict export controls. Exports are demonstrably no panacea to the kind of stop-start patterns of demand which have historically characterised Defence investment and it remains to be seen whether this changes under current defence industry policy settings and procurement plans.

3.7 Location

In 2008, of the total DMO's domestic purchases from the Top 50 defence suppliers, Queensland accounted for 25 percent of the total value of deliveries, South Australia 24 percent, NSW 19.5 percent, Victoria 14 percent, Western Australia nine percent, Northern Territory six percent, ACT two percent, and Tasmania one percent. These figures suggest that South Australia secures a disproportionately large share of Defence expenditure with defence industry located in several clusters including electronics in the Mawson Lakes precinct and adjacent to DSTO in Edinburgh, and at a shipbuilding/repair hub at Osborne. Such clustering seems to reflect a combination of political choice and economic incentive, occasionally criticised by other states.

3.8 Profitability

Historically intermittent Defence demand and the technical complexity could suggest that local defence suppliers face higher risks than many other areas of manufacturing. Nevertheless, the 2008 survey data suggests that defence suppliers enjoy relatively high levels of profitability: pre-tax accounting profit as a proportion of sales for specialised defence companies (those with 70 percent or more of total sales going to DMO) averaged 8.8 percent for the ten largest DMO supplier in 2008, 19.2 percent for seven specialised companies in the Top 41–50 group, and 9.3 percent for 17 specialised companies in the Top 50 group. This compares with the average pre-tax accounting profitability of 5 percent for defence-related areas of Australian manufacturing and 7.5 percent for Australian manufacturing as a whole (ibid.: 4). Overall, defence industry appears to be profitable despite the aforementioned threats of MOTS, COTS and overseas sourcing.

4. Conclusion: new defence industry policy agenda

At the time of writing, all four main elements of the current Government's defence industry agenda are in place: the Defence Industry Policy Statement, Naval Shipbuilding Plan, Defence Industrial Capability Plan and Defence Export Strategy. These comprise the new policy agenda that is to shape the development of the Australian defence industry over the next 20 years. The new agenda is intended to be radically different from the largely bipartisan policy of industry self-reliance that has evolved over the past forty years as it is underpinned by the concept of SICPs that transcends the previously highly selective and narrowly focused PICs "to cover virtually any industrial capability that might fall within Australia's technical reach" (Bourke 2019). While rebadged PICs "form the backbone of a new industrial sovereignty framework", it appears that "from around 20 percent of the (defence) industry covered by PICs", under the new approach "only 20 percent of the industry has been denied sovereign (SICP) status" (ibid.). This implies an import-replacement strategy aiming to build and stockpile in Australia a much larger proportion of military platforms and weapons systems acquired by ADF.

Clearly, the assurance of economic viability (health) of such broadly-defined industrial priorities could be immensely challenging in the years ahead. Nevertheless, the proponents of the new agenda see no problems in this respect given that Australia is about to embark on the largest build-up of its military capability in peacetime so that broadly defined industrial "must-have" capabilities will be utilised and sustained by the projected injection of A$200 billion of taxpayers' funds, which otherwise would leak abroad "to create jobs and manufacturing opportunities in other countries" (Minister for Defence Industry, *Defence Connect*, 14 May 2018). The associated demand smoothing and the more evenly dispersed workload should enhance the industry's productivity and, thus, substantially lower (possibly halve) the cost premia to be paid for import substitution despite the quadrupling of the protected defence industry base. The expected greater stability and continuity of workload is to increase the price competitiveness of in-country defence producers, which should not only lower the cost of home sourcing of military materiel for Defence but also make the industry more competitive in export markets. As a result, a virtuous circle of demand-supply interaction is to be engendered whereby demand smoothing is to reduce the variability of supply, which in turn will reduce the unit cost of home-made materiel to make them more affordable and demanded. Any shortfall of domestic demand is to be partly offset by increased exports, which will also help to enhance the productivity of Australian defence suppliers. And, if this is not sufficient, modest subsidies will make Australian exports more attractive for foreign buyers.

No evidence has been provided in support of all such claims and, not surprisingly, they have been received by defence economists with a degree of scepticism. As Davies et al. (2012: 1) – echoing earlier comments of the Productivity Commission (2016) – observe, the overall result of the proposed industry agenda is to:

> distort the allocation of resources, not only in the economy as a whole but also in defence itself, as the high cost of the program reduces the ability to fund the capabilities needed for the defence of Australia. Moreover, (our) analysis suggest the cost penalties associated with Australian production are unlikely to diminish in future. The goal of defence self-reliance does not provide a sensible justification for bearing these excessive costs.

Local defence industry advocates have long claimed that constructing new military platforms in Australia generates technological benefits for the rest of the economy. This was particularly the case in the 1980s and the 1990s with such high profile projects as the in-country assembly of F/18s and the COLLINS Class submarine program. Neither of these programs realised early expectations of significant technology spill-ins to the civilian sector. This is not surprising as military technologies are costly to transfer and adapt and the manufacturing sector that is likely to benefit most from such transfers is not as highly developed in Australia as in, say, Japan or South Korea (see Chapters 19 and 20). Further, to secure economy-wide benefits of technology transfers, the civilian sector must develop sufficient *absorptive capacity* to diffuse and adapt military know-how. There is, thus, little evidence of diffusion of dual-use and/or ex-defence technologies in the broader civilian economy. If anything, it is the civilian sector that has increased its capacity to support defence-specific industrial activities as demonstrated by a large number of SMEs acting as subcontractors for defence primes and OEMs. Nor is the predominantly foreign ownership of the largest defence prime contractors and military OEMs based in Australia likely to favour broader technology diffusion. Knowledge at the cutting edge of technology is highly proprietary and companies have no interest in making their technological crown jewels available to potential competitors. Nevertheless, the new industry agenda follows this well-trodden path of imputing high hope value to claims of potential economic gains to be realised by the civilian sector from the diffusion of imported and home grown military technology despite the wealth of experience, which suggests that a degree of healthy scepticism and caution is warranted.

The 2016 Defence Industry Policy Statement reiterates that "Australia's defence capability edge is based on Defence's ability to deploy, operate and sustain technologically superior capabilities (in the region)" (DoD 2016: 19). But as regional powers get more affluent, they not only increase their military spending but also invest in more technologically sophisticated war fighting capabilities. This is likely to intensify over the next twenty years as various regional powers are expected to acquire longer-range precision-guided missiles, including ship-based missiles. The 2016 Defence White Paper anticipates that

> Advanced intelligence, surveillance and reconnaissance systems, including both space and high-altitude capabilities, will be prevalent, reducing the effectiveness of stealth capabilities. The region will see more autonomous systems, such as unmanned combat vehicles, in operation in the sub-surface, surface and air environments.
>
> (Payne 2016: 49–50)

Other technological advances in the region will include "quantum computing, innovative manufacturing, hypersonics, directed energy weapons, and unmanned systems." Also, in the next twenty years, "half of the world's submarines" and "at least half of the world's advanced combat aircraft armed with extended range missiles and supported by highly sophisticated information networks will be operating in the region" (ibid.).

This technological perspective resonates well with scenarios offered in the broader military literature on the likely directions of military technological developments as the Fourth Technological Revolution unfolds (e.g., Hammes 2015, 2018). Fully autonomous weapons have been in US's inventory since the early 1980s when the Navy fielded a torpedo anchored on the bottom that launched when onboard sensors confirmed a designated target was in range (Hammes 2018). Lethal autonomous weapon systems (LAWS) using Artificial Intelligence (AI) have also been experimented for decades (Truffer 2018). However, it has been the operator who has had the final decision on the use of lethal force even though some systems, in particular air defences, have been nearly autonomous. It is therefore likely that future autonomous weapons will often operate under conditions that prohibit human oversight after launch. Technological advances rapidly expand the range of engagements that need to be conducted at machine speed excluding human operators (Hammes 2018). The US Navy recognized that 30 years ago when it developed the autonomous mode for its *Aegis Combat System*. At present, the United States holds a significant inventory of smart sea mines and torpedoes, autonomous micro-drones for carrying out small missions, and loitering munitions which can orbit prior to attacking their targets. All these systems comply with current US DoD policy that states "autonomous and semi-autonomous weapon systems shall be designed to allow commanders and operations to exercise appropriate levels of human judgement over the use of force" (ibid.). Other nations have paralleled the US investment in LAWS.[2] Smart weapons systems, drones and military robotics using AI devices are rapidly prototyped and gradually introduced into service in many countries, including China, Japan, Taiwan and South Korea in Asia-Pacific. As these systems may also operate in communications-denied environments, they are only restricted by the minimal sensor guidance to confirm the target autonomously when they decide to attack (ibid.).

Other developments include powerful but space-saving nano-explosives as well as additive manufacturing/3D printing that will allow the building and assembly of complex weapons systems, such as drones, and their elements fast and in remote locations. They could be used as rounds of ammunition and mobile detonators of potentially explosive systems located in enemy areas as well as sea and land platforms and aircraft on the ground. Surveillance and navigation satellites are already within reach of many small and medium powers (ibid.).

There is little public indication of how domestic innovation and indigenous capability developments might evolve in Australia in response to these developments. However, the following examples of priority areas of work for Defence's *Next Generation Technologies Fund* (NGTF), which forms a part of the new industry agenda, are suggestive:

- integrated intelligence, surveillance and reconnaissance,
- space capabilities,
- enhanced human performance,
- medical countermeasure products,
- multidisciplinary material sciences,
- quantum technologies,
- trusted autonomous systems,
- cyber,
- advanced sensors, hypersonics, and directed energy capabilities

(DoD 2016: 32).

These broadly defined transformational technology areas are intended to allow Australia to retain a technology "edge" against adversaries and provide "game-changing" Defence capabilities for the future. They are to be supported by a ten-year budget of A$730million, a rather modest outlay when compared with the projected expenditure on naval platform and land vehicle construction. Also, unlike the old defence R&D policy, which prioritised DSTO-based activities, the proposed NGTF targets more broadly defined R&D to be undertaken by industry and academic institutions as well as Defence.

On balance, it remains to be seen whether, given current policy settings, Australia's defence industry can make a meaningful contribution to the nation's response to bourgeoning military technological challenges in the Asia Pacific region. There are some parallels with the late 1980s and 1990s as the proposed platform building programs and the sustainment of legacy industry capabilities are set out to dominate the new industry agenda while the most technologically critical areas are likely to be associated with the development and diffusion of next generation technologies that will ride on numerous, low-cost platforms and make the future battlefield dominated by labour-saving and semi-autonomous warfighting equipment. As resources are to be diverted to legacy industry capabilities, it is likely that in future, as now, most of these cutting edge technologies will have to be imported.

Notes

1 Including that on Australian Signals Directorate, ASD, which became a statutory agency on 1 July 2018 that remains part of the Defence *portfolio* reporting to the Minister for Defence but is no longer part of the Department of Defence and has its own budget. This removes $827 million from the Defence Department's funding and, thus, presents some challenges for comparisons of defence spending over time (Hellyer 2018: 28).

2 For example, Israel has long fielded *Harpy*, a fully autonomous drone that is programmed before launch to fly to a specified area and then hunt for pre-specified targets using on-board sensors (ibid.).

References

Andrews, E. (2001) *The Department of Defence, Volume V of the Australian Centenary History of Defence*, Melbourne: Oxford University Press.

Beazley, The Hon K.C. (1987) *The Defence of Australia*, Canberra: Department of Defence, Australian Government Publishing Service.

Bourke, R. (2019) *Defence Projects and the Economy*, Canberra: Australian Strategic Policy Institute.

Brabin-Smith, R. (2005) 'The Heartland of Australia's Defence Policies', Working Paper no 396, Strategic and Defence Studies Centre, Australian National University.

Combet, The Hon G. (2010) *Building Defence Capability: A Policy for a Smarter and More Agile Defence Industry Base*, Canberra: Department of Defence.

Commonwealth. (1985) *Year Book 1984*, Canberra: Commonwealth of Australia, Australian Government Publishing Service.

Coulthard-Clark, C. (1999) *Breaking Free: Transforming Australia's Defence Industry*, Kew: Australian Scholarly Publishing.

Davies, A., Ergas, H. and Thomson, M. (2012) *Should Australia Build Warships? An Economic and Strategic Analysis*, Canberra: Australian Strategic Policy Institute.

Dibb, P. (1986) *Review of Australia's Defence Capabilities*, Canberra: Australian Government Publishing Service.

DMO. (2008) *Profile of Australian Defence Industry Major Australian-based Suppliers of Defence Materiel to DMO FY2007-08*, Canberra: Defence Materiel Organisation.

DoD. (2016) *Defence Industry Policy Statement 2016*, Canberra: Department of Defence, Commonwealth of Australia.

Hall, P. and Wylie, R. (2008) 'The Revolution in Military Affairs and Australia's Defence Industry Base, 1996–2006', *Security Challenges*, **4**(4): 57–80.

Hall, P. and Wylie, R. (2010) 'Arms Export Controls and the Proliferation of Military Technology', Chapter 4 in Goldsmith, B. and Brauer, J. (eds.) *Economics of War and Peace: Economic, Legal and Political Perspectives*, Bingley, UK: Emerald, 53–68.

Hammes, T.X. (2015) 'Small, Smart and Many: How Drones Will Defeat Legacy Platforms on the Battlefield', *RUSI Defence Systems*, 17(July).

Hammes, T.X. (2018) 'Reality in Autonomous Systems: It Starts the Loop', *The Cove*, available at www.cove.org.au/unit-pme/article-reality-in-autonomous-systems-it-starts-the-loop/, accessed 2 December 2018.

Hellyer, M. (2018) *The Cost of Defence, ASPI Defence Budget Brief 2018–19*, Canberra: Australian Strategic Policy Institute.

Hill, B.L. (1998) *Wirraway to Hornet – A History of the Commonwealth Aircraft Corporation*, Bulleen, Victoria: Southern Cross Publications.

Hinze, J. (2018) 'ADM's Top Forty Defence Contractors 2017', *Australian Defence Magazine*, available at www.australiandefence.com.au/top-40/adm-s-top-40-defence-contractors-2017, accessed 16 November 2018.

Holland, P. (2014) 'Reforming and Restructuring the Australian Workplace: A Study of the Williamstown Naval Dockyard 1983–1993', *Labour History*, **55**(3): 251–270.

Killen, The Hon D.J. (1976) *Australian Defence*, Canberra: Australian Government Publishing Service.

Kinnaird, M., Early, L. and Schofield, B. (2003) *Defence Procurement Review 2003*, Canberra: Department of Defence.

Macklin, R. (2017) *Rearming the ANZACS*, Canberra: Australian Strategic Policy Institute.

McIntosh, M., Michelmore, A., Brabin-Smith, R., Stone, J., Burgess, I. and Walls, R. (1997) *Future Directions for the Management of Australia's Defence – Report of the Defence Efficiency Review*, Canberra: Commonwealth of Australia.

Mortimer, D. (2008) *Going to the next level – The Report of the Defence Procurement and Sustainment Review*, Canberra: Commonwealth of Australia.

Nelson, The Hon B. (2007) *Defence and Industry Policy Statement 2007*, Canberra: Department of Defence.

Parliament (1999) 'The ADI Sale Process', Senate Standing Committee of Foreign Affairs, Defence and Trade, Canberra: Parliament of Australia, available at www.aph.gov.au/Parliamentary_Business/Committees/Senate/Foreign_Affairs_Defence_and_Trade/Completed_inquiries/1999-02/adi, accessed 5 Nov. 2018.

Payne, The Hon M. (2016) *Defence White Paper 2016*, Canberra: Commonwealth of Australia.

Productivity Commission. (2016) *Trade & Assistance Review 2014-15*, Canberra: Commonwealth of Australia.

Pyne, The Hon C. and Payne, The Hon M. (2018) *Defence Industrial Capability Plan 2018*, Canberra: Commonwealth of Australia, available at www.defence.gov.au/SPI/Industry/CapabilityPlan/Docs/DefenceIndustrialCapabilityPlan-web.pdf, accessed 5 Nov. 2018.

Ray, The Hon R. (1993) *Strategic Review 1993*, Canberra: Defence Publishing Service.

Ray, The Hon R. (1994) *Defending Australia – The Defence White Paper*, Canberra: Australian Government Publishing Service.

Tange, A. (1973) *Australian Defence – Report on the Reorganisation of the Defence Group of Departments*, Canberra: Department of Defence.

Truffer, P. (2018) 'Lethal Autonomous Weapon Systems and Artificial Intelligence in Future Conflicts', *The Cove*, October, available at www.cove.org.au/war-room/link-lethal-autonomous-weapon-systems-and-artificial-intelligence-in-future-conflicts-by-patrick-truffer-via-offizier, accessed 2 Nov. 2018.

Turnbull, The Rt Hon M. (2016) 'Australia's Future Fleet of Submarines', transcript of speech on 26 April 2016 available at www.malcolmturnbull.com.au/media.doorstop-australias-future-fleet-of-submarines.

Turnbull, The Rt Hon M. and Pyne, The Hon C. (2017) *Naval Ship Building Plan*, Canberra: Commonwealth of Australia.

Wylie, R. (2006) 'Supplying and Supporting Australia's Military Capability', in *CEDA (2006): The Business of Defence Sustaining Capability*, Melbourne: Committee for Economic Development of Australia, 50–63.

Wylie, R. (2007) 'A Defence Policy for Australian Industry: Are We There Yet?', *Security Challenges*, **3**(2): 53–71.

Wylie, R. (2008) 'Facilitating Defence Trade between Australia and the United States: A Vital Work in Progress', *Security Challenges*, **4**(3): 115–134.

Wylie, R. (2013) 'Defence Industry and Innovation Policy', *Security Challenges*, **9**(2): 107–119.

23 Brazil

Reassessing Brazil's arms industry

Diego Lopes da Silva

1. Introduction

Brazil is an intriguing case for defence economics. In the 1980s, the country became one of the largest exporters of military equipment in the world. By all measures, it was a successful case of how a Third World country could emerge as an arms producer. Notwithstanding, the favourable environment that drove Brazilian arms producers changed dramatically in just over a decade, leading the industry into a collapse in the 1990s. In an often-cited study on the industry's crisis, Conca (1997, p. 5) accurately wrote that "if Brazil's rise exposed the lack of consensus on what makes possible Third World military industrialization, its subsequent decline evidenced the poor understanding of what makes it sustainable".

Since the early 2000s, the Brazilian government has put forward a set of policies to recover and restore its once robust arms industry. A consensus among politicians and scholars emerged on the need for strengthening arms production capabilities in order to support Brazil's status as a rising power. The strategy was built upon four main guidelines: a) technology transfer from foreign defence partners; b) expansion of the defence industry; c) the restructuring of that industry; and d) the modernization of defence hardware and software. According to Gouvea (2015), Brazil's goal was to develop indigenous technologies in order to replace and compete with imported equipment.

Considering Brazil's recent efforts to rebuild its arms industry, the objective of this chapter is twofold. First, to provide an overview of Brazil's arms industry since 1980. However, greater attention shall be given to more recent developments regarding the sector's revival. The vast majority of the literature has been devoted to analysing Brazil's arms industry heyday, with most studies being published between the late 1980s and early 1990s. Despite the renewed scholarly interest since the mid-2000s, there is still a demand for studies comparing recent efforts to previous periods. Second, I also aim to reassess some of the predominant interpretations on past and current dynamics – mainly the role played by exports – with new data on Brazil's domestic arms procurement from 1960 to 2015.

The chapter will be structured as follows. The first section discusses some of the main features of Brazil's military expenditure. It illustrates how military spending has fluctuated according to Brazil's rather erratic economic performance and to political determinants, such as the return of democracy in 1985. A second section provides a brief background of Brazil's current and previous efforts to produce arms. The subsequent three sections discuss the structure, conduct, and performance of the Brazilian arms industry. A final section addresses the challenges and prospects for the sector.

2. Military spending

Military spending in Brazil is largely determined by political factors. When authoritarian rule came to an end in 1985, the military budget rose substantially from 1.4 to 2.7 per cent of Gross Domestic Product in 1989. The increase is in stark contrast with Brazil's fiscal behaviour during the dictatorship years. As Lowenthal and Stepan (1988) observe, the military burden in Brazil shrunk dramatically under military rule. In 1965, military spending corresponded to 3.4 per cent of Brazil's GDP, whereas by the end of the authoritarian period, it fell to 1.4 per cent. A declining military burden was offset by a spurt of economic growth: between 1967 and 1974, during what was later called the "Brazilian Miracle" (Veloso, Villela, and Giambiagi 2008), the economy grew by an astounding 10.15 per cent yearly on average.

The growth in military spending in the late 1980s defies the theoretical expectation that democracies spend less on their militaries. The argument – widely supported by empirical evidence (Albalate, Bel, and Elias 2012; Brauner 2015; Fordham and Walker 2005; Hunter 1997; Töngür, Hsu, and Elveren 2015) – posits that, to safeguard their tenure, politicians will reduce military spending as means to provide more resources for Education and Health. In tandem with this argument, Hunter (1997) claimed that the return of democracy in Brazil would weaken the Armed Forces' bargaining power for resources, thus leading to decreasing budgets, a position shared by Russet and Oneal (2001).

Nevertheless, as discussed in Zaverucha and da Cunha Rezende (2009), Brazil is an outlier to this pattern; despite the return of democracy, the military continued to increase spending either in absolute terms or in their relative share of the total expenditures. The handover of political power to civilians was largely controlled by the military, granting the Armed Forces enough bargaining power to retain influence over several key policy areas, especially on budget-making. To a large extent, Brazil's civilian governments increased the military budget as means of establishing control over the military (Zaverucha 2000).

In the 1990s, the spending pattern was somewhat different. There was a significant reduction in military spending between 1989 and 1992. Nevertheless, allocations quickly returned to pre-1989 levels by 1994. In the following years, military spending remained relatively stagnant until the end of the decade. During the 1990s, Brazil implemented a set of neoliberal policies that promoted privatization and budgetary constraints that affected military spending. Melo (2015) argues that the austerity measures put forward by neoliberal governments in the 1990s imposed a budget reduction that hindered long-term planning for Defence.

Nevertheless, the fiscal scenario changed significantly in the 2000s. An acute increase of commodities prices gave the Brazilian economy a renewed boost, reaching annual growth rates of 7.4 per cent. Brazil rode the Chinese demand-shock for commodities by growing its exports to Beijing fourfold between 2000 and 2010. This commodity-led growth spurt (Ocampo 2017, 2007) was also highly beneficial to the military sector. Indeed, export revenues provided enough resources to increase military spending substantially: 53.68 per cent between 2003 and 2014. In this economic environment, arms production projects were resumed and the Brazilian government designed a new set of policies to invigorate the arms industry.

Military spending endures severe constraints in Brazil. Firstly, the Brazilian economy suffers from structural macroeconomic vulnerabilities that affect the stability of the military budget. Arms production programmes require long-term planning and a steady provision of resources. Brazil's reliance on commodity exports renders its economy vulnerable to market fluctuations, from which the Brazilian government has not been able to shield itself. Since 2013, commodity prices fell, constraining the spending behaviour adopted by the Brazilian government thus far. The depreciation has already affected military spending, and the budget decreased by 7.2 per cent in real terms in 2016. With a worsening economic scenario, several military projects have been delayed due to lack of funds (see Figure 23.1).

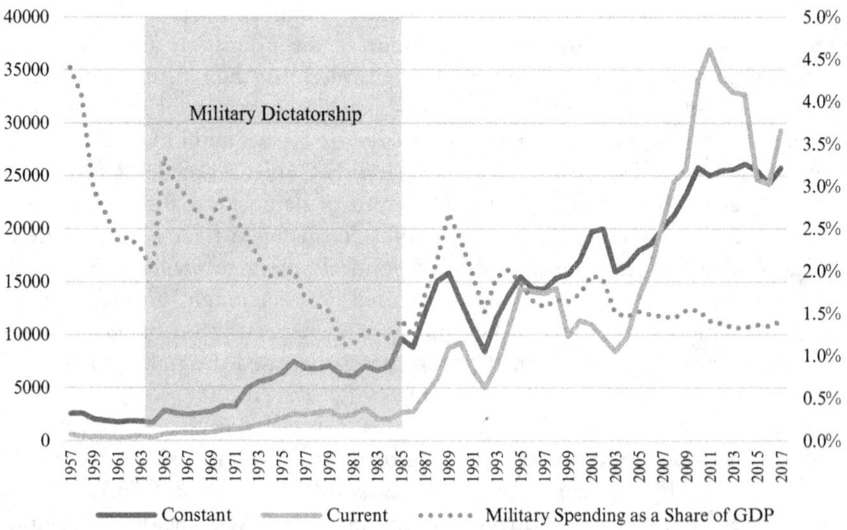

Figure 23.1 Brazilian military expenditure.

Source: SIPRI's military expenditure database. Values are in US$ millions at 2016 constant prices.

The second source of constraint is the overwhelming predominance of personnel costs within the military budget. Disaggregated data for military expenditures in Brazil is not available for an extended time-series. However, while limited, Table 23.1 provides some overview of the main features of defence spending. Personnel costs are the major expenditure category. As an average, personnel accounts for 77.3 per cent of all costs. Procurement has a small share, only 5.5 per cent. The limited procurement resources have rendered Brazil's arsenal largely obsolete and in poor condition.

Among all categories, Research and Development expenditure is the lowest: between 1992 and 2004, it accounted for less than 1 per cent on average. The scarce resources allocated to R&D investments in Brazil are far lower than those put forward by developed countries. Hartley (2007, p. 1154) shows that in 2001, Sweden invested 6.8 per cent of its military budget in R&D; Italy, a country with a GDP close to that of Brazil, spent 1.8 per cent. The paucity of resources attributed to defence R&D is one of the main obstacles to the development of Brazil's arms industry. As Krause (1990, 1992) puts it: most developing countries reach a plateau near the point where limited local R&D and limited independent production of advanced weapons should take place. Brazil is a clear example of such a pattern (see Table 23.1).

3. Rise, fall and rise again

Brazil defines the Defence Industrial Base as a

> set of state-owned and private companies that participate in one or more stages of research, development, production, distribution and maintenance of strategic defence products – goods and services that, given its peculiarities, may contribute to attaining goals regarding the country's security and defence.
>
> (Brazil 2005b)

Since the early 2000s, Brazil has made considerable efforts to promote this sector, especially during Luis Inácio Lula da Silva's first term as president (2002–2005) when defence affairs received renewed political attention. Besides allocating more resources to the Armed Forces, an institutional apparatus was conceived to foster military production. In 2005, the Brazilian government issued the National Defence Industrial Policy (NDIP: Brazil 2005b) and a revised version of the National Defence Policy (NDP: Brazil 2005a). Specifically concerning arms production, NDP sought "to qualify the national defence industry so that it conquers the necessary autonomy in indispensable technologies for defence purposes" (Brazil 2005a, 30). The enactment of the National Defence Strategy in 2008 (Brazil 2008), during Lula's second term (2006–2009), designed the policy instruments necessary to implement the goals set forth by NDP.

Table 23.1 Disaggregated military expenditure per cent shares

	1992	*1993*	*1994*	*1995*	*1996*	*1997*	*1998*	*1999*	*2000*	*2001*	*2002*	*2003*	*2004*	*Avg.*
Personnel Costs	72.46	72.67	71.52	75.69	81.75	56.27	80.51	73.86	81.22	81.20	85.01	87.00	86.17	77.33
Operation and Maintenance	18.58	19.07	12.92	12.50	11.32	23.63	13.60	20.36	12.20	11.21	9.58	10.50	11.50	14.40
Procurement	7.45	6.47	11.03	9.39	4.09	11.69	3.77	2.77	2.63	5.18	3.49	1.87	1.72	5.50
Military Construction	1.14	0.00	3.78	1.96	1.99	5.36	0.87	1.95	3.03	1.59	1.27	0.09	0.09	1.78
R&D	0.37	1.78	0.75	0.45	0.85	3.05	1.25	0.79	0.91	0.82	0.65	0.53	0.53	0.98

Source: SIPRI's internal database.

The efforts put forward during the past decade aimed at recovering Brazil's once robust arms industry. In the 1980s, Brazil emerged as a leading arms exporter among developing countries. Brazil's rise as an arms producer started in the mid-1970s when the government promoted international joint ventures as a means of increasing domestic capacity. Numerous licensing agreements were undertaken, leading large numbers of Brazilian firms to enter the Defence industry. Examples are the civil engineering firms Engesa and Avibrás, which started the production of armoured cars and missiles, respectively. Embraer produced the Xavante armed trainer under license from the Italian Aermacchi and the Seneca light planes licensed by the North American Piper. An important indigenous endeavour was the Astros II series of multiple rocket launchers, produced by Avibrás. The state was an active stakeholder in this process, providing robust financial support to Research and Development and the granting of extraordinary credits.

Notwithstanding, the auspicious environment changed dramatically in just over a decade: Brazil's arms industry collapsed in the 1990s. Several arms companies went bankrupt, while others were privatized. Created in 1969 as a public enterprise, Embraer was heavily hit by this new environment, where decreasing state support was combined with a demand downturn in the international civilian aviation sector. Until then, Embraer had received continuous public backing through budgetary allocations for research and procurement (Dagnino 1989). To cope with financial losses, the company was later privatized in 1994. Throughout that decade, Defence affairs received far less political attention and support, a setback from the remaining mistrust between civilians and the military due to Brazil's recent dictatorial past.

The industry's crisis in the 1990s makes the current revitalisation process a challenging enterprise. Brazil's ability to overcome the barriers faced in the 1990s is still uncertain. Furthermore, the current international arms industry structure is far different from that within which Brazil prospered as a producer. As highlighted by Gouvea (2015), Brazilian defence producers now face much fiercer competition in international defence markets than they did in previous times. The ongoing process of concentration in the arms industry (Bitzinger 2009; Devore 2013; Dunne 2009) could potentially hinder Brazil's competitiveness in foreign markets. This is a remarkable challenge and overcoming it will require solid planning from both the state and private sector.

4. Structure of the industry

The Brazilian arms industry can be divided into three categories (Imai 2011). First, state-owned firms – in principle – operate "at the technological ceiling by developing technologies that regular companies are unable to profitably achieve or obtain in the short or medium-term" (Brazil 2008). Hence, these companies must bear deficits to assure the supply of strategic equipment. Examples are the state-owned Empresa Gerencial de Projetos Navais (Emgepron), one of the main contractors involved in Brazil's navy modernization. Amazul, an Emgepron subsidiary created in 2012, oversees the Nuclear Propulsion Program (Brazil 2012), a critical project for Brazil's Defence. Also in the naval sector, the Arsenal da Marinha shipyard is a historically important shipbuilder. Another noteworthy state-owned company is the light weapons producer Imbel, in charge of the development of the iA2 5,56 mm rifle for the Brazilian Army.

The second group are private firms for which capital is primarily national. The most important firm in this group is Embraer. The KC-390 – a critical programme for Brazil's Defence strategy – is carried out by the company alongside BAE Systems. Another key company in this group is Avibrás, which oversees the Astros 2020 multiple launch rocket and is responsible for the commercial success of its predecessor, the Astros II. Odebrecht Defence and Technology, Agrale and Forjas Taurus are also important firms whose control is shared with the foreign capital.

Firms whose capital is primarily foreign comprise a third group. Iveco, a Fiat subsidiary, is responsible for the production of 2,044 units of the Guarani armoured vehicle for the Army. Moreover, Helibrás, an Airbus Group subsidiary, is involved in the production of the EC-725 helicopters, as part of the H-XBR Project. Currently, Helibrás is the sole helicopter producer in Latin America. Other companies in this group are Turbomeca do Brasil, a producer of small and medium power turbines for helicopters, and Daimler Chrysler do Brasil, manufacturing heavy-duty trucks and special vehicles for military use.

In 2013, a survey was conducted by the Institute for Applied Economic Research (IPEA in its Portuguese acronym) with a non-probabilistic sample of 202 companies that take part in the arms industry (Silva Filho et al. 2013: see Table 23.2). The data shed light on key aspects of the industry's structure, like capital composition and sources of income. Regarding the origin of the capital invested in the sector, 62.3 per cent was private national capital. Private companies with foreign capital were a minority, with less than 2 per cent. About 70 per cent of the companies were independent, whereas 28 per cent were part of a larger group.[1]

Also, the 2013 survey provided figures on market sectors. Less than 10 per cent of companies are highly dependent on the Defence markets. Mostly, companies try to diversify their activities, providing goods and services to the Public Security and Civilian sectors (see Table 23.3).

5. Market conduct

Over the past decade, Brazil has introduced a new set of fiscal incentives to foster domestic arms production. The enactment of the Special Regime for the Brazilian Aeronautic Industry (Retaero in its Portuguese acronym) in 2010 relieved the sector from several taxes. Whilst an important achievement, the Retaero was still confined to the aircraft sector. These incentives were enlarged in 2012 when the Law 12.598 established a comprehensive fiscal arrangement that encompassed the whole arms industry (Brazil 2012, 2013a,

Table 23.2 Source of capital

Capital composition	*Share (%)*
Independent, with national capital	62.3
Independent, with national and foreign capital	5.7
Independent, with foreign capital	1.9
Part of a group, controlled by national capital	13.2
Part of a group, controlled by foreign capital	15.1
No answer	1.9

Source: Silva Filho et al. (2013).

Table 23.3 End market

Market	*Share (%)*
Defence and Other	45.2
Defence, Public Security and Other	32.1
Defence	9.4
Other	3.8
Defence and Public Security	1.9
No answer	9.4

Source: Silva Filho et al. (2013).

2013b). The Special Tributary Regime for Defence Industry (RETID in its Portuguese acronym) sets forth special rules for procurement, contracting and product development.

To foster domestic procurement, RETID exempts what it defines as Strategic Defence Products (SDP) and Strategic Defence Firms (SDF) from a whole set of taxes and grants them priority in calls for procurement. To be covered by RETID, companies must have at least 70 per cent of their revenues from Defence-related activities. In 2014, 86 products were categorized as strategic under RETID; this number was increased to 103 in the following year. Currently, there are 63 Strategic Defence Firms covered by RETID. Tax exemptions encouraged civilian firms to open subsidiaries in the sector by offsetting the costs of conversion (Cepik and Bertol 2016, 12). A clear example is Odebrecht: the civilian infrastructure contractor created a defence branch, owning subsidiaries like Bradar and Mectron.[2]

It is worth noting that Brazil lacks a formal national procurement policy for all three Forces. Each branch of the military presents its own demands to the Secretary of Defence Products (SEPROD) under the Ministry of

Defence, which consolidates all requests for equipment acquisition. Among SEPROD's attributions is the proposition of the fundamentals for a future Defence Procurement Policy. In 2012, Brazil's Defence White Paper stated the intent to create such a policy and in 2015, Jacques Wagner, then Minister of Defence, prepared a draft for a Joint Procurement Policy for Defence Products; but so far, no significant progress was made.

One of RETID's objectives was to increase participation of national firms in Brazil's Defence Equipment Articulation Plan (PAED), a goal achieved with relative success (Brick 2012). Silva (2015) provides some interesting figures on the matter. Between 1999 and 2014, 63.2 per cent of all military contracts involving equipment modernization were signed with Brazilian companies: Embraer alone represents 12.9 per cent of this total (Table 23.4).

Whilst domestic contractors have been active in arms programmes, their participation is far from sufficient. Thus, Brazil has resorted to foreign firms to carry out projects specified by PAED. Data in Table 23.5, also found in Silva

Table 23.4 Top 15 Brazilian defence contractors 1999–2014

Company	*Number of contracts*	*City*	*State/Province*	*Ownership*
Embraer	12	São José dos Campos	São Paulo	Private
Avibrás	10	São José dos Campos	São Paulo	Private
Mectron	10	São Paulo	São Paulo	Private
Fundação Ricardo FRF	5	Rio de Janeiro	Rio de Janeiro	Private
Imbel	4	Brasília	Federal District	State-owned
Orbisat	4	Jacareí	São Paulo	Private
Atech	3	São Paulo	São Paulo	Private
Emgepron	3	Rio de Janeiro	Rio de Janeiro	State-owned
FUNDEP	3	Belo Horizonte	Minas Gerais	Private
Santos LAB	3	Santos	São Paulo	Private
FEMAR	2	Rio de Janeiro	Rio de Janeiro	Private
INACE	2	Fortaleza	Ceará	State-owned
Estaleiro Ilha S.A.	1	Rio de Janeiro	Rio de Janeiro	Private
Genpro Engenharia	1	São Paulo	São Paulo	Private
Bradar	1	São José dos Campos	São Paulo	Private

Source: P. F. da Silva (2014).

Table 23.5 Top 15 foreign defence contractors 1999–2014

Company	*Number of contracts*	*Country*
DCNS	4	France
Foreign Military Sales	4	USA
Ares Aeroespacial e Defesa/Elbit	3	Israel
IVECO/FIAT	3	Italy
SAAB	3	Sweden
BAE Systems	2	United Kingdom
Helibrás/Airbus Helicopters	2	France
EADS CASA/Airbus Group	2	Spain
CMN	1	France
AEL/Elbit	1	Israel
Agusta Westland	1	Italy
ARMSCOR	1	South Africa
ASK	1	Russia
Brunswick	1	USA
IAI	1	Israel

Source: P. F. da Silva (2014).

(2015), provides a measure of the extent to which Brazil's arms industry became internationalized. Since the late 1980s, excess capacity and a rising trend in research and development costs have led arms industries to increasingly rely on foreign direct investments and international cooperation to maintain their capacities (Bitzinger 1994; Dunne 2009; Sköns and Wulf 1994); a process that did not leave Brazil unscathed. Following this trend, recent arms production efforts were conducted with the considerable participation of foreign firms. The production of 16 EC-725 helicopters, for instance, is carried out by Helibrás, a subsidiary of Airbus Helicopters. The Baía de Sepetiba Consortium is a partnership between Odebrecht Defence and Technology and the French DCNS, and it is one of the main contractors involved in the construction of four conventional and one nuclear-propelled submarine.

Brazil's arms industry internationalization has also been boosted by offset agreements (Cepik and Bertol 2016). A new offset policy was launched in 2002 aimed at improving production capability (Brazil 2002). The strategy is not new, as Brazil has been seeking to advance its national industry through technology assimilation for decades. As highlighted by Perlo-Freeman (2004, 189), the production of the Xavante aircraft under license from the Italian Aermacchi in the 1960s was key to Embraer's early development. Recently, BAE Systems, signed a US$1.3 billion contract with Embraer for the Brazilian KC-390 medium light aircraft acquisition programme, agreeing to deliver commercial flight-control electronics and active side sticks for this aircraft as part of an offset package (see Table 23.6).

Table 23.6 Assessment of Brazil's offset policy

Sector	*Use of offsets*	*Technological success*	*Commercial success*
Fixed-wing aircraft (Embraer)	High	High	Mixed; military production hit trouble, saved by strong civil side
Helicopters (Helibrás)	High	Low	Fair
Missiles (Avibrás)	Low	High	Ran into serious trouble, but diversified and survived
Land vehicles (Engesa)	Low	High	Bankruptcy
Major naval vessels (AMJR; other)	High	Low	Very costly; private companies withdrew

Source: Perlo-Freeman (2004).

Another example of Brazil's offset policy is the acquisition of thirty-six JAS-39 Gripen-E multirole fighter aircraft from Saab in 2013. The Swedish company offered a significant offset package, valued at 175 per cent of the contract value. Additionally, Saab committed to transfer 100 per cent of technology and to build around 80 per cent of the fighter structure in Brazil. The Swedish bid won over the French Rafale, the F-35 Lightning, F/A-18E/F Super Hornet and the F-16BR offered by the United States, and the Russian Sukhoi SU-35 fighter (Herrera and Matthews 2014). Hence, Brazil's arms industry revitalization process is deeply tied to its offset policy. However, the net effects of this strategy are not clear. Previous analyses argue that economic benefits stemming from offsets in Brazil are negligible (Perlo-Freeman 2004): the costs of development and production are far higher when compared with off-the-shelf procurement. Furthermore, results concerning market performance and technological transfer have been mixed: offsets bore different results depending on the sector, with aircraft production being the most successful (Perlo-Freeman, 2004).

6. Performance

6.1 Contract performance

Several projects under the Defence Equipment Articulation Plan had cost overruns that will further complicate Brazil's arms industry modernisation. Table 23.7 below shows some estimates provided by Silva (2015) on contract performance. The modernization of the E-99 aircraft, for instance, had a 30 per cent cost escalation. Likewise, development costs of the VBR-MR

Table 23.7 Contract performance per project

Project	*Initial cost estimate*	*2015 cost estimate*
Modernization of the E-99 aircrafts	R$500,000,000.00	R$650,000,000.00
Modernization of 30 M113 vehicles	R$14,900,000.00	R$15,850,000.00
Building of Macaé Ships	R$2,200,000,000.00	R$2,200,000,000.00
PROSUPER	R$12,000,000,000.00	R$12,000,000,000.00
VBR-MR 8x8 armoured vehicles	R$84,694,040.00	R$110,000,000.00
VBTP-MR 6x6 armoured vehicles	R$6,515,904,080.00	R$4,424,694,169.00
iA2 5,56 mm rifle	R$ 55,000,000.00	R$ 110,000,000.00
Astros 2020 launching platform	R$1,246,000,000.00	R$1,411,000,000.00
VLS-1	R$305,500,000.00	R$303,700,000.00

Note:Figures are expressed in current values.

8x8 armoured vehicles increased by a similar measure. However, it must be acknowledged that the Brazilian government did not provide initial estimates on the number of units planned to be built; the revised 2015 cost figures for the VBR-MR 8x8 relate to the production of 408 units. Thus, the difference between the initial and 2015 costs could be related to an increase in the number of units produced.

Another project with cost overruns is the Astros 2020 launching platform. Designed to replace the Astros II, the Astros 2020 had its cost estimates revised by a value 13 per cent higher and its delivery postponed to 2019, rather than 2018 as initially planned. These cost and delivery slippages fit well within the analytical framework provided by Hartley (2007, p. 1157) to account for time-cost relationships. However, it is noteworthy that not all cost estimates rose: some projects, like the VBTP-MR 6x6 armoured vehicle, became cheaper. The revision was due to a decrease in the number of units to be produced reflecting an outcome of fewer resources.

Contract performance was directly affected by resource contingency. As mentioned earlier, due to an economic slowdown in recent years, several projects have received far fewer funds than planned. Although none of the projects are at risk of being cancelled, less resources will require adjustments in terms of units to be produced and deadlines. In 2013, the Integrated Border Monitoring System program (SISFRON), relied on a US$500 million budget; however, it received less than US$100 million. The cuts will certainly affect the 10-year deadline initially proposed. Likewise, the Proteger project, an initiative to secure Brazil's strategic infrastructures, had a massive cut in that same year: from an estimated US$400 million, it only received around US$20 million (Gouvea, 2015).

6.2 Productivity and profitability

The financial support provided by the Brazilian government, as well as its active stance in promoting sales abroad, bore some fruits in terms of company profits. Having been close to bankruptcy, Avibrás increased its gross revenue sixfold between 2012 and 2015. Around 90 per cent of the company's revenue comes from exporting (Magalhães 2018). The ammunition supplier CBC also benefited from the prosperous – albeit brief – economic moment experienced by Brazil. Table 23.8 shows the net revenue and profits of selected arms companies.

As seen in Table 23.8, Embraer is Brazil's biggest military firm. In SIPRI's 2017 top 100 Largest Arms Companies, Embraer ranks as the 81st (Fleurant et al. 2017). Created in 1969, Embraer had a vertiginous growth from the outset: between 1971 and 1976, the company's output increased from 5 to 469 units produced. Embraer managed to enlarge its production rather efficiently as the number of employees in the same period grew only fourfold, from 1,128 to 4,225 (Maldifassi and Abetti 1994, 46). After this initial growth spurt, Embraer's market performance fluctuated alongside Brazil's economy. Table 23.9 displays Embraer's losses in the mid-1990s. Throughout that decade, Embraer sales were reduced to only a fraction of its robust performance in the 1980's. However, the company managed to reverse the deficit it had accumulated, resuming profitability from 1998.

The role played by Embraer's military division has also varied. Until the mid-1990s, arms sales were a third of the company's total sales. During that decade, the company started to steadily decrease the economic importance of its military branch, reorienting its activities towards the civilian market; in 2000, arms sales comprised only 3.4 per cent of total sales, a figure in stark contrast to those reached in the 1980s or early 1990s. This proportion was enlarged throughout the 2000s, as the Brazilian government resumed public investments in the sector. However, it is noteworthy that whilst Embraer has been an important stakeholder in Brazil's arms industry revival, the share of arms sales in total sales reached in this period was far lower than in the 1980s or even the early 1990s. It seems that the company was wary of investing heavily in the sector as it had in the past.

Table 23.8 Net revenue and profits in 2016

Company	*Net revenue*	*Net profit*
Avibrás	1.344,7	236
CBC	729,7	122,2
Taurus	830,3	-103
Embraer	21.435,7	591,8
Helibrás	499,2	58,9
Agrale	539,3	-67

Source: Valor Econômico.

Note: Values are expressed in current 2016 millions of Reais.

Table 23.9 Embraer's market performance $ millions, 2016 prices

Year	*Total sales*	*Foreign sales*	*Arms sales*		*Arms exports*	*Profits*	*Employees*	*R&D*
			Total arms sales	*% of total sales*				
1994	344						3800	
1995	444	232	133	30.0		-375		
1996	438	283	132	30.2		-43		
1997	785	692	154	19.6		-13	3200	
1998	1391	1390	170	12.3		111	6737	
1999	3012	3269	211	7.0		367	8302	135
2000	4385		149	3.4	44	415		
2001	5303		224	4.2	147			
2002	5227		264	5.0	180			
2003	4074		497	12.2	329	258	12941	
2004	5941	11060	614	10.3		728	14648	
2005	4952	8430	511	10.3		384	16953	
2006	4341	8008	256	5.9		324	19265	
2007	5013	9484	331	6.6		330	21077	
2008	5582	11277	447	8.0		204	23509	
2009	4899	10056	430	8.8	160	406	16853	
2010	4070	8238	508	12.5		262	17149	55*
2011	3988	818	585	14.7		63	17265	
2012	4675		794	17.0		268	18032	
2013	4928	10772	940	19.1		281	19278	57*
2014	5076		1165	23.0		271	19167	
2015	6042		841	13.9		71		
2016	6218		932	15.0		168	18506	1269**

Source: SIPRI's internal database.
* Company funded.
** Externally funded by the National Development Bank.

6.3 Exports

Exporting arms is considered to be critical for defence industries as a means of diminishing fixed production costs through scale (Hartley and Sandler 2003; Kurç and Neuman 2017; Neuman 2006, 1984; Sandler and Hartley 1995). This rationale has been widely used in the literature to explain the rise and demise of Brazil's arms industry[3] (Gouvea 2015; Franko 2014; Kapstein 1991). It has been asserted that exports were the main driver of arms production in Brazil, as financial constraints did not permit larger domestic procurement. This assessment is corroborated by Gouvea (2015, 143), who argues that Brazil's arms industry had an export-led growth. Likewise, the industry's debacle in the 1990s is largely attributed to a demand decrease following the end of the Iran-Iraq war in 1988 (Moraes, 2012; Dagnino, 2010).

Brazil's arms export performance reached its peak in the mid-1980s with 0.65 per cent of the world total. Whilst negligible if compared with large arms exporters such as France or the United Kingdom, the figures were superior to those of other developing countries like India and Egypt. Exports appear in a rising trend from mid-1970s onwards, initially spurted by sales to Libya. After coming to power in 1969, Muammar al-Qaddafi sought to increase Libya's military might, having in Brazil a reliable partner. After becoming Libya's third largest arms supplier, behind the Soviet Union and France, Brazilian exports came to a halt after strained diplomatic relationships between the two countries in 1983 (see Table 23.10).

Table 23.10 Brazilian arms exports

1975–1988			*1950–2017*		
Country	*Total in TIVs*	*Share of total exports*	*Country*	*Total in TIVs*	*Share of total exports*
Iraq	609	28.12	Iraq	609	17.4
Libya	398	18.37	Libya	398	11.4
France	119	5.49	Colombia	245	7.0
Colombia	105	4.85	United Kingdom	221	6.3
Chile	105	4.85	France	201	5.7
Cyprus	99	4.57	Chile	163	4.7
Paraguay	95	4.39	Ecuador	122	3.5
Argentina	84	3.88	Indonesia	106	3.0
Egypt	67	3.09	Paraguay	99	2.8
Zimbabwe	65	3.00	Cyprus	99	2.8
Venezuela	59	2.72	Saudi Arabia	99	2.8
United Kingdom	43	1.99	Egypt	90	2.6
Peru	33	1.52	Afghanistan	88	2.5
Saudi Arabia	31	1.43	Argentina	85	2.4
Bolivia	31	1.43	Zimbabwe	65	1.9
Other	223	10.30	Other	815	23.3
Total	2166		Total	3505	

Source: SIPRI's arms transfer database. Figures are SIPRI Trend Indicator Values (TIVs) expressed in millions of dollars at 1990 constant values.

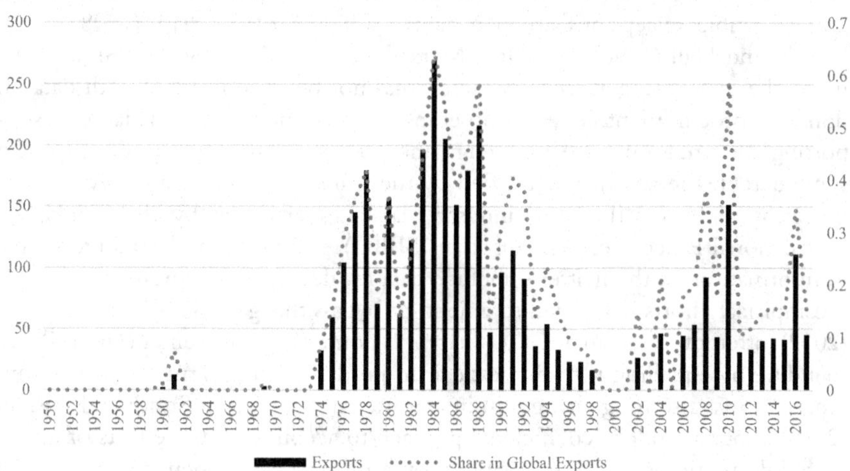

Figure 23.2 Brazilian arms exports.

Source: SIPRI's arms transfer database. Figures are SIPRI Trend Indicator Values (TIVs) expressed in millions of dollars at 1990 constant values.

Iraq was the largest recipient of Brazilian arms, having received over 48.3 billion TIV's throughout the war against Iran. Alongside the Soviet Union, China, and France, Brazil profited from this demand by exporting mainly armoured vehicles, such as the Cascavel and Urutu, and the Astros II system. The conflict became a convenient showcase for Brazilian-made military equipment (Dagnino 1989, p. 167). Consequently, Brazil became dependent on Iraq's procurement as exports became highly concentrated in that country. Between 1975 and 1988, 28.1 per cent of all arms transfers from Brazil went to Iraq. The abrupt fall in demand after the conflict came to an end was identified as the predominant factor in Brazil's arms industry crisis (Brigagão 1986; Dagnino 2010, 1989; Franko-Jones 1991; Moraes 2012: see Figure 23.2).

6.4 Domestic market

The export-dependence argument is frequently voiced in official documents and has been at the heart of Brazil's arms industry's revitalization process (Dagnino 2016, 2010). Magalhães (2016, 2018) shows how the military sector has used Brazil's arms export-dependence to lobby for larger fiscal incentives and a more active role of the state in promoting military sales abroad. Furthermore, Brazil's dependence on foreign markets has been used to justify a rather loose arms export control policy, leading to occasional divergences with the country's peace-promoting foreign policy guidelines (Magalhães 2018, p. 272).

The export-dependence argument demands a proper assessment. Indeed, there is considerable empirical evidence on the importance of exporting arms;

however, far less attention is given to the role played by domestic procurement. Some notable exceptions are Mouzakis (2002), Molas-Gallart (1998), Markowski and Hall (1998), and Hall, Markowski, and Thomson (1998). Surprisingly, the export-dependence argument has not been confronted with data on domestic procurement. There is no empirical account of the Brazilian case supporting the predominance of foreign markets vis-à-vis domestic demand. To some extent, the absence is justified by the scarcity of data. Currently, neither the arms trade nor the arms industry databases provided by the Stockholm International Peace Research Institute (SIPRI) – the most authoritative source of information on the matter – include data for domestic procurement.

Empirical efforts have tried to amend or bypass this gap. Bove and Cavatorta (2012) attempt to estimate the share of domestic procurement in military spending by equalling it to domestic arms production plus arms imports minus arms exports, assuming changes in inventories are negligible. Smith and Tasiran (2010) adopt a random coefficient approach to account for the effects of unobserved domestic production capability on arms imports propensity. Specifically for Brazil, Maldifassi and Abetti (1994) present data on domestic purchases between 1969 and 1988 based on a Minimum Costs per Soldier. Nevertheless, the estimates are imprecise as their base value are mostly assumptions.[4]

To address this dearth of robust figures related to domestic arms production, I introduce a new dataset of arms production in Brazil, between 1960 and 2015. Data were collected from numerous editions of specialized publications in military inventories, such as Jane's All the World's Aircraft, Jane's All World's Fighting Ships and Conway's All the World's Aircraft and the IISS Military Balance. It should be noted that SIPRI also uses most of these publications to populate its databases. Moreover, I had access to SIPRI's internal database, in which some domestic acquisitions are also listed, but not made publicly available.[5] The locally produced equipment identified in the publications mentioned above were transformed into Trend Indicator Values (TIV). TIVs are based on the known unit production costs of a core set of weapons, and it represents a transfer of military resources rather than financial values. Weapons for which the production costs are unknown are compared with core weapons based on size and performance characteristics. This method aims to provide a standard unit to allow the measurement of trends in the flow of arms to countries and regions over time. By using TIVs to track domestic procurement, an estimate of total arms production can be achieved by adding domestic purchases to exports. Regarding export values, equipment not locally produced or assembled was excluded.[6]

A few interesting trends stand out from the data. Firstly, Brazil's arms industry is bigger than usually depicted. As Figure 23.3 shows, our data shed light on an important domestic market so far unnoticed, highlighting the role played by the state in maintaining a stable demand for indigenously produced military equipment. As a matter of fact, the great majority of TIV transfers were conducted locally. In tandem with the predominant interpretation, Moraes (2012) argues that Brazil's arms industry had a deep historical dependence on foreign markets. To support his

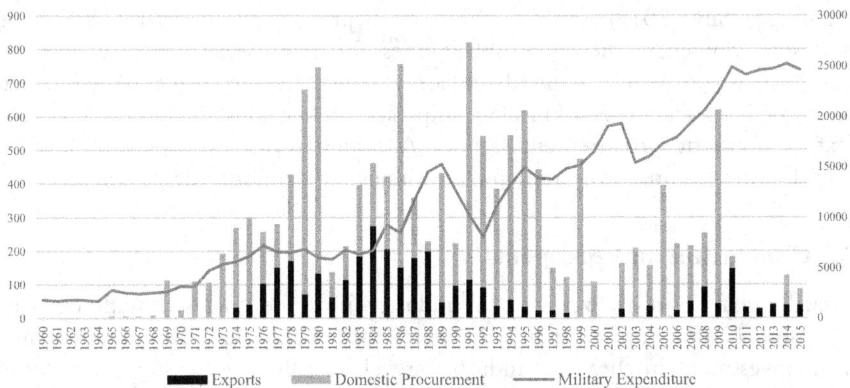

Figure 23.3 Brazilian arms production.

Source: SIPRI's arms transfer database, SIPRI's military expenditure database and author's own calculations. Figures for arms production are in SIPRI Trend Indicator Values (TIVs) expressed in millions of dollars at 2015 constant values. Military expenditure is expressed in millions of dollars at 2015 constant values.

argument, he uses data from Krause (1992, 164) on exports of military equipment as a share of total production in the mid-1980s. For Brazil, it ranges from 70 to 80 per cent, which is in line with our data. Notwithstanding, Moraes (2012) generalizes this figure for the whole time-series. Indeed, exports have fallen dramatically after the end of the Iran-Iraq war; however, the domestic market was able to absorb a large part of production until the mid-1990s. Certainly, Brazil's reliance on foreign markets is an important feature of its arms industry, as it is also the case in other developing arms producers. Nevertheless, its importance has been overestimated.

Our data allows for a comparison between the arms industry output of the 1980s, during its heyday, with the one reached from mid-2000 onwards. Despite governmental efforts, the industry's recovery is still incipient. Policy documents and part of the scholarly work published on the matter have displayed a marked optimism regarding Brazil's arms industry revival. Output levels have been modest and similar to those observed in the 1990s. One can argue that the revival was political rather than in actual production levels.

The estimates presented here must be considered with caution with some caveats kept in mind. First, although these are the best estimates available, I do not claim the dataset is complete. Certainly, there are domestic purchases for which reliable sources could not be found. However, I do argue that these unregistered transfers are small and would not change the general picture presented. Second, using TIVs to record domestic purchases does not add any new methodological problems, as it uses an instrument that is already in place and widely accepted by academia and decision-makers. However, it does reproduce some of its current shortcomings and fragilities, mainly the disregard of changes in the production costs of the same equipment (see Silva 2018). Finally, Table 23.10 presents the overall TIVs of the industry; however, there are specificities for each segment. Brazil's naval industry is primarily oriented inwards, while the majority of armoured vehicles is exported. As TIVs for ships are higher, this inflates to a certain extent domestic procurement figures. Although this is an aspect to bear in mind, arms exports measurements are subject to the same distortions.

7. Conclusion and prospects

Brazil's goal to revitalize its arms industry must be analysed with circumspection. Neither the costs nor the potential benefits stemming from significant investment in the arms industry are clear. Often, state support to arms production is justified by an alleged contribution to economic and/or technological development. This reasoning tends to underestimate crowding-out effects stemming from large resource allocations to military projects. Certainly, modernizing obsolete military equipment is an important goal governments should seek; however, Brazil is still a developing country with major social challenges. One must ponder defence affairs within this larger picture.

Current efforts to rebuild the Brazilian arms industry face significant challenges. Firstly, the economic conditions under which recent efforts to revitalize the industry were undertaken seem to wane. Amidst an institutional and economic crisis, Brazil's GDP growth rates have fallen significantly since 2010. As mentioned earlier, this leads to contingency measures that will severely restrict resources for military projects. As part of an austerity plan to curb the economic crisis that struck the country since 2014, Congress approved in 2017 the Constitutional Amendment 95 (CA 95), a new fiscal regime that limits government spending for the following twenty years. The financial ceiling established by the CA 95 is an overall limit that will increasingly stir even fiercer inter-bureaucratic competition for budget shares. The amount of resources necessary to continue the military modernization plans set out by Lula in the early 2000s is considerable. This scenario bounds the continuity of Brazil's military projects to CA 95s – rather questionable – effectiveness to foster economic growth. Otherwise, an increase in military expenditure will only come at the expense of other areas.

Another noteworthy challenge is the current process of deindustrialization Brazil is going through. Since late 1980s, the value added by the manufacturing sector as a share of GDP has been falling dramatically. The expansion of the primary sector in the 2000s had nefarious effects on Brazil's industrial capacity. As Ocampo (2017) puts it, Brazil, as well as other South American countries, has been unable to harvest the benefits of the commodity boom. On the contrary, it suffered from the negative structural effects of such dependence, notably deindustrialization. There is considerable empirical evidence on the importance of a robust industrial capacity for arms production

(Brauer 2003; Kinsella 2000; Neuman 1984; Yesilyurt et al. 2014). Certainly, the weakening of the industrial sector is a retarding aspect.

There is a perception that Brazil's plea for a more prominent role in international affairs should be matched by a robust arms industry. Hence, as argued by Cepik and Bertol (2016), Brazil faces a gap between its current military means and purported political ends. This gap will remain unless Brazil makes considerable changes in its economic policies. The acute deindustrialization the country has seen over the past 30 years poses a major challenge for the arms industry's survival. Likewise, recurrent macroeconomic instabilities affect the steadiness of resource allocation to the military. As discussed, budget cuts led to several delays in arms production projects. To make matters more difficult, Brazil entered its greatest economic recession in 2014, complicating even further any efforts to support military projects.

Political vicissitudes also play an important role. Recent events, such as the impeachment of former President Dilma Rousseff in 2016, brought great uncertainty into the political domain. Sudden economic and political shifts such as these have stricken defence affairs periodically in Brazil: the military coup in 1964; the "Debt Crisis" and its effects in the late 1980s and early 1990s; democratization in 1985 and the ensuing neglect of military matters are examples. If current trends remain on course, Brazil's arms industry future will be arduous, with erratic funds and political support. To rebuild its arms production capabilities and assure its sustainability, Brazil must address structural issues that go beyond defence affairs. This is the most fundamental challenge the country faces.

Notes

1 Defence covers supplies made to Navy, Army, Air Force and Ministry of Defence. Public Security covers supplies made to Civil Police, Military Police, Federal Police, Federal Highway Police, and Municipal Guards. Others cover supplies for markets other than Defence and Public Security markets.

2 Mectron was acquired by the Israeli Elbit Systems in 2016. The deal came after a financial crisis struck Odebrecht in the aftermath of corruption charges involving the company. Elbit will continue Mectron's projects in military communications, including the development of mission-based computers for drones.

3 There are contending hypotheses, however. Conca (1997) attributed the recession to the dismantling of the institutional structures once supporting arms production. Kapstein (1991, 595) diverges from Conca's stress on domestic factors by arguing that the reason for Brazil's relative success as an arms exporter was due to the opportunities and constraints provided by the international system. Nevertheless, the export-dependence argument is certainly predominant in the literature.

4 Maldifassi and Abetti (1994) calculate domestic arms production levels based on Dollars Per Soldier (DPS), which is given by $\text{DPS} = \frac{\text{defense budget} - \text{defense imports}}{\text{Number of military personnel}}$. For the 20-year period covered by their study, the minimum DPS value found was assumed to represent the minimum possible expenditures per soldier that would allow the Armed Forces to operate. The authors assume that when DPS was at its lowest point, defence spending was devoted to arms imports, minimum operational

expenses, military personnel salaries, and infrastructure maintenance, with no domestic arms purchases.

5 I would like to express my gratitude to the Arms Transfers and Military Spending Programme (AMEX) at SIPRI for all the help that has been provided to me while conducting this research. I was hosted at SIPRI as a Guest Researcher for 12 months. During this period, the AMEX Programme has assisted me in converting domestic purchases into TIV's, for which I am immensely grateful.

6 The use of TIV's to register domestic purchases does not add any new methodological fragilities, but it certainly reproduces the current ones, like its disregards for changing productions costs. For a discussion on the use of TIV's for domestic procurement and its limitations see Silva (2018).

References

Albalate, Daniel, Germà Bel, and Ferran Elias. 2012. "Institutional Determinants of Military Spending." *Journal of Comparative Economics* 40(2). Association for Comparative Economic Studies: 279–290. 10.1016/j.jce.2011.12.006.

Bitzinger, Richard A. 1994. "The Globalization of the Arms Industry: The Next Proliferation Challenge." *International Security* 19(2): 170–198.

———. 2009. *The Modern Defense Industry: Political, Economic, and Technological Issues*, edited by Richard A Bitzinger. Santa Barbara: Praeger.

Brauer, Jurgen. 2003. "Potential and Actual Arms Production: Implications for the Arms Trade Debate." *Arms Trade, Security and Conflict* 21–36. 10.4324/9780203477168.

Brauer, Jurgen, and John Paul Dunne. 2011. "Arms Trade Offsets: What Do We Know?" In *Handbook on the Political Economy of War*, 243–265. http://ideas.repec.org/p/uwe/wpaper/0910.html.

Brauner, Jennifer. 2015. "Military Spending and Democracy." *Defence and Peace Economics* 26(4): 409–423. 10.1080/10242694.2014.960245.

Brazil. 2002. "Portaria Normativa No 764/MD."

———. 2005a. "Decreto N° 5484."

———. 2005b. "Portaria Normativa N° 899/MD."

———. 2008. "Decreto N° 6703."

———. 2012. "Lei N° 12598."

———. 2013a. "Decreto N° 7970."

———. 2013b. "Decreto N° 8122."

Brick, Eduardo Siqueira. 2012. "Qual é o Plano de Articulação e Equipamentos de Defesa (PAED) Que o Brasil Necessita?" Niterói.

Brigagão, Clóvis. 1986. "The Brazilian Arms Industry." *Journal of International Affairs* 40 (1): 101–114.

Cepik, Marco, and Frederico Licks Bertol. 2016. "Defense Policy in Brazil: Bridging the Gap between Ends and Means?" *Defence Studies* 16(3): 229–247. 10.1080/14702436.2016.1180959.

Conca, Ken. 1997. *Manufacturing Insecurity: The Rise and Fall of Brazil's Military-Industrial Complex*. London: Lynne Rienner.

Dagnino, Renato. 1989. *A Indústria de Armamentos Brasileira: Uma Tentativa de Avaliação*. PhD thesis. Departamento de Economia, Universidade Estadual de Campinas, Campinas .

———. 2010. *A Indústria de Defesa No Governo Lula*. São Paulo: Expressão Popular.

———. 2016. "Sobre a Revitalização Da Indústria De Defesa Brasileira," no. January 2007.

Devore, Marc R. 2013. "Arms Production in the Global Village: Options for Adapting to Defense-Industrial Globalization." *Security Studies* 22(3): 532–572. 10.1080/09636412.2013.816118.

Dunne, John Paul. 2009. "Developments in the Global Arms Industry from the End of the Cold War to the Mid-2000's." In *The Modern Defense Industry: Political, Economic, and Technological Issues*, edited by Richard A Bitzinger. Santa Barbara: PRA.

Fleurant, Aude, Alexandra Kuimova, Nan Tian, Pieter D. Wezeman, and Siemon T. Wezeman. 2017. "SIPRI Top 100 Arms-producing and Military Services Companies." Stockholm.

Fordham, Benjamin O., and Thomas C. Walker. 2005. "Kantian Liberalism, Regime Type, and Military Resource Allocation: Do Democracies Spend Less?" *International Studies Quarterly* 49(1): 141–157. 10.1111/j.0020-8833.2005.00338.x.

Franko, Patrice M. 2014. "The Defense Acquisition Trilemma: The Case of Brazil." *Energy* (262): 1–12. 10.1111/j.1539-6975.2009.01318.x.

Franko-Jones, P. 1991. *The Brazilian Defense Industry*. Boulder: Wesview.

Gouvea, Raul. 2015. "Brazil's New Defense Paradigm." *Defense and Security Analysis*. 31(2). Taylor & Francis. 137–151. 10.1080/14751798.2015.1038452.

Hall, Peter, Stefan Markowski, and Douglas Thomson. 1998. "Defence Procurement and Domestic Industry: The Australian Experience." *Defence and Peace Economics* 9 (1–2): 137–165. 10.1080/10430719808404898.

Hartley, Keith. 2007. "The Arms Industry, Procurement and Industrial Policies." In *Handbook of Defense Economics Volume 2*, edited by Todd Sandler and Keith Hartley, 1139–1176. Amsterdam: Elsevier B.V.

Hartley, Keith, and Todd Sandler. 2003. "The Future of the Defence Firm." *Kyklos* 3: 361–380. 10.1080/1024269042000246666.

Herrera, Monica, and Ron Matthews. 2014. "Latin America in Step with Global Defence Offset Phenomenon." *RUSI Journal* 159(6): 50–57. 10.1080/03071847.2014.990815.

Hunter, Wendy. 1997. *Eroding Military Influence in Brazil*. Chapel Hill: University of North Carolina Press.

Imai, A. K. 2011. "Base Industrial de Defesa: Estratégias de Desenvolvimento Tecnológico." Rio de Janeiro: Escola Superior de Guerra. www.esg.br/images/Monografias/2011/IMAI.pdf.

Kapstein, Ethan B. 1991. "The Brazilian Defense Industry and the International System." *Political Science Quarterly* 105(4): 579–596.

Kinsella, David. 2000. "Arms Production in the Third Tier: An Analysis of Opportunity and Willingness." *International Interactions* 26(3): 253–286. 10.1080/03050620008434968.

Krause, Keith. 1990. "The Political Economy of the International Arms Transfer System: The Diffusion of Military Technique via Arms Transfers." *International Journal of the Canadian International Council* 45(3): 687–722.

———. 1992. *Arms and the State: Patterns of Military Production and Trade*. Cambridge: Cambridge University Press.

Kurç, Çağlar, and Stephanie G. Neuman. 2017. "Defence Industries in the 21st Century: A Comparative Analysis." *Defence Studies*. 17(3). Routledge. 219–227. 10.1080/14702436.2017.1350105.

Lowenthal, Abraham F., and Alfred Stepan. 1988. *Rethinking Military Politics: Brazil and the Southern Cone*. *Foreign Affairs*. Vol. 67. Princeton: Princeton University Press. 10.2307/20043828.

———. 2016. "A Política Brasileira de Exportação de Armas No Contexto Da Revitalização Da Base Industrial de Defesa." Pontifícia Universidade Católica de São Paulo.

Magalhães, D. A. M. 2018. *A Política Brasileira de Exportação de Armas (2003-2014)*. 1st ed. São Paulo: Cultura Acadêmica.

Maldifassi, José Alberto, and Pier Abetti. 1994. *Defense Industries in Latin American Countries: Argentina, Brasil and Chile*. Westport: Praeger.

Markowski, Stefan, and Peter Hall. 1998. "Challenges of Defence Procurement." *Defence and Peace Economics* 9(1–2): 3–37. 10.1080/10430719808404892.

Melo, R. 2015. *Indústria de Defesa e Desenvolvimento Estratégico: Estudo Comparado França-Brasil*. Brasília: Funag.

Molas-Gallart, Jordi. 1998. "Defence Procurement as an Industrial Policy Tool: The Spanish Experience." *Defence and Peace Economics* 9(1–2): 63–81. 10.1080/10430719808404894.

Moraes, Rodrigo Fracalossi de. 2012. "A Inserção Externa Da Indústria Brasileira de Defesa: 1975-2010." *Texto Para Discussão N° 1715*. www.ipea.gov.br/portal/images/stories/PDFs/TDs/td_1715.pdf.

Mouzakis, Fotis. 2002. "Domestic Production as an Alternative to Importing Arms." In *Arming the South: The Economics of Miltiary Expenditure, Arms Produciton and Arms Trade in Developing Countries*, edited by Jurgen Brauer and John Paul Dunne, 129–160. Hampshire: Palgrave Macmillan.

Neuman, Stephanie G. 1984. "International Stratification and Third World Military Industries." *International Organization* 38(1): 167–197. 10.1017/S0020818300004306.

———. 2006. "Defense Industries and Global Dependency." *Orbis* 50(3): 429–451. 10.1016/j.orbis.2006.04.004.

Ocampo, Jose Antonio 2007. "The Macroeconomics of the Latin American Economic Boom." *CEPAL Review* 93: 7–28.

———. 2017. "Commodity-Led Development Latin America." In *Alternative Pathways to Sustainable Development: Lessons from Latin America*, edited by Gilles Carbonnier, Humberto Campodónico, and Sergio Tezanos Vásquez Leiden: Brill Nijhoff.

Perlo-Freeman, Sam. 2004. "Offsets and the Development of the Brazilian Arms Industry." In *Arms Trade and Economic Development: Theory, Policy, and Cases in Arms Trade Offsets*, edited by Jurgen Brauer and John Paul Dunne. London: Routledge.

Russet, Bruce, and John Oneal. 2001. *Triangulating Peace: Democracy, Interdependence, and International Organization*. New York: W. W. W Norton.

Sandler, Todd, and Keith Hartley. 1995. *Handbook of Defence Economics Vol. 2*, edited by Todd Sandler and Keith Hartley. Vol. 2. Elsevier B.V.. 10.1016/S0221-8747(81)80028-8.

Silva, Peterson Ferreira da. 2015. "A política industrial de defesa no Brasil (1999–2014): intersetorialidade e dinâmica de seus principais atores". Ph.D. thesis. Instituto de Relações Internacionais, Universidade de São Paulo, São Paulo.

Silva, Diego Lopes 2018. "Filling Arms Production Data Gaps: South America as a Case in Point." *Economics of Peace and Security Journal* 13(2): 20–27. 10.15355/epsj.13.2.5.

Silva Filho, E. B., F. H. Schmidt, II. O. Andrade, and R. F. Moraes. 2013. "Base Industrial de Defesa Brasileira: Características Das Firmas e Percepção Dos Empresários Do Setor." 10. Brasília: Nota Técnica.

Sköns, Elizabeth, and Herbert Wulf. 1994. "The Internationalization of the Arms Industry." *The Annals of the American Academy of Political and Social Science* 535: 43–57.

Töngür, Ünal, Sara Hsu, and Adem Yavuz Elveren. 2015. "Military Expenditures and Political Regimes: Evidence from Global Data, 1963-2000." *Economic Modelling* 44. Elsevier B.V. 68–79. 10.1016/j.econmod.2014.10.004.

Veloso, Fernando A, André Villela, and Fabio Giambiagi. 2008. "Determinantes Do 'Milagre' Econômico Brasileiro (1968-1973): Uma Análise Empírica." *Revista Brasileira De Economia* 62(2): 221–246. 10.1590/S0034-71402008000200006.

Yesilyurt, Filiz, Bülent Güloğlu, Ensar Yesilyurt, and Şennur Sezgin. 2014. "The Determinants of Arms Production." *Defence and Peace Economics* 25(2): 205–211. 10.1080/10242694.2013.804670.

Zaverucha, Jorge. 2000. *Frágil Democracia: Collor, Itamar, FHC e Os Militares (1990–1998)*. Rio de Janeiro: Civilização Brasileira.

Zaverucha, Jorge, and Flávio da Cunha Rezende. 2009. "How the Military Competes for Expenditure in Brazilian Democracy: Arguments for an Outlier." *International Political Science Review* 30(4): 407–429. 10.1177/0192512109342689.

24 Indian defence industry

Will 'Make in India' turn it around?

Laxman Kumar Behera[1]

Introduction

Over the years, India has created a huge defence industrial base, presently comprising hundreds of production and R&D establishments. These establishments are engaged in design, development and/or production of arms varying from tanks to fighters, helicopters, submarines and other warships, defence electronics and missiles. However, in terms of innovation and efficiency, the Indian defence industry has not achieved its expectations, resulting in India's huge arms dependency, and belittling India's self-reliance objectives.

This chapter examines India's defence industry over a period spanning nearly four decades since 1980. In so doing, it also looks at the changing nature of Indian defence production from the public sector to the private sector; and the performance of the Indian industry. It also looks at the industry's future prospects keeping in view a host of reform measures taken by the Indian government in recent years, particularly those under the 'Make in India' initiative. The chapter begins with a survey of India's defence expenditure, focusing on research and development (R&D) and procurement spending, which are relevant for the industry's sustenance.

Defence expenditure

India's defence expenditure is not defined properly. In the absence of a formal definition, what is commonly referred to as India's official defence expenditure is the Defence Services Estimates (DSE), an annual publication of the finance division of the Defence Ministry. The DSE does not, however, cover the entire expenses incurred on national defence. As of 2018–19, it contains the spending details of two out of four Demands for Grants (DfG)[2] of the Ministry of Defence (MoD). The two DfGs included in the latest DSE cover the expenditure details of the three armed forces (army, navy and air force), as well as some other organisations, namely, the Ordnance Factories (OFs) and the Defence Research and Development Organisation (DRDO). Like every other expenses of the Indian government, all the expenses met through the DSE are provided under two categories: Revenue Expenditure and Capital Expenditure. While the former caters for the running or operating expenses (e.g. salaries, transport, maintenance, etc), the capital expenditure caters for asset creation. The main item of capital expenditure is what is commonly referred to as the modernisation budget or capital procurement.

The two DfGs which are outside the DSE but belong to MoD are: MoD (Miscellaneous) Expenditure and Defence Pensions. The former caters for the allocations of such organisation/elements as Border Roads Organisation, Coast Guard, Defence Estates Organisation, Military Firms and Ex-Servicemen Contributory Health Scheme. Besides, it also meets the secretariat general expense of various MoD offices. The defence pensions meet the retirement benefits of defence services personnel.

It may be noted that outside the MoD's purview, there are certain expenditures which have a direct bearing on India's defence but are provided separately through the Ministry of Home Affairs (MHA). The main expenditures pertain to four border guarding forces (BFG)– Assam Rifles (AR), Indo-Tibetan Border Police (ITBP), *Sashastra Seema Bal* (SSB) and Border Security Force (BSF), which are responsible for defending India's borders during peace time. The home ministry also provides certain other defence expenses relating to border management and infrastructure, and capital procurement of the BGF. If all these allocations are added to the MoD's larger budget, India's total defence expenditure (official and non-official) amounts to INR 4,394 billion (US$65.4 billion[3]) in current prices (Table 24.1), which makes India the world's fifth largest military spender. Total defence expenditure is 57 per cent higher than what is considered the official defence budget (or the DSE) and 9 per cent higher than the MoD's allocations.

For the purpose of simplicity and consistency of data, the Chapter uses the official defence expenditure as captured by the DSE. Figure 24.1 summarises the trends in expenditure between 1980–81 and 2018–19 along with annual growth and the defence's share in Gross Domestic Product (GDP) and the Central Government Expenditure (CGE). While the defence expenditure and annual growth are expressed in constant prices, the latter two are based on current prices. The constant price is calculated by applying India's GDP deflator.[4]

Between 1980–81 and 2018–19, India's defence expenditure in constant prices increased six-fold from INR 347 billion to INR 2075 billion, though there has been a great deal of annual fluctuations. Out of 38 years between 1981–82 and 2018–19, in 27 years the annual growth has been positive while the remaining 11 years have witnessed a decline. The decade of 1980s is the only decade in which the real annual growth rate has been 5 per cent or more for at least five years. It is also the only decade which recorded the highest annual growth rate (23 per cent in 1986–87). The high positive real growth in the 1980s was partly due to the massive military buildup that started in the last year of the 1970s following the USSR's invasion of Afghanistan and the ensuing US military assistance to India's arch rival, Pakistan.

Table 24.1 Size of India's official and non-official defence allocation, 2018–19

Ministry	*Elements*	*Current $ billion*
MoD	Defence Services Estimates (DSE)	41.55
	Other Expenses of the MoD of which:	18.61
	Pension	*16.19*
	MoD (Miscellaneous)	*2.41*
	Total MoD	60.16
MHA	Assam Rifles (AR)	0.83
	Border Security Force (BSF)	2.55
	Indo-Tibetan Border Police (ITBP)	0.82
	Sashastra Seema Bal (SSB)	0.73
	Border Infrastructure and Management	0.26
	BSF Air Wing, Aircrafts, River Boats and Helibase	0.03
	Total MHA	2.21
Grand Total (MoD & MHA)		65.37

Source: Ministry of Finance, *Union Budget 2018–19.*

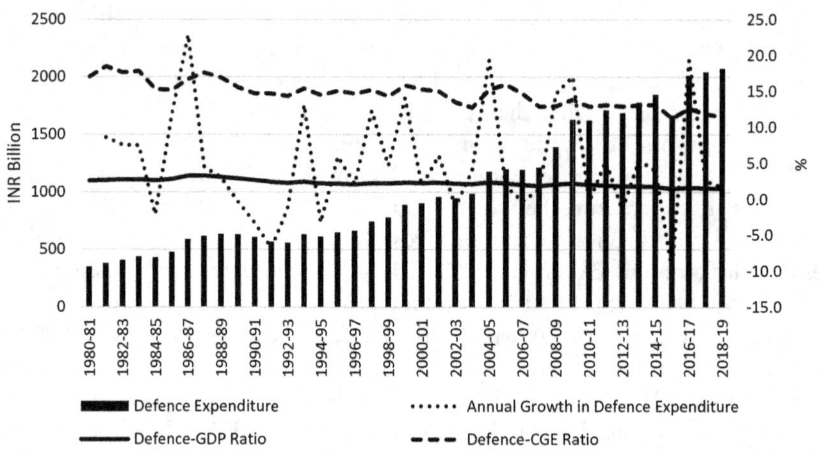

Figure 24.1 Defence expenditure, annual growth and share in GDP and CGE.

After a hefty growth in most of the years of the 1980s, defence expenditure contracted in the last year of that decade, and the negative growth momentum continued for the next three consecutive years of 1990s. Notably, the contraction in defence spending in the early 1990s was not due to the 'peace dividend' resulting from the end of Cold War that caused world military spending to fall for several years. The slowdown in India's defence spending was primarily due to economic reasons, with the country facing a severe balance of payment crisis in 1991 and two successive years of drastic devaluation of the rupee.

With India's primary security threats from its traditional rivals (Pakistan and China: see Chapter 3) remaining unchanged, defence expenditure rose again in 1993–94, this time being supported by the improvements in the economic conditions following the major revamp of the Indian economy undertaken in the early 1990s. Since then defence expenditure has contracted in some years, but the contraction has not extended beyond a year. However, all the major growths in post 1993–94 have not necessarily been driven by the modernisation of the Indian armed forces. Except for a 19.4 per cent growth in 2004–15, which was largely due to the hefty increase in procurement expenditure, all major growths have been largely due to increases in manpower costs. Incidentally, the manpower cost driven growth has been the recurring feature in India's defence expenditure in the recent past, most notably in 2008–09, 2009–10, and 2016–17 when defence expenditure grew substantially, primarily to accommodate the increases in salary arising from implementation of the Central Pay Commission recommendations. As discussed later, the increases in manpower costs have the most visible impact on the procurement budget whose share in defence expenditure has been significantly reduced over the last several years.

A noticeable feature of India's defence expenditure between 1980–81 and 2018–19 has been its near continuous declining share in both GDP and central government expenditure (CGE). While the share of defence in CGE has come down from a high of 18 per cent in early 1980s to 11 per cent in 2018–19, the defence-GDP ratio has declined from a high of 3.25 per cent in 1986–87 to 1.49 per cent in 2018–19. A primary reason for this drastic decline in the defence-GDP ratio is primarily due to faster growth in Indian GDP compared to defence expenditure[5]

Like defence expenditure, the procurement budget is not defined in the official documents. What is, however, widely understood as India's defence procurement budget is part of capital expenditure which is spent on procurement and the upgrade of weapons systems and other platforms such as tanks and other heavy vehicles, aircraft and helicopters, missiles, radars, ships, submarines and the like. It is, however, to be noted that even this loosely defined procurement budget has evolved over a period of time. Prior to 1987–88, a major part of expenditure, which is presently referred to as capital procurement, was included in the revenue expenditure. This is reason why a pre-1987–88 procurement data are not comparable with the data of later years. Figure 24.2 nonetheless provides a trend in the procurement budget and its share in defence expenditure since 1980. As can be seen, the procurement budget has grown by 65 times from INR 8.0 billion to INR 552 billion while its share has risen to an all-time high of 38 per cent in 2004–05 before declining to 26 per cent in 2017–18. Much of the decline in the latter years is due to the hefty growth in manpower costs which now account for

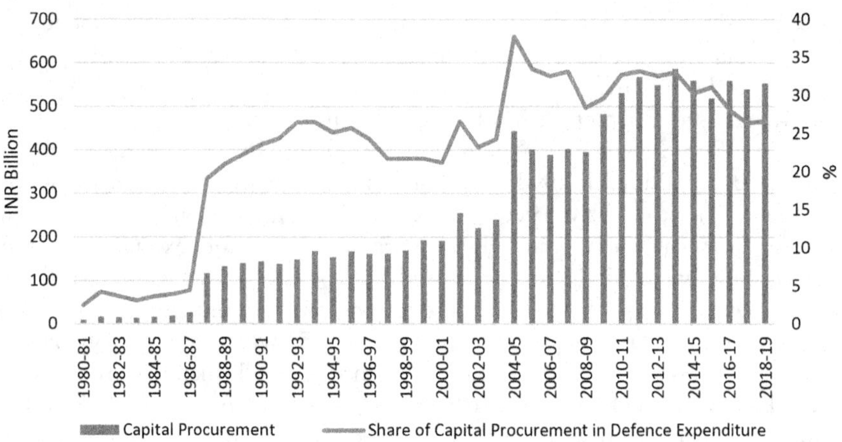

Figure 24.2 Capital procurement expenditure (in constant price) and its share in defence expenditure.

nearly half of defence expenditure, up from 26 per cent in 2007–08, the earliest year for which comprehensive manpower data is readily available.[6]

Much of India's defence procurement budget is spent on imports, though official statistics indicate otherwise. Part of the reason for this difference is due to the non-inclusion of what can be termed as India's indirect arms imports, which are undertaken by the domestic industry in the form of technologies, parts, components, sub-systems and raw materials for their production purposes. Based on India's latest official data, India's defence imports as accounted for by the three forces were in the range of 37–40 per cent between 2015–16 and 2017–18 (Table 24.2). What the official data hides is the indirect imports referred to earlier. According to a 2013 study, the indirect import of the DPSUs and the OFs, the main pillars of Indian defence production, amounts to nearly 35 per cent of their turnover.[7] If indirect imports from the domestic supplies are deducted, the net domestic share is around 40 per cent, which is much below the target of 70 per cent that was supposed to have been achieved by 2005 as per a plan articulated by a high level self-reliance committee set up in early 1990s.

The mammoth imports, both direct and indirect, have earned India the dubious distinction of being one of the largest importers of arms in the world. According to SIPRI, India with a 12 per cent share in global arms imports was the biggest importer during 2013–17.[8] For the period 1980–2017, India was also ahead of others with total imports amounting to 90 billion TIVs (Trend Indicator Values) or 8 per cent of the global total.

Table 24.2 India's defence capital procurement from domestic and foreign sources

Year	*Domestic source (current $ billion)*	*Import (current $ billion)*	*Total (current $ billion)*	*Share of domestic source (%)*	*Share of imports (%)*
2015–16	6.0	3.5	9.5	63	37
2016–17	6.2	4.1	10.3	61	39
2017–18	6.8	4.5	11.3	60	40

Source: Rajya Sabha, 'Indigenous Manufacturing of Defence Equipment', Unstarred Question No. 2097, Answered on August 06, 2018.

Note: Figures are converted from INR to US$ based on average annual exchange rate.

In comparison to defence expenditure or capital procurement, there is much greater clarity for defence R&D expenditure. Defence R&D expenditure, provided through the Ministry of Defence, is almost entirely accounted for by the DRDO, an organisation which came into existence in the late 1950s. Since its creation, the organisation has evolved over a period of time. Until the 1980s its expenditure was about 2 per cent or less of the defence budget. The share started to grow from the mid-1980s with the government sanctioning several high profile programmers, in a move to achieve self-reliance in areas of missiles and combat aircraft in particular. For 2018–19, it has a budget of INR 133 billion (INR 179 billion or $2.7 billion in current prices), representing 6.4 per cent of the defence budget (Figure 24.3). Together with capital procurement, defence R&D constitutes about INR 922 billion ($14 billion) in nominal terms, or about 33 per cent of defence expenditure in 2018–19.

Indian defence industry: an historical and statistical overview

Indian defence production dates back to early nineteenth century with the establishment of the Gun Carriage Agency in 1801. Since then, and especially after India's independence in 1947, the industry has grown both in size and competence. Presently, the industry consists of hundreds of public and private sector entities, though the former continues to play the dominant role in both R&D and production. The main players in the public sector are the Ordnance Factories (OFs), Defence Public Sector Undertakings (DPSUs) and the Defence Research and Development Organisation (DRDO), which function under the administrative control of the MoD. While the former two are involved in production, the latter is the dedicated defence R&D division of the MoD. In the private sector, there are numerous companies which are exposed to defence production, though there are 70-odd companies which are recognised license holders for the production of defence items.[9]

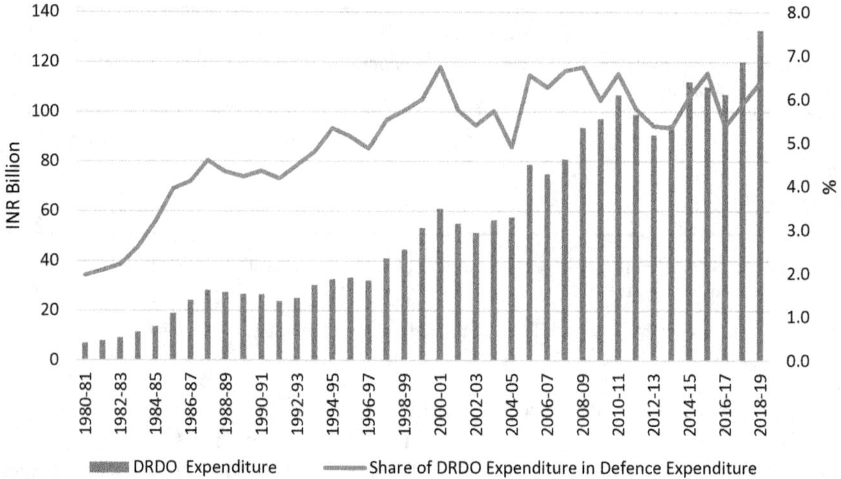

Figure 24.3 DRDO's expenditure (in constant prices) and its share in defence expenditure.

While the above entities are the main players in India's defence industry, they are supported by numerous other players, including small and medium enterprises, which play a critical role in supplying various parts, components and sub-systems to the established players in their production or developmental programmes. The DRDO alone works with over 1000 industries in its developmental programmes.[10] Among the big players outside the MoD's purview is the Cochin Shipyard Ltd, which functions under the administrative control of the Ministry of Shipping. It is presently building India's first indigenous aircraft carrier. In the private sector, BrahMos Aerospace, is a major player. Formed as a joint venture (JV) by DRDO with Russian collaboration with an equity share ratio of 50.5: 49.5, it manufactures highly potent supersonic cruise missiles. In 2017–18, its turnover was INR 21.2 billion ($328 million).

Ordnance factories

The OFs are the oldest departmentally run production agencies functioning under the Ministry of Defence. They operate under the Ordnance Factory Board (OFB), headquartered in Kolkata. The factories cater mostly for low- to medium technologies. Their origin dates back to 1801 when the colonial rulers opened the first factory in Kolkata. By the time the British left the subcontinent, 18 factories were set up, which by virtue of their location were inherited by India. Over the years, the number of factories has grown, though much of the expansion happened after India's military debacle in the 1962 war, in an effort to meet the increased defence hardware requirement.

Since 1962, 18 more factories, including eight after 1980, have been set up, taking the total number factories to 41. These factories are geographically spread at 24 different locations. The state of Maharashtra has the largest number of factories (10), followed by Uttar Pradesh (9). All the 41 factories are divided into five clusters or operating groups: Ammunition and Explosives (11); Weapons, Vehicles and Equipment (11); Materials and Components (8), Armoured Vehicles (6); Ordnance Equipment Factories (5). The principal customer of the OFs is the Indian Army, which accounted for nearly 80 per cent of its total output in 2017–18. Table 24.3 provides the latest fact-sheet of the OFB along with the DPSUs, while Tables 24.4 and 24.5 provide value of production and number of employees of these entities for the period 1980–81 to 2017–18.

Defence public sector undertakings

There are nine DPSUs: Hindustan Aeronautics Ltd (HAL), Bharat Electronics Ltd (BEL), Bharat Dynamics Ltd (BDL), BEML, Mishra Dhatu Nigam Ltd (MIDHANI), Mazagon Dock Shipbuilders Ltd (MDSL), Garden Reach Ship-builders and Engineers Ltd (GRSE), Goa Shipyard Ltd (GSL) and Hindustan Shipyard Ltd (HSL). Unlike the OFB which is a public arsenal functioning as a departmentally run organisation, the DPSUs are corporate entities, with six of them (HAL, BEL, BDL, BEML MIDHANI and GRSE) being listed on the stock exchange. Three DPSUs (HAL, BEL and BDL) figure in the SIPRI Top-100 arms companies in 2017[11] (Table 24.4).

Table 24.3 DPSUs and OFB: a factsheet

DPSU	*Year of incorporation*	*Turnover ($ million)*	*No. of employees*	*R&D expenditure ($ million)*	*Exports ($ million)*
HAL	1964	2837	29035	250	49
BEL	1954	1565	9726	153	27
BDL	1970	712	2788	6	0
BEML	1964	513	7722	16	4
MIDHANI	1973	103	850	2	0
MDL	1934	526*	8655	11	0
GRSE	1960	209	2214	1	0
GSL	1967	157*	1655	1	59
HSL	1952	94*	1352	1	0
OFB	1802	2300#	87474	16	37

Source: IDSA Database.

Note: Financial and employee figures of HAL, BEL, BDL, BEML, MIDHANI, GRSE and OFB for 2017–18 and those of MDL, GSL and HSL are for 2016–17. Financial figures are in current prices.
*: Revenue from operations. #: Value of Issues which are sales.

Table 24.4 Value of production of OFB and DPSUs, 1980/81–2017/18 (current $ million)

Name	*1980/81*	*1985/86*	*1990/91*	*1995/96*	*2000/01*	*2005/06*	*2010/11*	*2015/16*	*2016/17*	*2017/18*
HAL	200	476	499	475.0	569.8	1336	3611	2620	2550	2723
BEL	102	185	390	313.9	391.4	779	1212	1412	1378	1506
BDL	5	28	67	60.7	47.9	121	218	656	747	720
BEML	124	403	434	308.5	294.0	492	833	486	442	510
MIDHANI	3	18	26	27.5	25.0	40	106	110	109	109
MDL	110	282	172	107.0	155.9	117	573	627	525	–
GRSE	49	61	104	55.6	107.5	150	231	142	138	208
GSL	10	28	38	48.4	41.6	56	217	111	154	–
PTL	11	15	—	—	—	—	—	—	—	—
HSL	—	—	—	—	—	—	132	91	94	–
OFB	848	1111	1477	690.0	1208.7	1553	2461	1993	2210	2301
Total	1463	2606	3209	2087	2842	4645	9595	8248	8347	8077

Source: IDSA Database.

Notes:

i) HSL became a DPSU in 2010–11; PTL cased to be a DPSU from 1986–87 when it was transferred to HMT. -: Not available. —: Not applicable
ii) Value of production refers to financial value of items produced in a year and is different from sales. In some years, the industry especially shipyards, does not provide sales figures as they are less than the value of production. For example, a shipyard may build 10% of a submarine in a year; the sales figure for that year is zero but the value of production will be 10%.

Among the DPSUs, HAL is the biggest one, catering virtually for all aspects of India's military aircraft and associated avionics and accessories production, besides catering for some requirements of the space department. The company traces its origin to 1940 when visionary industrialist Walchand Hirachand set up Hindustan Aircraft Ltd with the objective of promoting the aviation industry in India. Two years later, the company was taken over by then British government ruling India, which in turn handed it over to the US Army Air Force for the duration of World War II for meeting the latter's requirement for aircraft repair and overhaul. Post-independence, the Indian government inherited the company and in 1954 it was placed under the administrative control of the MoD. In 1964, the Hindustan Aircraft Ltd was merged with Aeronautics India Ltd to form the present HAL.

Headquartered in Bengaluru in the state of Karnataka, HAL has 20 production divisions, 11 R&D centres and a facility management division spread across the country. It has also 14 JVs, in partnership with both Indian and foreign collaborators. Until now the company has produced 15 types of

Table 24.5 Number of employees in OFB and DPSUs, 1980/81–2017/18

Name	*1980/81*	*1985/86*	*1990/91*	*1995/96*	*2000/01*	*2005/06*	*2010/11*	*2015/16*	*2016/17*	*2017/18*
HAL	40903	42993	41530	35245	32642	29668	33681	30300	29526	29035
BEL	17229	18711	19357	17044	14177	12262	11180	9848	9716	9726
BDL	1255	1329	-	3123	3178	2814	2897	3132	3182	3095
BEML	11483	14526	-	-	14357	11975	11798	8827	8221	7722
MIDHANI	777	1532	1522	1456	1366	1319	1121	768	752	850
MDL	8324	16050	-	-	-	-	8090	8945	8655	-
GRSE	10750	10639	10080	8882	7350	5088	4117	2592	2401	2214
GSL	1459	2105	–	–	2047	1543	1667	1605	1655	-
PTL	2018	2005	…	…	…	…	…	…	…	…
HSL	-	–	—	–	–	–	3348	1548	1352	-
OFB	174000	185000	173340	162792	138551	115237	98914	88541	88474	-
Total	268198	294890	245829	228542	213668	179906	176813	156106	153934	52642

Note: -: Not available; … : Not Applicable.

aircraft from in-house R&D and 14 types under the transfer of technology from foreign sources. The first indigenous design was the HT-2 basic trainer in late 1940s, followed by the HPT-32, Kiran Mk I and Mk-II trainers. Post-1980s, HAL has been focussing more on the indigenous development and production of helicopters. The most complex design so far by the HAL is the HF-24 Marut, which first flew in the 1960s. HAL's present production portfolio consists of Su-30MKI fighter, the Hawk-Advanced Jet Trainer, the Light Combat Aircraft (LCA), Dornier-228 Light Transport Aircraft, Dhruv-Advanced Light Helicopter and Cheetal helicopters.

BEL was formed in 1954 with technical cooperation from France to manufacture defence electronics. Starting from the manufacture of basic communication equipment, the company has over the years diversified into areas such as radars, sonars, communication equipment, electronic warfare equipment, opto-electronics, tank electronics and C4I systems. Headquartered in Bengaluru, the company has nine production units, besides two subsidiaries and one joint venture with GE. Recently it has opened a new complex at Palasamudran in Andhra Pradesh to meet the business arising out of the missiles system and AESA radars. Among all the DPSUs, BEL is most proactive in R&D, with the first R&D activity dating back to 1958. With an R&D manpower of 2,162 personnel (of which 1,863 are engineers), its R&D spend in 2017–18 was close to 10 per cent of turnover, and it has also a high degree of indigenisation. Around 50–60 per cent of its turnover comes from its own design products and a further 20–25 per cent from other domestic players, with the balance 15–30 per cent coming from imported designs.

BDL was created from the DRDO and established as a DPSUs in 1970 with the purpose of building various missile systems, either under Transfer of Technology (ToT) or technologies supplied by the DRDO. It began production with the first generation anti-tank guided missiles (ATGMs), the French SS11B1, under ToT in the early 1970s. This was followed by the licensed production of 2nd generation ATGMs – the French Milan-2 and Russian Konkurs. The Company came into prominence with the launch of India's Integrated Guided Missile Development Programme in the early 1980s, under which the BDL was designated as the prime production agency. At present, it manufactures, besides ATGMs and strategic missiles, Akash surface-to-air missile, heavy weight torpedoes and decoys and test equipment. Besides the company is involved in the K-15 submarine-based ballistic missile (part of Indian's nuclear submarine, *Arihant* which made its first deterrence patrol in November 2018) and ASTRA air-to-air missiles. The company is headquartered in Hyderabad and has three production centers.

BEML (formerly Bharat Earth Movers Ltd) was formed in 1965, largely out of the rail coach division of HAL. The company has three business divisions, namely, mining and construction; defence; and rail and metro. Headquartered in Bangalore, the company has nine manufacturing units. In the defence sector, its prominent products include: high mobility trucks, recovery vehicles, bridge systems, vehicles for missile projects and tank transportation trailers. Among the DPSUs, BEML has the least exposure to defence. In 2016–17, the defence segment constituted less than 20 per cent of total gross revenue.[12] In 2016, the government gave in-principle approval for the privatization of the company, though till mid-September 2019, the progress on this front has been quite slow.

Among the four shipyards under the MoD, MDL is the most high-profile one. It was acquired by the MoD in 1960 from private owners. At the time of its takeover, MDL was mainly a ship repair yard. Since its acquisition, it has expanded to construct warships and submarines. Its major shipbuilding project started in the 1960s when it was entrusted to construct Leander class frigates with assistance from the UK. In the 1980s, MDL's shipbuilding capacity got a boost when the government decided to construct submarines for the Navy. Based on German technology it supplied two submarines, one in 1992 and the other in 1994.[13] Presently, it is constructing Scorpene submarines apart from a host of warships including missile destroyers and stealth frigates.

GSL was established in 1957 under Portuguese law as Estalerio Navais de Goa as a small barge repair facility. Following the liberation of Goa in 1961, the facility was transferred to the MDL from which it emerged as an independent defence shipyard in 1967. Over the years, the shipyard has moved to design and construct medium sized ships for the navy, coast guard and others. Between 1966 and 2017, it built over 200 ships.[14] The shipyard's product range for defence include offshore patrol vessels, missile craft, sail training ships and tugs. In 2016–17, the company's exports amounted to INR 4.0 billion ($ 59 million).

GRSE was taken over by the Indian government in 1960 to develop a second line of warship building facility. Located on the east coast of India in the state of West Bengal, the shipyard has the unique distinction of building the first indigenous warship for the Indian navy.[15] GRSE is also the only shipyard in India with has its own engineering and engine manufacturing division. Its major warship building activity has progressed from building patrol vessels, survey vessels and landing ship tanks in the 1980s to that of guided missile frigates, fast patrol vessels and portable steel bridges in the 1990s.[16] Presently it is building 19 warships which include three stealth frigates, two anti-submarine warfare corvettes, seven landing craft utility (LCU) ships, two water jet fast attack crafts (WJFAC) and five fast patrol vessels.[17]

HSL is the oldest and biggest public sector shipyard in India, located at Visakhapatnam, in the state of Andhra Pradesh. The shipyard was acquired by the Indian government from private owners in 1952, and placed under the MoD's control in 2010 with the purpose of building 'strategic assets and warships'. It has so far built 181 ships and repaired over 1960 vessels.[18] In the defence sector, its exposure has so far been limited to building minor ships (such as OPVs and tugs) and repairing submarines. Post-acquisition by the MoD, it has received several orders to build higher class warships. The MoD has already nominated HSL to build five fleet support vessels at a cost of INR 90 billion.

MIDHANI was established in 1973 to achieve self-reliance in special alloys which are required in the strategic sectors of defence, nuclear and aerospace. Headquartered in Hyderabad, the company has supplied more than 100 types of special metal alloys including super alloys, titanium and titanium alloys and special purpose steels.

Private sector

In comparison to the OFs and the DPSUs, the private sector is a relatively new entrant into India's defence production. It was barred from producing defence items until 2001 when the government decided to liberalise the defence industry and allow private participation through a licensing system. By June 2018, the government had issued 379 industrial licenses (ILs) to 230 Indian companies, of which 70 companies covering 114 licenses have reported commencing production.[19] The licenses issued cover almost all segments of defence production ranging from small arms to land systems, aircraft, naval platforms, missiles, radars and electronics. Unlike the OFB and DPSUs, the MoD does not however publish the turnover and other financial details of these private companies, making it difficult to assess precisely the contribution of this nascent sector to India's defence production.

Among the private sector companies, some of the big players are TATA, L&T, Bharat Forge, Mahindra, and Ashok Leyland, who have won defence contracts from the MoD, including a few in competition with global majors. TATA, for instance, won two significant contracts in global competition: one for modernising the air force's airfields in which it defeated an Italian company; and the other for providing an electronic warfare system to the Indian army by defeating Elta of Israel. The biggest order so far won by private companies is by L&T which defeated a Russian offer to win $750 million contract in 2015 for 100 howitzer guns for the Indian army.

Defence research and development organisation

The DRDO was established in 1958 by a merger of the Defence Science Organisation (DSO) with the Technical Development Establishments of the Army. At the time of its formation, the Organisation was a small entity with about 10 laboratories. Over the years it has evolved into a large Organisation with over 52 labs and other establishments. With a manpower of over 24,500, including 7,400 scientists, it has a budget of over $2.7 billion in 2018–19. Though the organisation was set up in late 1950s, it came into prominence in the 1980s when the government sanctioned a number of high profile R&D projects, principal of which are the Light Combat Aircraft (LCA), and Integrated Guided Missile Development Programme (IGMDP), under which the organisation was entrusted with the task of developing five different classes of missiles.

Presently, DRDO's interests transcend virtually all aspects of defence technologies from aeronautics; armaments; combat vehicles and engineering; electronics and computer sciences; materials; missiles and strategic systems; micro-electronics and devices; naval research and development; and life sciences. By the end of 2017, DRDO had a portfolio of 338 projects with a combined value of INR 700 billion ($10.4 billion). Some of its big projects each of which costs INR 1.0 billion or more are the LCA Navy, Rustom-II Medium Altitude Long Endurance (MALE) UAV, 155 mm/52 caliber towed artillery guns system, 1500 hp engine and AESA radar.

The huge portfolio notwithstanding, DRDO is often criticised for time and cost overruns besides performance shortfalls of many programmes it undertakes. Time and cost overruns are most visible in some of the most high-profile projects including the LCA, MBT Arjun, aero engine, Kaveri (for LCA), and air-to-air missile system (Astra). The criticism notwithstanding, the most notable contribution towards India's defence preparedness has been in the field of strategic systems, namely the long-range ballistic missiles. By 2017, the value of systems, which have already been inducted or cleared for production amounts to over $41 billion (Table 24.6).

Table 24.6 DRDO developed systems (as of December 2017)

Systems	*Inducted* (current $ billion)*	*Under induction # (current $ billion)*
Missile Systems	3.6	11.2
Electronic and Radar Systems	2.0	3.2
Advanced Materials and Composites	0.7	0.3
Armament Systems	1.3	3.0
Aeronautical Systems	0.2	12.1
Combat Vehicles & Engineering Systems	0.8	1.8
Life Science Systems	0.1	0.0
Naval Systems	0.2	0.6
Micro Electronics Devices and Computational Systems	0.04	0.0
Total	8.9	32.2
Grand Total	41.1	

Source: Standing Committee on Defence.

Note: Strategic systems not included in the systems mentioned.
*: Items already produced and inducted in defence forces. #: Items cleared for production but yet to be inducted into the services.

Industry structure and conduct

Historically, the OFB and the DPSUs have been the dominant players in India's defence production sector, though their respective importance have undergone a change over the years, at least from the perspective of value of production. In the 1980s, the OFs as a whole were the single largest defence entity in India, accounting for 59 per cent of total production. It has lost its pole position to HAL which now accounts for about 39 per cent of total production for all OFs and DPSUs and has emerged as the biggest defence company in India. Within the DPSUs, the relative importance of companies has also undergone a change. BDL, the manufacturer of missiles, has emerged as a strong player with a 12 per cent share in DPSUs' total production, up from just 1 per cent in 1980. BEL has also increased its share from 17 per cent to 22 per cent. The four shipyards together have, however, lost their share from 29 per cent to 15 per cent (Table 24.4).

Traditionally, defence production has been dominated by the DPSUs and OFB which had near exclusive monopoly in their respective domains: aircraft by HAL, ammunition, tank and light vehicles by the OFB, electronics by BEL, frigates and destroyers by the MDL, and OPVs by the GSL. In certain areas where capacity and capability overlapped, the MoD was the arbitrator in selecting the contractor and the size of its order. The MoD used its buying power to award defence contracts to these entities based on a capacity assessment and expertise. Most of the present orders of the OFB and DPSUs, such as main battle tank (MBT) Arjun, Infantry Combat Vehicle (ICV), SU-30MKI fighter, Mirage and Jaguar fighter upgrades, Hawk trainer, Akash Missile, Scorpene submarine, ASW Corvettes, are awarded to these entities by nomination, bypassing any sort of competition in awarding these contracts.

With the 2001 liberalisation, the structure of Indian defence industry is, however, beginning to change though resistance to reforms is firm and deep rooted. The private sector is now allowed to manufacture all types of defence equipment, though subject to official permission through licensing. Its participation is being increasingly facilitated through the periodic revision of the Defence Procurement Procedures (DPP) – the rule book of the MoD for the acquisition of weapons and platforms for the armed forces. This book was first articulated in the early 1990s and has been revised several times since then.

Since the turn of the present century, the DPP has expanded the procurement categories in an attempt to move away from direct import to indigenous production. In comparison to pre-2008 DPP, which was friendly to direct import and/or licensed production by the DPSUs/OFB, the DPPs since 2008 onwards have newer categories to support Indian private companies, which are also required to achieve a degree of indigenization in procurement contracts (see Table 24.7). Moreover, the DPP from 2013 onwards have listed all the categories in decreasing order of preference. Following the

DPP 2016, a new category, Buy (Indian – Indigenously Designed, Developed and Manufactured [Buy Indian – IDDM]) has been accorded the highest priority. This is followed by Buy Indian (in which 40 per cent has to be sourced from India), Buy and Make (Indian) – 50 per cent Indian content – Buy and Make and Buy (Global), which is given the lowest priority. The order of priority is intended to ensure that the authorities examine the higher category, which are friendly to the domestic industry, before moving to the lower category, which is less friendly to the local industry. Any exclusion of the higher category is to be documented on file and justified by the authorities. This puts an onus on the procurement authorities to examine all possibilities of using the domestic capabilities for equipping the Indian armed forces. This is a marked change from the earlier practice where import or licensed production by OFB/DPSUs was the default option.

However, despite the opportunity provided in the DPP for the private sector, its contribution has so far been marginal. In the 17 years since the liberalisation of the industry, the biggest order won by private sector companies has been that of L&T which won less than a US$1 billion contract for providing tracked artillery guns for the Indian army, whereas the OFB and DPSUs continue to receive much larger orders. The public sector entities still continue to enjoy a privileged position, which allows them to be awarded large orders without competition, while the private sector is required not only to compete for each contract but mostly has to wait inordinately long period to see the contract fruition if it happens at all.

Table 24.7 Salient features of defence procurement categories

Prioritised procurement category	*Year of incorporation*	*Minimum indigenous content requirement*	*RFP issued to*
Buy (Indian-IDDM)	2016	40% (if designed in-house) 60% (if manufactured in-house)	Indian companies Indian companies
Buy (Indian)	2015	40%	Indian companies
Buy & Make (Indian)	2008	50%	Indian companies
Buy & Make*	2003	Range and depth of ToT to be decided case by case	Foreign companies
Buy (Global)*	2002	Not Applicable	Foreign/Indian companies

Source: Table extrapolated from Ministry of Defence, Defence Procurement Procedures (relevant years).
Note:* Offset of 30 per cent is mandated in these categories when the procurement value is INR 20 billion or more.

Industry performance

Until 2001, the DPSUs and the OFs had a near monopoly of India's arms production. Even in the post 2001 period, the monopoly was still intact as the private sector is yet to make a dent due to various factors. Like in the other sectors, the monopoly of the DPSUs and OFs have bred inefficiency, reflected in their functioning and performance. Measured in terms of innovation, productivity, export success and timely execution of orders, they are gross underperformers.

Being the captive suppliers of the armed forces, the DPSUs and the OFs have hardly any incentive to obtain orders based on their innovation. Over the years, they have been confined to producing items based on the designs and technology supplied by others. The lack of focus on innovation is visible from their low R&D spending. The combined R&D spend of the nine DPSUs in 2016–17 was INR 30 billion, or a mere 5 per cent of their production value. Moreover, much of the R&D is spent by two entities, HAL and BEL with the others spending less than 1 per cent. The situation is similar in the OFs. In 2017–18, they spent only 0.5 per cent of their sales on R&D. With such a poor R&D orientation, it is a forgone conclusion that no new worthwhile products could be developed by them.

The combined labour productivity of the DPSUs as a whole is less than one-fourths of some of the leading global companies. This gross mismanagement of the labour force is also evident in the OFs, which employ two supervisors for every three direct industrial employees.[20] In essence, the poor labour productivity is a burden on the budget of the armed forces, effectively reducing their purchasing capacity and hampering their capability development.

Exports, a key indicator of the global competitiveness of any enterprise, are at best non-existent in DPSUs or OFs. Compared to 20–80 per cent revenues generated through exports by some of their global rivals, the DPSUs and OFs as whole hardly achieve 3 per cent of sales from exports. Not only have the DPSUs and the OFs failed to market their products in the global market but they have also failed miserably in sustaining whatever little success they had. The poor success in exports has prevented these entities from scaling up and achieving the benefits of scale and lower unit costs of purchase for the armed forces.

In a report presented to Parliament in July 2016, the Comptroller and Auditor General of India (CAG) castigated the DPSUs for their 'inordinate delay in supply of critical weapons and equipment … during XI Army Plan (2007–12),' hampering the 'modernisation and capability enhancement plan of the Indian Army.'[21] The CAG observed that contracts worth INR 301 billion amounting to 60 per cent of total value of contracts signed by the MoD with the DPSUs, were delayed. The CAG in his other reports has also castigated the OFs for severe delays in supply to the armed forces. In a report presented to Parliament in December 2015, the supreme auditor observed a shortfall of 61 per cent in the OFs' achievement of targets.[22] The poor target achievement along with the other poor performance indicators, reflect the gross inefficiency of these entities, which does not bode well for India's aspiration to become self-sufficient in defence production.

Make in India initiative

The defence industry has been identified as one of the 25 sectors under the Make in India initiative, launched by Prime Minister Narendra Modi in September 2014 with the aim of transforming India's manufacturing and innovation sectors. It is also one of the 10 'Champion Sectors' identified under the same initiative for focused attention because of their double-digit growth and significant employment potential.[23] Under the Make in India programme, the government has unleashed a host of reform measures including a set of ease of doing business measures, a number initiatives to provide a level playing field for the private sector vis-à-vis the DPSUs/OFB; domestic industry friendly procurement procedures, initiatives for reforming the public sector production entities and a host of measures for attracting investment.

The ease of doing business measures in defence production are intended to deepen the involvement, especially of Indian private sector entities and foreign companies in defence production. Towards this, the government has simplified the licensing process, relaxed the defence FDI cap, articulated a defence export policy, and opened the trials/testing facilities existing in the government set up for use by others. The simplification of the licensing process has removed some of the bureaucratic and procedural obstacles that had limited the grant of IL to the private sector in a time-bound manner. The simplified process has not only overcome this problem, but also led to a significant jump in the award of IL from a total of 107 ILs at the end of 2014–15 to 348 by 2017–18.[24]

The defence FDI cap, which had remained constant at 26 per cent for over a decade since the sector was first opened to foreign participation in 2001, was increased to 49 per cent under the automatic route and beyond 49 per cent to up to 100 per cent under the government approval route on a case by case basis. Though its impact has so far been muted, its potential for bringing in significant investment cannot be ruled out as several foreign companies have shown interest in investing in India in partnership with Indian companies.

In a move to allow Indian industry to benefit from scale economies and exploit the international arms market, the government has, for the first time, articulated a defence export policy. This policy, which also forms part of India's commitment to International export control regimes – particularly the Wassenaar Arrangement (to which India became a member in 2017), sets out a time- and procedure-bound process for the award of export license to Indian industry. The articulation of policy measure has led to some visible success, though the volume of exports still remains low in comparison to the world's major arms exporting countries. Total export by Indian industry has jumped from $317 million in 2014–15 to $726 million in 2017–18.[25]

The opening-up of trial and testing facilities run by the government agencies such as the armed forces, DPSUs, OFB and DRDO for use especially by private sector companies is a major boost for the latter as some of them were forced to take their equipment aboard for testing, resulting in time and cost escalation.[26] With the opening of these facilities, the private sector can now pay the necessary fees and test their equipment before its evaluation by the users or for exports.

To further encourage the private sector in defence production, the government has provided a much needed level-playing filed vis-à-vis the public sector undertakings in areas of taxes and payment terms. Previously, the private sector was required to pay certain taxes and duties while their public sector counterparts were exempted. This resulted in the private sector's potential bids being more expensive and uncompetitive. The government has now mandated everybody to pay the necessary taxes and duties, bringing every player to compete on an equal footing. Similarly, the government has extended the foreign exchange variation benefits in long-term contracts to the private sector which were previously only available to state-owned entities. The benefits will insulate them against the currency fluctuations and make their bids more competitive.

As part of the streamlining of DPP to align with the Make in India initiative, the government has taken two key steps. First, one of articulating a new procurement procedure, Buy (Indian-IDDM), as mentioned earlier. Second, related to the 'Make' procedure, which was first announced in 2006 with the objective of promoting design and development activities within the industry, especially the private sector. Under the 'Make' procedure, the government committed to provide financial assistance for prototype development of up to 80 per cent. However due to the procedural difficulties, not a single 'Make' project could be awarded. The government has not only simplified the whole procedure but also, articulated a list of projects for execution under the revised procedure, and extended financial assistance of up to 90 per cent. A new sub-category has also been introduced to allow industry to offer innovative solutions for evaluation by the government.

In one of the boldest measure to reform the state-owned defence production entities, the government initiated disinvestment/privatisation of DPSUs besides beginning to dismantle the monopoly of OFB in certain areas. In regard to the former, the government has already disinvested part of its equity stakes in HAL, GRSE, BDL and MDL by listing them on the stock exchange, and has given 'in-principle' approval for the privatization of BEML. The stock exchange listing is intended to infuse greater corporate governance, besides setting the stage for ultimate privatization (if such a decision is taken at all in the future). For the OFB, the government has identified 275 items out of 600-odd items produced by it as 'non-core' items. This would free the Indian army to procure these items through a competitive bidding process, and in the process end the monopoly of the OFB, which is now forced to compete with others to win tenders for these items.

Prospects for Indian defence industry

The Make in India initiative through a host of reform measures has undoubtedly brought a fresh lease of life to the otherwise moribund Indian defence production sector which has been known for its inefficiency and lack of innovation. All the reform measures taken in recent years are likely to have a positive impact on the Indian industry, especially the private sector, which despite having certain disadvantages vis-à-vis the OFB/DPSUs, has now a much better environment in which to operate. In particular, the private sector is expected to play a much greater role, particularly in land systems where it has greater expertise.

While the Indian industry is expected to play a larger role in the future, its contribution is unlikely to change India's self-reliance target in a dramatic manner. The primary reason is the lack of a strong R&D base and the Indian industry's excessive dependence on external ToT, especially those related to major platforms. A survey of India's current procurement plan reveals that India will remain dependent on external sources for major systems such as modern fighters, helicopters, conventional submarines and long-range missile defence systems. Considering 30–50 years of operational life of these systems, Indian industry's role in production of these platform will remain marginal at best.

Notes

1 The authour is a Research Fellow at New Delhi-based Institute for Defence Studies and Analyses (IDSA). Email: laxmanbehera@gmail.com
2 Demands for Grants contain the estimates of expenditure in respect of various ministries and departments and are required to be voted by the lower house of the Indian Parliament.
3 INR is converted to US$ based on the exchange rate of first nine months of 2018–19
4 International Monetary Fund, World Economic Outlook Database, October 2018
5 For a survey of India's Defence expenditure since 1947 see Laxman Kumar Behera, 'Changing Contours of Indian Defence Expenditure: Past as Prologue?', in Harsh V. Pant (ed.), *Handbook of Indian Defence Policy: Themes, Structures and Doctrines*, Routledge: New Delhi, 2016, pp. 235–251.
6 Ministry of Defence, *Defence Services Estimates* (relevant years).
7 Laxman Kumar Behera, 'Indian Defence Industry: Issues of Self-Reliance', IDSA Monograph, July 2013.
8 Pieter D. Wezeman et al., 'Trends in International Arms Transfers, 2017', SIPRI Fact Sheet, March 2018, www.sipri.org/sites/default/files/2018-03/fssipri_at2017_0.pdf.
9 http://pib.nic.in/newsite/PrintRelease.aspx?relid=180694, July 18, 2018.
10 DRDO Annual Report 2017, p. 107.
11 Apart from three DPSUs, OFs also figures in the Top-100 list. SIPRI, www.sipri.org/sites/default/files/2018-12/fs_arms_industry_2017_0.pdf
12 BEML, *Annual Report 2016–17*, p. iii.
13 Indian Navy, www.indiannavy.nic.in/content/submarines-active (accessed on 09 October 2018).
14 GSL, https://goashipyard.in/products/product-history/.

15 GRSE, http://grse.in/index.php/our-company/about-us.html (accessed on 09 October 2018).
16 GRSE, 'Achievement Highlights', http://grse.in/index.php/achievements/achievement-highlights.html (accessed on 09 October 2018).
17 Committee on Estimates 2018–19, p. 43.
18 HSL, 'Profile', www.hslvizag.in/content/7_1_Profile.aspx (accessed on 10 October 2018).
19 PIB, 'Privatisation of Defence Production', 18 July 2018, http://pib.nic.in/newsite/PrintRelease.aspx?relid=180694.
20 CAG, *Union Government (Defence Services): Army, Ordnance Factories and Defence Public Sector Undertakings*, Report No. 19 of 2016, p. 75.
21 CAG, *Union Government (Defence Services): Army, Ordnance Factories and Defence Public Sector Undertakings*, Report No. 19 of 2016, p. xi.
22 CAG, *Union Government (Defence Services): Army, Ordnance Factories and Defence Public Sector Undertakings*, Report No. 44 of 2015, p. 134.
23 Ministry of Finance, Government of India, *Economic Survey 2017–18*, Vol. 2, p. 125.
24 Ministry of Defence, 'India Stands Strong: Major Achievements of the Ministry of Defence in Narendra Modi Government', May 2018.
25 Ibid.
26 https://economictimes.indiatimes.com/news/defence/test-in-india-military-ranges-labs-opened-to-private-players-to-test-equipment/articleshow/50212027.cms.

25 Singapore's defence-industrial ecosystem

Ron Matthews and Collin Koh

1. Introduction

Singapore's defence-industrial origins date back to independence from Britain in 1965. Although colonisation had acted to suppress the island state's economic transformation, it had also implanted strong positive forces that would project the country forward to construct a powerful defence economy. These forces included a functioning civil service, the rule of law and adoption of the English language. In a country where 90 per cent of the population are of Chinese ethnic origin, the primary language is English, not Mandarin. In the defence domain, however, Britain had left precious little in the way of capability as arms had always been sourced from the colonial power. On final departure in 1968, Britain's military forces left independent Singapore with no air force and navy, and just a meagre army comprised of mostly Malay forces. Withdrawal was also combined with the closure of Britain's huge military base on the island, leading to the loss of 40,000 local jobs and a fifth of Singapore's national income.[1] This dealt Singapore a destructive economic blow, and also left it facing a strategic calamity. This was because surrounding the country was an arc of Islamic states that was, and is, perceived as an existential threat to Singaporean sovereignty. Such fears in the early decades following independence were fuelled by anti-Chinese riots and killings in both Malaysia and Indonesia. Additionally, Singapore suffered insecurity from intermittent regional frictions, including fishing and maritime territorial disputes, 'water wars' with Malaysia and actual military conflict with Indonesian armed forces during the latter's aggressive *Konfrontasi* era. It is little wonder, therefore, that Singapore felt vulnerable, and sought to quickly develop indigenous military capability, including defence-industrial capacity.

Singapore's response to such threats was strengthened by the election of Singapore's first prime minister, Lee Kuan Yew, who proved a strong and visionary leader. His view was that development must be defended, and resources were allocated for the build-up of Singapore's Armed Forces (SAF). A strategy of deterrence was crafted, whereby Singapore would be viewed by aggressors as a 'poisoned shrimp'; that is, notwithstanding the small size of the country, potential combatants would be deterred from attacking due to unacceptable casualties and damage that a powerful SAF would inflict upon them: 'easy to swallow but impossible to digest'.[2] An appropriate strategy was devised to overcome demographic constraints that would emphasise transformative defence innovation through niche military-technological 'force multipliers'.[3] Civil-military fusion was the intended result via high value dual-use technology synergies. Technology is a critical component of Singapore's success story, but accommodating the process of accelerating and intensifying innovation is investment into human capital. The energy and creativity of Singaporean engineers and scientists is a significant consideration, influenced partially by the strategic imperatives derived by the country's small size, but also by a Chinese socio-economic cultural that embraces such traits as *Mianzi* (saving and creating face).[4]

Singapore's small country defence-industrial model has proved remarkably successful in catapulting the industry from a position of dependence some 50 years ago to the present status of industrial, competitive and innovational maturity. Singapore's underlying defence-industrial strength has expanded, *pari passu,* with growth in the breadth and depth of its commercial economy. Table 25.1 evidences Singapore's contemporary and comparative success as a defence economic power. As a small nation bereft of natural resources, and with a population of around just six million people, Singapore has constructed a powerful economy, sponsoring an impressive military budget and housing the world's 40th biggest defence-industrial company. These defence economic metrics cast all other major Southeast Asian neighbours into the shade and compare favourably with the performance of other small countries, which have benefitted from a long history of industrial development and/or the possession of vast amounts of oil and energy resources.

By reference to Singapore's strategic and policy environment, the purpose of this chapter is to explore the development of the island state's defence-industrial base set against the broader defence economic context. Discussion begins with an overview of defence spending, procurement and defence-industrial development patterns. This is then followed by the articulation of a quadrilateral defence-industrial model that captures the principal influences affecting the development of Singapore's defence economy. Taking each in turn, the core components comprising strategic foresight, technological absorption capacity, exposure to trade and foreign partnerships and defence offset will be explained and analysed. The chapter closes by offering a brief prognosis on the future prospects of Singapore's defence industry.

2. Evolution of defence-industrial structures

Other than some basic in-country maintenance, repair and overhaul (MRO) provision for British and allied forces during WWII, Singapore possessed no defence-related manufacturing capacity until the late 1960s. The turning point was the election of Lee Kwan Yew and his determination that Independence would be defended, as far as was feasible by indigenous capability. Sovereignty would not be undermined by the capriciousness of foreign

Table 25.1 Singapore comparative defence economic performance, 2017

Country	*MILEX (US$ billion) current*	*GDP (US $ billion) nominal*	*Population (million)*	*GDP per capita (US$) nominal*	*MILEX/ GDP (%)*	*Defence firms in top global 100*
Singapore	10.1	324	5.6	55,236	3.3	1(40)
Southeast Asia						
Malaysia	3.5	315	31.6	9,945	1.1	0
Indonesia	7.9	1,016	264.0	3,847	0.8	0
Thailand	6.1	455	69.0	6,594	1.4	0
Vietnam	4.9	224	95.5	2,343	2.3	0
Brunei	0.3	12	0.43	28,290	2.9	0
Other Small States						
Kuwait	6.7	120	4.1	29,040	5.8	0
Norway	6.3	399	5.3	75,505	1.6	2(81 & 95)
Oman	8.4	73	4.6	15,668	12.1	0
Qatar	3.4	166	2.3	71,991	N/A	0
Sweden	5.5	538	9.9	53,442	1.0	1(32)
Switzerland	4.6	679	8.4	80,190	0.7	1(73)

Source: SIPRI, 2018 Database (MILEX, MILEX /GDP), World Bank 2017 (Population, GDP, GDP Per Capita) *Defense News*, 2018 (top 100 companies).

powers imposing arms embargoes when political considerations supersede strategic partnerships. It was inevitable, therefore, that defence industrialisation would be encouraged, but from the outset local defence companies would not benefit from direct government subsidies.[5]

The defence-industrial development process began in 1967, with the establishment of Chartered Industries (CI), the first of three divisions that would later (1989) become the state-owned Singapore Technology (ST) Corporation. Chartered Industries commenced production of several different types of ammunition and small arms, and gradually expanded capacity to include artillery shells and armour-piercing rounds for the AMX-13 tank's main gun. In 1976, CI purchased the rights of the SAR-80 assault rifle from Britain's Sterling Armament Company. The rifle was upgraded, and some 100,000 indigenously modified SAR-80s were produced for local and export use.[6] ST's second division was established in 1973, to locally design and produce mortars derived from a Finnish model. The division later produced the Israeli supplied M68 155mm howitzer, which was later locally modified and exported as the FH-88. Finally, in 1971, ST Automotive Engineering was launched to modify imported Mercedes heavy three-ton trucks to military spec standard. Foreign armoured personnel carriers, such as the US-supplied M-113, were additionally modified to serve as platforms for locally developed mortars and foreign supplied surface-to-air missile systems.

In 1974, the Singaporean government formed Sheng-Li Holdings to provide strategic oversight and management of the island state's rapidly expanding defence-industrial base. The policy focus was not only on land systems, but also the separate and rapidly evolving naval and aerospace entities. In the naval domain, Singapore Shipbuilding and Engineering was launched in 1968, and through overseas technology transfer agreements, quickly developed warship production. A major partnership was with West Germany's Lürssen Werft, leading to the license production in 1974–1975 of TNC-45 missile-equipped gunboats that accommodated Israeli-produced Gabriel missiles. In 1989, the same German company provided the design and a prototype vessel for the local construction of five corvettes that integrated US Harpoon ship-to-ship missiles. Aerospace was serviced by the Singapore Aerospace Corporation. The company was created in 1981 for local assembly of Italian supplied SIAI-Marchetti S-211 trainer aircraft, and also the provision of MRO for numerous types of military aircraft, engines and avionics equipment, including refurbishment of the American supplied A-4S Skyhawk fighter and depot-level maintenance of C-130 transport aircraft.

In 1990, in a move to promote organisational synergies, Sheng-Li Holdings was restructured and renamed Singapore Technologies (ST) Holdings. The thrust of this restructuring was to commercialise operations, with ST in 1994 coming under the control of the State Investment Company, Temasek. Through mergers and acquisitions, ST rapidly developed a commercial portfolio that included telecommunications, financial services, tourism and transportation. Singapore's defence industry was clustered into what was called ST Engineering (ST Engg), as part of a deliberate plan to diversify and cross-thread its functions into appropriate commercial activities across the expanding ST conglomerate. ST Engg became a publicly listed company, with Temasek Holdings owning a 51 per cent controlling share. ST Engg is presently structured into four major companies, namely – ST Aerospace, ST Marine, ST Electronics and ST Kinetics. The holding company has over the past five years derived most of its revenues and net profits from aerospace, followed by electronics, land systems and marine.[7] Significantly, ST Engg has evolved from a sole focus on the domestic market to operating as a global multinational defence company, with operations spread across the globe. In 2017, ST Engg employed 22,000 workers in 22 countries that generated S$6.62bn in revenue and S$511.9mn in profit.[8] The company is a success story, ranked 40th in the world's top 100 defence companies.

3. Procurement profile

Notwithstanding defence funding pressures, ST Engg has embarked on an ambitious post-2030 'Road Map' for a manpower-lean military capability aimed at doing more with less.[9] Detailed analysis of programme costs is not possible because Singapore's defence acquisition spending is secret, and thus the figures have never entered the public domain. It is clear, though, that the continuous and costly procurement of 'big ticket' platforms from foreign vendors, with whom ST Engg plays an important collaborative role, is a major undertaking. Aside from contributing to various programmes across land, air and naval systems domains through partnerships with foreign vendors, ST Engg has assumed the prime contractor role for major locally developed platforms. These include the Next-Generation Armoured Fighting Vehicle that will be an upgraded – more capable – version of ST Kinetics Bionix infantry fighting vehicle;[10] and there is a possibility of a local build for, firstly, the navy's Multi-Role Combat Vessel (MRCV), slated to replace the venerable (in-service since the late 1980s) *Victory*-class missile corvettes, and, secondly, the planned Joint Multi-Mission Ship (JMMS) that will offer larger and improved aviation capacity compared to the locally-built *Endurance*-class landing platforms dock vessels. The procurement process for these vessels will likely follow the conventional model of the lead ship being built in a foreign yard, with remaining units produced domestically under licence. Singapore's major arms procurements since 1980 are shown in Table 25.2. To date, there are no reported plans to initiate indigenous programmes for major platforms. This can be attributed to both the absence of economies of scale and less-than-guaranteed export prospects, with SAF the only secure client for such complex systems and platforms.

4. Unique defence-industrial 'ecosystem'

Singapore's defence-industrial ecosystem is framed by reference to an expanded definition of national security. The model was likely influenced by Japan's 'comprehensive' security approach that has been in place since the beginning of the 19th century Meiji era (1868–1912).[11] The Japanese interpreted security as a composite of economic, technological, military, diplomatic, political and related fields of competence. Comprehensive security embraces defence, including defence industrial capability, but this represents just one of multiple security competences, rather than equating to national security itself. Singapore has a similar Total Defence concept that has been forged on the same national security anvil, covering the conventional elements of economic, civil and military defence, but additionally there are elements of social and psychological defence, reflecting the country's diverse ethnic minority groupings. From the perspective of this chapter, Total Defence reflects the Singapore government's desire to interlace the defence (security) and economic (prosperity) objectives, to ensure that defence investment is not quarantined from the wider economic community. It is, therefore, instructive that across ST Engg's four subsidiary companies, only kinetics is dedicated to military outputs. The other three, aerospace, maritime and electronics, are civil-military, and functionally organised so that skills and

Table 25.2 Singapore major arms procurement, 1980–2017

Year purchased	*Supplier country*	*Item*	*Quantity*	*Remarks*
1980	USA	A-4S Super Skyhawk ground attack fighters	16	
1980	USA	F-5E Tiger II fighter-bombers	6	US$34 million deal
1981	USA	F-5F Tiger II fighter-bombers/trainers	3	US$16 million deal
1983	USA	A-4S Super Skyhawk ground attack fighters	8	
1983	USA	E-2C Hawkeye airborne early warning and control aircraft	4	US$437 million deal
1984	USA	F-5E Tiger II fighter-bombers	6	
1985	USA	F-16A/B Fighting Falcon multi-role fighters	8	US$280 million 'Project Peace Carvin I' deal
1986	Germany (West)	MGB-62 corvettes	6	
1986	USA	F-5E Tiger II fighter-bombers	5	
1986	USA	KC-130H Hercules refuelling aircraft/tactical transport	1	
1987	USA	C-130H Hercules tactical transport aircraft	1	
1987	USA	F-5F Tiger II fighter-bombers/trainers	3	
1989	USA	A-4B Skyhawk ground attack fighters	24	
1991	Sweden	Landsort-class mine countermeasures vessels	4	
1992	USA	F-16C/D Fighting Falcon multi-role fighters	18	US$890 million 'Project Peace Carvin II' deal
1994	USA	CH-47D Chinook heavy-lift helicopters	6	
1994	USA	F-16A/B Fighting Falcon multi-role fighters	8	US$280 million 'Project Peace Carvin I' deal
1995	Sweden	Sjöormen-class submarines	1	
1996	USA	F-16CJ Fighting Falcon multi-role fighters	12	First leased and then purchased
1997	Sweden	Sjöormen-class submarines	3	
1997	USA	F-16CJ/DJ Fighting Falcon multi-role fighters	12	US$350 million 'Project Peace Carvin III' deal

(*Continued*)

Table 25.2 (Cont.)

1997	USA	KC-135 Stratotanker refuelling aircraft	4	US$280–500 million 'Project Peace Guardian' deal
1998	USA	CH-47SD Chinook heavy-lift helicopters	6	
1999	USA	AH-64D Apache Longbow attack helicopters	8	Part of US$629 million 'Project Peace Vanguard' deal
1999	USA	CH-47SD Chinook heavy-lift helicopters	4	
2000	France	La Fayette frigates	6	US$750 million deal (part of US$1.6 billion 'Project Delta')
2000	USA	F-16D Fighting Falcon multi-role fighters	20	'Project Peace Carvin IV' deal
2001	USA	AH-64D Apache Longbow attack helicopters	12	US$617 million 'Project Peace Vanguard' deal
2005	Sweden	Västergotland-class submarines	2	US$128 million 'Project Northern Light' deal
2005	USA	F-15SG Strike Eagle multi-role fighters	12	US$1 billion 'Project Peace Carvin V' deal
2005	USA	S-70B Seahawk shipborne helicopters	6	
2007	Germany	Leopard-2A4 main battle tanks	182	
2007	USA	F-15SG Strike Eagle multi-role fighters	12	US$1 billion deal
2007	USA	G-550 airborne early warning and control aircraft	4	Ordered and delivered via Israel; mission systems fitted in Israel
2008	USA	M-142 HiMARS multiple rocket launcher	18	
2010	USA	F-15SG Strike Eagle multi-role fighters	8	
2012	Germany	Leopard-2A7 main battle tanks	12	
2013	Germany	Type-218SG submarines	2	
2013	USA	S-70B Seahawk shipborne helicopters	2	
2014	Spain	A330 MRTT refuelling aircraft	6	
2014	USA	F-15SG Strike Eagle multi-role fighters	8	
2016	USA	CH-47F Chinook heavy-lift helicopters	10	
2017	Germany	Type-218SG submarines	2	

Source: SIPRI Arms Transfers Database, at: www.sipri.org/databases/armstransfers (accessed on 22 October 2018). Note that the Carvin I-V programmes constitute the Republic of Singapore Air Force procurement of US F-16 fighter aircraft, including the provision of training at the Luke Air Force base in Arizona.

learning acquired on military programmes are transfused into ST's wider commercial and more profitable activities.[12]

Located within the Total Defence space is Singapore's 'defence ecosystem'. The concept was first coined by Quek Tong Boon (Deputy Defence Secretary for Technology and Transformation) in 2006. He defined it in terms of the interdependency and co-evolution between the country's users, developers and producers of defence equipment.[13] Although the 'users' (i.e. the SAF) do participate in the choice of system design, logistical requirements and other related issues, its absence of operational combat experience limits the extent of its contribution, and likely negatively impacts on defence export prospects, also. In the context of this chapter, therefore, perhaps a more relevant concept is a Singaporean 'defence-industrial ecosystem', reflecting the quadrilateral stakeholder relations between: firstly, policymakers and funders (government); secondly, developers, comprising the labyrinth of defence-related R&D organisations; thirdly, producers (defence industry); and, fourthly, the network of trading partners and collaborators, operating within a globalised environment. Whilst there also exists a high level of interdependence between each of these constituent parts, importantly, the defence industry assumes the role of pivotal player in transforming ideas and designs into 'teeth end' technological capability; indeed, it endorses the notion posited by Bilveer Singh that the defence industry is the fifth (military-related) arm of Total Defence.[14] At the core of Singapore's defence industry is ST Engg, sponsoring the cumulative and evolutionary incubation and then maturity of indigenous defence technologies into a 'secret technological edge' for use against potential aggressors.[15] This approach eschews the comprehensive development and production of platforms, but rather aims to develop high technology defence systems that can be integrated into platforms procured from overseas. However, to ensure this technological edge acts as a deterrent, its possession and deployment must be secret. This strategic posture was aptly described by Singapore's former President, S.R. Nathan, when he stated: 'we must develop indigenously … a technological edge … and this must be developed secretly – in strict secrecy – so that nobody knows the kind of defence-related technology and capability that we have developed'.[16] Yet, logically, the possession of a technological edge must be an 'open secret', as to deter potential aggressors they must be aware of the profound defence capability that faces them, albeit that the precise configuration and impact remains unspecified.

Figure 25.1, below, illustrates that the promulgation of an indigenous defence technological edge that emerges through internal interactions of the ecosystem's quadrilateral relations, particularly government-inspired strategic foresight and R&D investment. The defence-industrial ecosystem also comprises external drivers, such as overseas trading partners and collaborators (exposure to competitive pressures) and defence offset (technology infusion), which additionally contribute to the technological 'superiority' goal. A further influence comes from the aforementioned defence policy imperative that places

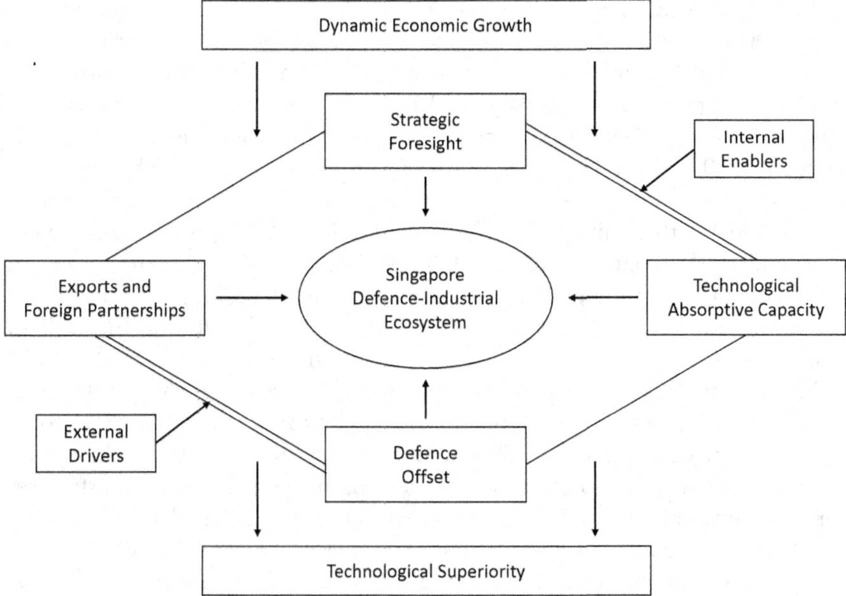

Figure 25.1 Constituent components of Singapore's defence-industrial ecosystem.
Source: authors.

a premium on technology multipliers through organic and overseas procurement of advanced weapons systems as a means of compensating for the restricted supply of military personnel. This search for technological superiority is a characteristic of Singaporean developmental strategy, implemented through the government's interventionist role. It is a process of proactive central planning in which the economy has been nurtured to progress rapidly through successive development stages from agriculture, manufacturing, services and finally knowledge-intensive transformation. The strategy encourages cultivation of incipient high technology industries, such as information, computer, telecommunications, defence and aerospace. The development of these 'strategic' industries has been catalysed through foreign direct investment and technological partnerships. Government policy emphasis has been on access to overseas technology to sustain and generate local skills and innovation. The result of this development strategy has been to secure a civil-military status best described by the metaphor, 'rich nation, strong army'.[17]

4.1 Strategic foresight

The Singapore government has always played a proactive role in identifying and sponsoring the growth and development of 'leading' sectors within the local economy. These may be described as growth poles, industrial pillars, champion industries, or most often 'strategic' industries. Such industries are viewed as powerful development catalysts, because of their important contribution to skilled employment, high sales, enhanced value added, knowledge-intensive output and strong backward industrial linkages. This interventionist development process goes back to the early post-independence era, but accelerated in 1991 by the launch of a Strategic Economic Plan.[18] The Plan highlighted eight strategic thrusts, including human resource development, international partnerships and investment, R&D and the promotion of industrial and technological clusters. Complementing the Strategic Plan was a Science and Technology Plan that invested billions of Singapore dollars into increasing the numbers of researchers and R&D capacity in both the civil and defence sectors. Defence and aerospace were viewed as integrative strategic industries, enjoying technological synergies that straddle the civil-military divide. The Economic Development Board (EDB) acted as the Singaporean equivalent of Japan's post-WWII MITI (Ministry of Trade and Industry) that sought to identify and orchestrate the development of strategic industrial sectors. For example, the EDB developmental model facilitated the creation of an advanced industrial aerospace cluster at the site of an old WWII Seletar airfield. This has attracted huge numbers of local and foreign high technology players, including global companies like General Electric (US), Lockheed Martin (US), Boeing (US), Thales (France), and Rolls-Royce (UK); the latter establishing assembly and testing facilities for its Trent family of aero-engines, creating over 2,000 skilled jobs.[19] EDB's 'visible hand' intervention in fostering the Seletar cluster proved a major instrumental factor in the project's success. Horizon scanning is a further crucial task of the EDB in its role of identifying the future emergence of new and dynamic military and/or civil strategic sectors.

A case in point is the space industry. Singapore was a late entrant into this high technology industry, but was attracted by the obvious high skill and capability spin-offs. Its entry started modestly with a 2003 locally built satellite X-SAT. Since then, Singapore has launched a series of different small satellites ranging from 1kg to 400kg in weight, and notably involving local university students in the R&D process.[20] Presently, the local space industry employs 1,000 people across 30 companies. Its principal sponsor is the EDB, which established an Office for Space Technology and Industry (OSTIn) in 2013. Following the tried and tested approach of harnessing local and foreign expertise, Singapore's space quest has enjoyed some early successes. For example, NTU scientists have developed a new tiny radar camera chip that is 100 times smaller than the current 200kg radar cameras, yet capable of capturing radar images regardless of light or weather conditions; it is touted to be about 20 times cheaper to produce and consumes 75 per cent less power.[21] In January 2018, DSO National Laboratories and NUS jointly launched the Satellite Technology and Research Centre (STAR) to develop distributed satellite systems capabilities, focused on multiple small satellites, each weighing a tenth of conventional satellites, either in formation or constellation. The new centre will also train undergraduates and graduate students to meet the manpower needs of the country's space industry.[22] DSTA and ST Egg have also partnered in early 2018 to acquire a new earth observation satellite, DS-SAR, with a synthetic aperture radar-imaging payload.

4.2 Technology absorptive capacity

The concept of technological absorptive capacity has regard to the spectrum of capabilities in an economy that facilitates local innovation. In the main, this includes possession of highly skilled scientists, engineers and design staffs, knowledge institutions, technology-based universities and specialised institutes, supply chains and R&D capacity. Since independence, Singapore has prioritised investment into human capital, created the development of world class universities, promoted overseas education of its best scholars and sought to nurture the rapid evolution of small medium size enterprises that act to deepen development of innovative supply chains and R&D. Due to its small size, and hence lack of scale opportunities, Singapore has pursued ambitious plans to elevate the role of technology progress, especially on the defence science and technology front. 'Singapore can lead in defence technology, even though we are small,' said Defence Minister Ng in 2017, revealing that the country has a 5,000-strong community of defence engineers and scientists, and has plans to fund a 40 per cent increase in scholarships and awards by 2025.[23] A critical push factor in positioning Singapore as a global player in defence technologies is the Defence Science and Technology Agency (DSTA). The Agency is a statutory board under MINDEF, whose aim is to harness and exploit science and technology to provide technological and engineering support for the defence and national security needs of Singapore. It implements defence technology plans, acquires defence equipment and supplies and develops defence infrastructure for the Ministry. DSTA works closely with DSO National Laboratories. This is Singapore's largest defence R&D organisation, aimed at developing technological solutions to sharpen the cutting edge of Singapore's national security. These R&D establishments operate as part of a technological web of local universities, the Agency for Science, Technology and Research (A*STAR), and other related government agencies, such as the Government Technology Agency of Singapore (GovTech), the Cyber Security Agency of Singapore, the National Research Foundation, and also the EDB.

The Singaporean Government does not disclose annual expenditure on defence R&D. However, in November 2001, the then Deputy Prime Minister and Defence Minister, Dr Tony Tan, revealed that Singapore spends about 4 per cent of its defence budget on long-term R&D endeavours.[24] This relatively high proportion seems about right, given Singapore's priority on the development of frontier defence technologies. The 4 per cent proportion applies to direct defence R&D through MINDEF's leading institutions, and in particular the DSTA and DSO National Laboratories. Additionally, ST Engg invests in R&D, though it is difficult to determine how this is split between the military and civilian sectors, especially given the advanced state of dual-use technologies developed and produced by the company. The ST Electronics CEO and President, Seah Moon Ming, stated in late 2007 that 7 per cent of the company's annual revenue was spent on customer-funded research; for instance, when SAF pays ST Engg to source and develop specific solutions and allows it to use the technology for purposes beyond the original project. Internally, ST Engg allocates about 3 per cent of its annual revenue for R&D, though certain divisions such as electronics spend more. Seah argues that R&D investment is a critical corporate dynamic, and if it falls below 5 per cent, then there is an inability to renew products, systems and capabilities.[25]

A third stream of defence-related R&D funding derives from the Singapore Government R&D allocations to university and polytechnic institutions. Since 2002, the budget supporting collaboration between premier local R&D institutions, such as A*STAR and ST Engg, was S$80mn. Additionally, DSTA established a S$20mn Technology Innovation Fund, extending defence-related R&D funding to small and medium enterprises.[26] More recently, in early 2014, MINDEF collaborated with Nanyang Technological University to establish an Office of Research and Technology in Defence and Security to coordinate the over 120 defence and security projects worth about S$130 million across five university research institutions.[27] ST Engg also collaborates with local universities in fostering R&D that has civilian and military applications. For example, in May 2012, ST Kinetics invested S$3 million in the Singapore Republic Polytechnic to establish the Advanced Composite Engineering Lab (ACEL). This laboratory specialises in composite material science research and production, and is possibly the first in Southeast Asia to specialise in natural fibre studies. The defence-industrial ecosystem also actively promotes overseas collaboration to obtain expertise from foreign research institutions. For example, the Campus for Research Excellence and Technological Enterprise (CREATE) was established at the National University of Singapore (NUS) in 2007 by the National Research Foundation to forge security-related R&D collaboration between local and premier foreign research institutions.[28] In February 2017, the National Cybersecurity R&D Laboratory (NCL) was launched at NUS with the support of the NRF's National Cybersecurity R&D Programme, serving as a test-bed for creative cybersecurity solutions and a one-stop platform providing ready-to-use tools and environments for cybersecurity research and training.

Contemporary R&D programmes reflect pragmatism regarding Singapore's long-term national security perceptions, foreseeable market opportunities and in no small part are driven by Singapore's long-term concern about its military manpower woes. Accordingly, policy emphasis on promoting capability in key niche R&D areas, covers, for instance: 1) emerging technologies including artificial intelligence (AI), robotics, cyber and additive manufacturing (or more commonly known as 3D printing); 2) unmanned systems; and 3) commercial space technologies. Towards the ultimate objective of indigenising R&D programmes, MINDEF initiated a seed grant of S$45 million per annum for DSTA and DSO National Laboratories to undertake AI and robotics R&D.[29] R&D programmes in these niche areas seek to exploit the latent expertise at the six local universities, especially in unmanned systems and related technological innovations, and there have been early successes. For example, NUS researchers have developed an Aerial Unmanned Vehicle – MantaDroid – that looks and swims like a manta ray, using only single motors and flexible fins to propel it through water.[30] NTU has been studying how to develop drones that act as air traffic management systems.[31] Separately, DSTA and ST Engg are collaborating to develop technologies to minimise manning requirements on board the navy's *Independence*-class Littoral Mission Vessels (LMVs). Additionally, DSTA and ST Kinetics unveiled in late 2016 a 10-variant Belrex family of Protected Combat Support Vehicles (PCSVs), tentatively targeted at the export market.[32] Finally, to publicise Singapore's niched capability in the development and production of unmanned aerial, ground and maritime systems, DSO National Laboratories is known to have developed the Meredith 400 autonomous underwater vehicle (AUV) for mine countermeasure operations.

4.3 Exports and foreign partnerships

Singapore is not one of the world's major defence exporters, not least because overseas arms sales have proved something of a balancing act, with the economic benefits derived from such exports often subordinated to the government's diplomatic imperative of maintaining a neutral stance in international affairs, generally, and conflict, specifically. As a result, export performance has been mixed. In the MRO field, Singapore is one of the world's leading providers, especially in aerospace, but across the broader military sectors performance has been less spectacular. Table 25.3 shows some notable patterns. During the Cold War, nearly all exports comprised ST Marine built naval vessels, such as simple coastal patrol and landing craft, along with other miscellaneous fleet auxiliaries; yet, the numbers built were modest. It was only after the Cold War ended that arms exports diversified beyond the naval sphere to include some land systems. This appeared to be at the cost of naval export volumes, even if some limited export successes were achieved in sales of more advanced vessels. For instance, one *Endurance*-class LPD (HTMS *Ang Thong*) was built for Thailand, but the option for a second unit was never exercised due to Bangkok's funding constraints. This was the largest warship ever exported by Singapore. A far smaller export programme was the four-ship *Al-Ofouq* class offshore patrol vessel sale to the Royal Navy of Oman, which was completed in 2016.

Table 25.3 Singapore's major arms exports

Year	*Recipient*	*Weapon*	*Quantity*	*Remarks*
1969	Malaysia	*Duyong*-class diving support tender	1	
1973	The Philippines	*Bataan*-class patrol craft	2	
1976	Brunei Darussalam	*Waspada*-class missile fast attack craft	3	
1978	Kuwait	LC-32m landing craft	3	
1979	Thailand	*Chula*-class fleet tanker	1	
1980	Oman	*Saba Al Bahr*-class landing craft	1	
1982	Oman	*Saba Al Bahr*-class landing craft	2	
	UAE	*Baracuda*-class support ship	1	
1983	Bangladesh	PB-46 patrol craft	2	
1984	Sri Lanka	*Abheetha*-class cargo ship	3	Second-hand
		Mahawele-class support ship	3	Second-hand
1985	Sri Lanka	LC-33m landing craft	2	
1986	India	*Tara Bai*-class patrol craft	6	Including 4 units built in India
	Sri Lanka	*Hansaya*-class transport craft	2	
	UAE	*Al Feyi*-class landing craft	1	
		Baracuda-class support ship	2	
1987	Brazil	*Grajau*-class patrol craft	4	
1988	Sweden	*Smit Manila* cargo ship	1	*Uto*
1990	Sri Lanka	LC-33m landing craft	2	
1993	Kuwait	*Al Tahaddy*-class landing craft	2	
1995	Papua New Guinea	Standard 120mm mortar	3	
1996	Indonesia	FH-88 155mm towed field howitzer	5	Possibly second-hand
	Papua New Guinea	Vosper Type-A/B	3	Second-hand
2000	Sri Lanka	Standard 120mm mortar	9	Second-hand
2002	Indonesia	*Jupiter*-class diving support tender	1	Second-hand
2007	Nigeria	FPB-38 patrol craft	2	From Malaysian production line
	UAE	SRAMS 120mm self-propelled mortar	48	
2008	Thailand	Bronco all-terrain tracked vehicle	10	
	Thailand	*Endurance*-class landing platform, dock	1	
	United Kingdom	Bronco all-terrain tracked vehicle	115	Designated Warthog

(*Continued*)

Table 25.3 (Cont.)

Year	*Recipient*	*Weapon*	*Quantity*	*Remarks*
2011	UAE	SRAMS 120mm self-propelled mortar	72	
2012	Oman	*Fearless 75*-class offshore patrol vessel	4	Project Al-Ofouq
	Unknown	SRAMS 120mm self-propelled mortar	25	
2015	UAE	SRAMS 120mm self-propelled mortar	24	

Source: Stockholm International Peace Research Institute (SIPRI), *Arms Transfers Database*, at: www.sipri.org/databases/armstransfers (accessed on 16 September 2018).

Other recent export successes include a major contract to supply a modified variant of the ST Kinetics' Bronco all-terrain tracked carrier (ATTC), designated Warthog, for the British Army's deployment in Afghanistan. Singapore's 120mm Super Rapid Advanced Mortar System (SRAMS) also found success with the United Arab Emirates, a return customer, ordering 96 units in total. There have also reportedly been unspecified sales, especially of small arms and light weapons (SALWs), to foreign clients. Singapore-made SALWs have seen some modest export successes, mainly to the developing world. But not all such sales have been properly documented, meaning that Singapore's SALW exports could be more than what have been reported thus far. For example, unknown quantities of Singapore-made SALWs, such as the Armbrust infantry light anti-tank and personnel weapons, found their way into the conflict-ridden Balkans in the 1990s.[33] In 1998, Chartered Industries of Singapore reportedly shipped a whole prefabricated arms factory to Myanmar and established, with Israeli consultancy assistance, the military junta-ruled country's SALW development and production capacity.[34] In 2005, Papua New Guinea authorities launched a probe into an illegal consignment of Singapore-built SAR-21 assault rifles along with six 30-round magazines and 500 rounds of 5.56mm SS109 ammunition, which were seized by Air Nuigini security personnel at Jacksons International Airport.[35]

In the late 1990s and early 2000s, Singapore embarked on a quest to carve out new overseas markets through a series of mergers and acquisitions. However, these efforts were characterised by a number of high profile failures to clinch major deals, such as the Bionix IFV bid for the US$7bn Army Interim Armored Vehicle programme. ST Engg also sought to acquire American firms, including ST Marine's 2002 acquisition of VT Halter Marine and the ST Engg 2009 acquisition of US subsidiary, VT Miltope. Such mergers and acquisitions reflect ownership of foreign entities that allow a direct 'in' to the US market. Another form of tie-up with foreign industrial capability is via technology partnerships. Singapore has performed exceedingly well, here, collaborating with other 'small' states, such as Israel, in niched business areas that include military aircraft retrofitting, upgrading and civilian conversion. ST Engg has been awarded open competition contracts to upgrade C-130J heavy lift aircraft belonging to the Turkish and New Zealand air forces. This is a capability that ST Aerospace has developed, even though it does not produce aircraft (with the notable exception of the EC-120 Colibri light helicopter through a joint venture with China and France, enjoying some export success). ST Aerospace has also achieved major successes in the upgrade of legacy fighter jets serving some foreign air forces. For example, it tied up with other foreign firms in 1999 to upgrade Brazilian and Turkish F-5 air force jets. Additionally, ST Aerospace worked with Thai Aviation Industries on the Falcon One cockpit and avionics upgrade programme to modernise part of the Royal Thai Air Force's fleet of F-16A/B Fighting Falcon multirole fighter jets in 2006.

4.4 Defence offset

Beginning in the 1970s, Singapore embarked on the task of constructing a strong and diversified domestic defence-industrial base, and the authorities quickly recognised the contribution that defence offset could make,[36] especially with respect to fostering the creation of capacity and enhancing worker skill sets. MINDEF followed a non-typical offset approach, and instead of designing and publishing a prescriptive policy, allowing overseas defence contractors sight of the regulations, the policy document was only available for internal consumption. This means that the offset authority and the offshore vendor commenced negotiations with a clean sheet of paper on each and every procurement programme. Predictably, the Singaporean bargaining position was always rigorous and demanding, but there would likely be greater opportunities for compromise, dependent upon the scale of procurement. From modest beginnings, Singapore's defence offset investments have grown considerably, and most offset observers would argue that the country now hosts one of the world's most successful offset regimes.

The earliest offset programme occurred in 1970, when Chartered Industries agreed a nine-year deal to license produce 80,000 American M16 assault rifles for the SAF.[37] In the decades since then, Singapore has engaged in far more ambitious offset agreements. For example, the naval programme to build six *Formidable* class stealthy frigates based on the French *La Fayette* design was linked to an offset arrangement that not only allowed Singapore to build five of these warships locally, under licence, but the country's primary defence technology institutions, the Defence Science and Technology Agency (DSTA) and Defence Science Organisation (DSO) National Laboratories, collaborated with their French partners on frontier stealth technology R&D. As would be expected, these 'silver bullet' defence R&D programmes are undertaken in complete secrecy. A further interesting maritime case study on the strategic approach MINDEF planners adopt when acquiring and then absorbing the overseas technologies in the local development of defence capability relates to submarine procurements. Singapore's initial acquisition of submarines were the A12 *Sjöormen* class, all acquired second-hand from the Royal Swedish Navy, mainly to serve as training platforms to support RSN attempts to build an undersea warfare capacity. The boats were refurbished and tropicalised for the local operating environment, and then recommissioned into RSN service as the *Challenger* class. The second batch of submarines acquired from Sweden was a pair of A18 Västergotland class boats, which were larger than the A12s, and built in the 1980s, hence newer. They were refurbished and modernised to the same standards as the Swedish Navy's *Södermanland* class, with an AIP section inserted midships, before being recommissioned as the *Archer* class. ST Engg Marine gained considerable expertise from interactions with Swedish submarine engineers, especially partnering on the integration of modern electronic systems. This progression of learning has enabled Singapore to scale the specialised submarine technology ladder in preparation for the next higher learning stage associated with the more recent acquisition of the navy's customised Type-218SG submarines built by the German shipbuilder TKMS.[38]

5. Future prospects

This chapter has explored and evaluated the principal attributes of Singapore's unique defence-industrial ecosystem. The successful push for defence industrialisation was spurred by strategic vulnerability. The interpretation of national security that highlights the contribution of economic, technological and military components ensured that the high cost of defence and aerospace development was funded by robust economic growth. Moreover, the search for technological security was facilitated by a parallel policy emphasis on promoting synergistic civil-military industrial and technological integration. The government's proactive support of strategic industries sponsored via intensive investment into the creation of deep technological absorptive capacity, especially high level R&D capability, has powered the defence and aerospace sectors into scaling higher technology stages. At the core of this defence-industrial ecosystem is ST Egg, which, through elevated levels of competitiveness and innovation, has catalysed rapid market expansion, and positioned the company at 40th in the world's top 100 defence companies. The development of Singapore's defence-industrial base has also been assisted by infusion of advanced technologies and learning through the process of defence offset. The diffusion and absorption of these offset-related technology transfers have proved effective principally because of the spectrum of diverse technology capabilities permeating Singapore's technology absorptive capacity. The one disappointing component within the quadrilateral defence-industrial ecosystem as conceptualised in this chapter is defence export performance. This will likely see dramatic improvement in future years, as ST Engg belatedly forges an international 'brand'. The company can be expected to pursue a nuanced and niched civil-military focus to capture not only the export of specialised high value upgrades, MRO and conversion programmes but also broader security-related sales of space, aerospace and artificial intelligence systems. There is no logic in tampering with the policy mechanics behind Singapore's defence industrial success, and through continued local and overseas strategic partnerships there is the expectation that the success story will endure. The chapter ends by asking the obvious question as to whether the model is transportable. It is possible, but would require emulation of not just the policy frameworks and institutional structures but also the cultural dynamics.

Notes

1 Ron Matthews and Nellie Zhang Yan, 'Small Country "Total Defence": A Case Study of Singapore', in Stefan Markowski, Peter Hall and Robert Wylie (eds), *Defence Procurement and Industry Policy – A Small Country Perspective, Routledge,* 2010, p. 255; original source: J. Drysdale, *Singapore: Struggle for Success*, North Sydney, George Allen & Unwin, 1984.

2 Bernard Loo, 'From Poisoned Shrimp to Porcupine to Dolphin: Cultural and Geographic Perspectives of the Evolution of Singapore's Strategic Posture,' in Amitav Acharya and Lee Lai To (eds.), *Asia in the New Millennium*: APISA First Congress Proceedings, 27–30 November 2003, Singapore: Marshall Cavendish Academic, 2004, pp. 352–375, and Evan A. Laksmana, 'Threats and Civil-Military Relations: Explaining Singapore's "Trickle Down" Military Innovation', *Journal Of Defense and Security Analysis* 33:4, 2017, p. 354; original source: Bilveer Singh, Arming the Singapore Armed Forces (SAF: Trends and Implications, Canberra: Strategic and Defense Studies Center, ANU, 2003, p. 26.

3 Michael Raska, 'Singapore's Next frontier: In Search of defence Innovation', *RSIS Commentary*, 105, 25 June 2018.

4 See, With Nellie Zhang, 'Small Country Total Defence: The Case of Singapore', *Journal of Defence Studies*, JSCSC, (September 2007).

5 Andrew T. H. Tan, 'Singapore's Defence Industry: Its Development and Prospects', *Security Challenges* 9:1, 2013, p. 80.

6 See, Singapore Defense Industries, www.globalsecurity.org/military/world/singapore/industry-defense.htm. Accessed 28 October 2018.

7 See, Singapore Technologies Engineering Ltd, *Annual Report 2017*, p. 3.

8 ST Engg 2017 Annual Report. www.stengg.com/media/520426/st-engineering-annual-report-engineering-your-future.pdf. Accessed 28 October 2018.

9 Thrina Tham, 'Doing more with less, SAF plans for smart platforms and tech: Dr Ng,' Ministry of Defence, Singapore, 30 June 2018.

10 In March 2017, MINDEF awarded a contract to ST Engineering for the production and supply of Next Generation Armoured Fighting Vehicles to replace the ageing ULTRA M113, with delivery slated to commence in 2019.

11 For an erudite explanation of this concept, see J. Chapman, R. Drifte and I. Gow, *Japan's Quest for Comprehensive Security: Defence, Diplomacy and Dependence,* London: Pinter, 1983.

12 For a discussion on the civilianisation of Singapore Technologies, see Tim Huxley, *Defending the Lion City – The Armed Forces of Singapore*, Allen & Unwin, 2000, p. 191.

13 Sourced from personal correspondence with Robert Karniol (1 November 2018), who supplied his seminal article, 'Industry Briefing: Singapore Defence Ecosystem', *Jane's Defence Weekly*, February 2006. It is also instructive that Quek Tong Boon interpreted the notion of a defence ecosystem as malleable. Citing from Karniol's 2006 article, Quek Tong Boon explained that …

> At the core [of this defence ecosystem] are MINDEF, the SAF, DSTA and DSO, then the two Temasek laboratories, our defence industry and dual-use R&D expertise that we can tap from our tertiary institutions and research institutes. We also consider our international partners and relevant parts of the private sector as integral to our defence *technology* ecosystem.[author emphasis added]

14 Bilveer Singh, Singapore's Defence Industries, Canberra Papers on Strategy and Defence, ANU, 1990, p. 49.
15 Evan A. Laksmana, 'Threats and Civil-Military Relations: Explaining Singapore's "Trickle Down" Military Innovation', *Journal Of Defense and Security Analysis* 33:4, 2017, p. 348.
16 S. R. Nathan, 'Creating the Technology Edge', *Singapore 1972–2003*, Singapore: DSO Laboratories, 2002.
17 See, Richard Samuels, Rich Nation, Strong Army: National Security and the Technological Transformation of Japan, Cornell Studies in Political Economy), May 1996.
18 Ron Matthews, 'Singapore's defence-Industrial "Model"', *Asia-Pacific Defence Reporter,* April/May 1999, p. 22.
19 *Rolls-Royce Commences Construction at Seletar Aerospace Park,* 1 February 2010. www.rolls-royce.com/media/press-releases-archive/yr-2010/100201-construction-seletar-aerospace-park.aspx. Accessed 28 October 2018.
20 An elaborate history and future plans for the development of Singapore's space industry can be found in a commentary penned by Professor Low Kay Soon who works at the National University of Singapore's faculty of engineering and helms the Satellite Technology and Research Centre located on the same campus. Low Kay Soon, 'Commentary: How Singapore can be a space power, with small satellites,' *Channel NewsAsia,* 8 October 2017.
21 'NTU scientists shrink 200kg radar camera technology into a tiny chip,' *Channel NewsAsia,* 22 February 2016.
22 Deyana Goh, 'Singapore's NUS and national defense research agency launch satellite centre,' *Space Tech Asia,* 25 January 2018.
23 *Speech by Minister for Defence Dr Ng Eng Hen at the Committee of Supply Debate 2017 on 3 March 2017,* Ministry of Defence, Singapore, 3 March 2017.
24 This figure does not include separate investments on R&D facilities in Singapore's universities such as Nanyang Technological University and National University of Singapore. See *Keynote Address By Dr Tony Tan Keng Yam, Deputy Prime Minister And Minister For Defence, At The Defence Technology Prize Presentation Ceremony Held On Tuesday, 6 November 2001 At Nanyang Auditorium, NTU,* Singapore Government Press Release, Media Division, Ministry of Information and The Arts.
25 Matthew Phan, 'Designing research at ST Engineering,' *Business Times Singapore,* 5 November 2007.
26 David Boey, 'Sharp rise in contenders for defence science awards,' *Business Times Singapore,* 30 November 2002.
27 Lee Jian Xuan, 'New office to oversee defence projects,' *Straits Times,* 16 January 2014.

28 For example, one of the latest projects mooted in collaboration with foreign institutions is to develop cyber-physical security systems to protect critical infrastructure. Lester Hio, 'New research programmes, governing council set up,' *The New Paper*, 2 December 2017.

29 The fund for DSTA would go towards expansion to include an analytics and AI laboratory aimed at exploiting real-time information derived from the Internet of Things and platforms, with significant application in the realm of maritime security. 'Singapore to invest S$45m a year in new defence tech labs for robotics, AI,' *Channel NewsAsia*, 3 March 2017.

30 Although not the first of its kind, NUS claims it is the first to use single motors for each fin and rely on the interplay of fluid and fin to mimic the animal's biolocomotion. 'Singapore: NUS-developed manta ray robot swims faster and operates up to 10 hours,' *New Vision*, 9 November 2017; 'Singapore researchers' underwater robot inspired by manta ray,' *Reuters News*, 4 December 2017.

31 'Singapore's NTU Developing ATM System for Drones,' *Aviation Week*, 6 February 2018.

32 'New Protected Combat Support Vehicles Enhances the Army's Precision Manoeuvre Capabilities,' Ministry of Defence, Singapore, 25 November 2016.

33 Steve Coll, 'Despite U.N. Embargo, Weapons Flood Into Balkans,' *The Washington Post*, 14 February 1993.

34 'Singapore ships arms factory to Myanmar: report,' *Agence France Presse*, 22 July 1998.

35 'Papua New Guinea police query import of firearms seized at airport,' *BBC Monitoring*, 1 June 2005.

36 Defence offset is best explained as reciprocal investment, whereby the purchasing country government demands economic benefits from the offshore vendor over and above the acquisition of the defence equipment.

37 See, Singapore Defense Industries, www.globalsecurity.org/military/world/singapore/industry-defense.htm. Accessed 28 October 2018.

38 Defence industry representatives declined requests for details of the submarine programme, emphasising the need to adhere strictly to contractual obligations that stipulated non divulgence of information.

26 South Africa and its defence industry

J. Paul Dunne, Guy Lamb and Eftychia Nikolaidou[1]

1. Introduction

South Africa is the second largest economy in Africa (after Nigeria) and one of the most industrialised countries in the African continent, ranked as an upper middle income economy by the World Bank. It is also the second largest military spender in Sub-Saharan Africa, according to the Stockholm International Peace Research Institute (SIPRI). Furthermore, it has the most developed arms industry on the subcontinent, with a range of capabilities and has seen considerable change since the end of the "apartheid"[2] regime that was in place over the period 1948–1994.

In the same way as one cannot understand the Cold War arms industry without understanding the Cold War context it developed from, so the South African defence industry is only understandable knowing the context of its "Apartheid" past. White minority rule was maintained by a high militarization of society and the economy, with partial trade sanctions imposed on South Africa over the period 1986–1991 and the UN arms embargo over the period 1977–1994. With the transition to democracy, the so called "Arms Deal" over the period 1996–1999 in which a supposed necessary upgrade of equipment was made through offset deals with international arms producers had a major impact on the industry and the level of state and corporate corruption (Dunne and Lamb, 2004; Feinstein, 2011). All these mean that the historical context is hugely important when analysing South Africa's defence industry.

This Chapter provides an overview of the evolution of the industry and an analysis of its present form. Section 2 considers the pattern of defence spending, arms exports and imports, through the aforementioned phases, while Section 3 focuses on the evolution of the defence industry, with Sections 4 and 5 considering the present nature of the industry and its performance and behaviour, respectively. Lastly, Section 6 provides some conclusions about the South African defence industry and offers some insights/recommendations about its future.

2. South Africa's military sector

From the 1960s until the beginning of the transition to democracy in 1990, South Africa maintained a high and increasing military burden in support of the apartheid state. The mid-1970s brought important developments to South Africa's defence industry and policy. Specifically, the United Nations arms embargo on South Africa in November 1977 motivated the South African government to move towards the restructuring of the domestic defence industry in order to achieve self-sufficiency in armaments. Armscor, the Armaments Corporation of South Africa was established in 1968 and assumed responsibility for the procurement and production of armaments for the South African Defence Force (SADF).

As Figure 26.1 shows, the military burden (military expenditure as a share of GDP) more than doubled between 1972–1977 (from just below 2.5% of GDP in 1972 to 5.3% of GDP in 1977) mainly because of growing external and internal opposition to apartheid, the independence of Angola and Mozambique in 1974, and the involvement of South Africa in their civil wars. This reflected the purchase of large amounts of imported weapons prior to the imposition of the mandatory UN arms embargo in 1977 and the implementation of a "Total Strategy" to combat the perceived "Total Onslaught" of communist expansionism in Southern Africa. With the growth in demand for weapons and equipment to maintain internal and external security and in anticipation of international sanctions, the apartheid regime invested heavily in the creation of a domestic defence industry. This saw domestic procurement expenditures increase six-fold in current prices in the 1970s (Dunne and Lamb, 2004).

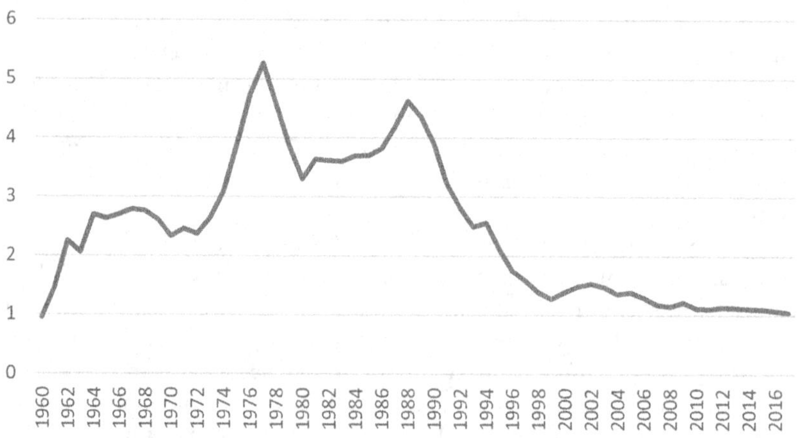

Figure 26.1 Military expenditure as a share of GDP (1960–2017).

Since the early 1980s, Armscor along with the private sector related industries expanded rapidly. Defence budgets allocated for procurement and armaments during the 1980s increased substantially given South Africa's involvement in a number of regional conflicts (i.e. Angola). The military burden continued to be high until 1988 (see Figure 26.1). Since then, there has been a gradual decline reaching 2.5% of GDP in 1994 (the end of Apartheid) with further reductions thereafter. So, the end of the Cold War was accompanied by a reduction in the various tensions and conflicts in many African countries as well as by the end of the apartheid regime in South Africa. These developments led to the resolution of most of the conflicts in the region and also led to reductions in military expenditure in real terms. This was particularly the case for South Africa that had moved to democracy and was facing reduced threats. Furthermore, South Africa withdrew its troops from Angola and Namibia (Batchelor, Dunne and Lamb, 2002).

As Figure 26.2 shows, South Africa's defence budget declined markedly from 1989. It fell by more than 50% in real terms between 1989/90 and 1997/98, with the acquisition budget declining by more than 80% in real terms. This had a dramatic effect on the country's defence-related industry, which downsized and restructured. The public sector was restructured and commercialised, with Armscor split in 1992 into Denel, a new state-owned industrial company and Armscor, which retained responsibility for procurement for the SADF. Since then the industry has had to deal with a trend of slowly declining military expenditure, both as a share of GDP and of central government expenditure, as other claims on resources took precedence (Figures 26.1 and 26.2).

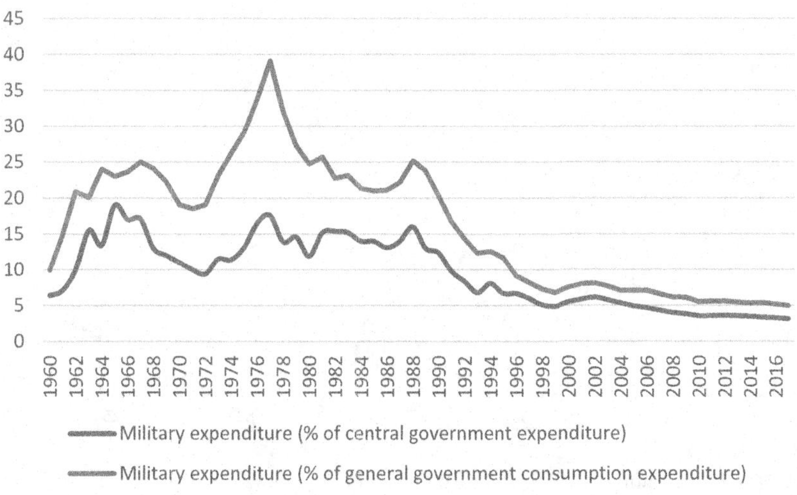

Figure 26.2 Military expenditure as a share of government spending (1960–2017).

Figures 26.3 and 26.4 present the SIPRI trend indicator values for imports and exports for South Africa. These are based upon the known unit production costs of a core set of weapons and are intended to represent the transfer of military resources rather than the financial value.[3] As Figure 26.3 shows, imports declined as the arms embargo became effective. Armscor entered the export market in 1982 and, as Figure 26.4 shows, the value of defence exports has increased substantially since the early 1980s. Defence related industries became some of the largest exporters of manufactured goods in the country.

With the end of Apartheid there was a loosening of restrictions and an increase in exports, though limited by engagement with the so called "Arms Deal". This saw foreign arms companies negotiating deals to provide major equipment orders for the South African National Defence Force (SANDF) with offsets (a form of countertrade). These were finalised in 1999 and have since been the subject of controversy. Defence exports saw a further dramatic increase after 2005, benefitting from the increasing international links achieved by the involvement of major British, French and German international arms companies in the domestic companies (see Figure 26.4).

There was not only an increase in the real value of South African arms exports from 2005 but also a significant increase in the number of countries that imported South African arms and defence-related equipment. That is, the number of export destinations (countries) increased from 50 in 2001 to 96 in 2009, as Figure 26.5 shows. However, the South African industry was highly dependent on a small number of importing states, particularly the US, which accounted for a quarter of the total value of arms exports between

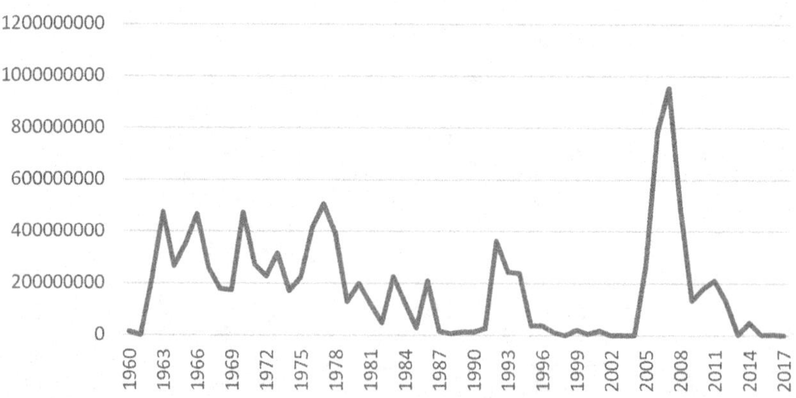

Figure 26.3 Arms imports 1990 US$ (SIPRI trend indicator values).

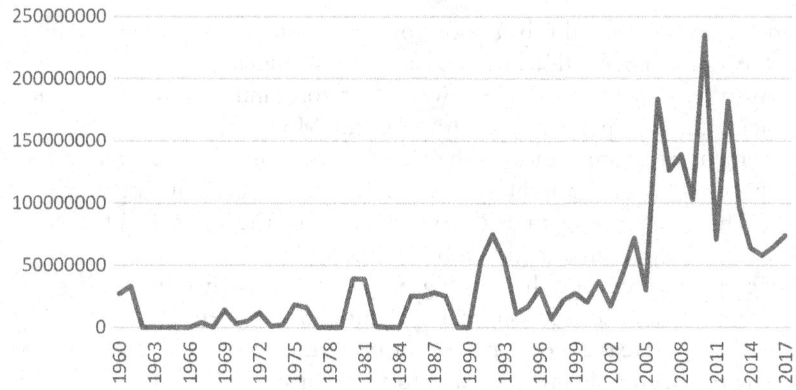

Figure 26.4 Arms exports 1990 US$ (SIPRI trend indicator values).

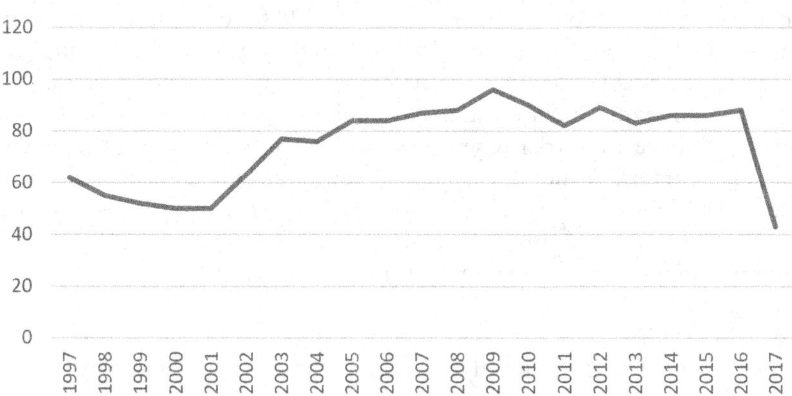

Figure 26.5 Number of export recipients.

1997 and 2017. Such dependence has resulted in considerable year-on-year variations in arns export revenue. Between 2007 and 2012 arms exports to the US accounted for 40% of the value of all South African arms exports but since 2013 onwards arms exports to the US have been insignificant, which is one of the key reasons there was a 41% decrease in the US$ value of South African arms exports between 2012 and 2013. Other major importers of South African arms have been India, Sweden, Germany, the United Arab Emirates and Saudi Arabia. Noticeably there was also an increase in arms imports at the start of this period (see Figure 26.3), so, net foreign income was not that impressive.

3. The evolution of the industry

From the 1960s until the beginning of the transition to democracy in 1990, South Africa maintained a high and increasing military burden in support of the Apartheid state. In 1972 growing external and internal opposition to apartheid, the independence of Angola and Mozambique in 1974, and the involvement of South Africa in their civil wars, led to large increases in military spending, with the military burden peaking in 1977 at just under 5% of GDP. The apartheid regime invested heavily in the creation of a domestic defence industry (Dunne and Lamb, 2004).

Such a large change had a big impact on the manufacturing sector, increasing its dependence on arms production between 1972 and 1979. It also led to the creation of what could be termed a military industrial complex (MIC) centred on the state-owned arms producer and procurer, Armscor, with private firms acting as sub-contractors. As a result of massive state investment, Armscor developed into one of the largest industrial groups in South Africa and by 1981 had assets of R2000 million, a yearly turnover of R1500 million in current prices and more than 25,000 employees. It was also contracting more than 900 companies in the private sector, which employed about 120,000 people. System development capabilities were established, with Armscor setting up operational research and systems engineering facilities and developing the idea of systems suppliers into the defence industrial base. Sophisticated products such as jet fighters, attack helicopters, armoured vehicles, communications systems, guidance systems, mobile artillery pieces, and reconnaissance drones had to be domestically produced or illegally sourced, so industrial policy favoured the arms industry and encouraged import substituting high technology production.

With the UN arms embargo, what had been produced under license became domestically produced independently and the capacity to develop components, undertake repairs and maintenance had to be developed. This led to the establishment of a level of technical sophistication and independence that was unique to arms production in developing countries (Batchelor, Dunne and Lamb, 2002). Resources flooded into the arms and other strategic industries creating growth but, as Batchelor, Dunne and Saal (2000) argue, leading to inefficient allocation of investment and inefficiencies that led to serious economic problems in the 1980s.

Things changed towards the end of Apartheid and between 1989 and 1997, when South Africa's defence expenditure declined by more than 50% in real terms. This started with the withdrawal of South African troops from Angola and Namibia and continued with South Africa's political transition and resulted in the downsizing of the South African military establishment. This had a dramatic effect on the country's defence-related industry, which downsized and restructured and, as we have seen, the public sector was restructured and commercialised, with Armscor split into Denel and Armscor, which retained responsibility for procurement for the SANDF (Batchelor, Dunne and Lamb, 2002).

Armscor's procurement policies, including more transparent and competitive procurement from both local and foreign suppliers, fundamentally altering the "cosy" relationship that was evident between the public and private sector industry during the Apartheid era. The African National Congress (ANC) led government's commitment to black economic empowerment from 1994. This resulted in a number of empowerment deals and equity partnerships between the (largely white) private sector defence companies.

South Africa's re-admittance into the international community and the lifting of the United Nations mandatory arms embargo in May 1994, allowed South Africa to legitimately purchase armaments from foreign suppliers for the first time since 1977. The decline in domestic procurement expenditure and the shrinking international market, led to considerable downsizing within both the public and the private sector, with the share of imports in total procurement spending remaining relatively constant.

In response to this decline in demand, the local defence firms pursued a number of supply-side adjustment strategies. Denel and the three largest private sector defence groups (Reunert, Grintek and Altech) experienced financial problems, but all reduced their dependence on their defence business to less than 20% of turnover and offset the declines in domestic defence with significant increases in non-defence work and export orders.

This downsizing and restructuring of the local defence industry took place in something of a policy vacuum, with the government adopting a "hands-off" approach to defence industrial adjustment as military spending declined. This changed in 1996 with the "Defence Review", a national review of South Africa's defence needs and capabilities. This set out four options for a force design for the SANDF. The option that emphasised reduced manpower and increased capital intensity was approved by Cabinet and Parliament in April 1998. This option recognised that there was no short or medium term military threat to South Africa, and that the defence budget would remain restricted for an extensive period of time. However, this option did envisage the acquisition of a wide range of major defence equipment for the SANDF due to aging equipment, but these purchases would require both Cabinet and Parliamentary approval. This subsequently laid the groundwork for what was to become known as the Strategic Defence Package (SDP) in September 1999, a R29.9 billion arms acquisition programme.[4]

To justify its decision to purchase arms from foreign suppliers and to win public support for the deal, the South African government stressed the potential positive effects of sellers' proposed industrial participation offers (offsets) on investment, job creation, and growth in South African defence related industry and the national economy at large. At the time of approving the program, the South African government indicated that foreign suppliers had made offset offers worth an extraordinary R104 billion, more than three times the value of the arms deal itself. This would result in the creation of more than 65,000 jobs over a period of 7 years. Since then the deal has been mired in controversy and has seen considerable debate and public scrutiny, to an extent unrivalled in any other country (Dunne and Lamb, 2003; Feinstein, 2011).

Leaving aside the issue of whether the expenditure on arms was necessary at all on security grounds, the choice of imports with offsets was risky. At the time, the purported economic benefits of offsets had been questioned and the little empirical evidence that was available already suggested that offsets tend to have a much smaller impact on the local economy than is usually promised (Brauer and Dunne, 2005). It was difficult to judge whether arms prices are reasonable since there are no standardised goods and fixed prices in the defence market. It was also unclear whether the work attached to offsets was genuine new work and whether it would be sustainable once the term of the arms deal expired. It is also worth noting that the offsets were skewed in favour of riskier civilian offsets and as was recognised in the August 1999 Affordability Report, civilian offsets were considered considerably more risky than direct defence offsets. Thus, there were considerable doubts about the benefits and concerns at the political costs (Dunne and Lamb, 2005; Feinstein, 2011; Holden, 2008; Sylvester and Seegers, 2008).

In 1999 the successful bidders were announced, with defence contractors in Britain, Sweden, Italy and Germany being selected. It was publicised that the total deal would cost R30 billion (in 1999 prices). Allegations of corruption, fraud and misconduct surfaced shortly thereafter, implicating both South African and foreign defence contractors (and their representatives). Given these allegations, investigations into the South African arms deal were pursued in Britain, Germany, South Africa and Sweden. The investigation by the United Kingdom's Serious Fraud Office into the actions of British Aerospace (BAE) Systems was arguably the most revealing in terms of the problematic role arms brokers had played in securing the contract for BAE. BAE, along with Saab (Sweden) had been awarded a tender to supply the South African Air Force with jet trainers and combat aircraft. This investigation revealed the existence of a group of arms brokers, who had allegedly been clandestinely contracted through front companies by BAE Systems to lobby the South African government on BAE's behalf.[5] Red Diamond Trading Ltd, established by BAE Systems in the British Virgin Isles in 1998 was allegedly one such company. Investigators have stated that there were reasonable grounds to allege that these brokers paid bribes and engaged in other corrupt activities to obtain significant advantage over their competitors in the tendering process.[6] In addition, it was suspected that the decision to award the tender to BAE/Saab was primarily the result of a deliberate intervention by the Minister of Defence (Joe Modise) at the time.[7]

In Sweden, Saab admitted that a payment of R24 million had been made through its South African subsidiary, SANIP, which they stated was by then under the control of BAE Systems, which was ultimately responsible for the payments.[8] In addition, a senior Swedish trade unionist was implicated in facilitating the payment of funds to an influential South African trade union, the National Union of Metalworkers of South Africa (which was aligned to the ANC).[9] In Germany, an audit of Ferrostaal (which was awarded the contract to supply the South African navy with submarines) conducted by a US law firm, Debevoise and Plimpton revealed that over R300 million in "questionable" payments was paid in relation to the South African submarine deal.[10] High ranking politicians in South Africa were implicated in receiving bribes, including former President Jacob Zuma. The controversy led to the establishment of the Seriti Commission in 2011. Nonetheless, the work of the Commission was dogged by controversy and its findings did not implicate ex-President Zuma in any wrongdoing. The work of the Commission has been widely criticised and is regarded by anti-corruption activists and commentators as a sham.[11]

Various investigations and legal challenges, by for example, Parliament and the Auditor-General, further exposed the problematic role of arms brokers.[12] Investigations and numerous media reports pointed to a host of other arms brokering individuals and entities allegedly involved in bribery (Feinstein, 2011).

Denel continued to dominate the domestic defence market, averaging 48% of the domestic market between 1992 and 2000, significantly lower than in the 1980s, when the former Armscor subsidiary companies (now part of Denel) accounted for nearly 70% of the domestic market. Denel also continued to dominate most of the seven major sectors of the domestic defence market, particularly aerospace, ammunition (small, medium and large calibre), weapons systems (including infantry weapons, cannons, artillery systems and missiles) and military vehicles (Dunne, 2006).

The other major sectors of the domestic defence market, namely electronics, maritime and support equipment were dominated by the three largest private sector defence firms, namely Reunert, Altech (now merged with ADS) and Grintek. In 1996, these three private companies accounted for over 80% of the private sector's share of the domestic defence market. Since the early 1990s these three firms have acquired many small and medium sized private defence firms in an attempt to consolidate their positions in the domestic market. These firms, like Denel, have also attempted to vertically integrate, by outsourcing far less of their defence business than in the past. Denel also dominated many of the sub-sectors of the domestic defence market such as information technology and testing.

The process of vertical integration had a negative impact on the hundreds of smaller defence firms, particularly those that acted as suppliers and subcontractors for the larger defence firms. Many small and medium sized private defence firms exited the defence market, merged with, or were acquired by, larger defence firms (e.g. Reunert acquired the armoured car division of TFM in early 1997). As a result, the domestic defence market (excluding imports) became increasingly concentrated. In 2000, Altech's defence interests were taken over by the black economic empowerment grouping African Defence Systems (ADS). ADS in turn became a subsidiary of French-based conglomerate Thomson CSF, which was renamed Thales in 2001.

Denel has, however, had a rather poor financial performance since its establishment in 1992. Over the period 1992–1996 its turnover declined by an average of nearly 6% per annum in real terms, while the three largest private sector companies, Reunert, Altech and Grintek, witnessed increases in real turnover during the same period. The late 1990's was more mixed, with the companies restructuring internally, and Reunert showing a decline in turnover (ADS's turnover, as a subsidiary of Thales, is now incorporated into the parent company's financial reports). Denel's total employment declined by nearly 9% between 1992 and 2000 from 15,572 to 11,090. The group has continued to shed jobs and employed around 10,000 in 2005 and almost half of that by 2017. This has been a major concern, given the high unemployment levels in South Africa.

The larger private sector firms performed well in the early and mid-2000s – a reflection in part of the impact of the defence offset programme. Reunert and Grintek yielded particularly impressive financial results for 2003 and 2004. During the second half of 2005, Saab took a majority stake in Grintek.

Clearly, the changes in the defence market reflected to some degree the changes taking place internationally, but there are also noticeable differences. As we have seen the end of apartheid led to substantial changes in the sector but also left it with a legacy of a large public sector producer and a strong grouping of private sector firms. Efforts from 1998 to restructure and privatise Denel came to be closely bound up with the arms procurement package (SDP) and the associated industrial participation programme, and the decision to find a large international defence company to take a strategic equity partnership in Denel. BAE Systems and Denel signed a memorandum of understanding in 1998 and in 2000, Cabinet approved BAE Systems as the preferred strategic equity partner for the Denel Aerospace and Ordnance Groups. It was hoped that the finalization of a strategic equity partnership with BAE Systems could be achieved by March 2001, but for various reasons the deal was not struck, leaving the two organizations in a formal and comprehensive but weakened partnership, with some degree of buy-in from BAE Systems, but without substantive equity and management participation. Within Denel Aerospace, Snecma/Turbomeca was approved as the strategic equity partner at division level for the business unit Airmotive. Similarly, within Denel Ordnance, the UK pyrotechnic manufacturer Pains Wessex Defence was confirmed as strategic equity partner for the Swartklip division (Dunne, 2003).

In 2006 the creation of Denel-Saab Aerospace was widely vaunted as being the great "pay-off" of the SDP. In return for \$1bn in (civilian) offset credits upfront, Saab agreed to take a stake in Denel Aerospace, integrate it into their supply lines and transform management. The project totally failed (Saab were still awarded their credits) and the management reverted back to Denel's control. It would appear that Saab agreed to get involved with Denel

Aerospace to get a huge whack of offset credits, but as these credits were not tied to any form of economic performance, little effort or investment was put into the new entity, and it exited after a number of disappointing years[13].

Up to the mid-2000s the level of revenue and assets increased little, if at all, in current prices and as Figure 26.6 shows they declined in real terms (adjusting for the CPI). Since 2011 they have increased, but in real terms are still lower than in 1997.

Figure 26.6 also shows that Denel was, not surprisingly, a loss-making enterprise for most of the period, reporting losses from 1998 to 2011, apart from 2001 when a small profit was reported. There was also a trend of increasing losses which bottomed out in 2006. It also had low revenue and was operating with ageing assets. One response in the early 2000s was to return to concentrating on the Group's perceived traditional strengths, although this is not without its contradictions, and to downsize in areas such as small arms. The Commercial and IT group were split off from Denel Aerospace and Denel Ordnance in 2001 and emerged as a separate entity. Denel's new business model positioned the company as a lead systems integrator in the domestic market and a domestic supplier and exporter of niche subsystems and components. The Group was consolidated into three manufacturing clusters or industrial parks as part of this strategy, namely, Denel Aerospace, Denel Land Systems, and Denel Commercial (Denel Reports, various).

With declining SA arms expenditures, Denel aimed to transform into a horizontally integrated global integrated supplier, rather than a vertically integrated local SANDF supplier and focussed on reducing costs (Denel, various, Annual Report, 2013). It saw the continuing problems as low revenue and was operating with ageing assets and continuing government subsidies. Various strategic, cost saving and restructuring initiatives from the mid-2000s led to positive

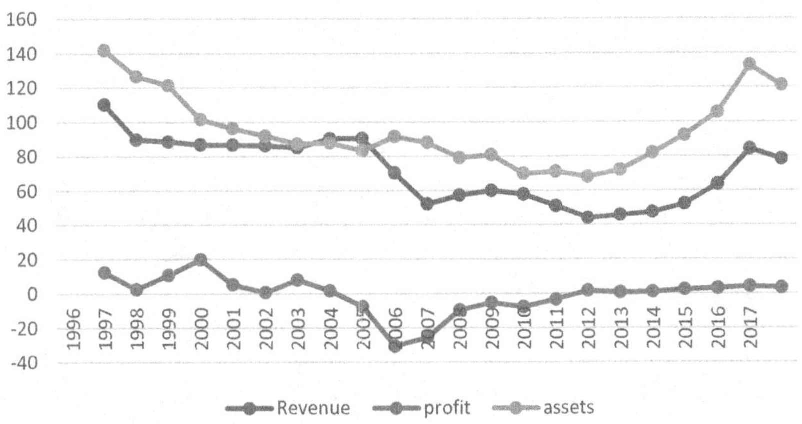

Figure 26.6 Denel's performance.

profits from 2011, but limited cash generation. Further, as noted in a report on the performance of state-owned enterprises in 2005, the Department of Public Enterprises, expressed concern that Denel's efforts to boost revenue through a focus on the export market had "resulted in an unfocused conglomerate" and there was "a lack of a clear strategy for global supply chain integration" (Department of Public Enterprises, 2005: 26). This remains a problem for the company, restricting investment in R&D and working capital and making it still dependent on government bail outs. For the 2017/18 financial year Denel reported a R1.7 billion loss, and was having difficulty paying staff salaries and fulfilling approximately R18 billion of outstanding orders (Reuters, 2018). In this regard, the South African government announced in October 2018 that it will provide a R3.43 billion guarantee to assist Denel with necessary restructuring and help towards its existing financial difficulties (Defence Web, 2018a).

It is also clear from Figure 26.8 that the move back to profitability has been linked to the growth of exports as a share of revenue and this raises a number of issues, with dependence on a number of countries and the tensions between the need to export and the existing arms export control regulations. Recently, the decline in exports to the USA, the growing importance of the Middle East which is increasingly controversial and the drop in the number of recipients does not suggest that prospects are good for future exports.

In terms of the industrial sectors, the market-driven processes of downsizing and restructuring led to a loss of capabilities, including skilled human resources. South Africa's maritime and naval shipbuilding industry, which is concentrated in Durban and Cape Town, downsized quite dramatically, with the attendant loss of valuable capabilities and skills. The country's only naval

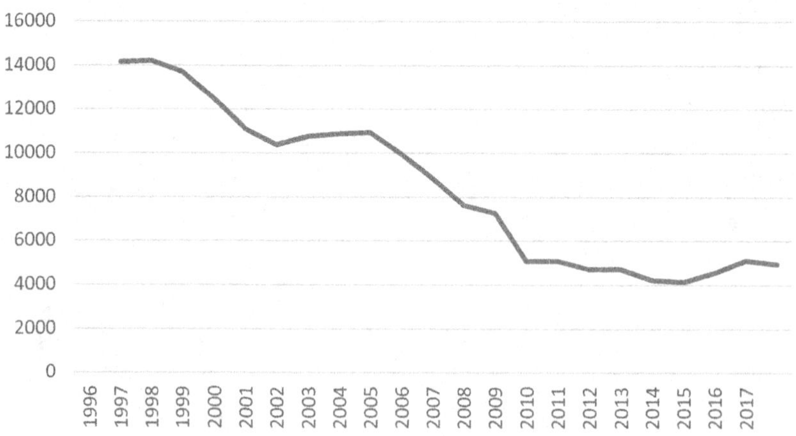

Figure 26.7 Denel employment.

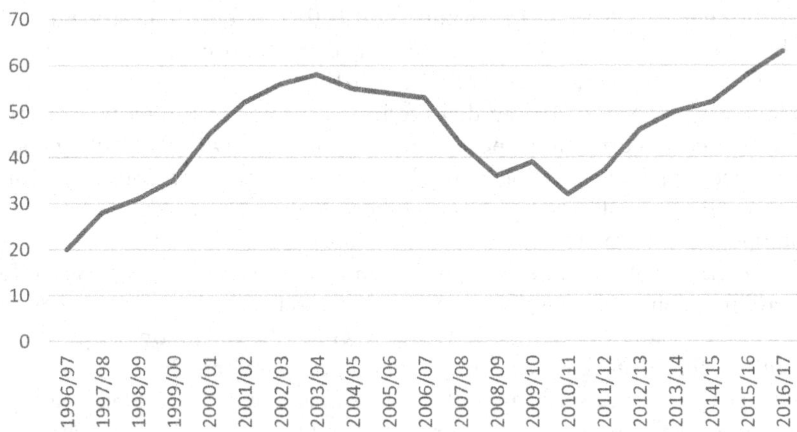

Figure 26.8 Denel exports share (% of turnover).

shipyard, Dorbyl Marine, closed down in the early 1990s because of poor trading conditions. The industry thus lacks the capacity to design and manufacture major naval ships including submarines, although a few companies have the capacity to design and manufacture small harbour patrol boats. However, the local maritime industry has a limited capacity in naval electronics (including shipborne radar systems), systems integration (combat suites), ammunition (including naval bombs and mines), research and development and ship repair and maintenance. Batchelor and Dunne (2000) suggested that this sector was not particularly well placed to benefit from the Navy's acquisition programmes without significant investments to upgrade and expand its existing capabilities. Some of these predictions have become reality.

In contrast, South Africa's aerospace industry, which is concentrated in a few companies in Gauteng, had a relatively well-developed capacity to design and manufacture missiles, aerospace engines and fixed and rotary wing military aircraft. The industry also had significant capabilities in electronics (including radar), avionics, systems integration, weapons systems, and ammunition. Again, Batchelor and Dunne's assertion that aerospace was well placed to benefit from the Arms Deal programmes has proved accurate.

The South African government remains committed to supporting the defence industry. In this regard, the 2015 Defence Review, stated that: "South Africa requires an effective defence capability, which includes, as an integral element, a defence industry to support sovereign capabilities and maintain an essential level of strategic independence" (Department of Defence, 2015:15–2). This, according to the Defence Review document, will include concerted assistance with the marketing of South African defence-related products and in gaining access to potentially profitable markets abroad (Department of Defence, 2015: 7–6). In this regard, the Defence Industry Fund was established in July 2018 to support small and medium enterprises to become more globally competitive (DefenceWeb, 2018b).

However, the South African defence industry remains tainted by allegations and evidence of corruption, mostly the result of the SDP offset arrangements. More recently, Denel has been implicated in the issue of "State Capture", which were allegedly corrupt dealings between former President Zuma and a number of associates, particularly the Gupta family, to illegally access and derive considerable income from state contracts[14]. Denel has lost two CEOs and a Chairman in the last few years over the setting up of a unit in Asia in cooperation with VR Laser Services, a Gupta owned company that has recently been declared bankrupt. These developments led to discussions within government, especially within the Parliamentary Joint Standing Committee on Defence, for the governance of Denel to be shifted from the Department of Public Enterprises to the Department of Defence (Parliamentary Monitoring Group, 2018).

4. Defence industrial structure at present

In the 2017 Denel Annual Report, the company reported progress in the consolidation of aerospace entities, maintenance of traditional areas in artillery, motorised infantry, munitions and precision guided weapons and the extension of capabilities, mainly into cybersecurity, command and control. The Denel aviation business was consolidated at the Kempton Park campus and Denel Aeronautics continued commitments to the Airbus A400M programme and is acquiring Turbomeca Africa to provide helicopter engine parts capabilities. There are also discussions with the DoD on upgrading of the Rooivalk attack helicopter (see Appendix). More than 60% of revenue was coming from exports and new collaboration with one of China's state owned defence firms in the local maritime sector. Denel Maritime also took over the management of the SA naval dockyards. This is an impressive range of capabilities, though considerably more limited than its earlier incarnation.

As Table 26.1 shows, Denel retains a relatively large number of divisions and they vary markedly in their dependence on export revenues, ranging from 99% of total revenue for LMT, which works on Airbus contracts, to 27% in Pretoria Metal Pressings. It also has large holdings, but less than 50% ownership, in 5 associated companies, including Rheinmetall Denel Munition, a joint venture with the German group and it is about to make full acquisition of Turbomeca Africa.

Denel remains the major player in the South African arms industry. It is supported by the state and has no local competition for its main products. The decline in procurement expenditure and the willingness to import has

Table 26.1 Denel structure 2017

	Employment	*Revenue**	*Exports (%)*
Denel Aerostructures	440	553	97
Denel Aviation	605	1092	33
Denel Dynamics	803	1627	62
Denel Land Systems	761	2675	73
Denel Vehicle System	654	1171	74
LMT Holdings SOC Ltd	204	152	99
Denel Overberg	158	137	31
Pretoria Metal Pressings	1093	583	27

Source: Denel Integrated Report 2016/17.
Note: *million rand, current prices.

led to an increasing importance of exports and a number of the private companies are really parts of large company international supply chains. Much of the industry is focused and it has become less of a burden on the State and focussed on niche markets.

A good indication of the nature of the defence industry is given by the membership of the Defence Manufacturers Association (AMD). This was created at the end of Apartheid and the break up of Armscor to operate as a lobby for the constituent parts of the industry. The membership consists of a range of relatively small companies in niche markets, often providing support, parts and components; foreign company subsidiaries; foreign company joint ventures; and companies associated with local firms. They range across a number of industrial sectors, including aerospace, marine, vehicles, engineering, clothing, logistics and consultancy services. Those with international linkages are usually part of international supply chains. Table 26.2 provides a full list of the companies that are claimed as members in 2018.

There are no systematic data about the changing size of the defence industry readily available, but figures presented in a recent defence industry strategy document give a snapshot. This suggests that using 2017 rand prices SANDF acquisition from the South African defence industry dropped from R26.2 billion in 1989/90 to R7 billion in 2017, Research and Development funding declined from R6.1 billion in 1989/90 to R850 million in 2017 and defence industry turnover has dropped from R31.6 billion in 1989/90 to R19 billion in 2016. Employment dropped from around 130,000 employees in 3,000 companies in 1990 (9% of manufacturing employment and 10% of manufacturing companies), to around 15,000 employees in 120 companies. This represents a considerable contraction in the sector and is argued to represent loss of both breadth and depth of capabilities, although the core capabilities are considered to remain intact.[15]

Table 26.2 Defence Manufacturers Association (AMD) companies 2018

Company name	*Specialism*
AMT: Advanced Maritime Transports:	Transport, logistics
Aerosud Aviation:	Aircraft maintenance repair parts emp 800
Hensoldt: Airbus DS Optronics	German: protection/surveillance emp 4000
Aselsan SA	Turkish: radio electronics. emp 5335
Aurecon SA	Engineering consulting emp 7500
Aztec Electronics	Power systems
BPL: Bidvest Panalpina	Logistics/supply chain
Bohlabela Ltd	Wheels
CCII Systems:	Naval systems
Cernofon CC	Technical advice offsets?
Compliance and Security	Advisory services
CSIR Defence Peace Safety	R&D
Cybicom Atlas Defence:	Naval systems
Damens Shipyards Cape	Shipbuilding and repairs
DCD Protected Mobility:	Armoured vehicles -mine detector
Denel SOC	Denel group emp 4941
Desert Wolf Consulting:	Engineering, projects
Emanzi Engineering	Consulting engineers
ETION (was Ansys)	Digital technologies
F&R Catai Transport	Transport solutions
Floida Engineering	Aerospace & defence; radar comms
FMM and TGT Construction	Recycling, construction
GEW Technologies:	Intelligence and security equip
Icarus Marine	Hydrofoil boats/patrol/interceptor
ILC Lerumo	Engineering support
Imperial Armour	Personal protection accessories
Integrated Convoy	Armoured personnel carriers RIVA
Intertechnic Contracting	Support services artillery
Katlego Global	Logistics
Lorris Duncker Consultancy	Arms control consultant/offsets
M-Tek	Electromechanical components subsystems
Megaray	Optical and Thermal. US
Milkor:	Multiple grenade launcher
MTU South Africa	Diesel engines
Natcom Group: Electronic Systems	Electronics (in business rescue 2014?)
Nautic South Africa	Shipbuilding support
North Park Group	Radar electronic warfare technology

(*Continued*)

Table 26.2 (Cont.)

Company name	*Specialism*
Offsets and Consulting	NIP and DIP advice
Optronics Africa CC	Import and export technology support
Osprea Logistics SA	Peacekeeping operations support
OTT Solutions	Support services?
OTT Technologies	Armoured and mine protection vehicles
Chute Systems	Parachutes
Paramount Group	Naval systems
Pearl Coral 1173 T/A TFASA	Security consultants
PGSI Group	BEEE investment
Protoclea Advanced:	Image engineering/surveillance
Reployable Camp Systems	Camp systems
Reutech:	Radar, comms, electronics
RGC Engineering	Precision engineering
Rheinmetal Denel:	Ammunition
Rippel Effect Systems	Grenade launchers
S Plane Automation	Control aerospace/unmanned
Saab South Africa	Electronics
Siemens	Engineering electronics
Southern African Shipyards	Shipbuilding, repair, maintenance
Tau Aerospace	Part of Safomar BEE aerospace
Tellumat Defence	Electronic systems
Thales South Africa Systems	Electronics/Engineering Frigate combat management, emp 160
TMI Dynamatics	Aerospace design and integration
Truvelo Manufacturers:	Weapons and Ammunition
Twiga Services and Logistics	Military vehicles
Vepac Electronics	Power supplies
Vliegmasjien	AUV plane
VR Laser Services	July 2018 went bust -Gupta owned, linked with Denel
ZD Investments T/A ZD Utilities	Engineering systems
Zebra Sun	Body armour

Source of information: members list on www.amd.org.za and individual company web sites.
Note: emp is employment.

5. Industry conduct

As we have seen, the industry started operating in the Apartheid state beset by arms embargoes. It then acted as the client for the government, with Armscor as the procurer and producer and a small number of private companies. It developed into a large industry with a level of sophistication unknown for a developing country, but at considerable economic cost. Its structure was that of a monopoly state owned supplier with some private sector procurement and little competition.

Changes occurred with the end of Apartheid leading to a decline in demand and a more hands off approach from the government, aside from splitting Armscor into separate procurement executive and producer (Denel). The existence of such technical skills at relatively low cost made South Africa of interest to the Western defence companies that were at the time internationalising their supply chains. So, companies downsized and developed links with foreign companies.

The major changes in the defence industry occurred from the early 2000s with the government's decision to procure weapons systems for the SANDF from foreign suppliers. This made explicit an already implicit government view that the maintenance of a general capability in military production was not feasible. Once this decision was made, a considerable amount of effort was put into attempts to obtain as much as possible from the potential supplier, both in the form of defence-related industrial participation, to maintain the competitive parts of the industry, and non-defence products. A major justification for the packages became the economic benefits through these offset deals.

The defence industrial participation (DIP) components, provided something of a lifeline to the South African defence industry, while at the same time undercutting any remaining aspirations for South Africa to maintain its own defence industrial base (Dunne and Haines, 2006). The initial response from the defence industry was generally favourable and they started to develop links with the foreign suppliers.

In the early stages of the implementation of the SDP, Batchelor and Dunne (2000) raised concerns about the capability of the local industry to benefit from the deals. They suggested that while the aerospace sector seemed best placed to benefit and to prove themselves attractive to foreign companies, the electronics sector might have a harder time and the maritime sector was likely to struggle. This seems to have been borne out (Dunne and Lamb, 2004). Certainly, it was the DIP side of the offsets that showed most success with the non-defence industrial participation (NIP) scheme tending to disappoint. Denel and some of the private companies were drawn further into the international networks of defence production through both direct and indirect DIP projects, but not much was seen of technology transfer or use of improved indigenous technology. Certain DIP contracts were of a nature that has obliged contractors to rethink their niche business and their form (e.g. Eloptro and Tellumat).

Most of the investment involved equity purchases, rather than fixed investment in plant and capital. These equity investments were linked to the arms purchases from countries such as Germany, Italy, Sweden and Britain, but also partly to larger initiatives by European governments to promote increased trade between South Africa and themselves. An increasing participation of European defence groupings and investors in the South African industry, at prime contractor and sub-contractor levels was part of the already ongoing restructuring and expansion plans of international defence groups, such as EADS, Thales and BAE Systems. This gave local companies opportunities to develop niches in the international market through their links with the foreign companies. Within the private sector, the SDP tended to favour the larger defence firms and in the end led to their takeover. There were a number of joint ventures between European and South African defence firms, allowing South African defence firms to become part of these European companies' global supply chains. Together with reduced domestic procurement, the defence sector shrank with attrition especially noticeable for the smaller firms.

Denel has also established joint ventures in the Middle East. In the UAE, it established a joint venture with the International Golden Group (IGG) in 2006, titled Denel Asia, which focused on the production and marketing of artillery and aerospace systems. In Saudi Arabia, Rheinmetall Denel Munition, which is joint venture with Rheinmetall Waffe Munition GmbH (Germany) of which Denel holds a 49% stake, built an ammunition manufacturing facility in partnership with the Saudi Military Industries Corporation in 2016[16]. Private sector defence companies have also established joint ventures with business entities in the Middle East, such as the partnerships established between the Paramount Group and IGG (in the UAE); and between the Paramount Group and the King Abdullah II Design Development Bureau and Jordan Manufacturing Services Solutions. There was also some evidence of a significant impact on South Africa's defence exports. Some European governments have been "prompted" to purchase South African defence products instead of their own products, despite criticism from their domestic defence industries. Some of the preferred European suppliers linked with South African defence firms in bids for foreign defence contracts[17].

In recent years the ailing Denel has attained profitability, but survives only with government support and is increasingly dependent on non-competitive contracts and exports through the linkages it has created. The only real competition is the willingness to buy foreign and this is limited by the desire to maintain Denel. The larger private companies are no longer purely local and a number of foreign companies have an important presence, though there are some newer local players, such as the Paramount Group. It is an impressively sophisticated industry for a country at South Africa's level of development, but it is in no way a comprehensive defence industrial base. It does however retain capabilities in most large weapon system technologies to allow SA to be an intelligent customer. A major problem is the dynamic between the internationalisation, growth of exports and impressive arms export controls that SA established. Despite the marked downsizing and restructuring, the SA defence-related industry remains highly capital, skill, import and research intensive, with relatively limited linkages to the civilian economy.

6. Concluding remarks

The South African defence industry has undergone considerable restructuring, reflecting to some degree the changes in the international environment. Military spending as a share of GDP declined markedly from 1989 to 1998 and although steadying it remains on a declining trend. The industry has certainly declined and changed considerably since the end of Apartheid and did see some benefits from the SDE offset deals, though at questionable cost. The Arms Deal has now been seen as fundamentally corrupt and has been corrupting to the young democracy. There has been an increasing involvement of foreign defence companies with SA companies becoming part of international supply chains, with state owned Denel, the only large comprehensive systems integrator in decline and struggling. Denel has also recently been mired in the state capture scandals. The declining domestic procurement has led to pressures to exports that have now led to problems and pressures on arms export control regulations.

What is left is an arms industry that is a shadow of its previous self but impressive for a country at the level of South Africa's development. It has companies that are internationally engaged with major contractors and act as suppliers in niche markets. Nevertheless, the defence industry represents a relatively small share of manufacturing output around half of which is Denel, which, while in profit, has serious liquidity problems. This puts pressure on the government to provide contracts to Denel, rather than to seek competitive bids, with the only potential competition usually coming from foreign contractors. Given the problems with the public sector resulting from state capture, relatively low economic growth, and the extremely high unemployment rate, the Government is unlikely to remove support from Denel anytime soon.

Appendix

Rooivalk

South African began the development of an attack helicopter, the Rooivalk in 1984. But it was still under development when the war in Angola ended in 1988 and the defence budget cuts started. Budget cuts inflicted further on the programme, and the planned acquisition was cut from 36 to only 12. This deprived the programme of the benefits of economies of scale.

The first prototype made its maiden flight only in 1990.But the delays meant it was obsolete aircraft when it finally began to be delivered to the SAAF in 1998. As a flying machine it is lauded, but its avionics system is outdated.

Only 12 production standard aircraft have been manufactured, all for the South African Air Force (SAAF) and no export orders have been won. This results from the fact that it is relatively expensive, given the lack of economies of scale; foreign worries about future support and the long-term viability of Denel; the fact that the Rooivalk is very heavily dependent on French technology, now owned by Eurocopter. Denel tried to get exports without Eurocopter's agreement and support, and potential customers were warned that they could not be guaranteed the support they would need for the engines and dynamics. This effectively killed off any remaining interest in the Rooivalk. Any recent interest has tended to come from countries that South Africa does not export to, based on its ethical arms trade policy[18].

Notes

1 We are grateful to Anthony Black, Keith Hartley and Paul Holden for comments, but the usual disclaimer applies.
2 Apartheid was the political and social system under white minority rule based on racial segregation.
3 See www.sipri.org/databases/armstransfers/background
4 In fact the approval of the Defence Review in 1998 was not an approval of the SDP, as it explicitly stated that every procurement would need Parliamentary approval. This was neither sought nor given and the SDP was merely presented to the house in December 1999.
5 Stefaans Brümmer and Sam Sole, How arms "bribes" were paid, *Mail and Guardian*, 5 December 2008, 2–3.
6 Indeed, it was through Red Diamond Trading that payments were made to middlemen and agents in South Africa, including the special advisor to Joe Modise. In total, the SFO tracked £115m that was transferred to agents on the deal through overt and covert (Red Diamond) avenues.
7 William John Downer, Founding affidavit, In the High Court of South Africa (North Gauteng High Court, Pretoria) in the matter between the National Director of Public Prosecutions (applicant) and Fana Hlongwane (respondent) for an ex parte order in terms of section 38(1) of the Prevention of Organised Crime Act 121 of 1998, Cape Town, 2 March 2010.
8 See "Saab completes internal investigation regarding consultant contract in South Africa", Saab Press Statement, 16 June 2011, https://saabgroup.com/media/news-press/news/2011-06/saab-completes-internal-investigation-regardingconsultant-contract-in-south-africa/and Saab admits R24-million bribe paid to clinch arms deal, Mail and Guardian, 16 June 2011.
9 Tabelo Timse et al., Swedish TV reveals fresh claims in South Africa's arms deal, Mail and Guardian, 22 November 2012.
10 Paul Kirk, The Citizen, More dirty arms deal money, 5 August 2011.
11 www.corruptionwatch.org.za/corruption-blind-seriti-commission-zero/
12 Schabir Shaik was one such brokering persona. At the time of the arms deal he was a financial advisor to Jacob Zuma, a key arms deal government decision-maker and from 2009 to February 2018, the President of South Africa. In 2005 Shaik was convicted of corruption and fraud relating to the solicitation of bribes from a French arms manufacturer, Thompson-CSF for Jacob Zuma (J. Squires, The State versus Schabir Shaik and 11 other, Judgment, 31 May 2005, Durban.) Shaik was imprisoned in 2008 with a 15-year sentence, but was released on medical parole the following year.
13 "Final Report of an Impact Assessment Undertaken at Denel Saab Aerostructures (Proprietary) Limited Related to an Aerospace Project Within the National

Industrial Participation Program", NAD Auditors, 2010'. And Joint Submission of Paul Holden and Andrew Feinstein to the People's Tribunal on Economic Crime, February 2018, pp. 237–238, https://corruptiontribunal.org.za/site/wp-content/uploads/2018/02/AD1-Joint-Submission-to-the-Peoples-Tribunal-Paul-Holden-and-Andrew-Feinstein-final.pdf

14 The Gupta brothers are wealthy Indian businessmen who, through their links with the then president, gained influence in South Africa to the extent of what is termed "state capture". The extent of this is becoming apparent with the statements being made to a Commission and the damaging impact of the resulting corruption with ongoing power cuts. See www.businesslive.co.za/fm/features/2018-09-06-counting-the-cost-of-state-capture/

15 See www.dod.mil.za/advert/ndic/doc/Defence%20Industry%20Strategy%20Draft_v5.8_Internet.pdf and www.defenceweb.co.za/index.php?option=com_content&view=article&id=52310:sa-defence-industry-fund-officially-launched&catid=7:Industry&Itemid=116

16 In fact Rheinmettall has been explicit in stating that they have invested in Denel (and other subsidiaries) so that they can avoid German export law, specifically the fact that German exports to Saudi Arabia are forbidden. RDM allows Rheinmettall to sell to Saudi Arabia from South Africa, taking advantage of the fact that SA arms exports are barely monitored and may involve corruption. Indeed Saudi Arabia's government made serious moves towards buying a share of Denel (www.reuters.com/article/us-saudi-safrica-arms-exclusive/exclusive-saudi-makes-1-billion-bid-for-partnership-with-south-africa-defense-group-denel-idUSKCN1ND14Q). With growing concerns and the atmosphere created by the investigations into state capture, this has been stopped by government.

17 Local industry is integrated into the global aerospace industry OEM supply chains, including Augusta Westland, the Airbus group, Alenia Aeronautica, BAE Systems, Boeing, Dassault, Gulfstream (part of General Dynamics), Lockheed Martin, Rolls-Royce, Saab and Safran. Another example is Denel Land Systems links with Patria and BAE Systems. www.engineeringnews.co.za/print-version/south-african-defence-industry-moves-to-collaborate-at-home-and-abroad-to-thrive-2014-10-24

18 Keith Campbell (2017) What went wrong with the Rooivalk? Engineering News www.engineeringnews.co.za/article/what-went-wrong-with-the-rooivalk-2007-06-08-

References

AMD (various) "Defence Manufacturers Directory". www.amd.org.za/

Batchelor, Peter and J Paul Dunne (1998) "The Restructuring of South Africa's Defence Industry", *African Security Review*, Volume 7, No. 6, pp. 27–43.

Batchelor, Peter and J Paul Dunne (2000a) "Industrial Participation, Investment and Growth: The Case of South Africa's Defence Related Industry", *Development Southern Africa*, Volume 17, No. 3, September, pp. 417–435.

Batchelor, Peter and J Paul Dunne (2000b) "The Peace Dividend in South Africa", Chapter 2 in Joern Broemmelhorster (ed.) *Demystifying the Peace Dividend*, Bonn International Conversion Centre and Baden-Baden, Nomos Verlagsgesellschraft, pp. 25–46.

Batchelor, Peter, J Paul Dunne and Guy Lamb (2002) "The Demand for Military Spending in South Africa", *Journal of Peace Research*. Vol. 39, No. 3, pp. 315–330.

Batchelor, Peter J Paul Dunne and David Saal (2000) "Military Spending and Economic Growth in South Africa", *Defence and Peace Economics*, Volume 11, No. 6, pp. 553–571. ISSN 1024 2694.

Batchelor, Peter, J Paul Dunne and Sepideh Parsa (2000) "Corporate Performance and Military Production in South Africa", *Defence and Peace Economics*, Volume 11, No. 6, pp. 615–641. ISSN 1024 2694.

Birdi, Alvin, J Paul Dunne and David Saal (2000) "The Impact of Arms Production on the South African Manufacturing Industry", *Defence and Peace Economics*, Volume 11, No. 6, pp. 597–613. ISSN 1024 2694.

Brauer, Jurgen and J Paul Dunne (2005) "Arms Trade Offsets and Development", *Africanus: Journal of Development Studies*, Volume 35, No. 1, pp. 14–24. ISSN 0304-615X.

Brauer, Jurgen and J Paul Dunne (eds.) (2004a). *Arming the South: The Economics of Military Expenditures, Arms Production and Trade in Developing Countries*. Basingstoke: Palgrave, April 2002. ISBN: 0-333-75440-9.

Brauer, Jurgen and J Paul Dunne (eds.) (2004b). *Arms Trade and Economic Development: Theory, Policy, and Cases in Arms Trade Offsets*, September 2004. London: Routledge. ISBN: 0-415-33106-4.

DefenceWeb. (2018a). "Denel's government guarantee extended to 2023", DefenceWeb, 30 October 2018, www.defenceweb.co.za/index.php?option=com_content&view=article&id=53567:denels-government-guarantee-extended-to-2023&catid=7:Industry&Itemid=116.

DefenceWeb. (2018b). "SA Defence Industry Fund officially launched", 6 July, www.defenceweb.co.za/index.php?option=com_content&view= article&id= 52310&&catid=74&Itemid=30.

Denel (various) "Annual Reports".

Department of Defence. (2015). *South African Defence Review 2015*. Pretoria: Department of Defence.

Department of Public Enterprises. (2005). *An Analysis of the Financial Performance of State Owned Enterprises*. Pretoria: Department of Public Enterprises.

Dunne, J Paul (2003) "The Making of Arms in South Africa", *Economists Allied for Arms Reduction (ECAAR) Review*, Volume 1, January.

Dunne, J Paul (2006) "The Making of Arms in South Africa", *Economics of Peace and Security Journal*, Volume 1, No. 1, January. ISSN 1749-852X.

Dunne, J Paul and Eamon Surry (2006) "Arms Production", Chapter 9 in *The Stockholm International Peace Research Institute (SIPRI), Yearbook, 2006: Armaments, Disarmament and International Security*, Oxford: Oxford University Press, pp. 387–418.

Dunne, J Paul and Guy Lamb (2004). "Defence Industrial Participation: The Experience of South Africa", Chapter 19 in Jurgen Brauer and Paul Dunne (eds.) *Arms Trade and Economic Development: Theory Policy and Cases in Arms Trade Offsets*, London, Routledge, September 2004, pp. 284–298. ISBN: 0-415-33106-4.

Dunne, J Paul and Richard Haines (2006) "Transformation or Stagnation? The South African Defence Industry in the Early 21st Century", *Defence Studies*, Volume 6, No. 3.

Feinstein, Andrew (2011). *The Shadow World: Inside the Global Arms Trade*. London: Hamish Hamilton/ Penguin.

Holden, Paul (2008). *The Arms Deal in Your Pocket*. Jeppestown, RSA: Jonathan Ball.

Holden, Paul (2017). *Indefensible: Seven Myths that Sustain the Global Arms Trade*. Chicago: Zed Books and University of Chicago Press. Collected by Paul Holden.

Parliamentary Monitoring Group. (2018). NCACC Annual Reports: 2016 & 2017, with Ministers of Defence & Energy; Deployment resources funding; Mozambique Channel piracy, Department of Military Veterans status, 7 June 2018, https://pmg.org.za/committee-meeting/26606/

Reuters. (2018). "Union Demands Bailout for Denel", DefenceWeb, 12 November 2018, www.defenceweb.co.za/index.php?option=com_content&view=article&id=53718:union-demands-bailout-for-denel&catid=7:Industry&Itemid=116

SIPRI (various years) *SIPRI Yearbook: Armaments, Disarmament and International Security*. Oxford: Oxford University Press.

Sköns, E. and J Paul Dunne (2007) "Arms Production, Economics of", in Lester Kurtz (ed.) *Encyclopaedia of Violence, Peace and Conflict*, 2nd edition. Amsterdam: Elsevier.

Sköns, E. et al. (1998) "Military Expenditure and Arms Production", in *SIPRI Yearbook 1998: Armaments, Disarmament and International Security*, Oxford: Oxford University Press, pp. 185–213.

Smith, Ron P. (2009). *Military Economics*. Basingstoke: Palgrave.

Sylvester, Justin and Annette Seegers (2008) "South Africa's Strategic Arms Package: A Critical Analysis", *Scientia Militaria, South African Journal of Military Studies*, Volume 36, No. Nr 1. doi:10.5787/36-1-45

27 North Korea's defense industry

Namhoon Cho

Introduction to North Korea's defense industry

Definitions

Generally, a defense industry refers to the industry that manufactures weapons, equipment and materials used by the military that are needed for the defense of a state. Defense industry, therefore, encompasses various types of industries – not only the weapons industry but several other industries as well, including consumer goods industries which supply clothing and food. Nevertheless, when we say defense industry, it typically refers to the munitions and military supplies industries that process and manufacture weapon systems, munitions or military supplies including military clothing, shoes and food.

North Korea's definition of defense industry is similar. It defines defense industry as a manufacturing of military supplies which are required to strengthen national defense capability. North Korea claims that the development of the defense industry is an essential requirement stemming from the basic function of a proletarian dictatorship. It also characterizes the defense industry as an inevitable requirement for building socialism and communism. North Korea argues that this is due to the fact that the building of socialism and communism is being carried out under the constant threat of invasion by the US-led imperialists.[1] Based on this recognition, North Korea has maintained a level of weapon systems production that may counter the threats from the imperialists, irrespective of the past economic crisis. Worden (2008) argues that "North Korea's extensive defense production capability reflects its commitment to self-reliance and its military-first (Songun) policy." He analyzes that "as it relates to the defense industry, emphasis on the military-first policy has two foci: preferential development of defense articles and accomplishment of announced economic priorities executed in the revolutionary military spirit."[2]

North Korea is a socialist country "with a planned economic system rooted in the socialist ownership system, whereby the means of production and output are vested in society-wide public ownership and cooperative ownership."[3] North Korea's constitution stipulates that the means of production are owned by the state and social cooperative organizations. State ownership is equivalent to ownership by the general masses, and applies to natural resources, railways, aircraft, roads, postal networks, major factories, enterprises, ports and banks. On the other hand, ownership by social cooperative organizations denotes collective ownership by workers of an organization, and applies to land, agricultural machinery, ships, smaller factories and enterprises.[4] Since defense factories and enterprises are one of the most important production facilities in North Korea, it is natural that they be owned and operated by the state and the public sector just as most of other means of production and output in the country are owned by the state and cooperative organizations.[5]

A 1998 revision to North Korea's constitution recognizes private ownership and inheritance of "income from legal financial activities," leading to an expansion of private ownership for both social organizations and individuals.[6] Also, the severe economic downturns transformed the central planning and management practices that had been enforced in the past.[7]

However, this phenomenon is not seen in the defense industry. Since the mid-1990s, the State Planning Commission has been devising and managing performance indicators in such areas as infrastructure and leading economic sectors, areas that are strategically important and thus need to be handled at the state level. Performance indicators in the defense industry are also handled at the state level since the output should satisfy North Korea's military requirements. Other indicators are left to the discretion of relevant institutions, factories and enterprises so that they make up their own indicators under the modified planning system.[8] The Central government, in the past, imposed a real or volume index, such as "production targets". However, following the 7·1 economic measures (2002), a currency or monetary index, such as "target net income", is being imposed, allowing companies greater independence in setting types of goods produced and their quantity.[9]

North Korea has promoted a socialist style of industrialization since 1960s when Kim Il-sung ruled North Korea. This process was guided by three basic policies for economic development: first, a self-sufficient national economy; second, heavy industry-led development; and third, parallel development of the military and the economy. Among these, with the goal of simultaneously achieving economic development and military build-up – the parallel development of the military and the economy – led to the establishment of the military-industrial complex in North Korea, thereby establishing the military economy as an independent economic sphere outside of the people's economy.[10] It is called the "Second Economy" and is handled by different organizations from that of the "People's Economy." The adjustments to this framework in the 1990s wrought by economic factors notwithstanding, little effort was made to implement a fundamental policy reform. This continues to hold in the Kim Jong-un era, marked by adherence to the dual-track development of the economy and nuclear weapons.[11]

Control and operation

Defense factories and enterprises in North Korea are owned by the state and are guided and controlled by the Worker's Party of Korea (WPK) and the Cabinet as shown in Figure 27.1.

The Second Economic Committee directly controls defense factories and enterprises. However, the Second Economic Committee exercises control on guidance by the higher authorities.

The defense industry is controlled by the State Affairs Commission, the Worker's Party of Korea and the Cabinet through a hierarchical association.[12] Each year, the Ministry of People's Armed Forces determines the defense requirements and submits them to the State Affairs Commission for approval. The State Affairs Commission, in conjunction with the party Central Military Commission, then establishes the defense priorities and issues directives, which are then disseminated by the Cabinet and the party Central Military Commission.[13]

The Cabinet forwards these defense requirements to the appropriate agencies for execution. First, the State Planning Commission uses defense requirements to help inform budget appropriations, which are approved by the Supreme People's Assembly.[14] Second, these defense requirements are used for the Ministry of Finance to administer financial affairs. North Korea has a single funding system by which the government takes the sole responsibility for distributing the funds necessary for the operation of defense industry factories and enterprises. All funds required in the execution of the government's plans are guaranteed by the state's fiscal plan.[15] Third, they are used for other agencies to be directed to supply energy and material resources. The Central Military Commission, working through the WPK's Machine-Building Industry Department[16] establishes the defense industry policies which are then tasked to the Second Economic Committee for implementation.[17]

The Second Economic Committee, a subordinate organ of the State Affairs Commission, directs the defense industry with oversight and guidance provided by the party Machine-Building Industry Department. The Second Economic Committee is organized into nine bureaus and it exercises responsibility for the defense industry plans, finances, production, distribution and foreign military sales.[18]

The Second Economic Committee oversees all R&D and production activities of the defense industry and R&D institute. It consists of one general bureau, seven machine industry bureaus, one R&D institute and one trading bureau. The general bureau is responsible for defense industry plans, budget compilation, resource procurement and distribution. On the other hand, the seven machine industry bureaus direct and manage procurement, development and production of defense factories and enterprises. The First Machine Industry Bureau oversees small and light arms, ammunitions and general-purpose equipment. The Second Machine Industry Bureau commissions

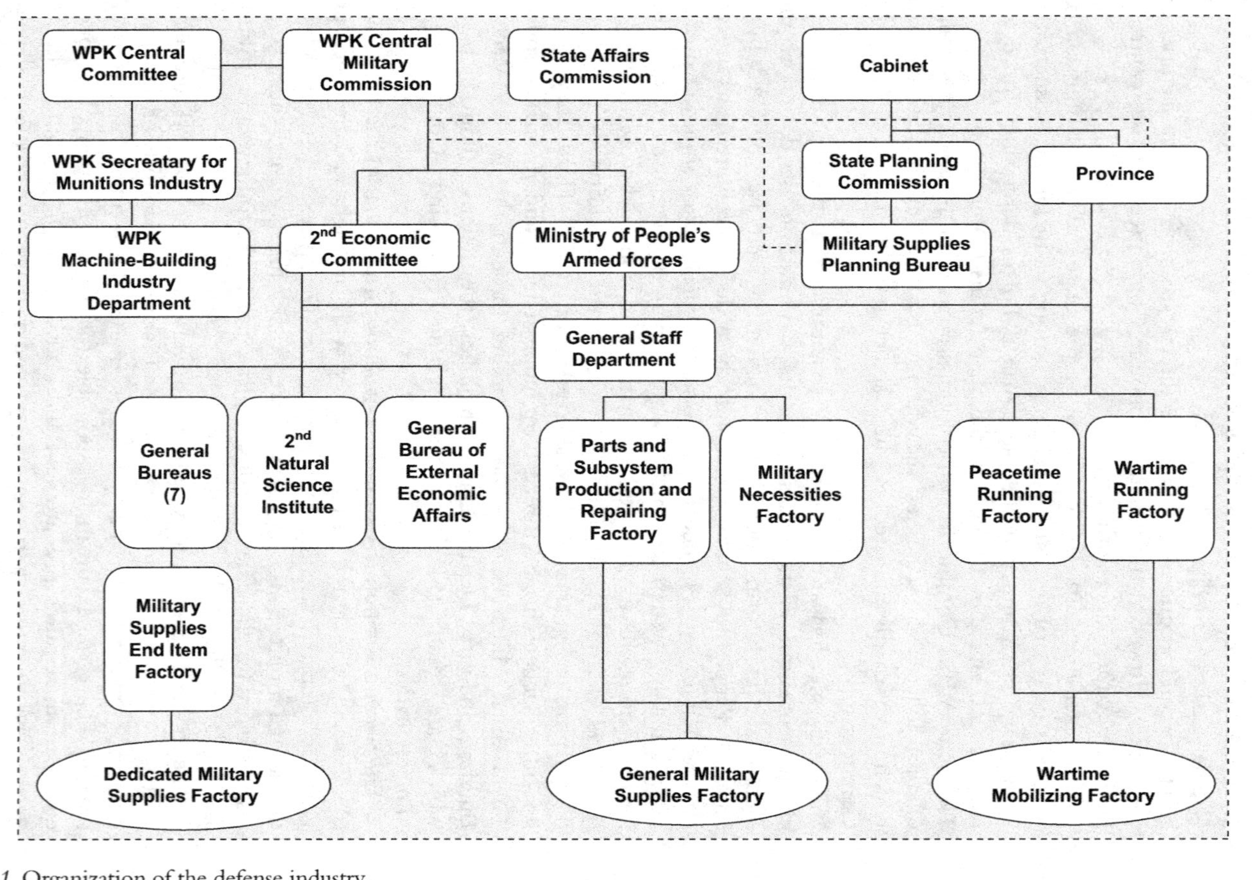

Figure 27.1 Organization of the defense industry.

*Data: Korea Finance Corporation (2010).

tanks, armored vehicles and trucks. The Third Machine Industry Bureau manages artillery and anti-aircraft artillery systems. Rockets and missiles are managed by the Fourth Machine Industry Bureau while the Fifth Machine Industry Bureau controls nuclear, biological and chemical weapons. The Sixth Machine Industry Bureau is responsible for naval vessels, and finally the Seventh Machine Industry Bureau produces aircraft and communication equipment.

The Second Natural Science Institute directs all defense industry research and development. The machine industry bureaus supervise defense factories and coordinate internally with Defense National Science Institute and the corresponding Ministry of Armed Forces bureaus and commands. The External Economic Affairs Bureau is the Ninth Bureau of the Second Economic Committee and has the primary responsibility for foreign military sales and shared responsibility with the machine industry bureaus for defense equipment procurement. A number of trading companies are under this bureau. The foreign currency earned by the External Economic Affairs Bureau from foreign military sales either funds the defense industry or supplements its spending.

The current position

The Munitions industry is at the center of the North Korean defense industry. It is divided into dedicated munitions factories that assemble and manufacture guns, artillery, ammunition, tanks and warships; munitions parts factories that manufacture weapons parts; and ordinary military supplies factories that manufacture military supplies such as military uniforms, military shoes and accessories.

Military supplies factories in North Korea are typically large-scale manufacturing complexes that manufacture goods not only for the military but for the non-military as well. This is due to several reasons, including the creation of an operating fund for the factories through sales of civilian goods. Another purpose is to promote efficiency through hierarchy. In cases where the purpose of a factory complex is to disguise the military supply factory, a civilian goods factory is located on the ground level while a military supplies factory is located underground. In addition to dedicated military supplies factories that manufacture military supplies exclusively, there are wartime mobilization factories that normally produce civilian supplies but are transformed into military supplies factories during wartime (Table 27.1).

It is not clear how many military supplies factories there are in North Korea. Estimates suggest that there are approximately 44 dedicated munitions factories, about 136 parts factories and 190–200 military supplies factories. Of the dedicated munitions factories, approximately 8 are thought to produce guns and artillery while some 2 factories are thought to manufacture armored vehicles and some 19 factories produce ammunitions and explosives. About two factories are thought to manufacture warships while some two factories are thought to assemble aircraft.[19] Some 500,000 workers are estimated to be working at dedicated munitions factories while approximately 2 million workers are estimated to be employed in the defense industry.[20]

North Korea's representative military production factories by sectors are shown in Table 27.2.

The development of the North Korean defense industry

The first munitions factory in the North Korean region was a weapons repair factory in Pyeongchon district of Pyongyang built during the Japanese colonial period. Japan constructed a factory to supply the weapons necessary for the invasion of Manchuria. Following the liberation, North Korea restored the factory which produced automatic rifles, ammunition, mortars and mortar munition.

During the Korean War, this factory was relocated to an underground space in the mountainous region of Gunjari, Seongcheon-gun in South Pyeongan Province in order to escape US bombing. The phrase "Gunjari Spirit" frequently used to encourage production, refers to the ceaseless weapons production of the Gunajri factory during the period, urging the people to follow the example.

Following the retreat of the North Korean military, the factory was relocated to the mountainous rear area of Janggang-gun in Jagang Province. Based on the experience during the Korean War, North Korea constructed most munitions factories underground in mountainous rear areas. This is why more munitions factories are located in Jagang Province than in other regions.[21]

Table 27.1 North Korea's defense factories

Item	*Dedicated factory*	*Parts & subsystem factory*	*Total*
Guns & Artillery	8	35	43
Armored Vehicles	2	10	12
Vessels	2	10	12
Aircraft	2	7	9
Rockets & Missiles	5	3	8
Ammunitions	19	36	55
C3	6	8	14
Bio & Chemical Weapons	0	16	16
Others	0	11	11
Total	44	136	180

* Data: Korea Finance Corporation (2010), *The North Korea Industry*, p. 175.

Table 27.2 North Korea's major defense factories

Fields	*Factory name*	*Characteristics*	
Guns & Artillery	2·8 Machine Factory (No. 65 Factory)	Location	Junchon, Jagang Province
		Products	Pistols, Rifles, Machine Guns, Mortars
		Employees	12,000
Aircraft	Panghyon Aircraft Factory	Location	Kusong, N. Pyongan Province
		Products	UAV, Aircraft parts & components, Aircraft assembly
		Employees	3,000
Tanks & AFV	No. 95 Factory (Kusong Tank Factory)	Location	Kusong, North Pyongan Province
		Products	TEL Support Vehicles, Tanks, AFV
		Employees	8,000
Warships	Najin Shipyards	Location	Najin, N. Hamkyong Province
		Products	Najin/Soho Class Frigates
		Employees	NA
Sub-marines	Bong-Dae Boiler Shipyards	Location	Shinpo, S. Hamkyong Province
		Products	Sang-O/Gorae Class Submarines
		Employees	NA
Missiles	No. 26 Factory (Kanggye General Tractor Plant)	Location	Kanggye, Jagang Province
		Products	Mortar Warheads, Missile Warheads
		Employees	12,000
	No. 81 Factory	Location	Songgan, Jagang Province
		Products	Missile components
		Employees	NA
	No. 11 Factory	Location	Jonchon, Jagang Province
		Products	Missile launch assembly
		Employees	NA
Engines	1·18 Machine Factory	Location	Kaechon, S. Pyongan Province
		Products	SCUD missile engine, rocket engine
		Employees	NA

During the period 1951–1953, North Korea fought a fierce war with South Korea and the multinational forces led by the UN. As a result, by the 1953 signing of the Armistice Agreement, North Korea had virtually no weapons and military supplies remaining. During the Cold War, however, North Korea came to possess massive military power and weapon systems through an intense arms race with South Korea.

Most of the weapons that North Korea acquired during the period were assembled and manufactured by North Korea on its own. From early on, North Korea succeeded in domestically producing weapons through reverse-engineering and licensed production under the motto "self-reliance in defense industry." As a result, the weapon systems of North Korea are mostly domestically assembled or developed and manufactured, with the exception of some weapons from China and the former Soviet Union that were acquired in the early stage.

Following the end of the Korean war and the subsequent recovery process, North Korea began to focus on weapons production in the 1960s. At the time, North Korea promoted the production of basic conventional weapons imitating weapons from the former Soviet Union and China. As a result, North Korea manufactured rifles, light machine guns, heavy machine guns, mortars, anti-aircraft machine guns, recoilless rifles, anti-tank rocket launchers and 107mm rockets. In the latter part of the 1960s, North Korea also built small sized torpedo boats and high-speed boats such as the P-4 and P-6.

North Korea's weapons production at the time was tied to the country's industrialization. North Korea's first 7-year Plan (1961–1967) was launched in 1961. Heavy and chemical industry formed the core leading sector of North Korea's economic development at the time and the heavy and chemical industry provided the basis for the development of steel, machinery and shipping sectors that are necessary for the production of weapons. There were negative impacts as well, however. The concentration of significant resources in the munitions industry led to an imbalance among industries, resulting in the consumer goods industry and the automobile industry falling behind.

In the 1970s, North Korea began undertaking the mass production of various weapons, including mobile weapon systems. In the 1970s, North Korea's defense industry capability grew such that it was producing ground weapons such as tanks, self-propelled rockets, armored vehicles, as well as various vessels and submarines. North Korea began production of a variety of field artillery, rocket launchers, launch vehicles, M-1973 armored vehicle and the K-61 amphibious armored transport vehicle. In 1973, it began manufacturing an imitation of the Chinese T-59 armored vehicle and in 1978, it started producing T-62 armored vehicles with technological support from the former Soviet Union. At this time, North Korea began manufacturing SA-2 portable guided anti-aircraft missiles of the former Soviet Union; and it also built 1,500 ton patrol boats and 1,400 ton submarines.

North Korea's defense industry continued to grow in the 1980s. During this period, North Korea placed emphasis on improving the quality of its weapons systems while focusing on the production of precision weapons. Production also started of guided weapons, such as AT-3 anti-tank guided missile, SA-7 surface to air guided missile, and the assembly and the manufacture of various aircraft, including the Soviet MI-2 helicopter, MIG-21 jet fighter and the Yak-18 jet trainer.

At the same time, North Korea focused on investing in technology development and facilities expansion. The quality of its tanks was improved during this period and North Korea began mass production of its self-developed Cheonmaho tanks. The 1990s saw the development and deployment of Pokpungho tanks while Songunho tanks were developed and deployed in the 2000s. All these tanks are thought to be upgrades of the Soviet T-62 tank.

In the 2000s, North Korea focused its efforts on the development of nuclear weapons and medium- and long-range missiles. After the Korean War, South Korea and North Korea engaged in an intense conventional weapons arms race but North Korea was unable to catch up with South Korea in such an arms race. Based on the mobilization of resources necessary for the arms race and economic growth, South Korea technologically overwhelmed North Korea. Therefore, North Korea pursued other means so as not to fall behind in the arms race and it resorted to developing nuclear weapons and missiles. For this reason, in the 1990s, North Korea embarked on the development of nuclear weapons and missiles and it began the independent production of missiles in the 1980s. North Korea had been producing Scud missiles at the time with outside technological assistance especially from the Soviet Union.[22] Missile development began in earnest with the successful test launch of medium-range missiles such as Rodong in the 2000s. In 2017, North Korea successfully test launched medium- and long- range missiles, namely, the Hwasong 14 and Hwasong 15. At the same time, North Korea actively engaged in the development of nuclear weapons, holding six nuclear tests beginning with the first nuclear test in 2006. The most recent nuclear test took place in 2017.

Characteristics of the North Korean defense industry

The first characteristic of North Korea's defense industry is location. Military supplies factories are dispersed throughout the country, but many of them are concentrated in Jagang Province and areas near Pyongyang. Ease in supplying raw material is an important factor in determining the location of a military supplies factory. For example, missile factories are located near aluminum mines and nuclear weapons facilities are located close to uranium mines. Factories that share weapons production processes are concentrated in a particular area such as the missile factories near Pyongyang.[23]

Most North Korean military supplies factories are located near railways. This is not surprising given the state of North Korea's transportation system. Military supplies factories manufacturing mostly heavy and large products, requiring them to be in places with convenient transportation so as to facilitate transportation. Due to the poor road conditions in North Korea, trains are the main mode of freight transportation. It is thus inevitable that military supplies factories are located near railways. Satellite imageries show factories connected to railway branch lines and most of these are thought to be military supplies factories.

Most military supplies factories in North Korea are located underground. As previously mentioned, this stems from the experience of the Korean War and is aimed at minimizing damage from enemy attacks. North Korea, faced with the overwhelming surveillance capability and air power of the United States, felt it was a prudent move to locate military supplies factories in mountainous areas or underground.

The second characteristic of North Korean military supplies factories is the comparatively better treatment of workers. Rations for laborers at these factories are distributed relatively smoothly and their wages are thought to be higher than the average wage in North Korea. This is so that military supplies factory workers may focus only on the production of munitions.

North Korea is a socialist country where private property is banned and the state distributes rations as compensation for labor. However, such state ration system collapsed in the mid-1990s and now exists in name only. The only groups that continue to receive rations are party, military and the Cabinet members and Pyongyang citizens; but ration systems for military supplies factories remain partially in operation if on an unstable basis.

There are believed to be two reasons for providing relatively stable rations to military supplies factories. First, military supplies factories, which are able to produce consistently, have relatively higher rates of operation compared to other factories. Second, military supplies factories which are part of the military sector is one of the priority sectors, and military supplies production is encouraged by providing relatively stable ration supplies.

The rate of operation of North Korean military supplies factories is higher than that of civilian supplies factories. Take the example of tank factories. Starting in the 1980s, North Korea produced a significant number of new tank models. From 1980 to 2013, North Korea produced about 1,200 Chonmaho tanks.[24] From 1992 to 2013, about 250–500 Pokpungho tanks were manufactured.[25] From 2005 to 2012, the country produced about 900 Songunho, an improved version of existing tank models. In the 34 year-period from 1980 to 2013, a total of 2,350 to 2,600 tanks were manufactured.

Such example applies to recent missile production as well. The frequent test launching of North Korean missiles between 2015 and 2017 is thought to have provided the condition for maintaining the high rate of operation at the missile factory. However, such preferential treatment of military supplies factories is gradually disappearing as the country's economy worsens. For example, the North Korean authorities which allot foreign currency earning projects to ordinary factories and businesses have begun allocating such projects to military supplies factories as well.[26]

As a priority sector, North Korea's military supplies factories enjoy priority in the provision of raw materials, which guarantees production. Such priority in provision also applies to the provision of energy, such as electricity. A significant number of North Korean military supplies factories have coal mines and oil provision facilities that supply energy exclusively for their use. For example, Kaechon mine in South Pyongan Province and Kujang district mine in Kujang County supply coal exclusively to military supplies factories under the supervision of the Second Economic Committee.

Following the period of "Arduous March" sparked by the collapse of Soviet communism in the mid-1990s, the rate of operation at North Korean factories began to fall rapidly. The collapse of the socialist system of the international division of labor led to a reduced demand for products that North Korea supplied to other socialist countries and subsequently, the rate of operation at factories fell rapidly. However, military supplies factories were somewhat removed from such a trend. North Korea's own domestic demand for weapons and military supplies and overseas demand, mainly from the Middle East and Africa, continued.

Third, modernization and restructuring is underway at North Korean military supplies factories. During his recent onsite inspections of military supplies factories, Kim Jong-un has been emphasizing modernization. CNC machines in defense factories are being rapidly modernized under Kim Jong-un's guidance.[27]

Conversion of a civilian supplies factory to a military supplies factory is a frequent occurrence. For example, Chongjin Shipyard, one of North Korea's three largest ship yards was converted into a military supplies factory around 2013, combining an existing military supplies factory and a civil supplies factory, civilian shipbuilding work became scarce. However, Chongjin Shipyard has been actively manufacturing military patrol boats and semi-submarine boats, maintaining a relatively higher rate of operation than before the conversion.[28]

Another example is Factory No. 29 (Chongsu Chemical Plant) located in Sakchu, North Hamgyong Province. This was a nearly-abandoned chemicals factory but has since been converted into a factory producing battery parts for submarines in 2016.[29] One of the reasons this former chemical factory was converted into a battery factory is the existence of a nickel mine near the factory, nickel being the main raw material for batteries.

The 6·4 Rolling Stock Works (6·4 Charyang Chonghap Kiopso), which manufactures rail-transport medium range missiles, is another example. The plant originally manufactured trains for civilian use. However, it was converted to a military supplies factory in 2014, the year North Korea announced the five-year plan to modernize the military. Previously under the Korea State Railway in the Ministry of Railways, the plant is now under the Second Economic Committee which oversees the defense industry. Following Kim Jong-un's directive in March 2016 to diversify the means of nuclear attack, this factory has been producing rail-transport medium range missile launchers.[30]

The defense industry of North Korea is thought to have attained a high level of technology. At the 7th Congress of the Workers' Party of Korea, Kim Jong-un declared that North Korea was able to manufacture military machinery at will. However, North Korea's capability in the latest electronics and aircraft manufacture appears to remain low.

Estimation of North Korea's annual defense industry production

It is impossible to work out the size of the annual production of North Korea's weapons systems as the North Korean authorities do not release such data. However, it is partially possible to estimate a changing trend in the size of North Korean weapons system production from some of the limited information and data available. For this, it is necessary to divide the demand for North Korean weapons system into domestic demand and overseas demand, and then examine the characteristics of each type of demand. Here, we attempt to look at the domestic demand for North Korean weapons systems: its military requires North Korean weapons systems. Therefore, the demand for North Korean weapons systems will be determined by North Korea's military characteristic and demand.

The Defense White Paper issued by Korea biennially contains North Korea's weapons system quantities for a specific year. This quantity can be expressed as follows:

$$WQ\ (year\ i+1) = WQ\ (year\ i) - RQ\ (year\ i) + PQ\ (year\ i) \tag{1}$$

where WQ (year *i*): quantity of weapons system in year *i*
RQ (year *i*): quantity of weapons system retired in year *i*
PQ (year *i*): quantity of weapons system produced in year *i*

The quantity of weapons systems produced in year *i,* is as follows;

$$PQ\ (year\ i) = WQ\ (year\ i+1) - WQ\ (year\ i) + RQ\ (year\ i) \tag{2}$$

If it is possible to know RQ (year *i*), the quantity of retired weapons systems, we can obtain PQ (year *i*), the quantity produced to meet the domestic demand for weapons system because WQ (year *i*+1) – WQ (year *i*), the change in weapons system quantities is shown in the Defense White Paper. Let's calculate the production quantity for domestic demand purposes by calculating the rate of retirement of tanks obtained from the data on tank production quantity and using it as a proxy for the rate of retirement of other weapons systems.[31]

Let us first calculate the rate of retirement. To calculate the rate of retirement, we estimated the annual production quantity of North Korean tanks using production data for a new type of tank. It is assumed that an equal quantity was produced every year in calculating the annual production quantity. Data on the estimated production quantities for the Chonmaho, Pokpungho and Songunho tanks are shown in Table 27.3. Using these data in the formula above, it is possible to calculate the rate of retirement of tanks each year. Table 27.3 shows the author's estimates of the annual number of tanks retired and the average rate of retirement during the period 1980 to 2013.

In 1988, South Korea's Ministry of National Defense White Paper began to include data on the size of North Korea's weapons systems. Hence, although data on North Korean tank production exists starting in 1980, only data from 1988 to 2016 were used in calculating the annual rate of retirement of tanks. The resulting rate of retirement of tanks during the period is 1.113%. (=2067.65/111,900), as shown in Table 27.4.

Production quantities for different weapons systems for each year from 1988 to 2016 are calculated in Table 27.5 using the annual rate of retirement for tanks. The annual rate of retirement of tanks was applied to each weapons system as production data on other weapons do not exist.[32] Table 27.5 shows various weapons systems' production quantities per year, total production quantity, average annual production quantity and average annual change in retained quantity calculated over 1988–2016 using the annual retirement rate for tanks.

Table 27.5 shows some negative figures in the annual production quantities; but negative production is not possible. Negative figures arise from the use of the average rate of retirement during the 1988–2016 period. The negative figures will be eliminated if the average rate of retirement could be replaced by individual rates of retirement for each year.

The estimates show North Korea's annual weapons systems production for various categories to be about three to 355. In the case of submarine, it is estimated to produce three units a year. An annual average of five to seven battleships, landing craft and supporting vessels are estimated to be built. As for aircraft and helicopters, an annual average output of some 16 units and about four units are estimated, respectively. Land-based weapons systems show the largest annual production quantities with an annual average of 45 armored vehicles, about 71 tanks and about 355 field artilleries being produced.

Such annual average production quantities exceed the annual average quantity change. The difference reflects the quantity retired. Fighter aircraft have a higher number of retired units compared to the production quantity. Since the 2000s, North Korea has not been able to acquire aircraft from abroad, resulting in continued decrease in the number of aircraft retained while the aviation industry production is limited to the production of some parts and maintenance.[33]

Production for the domestic demand have been estimated. What about production for foreign demand? How much of weapon systems has North Korea produced for overseas demand and who are the importers? Countries in the Middle East and in Africa are the main buyers of North Korea's

Table 27.3 Estimates of North Korea's tank production (1980–2013)

Item	*Production*				*Production quantity in each phase*			
	Period	*Time span (Year)*	*Total quantity*	*Average annual quantity*	*1980–1991*	*1992–2004*	*2005–2012*	*2013*
Chonmaho	1980–2013	34	1,200	35.29	35.29	35.29	35.29	35.29
Pokpungho	1992–2013	22	250	11.36	11.36	0.00	11.36	11.36
Songunho	2005–2012	8	900	112.50	112.50	0.00	0.00	112.50
Total	1980–2013		2,350	69.12	69.12	35.29	46.66	159.16

* Note: Average Annual Quantity is the average number of tank units produced annually over the given time span (=Total Quantity/Time Span).

Table 27.4 Estimates of annual retirement quantity of North Korea's tanks

Year	*Tank quantity*				*Year*	*Tank quantity*			
	Retention	*Change*	*Production*	*Retirement*		*Retention*	*Change*	*Production*	*Retirement*
–1987			282.40		2002	3700	-50	46.66	96.66
1988	3500	0	35.29	35.29	2003	3700	0	46.66	46.66
1989	3550	50	35.29	-14.71	2004	3700	0	46.66	46.66
1990	3600	50	35.29	-14.71	2005	3700	0	159.16	159.16
1991	3650	50	35.29	-14.71	2006	3700	0	159.16	159.16
1992	3700	50	46.66	-3.34	2007	3800	100	159.16	59.16
1993	3750	50	46.66	-3.34	2008	3900	100	159.16	59.16
1994	3800	50	46.66	-3.34	2009	4000	100	159.16	59.16
1995	3800	0	46.66	46.66	2010	4100	100	159.16	59.16
1996	3800	0	46.66	46.66	2011	4150	50	159.16	109.16
1997	3800	0	46.66	46.66	2012	4200	50	159.16	109.16
1998	3800	0	46.66	46.66	2013	4250	50	46.66	-3.34
1999	3800	0	46.66	46.66	2014	4300	50	0.00	-50.00
2000	3800	0	46.66	46.66	2015	4300	0	0.00	0.00
2001	3750	-50	46.66	96.66	2016	4300	0	0.00	0.00
					A	111,900	800	2067.60	1267.60
					B			2350.00	
					C				1.133%

A: Quantity Change (1988–2016), B: Quantity Change (~2016), C: Annual Rate of Replacement.

Table 27.5 DPRK's annual average production quantity by weapon systems

Year	*Tanks*	*APC*	*Artillery*	*Battle ship*	*Landing craft*	*Supporting ship*	*Sub-marines*	*Fighter aircraft*	*Support aircraft*	*Rotary wing*
1988	39.6	22.2	88.4	4.9	2.3	2.3	0.0	9.3	5.7	3.2
1989	90.2	194.1	897.4	2.8	22.5	22.5	24.3	24.5	-4.4	8.2
1990	90.8	196.1	906.5	2.8	22.7	22.7	0.3	24.6	-4.6	8.3
1991	91.3	127.2	308.8	14.4	17.9	17.9	0.8	9.6	5.4	3.3
1992	91.9	128.3	311.0	14.5	18.1	18.1	0.8	9.6	5.4	3.3
1993	92.5	28.3	616.7	-0.5	28.3	28.3	0.8	9.6	5.4	3.3
1994	93.0	28.3	622.3	-0.6	28.6	28.6	0.8	9.6	5.4	3.3
1995	43.0	180.0	223.5	2.9	11.2	11.2	4.8	4.6	20.6	3.3
1996	43.0	181.7	224.6	2.9	11.3	11.3	4.9	4.5	20.8	3.3
1997	43.0	-221.1	630.3	9.9	92.3	92.3	2.9	14.6	10.8	18.5
1998	43.0	-223.9	635.9	10.0	93.3	93.3	3.0	14.6	10.9	18.6
1999	43.0	26.1	388.8	-0.1	-14.4	-14.4	25.7	19.7	5.9	3.6
2000	43.0	26.1	391.6	-0.1	-14.7	-14.7	26.0	19.9	5.9	3.6
2001	-7.5	-24.5	242.7	4.9	5.3	5.3	1.0	9.9	5.9	8.7
2002	-8.1	-25.1	243.9	4.9	5.3	5.3	1.0	9.9	5.9	8.7
2003	41.9	-25.6	447.3	4.9	-100.9	-70.5	-9.1	-10.4	21.1	-1.3
2004	41.9	-26.2	450.7	4.9	-102.1	-71.4	-9.2	-10.6	21.2	-1.4
2005	41.9	23.8	150.7	-0.2	2.9	3.6	-4.3	4.3	1.2	-1.4
2006	41.9	23.8	150.7	-0.2	2.9	3.6	-4.3	4.3	1.1	-1.5
2007	143.0	23.8	302.4	4.8	2.9	3.6	5.7	19.4	6.1	3.5

2008	144.2	23.8	304.1	4.8	2.9	3.6	5.8	19.5	6.1	3.5
2009	145.3	23.8	154.1	4.8	2.9	3.6	0.8	-0.6	1.1	-1.5
2010	146.4	23.8	154.1	4.8	2.9	3.6	0.8	-0.7	1.0	-1.6
2011	97.0	74.4	52.9	4.8	2.9	3.6	0.8	9.3	6.0	3.4
2012	97.6	74.9	51.8	4.8	2.9	3.6	0.8	9.3	6.0	3.4
2013	98.1	176.6	505.8	9.8	2.9	3.6	0.8	9.3	6.0	3.4
2014	98.7	178.3	509.7	9.9	2.9	3.6	0.8	9.3	6.0	3.4
2015	48.7	28.3	159.7	4.9	-2.1	-1.4	0.8	4.2	6.0	-1.7
2016	48.7	28.3	159.7	4.9	-2.2	-1.5	0.8	4.2	6.0	-1.7
Total Prod.	2,067.6	1,295.5	10,285.9	140.9	152.2	221.4	88.1	265.3	200.0	109.6
Annual Prod.	71.3	44.7	354.7	4.9	5.2	7.6	3.0	9.1	6.9	3.8
Annual Change	28.6	19.3	225.0	0.0	1.8	3.9	1.6	-0.4	1.1	0.4

weapon systems. Iran is the biggest customer having bought 1.527 billion US dollars (current value) until 2016, while Syria is the second biggest buyer having bought 515 million US dollars (current value) during the same period.[34]

The biggest export item is missiles while the second biggest is artillery. It should be remembered that until the 1980s, artillery was North Korea's most popular export item until missiles replaced them as the biggest export item after the 1990s, as shown in Table 27.6 (data in current prices).

Because of international arms controls and sanctions, North Korea's arms exports have diminished over the years. After the peak of the 1980s when the average annual export reached 110 US million dollars, it has declined slowly from 68 US million dollars in the 1990s to 57.4 million US dollars in the 2000s and 0.14 US million dollars in the 2010s. North Korea's annual arms export trends are shown in Figure 27.2 (data in current prices).

North Korea's weapon systems production for both domestic and overseas demands are examined. Total production of North Korea's defense industry may be estimated by adding the two figures. To get that figure, first, acquire North Korea's annual export quantities by weapon systems. Data from SIPRI Armstrade DATABASE are used to obtain North Korea's export data set.

North Korea exported a small amount of weapon systems after the 2000s compared with significant amounts in the 1980s. In the 1980s, North Korea's artillery were the most popular item while in the 1990s, its missiles were the most popular item in the international weapons market. North Korea's export quantities by weapon systems are shown in Table 27.7.[35]

North Korea's annual production quantity can be acquired by summing the production for domestic demand in Table 27.5 and that for overseas demand in Table 27.7. The result is shown in Table 27.8.

Tables 27.7 and 27.8 show that the number of annual production quantities for overseas demand is just about 1% of the total production quantities of both domestic and overseas demands. This means that arms exports did not contribute much to the increase in North Korea's weapon systems production. However, missile exports are not included in Tables 27.7 and 27.8 and they played a significant role in increasing North Korea's weapon systems production after the 1990s.

Future research direction

North Korea is a country that is kept hidden. There are virtually no official statistics released by the government and accessing concrete material is not easy. North Korea research, therefore, requires continued collection of reliable material and data analyses. Such attempts and efforts are not only required also for the study of North Korean defense industry, but they must be conducted more rigorously. This is because it is even more difficult to obtain material related to the North Korean defense industry that deals with issues of the North Korean military troops.

Table 27.6 DPRK's annual average export by decades (in million US dollars)

Item	*1970s*	*1980s*	*1990s*	*2000s*	*2010s*	*Total export (1974–2017)*
Aircraft	1.00	1.20	0.00	0.00	0.00	18
Armored vehicle	0.00	27.00	0.00	0.30	0.00	273
Artillery	1.17	52.90	6.70	0.00	0.00	603
Missiles	0.00	24.60	61.30	31.40	0.14	1,174
Ships	5.17	4.40	0.00	25.70	0.00	332
Total	7.33	110.10	68.00	57.40	0.14	2,400

* SIPRI Arms Transfer DATABASE (http://armstrade.sipri.org/armstrade/page/values.php).

A significant amount of material concerning the North Korean defense industry relies on material from Japan. This is because most of the defense industry factories in North Korea were built by the Japanese during the Japanese occupation of the Korean Peninsula for the purpose of invading Manchuria. As a result, much of the material that exist are based on material from a long time ago. Recent material rely mainly on North Korean media such as Rodong Sinmun and defector testimonies but most of them do not provide a full picture and are not very credible.

It is now necessary to form a data base on North Korean defense industry and to generate and accumulate secondary material based on the existing material. The present study attempted to estimate the production size of the North Korean defense industry based on the production quantity of a new

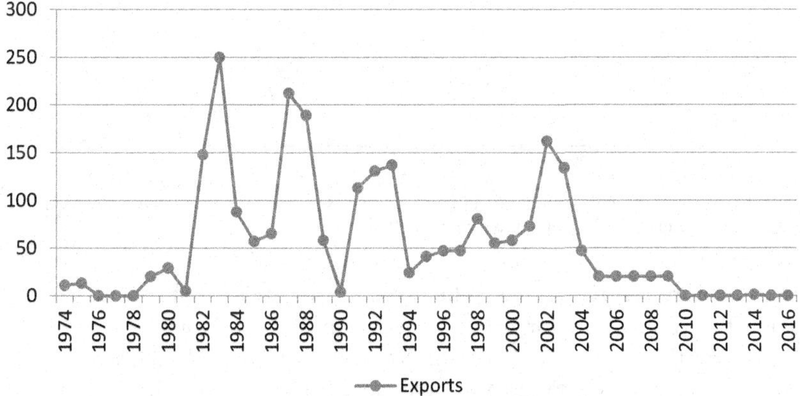

Figure 27.2 North Korea's volume of annual exports (unit: million US dollars).

Table 27.7 DPRK's annual export quantity by weapon systems

Year	*Tanks*	*APC*	*Artillery*	*Battle ship*	*Landing craft*
1978					4.0
1979			22.0		4.0
1980					
1981	75.0		16.7		
1982	75.0		102.7		
1983			218.9		
1984			202.3		
1985			202.3		
1986			162.3	3.0	
1987			125.1		
1988			9.1		
1989			9.1		
1990			9.1		
1991			9.1		
1992			9.1		
1993			9.1		
1994			9.1		
1995			9.1		
1996			9.1		
1997			9.1		
1998			16.0		
1999					
2000		10.0			
2001				7.5	
2002				18.5	
2003				5.0	
2004 – 2016					
Total Prod.		10.0	106.9	31.0	
Annual Prod		0.3	3.7	1.1	

SIPRI Arms Transfer DATABASE (http://armstrade.sipri.org/armstrade/page/values.php)
* Note: the export of second- hand items and missiles are not included. There are no export data for supporting ships; submarines; fighter and support aircraft and rotary wing.

model of North Korean tanks. The continuation of this type of research will provide the foundation for a better understanding of North Korean defense industry. Furthermore, when North Korea is denuclearized, research on the North Korean defense industry would need to pay attention to the changes in the North Korean policy on military capability building.

Table 27.8 DPRK's annual total production quantity by weapon systems

Year	*Tanks*	*APC*	*Artillery*	*Battle ship*	*Landing craft*	*Supporting ship*	*Sub-marine*	*Fighter aircraft*	*Support aircraft*	*Rotary wing*
1988	39.6	22.2	97.5	4.9	2.3	2.3	0.0	9.3	5.7	3.2
1989	90.2	194.1	906.5	2.8	22.5	22.5	24.3	24.5	-4.4	8.2
1990	90.8	196.1	915.6	2.8	22.7	22.7	0.3	24.6	-4.6	8.3
1991	91.3	127.2	317.9	14.4	17.9	17.9	0.8	9.6	5.4	3.3
1992	91.9	128.3	320.1	14.5	18.1	18.1	0.8	9.6	5.4	3.3
1993	92.5	37.4	616.7	-0.5	28.3	28.3	0.8	9.6	5.4	3.3
1994	93.0	37.4	622.3	-0.6	28.6	28.6	0.8	9.6	5.4	3.3
1995	43.0	189.1	223.5	2.9	11.2	11.2	4.8	4.6	20.6	3.3
1996	43.0	190.8	224.6	2.9	11.3	11.3	4.9	4.5	20.8	3.3
1997	43.0	-212.0	630.3	9.9	92.3	92.3	2.9	14.6	10.8	18.5
1998	43.0	-207.9	635.9	10.0	93.3	93.3	3.0	14.6	10.9	18.6
1999	43.0	26.1	388.8	-0.1	-14.4	-14.4	25.7	19.7	5.9	3.6
2000	43.0	26.1	391.6	-0.1	-14.7	-14.7	26.0	19.9	5.9	3.6
2001	-7.5	-24.5	242.7	12.4	5.3	5.3	1.0	9.9	5.9	8.7
2002	-8.1	-25.1	243.9	23.4	5.3	5.3	1.0	9.9	5.9	8.7
2003	41.9	-25.6	447.3	9.9	-100.9	-70.5	-9.1	-10.4	21.1	-1.3
2004	41.9	-26.2	450.7	4.9	-102.1	-71.4	-9.2	-10.6	21.2	-1.4
2005	41.9	23.8	150.7	-0.2	2.9	3.6	-4.3	4.3	1.2	-1.4
2006	41.9	23.8	150.7	-0.2	2.9	3.6	-4.3	4.3	1.1	-1.5
2007	143.0	23.8	302.4	4.8	2.9	3.6	5.7	19.4	6.1	3.5
2008	144.2	23.8	304.1	4.8	2.9	3.6	5.8	19.5	6.1	3.5
2009	145.3	23.8	154.1	4.8	2.9	3.6	0.8	-0.6	1.1	-1.5
2010	146.4	33.8	154.1	4.8	2.9	3.6	0.8	-0.7	1.0	-1.6

(*Continued*)

Table 27.8 (Cont.)

Year	*Tanks*	*APC*	*Artillery*	*Battle ship*	*Landing craft*	*Supporting ship*	*Sub-marine*	*Fighter aircraft*	*Support aircraft*	*Rotary wing*
2011	97.0	74.4	52.9	4.8	2.9	3.6	0.8	9.3	6.0	3.4
2012	97.6	74.9	51.8	4.8	2.9	3.6	0.8	9.3	6.0	3.4
2013	98.1	176.6	505.8	9.8	2.9	3.6	0.8	9.3	6.0	3.4
2014	98.7	178.3	509.7	9.9	2.9	3.6	0.8	9.3	6.0	3.4
2015	48.7	28.3	159.7	4.9	-2.1	-1.4	0.8	4.2	6.0	-1.7
2016	48.7	28.3	159.7	4.9	-2.2	-1.5	0.8	4.2	6.0	-1.7
Total Prod.	2,067.6	1,305.5	10,395.8	171.9	152.2	221.4	88.1	265.3	200.0	109.6
Annual Prod.	71.3	45.0	358.4	6.0	5.2	7.6	3.0	9.1	6.9	3.8

Notes

1 The Institute of Economics (1985), North Korea's Academy of Social Science, *Economic Dictionary*, p. 225.
2 Worden, Robert L. eds. (2008), *North Korea: A Country Study*, U.S. Government Printing Office, p. 271.
3 Institute for Unification Education (2017), *2017 Understanding North Korea*, Ukgo Publishing Company, p. 171.
4 ibid.
5 Only farming lands and cultivating tools are owned by cooperative organizations while other lands and facilities including defense factories, are owned by the state. The dominant form of ownership in the North Korea's economy is state ownership. However, in the agriculture sector, where cooperative farms accounted for 80% of all farms, co-ownership is the dominant type of ownership. Lim, Soo-ho (2008), *Coexistence of Planning and Market*, SERI, p. 35.
6 Institute for Unification Education (2017), p. 172.
7 ibid., p. 173.
8 Korea Institute for National Unification (2009), *North Korea Overview 2009*, KINU, p. 183.
9 Lim, Soo-ho (2008), p. 183.
10 Institute for Unification Education (2017), p. 174.
11 ibid.
12 The State Affairs Commission (SAC) of North Korea is defined by the 2016 constitution as "the highest guiding organ of the material managing organ of matters". During the 4th plenary session of the Supreme People's Assembly in June, 2016, the SAC officially replaced the National Defense Commission with an extended focus towards other national concerns aside from defense and security. Kim Jong-un is the current chairman of the SAC. (Wikipedia).
13 Worden, Robert L. eds. (2008), p. 270.
14 Yang, Mun-su (2015), *North Korea's Planned Economy and Marketization*, Ministry of Unification, p. 11.
15 Yang, Mun-su (2015), p. 11.
16 In the past, it is called Munitions Industry Department.
17 Worden, Robert L. eds. (2008), p. 270.
18 Worden, Robert L. eds. (2008), pp. 270–271.
19 Korea Finance Corporation (2010), *The North Korea Industry*, p. 175.
20 Shin, Beom-chul et al. (2012), *Research on North Korea's Military*, Korea Institute for Defense Analyses, p. 278.
21 Choi, Sung-bin et al. (2005), *Outline of North Korea's Defense Industry*, Korea Institute for Defense Analyses, October 2005, pp. 26–33.
22 Financial Times, "North Korea can make its own ballistic rocket engines, say US," 16 August 2017. "Ukraine his pointed the finger at Moscow, which throughout the 1980s and 1990s funneled Scud missile technology to Pyongyang."
23 RFA, "North Korea Places Strategic Defense Zone within Pyongyang's Administrative District," 6 March 2018.
24 Kang, In-won (2013), *Acquisition Trend of World Main Battle Tank*. Defense Agency for Technology and Quality, p. 195.
25 ibid., p. 197.
26 RFA, "North Korea Munitions Factories Turn to Fishing to Generate Foreign Currency," 9 August 2017.
27 The Korea Herald, "Kim, Jong-un calls for modernized production in visit to glass factory," 18 November 2018.

28 RFA, "North Korea Shipyard Producing Troop Transport Submarines," 10 December 2015.
29 RFA, "Sanctions Force North Korea to Shutter Chemical Factory," 19 April 2018.
30 RFA, "North Korea Manufactures Rail-Transport Medium Range Missile Launcher," 30 August 2016.
31 It is a heroic assumption. However, it is the best assumption at this moment because the production data on weapon system other than that of tanks is not available.
32 If in the future, it is possible to obtain data on the production quantity of each weapons system, it will be possible to obtain more accurate production quantities per year.
33 On the other hand, in the aviation industry, rocket production is very active.
34 SIPRI Arms Transfer DATABASE (http://armstrade.sipri.org/armstrade/page/values.php)
35 Missiles exports are excluded in Table 27.7 because data on missiles are not shown in the ROK Defense White Papers.

References

Choi, Sung-bin et al. (2005), *Outline of North Korea's Defense Industry*, KIDA Research Report, Mu05-2136, Seoul: Korea Institute for Defense Analyses.

Institute for Unification Education (2017), *2017 Understanding North Korea*, Seoul: Institute for Unification Education.

The Institute of Economics (1985), *Economic Dictionary*, Pyongyang: North Korea's Academy of Social Science Publishing House.

Kang, In-won (2013), *Acquisition Trend of World Main Battle Tank*, Seoul: Defense Agency for Technology and Quality.

Korea Finance Corporation (2010), *The North Korea Industry*, Seoul: Korea Development Bank.

Korea Institute for International Economic Policy (2002), *2003/04 North Korea's Economy Whitepaper*, Seoul: Korea Institute for International Economic Policy.

Korea Institute for National Unification (2009), *2009 North Korea Overview*, Seoul: Korea Institute for National Unification.

Lee, Suk, eds (2018), *2017 The DPRK Economic Outlook*, Sejong-si: Korea Development Institute.

Lim, Soo-ho (2008), *Coexistence of Planning and Market*, Seoul: SERI.

ROK Ministry of National Defense (1988–2016), *Defense White Paper*.

Shin, Beom-chul et al. (2012), *Research on North Korea's Military*, KIDA Research Report AN11-2199, Seoul: Korea Institute for Defense Analyses.

SIPRI Arms Transfer DATABASE (http://armstrade.sipri.org/armstrade).

Worden, Robert L., eds (2008), *North Korea: A Country Study*, Washington DC: Federal Research Division, Library of Congress.

Yang, Mun-su (2015), *North Korea's Planned Economy and Marketization*, Seoul: Ministry of Unification.

28 Overall conclusion

Keith Hartley and Jean Belin

We started by posing three questions about what is known, not known and what we need to know for a better understanding of the world's defence industries. This book is proof of what is known. There is a considerable amount of information on the world's defence industries as displayed in each of the Book's Chapters. These contain information about the size, structure, conduct, performance and ownership of the industries. Challenges and future prospects are also reviewed.

Data

A major finding concerns the general absence of *government-supplied* data on the size of their defence industries. Authors have provided available data from a variety of sources on industry size as measured by sales and employment. However, it is not possible to ensure that all size data are based on a standard and uniform definition of defence industries, their arms sales and identical definitions of employment. Sales data need to comprise standard definitions of sales to national armed forces and exports sales. Employment data vary between numbers based on direct, indirect and induced jobs and it is not always clear which definitions are used.

For employment numbers, the UK is an exception with defence industry employment data provided by the national government. Japan is a complete contrast lacking any consistent employment data set reflecting the Japanese defence production model where arms production is embedded within the civilian sector (e.g. tank production in MHI where workers who make tanks will then shift to make bulldozers in the same plant).[1]

To indicate relative and absolute size, Table 28.1 presents a summary of defence industry employment numbers for the nations in this study. Estimating industry size based on sales is more difficult since sales to national defence ministries need to be combined with defence export sales all using standard definitions. The major employers are the USA, China, Russia and North Korea accounting for a total of between some six million to over nine million defence industry jobs. The European total is misleading since it represents the aggregate total for all European Union member states and not for the trans-European companies only. Overall, the

Table 28.1 Defence industry employment

Country	*Employment numbers*
USA	2.3–4.141 million
China	1.7 million
Russia	1.3million – 2 million
UK	260,000
France	200,000
Trans-European	1.513 million
Italy	50,000
Germany	90,000–120,000
Spain	40,000
Greece	5,210+
Poland	20,000
Switzerland	10,000
Ukraine	80,000
Sweden	30,000
Norway	6,700
Turkey	44,740
Israel	45,000+
South Korea	28,000+
Japan	NA
Canada	27,000–59,800
Australia	20,343+
Brazil	18,506+
India	153,934
Singapore	22,000+
South Africa	15,000
North Korea	500,000–2 million
TOTAL	**7 million to 11.1 million**

Notes:

i NA = data not available
ii (+) shows numbers are larger
iii Data are for 2016/17. Trans-European numbers are excluded from the total since separate national numbers are used.
iv Range of numbers shows direct numbers (lower figure) and direct plus indirect employment. Figures are rounded.
v Numbers based on Country estimates presented in this book.

industries in this study employed some seven million to 11 million personnel; and there are arms industries in other countries not included in this book. These are large numbers showing that the global defence industry employs substantial numbers of scarce labour resources with alternative uses.

Structure, ownership and nationality

Typically, national defence industries are domestic monopolies, but the *major* arms industries are more competitive *within* their national defence markets shown by duopoly and oligopoly (e.g. Russia; USA). In contrast, *world* markets are more competitive. The long-run trend has been towards a smaller number of larger firms and this trend is likely to continue. Within the world, there is a mix of private and state ownership.

Private ownership of arms firms exists in counties such as Australia, Canada, Germany, Japan, Singapore, Switzerland, the UK and the USA. State ownership of arms firms is prevalent in China, Greece, India, Russia and North Korea and these firms are likely to pursue various non-profit objectives (e.g. sales; employment; growth; regional locations; national prestige projects). But the private/public sector distinction is much more complex. The private sector embraces national and foreign individuals and firms, families and financial institutions, public joint stock companies and owner-managed firms. For example, the privately-owned Swedish and Swiss defence industries have substantial foreign ownership. Similarly, the state sector ranges from government departments to agencies such as trading funds as well as public corporations and nationalised firms and industries. There are further dimensions adding to the complexity of the private/public sector distinction. Capital and product markets provide efficiency incentives. In private capital markets, shareholders usually pursue profit objectives which limit managerial non-profit behaviour. Public sector organisations are more likely to be managed by politicians and government-appointed managers focused on public service accountability and life-time tenure which might not be conducive to entrepreneurial activity. Public and private ownership might also operate in product markets with varying degrees of competition and monopoly. Examples include state and privately-owned monopolies as well as private firms in competitive markets.

Firms in national defence industries display a variety of organisational forms. Privately-owned and profit-seeking firms will adopt organisational structures which minimise their transaction costs (e.g. vertical integration; multi-divisional firms). These firms are also subject to capital market constraints in the form of take-overs and threats of bankruptcy. In contrast, state-owned firms are not subject to such capital market constraints: they are likely to face 'soft budget' constraints and they will select organisational forms which are not necessarily efficient. Future trends towards a smaller number of larger firms is likely to lead to increased concentration *within* nation states with more international mergers and alliances *between* nations and governments will be central in approving international mergers.

Role of government

Whether privately or state-owned, governments are a key determinant of industry size, structure, conduct, performance and ownership. Governments determine technical progress by specifying the operational requirements for their national armed forces; they determine whether their national orders are allocated to national arms firms or to overseas rivals (new entry); their orders determine industry size; they determine the form of competition; and they 'police' industry performance (state controls on profits and exports); they also allow or prevent both national and international mergers.

Industry future

Governments are also central to the future of arms industries and governments add a nationality dimension to the analysis. For example, the governments of India, Israel and North Korea have specific national dimensions affecting their arms industries: they are willing to support their national industries for reasons of security and independence almost regardless of costs. Similarly, Sweden and Switzerland have defence economies determined by their commitment to neutrality. The nationality dimension is also reflected in the location of company headquarters and the opportunity for foreign ownership. Some governments prefer state ownership with no opportunities for foreign ownership of their arms industries.

A government's role is to protect its citizens and their property from external threats. Governments provide the buying power affecting their arms industry's future where more sales offer prospects for industry survival. Threats are likely to continue meaning a future for arms firms. But future threats are difficult to predict. They take different and varying forms. For example, the period 2000 to 2019 was dominated by terrorist threats with different types of terrorist organisations (e.g. al Qaeda; IS; Hamas; Real IRA) of varying size and military specialisms (e.g. bombings; suicide attacks; kidnapping). There were also regional conflicts such as Afghanistan, Iraq, Libya and Yemen. Technical progress leads to new weapons systems which will generate new threats and new demands for arms (e.g. uninhabited air, land and sea systems). Nuclear proliferation will continue, especially if new technology leads to cheaper nuclear systems. Nor can space be ignored: there will be incentives to develop and deploy space weapons, including military bases in space (e.g. moon bases). Whilst known, unknown and unknowable threats exist, there will be corresponding incentives for peace-making (e.g. nuclear threats from Iran and North Korea). However, efforts at peace-making require international collective action which involves substantial transaction costs and 'free rider' problems. Peace is not costless and will create new demands for arms to equip peace forces (e.g. surveillance systems).

Predictions about the future are notoriously uncertain and most likely to be wrong! However, some broad generalisations are possible. The future will involve transformation in a nation's armed forces. The army, navy and air forces after next will be radically different as they embrace new technologies and respond to new threats. By 2050, the armed forces will have new types of equipment, new skill requirements and new roles. Such changes will affect defence industries as they adjust to new demands from the armed forces leading to the defence industry after next. This future defence industry is likely to have an even smaller number of larger firms with larger R&D divisions. An increasing dependence on defence business might lead to arms firms merging with civil firms, but actual responses might differ between the air, land and sea sectors. New technology might lead to new entrants to the arms industry as well as exits of established firms, particularly firms which fail to adjust to new technology (Dombrowski et al., 2002). New technology will be costly.

Rising costs

The trend of rising equipment costs is likely to continue, leading to the vision of a single tank army, single ship navy and Starship Enterprise for the air force. Rising costs and limited defence budgets mean smaller numbers of equipment ordered and reduced output volume for arms industries; but higher real values of sales.

The historical trend of rising real unit equipment costs was identified by Norman Augustine (Augustine, 1987). Two of his Laws are relevant. First, 'the last 10% of performance generates one-third of the cost and two-thirds of the problems' (Augustine, 1987, p. 138). Second, the Law of impending doom or economic disarmament:

> in the year 2054, the entire defense budget will purchase just one aircraft. This aircraft will have to be shared by the Air Force and Navy … except for a leap year, when it will be made available to the Marines for the extra day.
>
> (Augustine, 1987, p. 143).

Rising unit costs have followed an historical upward trend and have affected all types of defence equipment. Examples of inter-generational cost escalation include aircraft carriers with 6% annual real cost growth, combat aircraft at 8% and tanks at 11% (Kirkpatrick and Pugh, 1983). Rising unit costs reflect higher development costs and higher unit production costs. For example, for combat aircraft, development costs might be 100–200 times unit production costs (Pugh, 2007).

There are various solutions to rising unit costs. To offset the rise in unit production costs, the armed forces will buy fewer aircraft, ships and tanks and will respond to rising development costs by funding fewer new programmes. Equipment will be retained longer in service resulting in higher maintenance costs and reduced operational effectiveness. Or, collaboration appears to offer cost savings but often fails to reduce the long-run trend to higher unit costs. Alternatively, increased exports might offer cost savings from longer production runs and export levies to reduce development costs; but the contribution of exports is usually small. Another option is for a nation to abandon a major and costly military capability. For example, New Zealand abandoned buying new fighter aircraft for its air force. Or, new technology in development and production work might offer cost savings (Kirkpatrick and Pugh, 1983). There will also be optimistic claims of new procurement policies which will appear to 'solve' the problem. Whatever the solutions, continued rising unit costs have major implications for both the armed forces and national defence industries.

Arms firms will focus increasingly on acquiring new technology (R&D) and developing the skills of their production labour. Firms will also change and adopt new forms of organisation and methods of 'doing business' in an effort to reduce costs. For example, arms firms will merge both within and between nations. The USA will remain a major and attractive defence market, so increasing the inducements for firms to merge with American arms firms. Similarly, if the European Union develops its Single Defence Equipment Market, it will provide incentives for trans-European mergers.

Conclusion: a research agenda

There remain considerable opportunities for new research into Defence Industries. Examples include:

1) More in-depth studies of the Industries included in this volume. Examples include theoretical and empirical studies of structure and conduct and their impacts on firm and industry performance. There is massive scope for theoretical and empirical work based on game theory models of defence industries and market inter-action between industry and government. More information is needed on the labour force of defence industries: for example, the human capital composition of defence industry labour (numbers, types and skills of scientists and technologists).
2) Extending the coverage to include more countries. Examples include the arms industries of Africa, South and Central America, the Middle East and other European countries. Iran is an obvious unknown.
3) New threats, including the extent to which terrorist groups form defence industries and represent novel forms of military capability. For example, the 9/11 attacks in the USA were made by a terrorist air force with airliners used as accurate cruise missiles ('flying bombs'). Similarly, terrorist groups often adapt civil equipment for military use: for example, small trucks used as armoured fighting vehicles. Furthermore, terrorist groups create their own sources of arms supply comprising homes, garages and village communities manufacturing small arms, suicide vests and improvised explosive devices. Terrorist groups are of varying size and acquire weapons illegally through theft and illegal (black market) purchases.
4) Retaining defence industrial capability. Future prospects of fewer new development projects and shorter production runs raises questions about how nations will retain their defence industries during 'troughs' in development and production work. Solutions have included additional

production orders to maintain capacity and retain skilled labour; demonstrator projects to sustain development teams; and export orders to provide work during periods of excess capacity. More radical solutions have evaluated 'mothballing' where industrial capacity is maintained until demand revives. Examples occur in industries such as steel and cement plants and shipbuilding where docks are mothballed. But mothballing is not costless and involves policing and maintenance costs: physical plant and machinery need to be maintained and premises have to be protected from vandalism. More importantly, mothballing retains physical capital but not the required human capital. For example, aircraft assembly plants can be mothballed but the skilled labour required for development and production has to be recruited and trained which involves costs and takes time.

5) Scope for international collective action. Retaining defence industrial capacity can be viewed as an opportunity for international collective action. For example, efforts to create a European defence industry will encounter the challenge of retaining defence industrial capacity which is not costless. Such costs might be shared between Member States of the EU although it is recognised that international collective action encounters problems of burden-sharing and free-riding.

Uncertainty cannot be ignored. The future is uncertain and no one can predict it accurately: today's growing industries could be tomorrow's declining sectors. New technology will affect both military forces and defence industries and much depends on the willingness and ability of their agents to adapt to change. Historically, military forces and arms industries had to adjust to tanks replacing horse cavalry and aircraft carriers replacing battleships. In conflict, the failure to adapt is likely to lead to defeat. This suggests the scope for studies of arms industries responding to new technology. For example, does new technology require state funding or can it be left to private markets; does technology require larger firms or is there scope for small firms; and does revolutionary technical change emerge outside the established defence industry?

Change is inevitable and is a feature of defence industries. Which market structure and firm size is most conducive to technical change and does ownership matter? For example, does technical change in defence industries require large state-owned monopoly firms or privately-owned firms in oligopoly industries? Or, are new entrants from civil industries more likely to promote technical change in defence industries (via technology spin-ins)? If so, which civil industries offer new technologies for arms industries (e.g. electronics; motor vehicles)? There is no shortage of research questions requiring theoretical and empirical work on defence industries.

Note

1 These remarks are based on correspondence with Chris Hughes.

References

Augustine, N.R. (1987). *Augustine's Laws*, Penguin Books, Harmondsworth, England.

Dombrowski, P.J., Gholz, E. and Ross, A.L. (2002). *Military Transformation and the Defense Industry After Next*, Naval War College Newport Papers, Newport, Rhode Island.

Kirkpatrick, D.L. and Pugh, P.G. (1983). "Towards the Starship Enterprise" *Aerospace*, 16–23, May.

Pugh, P.G. (2007). *Source Book of Defence Equipment Costs*, Dandy Booksellers, London.

Index

Printed in the United States
by Baker & Taylor Publisher Services

Printed in the United States
by Baker & Taylor Publisher Services